THE COLD WAR'S KILLING FIELDS

THE COLD WAR'S KILLING FIELDS

RETHINKING THE LONG PEACE

PAUL THOMAS CHAMBERLIN

HARPER

An Imprint of HarperCollinsPublishers

FIRST EDITION

DESIGNED BY WILLIAM RUOTO

Library of Congress Cataloging-in-Publication Data has been applied for.

ISBN 978-0-06-236720-4

18 19 20 21 22   LSC   10 9 8 7 6 5 4 3 2 1

To Lien-Hang Nguyen

CONTENTS

THE COLD WAR'S KILLING FIELDS

INTRODUCTION: A GEOGRAPHY OF COLD WAR-ERA VIOLENCE

This is a history of the deadliest military theater of the Cold War age. It focuses on a nearly contiguous belt of territory running from the Manchurian Plain in the east, south into Indochina's lush rain forests, and west across the arid plateaus of Central Asia and the Middle East. Seven out of every ten people killed in violent conflicts between 1945 and 1990 died inside this zone. These killing fields skirted the frontiers of the Communist world and, together with Europe's Iron Curtain, formed the front lines of the Cold War. Here, along Asia's southern rim, superpower armies, postcolonial states, and aspiring revolutionaries unleashed three catastrophic waves of warfare that killed more than fourteen million people. The superpowers flooded these lands with foreign aid—eighty cents out of every dollar Washington and Moscow sent to the Third World ended up here. Ninety-five percent of Soviet battle deaths occurred inside this stretch of territory. For every thousand American soldiers killed in combat during the period, only *one* died elsewhere.[1]

The territory itself has been known by a number of names. It roughly corresponds to the overland trade routes of the ancient Silk Road and the southern borders of the Mongol Empire. In the twentieth century, geographer Nicholas Spykman would name this area the "rimland." Officials in the Dwight Eisenhower administration spoke of East Asia and the Northern Tier, while Soviet officials would later make plans for the Southern and Eastern Theaters. The term *southern Asia* is perhaps most accurate, but it, too, risks confusion both because of its similarity to South Asia (the Indian subcontinent) and because the so-called Middle East is often treated as if it were somehow separate from Asia. For the purposes of the Cold War, this stretch of territory served as the killing fields, home to the bloodiest fighting of the post-1945 era.

Despite serving as the era's central axis of warfare, these Cold War bloodlands are not mentioned in conventional histories as a defined space—the area has not been mapped, and many of its constituent conflicts are little more than footnotes in the story of post-1945 international relations. As a result, the global picture of Cold War–era violence remains shapeless and is all too often overlooked outside scholarly circles.[2] Instead, most of us tend to see the period from the perspective of the industrialized world: as a time of relative peace. Indeed, the most influential historian of the Cold War, John Lewis Gaddis, would call the Cold War a "long peace," an apt reference to the near absence of Great Power warfare during the era. For Gaddis, Third World conflicts shifted the superpower competition to the level of proxies, helping to ensure that the Cold War remained mostly cold and providing a measure of stability to the larger international order. Yet, for millions of people throughout the postcolonial world, the post-1945 era was marked by brutal warfare. What would a broad history of the Cold War age look like, I wondered, if told from the perspective of the period's most violent spaces?[3]

This book seeks to tell this story. It follows the course of the era's deadliest conflicts and examines how this violence shaped the Cold War and the decades that followed. The most concentrated violence of the age did not occur when or where I had expected. The killing focused on certain places and certain times, and it followed identifiable patterns. As the process of decolonization ran headlong into superpower struggles for regional dominance, the era's bloodiest battlefields traversed the southern rim of Asia. Across these Cold War bloodlands, postcolonial revolutionaries struggled to make a new world while Great Power armies launched brutal campaigns aimed at holding the line. It is a side of the Cold War age about which we know surprisingly little: a long chain of vicious conflicts fought across southern Asia to mark the transition from a world of colonies to a world of nation-states, to lay down the far frontiers of the Cold War order, and to reshape international politics.

Far from being incidental to the superpower struggle, violence played a fundamental role in shaping the contours of the U.S.-Soviet rivalry and international politics after 1945. If Latin America was Washington's imperial workshop and Eastern Europe was Moscow's laboratory of socialism, the contested borderlands of southern Asia served as the staging grounds for both superpowers' containment strategies and for new modes of revolution and resistance.[4] As decolonization destroyed a centuries-old European colonial order, Washington and Moscow rushed to fill the vacuum. Both superpowers sent their armies to battle guerrilla fighters on the far frontier; both scoured the globe in search of allies that might serve as proxies in the struggle to contain their adversary. Rarely did these conflicts carry geopolitical significance commensurate with the resources that Washington and Moscow devoted to them. But Cold War strategies (Washington's bid to contain Soviet influence and Moscow's parallel campaign to breach a feared capitalist encirclement) magnified the importance of these conflicts and led both superpowers into interventions that frequently ran counter to their long-term interests.[5]

While the drive to contain their rival's influence dragged Washington and Moscow into the postcolonial world, Third World revolutionaries and political leaders fought to realize their own visions of decolonization and liberation. Local forces joined the struggle along the Cold War frontiers in complex patterns of collaboration, co-optation, and resistance in bids to assert their own influence while manipulating superpower anxieties to win vital assistance for their local struggles. As they did so, regional players disrupted superpower designs and redirected the currents of international power. These postcolonial battlefields emerged as new political spaces in which superpowers, local governments, and revolutionaries refined techniques of mass violence, rewrote the politics of revolution, and reshaped the structures of world power. In the process, the battles for the Cold War borderlands forged many of the greatest geopolitical transformations of the twentieth and twenty-first centuries—these lands witnessed the consolidation of a new system of postcolonial states, the rise and fall of Third World communism, and the emergence of a new politics of sectarian revolution.[6]

My purpose is not to argue that the conflicts covered in this book are best understood as proxy battles of the Cold War; nor is it to suggest that the Cold War was in fact the sum total of wars in the Third World. The book does not claim to offer a full or encyclopedic account of Third World conflicts during the post-1945 era. Rather, it tells the history of the most intensely violent theater of the superpower struggle: the Cold War's postcolonial borderlands along Asia's southern tier. In doing so, it examines the bloodiest encounters of the era and considers how they shaped the course of world affairs in the second half of the twentieth century. It argues that the Cold War forged a network of connections that linked these struggles together and increased their destructive potential by an order of magnitude. Although each individual conflict may not have been a direct outgrowth of the Cold War, each was shaped in important ways by the larger structure of superpower relations during the period. While a case may be made for treating the superpower conflict separately from these conflicts along the periphery, such an approach obscures the rivalry's global impact and overlooks the influence of non-Western societies on the dynamics of the East-West struggle. Conversely, local studies that downplay the Cold War tend to gloss over global influences and place their subjects in a sort of regional vacuum. Instead, this book approaches the Cold War as a worldwide phenomenon—a complex, interconnected web of regional systems stretching around the world and connected to the global latticework of U.S. and Soviet power.

Although parts of this story will sound familiar to many readers, our understanding of it remains surprisingly limited. Conventional wisdom tells us that the Third World experienced violence during the Cold War, but the precise shape of that violence remains indistinct. We remember a few large wars such as Vietnam, Korea, and Afghanistan, but these accounted for less than half the era's war deaths.

Beyond these better-known conflicts, we have a tendency fall back on generalizations—wars took place in the Third World or in Asia, Latin America, or Africa—but these are enormous regions, and only a fraction of the countries in the developing world suffered such massive bloodletting. These vague characterizations are insufficient for understanding such weighty issues.

Our understanding of post-1945 warfare remains strangely shapeless; it contains virtually no sense of scale, timing, or geography. And this lack of structure is troubling. Consider, for example, histories of World War II in Europe that gloss over the fact that the overwhelming majority of the casualties took place on the Eastern Front—that ignore Stalingrad to focus on Normandy. Such works obscure the enormous role that the Soviet Union played in the war and lionize American contributions. Likewise, how seriously can we take a study of the Vietnam War that downplays the fact that far more Vietnamese were killed than Americans? Such a history would mask the incredibly brutal impact of the war on the civilian population of Vietnam. Why should we not apply the same logic to the Cold War era? By ignoring the spatial and temporal dimensions of post-1945 warfare, or approaching them in a piecemeal fashion, we conceal core dynamics of power and violence in the Cold War international system. Put simply, by avoiding a systematic examination of the period's wars and massacres, we whitewash the inherently violent history of the post-1945 era.

I therefore chose to let the numbers be my guide. Mortality figures, imprecise as they may be,[7] provide the most straightforward means of gauging the scale and intensity of mass violence across disparate societies; they allow us to establish a rough map of mass killing across both time and space. When we do so, a startling picture of Cold War–era violence emerges.

The post-1945 era's conflicts were neither random nor evenly distributed across the developing world. Although historians tend to treat Third World clashes indiscriminately, Africa, Latin America, Asia,

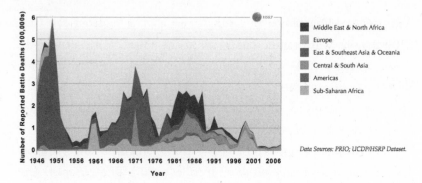

The Three Waves of Cold War–Era Violence

(Courtesy of Andrew Mack, director, Human Security Report Project, Simon Fraser University)

and the Middle East suffered dramatically different levels of violence over different periods. As a result, the incidence of Third World conflicts during the Cold War followed discernible geographic and historical logic. Indeed, more than 70 percent of the people killed during the Cold War died along the eastern, southern, and western periphery of the Asian landmass. Superpower interventions tell a similar story. Soviet forces lost 722 soldiers in their 1956 invasion of Hungary and 96 in the 1968 invasion of Czechoslovakia; nearly 15,000 died in the Soviet-Afghan War. Washington's invasions of the Dominican Republic, Grenada, and Panama resulted in 80 to 90 U.S. deaths; about three times that number died in the 1983 intervention in Lebanon alone; and around 95,000 U.S. troops were killed in Korea and Vietnam. All told, Soviet and U.S. military forces suffered 95 percent and 99.9 percent of their combat deaths, respectively, inside these Cold War bloodlands.

Likewise, the flow of foreign aid to the Third World reveals the importance the superpowers placed on the Asian rim. According to the United States Agency for International Development, between 1946 and 1992 the U.S. government allocated over $106.5 billion in loans and grants to Middle Eastern countries. During the same period, Washington sent just under $20.2 billion to sub-Saharan

Africa, and $32.6 billion to Latin America. Asia received just over $100 billion. Washington sent five times as much aid to the Middle East during the Cold War as it did to sub-Saharan Africa and over three times as much as it sent to Latin America. In other words, about 79 cents out of every dollar the U.S. government sent to the non-Western world during the Cold War went to either the Middle East or Asia.[8] Soviet aid figures are somewhat more difficult to obtain, but the CIA estimated that between 1955 and 1965, Moscow sent just over $2 billion in economic aid to the Middle East, $729 million to Africa, $115 million to Latin America, and $2.1 billion to Asia. If correct, this means that, for every dollar the Soviets spent in Africa, they spent three in Asia; for each dollar they sent to Latin America, they spent $17 in the Middle East. As such, around 82 cents out of every dollar Moscow sent to the developing world during the period ended up in either the Middle East or Asia.[9]

It was no coincidence that the fiercest battles of the Cold War era raged along the borders of what would become the world's two great Communist powers. These Cold War borderlands constituted the most hotly contested terrain of the superpower struggle. It was here along the postcolonial frontiers of their respective spheres of influence that the superpowers felt most vulnerable: unlike Latin America, Europe, and Africa, each of the regions along the Cold War borderlands would swing between strategic alignment with Washington and Moscow. It would be here that the United States deployed its containment strategies against the expansion of Communist power, sending its forces to distant stations overseas along the front lines of the Communist world. And it was here that the Soviet Union and its allies sought to breach a perceived capitalist encirclement. By projecting their power and influence into these postcolonial societies, Washington and Moscow followed in the footsteps of their imperial predecessors. Even as World War II and the global process of decolonization destroyed the old imperial order, it set the stage for a new Great Power struggle that would unleash new waves of violence across the postcolonial world.

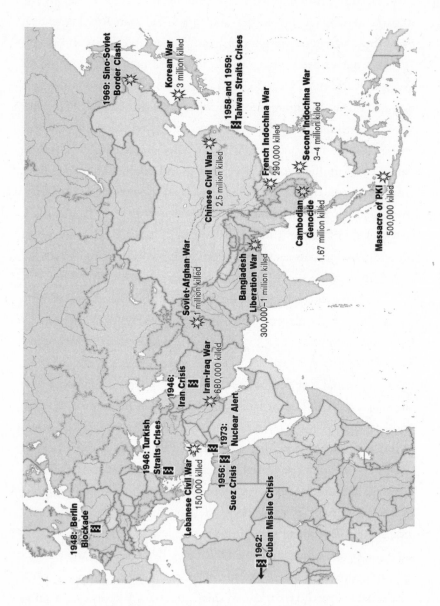

The Geographical Concentration of Violence Around the Southern Rim of Asia

THREE FRONTS

Mapped over time, the killing followed a defined path through the developing world, converging along three broad battlefronts that together accounted for more than 70 percent of war deaths during the Cold War era. Each battlefront was made up of local struggles linked to one of three regional clusters of warfare that were in turn connected to the global networks of the Cold War. Each front cut along the borders of the Soviet Union and China. Each centered on the rise of a regional power. Each unfolded in the wake of decolonization. While the heavily garrisoned frontier in Central Europe remained relatively peaceful, vicious conflicts raged in the east.

The first major front emerged in the immediate aftermath of World War II. The sudden collapse of Japan's empire created the necessary conditions for a string of interconnected revolutions in East Asia. At the center of this first wave of conflicts sat the Chinese Revolution. Communist forces led by Mao Zedong launched a series of bloody campaigns that transformed the world's most populous nation into a revolutionary power and a patron of insurgencies throughout East Asia. This East Asian Communist offensive inspired revolutionary fighters around the postcolonial world and redrew the map of the Cold War, bringing the superpower struggle to the developing world and setting the stage for Korea and Indochina to become critical theaters in an increasingly global struggle.

A second front coalesced at the beginning of the 1960s, along the Indian Ocean rim as North Vietnamese Communists resumed their war against the now-U.S.-backed regime in Saigon. Hanoi's rise exacerbated the growing split in the Communist world between Moscow and Beijing at the same time that it touched off a creeping U.S. intervention in Vietnam. The triangular struggle among Washington, Moscow, and Beijing intensified local violence throughout the region as a series of bloodbaths washed over the Indo-Asian lands of Vietnam, Indonesia, Bangladesh, and Cambodia. Although the United

States eventually abandoned the collapsing regime in South Vietnam (which led to a resounding victory for the Vietnamese Communists), the rifts in the Communist world among Moscow, Beijing, and Hanoi devastated hopes for a wider progressive revolution in Asia and much of the rest of the developing world. Here, in the war zones of South and Southeast Asia, the character of the killing began to change. Whereas Chinese, Korean, and Vietnamese revolutionaries had fought under the banner of communism, fighters in Indonesia and Bangladesh began killing in the name of religion and in defense of ethnic identity.

This transformation in the politics of revolution became more pronounced after 1975, when a third wave of warfare washed across the greater Middle East. Egypt's break with Moscow and realignment with the United States removed the most important progressive power in the Arab world and triggered a struggle for regional leadership among would-be successors. The Lebanese Civil War emerged as a central arena in this regional contest as clashes erupted among Palestinians, Syrians, Israelis, and local militias. Rapidly rising oil prices triggered a second geopolitical shock, expanding the influence of oil-rich Gulf states and unleashing catastrophic inflation in Iran. The subsequent outbreak of a theocratic revolution in Iran in 1979 plunged the wider region into conflict and led both superpowers to expand their military deployments in Southwest Asia. Notably, the Marxist revolutionaries so prominent in earlier decades were all but absent from these late–Cold War clashes. Instead, a new generation of fighters took the offensive in a series of sectarian revolts that placed secular forces on the defensive. A disparate array of political forces recognized that religious and ethnic identity (often in competing forms) provided the most potent means of mobilizing support for their separate causes. As the Cold War entered its final decade, sectarianism and ethnocentrism supplanted secular liberation as the primary vehicles of revolutionary politics in the developing world.[10]

Put together, these three stages chart the rise and fall of the Third

World Communist revolution from Mao's initial victories in East Asia, through the Sino-Soviet split and the Indo-Asian bloodbaths of the 1960s and '70s, and on to Southwest Asia's sectarian wars of the 1980s. As secular Marxist guerrillas gave way to ethno-religious warriors, the face of global revolution was transformed. Each wave of liberation fighters crafted their own model of revolutionary struggle. Mao's blueprint for revolutionary war relied on extensive efforts to build a political base among the population and the construction of a cult of personality focused on a central political leader. The Chinese, North Korean, and Vietnamese revolutions all followed this rough design. Moscow and Beijing served as the principal sources of foreign aid for this first wave. By the 1960s, however, aspiring liberation fighters had introduced a number of innovations. Moscow's attempts to dismantle Stalin's cult of personality and the Sino-Soviet split both challenged the Great Leader mythos. In its place, a new generation of revolutionaries celebrated the rank-and-file guerrilla fighter: a heroic, self-sacrificing radical capable of spectacular feats. Likewise, the Maoist focus on careful political work lost favor as revolutionaries increasingly looked to armed struggle as the engine of political organization. The Cuban *foco* model, which looked to small groups of elite guerrillas to create the conditions for a broader revolution, Le Duan's General Offensive–General Uprising strategy, and Palestinian commando operations each emphasized military action over political spadework. These second-wave revolutionaries could draw on an extensive, if sometimes shallow, network of support from Third World revolutionary states such as Algeria, Vietnam, and Cuba. By the late 1970s, a new generation of revolutionary fighters appeared. The de facto partnership between Beijing and Washington and the Third Indochina War's Communist fratricide (whereby Chinese, Vietnamese, and Cambodian Communists went to war against one another) undercut the appeal of progressive, postcolonial revolution. In place of the secular left-wing guerrilla, this third wave embraced the mythos of the holy warrior: a humble, pious fighter driven by devotion to both faith and clan. These third-wave fighters, in all their ethnic and religious diversity, focused less on the creation of new political bases of support than on consolidating control over existing sectarian and ethnic networks of social organization. The United States, Pakistan, Saudi Arabia, and Israel would serve as the principal sources of foreign support for this third wave of liberation fighters.

The Cold War between Washington and Moscow was integral to this story. Both superpowers marshaled enormous resources, both claimed the mantle of world leadership, both embraced totalizing visions of world order, both defined their security interests as global, and both feared the rising global power of their adversary. Driven by these fears, leaders in the White House and the Kremlin implemented strategies designed to contain the expanding influence of their rival. Though their initial campaigns aimed at fortifying postwar Europe, upheavals in the wider world led the superpowers to send massive flows of weapons, cash, and soldiers to war zones across the globe. In doing so, they transformed local wars into proxy battles in the superpower struggle. Conflicts that might have ended in quick, decisive victories instead became drawn-out campaigns fought by local forces armed and funded by outside powers. The Cold War confrontation functioned as a central nervous system, linking disparate societies and distant battlefields into a global network through which flows of arms, capital, tactical knowledge, soldiers, and political ideologies circulated.[11] Superpower containment strategies fueled a series of regional wars along the contested frontiers of the Cold War international order. Tellingly, global levels of violence markedly declined after the end of the Cold War. The only regions that witnessed an increase in violence after 1990 were Africa and Eastern Europe.

Furthermore, the Cold War spawned a uniquely syncretic form of warfare that placed superpower expeditionary forces on the same battlefields with guerrilla fighters and postcolonial armies. The largest wars of the period combined the dynamics of the East-West conflict with indigenous struggles and moved seamlessly from guerrilla rebellions to civil wars to superpower interventions. The conflicts of the Cold War age were characterized by extreme asymmetry, staggering diversity, and high volatility. The technologies of violence proved as varied as those who wielded them. Rebels carrying antiquated colonial rifles squared off against American and Soviet soldiers armed with state-of-the-art weapons systems while Third World states launched armored assaults against enemy governments. Khmer Rouge executioners bludgeoned thousands of Cambodians to death using iron ox-cart axles. Iraqi commanders directed poison gas attacks on Kurdish villagers. All the while, the specter of nuclear war loomed. The era's conflicts were all the more devastating because most took place inside the most heavily populated sections of Third World societies. Postcolonial cities such as Seoul, Dhaka, and Beirut became war zones while their surrounding hinterlands teemed with guerrillas.

As the superpowers built global alliances, Third World liberation fighters formed a mirror network of international relations during the Cold War. From the late 1940s to the mid-1970s, Beijing sat at the center of this revolutionary international. Chinese officials brought in thousands of insurgents to receive training in political strategy and military tactics. Guerrilla leaders from Algeria, Cambodia, Korea, Indonesia, Palestine, sub-Saharan Africa, and Vietnam all made the journey to PRC-run training camps to study the art of revolution. Beijing also furnished fellow revolutionary forces with military aid. Although this support mostly consisted of small arms, such aid often provided a vital shot in the arm to struggling liberation fighters, as did the attendant entrée to the broader revolutionary world. By the 1960s and '70s, the Algerians, the Palestine Liberation Organization, the North Koreans, and the Vietnamese had joined the Chinese in establishing their own camps, promoting their own military strategies, and sending their own advisors as part of the Third World revolutionary international. Yet, following the collapse of the Sino-Soviet alliance and China's rapprochement with the United States, Beijing's enthusiasm for supporting Third World revolutionaries waned. From the mid-1970s onward, the center of world revolution passed from China to a scattered collection of groups in Central and Southwest Asia. The revolutionary infrastructure of the late Cold War comprised training camps in Afghanistan, Iran, Lebanon, and Pakistan. By the mid-1980s, with Washington pumping hundreds of millions of dollars of Reagan Doctrine aid to insurgents in Afghanistan, Nicaragua, and Angola, the CIA may have been the largest patron of rebel armies in the world. While Chinese revolutionaries pushed a Maoist ideology, this new generation of radicals increasingly mobilized around ethnic and sectarian lines.[12] In this way, the twenty-first-century dynamics of insurgency and counterinsurgency were born on the postcolonial battlefields of the Cold War.

Tragically, Cold War–era conflicts proved particularly lethal for noncombatants. In every major conflict, civilians made up the majority of casualties. Millions were caught in the crossfire or became victims of planned massacres. Virtually no side remained blameless. Chinese armies starved entire cities into submission, and American soldiers slaughtered Vietnamese villagers. Pakistani soldiers massacred Bangladeshi intellectuals, and the Khmer Rouge transformed Cambodia into a massive labor camp. War crimes and civilian atrocities were no mere aberrations; nor were they instances of collateral damage. Rather, the history of the Cold War era is saturated with examples of the deliberate and strategic use of mass violence against noncombatants. Civilians were slaughtered because they lived in villages controlled by the wrong political faction; because they were members of the wrong ethnic or tribal group; because they followed the wrong religion. Ultimately, the Cold War era must also be remembered as an age of systematic civilian atrocities.

Generations of war and outside intervention fueled the radicalization and militarization of politics across much of the Third World. Washington and Moscow employed a Cold War calculus to choose allies in societies across Asia, Africa, and Latin America, supporting friendly regimes, rebel fighters, and political parties. In dramatic examples such as Iran, Guatemala, and Afghanistan, superpower-engineered coups toppled leaders and replaced them with regimes beholden to Washington or Moscow. More often, infusions of outside aid allowed unpopular and corrupt Third World governments to hold on to power without instituting popular reforms. Military assistance programs enabled dozens of Third World regimes to build fearsome security forces that were more likely to attack their own populations than neighboring states. Washington and Moscow prized ideological loyalty in their Third World allies over democracy, human rights, and even competence. In practice, these policies amounted to decades-long campaigns against political moderates in the Third World. By the end of the Cold War, states across the developing world had been armed to the teeth, their political centers ravaged, and the populations terrorized.

Yet Third World players were no mere pawns in a superpower game. They fought not to defend superpower-endorsed political ideologies but to advance their own strategic interests. Inside the newly formed states of the postcolonial world, leaders and their rivals faced the challenge of forging new national armies, economies, and identities. In the wake of decolonization, former colonial subjects had to be transformed into citizens, prompting the question of who, precisely, deserved to be included. Political ideology, ethnicity, and religious affiliation cut through postcolonial societies and formed the basis for many of the coming conflicts. Across the febrile landscape of the newly decolonized world, warlords, revolutionaries, and political leaders surged forward to lay claim to power and territory. Nationalists and Communists launched purges against one another, feuding ethnic groups slaughtered outsiders, and sectarian rivalries escalated into full-blown wars. Violence became a key instrument of state building in much of the postcolonial world, a means of securing power, defending regimes, eliminating rivals, and imposing order over volatile societies.

Superpower patronage served as another weapon in the arsenal of postcolonial leaders. U.S. and Soviet agents crept through Third

World capitals, promising guns and cash to governments and rebels alike, all in the name of containing the nefarious influence of their superpower adversary. This foreign patronage could propel aspiring revolutionaries to national power and push ambitious leaders to regional prominence. Seizing this opportunity, local forces joined the Cold War struggle not as puppets but as willing participants, eager to manipulate the global networks of superpower influence for their own purposes. Yet foreign patronage presented an array of dangers. If too obedient, superpower clients risked being branded as puppets by their rivals. If too rebellious, they risked provoking a superpower intervention. Also, nothing precluded one's rivals from cutting their own deals with outside powers. In this way, the web of Cold War patron-client relationships transformed postcolonial societies into sites of contest among local governments, rebel fighters, and the superpowers.

The Cold War international order, then, was never truly bipolar. By 1947, when President Harry Truman announced the doctrine that was to bear his name and initiate a decades-long policy of anti-Soviet containment, Mao's Communist forces were only months away from overturning the regional order in Asia and remaking China as a third Great Power. Over the next four decades, Beijing played a critical role in shaping world affairs. Similar bids for power—some successful, some failed—arose from such distant capitals as Cairo, Algiers, Havana, Hanoi, Baghdad, and Tehran. These challenges, rather than the grand strategies of U.S. presidents and Soviet premiers, determined the timing and location of the era's largest conflicts. These war zones, as much as the conference rooms in the White House and the Kremlin, determined the shape of world politics in the decades to come. Leaders such as Mao, Suharto, and the Ayatollah Khomeini held the initiative in what was truly a global struggle. To characterize the post-1945 era as bipolar or even tripolar is to gloss over the reality that, as historian John Lewis Gaddis explains, "the diversification of power did more to shape the course of the Cold War than did the balance of power."[13]

Nor did the Cold War give rise to a Pax Americana in which the United States dominated the post-1990 international system. To win the Cold War in the Third World, the superpowers recruited fearsome allies across Asia, Africa, Latin America, and the Middle East. Yet, having stoked the fires of Third World revolution, Washington and Moscow found them difficult to control. The Kremlin would come to regret its aid to Mao's Communist forces in China after the Sino-Soviet split. Chinese leaders faced similar questions about their support for Vietnamese revolutionaries after the two countries went to war in 1979. Washington's reckoning arrived a decade after the end of the Cold War, when Islamic militants, nurtured by American officials during the Soviet-Afghan War, turned their fury against the United States. Like Dr. Frankenstein's monster or the Golem of Prague, many of these superpower proxies turned against their creators.

Indeed, placed in a larger historical context, the wars of the post-1945 era showcased the relative decline of Western power in world affairs as decolonization created a new global order. Where military might and political influence had been concentrated in the hands of Western states and Japan prior to 1945, the Cold War era witnessed the diffusion of power across the international order. Although Washington and Moscow still commanded the world's most formidable armed forces, rising powers in the Third World (such as Beijing, Hanoi, and Tehran) mounted challenges to Western authority that would have been unthinkable in earlier generations. This convergence of superpower containment policies and postcolonial power struggles reshaped dozens of societies across the globe and generated the largest wars of the post-1945 era. In this way, Asia's Cold War bloodlands formed the crucible out of which the Third World and the contemporary international system emerged.

This book connects these seemingly disparate histories into one cohesive story for the first time. The following chapters map the trail of deadly liberation wars as they swept south and west along the Asian periphery. Although my focus is international, much of the narrative centers on the United States, which remained the most powerful player on a global field crowded with rival Great Powers, ambitious Third World states, and rebel fighters. The book is divided into three parts corresponding to each of the three major waves of killing during the Cold War. Together, these sections chart the rise and fall of the Third World Communist revolution and the resurgence of ethnoreligious warfare in the developing world.

A project of this scope draws, by necessity, on a diverse range of sources and documents. It makes extensive use of declassified U.S. government documents and Soviet and Chinese documents released by the Cold War International History Project and the National Security Archive, both based in Washington, DC, and special use of newly declassified CIA files. Yet it also seeks to reach beyond official government records. To that end, it uses collections held by nongovernmental and human rights organizations, oral histories, eyewitness accounts by journalists, and a small number of interviews. It draws on documents from a number of Third World countries as well. No scholar could possibly become a specialist in Afghan, Bangladeshi, Chinese, Korean, Indonesian, Iranian, Iraqi, Lebanese, Soviet, U.S., and Vietnamese history. A book of this topical breadth would not have been possible, therefore, without the work of hundreds of historians and area studies specialists.

The wars of the post-1945 era were by their very nature protracted and diffuse. They connected many societies across multiple regions, and these linkages were not always clear. As a result, it has been far too easy to overlook the scale of destruction generated by these conflicts. The book makes the case that it is time to move beyond regional and local histories of these terrible events to take a global view of mass violence during the Cold War era. Consider perhaps the best-known atrocity of the period, the 1968 My Lai Massacre, which left some four hundred Vietnamese children, women, and men dead. My Lai came to epitomize the specter of a superpower military run amok.

Although the perpetrators were identified and brought to justice, for the war's supporters, the massacre was an appalling war crime, a black mark on an otherwise noble war. For critics of U.S. policy, My Lai served as an allegory for the larger Vietnam War, a savage imperial adventure waged by a country that had lost its way.

This book challenges both interpretations because each ultimately treats My Lai as exceptional. Approached in isolation, the massacre of Vietnamese civilians or the Vietnam War itself can be dismissed as an aberration—in the same way that countless slaughters throughout the Cold War period have been treated as horrific singularities. As long as these stories continue to be told separately, we risk falling into the trap of treating them as anomalies. Yet if we place them in context, a larger landscape of Cold War–era violence emerges. Between the end of World War II and 1990, more than 20 million people died in violent conflicts. Broken down, that means that an average of more than 1,200 people died in wars of one type or another, every day, for forty-five years. Most of them were civilians. In raw numerical terms, this death toll equals more than three My Lai massacres every day for forty-five years. Nearly all of them have been forgotten. This book argues that this violence was not simply an accidental consequence of local wars or superpower meddling. Rather, massacres such as My Lai were integral components of the Cold War world. This book is a humble attempt to construct a broader history of some of those tragedies and an effort to explain, at least in part, why they occurred and why they matter for the world today.

THE IRON CURTAIN DESCENDS

1945 – 1947

Three hours past midnight on April 16, 1945, approximately nine thousand Soviet guns opened fire on German positions along the Seelow Heights guarding the eastern approaches to Berlin. "Along the whole length of the horizon it was bright as daylight," a Russian engineer remembered. Soviet troops were forced to cover their ears to avoid burst eardrums from the bombardment. In the sky above, flocks of birds wheeled amid clouds of smoke that poured up from the German lines. Forty miles from the front, terrified residents waited as their walls trembled from the distant barrage. After nearly six years of war, Adolf Hitler's capital lay besieged before the Red Army. Three Soviet fronts comprising 2.5 million men closed around the last fortress of the Third Reich. In the coming days, Soviet commanders would unleash a crushing assault that devastated Berlin. Savage street fighting tore through city blocks as the last of the Wehrmacht fell before the Soviet onslaught. Russian forces stormed the capital, raping and pillaging in an orgy of mass violence. "A ghost town of cave dwellers was all that was left of this world metropolis," reported a representative from the Red Cross. Seventy-five miles to the west, American forces camped along the Elbe River waited to meet the advancing

Red Army. Joseph Stalin, the Soviet premier, had built the mightiest army the world had ever seen, one that outnumbered American and British forces by a factor of four to one. Though they celebrated the Third Reich's collapse, no one could have blamed the American commanders for feeling anxious. If Stalin chose not to halt his legions in Germany but to send them into western Europe, perhaps no force on earth could stop the Communist juggernaut. That was about to change.[1]

Less than four months later, a brilliant light flashed across the skies above Hiroshima, followed by a crushing shock wave that ripped out across the city, accompanied by a burst of intense heat. At ground zero, the courtyard of Shima Hospital, temperatures reached 5,400 degrees Fahrenheit. People near the epicenter of the explosion were instantly vaporized. The explosion reduced human bodies, historian Richard Rhodes would write, "to bundles of smoking black char in a fraction of a second as their internal organs boiled away." The heat from the bomb ignited thousands of fires around the city, which set off a vortex of air currents that took the form of a firestorm. Ninety-two percent of Hiroshima's 76,000 buildings were destroyed. The stunned survivors found themselves lost in a burned-out wasteland. Corpses clogged the Ota River as a radioactive black rain spattered across the charred ruins of what had been, only hours before, Japan's seventh largest city. Approximately 130,000 people were killed instantly; 110,000 of them were civilians. Another 140,000 died by the end of the year. Soon after, President Harry Truman announced the bombing. If the Japanese leadership did not surrender, he explained, "they may expect a rain of ruin from the air, the like of which has never been seen on this earth." More bombs were in production, and the United States intended to use them. Three days later, Truman made good on his promise and dropped a second atomic bomb, on Nagasaki. On August 14, 1945, the Japanese Empire surrendered, and the largest war in human history came to an end.[2]

More than sixty million people died in the Second World War.

Cities across Europe and Asia lay in ruins. As survivors wandered through the irradiated ruins of Hiroshima and Nagasaki, Allied troops in Europe picked their way through the ghastly remains of Nazi concentration camps, where Hitler's minions had slaughtered millions as part of a genocidal campaign against Jews, Soviet POWs, Poles, Romani, and others deemed undesirable. The discovery of mass graves scattered across the countryside to the east would soon drive the grisly toll even higher. In China, between ten million and twenty million people had died as a result of Japan's bid to carve out its own empire in Asia. Japan's murderous campaigns destroyed decades of European colonial rule throughout the region, replacing it, briefly, with an empire centered in Tokyo that rivaled Berlin in its brutality. Much of the war had been a clash between authoritarian governments—Germany, Japan, and the Soviet Union.

On the other side of the Eurasian landmass, a massive stream of refugees moved out across Europe. "The roads, footpaths, tracks, and trains were crammed full of ragged, hungry, dirty people," writes historian Anne Applebaum. "Starving mothers, sick children, and sometimes entire families camped on filthy cement floors for days on end."[3] A report from the International Labour Office estimated that the war in Europe had driven more than thirty million Europeans from their homes.[4] Many of the war's survivors now sought revenge. Soviet forces in the east unleashed a vicious campaign of ethnic cleansing designed to carve off the eastern territories of Germany. After seizing valuables, Polish troops forced German civilians into cattle wagons headed west to the new borders of Germany. The German population of East Prussia was reduced from 2.2 million to 193,000. An estimated 200,000 Germans were corralled into labor camps; another 600,000 were sent east to labor in the USSR. Czechoslovakia drove 3 million Germans from their homes, killing 30,000. Another 5,558 committed suicide.[5]

Yet the scale of destruction reached beyond the horrifying human toll. The greatest war in human history laid waste to a world order that had existed for centuries. For nearly five hundred years, the Great Powers of Europe (and, more recently, Japan) had pursued a relentless campaign of expansion that divided most of the world into colonial possessions. While colonized peoples often exercised significant autonomy at the local level, the imperial powers dominated the world stage. The Second World War dealt a deathblow to this old order. While the United States had crushed Japan's empire in the east, the battle for Europe broke Britain's and France's holds on their colonies. Though victorious governments in London and Paris sought to reconstruct ties to their colonies, the twilight of their empires had long since fallen.* The world now entered one of the greatest geopolitical transformations in history. As the tide of imperial power receded, the shape of the postwar global order remained unclear. If the end of the war marked the twilight of the imperial era, it also signaled the beginning of a general crisis in world affairs.

The battle for control of this new global order would take place amid the ruins of empire.[6] The two most powerful rivals for succession, the United States and the Soviet Union, commanded massive armed forces. The battle-hardened Red Army represented the largest military force ever assembled. While numerically smaller, the U.S. Army wielded nuclear weapons capable of instantaneously incinerating entire population centers. Having built these awesome forces, the superpowers faced the choice of whether to sheath their weapons or to embark on a new campaign to achieve global preeminence. Although Washington and Moscow were the strongest contestants in the struggle for supremacy, they were not the only ones. As the imperial powers' ability to control their empires failed, a host of nationalists, revolutionaries, and warlords surged forward to claim power throughout the colonized world. What these postcolonial forces lacked in military might, they sought to make up for in revolutionary zeal. In the months following the end of World War II, the broad

---

* In 1974, Portugal would be the last European empire to relinquish its hold on its colonies.

shape of the world crisis came into view. While the two superpowers engaged in an increasingly tense struggle for global power that would soon become known as the Cold War, the peoples of the developing world fought to establish their own states in a sweeping and often violent process of decolonization. Meeting upon a rapidly shifting geopolitical landscape, superpowers, revolutionaries, and small states would each play a role in the post-1945 world crisis and in shaping the world that followed.

TREACHEROUS ALLIES

On May 24, 1945, sixteen days after Germany's surrender, British prime minister Winston Churchill commissioned a top-secret study titled "Operation Unthinkable" to investigate the possibility of launching a joint U.S.-British attack on the Red Army to begin on July 1. Churchill hoped to force Stalin to relax his grip on Eastern Europe. British military planners warned that such an action could prove disastrous. Anglo-American forces could draw on 47 divisions for an offensive, leaving 40 divisions for reserve and defensive operations. The Soviets could respond with 170 divisions "of equivalent strength" and muster a two-to-one advantage in armor. In order to counter this advantage, military planners suggested rearming German units (recently defeated Nazis) and sending them once again into battle against the Red Army. Furthermore, they did not expect Anglo-American strategic bombing to provide a decisive advantage given the dispersal of Russian industry. Likewise, British strategists warned that there was "virtually no limit to the distance to which it would be necessary for the Allies to penetrate into Russia in order to render further resistance impossible." The British chief of the Imperial General Staff therefore concluded that the "chances of success [were] quite impossible." Although Churchill insisted that the operation was nothing more than a contingency study, generals in the Red Army (whose spies had informed them of the study almost immediately) were not so sure.[7]

The behavior of Moscow's wartime allies hardly inspired confidence in the Kremlin. After all, Britain and France had been the first to appease Hitler's ambitions in 1938 at Munich, where Neville Chamberlain had proclaimed "peace in our time." Chamberlain's successor, Churchill, was an inveterate anticommunist. In 1941, as millions of Russians were being slaughtered by the Germans, a junior senator from Missouri had suggested that the United States sit back and feed the flames of war in Europe: "If we see that Germany is winning we ought to help Russia and if Russia is winning we ought to help Germany, and in that way let them kill as many as possible." That junior senator, Harry Truman, was now president of the United States. Even after Washington entered the war, the Americans and the British proved lukewarm allies. While the Wehrmacht rampaged through Western Russia, leaders in Washington and London bided their time. Stalin's pleas in 1942 for his allies to open a second front in western Europe went unheeded. Instead, the British and Americans launched an invasion of North Africa—seemingly aimed at preserving British imperial possessions in the Mediterranean. Rather than striking at Nazi power in France and Germany in 1943, Roosevelt and Churchill chose to invade Italy. The Allies would not open a true second front until June 1944, nearly a year and a half after the Soviet Union turned back the German invasion at the Battles of Stalingrad and Kursk. By the time British and American soldiers stormed the beaches at Normandy in June 1944, the Red Army had the Wehrmacht on its heels. Even worse, Washington and London refused to share the secrets of the atomic bomb with Moscow. While American and British scientists hurried the weapon to production, Stalin relied on an extensive network of spies to provide news of its development. Such a betrayal could hardly have surprised the Soviet leader. The Americans and the British had launched a clumsy intervention in 1917 at the Russian port of Archangel in a bid to prevent a Communist victory in the Russian Civil War. That the capitalist governments should prove treacherous allies in the great battle against Nazism was no great shock.

American and British leaders were equally suspicious of Stalin. Although their wartime propaganda lauded "Uncle Joe" as a stalwart ally in the fight against Hitler, officials in Washington and London had few illusions about the Communist dictator. As the shadow of war loomed over Europe in 1938, Moscow signed the Molotov-Ribbentrop Pact, in which Germany and the Soviet Union pledged not to attack one another and agreed to divide Poland, a tragic casualty of Great Power diplomacy.

While Hitler struck at France and Britain in 1940, Stalin stood aside. It would take a full-scale German invasion of the Soviet Union to draw Stalin into the war. The Russian people paid dearly for Stalin's misplaced trust in Hitler. More than twenty million Russians would die in the heaviest fighting of the war. To turn the tide, Stalin assembled a massive war machine that had smashed its way to the Elbe, crushing all resistance in its path. Leaders in Washington and London now had every reason to believe that Stalin would maintain his hold on eastern Europe. Furthermore, if any wondered what Soviet dominion over eastern Europe might look like, they needed to look no further than Stalin's brutal reign in the Soviet Union itself. In the decade before the outbreak of the Second World War, the Soviet regime had unleashed a campaign of violence against its own people. Some 5 million people died as a result of forced collectivization in the early 1930s; 750,000 were shot as part of political purges; another million were sent to the Gulag.[8] Stalin was just as harsh toward eastern Europeans. In March 1940, on the recommendation of his chief of security, Lavrenty Beria, Stalin ordered the mass execution of at least 25,000 Polish prisoners (many of them military officers) as a means of quashing any resistance to Soviet occupation. Soviet officials dumped their corpses in mass graves in Katyn Forest in Russia.[9]

Yet the animosity between Washington and Moscow ran deeper than wartime disputes. At its heart lay an ideological clash between competing American and Soviet visions for a postwar international order. As the world's largest capitalist country, the United States hoped to lead the way in creating a world of nation-states with free-market economies and linked by a common global market across which goods and capital flowed largely unimpeded. Washington also supported liberal-democratic political systems, although political freedom was secondary to free trade. As the world's largest economy and manufacturer circa 1945, the United States had much to gain from such a world. In contrast, the Soviet Union, as the world's first successful socialist state, looked to lead a postwar world marching toward communism. Stalin and his comrades were convinced that, while the capitalist and imperialist powers of the world would resist revolution, their exploitative socioeconomic models were bankrupt—as evidenced by the Great Depression and the rise of fascism and Nazism in the preceding decade. Having crushed the Third Reich, the Soviets hoped to encourage the rise of fellow Communist states around the world.[10]

PROBING ACTIONS

Such ideological rivalries might have remained academic had it not been for the scale of destruction wrought by the Second World War. The collapse of the old imperial order left a massive power vacuum throughout swaths of Eurasia and opened the door to superpower competition to fill the void. At the center of this emerging struggle sat the city of Berlin and the so-called German question. The Allied powers divided a prostrate Germany into zones of occupation at the close of the war. British and American leaders, and the somewhat less enthusiastic French, hoped to rebuild Germany as one of the cornerstones of a stable, prosperous postwar Europe. Failure to integrate Germany into the emerging western European capitalist system would not only strip that system of one of its strongest members but also sow deep resentments among the German people. But Moscow, which had suffered the brunt of the Nazi assault, favored a policy of repression. Stalin was adamant that Germany never regain the ability to threaten the USSR. In the months following the end of the war, the differences between the Allied victors fell into increasingly sharp relief. By the end of 1945, leaders in both Moscow and Washington came to embrace the idea of separate spheres of influence in Germany and, ultimately, Europe. "Whoever occupies a territory also imposes on it his own social system," Stalin told Yugoslav Communists in April 1945. "Everyone imposes his own system as far as his army can reach. It cannot be otherwise." If this arrangement appeared to settle the matter of superpower influence in Europe, it left open the question of superpower influence in the rest of the world. British and American leaders hoped that Stalin, having been granted a sphere of influence in Eastern Europe, would be content to leave the Middle East and the Mediterranean to the Anglophone powers. But Stalin was hardly content with dominion in Eastern Europe. The United States and Britain each had spheres of influence outside Europe, but the Russians, Stalin complained to British foreign secretary Ernest Bevin, "had nothing." A stunned Bevin protested, explaining "that the Soviet sphere extended from Lübeck to Port Arthur." The Western powers were about to discover just how eager the Kremlin was to change this situation.[11]

Soviet leaders had already begun drawing up plans to consolidate what they perceived to be their well-deserved geopolitical gains as victors in the global conflict, realizing strategic ambitions that predated the Bolshevik Revolution. Having secured his European frontiers, Stalin turned to his southern flanks, which ran through Turkey, Iran, and into the Far East.[12] The Kremlin's first tentative moves focused on Azeri tribes in the northern provinces of Iran. The region had been under the control of the Red Army since 1941 as part of a joint Allied operation in which Soviet and British forces occupied the north and south of Iran, respectively, in order to prevent Tehran from aiding the Axis powers. In June 1945, Stalin issued a top-secret decree creating a mission for the geological survey of oil fields in northern Iran with the assistance of the Soviet Army, with the goal of establishing at least ten oil wells in seven different locations.[13] These were just the beginning of Moscow's plans for the Azerbaijan province. The following month, the Politburo sent a message to the Communist Party leadership in northern Iran calling for the creation of a separatist movement in the province, with the goal of forming a "national autonomous Azerbaijan district [oblast]" in northern Iran. The instructions called for the organization of the Azerbaijan Democratic Party (ADP), which would represent the leadership of the separatist movement, with its headquarters in Tabriz. The Kremlin was creating a puppet separatist movement in the Soviet zone of occupation.[14] It was doing so, moreover, in a way that circumvented the power of the Iranian Communist Party, the Tudeh. At the end of August, an unseated representative to the Iranian Parliament, the Majlis, Ja'afar Pishevari, from Tabriz, founded the ADP.[15] Though it was cloaked in the mantle of Azeri nationalism, the ADP was controlled by the Kremlin. As Stalin himself would admit, the "deep revolutionary crisis" in Azerbaijan was manufactured in Moscow.[16]

Encouraged by Soviet agents, Azeri nationalists staged an uprising in November 1945. Red Army officers, acting on orders from Moscow, created a closed area in the north, refusing the admission of Iranian and foreign officials without special permission and blocking the central government's efforts to reinforce its police units in the north.[17] Meanwhile, the Red Army worked to shield the party's efforts to organize. By late November 1945, some six thousand Soviet troops in plainclothes had entered Tabriz, threatening the city's Iranian garrison. The garrison's commander had orders to defend his post and the city's public buildings "to the last man." Meanwhile, the Soviets appeared to be distributing weapons to rebel groups among the local population. Soviet forces had created similar situations in other cities throughout northern Iran.[18] On November 20, Soviet forces stopped a column of Iranian soldiers headed for Tabriz to reinforce the city's garrison. Iran's Ministry of Foreign Affairs complained to the U.S.

State Department that Moscow was fomenting a rebellion in the north of the country. If the United States remained "quiescent while the Soviet Union carries out what seems to be a carefully laid plan to deprive Iran of its independence or infringe upon its integrity," Loy Henderson, director of the Office of Near Eastern and African Affairs, warned, "no small country in the world can in the future have any confidence in promises made by the Great Powers."[19]

Watching the mounting crisis from Moscow, the U.S. embassy's chargé d'affaires, George Kennan, argued that Moscow's moves were part of a larger strategy: "The basic motive of recent Soviet action in northern Iran is probably not the need for the oil itself but apprehension of potential foreign penetration in that area coupled with the concern for prestige which marks all Soviet policy these days." Azerbaijan was dangerously close to the massive Soviet oil installations at Baku, which had "so closely escaped complete conquest" by Hitler's armies. Kennan warned that Soviet leaders, preoccupied with the "methods as well as the aims of Tsarist diplomacy," were working to carve out a buffer state in northern Iran.[20]

The crisis came to a head in March 1946, when the UN Security Council turned its attention to Soviet actions in northern Iran. Unwilling to risk an international showdown, Stalin agreed to withdraw his forces, and the Truman administration declared victory. As the president later recalled, "The world was now able to look more hopefully toward the United Nations. But Russia's ambitions would not be halted by friendly reminders of promises made. The Russians would press wherever weakness showed—and we would have to meet that pressure wherever it occurred, in a manner that Russia and the world would understand."[21] Soviet leaders were taken aback by the reaction at the United Nations and in Washington. As Molotov explained, "We began to probe [on Iran], but nobody supported us."[22] The Iran crisis helped cement Washington's approach to the emerging Cold War and shape its actions in the year to come. By standing firm in the face of Soviet pressure in Iran, rather than conceding as Franklin Roosevelt's administration had done in Eastern Europe, Washington had prevailed. The Iran crisis seemed to provide a blueprint for future engagement with Moscow.[23]

PATIENT BUT DEADLY STRUGGLE

The superpower face-off in Iran cast a shadow over the already darkening relationship between Washington and Moscow. On February 13, 1946, the State Department sent a request to the U.S. embassy in Moscow for an assessment of one of Stalin's recent speeches. In response, Kennan sent back a five-thousand-word telegram, the longest in State Department history. In five sections, Kennan's so-called Long Telegram laid out a damning appraisal of Soviet policies and likely actions in the future. Soviet leaders maintained a "neurotic view of world affairs" rooted in a "traditional and instinctive Russian sense of insecurity," Kennan wrote. The "USSR still lives in antagonistic 'capitalist encirclement' with which in the long run there can be no permanent peaceful coexistence." The Kremlin would do everything in its power short of outright military aggression to advance its interests at the expense of the capitalist world. Over centuries, Russian leaders "have learned to seek security only in patient but deadly struggle for total destruction of rival power, never in compacts and compromises with it." In the developing world, Moscow would work to weaken the influence of the Western powers, in the hope of creating "a vacuum which will favor Communist-Soviet penetration." He explained that coping "with this force [is] undoubtedly [the] greatest task our diplomacy has ever faced and probably [the] greatest it will ever have to face." There was reason for hope, however. Kennan argued that, unlike Nazi Germany, the USSR sought to avoid risks. Soviet leaders would stage probing actions, but upon encountering resistance, they would withdraw. Furthermore, the Soviet Union was far "weaker" than the United States and, like czarist Russia before it, beset by internal challenges. "World communism is like [a] malignant parasite which feeds only on diseased tissue," Kennan insisted. If the United States and its allies remained strong, they would prevail.[24]

Kennan was not the only individual thinking along these lines. Two weeks after the Long Telegram came over the wires, Winston Churchill delivered a speech at Westminster College in Fulton, Missouri. The former prime minister warned of the descent of an "iron curtain" across Europe, separating the Soviet-controlled east from the free nations of the west. "From Stettin in the Baltic to Trieste in the Adriatic, an iron curtain has descended across the Continent," he warned.

> Behind that line lie all the capitals of the ancient states of Central and Eastern Europe. Warsaw, Berlin, Prague, Vienna, Budapest, Belgrade, Bucharest and Sofia; all these famous cities and the populations around them lie in what I must call the Soviet sphere, and all are subject, in one form or another, not only to Soviet influence but to a very high and in some cases increasing measure of control from Moscow.[25]

The situation in Iran seemed to vindicate Kennan and Churchill's warnings about Soviet ambitions and to represent a test case for American resolve. It would be only a matter of months before leaders in Washington had a chance to apply the lessons they had taken from Iran to another crisis in the Middle East.

While Kennan and Churchill sounded the alarm in the United States, the Kremlin kept a wary eye on the Western powers. On September 27, 1946, the Soviet ambassador to Washington, Nikolai Novikov, cabled Moscow with a scathing assessment of American policy. Novikov's cable warned of a U.S. crusade for "world domination." The United States had sat out for much of World War II, he explained, hoping that rival Great Powers would destroy themselves and create an opening for Washington to step into the vacuum. While Europe was devastated, the Soviet Union emerged much stronger than American leaders anticipated. At the same time, the transition from Roosevelt to Truman had brought into power "a politically unstable person with certain conservative tendencies." Under this new leadership, the most "reactionary circles" of the Democratic Party focused on a massive military buildup. "According to available official plans," he explained, "in the coming years 228 bases, support bases, and radio stations are to be built in the Atlantic Ocean and 258 in the Pacific." The Americans occupied or were building bases in "Newfoundland, Iceland, Cuba, Trinidad, Bermuda, the Bahamas, the Azores, and many others; in the Pacific Ocean: former Japanese mandated territories—the Marianas, Caroline and Marshall Islands, Bonin, Ryukyu, Philippines, and the Galapagos Islands."

The inescapable conclusion, according to Novikov, was that U.S. "armed forces are designed to play a decisive role in the realization of plans to establish American world domination." He added that some fifty thousand U.S. troops were already involved in the Chinese Civil War (a struggle between Communist rebels led by Mao Zedong and the government of Chiang Kai-shek) and that Washington was actively seeking to expand its influence in the Middle East. Meanwhile, the United States had initiated a campaign to undermine Moscow's influence in countries along the borders of the USSR through infiltration of financial markets and "weakening and disbanding [razlozhit'] the democratic governments in power there which are friendly to the USSR and then replacing them with new governments which would obediently carry out a policy dictated from the US." Within the United States, American officials had created an atmosphere of anti-Soviet hysteria designed to persuade the American people to support this unprecedented military buildup. Novikov concluded: "It ought to be fully realized that American preparations for a future war are being conducted with the idea of war against the Soviet Union, which in the eyes of American imperialists is the chief obstacle in the American path to world domination."[26]

ANOTHER WAR IN THE MAKING

The next confrontation would take place in the Eastern Mediterranean. Control over the Straits of the Bosporus and the Dardanelles had been a goal of Russian leaders dating back to the era of the czars. Command of the strategic straits, which linked the Black Sea to the Mediterranean, would give Russia a platform to exert influence throughout the Mediterranean. In March 1945, the Soviet Union rejected its treaty of neutrality with Ankara in the hope of negotiating a new arrangement that would revise Turkey's frontier with the Soviet Union and grant Moscow basing rights and joint control over the straits. As had been the case with Iran, Stalin viewed Turkey as part of the Soviet Union's security perimeter. In the wake of its decisive victories in World War II, Moscow expected to project its sphere of influence over Turkey. Further, in 1943 both Churchill and Roosevelt had agreed, in principle, to some sort of revision of the treaty that governed control of the straits. In preparation for his bid to take the straits, one KGB agent recalled, Stalin hoped to probe "exactly how far the West would go to defend this part of the world."[27]

By late 1945, American leaders were increasingly coming to the conclusion that Stalin was making a bid for control of the Northern Tier, a line of states along the borders of the Soviet Union from Turkey through Iraq, Iran, and Pakistan. Kennan identified Turkey as the weak link in the Soviet western defense chain. In December, the U.S. ambassador to Turkey, Edwin Wilson, predicted that a major crisis would break out in the Middle East in the coming months. In particular, he warned that Moscow was trying to use the issue of the straits as a means of extending its control over Ankara. Truman was also coming to the conclusion that some sort of action must be taken. "There isn't a doubt in my mind," he wrote in early January 1946, "that Russia intends an invasion of Turkey and the seizure of the Black Sea Straits to the Mediterranean. Unless Russia is faced with an iron fist and strong language another war is in the making."[28] Reflecting on the importance of Turkey and the straits, Wilson explained that the "maintenance [of] Turkish independence has become [a] vital interest [to the] United States. If Turkey falls under Soviet control[, the] last barrier [would be] removed in [the] way [of a] Soviet advance to Persian Gulf."[29]

As Stalin increased the pressure on Ankara, Truman and the Departments of State and War came to share this view. On August 15, 1946, the White House approved a joint memo from War and State that read, "In our opinion, the primary objective of the Soviet Union is to obtain control of Turkey." Should Moscow succeed in this, "it will be extremely difficult if not impossible, to prevent the Soviet Union from obtaining control over Greece and over the whole Near and Middle East. It is our experience that when the Soviet Union obtains predominance in an area, American, and, in fact, all Western influences and contacts are gradually eliminated in that area." U.S. leaders would interpret a Soviet victory on the issue of the straits as the first stage of a larger campaign to seize control over the entire Middle East. Ultimately, the "only thing which will deter the Russians," the report concluded, "will be the conviction that the United States is prepared, if necessary, to meet aggression with force of arms."[30]

In a subsequent memorandum, the Joint Chiefs of Staff concluded that Moscow's demands vis-à-vis the straits would give the Soviet Union a bridgehead in the region that could be reinforced within a matter of "days or hours" and set Turkey on a path to becoming a Soviet satellite. "Strategically," they explained, "Turkey is the most important military factor in the Eastern Mediterranean and the Middle East." The Kremlin's success in projecting its power into Turkey would make the Western position in the region untenable in the event of a major military crisis. For these reasons, the JCS recommended that military and economic aid be extended to Ankara along with U.S. technicians and military advisors.[31] The Near Eastern Affairs desk at the State Department agreed, explaining that, as one of the few nations on the Soviet Union's borders that had not fallen under the Kremlin's influence, Turkey was a prime target for subversion. Moscow sought to weaken the regime in Ankara and bring it under Soviet influence with the object of using "Turkey both as a defense against possible outside attack from the Mediterranean and as a springboard for political and military expansion by the USSR into the Mediterranean and the Near and Middle East." Turkey represented "the stopper in the neck of the bottle through which Soviet political and military influence could most effectively flow into the Mediterranean and the Middle East." Officials warned that a "Russian-dominated Turkey would open the floodgates for a Soviet advance into Syria, Lebanon, Iraq, Palestine, Transjordan, Egypt, and the Arabian peninsula," and into Greece and Iran. The political fallout from a Soviet victory in Turkey would be even more far-reaching, convincing the many governments around the world that currently feared Moscow's designs to come to terms with the Communist superpower for fear of being next on the list. "Turkey cannot stand in the face of the USSR if left entirely alone," officials explained. Rather, Washington should give diplomatic, economic, and military backing to Ankara for the purpose of resisting the further expansion of Soviet influence.[32]

Plans for such a response had already been prepared. In the summer of 1946, the JCS had drawn up a prospective war plan against the Soviet Union code-named PINCHER. The Middle East sat at the center of the plan, which envisioned a Soviet thrust through Europe while the Western powers regrouped and launched a strategic bombing campaign from British air bases in the Middle East. Should this aerial campaign prove insufficient to halt the Soviet offensive, the Western powers would prepare a ground assault through Turkey and the Eastern Mediterranean north into the Soviet Union, thereby avoiding the tortuous route through Eastern Europe that had proved fatal for both Napoleon and Hitler. Officials in Washington therefore concluded that the most viable corridor to attack the Soviet Union, in the event of a war, would be through the Middle East from bases in Turkey. Both Moscow and Washington recognized that the region, and Turkey in particular, represented the soft underbelly of the Soviet Empire.[33] After learning of the PINCHER plans through its network of spies in the West, the Kremlin backed off, seeking to assuage the war scare in Washington. One KGB officer suggested that the agency might have helped prevent a war between the superpowers. Molotov later explained, "It was good that we retreated in time or [the situation] would have led to joint aggression against us."[34]

Moscow ultimately hoped to create a rim of buffer states that would help ensure Soviet security. Stalin had launched a "war of nerves" along the Soviet periphery designed to breach the "hostile capitalist encirclement" of which Lenin had warned. The goal was not to start a confrontation with the Western powers but, rather, to establish a security buffer along the USSR's frontiers, a privilege that Soviet leaders felt they had earned as a result of their decisive role in World War II. "We were simply on the offensive," Molotov later argued. "[Washington and London] became angry at us, of course, but we had to consolidate what we [had] conquered." In the process, Stalin was testing the limits of international diplomacy, but in doing so, he wasted the political capital that the USSR had built up during the war. Stalin appears to have overestimated the divisions between the capitalist powers. Far from taking advantage of Anglo-American disagreements, Stalin's moves in both Iran and Turkey served to unify British and American leaders against a perceived Soviet threat, sparking a war scare in Washington and convincing the Truman administration to commit to the defense of the Eastern Mediterranean and the Middle East.[35]

SATELLITES, CLIENTS, DEPENDENTS, AND PUPPETS

Placing a region as volatile as the Middle East at the center of Anglo-American strategic plans, however, carried its own risks. As Prime Minister Clement Attlee explained in January 1947, these war plans required "very careful consideration." By crafting the Middle East as a bastion arrayed against the Soviet Union, the Western powers would be relying on "weak, backward and reactionary states." Compounding matters, "We shall constantly appear to be supporting vested interests and reaction against reform and revolution in the interests of the poor," Attlee stated. Such a policy would be not only costly but also potentially dangerous.[36] If the Middle East and the Mediterranean were to form the linchpins in the West's defense against the Soviet Empire, London would need Washington's help in carrying the burden. On February 24, 1947, the British ambassador to the United States, Lord Inverchapel, notified Loy Henderson and Undersecretary of State Dean Acheson that his government could no longer maintain its commitments in the Eastern Mediterranean. Great Britain, in the midst of economic and financial crisis, could no longer provide the levels of economic aid necessary to ensure Greek and Turkish independence in the face of Soviet encroachments. The announcement, Acheson argued, presented the United States with "the most major decision with which we have been faced since the war."[37] The British government was in fact in the process of liquidating many of its imperial possessions, having announced its planned withdrawal from Burma, Palestine, and India. Undersecretary of State William Clayton observed that the "reins of world leadership are fast slipping from Britain's competent but now very weak hands. These reins will be picked up either by the United States or by Russia. If by Russia, there will almost certainly be war in the next decade or so, with the odds against us. If by the United States, war can almost certainly be avoided."[38]

On February 24, 1947, Henderson convened the Special Committee to Study Assistance to Greece and Turkey to discuss the U.S. response to the news. The committee concluded that, owing to the strategic importance of the two nations, the United States must step forward to assume this new responsibility. Moreover, the participants recognized that this "might be only one of many instances" in which

Washington would be called upon to take up London's responsibilities. The committee suggested that "the financial part of the problem be approached on a global basis, urging that it must be presented to Congress as part of a worldwide program . . . to electrify the American people."[39] Two days later, on February 26, Secretary of State George Marshall met with the secretaries of war and the navy to discuss the situation. All agreed that the Eastern Mediterranean represented a strategically vital region that could not be allowed to fall under Soviet domination. Moreover, the secretaries agreed that the "Greek and Turkish problems were only part of a critical world situation confronting us today in many democratic countries and that attention must be given to the problem as a whole."[40] If Communist forces were to prevail in Greece and Turkey, Kennan predicted, "the military-economic potential of the area of the world which we had abandoned to hostile forces would be several times greater than that of the area which would be left to us."[41]

Marshall took the matter to President Truman the following day, warning the president that an urgent crisis with "direct and immediate relation to the security of the United States" had arisen in Greece and Turkey. With the withdrawal of British support, it now seemed clear that the two nations could not hold out against Soviet encroachment and eventual domination. "There is no power other than the United States which can act to avert this crisis," Marshall explained.[42] Truman found the argument persuasive and moved immediately to convene a meeting with congressional leaders. But the congressmen were not eager to expand American commitments overseas. As the president struggled to explain to them the gravity of the situation, Acheson spoke up with a well-rehearsed characterization of a worst-case scenario:

> In the past eighteen months, I said, Soviet pressure on the Straits, on Iran, and on northern Greece had brought the Balkans to the

point where a highly possible Soviet breakthrough might open three continents to Soviet penetration. Like apples in a barrel infected by one rotten one, the corruption of Greece would infect Iran and all to the east. It would carry infection to Africa through Asia Minor and Egypt, and to Europe through Italy and France. . . . The Soviet Union was playing one of the greatest gambles in history at minimal cost. It did not need to win all the possibilities. Even one or two offered immense gains. We and we alone were in a position to break up the play.[43]

Acheson's summary stunned congressional leaders. After a moment of silence, Senate Majority Leader Arthur Vandenberg told Truman, "Mr. President, if you will say that to Congress and the country, I will support you and I believe that most of its members will do the same."[44] If Acheson's language was calculatedly alarmist, it nevertheless reflected a strong sentiment among many in Washington about the dangers of further Soviet encroachment in the Eastern Mediterranean and the wider Middle East.

On March 12, 1947, Truman addressed a joint session of Congress. The president outlined the dangers facing Greece and Turkey and then turned to the global context:

At the present moment in world history nearly every nation must choose between alternative ways of life. . . . One way of life is based upon the will of the majority, and is distinguished by free institutions, representative government, free elections, guarantees of individual liberty, freedom of speech and religion, and freedom from political oppression. The second way of life is based upon the will of a minority forcibly imposed upon the majority. It relies upon terror and oppression, a controlled press and radio, fixed elections, and the suppression of personal freedoms. I believe that it must be the policy of the United States to support free peoples who are resisting attempted subjugation by armed minorities or by outside pressures.

In fewer than 150 words, Truman had outlined the basic premise of American grand strategy for the next half century. The United States prepared to embark on a global crusade against communism.[45]

As part of a broad campaign to convince the American people to throw their support behind this global crusade, in July 1947, George Kennan, under the pseudonym "X," published an article in *Foreign Affairs* that expanded on the ideas put forward in his Long Telegram. Soviet leaders, he argued, were driven by deep insecurities, ideological faith in the eventual demise of capitalism, and a need to manufacture foreign enemies to justify absolutism at home. Washington must treat Moscow not as a partner, Kennan wrote, but as a rival. Soviet leaders were patient and calculating, their policies aimed at bringing "persistent pressure toward the disruption and weakening of all rival influence and rival power." While the Kremlin would not initiate a dramatic conflict to achieve its goals, it would also not be deterred by single reverses. "In these circumstances," Kennan argued, "it is clear that the main element of any United States policy toward the Soviet Union must be that of a long-term, patient but firm and vigilant containment of Russian expansive tendencies." He called upon the United States to "confront the Russians with unalterable counterforce at every point where they show signs of encroaching upon the interest of a peaceful and stable world." Kennan's vision would come to form the basis of Washington's containment strategy.[46]

NOT EVERY AMERICAN AGREED. WALTER LIPPMANN MAY have been the most widely read man in America. Since 1931, his column, Today and Tomorrow, had run in scores of newspapers around the country. In 1947, he devoted a series of columns (which would ultimately give the Cold War its name) to responding to Kennan's

Foreign Affairs article. Containment worried Lippmann because it represented an entirely different commitment than earlier wartime buildups. He warned Americans that containment entailed a massive expansion of American security interests for a prolonged period of time. Moreover, it would force the United States to scour the globe in search of allies, many of whom would not share American values. "The policy can be implemented only by recruiting, subsidizing, and supporting a heterogeneous array of satellites, clients, dependents, and puppets," he explained. "The instrument of the policy of containment is therefore a coalition of disorganized, disunited, feeble and disorderly nations, tribes and factions around the perimeter of the Soviet Union." To maintain this coalition, the United States would be forced to intervene frequently in the affairs of states scattered along the frontiers of the Soviet Union. Success, for Washington, would require the creation of stability in this region. "The Russians," he warned, "can defeat us by disorganizing states that are already disorganized, by disuniting peoples that are torn with civil strife and by inciting their discontent which is already very great." Lippmann offered a prescient critique of containment:

As a matter of fact, this borderland in Europe and Asia around the perimeter of the Soviet Union is not a place where Mr. X's "unassailable barriers" can be erected. Satellite states and puppet governments are not good material out of which to construct unassailable barriers. A diplomatic war conducted as this policy demands, that is to say conducted indirectly, means that we must stake our own security and the peace of the world upon satellites, puppets, clients, agents about whom we can know very little. Frequently they will act for their own reasons, and on their own judgments, presenting us with accomplished facts that we did not intend, and with crises for which we are unready. The "unassailable barriers" will present us with an unending series of insoluble dilemmas. We shall have either to disown our puppets, which would be tantamount to appeasement and defeat and the loss of face, or must support them at an incalculable cost on an unintended, unforeseen and perhaps undesirable issue.

In sum, Lippmann blasted containment as a "strategic monstrosity" that would be expensive, unwieldy, and likely to drag the United States into the affairs of far-flung nations throughout the Cold War periphery.[47]

Washington's emerging formulation of its containment strategy bore a striking resemblance to the work of one of America's most prominent scholars of international relations, Nicholas Spykman. The director of the Yale Institute of International Studies, Spykman had finished a seminal work on geopolitics just before his death in 1943, at age forty-nine. Published posthumously, *The Geography of the Peace* argues for the strategic importance of what Spykman called the rimland, a wide belt of territory running from the Atlantic Littoral, through the Middle East, and into the Asian monsoon lands. Prevailing theories, based on the work of another giant of twentieth-century geopolitics, Halford Mackinder, looked to the Eurasian heartland as the pivot of world politics. This same Eurasian heartland had hosted the largest battles of the Second World War between the Wehrmacht and the Red Army. But Spykman disagreed with Mackinder's thesis. The rimland, he explained, commanded the principal approaches into the heartland and "formed a vast buffer zone of conflict between sea power and land power." This vast intermediate zone held the key to global power in the post-1945 world. "Who controls the rimland rules Eurasia," Spykman explained; "who rules Eurasia controls the destinies of the world."[48]

THE PERILS OF DECOLONIZATION

Yet the societies in Spykman's rimland, Kennan's containment zone, and Lippman's Cold War borderlands were not merely an arena for superpower ambitions. Even as the Cold War between Washington and Moscow took shape, a larger geopolitical transformation was · under way. As the old European empires that had dominated global affairs for centuries collapsed, dozens of new, postcolonial states emerged. This global process of decolonization, rather than the superpower struggle, would give birth to the first large-scale bloodletting of the Cold War era. On the evening of August 14, 1947, as the last British viceroy of India, Louis Mountbatten, and his wife watched the Bob Hope movie *My Favorite Brunette*, violence erupted across India. The previous June, Mountbatten had designated August 15, 1947, as the date for the formal termination of the British Empire in India. At midnight, power would be transferred from the British Raj to two new states, the Dominion of India and the Dominion of Pakistan. India would be a majority-Hindu state, and Pakistan would be majority Muslim. The announcement of Partition set off a wave of violence as millions of people took flight in an effort to relocate. British officials heading to the train station in Lahore reported bodies thrown in the streets and pools of blood soaking the train platform. Flames rose from burning villages along the tracks heading south. Refugees faced repeated assaults from guerrillas who "culled them like sheep." "Religious fury has transgressed every civilized bound," one American journalist wrote. "Men, women and children are . . . commonly beaten to death with clubs and stones or butchered with knives, spears or axes and left to die slowly with their agony intensified by heat and flies." Brutal sectarian violence ravaged the subcontinent, leaving at least half a million people dead.[49]

If the crises in Iran, Turkey, and Greece showcased the ideal execution of America's containment strategy, the violence of Indian Partition revealed the strategy's gaps. Indeed, the violence unfolding on the subcontinent was only a taste of conflicts still to come. The transition from a world of empires to a world of nation-states would be bathed in blood. In many cases, ethnic and sectarian conflicts would become entangled with Cold War politics as rival factions sought superpower patronage in their local struggles. Neither Washington nor Moscow was prepared for the new postcolonial conflicts with which it was now confronted. It would take two massive civil wars in Asia to convince Truman and Stalin of the stakes in the coming struggle for the postcolonial world. Unbeknownst to Truman and Stalin, by 1947 the twin forces of the Cold War and the struggle for decolonization were on a collision course.

In the two years following the end of the Second World War, the victorious alliance had collapsed into a fog of mutual suspicion. From their offices in Washington, American leaders gazed out upon a world in which the Red Army sat camped along the rimland. Churchill's warnings of the Iron Curtain echoed through the halls as the Truman administration prepared to implement a policy based on Kennan's vision of containment. Nearly five thousand miles away, Soviet leaders peered west from the Kremlin at a nuclear-armed capitalist superpower scrambling to set up hundreds of military bases around the world. The former Great Powers of Europe were well on their way toward rebuilding their ruined capitals, but they would never reclaim their world empires. The European frontier between Soviet-controlled states and pro-Western regimes began to harden into a heavily fortified zone with the divided city of Berlin at its core. Meanwhile, in dozens of societies throughout Asia, Africa, and the Middle East, aspiring leaders and ardent revolutionaries rushed forward to claim power from the departing imperial authorities. They were not alone. The two superpowers, ever watchful, sent their agents into the developing world with orders to prevent these new states from falling into their rival's sphere of influence. To do this, they set about recruiting legions of satellites, puppets, and clients of which Lippmann had warned. Washington and Moscow's "unassailable barriers," which Lippmann had critiqued, were now set to become the central battlefields of the Cold War era. The horrors of the Second World War were over, but the wars of containment were just beginning.

PART I

THE EAST ASIAN OFFENSIVE AND THE RISE OF THIRD WORLD COMMUNISM

1945–1954

THE FIVE YEARS FOLLOWING THE END OF THE SECOND World War witnessed the unraveling of the Grand Alliance and the rise of the superpower confrontation. By the end of the 1940s, American hopes for a new world order based on peace and cooperation had been replaced with a sense of foreboding. Nowhere was this truer than in the Far East. Leaders in both Washington and Moscow watched as East Asia unexpectedly became the most violent region in the world. While the superpowers initially focused on a budding rivalry in Europe, a series of local wars in China, Korea, and Indochina transformed the region into a pivotal Cold War battlefield. These conflicts reached beyond individual nations to tilt the balance of power in the wider world and fundamentally change the superpowers' geostrategic calculus.

The Third World had become a key theater of superpower competition. For a time, the battle for Asia looked as if it might determine the fate of the broader world. "Throughout the Orient there was war, or the talk of war," wrote Hanson Baldwin, military affairs editor for the *New York Times*, on Christmas Eve 1950. "[T]he gauntlet has been thrown down in Asia and thousands of men from scores of different

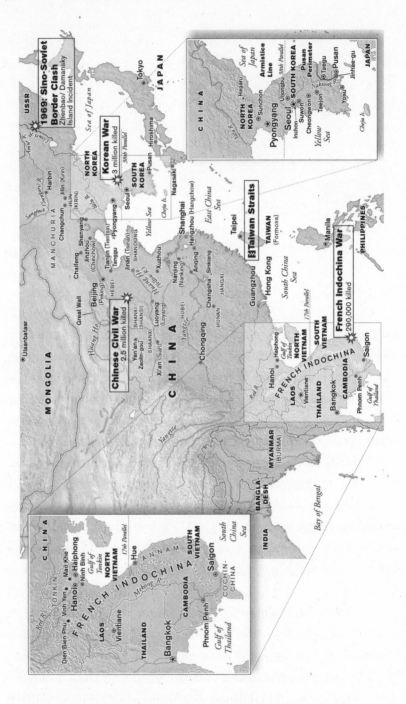

Rough Map of East Asian Offensive, 1945–1954

races march and shoot and die—from the sub-Arctic cold of Korea to the sticky tropical heat of Indo-China's river deltas." The shadow of "Red China" was spreading across the Pacific Rim nations of Korea, Japan, Taiwan, and Vietnam, he explained, over "the fecund, teeming millions" of East Asia. Beijing was "the brooding, ominous giant that looms over the rimlands; this is the mysterious, almost primeval, force which now shapes the destiny of the Orient."[1]

Americans such as Baldwin had good reason to be fearful as they watched what appeared to be a creeping Communist offensive in East Asia. Beneath the banner of Marxist revolution, the first wave of mass violence in the Cold War era swept through East Asia as Communist forces launched a series of bloody campaigns in China, Korea, and French Indochina. The resulting wars appeared to the Western powers as a coordinated Communist assault aimed at linking East Asia to the Soviet bloc. As a 1949 report from the U.S. National Security Council explained, "If Southeast Asia is also swept by communism, we shall have suffered a major political rout the repercussions of which will be felt throughout the rest of the world, especially in the Middle East and in a then critically exposed Australia. . . . The colonial-nationalist conflict provides a fertile field for subversive Communist movements, and it is now clear that Southeast Asia is the target for a coordinated offensive directed by the Kremlin."[2]

Such fears were stoked by a trickle of intelligence that seemed to confirm the existence of a coordinated East Asian offensive. In December 1951, the CIA reported on a Sino-Soviet military conference held in the Biyun Temple, in the western hills outside Beijing, to draw up global war plans. The attendees included Mao Zedong, chairman of the Chinese Communist Party; Chinese premier Zhou Enlai; the supreme commander of Soviet Far Eastern forces, Marshal Rodion Malinovsky; North Korean premier Kim Il-sung; and representatives from Vietnam, the Japanese Communist Party, Burma, and Mongolia. Moscow would continue its efforts to aid Chinese military programs as Beijing amassed a 2.5-million-man army. China would continue its military aid to Vietnamese Communist forces and to North Korea in its war against Washington and Seoul. Both Moscow and Beijing would work with Japanese Communist forces to build an exile army in the Soviet Maritime Provinces, at the far eastern edge of the Soviet Union. In the event of a global war, Beijing would assume command of military operations in Southeast Asia while Soviet forces would take the lead in the North Pacific war district, which included Northeast China (Manchuria), Korea, and Japan. A Soviet general would serve as commander in chief of all Communist forces in the Far East.[3]

The Chinese Revolution (1945–1950) set the stage for the emerging battle for East Asia. The military offensive launched by Mao's forces disrupted the Cold War stalemate and pulled superpower attention east into Asia as the decades-old civil war between Communist guerrillas and the Chinese government roared back to life. As the guerrillas gained ground, they threatened to remake the most populous nation on earth and reshape much of the developing world. Between 1945 and 1954, the shock waves from the Chinese Revolution reverberated across the Pacific Rim in societies already shaken by the destruction of the Japanese Empire and the impending collapse of European colonialism. By 1954, Communist forces were perched on the brink of achieving a decisive victory in the developing world.

The battle for East Asia brought the superpower struggle to the Third World. Ferocious conflicts across the region convinced American leaders that they were witnessing a Communist bid for world domination. The months between October 1949 and June 1950 were pivotal in the formation of what would become the Cold War in the Third World. China's emergence as a Communist giant in October 1949 overturned the balance of power in East Asia and raised the prospect of Marxist revolutions across the developing world. The string of Asian revolutions raging in China, Korea, and Indochina coalesced into a coherent front in the strategic calculations of Cold War leaders in both Washington and Moscow. Meanwhile, Communist victories in the east pushed reluctant Soviet leaders to throw their support behind Asian revolutionaries. Mao and his comrades redirected the course of the Cold War struggle away from Central Europe and into the postcolonial borderlands of East Asia and beyond.

The Communist victory in China touched off a scramble in both Washington and Moscow to adjust to the new balance of power in East Asia. While U.S. leaders agonized over the apparent loss of China, Soviet officials retooled their strategies to account for a new revolutionary power center in the east. By the time North Korea launched an assault across the Thirty-Eighth Parallel and into South Korea in June 1950, Moscow and Beijing were working as reluctant patrons in extending the sphere of Communist influence. But officials in Washington had also revamped their plans and were now ready to meet the North Korean thrust with a full-scale military intervention backed by the mandate of the young United Nations. Meanwhile, French expeditionary forces fought a bloody colonial war against Communist guerrillas in the jungles of Indochina. Together, this cluster of wars in China, Korea, and Indochina killed between five million and six million people and represented the first stage of mass violence in the Cold War era.[4] The combined impact of these conflicts tilted the strategic balance of power in East Asia firmly in favor of Communist forces and heralded the rise of Communist China as a major player in world affairs.

THE COLD WAR COMES TO CHINA

1945 – 1946

A visitor to Yan'an in 1946 would have found it an unlikely base for a movement poised to change the course of modern history. Tucked into the treeless hills of Shaanxi Province in north-central China, much of the city consisted of small caves carved into the sides of the Yellow River Valley. Heavy rains turned Yan'an's dirt roads to mud into which people could sink up to their knees. The fifty-foot-thick walls that encircled the old city were almost all that remained of ancient Yan'an; the rest had been flattened during the war with Japan. Much of the population lived in the honeycomb of cliffside caves, which contained schools, an army headquarters, and a hospital. The residents of the city lived an egalitarian if austere existence. Party leaders, military commanders, and professors ate the "No. 1 meal," which was, according to a Western reporter, "only slightly better" than the No. 2 meal served to the rest of the population. Both consisted of "meat, rice, potatoes, Chinese cabbage and other locally grown vegetables, eggs and bean curd." Milk was reserved for hospitals and nurseries. Such modesties masked the true power hidden in this remote corner of China: Yan'an was the stronghold of the Chinese Communist Party (CCP).[1]

From these humble foundations, the CCP launched a revolution that would shake the world. Led by Mao Zedong, whose ordinary appearance masked a brilliant political leader and military theoretician, the CCP pioneered a punishing new strategy of guerrilla war that promised to tilt the scales of military power in favor of revolutionaries throughout the Third World. Mao's eventual victory in 1949 over the Nationalist government would rank among the greatest of the twentieth century, bringing the world's most populous country under Communist rule. It is difficult to overstate the historical significance of the Chinese Civil War for the Cold War. With the CCP's triumph, one-fifth of the world's population effectively switched sides in the nascent superpower struggle. Furthermore, Mao's model of revolutionary war became the prototype for dozens of other national liberation movements around the Cold War world. Mao's guerrillas would be fish swimming in a sea of the people. Less celebrated, but perhaps just as significant, was the CCP's formula for siege warfare and massive offensives against cities. During the last stage of the civil war, Communist forces successfully transitioned guerrilla warfare to conventional operations and managed to bring their rural tactics into China's largest cities. By deploying siege tactics against Nationalist-held population centers, the CCP slowly gained the upper hand.[2] In this mode of conflict, civilians formed part of the battlefield. Mao's success created a dilemma for the superpowers. Neither Washington nor Moscow had expected to see mainland China in play in the developing East-West rivalry. Nor, for that matter, were American and Soviet leaders seeking to push the developing Cold War into East Asia. Rather, both superpowers remained focused on tensions along the borders of their respective spheres of influence in Europe and the Near East. Yet, not for the last time, local leaders in the Third World transformed the dynamics of the Cold War struggle and, in doing so, changed the course of twentieth-century history.

THE GUERRILLA AND THE GENERALISSIMO

In 1934, the Communists had been on the verge of annihilation. China's central government had launched a campaign, spearheaded by General Chiang Kai-shek, chairman of the National government, aimed at crushing the Chinese Soviet Republic in Jiangxi, in southeast China. Chiang's vicious attacks drove the Communists underground, cutting them off from the cities and forcing them to rely on only meager support from peasants in the countryside. Chiang's troops were now moving to encircle and destroy what was left of the CCP. "Within the areas that Chiang controlled," one journalist wrote, "police butchered Communist leaders; families of known Communist leaders were wiped out; students were watched and spied on, and possession of Communist literature was made a crime punishable by death." In October 1934, the remnants of the CCP staged a desperate breakout from Chiang's blockade, beginning what became known, in Communist lore, as the Long March. Some eighty-six thousand men and women embarked on a six-thousand-mile trek that wound through some of southern China's most rugged territory and ended in Yan'an. Hunted by government forces, beaten down by the elements, and suffering from disease and desertion, only one in ten remained by the end of the march one year later. What became one of the greatest strategic retreats in history saved the CCP and propelled a new leader to the head of the party.[3]

Short and stout with a round face that curved up to a receding hairline, Mao cultivated an air of peasant simplicity. Born into the family of a wealthy Hunanese farmer in 1893, the young Mao had watched the rise of Chinese nationalism and the Revolution of 1911, which overthrew the Qing dynasty. Radicalized in his youth, he helped establish the Changsha branch of the CCP in the early 1920s. For the next five years, the Communists worked alongside the ruling Guomindang Party (GMD) under the leadership of Sun Yat-sen. Chiang, Sun's successor, broke the alliance, however, launching a savage assault on CCP units in Shanghai in 1927 that marked the beginning of the Chinese Civil War. Mao joined his comrades in the Jiangxi Soviet, where he became the most vocal advocate for the use of guerrilla operations against government troops. Party leaders overruled him, however, choosing instead a strategy of frontal confrontation. When that policy failed and the remnants of the CCP were forced to flee in 1934, Mao stood ready to assume command. By the end of the Long March, his leadership was unchallenged. Casting himself as a tireless man of the people, Mao sought to serve as a bridge between China's Confucian past and, he hoped, its Communist future.

In his new headquarters in Yan'an, Mao transformed the remains of the CCP into a cohesive movement with a clear political ideology and leadership structure. He codified party doctrine and consolidated personal control. In a series of lectures held in 1936, he outlined his strategy of revolutionary war, which called for a modification of the Soviet example. "China's revolutionary war," he explained, "is waged in the specific environment of China and so has its own specific circumstances and nature. . . . Although we must value Soviet experience . . . we must value even more the experience of China's revolutionary war, because there are many factors specific to the Chinese revolution and the Chinese Red Army." Likewise, the CCP would not be Moscow's puppet: China and Russia would work together only when their interests coincided. Mao was in the process of breaking with Stalinist orthodoxy, molding the CCP into an autonomous movement that would tailor Communist doctrine to suit the needs of the Chinese Revolution.[4] Yet he would not be the only contender for control of China.

As the winter chill fell over China in late 1946, a second leader laid plans for the nation. At sixty years old, Chiang Kai-shek could count himself among the victors in the largest conflict in human history. Eight years of brutal warfare with Japan had torn through large sections of the country. Japan had occupied parts of China since the 1931 invasion of Manchuria, and the Second Sino-Japanese War

(1937–1945) had left between fifteen and twenty million dead. Over half the nation's industry lay in ruins, along with two-thirds of its shipping and almost all its rail lines. Still, the Generalissimo (as the Western media called Chiang) had every reason to expect a brighter future. In contrast to Mao's proletarian image, Chiang projected an air of aristocratic elegance. A decorated soldier, he maintained a carefully manicured mustache and posed for portraits in a crisp dress uniform festooned with medals. Crucially, he enjoyed strong support among influential political and business leaders in the United States. Leading the GMD government from his wartime capital in the city of Chongqing, he appeared the very picture of a reliable Western ally.[5]

Yet not everyone was so enamored with the Generalissimo. His American military advisor, Joseph Stilwell, judged Chiang to be little more than an ignorant dictator. He seemed to have "no intention of doing a thing or else he is utterly ignorant of what it means to get ready for a fight with a first class power." As Chiang's biographer explained, the American general saw the Generalissimo as having "no values; no skills in government or generalship; no real interest in modernization and welfare of China except to the extent it increased his power; no human qualities worth noting such as patriotism, bravery, loyalty, or a sense of duty and honor; and no valid intellectual or cultural interests." For his part, Chiang found Stilwell—a man whose nickname, Vinegar Joe, said much about his personality—abrasive; it was hardly an auspicious alliance at the interpersonal level.[6]

Nevertheless, most observers assumed that Chiang would lead China in the postwar world. As for the Communists, they appeared, in historian John Lewis Gaddis's words, to be "little more than an obscure group of revolutionaries who engaged in long marches, lived in caves, and lectured one another on their own peculiar understanding of Marxist-Leninism."[7] Yet the war with Japan dramatically changed the playing field in the Chinese Civil War. Both the CCP and the GMD had fought against the Japanese occupation, but the Communists were able to make the most of the situation. Chiang's decision to retreat from the coastal regions into the southwest and establish a new headquarters in Chongqing gave the impression that the regime was biding its time for the Allied powers to defeat Japan. Communist leaders pushed this narrative in a bid to discredit the GMD while simultaneously exaggerating the impact of their guerrilla operations against the Japanese. Likewise, the Japanese occupation highlighted Chiang's inability to liberate China at the same time that it created room for Mao's forces to amass greater power. As Chiang's strength slowly bled out over the course of the Japanese occupation, Mao seized the opportunity to become a potent challenger to the GMD.[8]

As the Nationalists retreated in the face of Japanese conquest, Communist cadres infiltrated towns and cities throughout Northeast China. Inside the zones controlled by the Japanese, the Communists created political organizations and laid plans to launch a more extensive campaign of resistance. Convinced that the CCP was the greater threat to his regime, Chiang stationed his best forces around Yan'an in an attempt to block the rising power of the Communists, a fact that irritated Stilwell. "For me," Chiang explained, "the big problem is not Japan, but the unification of my country." The United States would eventually defeat Japan, but if Mao and the CCP were able to take control, "we run the risk—and so do you Americans—of winning for nothing. . . . Behind Mao there is the religion of Communism—and in consequence, Russia." Indeed, when the Japanese surrendered in September 1945, Mao's forces, which had grown to approximately nine hundred thousand troops, controlled nearly four hundred thousand square miles of territory (10 percent of the country) inhabited by some one hundred million people.[9]

AFTER THE ATOMIC BOMBING OF HIROSHIMA AND NAGA-saki convinced the Japanese to surrender, Chiang's regime had gained a chance to redeem itself, reassert control over lost territory, and purge its ranks of officials who had collaborated with the occupation.

Chongqing failed in all these tasks. At the close of the war, the GMD regime controlled only about 15 percent of the nation. Nationalist troops increased this number to 80 percent by the end of the following year, but the reestablishment of centralized political authority was accompanied by rampant corruption. GMD officials rushed back into China's cities eager to line their pockets at the expense of the newly liberated populations. Public resentment over this perceived exploitation swelled in the months following the end of the war. Making matters worse was the failure of the Nationalists to identify and punish collaborators. Rather, Chiang and the GMD were more concerned with the threat posed by the Communists; collaborators and even Japanese troops might be considered allies against the CCP. On August 23, 1945, the Nationalist regime issued orders to the Japanese troops who had surrendered but had yet to be evacuated to maintain their positions until they could be disarmed by the GMD; under no circumstances should they surrender to Communist forces. Chiang's government even went so far as to order Japanese troops to recover positions that had been taken by the CCP. If the GMD's behavior during the war undermined its credibility, its actions following the Japanese surrender dealt an even worse blow.[10]

As U.S. secretary of state James Byrnes noted in December 1945, some three hundred thousand Japanese soldiers were still armed and in place because the GMD lacked the forces to reoccupy territory. An immediate Japanese departure, he argued, "would merely mean that the [Communist] revolutionary forces . . . would move in and occupy these areas before the [N]ationalist troops could get there, thus cutting Chiang Kai-Shek's communications with Manchuria and setting the stage for a large-scale civil war." But the presence of Japanese troops gave Moscow an argument to leave its own forces in place. Soviet foreign minister Vyacheslav Molotov "found it very abnormal that four months after the surrender there were still fully armed Japanese troops" in China.[11]

Mao and the CCP leadership saw their opportunity. In the wake of Tokyo's surrender, Communist forces surged forward to take whatever territory they could from the defeated Japanese occupiers as part of a general offensive designed to seize key positions. In the following weeks, more than one hundred clashes were reported between Communist forces and Japanese troops. Meanwhile, the Communist press blasted the GMD for failing to eliminate collaborators and retake Chinese territory from the occupiers. Reporters who reached the capital of the Japanese puppet government in Nanjing at the end of August observed that there was nothing "that indicates its liberation. . . . [Japanese general] Okamura is still enthroned in the Foreign Ministry Building. . . . Japanese sentries are posted everywhere, with orders to maintain peace and protect their compatriots." As Mao and an energized CCP pushed out from Yan'an in a bid to play a central role in postwar China, Chiang and the GMD racked up enemies among the population. The stage was set for the resumption of civil war.[12]

THE COLD WAR MOVES EAST

Yet China's fate would not be decided by indigenous forces alone. In the months following Japan's surrender, the escalating tensions between the Communists and the Nationalists pulled superpower influence into the region. Leaders in both Washington and Moscow saw Chiang's regime as integral to their plans for postwar international security. They expected China, the largest state in Asia, to function alongside the United States, the Soviet Union, and Great Britain as one of the world's four policemen, the principal allies in World War II that would work to maintain peace and stability within their respective spheres of influence in the postwar world. The general outlines of this agreement emerged at the Yalta Conference in February 1945: the United States would recognize Soviet rights and privileges in Asia if Stalin joined the war against Japan and recognized Chiang's position in China. Given the choice between supporting his fellow Communists and securing Russian interests in Asia, Stalin opted for the latter. The CCP greeted news of Moscow's entry into the war with joy, assuming that Soviet forces would now cooperate with the Chinese Communists in the coming battle against the GMD. But the Soviet leader refused to compromise his own interests to aid Marxist revolutionaries in China. "If a civil war were to break out," Stalin warned the CCP, "the Chinese nation would face self-destruction." The signing of a treaty of alliance between Moscow and the GMD on August 14, 1945, made official Stalin's betrayal of his ideological comrades.[13]

Though Stalin's decision shook the CCP, Mao was not taken completely by surprise. This was not the first time that the Kremlin had disappointed the Chinese Communists. Indeed, Stalin's capriciousness had helped convince Mao of the need to develop the CCP as an autonomous entity that placed priority on its own interests. He also recognized the cruel nature of Great Power politics. "Confined by the need to maintain international peace, as well as by the Sino-Soviet treaty," Mao told his comrades, "the Soviet Union is not in a position to act freely to support us." Such a move might touch off a proxy war in China between Moscow and Washington. Rather, Mao insisted that the Communists must adapt to this new situation: the GMD would take control of China's large cities, and Mao would begin negotiations with Chiang. As the CCP's Central Committee stated, "neither the Soviet Union nor the United States favors a civil war in China. . . . The party therefore has to make major concessions." With this in mind, Mao and his advisor Zhou Enlai grudgingly agreed to journey to Chongqing in late August 1945 to begin talks with Chiang and the Nationalists about the possibility of papering over differences and establishing coalition rule over the country.[14]

To all outward appearances, Chiang had triumphed. The Japanese Empire was defeated, and its forces were being driven out of the country; both the United States and the Soviet Union recognized the GMD's authority over the nation; and China was to be one of the four Great Powers in the postwar era. Nationalist military forces were, on paper, vastly superior to those of the Communists, but Chiang faced extensive internal challenges. China had been ravaged by decades of war, and its economy was beset by problems. Chiang presided over a political-economic system badly in need of reform, but the engine of that reform, the GMD regime, was rife with corruption, marked by nepotism, and seemed unable to implement the political and economic programs necessary to put the nation back on course to postwar prosperity and stability.[15]

American officials were well aware of these problems in Chiang's regime. The previous summer, Washington had sent a delegation to Yan'an (the "Dixie Mission") led by State Department officer John Service and Col. David Barrett of the U.S. Army, to investigate the possibility of military cooperation between Washington and the CCP. Service remembered that upon arriving in July 1944, the delegation had been immediately struck by "the difference in attitude in Yenan. [Chiang's government in] Chungking was simply waiting for the end of the war to come. Here up in Yenan—they had nothing, and they were poor as anything, off in the boondocks—the whole atmosphere was just full of confidence and enthusiasm. They were absolutely sure that they were winning." Added to this sense of optimism was the efficiency with which affairs in Yan'an were run. In contrast, the GMD seemed disillusioned, inefficient, and incompetent. "Chungking was discouraging," Service explained, "a gloomy place to be. People were waiting for the end of the war, or they were trying to do as little as possible in prosecuting the war. There was rampant inflation with all the suffering and dissatisfaction, complaining, that that caused."[16]

It was Yan'an, not Chongqing, that seemed to be the most vibrant center of political activity in China. Perhaps even more important, as far as the United States was concerned, was the fact that unlike the GMD, the Communists were fielding a credible armed resistance to the Japanese occupation. While Chongqing appeared to be waiting for Washington to defeat Tokyo, Yan'an had launched a series of successful guerrilla campaigns that interfered with the Japanese operations and forced the occupation to take added security measures. Service recommended that American military support be extended to the Communists as part of a coordinated effort against the Japanese. Moreover, considering that the Japanese had been unable to defeat Mao and the CCP, Service saw no reason to assume that Chiang and the GMD would be more successful in fighting the Communists after the war. "The Communists are certain to play a large, if not dominant, part in China's future," he concluded. "In other words . . . Chiang Kai-shek is not China, and we should not limit ourselves to talking to Chiang Kai-shek."[17]

Still, prevailing opinion in Washington favored the GMD. In early October 1945, a force of fifty thousand American marines landed on the north coast of China to assist the GMD in the takeover of Japanese-occupied territory. American troops established virtual control over Beijing and Tianjin. U.S. forces also provided logistical support for Nationalist troop movements into major cities in Manchuria. But re-establishing central authority would not be easy. In Beijing, American observers reported that while the marines had taken control of the city, the surrounding countryside was still "filled with communists." Moreover, CCP resentment toward the United States, now openly working with the GMD, was building. Meanwhile, Stalin was working to secure Moscow's position in postwar China. Though he still suspected that a Soviet-GMD alliance remained his best bet for securing Moscow's influence in China, he also ordered Soviet forces to turn over captured Japanese weapons to Communist units and began sending Soviet military advisors to the CCP. The commander of the U.S. Army observer group at Yan'an warned that Soviet forces were transferring "large stores of captured Japanese war material, including ammunition and weapons," to the CCP and that "the withdrawal of the Soviet occupational forces [was moving] on a schedule favorable to the Chinese Communist forces[,] thus enabling the latter to make timely and accurate tactical consolidations." Though both superpowers had initially hoped to focus on interests elsewhere and remain aloof from the escalating conflict in China, neither was able to do so. As Mao's biographer noted, "The Cold War, conceived in Europe, was rapidly spreading east."[18]

Watching events from the White House, Harry Truman remained wary of the mounting dangers in China. In a public statement on December 15, 1945, the president explained that he intended to use American power to support the Nationalist government in China, but he urged a political resolution to the ongoing strife in that nation. Above all, he insisted that he did not intend to intervene militarily "to influence the course of any Chinese internal strife."[19] But political negotiations between the GMD and CCP were at an impasse. Both sides believed their positions to be strong, and neither was eager to compromise, particularly on issues of territorial control and the representation of Communist forces in the military. Even as Mao and Chiang negotiated in Chongqing, their preparations for civil war continued. On October 11, 1945, Mao returned to Yan'an, leaving his deputy, Zhou Enlai, to continue the fruitless talks with Chiang.[20]

In an effort to salvage the negotiations, in December 1945, Truman sent Gen. George Marshall, chairman of the Joint Chiefs of Staff during World War II, to Chonqing. Marshall faced a daunting task. Not only did the Communists and the central government appear to be on the brink of civil war, but Marshall was the envoy of an outside power that had clearly aligned itself with the GMD. American marines occupied several major cities in China and were working with Nationalist forces and even some Japanese troops to maintain security over strategically important areas in China.[21] Marshall confronted the added challenge of repairing the damage wrought by the abrupt departure of the U.S. ambassador to China, Patrick Hurley, who had just resigned, causing an uproar in the United States. Hurley publicly blamed Communist sympathizers in the State Department for both his departure and the failure of the negotiations in China. Compounding matters, Marshall understood that he had very little leverage over Chiang. Washington had already committed itself to the GMD. The United States simply could not afford to cut off aid to the Nationalists and retain its influence in China. Marshall could plead with Chiang to introduce reforms, but the diplomat carried no sticks with which to compel cooperation.[22]

Both Washington and Moscow had come to view the situation in the Far East through the prism of their respective interests. Neither wanted war, but each reached for geopolitical advantage in the region. A joint committee of the U.S. Departments of War, Navy, and State would conclude in June 1946 that a Communist victory would bring the region into the Soviet economic sphere, giving the USSR "the greatest agglomeration of power in the history of the world," stretching from Central Europe to North Asia. Marshall endeavored to broker a lasting settlement between Mao and Chiang that would have the effect of driving Soviet influence out of Manchuria and pacifying the CCP. While, with one hand, he pushed Chiang to enact political reforms, he used the other to direct military aid to the GMD regime that would allow the Nationalists to reassert control over Manchuria. The Generalissimo chafed under Marshall's pressure. As one of the four great victors of World War II, he expected to be giving the orders rather than receiving them. In contrast, Washington sought a compliant regime in China that would obey its commands. Chiang's resistance to Marshall's reform programs served as an unwanted complication. But in the face of the Communist threat, there was little Chiang could do.[23]

MANCHURIA

Henry Lieberman arrived in Chifeng in the final, frigid days of January 1946. The thirty-one-year-old St. Louis native was among the first Western journalists admitted to Soviet-occupied territory in northern China. Lieberman had joined the Office of War Information in 1942 and been stationed in China. After Japan's surrender in 1945, he took a job with the *New York Times*, where he would spend the rest of his career. Now, standing face-to-face with Soviet soldiers amid Chifeng's weather-beaten mud huts, Lieberman found the Russians cordial. The burly blond soldiers wore sheepskin coats, wool-trimmed hats, and felt boots to guard against the frosty air. They carried submachine guns but "smiled easily" for photographs and puffed on American cigarettes. Although relations between Moscow and Washington had grown increasingly tense in the months since the end of the war, Lieberman found palpable warmth amid the winter cold.[24]

Lieberman had stepped onto the front lines of what was to be the first great battle of the Cold War, the ancient imperial frontier of Manchuria. To the north lay Siberia and the Soviet Union; Mongolia stretched out to the west; Korea and the Yellow Sea lay to the south. Known for its hot, humid summers and cold, subarctic winters, the region was a strategic crossroads in East Asia. In all, Manchuria represented five hundred thousand square miles of territory and was home to no fewer than forty-five million people along with 70 percent of China's heavy industry. Manchuria's mills smelted millions of tons of steel and pig iron each year while its factories churned out machinery, automobiles, and aircraft. The region's soil contained large mineral deposits, and its irrigated river valleys produced bountiful quantities of wheat, millet, rice, and soybeans. While Manchuria's interior was crisscrossed by navigable rivers teeming with fish, its coastline was scattered with deep harbors and key ports linking the region with the wider Pacific world. These highlands served as a natural defense for the region over the centuries and a formidable barrier for armies invading from the south and west. By the early decades of the twentieth century, a network of railways connected the region's major cities, Shenyang, Siping, Changchun, and Harbin, helping make Manchuria an important center for industrial production.[25]

Manchuria sat at the juncture of Siberia and China, Russia and the Far East. Native Manchurians, who made up 80 percent of the population, tended to be taller than other Chinese, with long, oval faces and ruddy complexions. The region was also home to one million

Mongols, many of whom still lived a nomadic, tribal existence. Seven hundred fifty thousand Japanese also lived in Manchuria, along with two million Koreans brought in to grow rice under the Japanese occupation. Another twenty-five thousand Cossacks lived in the White Russian colony in Harbin. In the hot summers, most Manchurians tilled the rich soil using methods not much different from those of their ancestors. In the frigid winters, peasants searched for other means of work. Sanitation remained poor through much of the countryside. Venereal disease was rampant. Nine out of ten Manchurians were illiterate. Japan's imperial armies had seized the region in 1931, creating the puppet state of Manchukuo. With the collapse of the Japanese Empire fourteen years later, Manchuria was set to become the battleground that would decide China's fate in the postwar world.[26]

The Generalissimo understood the importance of Manchuria and had every intention of taking it back from the Communists. Convinced that Stalin was aiding the CCP, Chiang was growing increasingly frustrated that the rest of the world appeared oblivious to the rising threat of the Communists. Making matters worse, Chiang suspected General Marshall of favoring appeasement of the USSR over the defense of China. Caught between the two superpowers, Chiang made preparations for the reconquest of Manchuria as soon as the international situation presented an opening. Indeed, the battle for Northeast China was already under way, with Soviet forces providing limited aid to the CCP while sporadic fighting continued despite Marshall's negotiations. Finally, in February 1946, Chiang's government formally requested a Soviet withdrawal from Manchuria. Soviet officials stalled for nearly three weeks, buying time for Communist forces to prepare to seize their about-to-be evacuated positions. By the time the Soviets departed, Communist troops were camped outside major cities, poised to assume control over much of the region. Chiang was not willing to wait any longer: in March, he ordered his commanders to advance into Manchuria and push the Communists back. On March 13, in the first major battle of the struggle for Northeast China, Nationalist troops drove Communist troops away from Shenyang, capturing the city one day after the Soviet evacuation.[27]

Mao had hoped that the Marshall negotiations might provide an avenue for the CCP to survive and, over time, increase its influence in the regime. But the GMD's assault forced the Communist leader's hand. In late March, the Communists outlined their new strategy: "Our party's policy is to go all out to control Changchun and Harbin, and the entire Changchun Railroad. We should prevent Chiang's troops from advancing there at any price." Mao ordered Lin Biao, commander of the Communist Northeastern Military District, to counterattack. A decorated field commander, Lin was the son of a merchant from Hubei Province of central China and a 1926 graduate of the prestigious Whampoa Military Academy. Lin had played an important role in the resistance against Chiang's encirclement campaigns of the 1930s, and then was a key leader in the Long March that brought the CCP to Yan'an. His distinguished military record continued through the war with Japan with a celebrated victory at the Battle of Pingxingguan Pass in 1937. In 1945, after the Japanese surrender, Lin moved to Manchuria to assemble the Northeast Democratic Alliance Army and prepare for the coming war with the GMD. A young man still in his late thirties, Lin was, according to an American journalist, "slight, oval-faced, dark, handsome." Efficient and business-like, he was a fiercely loyal member of Mao's inner circle and a strong advocate of guerrilla operations designed to bleed his enemy over a long, drawn-out campaign.[28]

Lin struck at Changchun and Harbin, taking both cities in April. Changchun and its population of some eight hundred thousand fell on April 18, after a five-day siege that left large portions of the city in ruins. After capturing the rail station on April 16, some twenty thousand People's Liberation Army (PLA) troops (the CCP's military forces), armed with Japanese machine guns, mortars, and grenades, began a block-by-block assault on the government garrison. Desperate street fighting broke out amid bank buildings, police stations, broadcast centers, and City Hall and left thousands dead. An American reporter who witnessed the fall of Changchun called it the "most important prize" yet taken by the CCP in the war.[29] The Communist army, Henry Lieberman observed, "is not rabble but a disciplined, trained, organized, well-officered fighting machine." While commissars ensured a level of ideological dedication among the rank-and-file, young women served as propaganda officers seeking to win the support of the local population. Living on a diet of rice and cabbage, PLA soldiers received a monthly salary of three Manchurian dollars—less than two American cents.[30]

But these initial victories proved misleading. Fighting continued into May, and the larger, better-equipped Nationalist forces began to push the Communists back. However, as Chiang's troops drove deeper into Manchuria, Marshall's patience with the Generalissimo ebbed. Rather than focusing on the ongoing mediation efforts, Chiang traveled to the front to oversee the offensive that he hoped would destroy the CCP's main forces. The government assault on Manchuria further undermined U.S. attempts to act as a mediator and jeopardized the entire process of negotiation. By the time that Marshall was able to establish a cease-fire in early June, the Nationalist regime appeared to have the upper hand. In less than a year, the Japanese had been defeated, Soviet forces had evacuated Chinese territory, Chiang had reemerged as the recognized leader of China, and GMD forces were driving into Manchuria. Although he still had concerns about whether his American allies might compromise GMD interests to seek accommodation with Communists in both Yan'an and Moscow, Chiang had good reason for optimism. In March, Winston Churchill had delivered his "Iron Curtain" speech in Fulton, Missouri, in the midst of deteriorating relations between the United States and the Soviet Union. As the global threat of communism came into focus, Chiang expected Washington to increase its support for the GMD. Accordingly, the Generalissimo stoked the fires of anticommunism by feeding the Americans reports of Soviet arms shipments to the CCP. While Marshall struggled to regain momentum in the negotiations, his mission received another blow: in June, the U.S. Congress voted to continue Lend-Lease aid to the Nationalist regime. Far from a neutral arbiter between the two sides, the United States was acting as Chiang's biggest backer. It was becoming increasingly apparent to all sides that the Marshall Mission was in trouble.[31]

In May 1946, Chiang had moved his capital back to Nanjing, reestablishing the GMD government in the former seat of the Japanese puppet state. With its busy streets packed with noisy traffic and hurried pedestrians, Nanjing appeared as a city resurgent. Few could have predicted that the Generalissimo and his government would flee the city in less than three years. Both the Nationalists and the Communists used the June truce to prepare for what would be an even fiercer round of fighting. The GMD offensive had succeeded in taking the Manchurian capital of Changchun in May and, at the time of the cease-fire, moved into a position to threaten Communist-held Harbin. While the two sides argued at the negotiating table, both Mao and Chiang concluded that their opponent had the weaker hand. The success of the Nationalist offensive in Manchuria seemed to convince Chiang that a military victory against the CCP was within reach. Conversely, Communist commanders concluded that, with the exception of those units that were being strengthened by the Americans, the Nationalist forces were in poor shape. The numerically superior Nationalist forces succeeded in pushing the Communists back, but a disordered command structure and low morale among the troops hinted at larger problems. The CCP, for its part, continued launching guerrilla attacks against Chiang's advancing armies as the government offensive continued.[32]

Meanwhile, tensions between the CCP and the United States continued to mount. On July 29, 1946, at Anping, Communist forces ambushed a convoy of forty American marines on its way to Beijing.

The guerrillas blocked the road with boulders and farm carts, halting the convoy and then opening fire on it. The marines were pinned down under Communist fire for some time before they were able to counterattack, only to find that the guerrillas had retreated. Villagers from the area then refused to provide the marines with information as to the whereabouts of the Communists. As furious American officials sought explanations from Communist leaders, the attack came to showcase the degree to which the United States had become embroiled in a bloody guerrilla war in a massive Asian country. Indeed, American leaders had no stomach for such a course of action so soon after the end of World War II. Truman sent signals through Marshall that there were limits to what the United States was willing to do. A "China disunited and torn by civil strife could not be considered realistically as a proper place for American assistance," he would explain. If Chiang was unable to gain control over the situation or reach accommodation with the CCP, he should not expect the United States to intervene on behalf of the Nationalist government. The rape of a female student at Beijing University on Christmas Eve 1946 by an American serviceman fueled resentment against the U.S. presence. Left-wing propaganda and accusations of American imperialism quickly transformed the assault into a major international incident that became yet another indication of the degree to which the U.S. position in China was becoming untenable.[33]

Although few recognized it, the pieces were now in place for China to become a Cold War battlefield. The local struggle between Mao and Chiang that had destabilized one of the Great Powers of the postwar world and now threatened to dramatically expand the borders of the Communist bloc was pulling Washington and Moscow into the Chinese Civil War, a conflict that would soon emerge as a sort of archetype for future conflicts in the Third World. In the coming decades, local Nationalist fighters, backed but not controlled by foreign Communist powers, would rise up against faltering conservative regimes aligned with Western governments across the postcolonial world. Moscow would seek to modulate its support to left-wing rebels so as not to invite direct intervention from the Western powers, while Washington grappled with the challenge of creating viable, pro-Western postcolonial regimes that could withstand the threat of revolution. But first, the force of revolution prepared to transform China.

THE COLD WAR'S FIRST BATTLEFIELD

1946–1949

The winter of 1946–47 proved pivotal to the civil war in China and the broader Cold War. As fighting intensified between Chiang and Mao's forces, Washington and Moscow drifted toward greater involvement. Even as the Cold War took shape in Central Europe, fighting along the eastern reaches of Asia began to transform the superpower confrontation.

Frontline Nationalist soldiers in Manchuria battled the Communists and the bitter cold amid a landscape of frozen brown earth broken by the occasional grove of trees or earthen hut. At the village of Halahai, north of Changchun, troops huddled in an ancient moat and in trenches dug behind barbed wire. Enlisted men wore thick quilted coats, wrapped leggings, and canvas sneakers. Their breath hung in swirling clouds in the frosty air. GMD forces tied cotton blankets lined with dog fur to the hoods of their vehicles in an attempt to keep the motors from freezing. The fighting, one commander told American reporter Henry Lieberman, was "hit and run": "We are having a difficult time holding them off. They have the initiative of attack. . . . They travel light, strike across country, and often come at night. They never try to stand up to us, but retire swiftly and content themselves mainly with railway and other demolitions."[1]

It was a difficult type of war to describe. As Lieberman explained, "There are hundreds of thousands of troops in the field but no large-scale battles, and it is virtually impossible to draw lines on a military map." While government troops garrisoned major cities, patrolled roads, and defended rail lines, Communist guerrillas stole through the countryside. From hidden bases, they launched raids against ramshackle government fortifications before retreating into the hinterland.[2]

With the Marshall Mission's failure, Chiang and Mao prepared for all-out war. Mao's forces now had the chance to test his theories of guerrilla revolution on a massive scale in the world's most populous nation. The trickle of arms and support from Moscow had slowly increased while, at the same time, it appeared that Washington was unwilling to intervene in force on the Guomindang's side. Likewise, Marshall's inability to achieve a diplomatic solution hinted at the limits of American power in Asia. The United States might have had the world's largest economy and a monopoly on atomic weapons, but its leaders could do little to change realities on the ground in China. As Mao and his commanders began racking up victories, they presented the superpowers with a fait accompli: whether Washington and Moscow liked it or not, the Cold War had entered the Third World. The time had come to choose sides.

THE FIRST STAGE: DEFENSIVE OPERATIONS AND GUERRILLA WAR

In the closing days of 1946, few signs of the war were apparent in the metropolises in the GMD-controlled areas south of the Great Wall. The American community in Beijing celebrated the Christmas holiday, one American journalist wrote, beneath the "clear, cold skies of winter in North China." Streetcarts stacked with food steamed in the frigid air as shoppers shuffled past the windows of stores packed with wares. As expatriates celebrated inside the city, Communist forces used the cover of a thick snowstorm to attack a garrison at the town of Luchungstun, five miles north of the Beijing defensive perimeter. In Shanghai, a city of four million, pedestrians battled with swarms of street vendors, rickshaws, and money changers on the crowded sidewalks. Neon signs fed by intermittent currents of electricity lit the entrances of cabarets filled with Russian dancers. Smugglers ran a lucrative trade while the black market continued to thrive amid the chaotic financial scene.[3]

For the time being, Chiang still appeared to have the upper hand. The Nationalists fielded greater numbers of men and more firepower than their CCP counterparts and used both to crushing effect against Communist-controlled cities. Chiang's strategy aimed at retaking Manchuria's major cities and establishing control over the region's rail lines. The surrounding countryside could be dealt with later. Recognizing that he was outgunned, Mao ordered his troops to retreat, abandoning all the major cities in Manchuria except for Harbin. As the Communists melted away before the GMD advance, Chiang and his commanders predicted a quick victory. In reality, Mao had concluded that his armies must assume a defensive posture in this first stage of the war. The Communists sought to avoid pitched battles, choosing to confront government troops only when they were assured of enveloping and destroying the forces they encountered. Mao insisted that his commanders must only engage government forces when the Communists enjoyed overwhelming superiority and were able to annihilate entire units. "When we wipe out one regiment," he explained, "[the enemy] will have one regiment less. When we wipe out one brigade, he will have one brigade less. . . . Using this method we shall win. Acting counter to it we shall lose." Government troops who surrendered, furthermore, were incorporated into the Communist armies. Following this strategy, the Communists would destroy some fifty Nationalist brigades in early 1947. In lieu of a set-piece battle with Chiang's forces (which he knew he would lose), Mao pursued a punishing strategy of attrition. These tactics of envelopment, isolation, and annihilation were designed to create massive casualties and sap the enemy's will to fight. They would prove brutally effective.[4] U.S. officials noted that Mao's forces enjoyed a number of advantages: "[T]hey have had long experience in guerilla warfare and have almost unlimited room in which to maneuver. Consequently, while they cannot risk a decisive engagement with the National Govt forces, the latter have never been able to fix the former into position and administer an annihilating blow."[5]

Indeed, late 1946 marked the high tide of Nationalist power in Manchuria. Despite its victories on paper, the GMD was unable to dislodge the CCP from Northeast China. All the while, Chiang's army was forced to maintain a costly occupation of Manchurian cities under increasingly complacent commanders who avoided risky operations. Rank-and-file soldiers fell into the "fleshpots of the cities" while their officers speculated on the local commodity markets. Communist cadres, meanwhile, continued a guerrilla campaign and propaganda operations that targeted government forces. Any illusions that the government had control of the situation were shattered in the first half of 1947 when Communist general Lin Biao launched a series of five offensives across the Songhua River. Lin's goals were to present a credible challenge to the government presence in Manchuria and to capture Nationalist weapons and supplies. With 400,000 troops, Lin struck at government-held territory, capturing dozens of towns before laying siege to the city of Siping. There, GMD forces halted the Communist offensive, inflicting some 40,000 casualties, but the campaign had accomplished its strategic objectives. The Communists claimed to have seized large stores of government arms and supplies, annihilated some 82,000 government troops, and liberated nearly half of Nationalist-held Manchuria along with the 10 million people who lived in it. Most important, wrote historian Steven Levine, the campaign "demonstrated that the strategic initiative [in Manchuria] now lay with the" Communists.[6]

As the slaughter in Manchuria intensified, the Marshall Mission teetered on the brink of collapse. The American diplomat was exasperated with what he viewed as Chiang's insistence on seeking military victory against the CCP and his refusal to enact political and economic reforms in his own regime. Marshall was convinced, first, that the Communists could not be defeated through military force and, second, that corruption and political rot were eating away at the GMD regime from within. Chiang had decided, Marshall complained in a message to President Truman, "in the midst of a deplorable currency and financial situation, [to use his] capital resources for the conduct of the present fighting" against the CCP.[7] Chiang's campaign in Manchuria was threatening to bankrupt his government. Marshall warned the Generalissimo that hostilities in Manchuria would quickly spread to the rest of the country, opening the door to Soviet-backed Communist subversion throughout China. The Nationalist regime, Marshall explained in August 1946, "had little, if any, prospect of gain by pursuing hostilities at the present time and a very definite prospect of a great loss with the possible collapse of the government and the almost certain collapse of its economy." The Manchurian campaign would draw the GMD into a prolonged war with an experienced guerrilla army and stretch Nationalist lines of supply and communication over untenable distances. Marshall insisted that a military confrontation with the CCP under these circumstances was "ruinous." The only other option was for Chiang to "swallow the Communist Party—which was too large and powerful to ignore."[8]

Ultimately, Marshall worried that American aid served to encourage Chiang's disastrous course of action and discourage the leader from making necessary political changes. The regime was still marked by corruption and inefficiency. Ambassador John Leighton Stuart noted:

Perhaps the most serious feature is what is usually spoken of as the widespread corruption and inefficiency of the Government. This is even worse than the references in print which have come to my notice. It includes misrule, exploitation, graft, favoritism, incompetence and callous indifference to the welfare of the masses. There is also much ruthless and irresponsible repression, savoring strongly of fascist methods, and inspiring fear and resentment quite generally among intellectuals. The great majority of those in positions of authority are military rather than civilian officials.[9]

A CIVILIAN ADVISOR, COLUMBIA UNIVERSITY'S NATHANiel Peffer, warned the U.S. ambassador to China that "the United States is causing civil war, since without U.S. assistance, the Government could not continue its military operations." Continued aid to the GMD, he argued, was the equivalent of "[p]umping blood into a corpse."[10] Worse still, the continued American presence in China might provoke Stalin to increase Soviet influence in the region, risking a superpower proxy war in East Asia. For all these reasons, Marshall concluded that U.S. involvement in China should be reduced. This view was not universal in the U.S. government, however. Secretary of the Navy James Forrestal disagreed with Marshall's assessment, insisting that Moscow still had designs on the region. The U.S. Army concurred, predicting that an American withdrawal would allow the region and its industrial potential to fall under the influence of the USSR. "The United States and the world might then be faced . . . with a Soviet power analogous to that of the Japanese in 1941, but with the difference that the Soviets could be perhaps overwhelmingly strong in Europe and the Middle East as well." Meanwhile, State Department officials echoed Marshall's assessment. If American aid could be used as a lever to induce Chiang to reform his government, the risk of pushing the CCP into Stalin's arms would diminish. What was needed in China, they argued, was not a military approach, which risked provoking Soviet intervention and was not likely to work, in any case, but a flexible political program that would address the roots of the CCP-GMD dispute.[11]

Yet Chiang rejected this advice. Relations between Marshall and the Generalissimo continued to deteriorate as the Nationalist offensive dragged into autumn. Marshall remained focused on brokering a political settlement and was deeply skeptical of the idea that the GMD could defeat the CCP with military force. Conversely, Chiang was bolstered by a string of Nationalist victories in Manchuria and adamant that Mao and the Communists would never accept a political settlement that left the GMD in control. In early October, a furious Marshall threatened to return to the United States as Chiang continued his campaign in the north. The Generalissimo received further encouragement in November, when midterm elections in the United States returned control of Congress to the Republican Party, which the Generalissimo expected to be more sympathetic to his Nationalist government. Marshall continued to press Chiang for reforms, however, warning that the GMD could not expect Washington to continue "to pour money into the vacuum being created by the military leaders in their determination to settle matters by force." The Nationalists would bankrupt themselves long before they defeated the Communists, he warned the stubborn Generalissimo. Chiang shrugged off the warning, however, insisting that military force was the only solution to the struggle with the CCP. On January 7, 1947, the White House announced that General Marshall would be returning to the United States. Diplomacy had failed.[12]

Immediately following his departure, Marshall (who would become secretary of state on January 21, 1947) published a statement insisting that the "greatest obstacle to peace has been the complete, almost overwhelming suspicion with which [the CCP and GMD] regard each other." While each party contained honorable members with genuine interest in China's future, both were overrun with extremists. "On the side of the National Government," Marshall said, "which is in effect the Kuomintang, there is a dominant group of reactionaries who have been opposed, in my opinion, to almost every effort I have made to influence the formation of a genuine coalition government." The Communists, for their part, had undermined negotiations through the dissemination of "vicious" propaganda that, beyond being entirely false, held "a determined purpose to mislead the Chinese people and the world and to arouse a bitter hatred of the Americans." Both sides had refused to make genuine political concessions. The GMD, intent on "their own feudal control of China" and dominated by the military, was utterly resistant to reform and seemingly convinced that American aid would continue "regardless of their actions." On the other hand, the Communists were now "counting on an economic collapse to bring about the fall of the Government, accelerated by extensive guerilla action . . . regardless of the cost in suffering to the Chinese people." The government's only hope for salvation, Marshall concluded, lay in the adoption of political reforms and the shift away from one-party rule. Marshall's condemnation of both sides hinted at the hopelessness of the situation in China and the general's doubt as to whether any amount of American support could influence the ultimate outcome.[13]

The final collapse of Marshall's negotiations came as no surprise to Communist leaders. Responding to Marshall's statement on January 10, Zhou Enlai delivered an address on Yan'an radio, explaining that the American diplomat "admitted that there is a reactionary group in the Kuomintang which constitutes a dominant one in the Kuomintang government. . . . They oppose a coalition government, have no confidence in internal cooperation, but believe in the settlement of problems by armed force." Zhou added, however, that it was Chiang himself who sat at the head of this reactionary clique and was intent on waging full-scale war against his challengers from the CCP. Meanwhile, the CCP's information chief, Lu Ting-yi, published a memorandum in Yan'an's *Emancipation Daily* laying out the Communist view of the postwar international system. Citing Mao, Lu explained that the great war against fascism (World War II) had been won, but he pointed to a coming clash between the democratic, antifascist peoples of the world and the antidemocratic forces and remnants of fascism. While the USSR fought on the side of the democratic forces, "the American imperialists took the place of the Fascist Germany, Italy and Japan [following World War II] becoming a fortress of the world reactionary forces." Allied with China's Chiang Kai-shek, Britain's Winston Churchill, and France's Charles de Gaulle, the United States was intent on "enslaving the American people and [seeking] world domination." The democratic forces of the world should take heart, however, as the "international position of the most progressive nation in the world, the U.S.S.R. has greatly improved." "It can be categorically predicted," Lu concluded, "that within three to five years at the most, the face of China and the world will be completely changed."[14]

On the global stage, it was clear that the wartime alliance between the United States and the Soviet Union had come unraveled. An atmosphere of mutual suspicion now pervaded superpower relations as diplomats such as George Kennan and Soviet ambassador to the United States Nikolai Novikov warned of a coming rivalry between Washington and Moscow. In light of the emerging Cold War, the struggle for China took on a new importance. If Truman's containment strategy was to be a global doctrine, the China theater would be critical. The soon-to-be-created Central Intelligence Agency (CIA) would warn that Soviet moves in China were in keeping with their larger strategy of extending "control and influence . . . wherever and whenever possible by all means short of war, and [reducing] the control and influence of other major powers." Chinese victories in Manchuria brought resources, industries, and a "vital strategic link with Korea" into the Soviet orbit. The CCP represented "the most effective instrument of Soviet policy toward China." As long as the civil war continued, the CCP would remain aligned with Moscow. Therefore, ongoing civil war and instability ultimately favored Soviet policy in East Asia.[15] Stalin and his comrades in Moscow had indeed come to recognize the potential importance of the CCP. In June, Stalin, writing under the pseudonym "Fyodor Kuznetsov" (a former Red Army commander), had written to the Kremlin's agent in Yan'an with instructions to arrange a meeting with Mao. Stalin offered to send a plane to Harbin to bring the Chinese leader to Moscow.[16]

All but the most hopeful parties now recognized that diplomacy had failed; the struggle for China would be settled on the battlefield. In Manchuria, Lin Biao's army continued its campaign against the GMD, and even Chiang was becoming aware of the dangers of a protracted war against the Communists. Eager to deal a decisive blow to his adversaries, the Generalissimo signed off on a plan to attack the Communist capital itself at Yan'an. In March 1947, Gen. Hu Zongnan was given 150,000 men and 75 aircraft and charged with taking the enemy capital. By March 16, government troops were close enough to observe the panic in the city through binoculars. With the GMD army closing in, the CCP was forced to abandon its capital. On May 19, Hu took the city along with 10,000 prisoners. Back in Nanjing, Chiang celebrated the news, predicting that the fall of Yan'an signaled the beginning of the end of the war with the Communists. In fact, the apparent defeat of the CCP was far from decisive. General Hu's personal secretary, a Communist spy, had informed the CCP of the government offensive, giving Mao time to prepare. Although he was reluctant to abandon Yan'an, Mao refused to divert forces from the campaign in northern China to defend it. As Chiang and Hu finalized their preparations for the attack, the Communists began their evacuation. The party leadership retreated from Yan'an, moving to the north and east and regrouping in the village of Zaolin'gou, in Shaanxi. With Hu in pursuit of the Communist leadership, Mao launched a counteroffensive consisting of guerrilla attacks, ambushes, and strategic retreats designed to isolate and destroy sections of the Nationalist army. As an American reporter wrote, "Yanan was worse than worthless to the [GMD]. It sucked one of their crack army groups into a desolate, semidesert country where there were no rations, ammunition, or supplies to replenish their stocks, and where the people were bitterly hostile." This cat-and-mouse game pulled GMD forces deeper into Communist-controlled territory and served as a further drain on government resources.[17]

Indeed, Chiang's triumph in capturing Yan'an proved to be a Pyrrhic victory. Even as the government hurled its best troops at the abandoned CCP capital, the Communists continued their defense of Manchuria, which was developing into a "strategic trap" for government troops as Chiang poured divisions into the region. Communist forces staged a series of feints that drew the Nationalist armies deeper into Manchuria, stretching out tenuous lines of supply and draining Nanjing's reserves. Relying on guerrilla tactics and spurning large engagements, Communist commanders followed a strategy designed to bleed the numerically superior government forces slowly through attrition. "The capture of the town of Houma," noted a French observer, "cost the Reds two hundred killed and wounded, but brought them eighteen hundred prisoners, including a brigadier general. The capture of the town of Sinkiang cost them four wounded, and they took six hundred prisoners from the seven hundred militia who tried to defend the place. The capture of Kuwo, defended by two Nationalist regiments and attacked by three Red regiments, yielded the Communists two thousand prisoners—the entire garrison."

While the Communists enjoyed high morale and were able to launch coordinated, well-executed attacks, the "lack of fighting spirit shown by the common [government] soldier demonstrates the degree to which the Nationalist army has disintegrated." Thereafter, the prisoners that the Communists took were given "indoctrination and political instruction" and incorporated, along with captured weapons, into the CCP armies. As a result, the ongoing attacks against government forces in North China became "paying propositions" for the Communists. Mao's strategy was working, depleting the Nationalist armies and increasing the numerical and material strength of CCP forces.[18]

THE SECOND STAGE: LIMITED COUNTEROFFENSIVE

By mid-1947, Mao and his generals were ready to abandon the defensive stage of the war, which had relied on strategic retreat and guerrilla operations, and to launch a new phase of limited offensives in the struggle against the GMD. That summer, Mao sent his general Liu Bocheng to stage an offensive against Nationalist forces in the Central Plains, a region stretching from Hebai, across the Yellow River, to the ocean at Shandong. In the spring of 1947, the GMD, working with American engineers, had redirected the flow of the Yellow River into a new bed, flooding some five hundred villages and forcing over one hundred thousand people to relocate. While the diversion of the river was a technical success, it multiplied the hardships of the already suffering population, sowing the seeds for widespread unrest. Communist forces discovered just how soft GMD positions were in the area during a series of attacks in the spring that led Mao to decide that the Central Plains represented the "underbelly" of the government's position. Liu's army would cross the river with the objective of surprising government forces and inflicting as many casualties as possible. After the crossing, Communist forces found a peasantry that was eager to support the assault against the GMD. With the help of thousands of locals, Liu's troops cut into Chiang's Second and Fourth Armies, killing nearly eighty thousand. As panic swept through the Nationalist forces, Liu's troops continued their assault, turning the Central Plains into a bloodbath before staging a retreat in which they were forced to abandon many of their heavy weapons. Nevertheless, in late July, Mao heralded the campaign as the turning point of the war and announced that Chiang would be defeated in the space of five years.[19]

Meanwhile, in Manchuria, Lin Biao launched two major offensives against the Nationalist-controlled cities of Changchun, Kirin, and Shenyang. Lin's strategy aimed at isolating the cities and cutting off the GMD garrisons. After conducting sustained sabotage operations against the railway that connected Beijing and Shenyang, which served as the lifeline for Nationalist troops in much of Northeast China, Lin's troops captured the line, severing the GMD's supply chain in September. Communist armies continued their offensive through October, surrounding Changchun, Kirin, and Shenyang and besieging the government forces within. The Nationalists were able to reestablish a supply route to Shenyang and Kirin, but Communist generals now held the initiative. As 1947 came to an end, the CCP's growth, coupled with and fed by the attrition of the GMD's armies, was fast erasing the government's numerical and material advantages. On the heels of these successful campaigns in Manchuria and the Central Plains, the Communists stood poised to stage a new round of offensives against the GMD regime. Some U.S. officials still held out hope, however, even if it meant downplaying the threat. "[F]rom [a] purely military viewpoint at least," the vice consul at Changchun reported, Mao's forces were "still essentially guerrillas."[20]

Even as the military tide began to turn through the second half of 1947, the GMD regime found itself beset by deteriorating economic conditions. Since the end of World War II, Chiang's government had been battling a mounting economic crisis. The GMD badly mismanaged the transition from the economic situation during World War II, in which much of the country sat under Japanese occupation and the control of puppet businesses, to the post-1945 system. Shortages in currency prompted Chiang's government to begin printing more money, which touched off a dramatic rise in inflation. By early 1947, wholesale prices in Shanghai had risen thirtyfold. Further, unemployment was on the rise throughout the country. This dangerous economic situation, in turn, generated labor unrest in the form of more than 1,700 strikes in 1946 alone. The presence of Communist infiltrators in many labor organizations exacerbated the GMD's problems. Chiang's determination to continue his military campaigns in

Manchuria sapped GMD resources and shifted the regime's attention away from addressing its worsening economic situation at home.[21]

In late 1947, American and GMD leaders confronted a series of setbacks that had taken place over the previous year. Communist forces had taken the offensive in Manchuria, and government control of the key cities of Changchun, Kirin, and Shenyang was in jeopardy. Ambassador Stuart warned that CCP divisions appeared to be in a position to "take either [Changchun or Kirin] at will." The Communists threatened to cut off Shenyang and Changchun, leaving the garrisons there with no more than six months of supplies. The civilian population of Shenyang had a month's supply of food, by the most optimistic estimates: reports of starvation among the population had already started to surface. American diplomats and GMD commanders concluded that the most recent Communist offensive had been a complete success. The CCP had cut strategic communications and transportation links between Shenyang, Changchun, and Kirin and seized government supplies. Government commanders concluded that the "Communists have permanently established themselves" south of the Songhua River and were now gearing up for a seventh offensive. The GMD admitted to some twenty-eight thousand casualties in the latest offensive, but American observers warned that this was a low estimate. At the same time, supply shortages undermined the effectiveness of government troops that remained in Manchuria. The CCP was in a strategically stronger position heading into 1948, having consolidated control over 95 percent of Northeast China.[22]

In mid-December, Lin Biao sent his troops across the frozen Sungari River to attack Chiang's Fifth Army south of Shenyang. Hampered by a shortage of supplies and ammunition, government forces were pushed to the breaking point. On Christmas Day 1947, Mao forecast the imminent collapse of Chiang's regime, "America's running dog," and announced that the strength of "the world anti-imperialist camp had now surpassed that of the imperialist camp." The Communist leader outlined his strategy of revolution, including a program of agrarian reform that aimed to give China's peasants a stake in the revolution and establish state control over the economy. On the battlefield, Mao called again for a phased struggle that would build strength over time. The revolutionaries must engage government forces only when they are assured of victory, fighting a "war of movement" that used tactical retreats to avoid battles of attrition and aimed to secure weapons and supplies from enemy forces. At the same time, Mao lashed out at "American imperialism" and its support for Chiang's regime and called for solidarity with the forces of global communism. "[A]ll anti-imperialist forces of the various Eastern countries should also unite," Mao insisted, "taking as the objective of their struggle the liberation of the more than 1,000,000,000 oppressed people of the East." Chiang's generals responded with their own announcement that the Manchurian crisis was now over, ignoring the fact that the Nationalists controlled no more than 3 percent of Northeast China.[23]

While CCP and GMD leaders hurled rhetorical attacks at one another, the Communists' Winter Campaign continued. Communist forces had surrounded Changchun and were on the verge of encircling Shenyang, further straining government efforts to supply its garrisons. Nationalist troops in Shenyang braced themselves for a frontal assault as Communist forces fought their way into the western suburbs of the city. The defenders had raised brick-and-concrete pillboxes, created ice redoubts, and set up barbed-wire barricades in preparation for a vicious battle on the city streets. The government garrison was on the brink of being cut off, and the situation, according to military analysts, "was rapidly approaching the hopeless stage."[24]

Meanwhile, civil and labor unrest gripped the country. "The people are losing confidence everywhere," Chiang wrote. The *Far Eastern Economic Review* marveled at the growing support for the CCP. Even businessmen, the magazine noted, "feel now that life under the relatively honest totalitarianism of the Communists could not be worse than it is under the corrupt inefficiency of the Kuomintang." Over

$400 million in promised aid from the United States was approved too late to reverse the tide of the war in Manchuria, and the CCP's military offensive continued. By March 1948, the government controlled less than 1 percent of Manchuria. The government's "military position [is] gravely critical," U.S. ambassador John Leighton Stuart explained, "with general military collapse in [the] north becoming increasingly possible." Kirin and Ssupinkai had fallen; Shenyang and Tsinan were threatened; the losses of Luoyang and Xi'an were likely; Shanxi faced famine. Chiang had virtually no reserves. "In most areas material shortages further weaken Government capabilities. . . . Troop attrition proceeds at rapid rate." New recruits, when available, arrived "virtually untrained." Perhaps worse of all, Stuart warned, the "present Government leadership has apparently no overall plan to organize and commit its few remaining resources in any effective manner." Having lost their faith in an American rescue, a growing number of GMD leaders were coming to see the loss of the civil war as "probably inevitable." In short, the ambassador concluded, the "deterioration of the Government's military position is accelerating and . . . the time when any assistance can be effective is rapidly running out."[25]

Meanwhile, over the winter and spring of 1948, Communist forces continued their offensive, retaking Yan'an in April. The following month, Mao predicted victory by mid-1951. CCP troops enjoyed considerable advantages on the battlefield. In one battle after another, GMD units proved inferior to their Communist counterparts. "Our troops . . . became soft and concerned only with pleasure," one government commander lamented. "[They] lacked combat spirit and there was no willingness to sacrifice." American military officials blamed the incompetence of the officer corps. Moreover, while a brutally efficient counterintelligence operation kept GMD spies out of Communist units, CCP spies were able to penetrate much of the Nationalist leadership. Nationalist morale continued to deteriorate, and the government began forcing men into service. Many conscripts died of disease or starvation before ever reaching their units. Desertion was rampant.[26]

Mao had already begun planning for a new, postrevolutionary China. The previous November, the guerrilla leader sent a message to Moscow asking advice for how to handle opposition parties after the CCP's victory. That it took nearly six months for the Kremlin to reply was perhaps an indication of Stalin's continuing reluctance to commit to the Chinese revolutionaries. Though he applauded Mao's zeal, Stalin encouraged him to allow opposition groups to remain as representatives of the "middle strata of the Chinese population," provided that they opposed the GMD. But Moscow was now moving toward more substantial support for the CCP. In May, Soviet military commanders ordered their officers to begin drawing up a list of supplies needed by the People's Liberation Army. "It is clear," they explained, "that without the extensive material assistance of America, the resistance against those who fight for the real liberation of China would have already been compelled to cease long ago." Moreover, "the success of the Chinese reactionaries would greatly enhance the position of American imperialists in East Asia." Soviet leaders had decided to increase assistance to CCP forces, sending armor, motorized artillery, and Chinese crews trained in the USSR. "To us," the message concluded, "China is an old neighbor, with whom we wish to maintain friendly relations, but to the Americans, it is a base for advancing opposition to the Soviet Union." The time had come to "give to the Chinese people the feeling that after thousands of years of unscrupulous exploitation and slavery, a new era has come to them and their destiny is now at last in their own hands."[27]

Not all those who experienced liberation found cause to rejoice. As the Communist offensive swept into the cities, it took a horrific toll on the civilians caught inside. In May, the PLA began a five-month siege of Changchun designed, in Lin's words, to "[t]urn Changchun into a city of death." The Communist strategy displayed the full brutality of the civil war: aware that Changchun's defenders had only enough food to last through July, Lin blocked civilians from evacuating the city. Lin's troops planned, in the words of two historians, to "starve the city into surrender." Sentries were ordered to turn refugees back into the starving city. By late summer, Lin reported that a "grave famine" had broken out. "The civilian inhabitants are mainly living on tree leaves and grass, many have died of starvation." Refugees who managed to escape the CCP's "starvation blockade" gave macabre descriptions of the situation. Bodies littered the streets of the once-beautiful capital. Trees were torn down and houses pulled apart as survivors scoured the city for any remaining sources of firewood. The going price for a pound of millet had topped fifty dollars. By the time Changchun finally fell in October, the city's population "had dropped from half a million to 170,000." According to one Communist general, these siege tactics were used on other GMD-held cities as well. The war for China had begun to shift from the countryside to the cities.[28]

STAGE THREE: FINAL OFFENSIVE

In the fall of 1948, Mao and his commanders decided that the time had come to launch the third and final stage of their revolutionary war, a full offensive against government forces. This would take the form of two major thrusts, the Liaoshen and Huaihai campaigns. The Liaoshen campaign began in September, when Lin Biao sent some 700,000 troops to attack the approximately 450,000 government troops in the Manchurian cities of Jinzhou, Shenyang, and Changchun. Rail lines to the Nationalist garrisons had been cut off by CCP attacks, and Nanjing was forced to airlift supplies to the nearly half a million government forces inside the three cities. Communist leaders hoped the campaign would deal a decisive blow to Chiang's attempt to retake Manchuria.[29]

Dire reports flowed in from the U.S. consulates in Northeast China. Officers in Beijing warned that the GMD's position in the area was "untenable." Changchun was about to fall. "It is already well past [the] eleventh hour in North China. But if North China stands at this date on [the] brink of disaster it is due in large part to Nanking's consistent selfish suspicious neglect in [the] past."[30] The following day, officers in Shenyang reported "[b]ewilderment and slight hysteria" in the wake of the fall of Jinzhou and Changchun. The population believed that the "end [of] Government tenure [in] China [was] rapidly approaching, if not already in sight."[31] Ambassador Stuart warned that Manchuria was on the brink of falling to the Communists. Government forces lost twenty-six divisions with the fall of Jinzhou and Changchun. "Together with [government] losses suffered south of [the] Great Wall since [the] People's Liberation Army launched its autumn offensive, [GMD] losses to date total 450,000 or almost half [a] million men." The Communists now had almost total command of Manchuria.[32]

The rapid collapse of Chiang's forces in Manchuria convinced Mao and his generals to gamble and extend their offensive in a bid to seize all of China north of the Yangtze River and destroy the Nationalist armies they encountered. The result would be the Huaihai campaign, the largest military operation since the end of World War II. At its height, Huaihai involved nearly two million soldiers spread across a twelve-hundred-mile front line. Much of the fighting would focus on the city of Xuzhou, which Chiang had transformed into a regional headquarters. After the Communist successes in September and October, Xuzhou stood exposed as a salient jutting north into CCP-controlled territory. One American journalist described the city: "We found [Xuzhou], an ugly old market town of rutted roads and dilapidated two-story buildings, overrun with refugees, the hospitals jammed with untended wounded, the airfield crowded with panicky civilians battling each other and attempting to bribe their way into the outgoing transports which had brought in supplies."

The city formed the "pivot" upon which "the fate of Nanking and Shanghai would turn." Mao and his generals chose to send units commanded by Deng Xiaoping south of the city, cutting off the Nationalist line of retreat from Xuzhou. Chiang's commander in Xuzhou recognized this danger and suggested an attack against Deng's smaller force in the south, but the Generalissimo refused, insisting on an assault against the CCP's main forces to the north. By mid-November, Deng's operation was successful: the massive GMD garrison in Xuzhou was isolated. The CCP's news agency announced that the balance of military forces in China had tilted: "The PLA, long superior in quality, has become superior in numbers as well. This is a sign that the victory of the Chinese revolution and the realization of peace in China are at hand." Communist commanders used their troops to encircle and isolate government units. Once they had cut off a body of GMD troops, the Communists launched a wave of poorly trained militiamen against their foes. After this first wave had taken the brunt of the GMD's defensive fire, a second wave of seasoned regular soldiers attacked their lines.[33]

As the fighting drew closer, despair gripped Nanjing. The government's desperate attempts to regain control of the economy by setting price controls sparked massive buying sprees followed by a precipitous drop in purchases. In the space of a month, shopkeepers had gone from hiding their goods to complaining about the lack of customers. Meanwhile, the more affluent citizens of the capital prepared to evacuate to havens in Hong Kong and Shanghai in the likely event of a Communist victory in the war. A second exodus of foreign nationals had created a glut in the housing market. An American correspondent described the mood in Nanjing as "eerie." Power blackouts were commonplace. Policemen with fixed bayonets patrolled the streets, enforcing martial law and a government curfew of 11:00 p.m. Most residents were headed for home by the time the sun began to set at 5:30 p.m. Indeed, the only apparent scenes of activity were the cinemas, which remained crowded with Chinese eager to escape the tumultuous reality that surrounded them.[34]

Government troops in Beijing also braced for a Communist assault. As the sound of mortar fire rumbled in the distance, GMD soldiers prepared defensive lines on the outskirts of the encircled city.

Demolition crews razed shops along the approaches to the city to prevent them from falling into enemy hands. Meanwhile, Nationalist officers stopped groups of refugees outside the city gates to search their ranks for CCP infiltrators. Inside the city walls, life ground to a halt. Along with electricity cutoffs, an 8:00 p.m. curfew cleared the darkened streets. Beijing's grand hotels stood mostly empty, and trolley service had been suspended. Still, residents could be grateful that supplies of food remained plentiful and water still ran through the taps.[35]

In a cable to Stalin written at the end of 1948, a confident Mao reported impressive gains. The CCP commanded some 900,000 soldiers along with 400,000 support personnel in a massive campaign aimed at encircling 33 GMD divisions and taking control of Beijing, Tianjin, and the Tanggu seaport. From there, Communist forces would be in a position to launch a full-scale assault on Chiang's strongholds in the south. Nationalist rule was crumbling, he wrote, as the masses defected to the Communists. Meanwhile, he told Stalin, the "blatantly aggressive policy of the US government has already bankrupted itself." In light of these successes, Mao predicted victory within three and a half years. His assessment would prove too pessimistic.[36] By the end of January 1949, the CCP controlled an area with a population of 210 million people in comparison with the 260 million in GMD-controlled territory. Mao's armies comprised some 2.2 million soldiers—twice as many as the GMD. As he told a Soviet official in January 1949, "the military stage of the Chinese Revolution must be considered complete." Despite reaching the brink of victory in a twenty-year struggle, Mao remained humble—at least when speaking to the Kremlin's representatives. Nevertheless, Soviet officials had come to see the value of the CCP's contributions. "The Chinese Revolution has its own road," they explained, "which gives to it the look of an anti-imperialist revolution." The Chinese Revolution, they concluded, was sure to carry "a theoretical value for the revolutionary movement of the countries of Asia."[37]

Mao now turned his attention to attacking the GMD's Twelfth Army, which was marching north in a bid to reestablish links with the besieged garrison in Xuzhou. CCP forces laid a trap for the Nationalists along the banks of the Huai River and managed to corner the GMD force between the river and the hills to the north and east. GMD commanders now realized the impending danger of their situation and ordered their forces to stage a retreat. Nationalist troops pulled out of the city before dawn on December 1, 1948. On December 15, after fierce fighting, the PLA forced the surrender of the Twelfth Army, eliminating a force of 120,000 Nationalist soldiers. On January 6, 1949, CCP commanders began their final assault on the Xuzhou garrison, forcing the surrender of some 200,000 government troops four days later. The decisive Communist victory in the Huaihai campaign arrived with startling speed. Mao and his commanders were "overjoyed," but they now faced the dual challenge of ruling over the massive territory they had conquered and moving their revolution from its origins in the countryside to its future in the cities.[38]

As news of the defeats in the northeast made its way to Chiang in Nanjing, the Generalissimo came to realize the scale of the disaster he now faced. "Reports of lost battles swirl in like falling snow," he lamented. "North China and the below-the-wall region are on the brink of collapse." Chiang now began to consider two drastic actions: moving his government from Nanjing to Taiwan and tendering his own resignation. There was little standing between Mao's forces and Chiang's capital. The island of Taiwan, some 112 miles off the coast of mainland China, would be Chiang's final fortress. His last resort, politically, would be his resignation. By stepping down, Chiang wrote, he might be able to "shake up the inept party, military, and government machines; break up the stalemate in politics, and be ready to regroup for a new start from zero." The first weeks of 1949 witnessed the growing exodus of Nationalist resources and officials from China's ports. "Government officials, merchants, businessmen, and their families crowded aboard freighters, ferries, tugboats, and any other type of vessel available for the trip across the Taiwan Strait," explained one of Chiang's biographers. "Huge army units with their weapons crowded the docks as well."[39]

Even as Mao's commanders delivered a crushing blow to Chiang's armies with the Huaihai campaign, Lin Biao continued his offensive in the north. The last pocket of Nationalist control to the north of the Yangtze consisted of the great cities of Tianjin and Beijing, held by Gen. Fu Zuoyi and some of the best remaining GMD forces. Both Fu and Lin recognized that, following the crushing government defeat to the south, the fall of the two cities was inevitable. The Communists had no desire to destroy the industrial infrastructure of the two cities, and Fu was reluctant to subject the ancient capital of Beijing to the ravages of battle. Fu therefore began negotiations with the CCP for an honorable surrender. On January 15, 1949, Tianjin fell to Communist forces. Six days later, Fu accepted a "compromise" with Lin that gave Beijing to the Communists virtually untouched. Fu's army was incorporated into the PLA, and the general himself became a CCP commander.[40] In Nanjing, Ambassador Stuart reported that Communist forces could likely take that city in a week, if they chose to do so. The Communists were on the verge of moving south, and it appeared as if nothing could stop them, Stuart explained.[41]

With the Communists in firm control of the North China Plain, Chiang had few cards left to play. He could try to maintain a regime in southern China, using the Yangtze as a line of northern defense; he could retreat to the southwest and stage a resistance against Mao's regime; or he could flee to Taiwan. Although the Generalissimo issued valiant proclamations about his decision to defend Nanjing, the regime's flight to Taiwan was already well under way. Since the end of World War II, the GMD had been consolidating control over the former colony. Beginning in February 1947, in response to anti-GMD riots, Chiang's forces staged a brutal crackdown on Taiwanese protestors, purging the island of thousands of intellectuals and community leaders. By the beginning of 1949, Chiang had transformed the island into his last redoubt. Meanwhile, the mainland had been ravaged by war. Henry Lieberman described a landscape of utter devastation: "Smoking villages, pounded by artillery, with primitive mud-and-thatch houses deserted and fields untilled. The dead uniformed illiterates on the battlefields of Kiangsu, Anhwei and Honan, whose twisted corpses left one wondering whether they knew what they had been fighting for. The wounded, crawling and hobbling back to their lines, lying uncared for in long rows on the cold bare floors of schoolhouses commandeered by the army, or begging in the streets of Tientsin and Shanghai."

After regrouping in the north, the CCP began a series of strained negotiations with Chiang's short-lived presidential successor, Li Zongren. Chiang had resigned the presidency on January 1, 1949. On April 15, the Communists gave Li a list of ultimatums; five days later, he rejected them, and Mao's commanders prepared to resume their drive toward the Nationalist capital.[42]

The greatest remaining obstacle to Communist forces was the Yangtze River, a nearly four-thousand-mile-long waterway that drained one-fifth of China's total landmass. Mao's troops held the northern banks. On the southern banks sat Chiang's capital of Nanjing. On April 20, Mao ordered his armies to cross the river and take the city. Communist troops, wrote an American reporter, "jammed aboard thousands of junks, sampans and motor launches," breached the Yangtze line along a front that was 325 miles long. The nearly 325,000 Nationalist soldiers in the area put up a token resistance, but CCP commanders accomplished the crossing with minimal losses. Western journalists in Nanjing awoke to the sound of gunfire on the morning of April 23. The Nationalist garrison had abandoned Nanjing. The city's northern gates stood open and unguarded as looters swept through the GMD's capital. City policemen stripped off their uniforms and melted into the crowds, sparking chaos on the streets. As local leaders scrambled to restore order until authority could be handed off to the Communists, fires set by retreating Nationalist troops burned in ruined buildings.

Explosions shook the shoreline of the Yangtze as GMD commanders destroyed ammunition and fuel dumps. Meanwhile, the last remaining Nationalist officials scrambled to board planes bound for Shanghai, with valuables, luxury furniture, and even a piano in tow. The U.S. ambassador complained that the "[r]idiculously easy Communist crossing of [the] Yangtze [had been] made possible by defections at key points, disagreements in High Command and [the] failure [of the] airforce [to] give effective support."[43]

The PLA offensive continued, taking Hangzhou on May 3 and closing in on the commercial metropolis of Shanghai. Chiang's commanders in Shanghai announced their intention to turn the city into "a second Stalingrad," digging ditches and erecting a ten-foot-high palisade. Demolition teams leveled a half-mile strip of territory in Shahghai's suburbs containing "some of the finest estates in China," according to an American journalist. The Nationalists, in their effort to create a "Maginot Line" of fortifications, razed pagodas, mansions, greenhouses, bridges, and gardens along with peasant villages. Still, the majority of Nationalist units in the city were more concerned with evacuation than resistance. On May 25, the CCP marched into Shanghai, seizing more than a hundred thousand prisoners. Nationalist defensive positions at police stations and pillboxes put up white flags. As red flashes spread across the night sky—the result of gasoline fires raging at the abandoned airport—workers at the American consulate watched the last skirmishes along the banks of Suzhou Creek. In the roughly four weeks since crossing the Yangtze, the PLA had captured a combined territory larger than the total area of France.[44]

Three weeks later, Mao cabled Stalin to report the military progress of his forces. In three years of fighting, he boasted, the PLA had killed "5 million 590 thousand people." Mao estimated that no more than 500,000 GMD forces remained. "These are insignificant remnants of the Guomindang forces," he wrote. "It will not take too much time to destroy them."[45] CIA officials more or less agreed. A report written in April 1949 warned that Moscow was seeking to bring

China into the Soviet orbit as part of its quest for "world domination." The Kremlin, the report continued, hoped to use "China as an advance base to facilitate Soviet penetration of Southeast Asia . . . the outflanking of India-Pakistan and the strategically important areas of the Middle and Near East; and eventually control of the entire Asiatic continent and Western Pacific."[46]

The Nationalist defenses had collapsed. With government forces fleeing to the southwest and to Chiang's Taiwan base, Mao and the Communists faced four new challenges. The first concerned the task of moving what had been a primarily rural revolution into China's great cities. Mao and his commanders feared that their troops might be corrupted in this new urban environment, facing an array of new, insidious dangers. The CCP leadership also worried that U.S. intervention in the war might be imminent: the crossing of the Yangtze, the fall of Shanghai, and the collapse of GMD power might push American leaders into the fray in a last-ditch effort to "save" China from the Communists. Furthermore, Mao was convinced that he could not simply abandon the southern and western reaches of the country to the remnants of Chiang's regime. Doing so raised the risk of Chiang or other Nationalists creating independent regimes on China's periphery, which would represent a constant threat to Mao's revolution. The hunt for Chiang's forces would not be bloodless, however. In June, a CCP expedition to Shaanxi was nearly annihilated, losing fifteen thousand soldiers. Finally, a final assault on Chiang's fortress of Taiwan (which was compounded by the CCP's failure to take the island of Quemoy in 1949) presented a daunting challenge for Mao and the PLA. Nevertheless, it was clear to even the most ardent of Chiang's supporters that the war was lost. Mao and the CCP had achieved victory.[47]

FROM YAN'AN TO THE WORLD

On October 1, 1949, an audience of one hundred thousand packed into the square before Beijing's Forbidden City to listen to Mao, the victorious guerrilla commander, announce the victory of the Communist revolution. As the afternoon sun streamed down over the crowd, Mao proclaimed, "We, the 475 million Chinese people, have stood up and our future is infinitely bright." The assembled crowd watched as the PLA staged a military parade, with shouts of "Long live Chairman Mao." Later, after night came to the city, fireworks sparkled in the sky in celebration of the birth of a new China. The following day, the Soviet Union recognized the People's Republic of China, and congratulations began to filter in from Communist parties around the world.[48] All told, more than two million people had died in this last phase of the Chinese Civil War after 1945, but the revolution was not yet secure. Mao worried that the PRC represented the weakest front in the Communist world, and the most likely target of Western intervention. Chiang, too, forecast a coming clash between the superpowers. Telling his lieutenants to take heart, the Generalissimo promised that World War III, which was imminent, would liberate China from the grips of the CCP. Both Mao and Chiang, then, recognized that the stakes in the civil war were greater than the political fate of China itself. Indeed, the fate of China was of concern to the entire international system.[49]

Mao's forces had demonstrated that small, well-organized cadres of committed revolutionaries could challenge numerically superior government forces with access to far greater resources. Even so, the CCP's victory was dependent largely on the inefficiency and incompetence of Chiang's regime, but the message to aspiring revolutionaries around the world seemed clear: the tides of history were moving in favor of national liberation. Translated into the context of the nascent Cold War struggle, the Chinese Civil War appeared to signal a clear victory for international communism. As Mao laid plans for the PRC's role in international affairs, he envisioned a partnership between Moscow and Beijing: while the former remained the center of the international Communist movement, the latter took responsibility for spreading communism throughout East Asia. China, in Mao's mind, assumed the lead in spreading socialist revolution in places such as Japan, Korea, Burma, and the Philippines. At the top of Mao's list sat Indochina and the sixty-year-old leader of the Vietnamese Communist Party, Ho Chi Minh.[50] In January 1950, the CIA warned of indications that the Chinese Communists had accepted Moscow's encouragement to "activate immediately their revolutionary program for Southeast Asia."[51] The CCP's victory had changed the dynamics of the Cold War not only in China but also in the wider world.

Superpower intervention in China's civil war was both limited and reluctant. Neither Truman nor Stalin sought extensive involvement in the civil war; nor did they want to scrap the provisions of the Yalta Agreement that treated China as one of the world's four policemen. Indeed, as of 1946, Washington and Moscow were allied with the GMD, at least on paper. Both governments, moreover, were wary of taking any action that would provoke their rival into greater involvement in China. In the early years of the Cold War, it was not certain that the superpower rivalry would spread into corners of the world such as China. In this sense, it was Mao and Chiang, rather than Truman and Stalin, who put the Third World in play in the Cold War struggle. Both Chinese leaders sought to gain and maintain the patronage of the superpowers, bending them to the will of their respective parties. Although crises had broken out in Iran and Turkey, China was the first truly decisive battle of the Cold War in the postcolonial world, and local actors played a pivotal role in drawing the U.S.-Soviet rivalry into new regions of the globe.

Though local players held the initiative in the civil war, the conflict carried dramatic repercussions for both superpowers. The collapse of Chiang's regime sent shock waves through the American political system, generating accusations that the Truman administration and the Democratic Party had "lost" China. Prominent Republicans in Washington such as Richard Nixon (and, later, Joseph McCarthy) exploited the situation for domestic political gain, in the process generating a Red Scare in the United States. This atmosphere of paranoia would have the long-term impact of purging a significant number of regional experts from the State Department, hampering future American diplomacy in Asia. It also helped to create a political environment in Washington that placed added pressure on the Truman administration to take an increasingly confrontational posture with regard to communism in East Asia and to the Soviet Union in general. While a large-scale military intervention in China had been all but unthinkable in 1948, the United States would be ready to launch just such an action in Korea by 1950.

The victory of the Chinese Communists surprised Moscow as well. While Soviet leaders could not but applaud the turn of events in the East, Mao's triumph appeared to turn Marxist theory on its head. China was not a heavily industrialized nation, and its revolution had not been proletarian. Moreover, the CCP did not function as the Chinese wing of the Communist Party of the Soviet Union. Mao's revolutionaries operated independently of Moscow, a fact that troubled Stalin and gave hope to some U.S. officials. As the U.S. consul general in Shanghai argued,

> Chinese Communists are not 100% subservient to [the] Kremlin. . . . [T]heir party is not monolithic in basic thinking on such vital points as relations with [the] west and . . . [the] Soviets themselves are not too pleased with Chinese Communist successes. . . . Viewing [the] situation in historical perspective it seems to me inherently improbable that [the] Soviets can indefinitely exert control over China through [the] Chinese Communists[,] who have risen to power largely through [their] own efforts and can scarcely be brought to heel by force. Vital question is whether break will come in 2 years or 200. Our own policies may profoundly influence this.[52]

It would take another two decades for U.S. leaders to exploit this rift between Beijing and Moscow. For the time being, the CCP's victory compelled Moscow to extend its protection and support to Beijing, thereby expanding the defensive perimeters of the communist bloc. In the coming years, China would emerge as a powerful player on the world stage in its own right, commanding a formidable army of several million soldiers.

ULTIMATELY, THE CCP'S JOURNEY FROM YAN'AN TO BEIjing carried a global significance. Mao brought the Cold War to the Third World. In doing so, the CCP-GMD clash, one historian explains, made "East Asia *the* main battlefield of the Cold War." Mao's triumph marked the first great turning point. The resurgence of the Chinese Revolution after 1945 helped ignite the first major front in the Cold War's killing fields, which appeared, to the Western powers, as a general Communist offensive in East Asia. Just as important, the CCP's revolution linked the Cold War to the global struggle for decolonization. Mao's version of socialist revolution became a weapon for those struggling against colonial oppression. In Mao's formulation, calls for decolonization and national liberation replaced the rhetoric of class struggle.[53]

In the wake of the CCP's triumph, anticolonial revolutionaries in Korea, French Indochina, Algeria, the Middle East, Africa, and Latin America all turned to Mao's model of guerrilla war as a source of inspiration for their own armed struggles. The CCP's victory rang out around the Cold War international system, signaling the rise of Beijing as a major player and heralding the appearance of a new mode of socialist revolution tailored for the developing world. The string of postcolonial liberation wars that would arc through the southern rim of Asia began with the CCP's victories in China. From their humble beginnings in Yan'an, Mao's revolutionary forces had unleashed a movement that was now set to transform the world.

INTERVENING IN KOREA

1945–1950

In the summer of 1950, the forces unleashed by the Cold War and the Chinese Revolution converged on a most unlikely place: Korea. Dubbed the Hermit Kingdom by outsiders, pre-twentieth-century Korea was largely isolated from the outside world. One Western reporter described the peninsula as a "tangled, twisted mass of rugged mountains stubbled with small timber, snow capped in the north, laced with many streams and rivers . . . and in the valleys and up the terraces of the hills the fantastic patterns of the rice paddies, green and golden and yellow, broken now and again by wasteland, red as the clay of Georgia, corrugated like the mountains of the moon."[1] The Japanese seizure of Korea in 1910 replaced this isolation with four decades of brutal colonialism. In 1945, American and Soviet forces occupied the newly liberated peninsula. Neither superpower had ambitious plans for what it believed was a strategically insignificant corner of the world. Tragically, though, the shock of the Chinese Revolution and the rising stakes of the Cold War struggle would dramatically change Korea's place in world affairs.

Between 1950 and 1953, the peninsula served as the central theater in America's war against communism in Asia and the first instance of a direct superpower military intervention in the developing world during the Cold War. The Chinese Revolution had awakened both Washington and Moscow to the high stakes of the nascent Cold War in Asia. While Stalin and Mao worked to harness nationalist elements in Korea and the postcolonial world, Truman and his advisors prepared to fortify key bulwarks against what they feared was a broader Communist onslaught. Neither Washington nor Moscow initially saw the peninsula as a vital interest, yet viewed through the lens of the Cold War, Korea came to appear pivotal. The Koreans would fight their ongoing civil war amid the carnage of a superpower intervention and an invasion from the most populous nation in the world.[2] Truman's decision to intervene pulled the United States into the first in a series of wars in the developing world during the post-1945 era. The Korean War effectively militarized America's containment policy and helped to ensure that the Cold War would be fought on Third World battlefields.

The fighting unleashed perhaps the most intense violence of the post-1945 era, killing more than three million people (equivalent to 10 percent of the peninsula's population) in the space of three years. Both sides slaughtered civilians by the thousands and committed vicious atrocities. In Korea, two of the world's Great Powers would clash, and one, the United States, would contemplate the use of atomic weapons for a second time in less than a decade. Tens of thousands of infantry were killed in human-wave attacks, urban and trench warfare, long campaigns, and bloody retreats that stretched up and down the length of the Korean Peninsula. Seoul, seat of the South Korean government, was transformed from a bustling capital to a maze of smoking ruins. Three years of brutal ground combat and aerial bombing wiped dozens of towns and villages off the map.[3] Here, at the edge of the Pacific Ocean, Washington mounted its first full-scale intervention to halt the expansion of communism in the developing world.

DIVISION AND CIVIL WAR

No one could have predicted this calamity in the autumn of 1945, when American GIs entered Seoul, a city five and a half centuries old, surrounded by mountains and inhabited by more than a million people. "The autumn air was brisk and clear," a Western journalist wrote. "Eagles wheeled overhead against white clouds, their shadows crossing palaces and hovels, crumbling temples and Western buildings." American military vehicles pushed through streets packed with carts, bicycles, and pedestrians while soldiers on leave wandered among a labyrinth of alleyways and side streets.[4]

Like the war in China, the conflict in Korea predated the Cold War and the involvement of the superpowers. In its inception, the Korean War was a revolution brought on by the collapse of the Japanese Empire. The Japanese had established military control over the Korean Peninsula in 1910 as part of their bid for Pacific empire. For the next four decades, Tokyo ruled over a largely impoverished, undereducated, agrarian society in which the native language was suppressed and millions of peasants became little more than slaves. Inside occupied Korea, nationalists and Communists slowly built their political bases, fighting the Japanese at the same time that they were laying the foundations for what would become a civil war after 1945. The American destruction of the Japanese Empire in World War II brought this colonial rule to an abrupt end, however, and left the Allied powers in control of the peninsula.[5]

American and Soviet leaders had given little thought to the postwar occupation. Late on the evening of August 14, 1945, the day of the Japanese surrender, two American officials, Dean Rusk and Col. Charles Bonesteel, stepped out of a meeting and into an adjacent room to hastily draw up a proposal for the division of Korea between Soviet and American occupation forces. Lacking extensive knowledge of Korea, they used a map from the magazine *National Geographic* to bisect the nation in such a way as to leave Seoul under American control.

The Thirty-Eighth Parallel, Rusk would recall, "made no sense economically or geographically," but time was of the essence. Rusk and
Bonesteel proposed the plan, and both their superiors and the Soviets
accepted. Moscow and Washington each feared the expansion of its
rival's influence in the region, and each was amenable to the concept
of a joint trusteeship in what it considered a north Asian backwater.[6]

But U.S. authorities in the south were not well prepared to begin
the complex task of postcolonial state building. Four decades of Japanese rule had left a society on the brink of revolution. As Japanese
forces stood down, people's committees coalesced throughout the
peninsula, demanding independence and massive political and economic reforms. The American occupation forces confronted a rapidly
changing social landscape: tenants battled against landlords in the
countryside while competing political factions jockeyed for power in
the cities. Gen. John Hodge, commander of the occupation, described
southern Korea as "a powder keg ready to explode." He judged the
greatest threat to come from the possibility of collaboration between
the Kremlin and left-wing elements in Korea. Fearful of mounting
radicalism, Hodge sidelined Korean nationalists, choosing instead to
work with the remnants of the Japanese Army and local collaborators. Further, he began setting up separate administrative and defense
apparatuses for the southern half of the country, which left some officials in Washington to worry about the danger of a permanent division that would leave northern Korea under Soviet influence.[7]

In short order, ad hoc administrative measures became the foundation for the permanent division of Korea between North and South.
After their attempts to establish a coalition government in the South
composed of moderates and conservatives failed, U.S. officials settled on a pro-Western politician, Syngman Rhee, as the leader of the
new regime. The seventy-year-old nationalist had studied at George
Washington University, Harvard, and Princeton. An advocate for
Korean independence from Japan, Rhee had been active in politics
since 1896. With the American victory over Japan, he returned to his

homeland eager to play a role in shaping a new, independent Korea. Rhee proved to be no American puppet, however. He worked assiduously to establish support among bankers and landlords, becoming one of the most influential conservative leaders in the country. From this position, he sought to undermine U.S.-Soviet negotiations for the creation of a unified Korea between 1946 and 1947. By attacking the prospect of a broad-based coalition, Rhee helped to force the United States into a position of choosing between a joint Korea led by a left-wing regime or a divided Korea with a conservative government in Seoul. Faced with this proposition, Washington acquiesced to the creation of a South Korean state under Rhee's leadership, the Republic of Korea (ROK), in 1948.[8]

While the Americans created a pro-Western regime in the South, Moscow laid the foundations for a Communist system in the North. The man who would rise to leadership in Pyongyang was Kim Il-sung. Although the precise details of Kim's early life are murky, distorted by both North Korean hagiography and South Korean anticommunist propaganda, the general story is well known. Born in the picturesque village of Mangyongbong outside Pyongyang in 1912, Kim moved with his family to Manchuria in 1920. By 1932, Kim had joined a band of guerrillas operating against Japanese military forces in Manchuria and Korea. While fighting in China, he received a political education in Maoism from his Chinese superior officer, Wei Zhengmin. Kim distinguished himself as a guerrilla commander and earned fame for leading a raid against the Japanese-occupied Korean town of Poch'onbo in June 1937. Kim's rebels killed a number of Japanese police, destroyed several government buildings, and made off with four thousand yen. His success earned him the distinction of having a bounty placed on his head by Japanese officials. Hunted by the Japanese, Kim and what remained of his guerrillas escaped across the Amur River into the Soviet Union in 1940 or 1941, where he received further training from the Red Army. After the end of World War II, officials in the Soviet occupation placed Kim in power.[9]

Yet Kim and the party leadership in Pyongyang were not Kremlin puppets. They proved adept at transposing Communist political structures onto Korean culture and society. Kim worked to bring the North Korean peasantry into the party system, mobilize the population, institute radical land reforms, and nationalize heavy industry. In the coming years, the regime would establish an enduring cult of personality behind the person of Kim Il-sung and use the educational system, publishing houses, and film industry to promote a powerful strain of nationalism among the population. Finally, the regime created a large and efficient state security apparatus. The result was a sweeping Communist revolution in the North that proved surprisingly successful at marrying Korean nationalism to a Stalinist political and economic system.[10]

If the division of Korea between a Communist North and a noncommunist South served superpower interests, it had no basis in Korean history. Indeed, the country had existed as a cohesive cultural entity for centuries. Seoul and Pyongyang were all but destined to contest an artificial boundary bisecting the country. The existence of an active left-wing movement in the South only added fuel to this political discontent over division, pushing the country closer to civil war. As Koreans watched the revolution unfolding just over the border in China, many longed to replicate the process on the peninsula. Conflict would break out even before the official establishment of the Republic of Korea, in the form of guerrilla warfare.

The first major flashpoint of this war appeared in April 1948, when a left-wing uprising broke out on the southwestern island of Cheju. The revolt was led by the people's committees that had run the Cheju government since 1945. While the American military occupation had marginalized left-wing forces, Seoul's attempts to reestablish control over the island sparked a rebellion, which Seoul resolved to crush using brutal and overwhelming force. As the counterinsurgency mounted, the interior of the island was designated an enemy zone and government troops began forcing peasants to the coastal regions and

burning villages in insurgent areas. U.S. officials noted that Pyongyang radio had cheered the insurgency as "the forerunner of the widespread armed resistance which is destined to sweep the country as
soon as American troops have been withdrawn. . . . It is clear from the
nature of the propaganda emanating from the Soviet-controlled radio
that Cheju Island has been chosen as the spot for a major Soviet effort
to sow confusion and terror in southern Korea."

Soviet agents were infiltrating Cheju on small North Korean fishing boats while Soviet ships and submarines lurked offshore. U.S. officials warned, "Photographs of operations on Cheju indicate unusual
sadistic propensities on the part of both Government and guerrilla
forces. Signal atrocities have been reported, indicating mass massacre
of village populations, including women and children, accompanied
by widespread looting and arson. In some cases the Army has been
guilty of revenge operations against guerrillas which have brought
down vengeance on unarmed villagers."

Individuals suspected of aiding the revolt faced the threat of government reprisal, torture, and even massacre. By the time government
forces gained the upper hand in the spring of 1949, nearly 70 percent
of Cheju's villages had been burned and a third of its population had
been forced into government-controlled villages. While official casualty estimates projected just under twenty-eight thousand killed in
the uprising, Cheju's governor told American officials that the actual
number was closer to sixty thousand—one out of every five residents.[11]

As the bloodshed in Cheju neared its peak, another incident seized
international headlines and threatened to cut the feet out from under
Rhee's newly formed regime. With South Korean police struggling
to put down the insurrection in Cheju, Seoul ordered the army to
reinforce the counterinsurgency against Communist rebels inside the
country. On October 19, 1948, a mutiny broke out in the Fourteenth
Regiment of the South Korean army, which had just received orders
to move to Cheju. The mutineers seized the southern city of Yeosu,
taking possession of thousands of weapons and executing some five

hundred police, soldiers, government officials, and civilians. The uprising then spread to the nearby city of Sunchon, which also fell to the rebel troops. The regime in Seoul responded with decisive action, ordering eleven battalions with some five thousand loyalist troops to surround Yeosu and Sunchon and crush the mutiny. In a week of vicious urban fighting, government troops were able to retake the rebel strongholds, though the counterattack left entire city blocks in ruins. American forces provided support, reconnaissance, resupply, and planning for the government assault. By October 27, the mutiny had been put down. "The city stank of death and was ill with the marks of horror," one American journalist in Sunchon recalled. Corpses littered the streets, and relatives were unwilling to claim the bodies for fear of facing retribution from ROK police. Meanwhile, long lines of men and boys waited to be interrogated at public buildings. Between twenty-five hundred and five thousand people had been killed in the rebellion.[12]

The uprisings in Cheju, Yeosu, and Sunchon convinced Rhee that the time had come to dramatically expand his security forces. In November 1948, the regime passed the National Defense Act, authorizing the creation of a one-hundred-thousand-man army and a ten-thousand-man navy. Meanwhile, the size of the South Korean National Police was increased to fifty thousand, twice the size of the Japanese forces that had occupied the entire peninsula. Rhee used these forces to crush the regime's political opponents and tighten his grip over South Korean society. In December, the regime passed the National Security Law, which gave Rhee the power to use ROK military forces against political dissidents. "Every observer with long experience of Korean affairs," explained an Australian diplomat, "holds the opinion that we have at present in South Korea a reactionary government closely associated with unscrupulous landlords and bolstered by a vicious police force." Rhee's massive security apparatus would not come on the cheap. As the size of Seoul's forces swelled, the ROK issued some two hundred million dollars in requests for

U.S. military assistance. After Washington rebuffed these requests, Seoul began taking out extensive loans from the Bank of Korea and printing more currency. As its ostensible ally in Seoul moved into an increasingly precarious position, the U.S. government was approaching the moment when it would be forced to commit to the ROK or cut its losses.[13]

Even as Rhee's forces struggled to put down the insurgency in the South, border clashes raged along the frontier with North Korea, particularly between May and December 1949. Both regimes looked toward the eventual reunification of Korea, and both launched raids across the border. South Korean forces were the aggressors in the majority of these incidents, but they were restrained by U.S. refusals to provide the ROK with the heavy weapons necessary to launch a full-scale invasion of the North. With a goal of deterring a civil war in Korea, U.S. diplomats explained to Rhee that he should not expect Washington to save his regime if he were to provoke a showdown with North Korea. The Soviet Union was similarly reluctant to back a Democratic People's Republic of Korea (DPRK) invasion of the South, fearing the larger repercussions of such a clash for the Cold War struggle. Furthermore, with tens of thousands of North Korean troops fighting in the Chinese Civil War, Pyongyang was not in a position to begin a war with the ROK. With the end of the civil war in China, however, the situation began to change.[14] In December 1949, CIA officials warned that North Koreans were returning across the border with Manchuria and that the Soviets were preparing an arms shipment to be smuggled into South Korea in mid-January. The report warned that guerrilla activities in South Korea were likely to increase.[15]

Kim was convinced that the only way to reunify Korea was through military force: "[W]e will be victorious," he proclaimed, "but victory does not come on its own; victory must be won." Korea, he argued, must take the Bolshevik Revolution and the recent victory of the CCP in China as models for the struggle against the regime in the South. The failure of the southern uprisings bolstered the argument for large-scale military operations. With this in mind, Kim enlarged the North Korean military and began building an arms industry to supply it. Aiding in this drift toward war was the failure of the North's 1949 two-year development plan and the feared stagnation of the DPRK economy. Kim was also mindful of domestic rivals (most notably the southern Communist leader Pak Hon-yong), who would reap the greatest gains from a popular uprising in the South: the best way for Kim to ensure his leadership over a reunified Korea was to conquer the South through military force. Furthermore, by mid-1950, North Korea had reached the third stage of Mao's theory of revolutionary war. Korean Communists had staged guerrilla operations in the South in the preceding years as the DPRK built up its military power north of the Thirty-Eighth Parallel. Limited border clashes had transpired during the period of equilibrium between the two Koreas. By the summer of 1950, North Korea had become strong enough to launch a final offensive designed to topple Rhee and reunify the peninsula.[16]

Changing attitudes in Moscow also helped convince Kim that the time had come to attack. Prior to 1949, Stalin had been skeptical of the potential for Communist success in East Asia. Much like his American counterparts, he preferred to focus on extending his country's influence into Europe. Some Soviet officials doubted that North Korean forces were strong enough to win a war against the South. "Even taking into account the help which will be rendered to the northern army by the partisans and the population of South Korea it is impossible to count on a rapid victory," they noted in mid-September 1949. They warned that

a drawn out war gives the possibility to the Americans to render corresponding aid to Syngman Rhee. After their lack of success in China, the Americans probably will intervene in Korean affairs more decisively than they did in China and, it goes without saying, apply all their strength to save Syngman Rhee. . . .

Moreover, a drawn out war in Korea could be used by the Americans for purposes of agitation against the Soviet Union and for further inflaming war hysteria. Therefore, it is inadvisable that the north begin a civil war now.

But Mao's unexpected triumph in China changed the playing field and led Stalin to ignore these recommendations. In January 1950, Stalin told Mao that he was no longer interested in maintaining his wartime agreements with the Western powers. "To hell with Yalta!" he thundered during the negotiations that would lead to the Sino-Soviet Treaty of Friendship in February. Moscow was prepared to turn its attentions east. The Kremlin would now treat Mao and the CCP as partners and begin to provide substantial amounts of aid to the Viet Minh forces in French Indochina. Furthermore, Stalin decided to increase aid to the regime in Pyongyang and gave Kim Il-sung the go-ahead to prepare for an attack against the South. Heartened by Mao's victory and the successful test of a Soviet atomic bomb the previous August, Stalin was ready to challenge America's position in East Asia.[17]

Stalin also had new reason to doubt Washington's commitment to Seoul's defense. Even as Soviet and Chinese leaders met to negotiate the Sino-Soviet Treaty in January 1950, U.S. secretary of state Dean Acheson outlined a vision for U.S. security interests in the Pacific that excluded Korea. "This defensive perimeter," he told reporters, "runs along the Aleutians to Japan and then goes to the Ryukyus . . . [and] from the Ryukyus to the Philippine Islands."[18] South Korea's security, he explained, could be provided by the United Nations. That same month, the U.S. Congress voted down a bill that would have provided economic aid for the regime in Seoul. And if Washington's actions in regard to the Chinese Civil War were any guide, it now seemed unlikely that the Truman administration would intervene to save the ROK. But these signals were misleading. Washington had in fact entered a period of profound insecurity. As American officials surveyed the international scene in 1950, they saw a number of alarming signals: the Soviets had detonated their first atomic weapon in August 1949; weeks later, Mao announced a Communist victory in the world's most populous nation; the French seemed unable to gain the upper hand in their war against Communist guerrillas in Indochina; and Communist rebels were on the march in the Malaya Peninsula and the Philippines. Making matters worse, President Truman's domestic opponents in the Republican Party had begun to attack the Democrats for the "loss" of China.[19]

No document better reflected this atmosphere of heightened insecurity than National Security Council Paper 68 (NSC-68), drafted in April 1950. The report laid out a vision of a polarized international system in which the forces of democracy and capitalism confronted the rising power of an authoritarian state, driven by a "fanatic [Communist] faith" and bent on world domination. The United States, the report insisted, was the only power standing between the Kremlin and its goal of enslaving the world. In its most dire warning, the report argued, "The assault on free institutions is world-wide now, and in the context of the present polarization of power a defeat of free institutions anywhere is a defeat everywhere."[20] Using this logic, areas and countries of seemingly little strategic significance could be transformed into vital interests. In a zero-sum game, any victory for communism was a defeat for the forces of freedom and democracy. In practical terms, NSC-68 called for a dramatic expansion of U.S. global commitments in an effort to halt the spread of communism and for a sharp increase in defense spending. Whereas George Kennan's earlier formulation of containment strategy called for the use of concerted diplomatic pressure to block the spread of Soviet influence, NSC-68 proposed the use of military force, when necessary, in the form of limited war. Washington must be prepared to fight along the front lines of the Cold War around the world. While many areas might not be so vital as to justify the risk of nuclear war, they were still worth defending using more limited means. In short, NSC-68 called for the militarization of Cold War containment policy. But Truman remained skeptical. Although recent months had seen a steady stream of troubling developments in the Cold War, the president was hesitant to commit American resources to the massive undertaking outlined in the report. This was about to change.

THE ATTACK

At 4:00 in the morning on June 25, 1950, as a steady drizzle of rain fell from the predawn sky, some ninety thousand soldiers of the North's Korean People's Army (KPA) lurched forward as their artillery opened up on targets in the South. North Korean troops crossed the Thirty-Eighth Parallel at six points along a 150-mile-wide front. South Korean and American troops near the front were caught by surprise. There had been fighting along the border for months, with each side launching raids against the other, but nothing of this scale had yet taken place. Syngman Rhee, the president of South Korea, did not learn of the attack until 6:30 a.m., and he waited ninety minutes before notifying American officials. It took several more hours for the reality of what was happening to sink in: North Korean troops had crossed the border en masse and were rapidly pushing South Korean forces back toward Seoul. Their plan was to launch assaults along the length of the Thirty-Eighth Parallel, with the main assault aimed at sweeping down the Uijongbu Corridor and enveloping the capital. Kim Il-sung, president of North Korea, anticipated the collapse of South Korean forces in one week, the capture of Seoul, and the end of the war. Gen. Douglas MacArthur, commander of the U.S. occupation forces in Japan, downplayed the severity of the situation. "This is probably only a reconnaissance-in-force," he announced. "If Washington only will not hobble me, I can handle it with one arm tied behind my back."[21]

The initial North Korean assault across the Thirty-Eighth Parallel on June 25 achieved startling success, driving the South Korean defenders south and opening the approaches to the capital. In the coming days, it looked as if Kim's gamble would pay off and the peninsula would be reunified under Communist control. The residents of Seoul, less than thirty miles from the front, listened anxiously for reports of the fighting and watched ROK soldiers moving north to confront the attackers. On the afternoon of June 26, radios across the city announced a victory for South Korean forces north of Uijongbu. The celebrations ceased by evening, however, as refugees reached the northern stretches of the city and residents began to hear the muted rumble of heavy guns. In the early morning hours of June 27, American officials received orders to evacuate Seoul. Fear swept through the city as the flow of refugees increased and thousands of civilians tried to flee across the Han River bridges. The first North Korean forces reached Seoul around 7:30 p.m. but were held off by the city's defenders for several hours. The flow of refugees continued through the night and into the next morning. At 2:15 a.m., panicked ROK officials detonated explosives on the bridges, killing around a thousand civilians and South Korean soldiers crossing the river and stranding another 44,000 ROK troops on the northern bank. By the third day of the attack, some 76,000 ROK troops were unaccounted for; South Korean commanders could locate only 22,000 soldiers of their remaining force.[22]

As increasingly dire reports of the situation in Korea poured into Washington, Truman administration officials moved quickly toward intervention. Convinced that North Korea was a Soviet puppet state, Truman and Acheson feared they were watching the beginning of a general Communist offensive against Western security interests. U.S. forces in Asia would have to prepare for a larger attack. Meanwhile, the president authorized American air strikes against North Korean forces and ordered U.S. troops to defend South Korean airfields and ports. Visiting the front, General MacArthur issued a soberer appraisal, saying that U.S. ground forces would be needed to reverse the DPRK's offensive. On June 30, Truman agreed to the general's request to send two of his four divisions from Japan to Korea. "If we let Korea down," Truman argued, "the Soviet[s] will keep right on going and swallow up one piece of Asia after another. . . . If we were to let Asia go, the Near East would collapse and no telling what would happen in Europe." In July, Acheson would tell the Senate Foreign Relations Committee that the attack had been "an open, clear, direct challenge" to the United States. The Kremlin believed that the United States would not defend South Korea, he concluded, and now hoped to advance on the earlier Communist victory in China. "The attack," he would write that same month, "makes amply clear centrally directed Communist Imperialism has passed beyond subversion in seeking [to] conquer independent nations and [is] now resorting to armed aggression and war."[23] A State Department intelligence assessment was even more dramatic, warning that the North Korean attack was part of a global Soviet-backed offensive with repercussions for Western interests in Japan, Formosa, Indochina, Burma, and Malaya. It might even be the prelude to "possible Soviet moves in Germany or Iran." The destruction of "the US 'salient' in Korea would deny to the US any area where land forces could be staged for an attack" on the eastern reaches of the USSR or China. Moreover, control over the entire peninsula threatened Tokyo and effectively neutralized "the usefulness of Japan as an American base" in the event of a war in the Far East.[24] "To sit by while Korea is overrun by unprovoked armed attack," warned the U.S. political advisor in Tokyo, "would start [a] disastrous chain of events leading most probably to world war."[25]

But American officials overestimated Moscow's influence over North Korea. As Soviet leader Nikita Khrushchev later explained, "the war wasn't Stalin's idea, but Kim Il-song's. Kim was the initiator." As Stalin would tell Kim, "If you should get kicked in the teeth, I shall not lift a finger. You have to ask Mao for all the help." The Kremlin, hoping to secure long-term access to warm-water ports, had concluded that the best option lay in supporting Kim's attempts to reunify the peninsula. A North Korean victory would grant Moscow access to the harbors at Inchon and Pusan and represent another step in the expansion of communism through East Asia. Washington, in any case, had excluded South Korea from its defensive perimeter in the Pacific. Kim's move was a gamble, but not an unreasonable one.[26]

While Stalin reluctantly supported Kim, Mao's role was more complicated. Mao and his comrades had expected a U.S. military intervention in Asia since 1949. U.S. involvement in Korea also gave the CCP an opportunity to further consolidate its hold on mainland China. As Beijing wrote on June 29, 1950, "The United States has . . . exposed its imperialist face, which is not scary at all but is favorable for the further awakening of the Chinese people and the world."[27] At the same time, the American military intervention in Korea represented a dire threat to Beijing. "If the U.S. imperialists win [in Korea]," Mao would warn in August, "they may get so dizzy with success that they may threaten us. We therefore must come to [North] Korea's aid and intervene in the name of a volunteer army, although we will select the best timing." Moreover, the chance to confront Washington's armies on an Asian battlefield also presented a tremendous opportunity to showcase the military might of the PRC. The United States could send as many as forty divisions to Korea, Mao bragged to a Soviet diplomat, but Chinese forces would "grind" them up. He later told Stalin that his goal in Korea was "to spend several years consuming several hundred thousand American lives." The peninsula could be transformed into an enormous killing field that might tilt the global balance of power in the Cold War. More than just sucking the United States into a bloody quagmire in a war against Mao's battle-hardened guerrillas, a war between American and Chinese armies in Korea would place substantial pressure on Stalin to send even more support to Beijing.[28]

Stalin was happy to see the United States engage in what promised to be a bloody intervention in Korea. As he wrote in August 1950, the United States had become "entangled in a military intervention in Korea and is now squandering its military prestige and moral authority. Few honest people can now doubt that America is now acting as an aggressor and tyrant in Korea and that it is not as militarily powerful as it claims to be. In addition, it is clear that the United States of America is presently distracted from Europe in the Far East. Does it not give us an advantage in the global balance of power? It undoubtedly does."

Moreover, if the United States managed to drag China into the war, it would find itself battling massive armies in hostile terrain. If this happened, Stalin continued, "America would be incapable of a third world war in the near future. Therefore, a third world war would be postponed for an indeterminate period, which would provide the time necessary to strengthen socialism in Europe, not to mention that the struggle between America and China would revolutionize the entire Far East. Does all this not give us an advantage from the perspective of the global balance of power? It unquestionably does."[29]

MAO'S ACTIONS ALSO PLAYED INTO STALIN'S HANDS. The Soviet leader approved Kim Il-sung's plans but gave Mao primary responsibility for protecting North Korea. In doing so, Stalin created a win-win situation for the Kremlin. If the North Koreans won the war, the peninsula would fall under full Communist control. Conversely, if the North Korean offensive bogged down and China intervened, Mao would be forced to turn to Stalin for support, thereby increasing Beijing's dependence on Moscow. All the while, the United States would be pouring its resources into a vicious war in a region of negligible strategic value. The war in Korea greatly benefited the Soviet geopolitical position.[30]

The controversy over Soviet and Chinese involvement has led to two basic historical interpretations of the war. The first, embraced by Truman and his advisors, saw the war as an international conflict. The North Korean invasion of South Korea was an act of Communist aggression by one state against another state. The war began with this invasion in 1950 and ended in 1953 with an armistice. The second interpretation, put forward by the Communist states and a number of Western scholars, argued that the Korean War was, at heart, a civil war. The war began in 1945, or even as early as 1932, and had killed some one hundred thousand Koreans by June 1950. The DPRK's attack in June was not an *invasion*—for how could Koreans invade Korea? Rather, it was one stage in a larger conflict. Neither Kim nor Rhee accepted the legitimacy of the Thirty-Eighth Parallel as an international boundary, and both were fighting to reunify Korea.[31] Both these interpretations have some validity, but it is difficult to dispute the notion that the conflict in Korea began as, and in many respects remains, a civil war. The reality of foreign intervention does not change the underlying nature of the conflict as a war between two competing Korean regimes.

In the end, what ultimately distinguished the war in Korea from the conflict that had just ended in China was the Truman administration's decision to launch a massive intervention in the war. This would mark the first instance of large-scale superpower intervention in the developing world during the Cold War, and it would dramatically change the course of the East-West conflict. The Truman administration elected to approach the UN Security Council to request international sanction for intervention. The Security Council passed two resolutions on July 25 and 27, which, respectively, demanded that Pyongyang withdraw its forces and called for UN member states to come to the aid of the ROK. American officials were able to take such a commanding role in the Security Council due to the absence of the Soviet ambassador, who had received instructions from Stalin himself not to attend the meeting on Korea. Faced with little opposition, the Truman administration was able to secure the backing of the United Nations for its intervention to save Rhee's pro-Western regime. The U.S. intervention in Korea would take place, as Gen. Omar Bradley noted, "under the guise of aid to the UN."[32]

The scale and speed of Truman's response to the situation in

Korea surprised observers around the world. General MacArthur, commander of the U.S. occupation in Japan, was "amazed" that the president was taking the nation to war in Korea without submitting the matter to Congress, a disturbing precedent for later Cold War conflicts. Stalin, too, was surprised at the American decision to intervene in a country that Washington had chosen to leave outside its security perimeter only months before. Even Mao seems not to have expected Truman to act so quickly. The Truman administration's fear of a global Communist offensive, of which Korea might represent only the spearhead, led Washington to take drastic and reckless action. Truman led the United States into a war not to defend American lives but to reestablish a Western defensive line at the Thirty-Eighth Parallel. "Harry Truman had ordered troops into action on the far frontier," one historian later wrote. "This was the kind of war that had bleached the bones of countless legionnaires on the marches of the [British] empire, and had dug the graves of numberless Britons, wherever the sun shone." With the decision to intervene in Korea, the United States had taken up the mantle of a global power.[33]

INTERVENTION

General MacArthur, one of the most decorated military leaders in American history, would command UN forces. Son of Arthur MacArthur, an officer in the U.S. Army and a Medal of Honor recipient, Douglas spent his childhood on military bases around the American West. After graduating first in his class at West Point, MacArthur served in the Philippines and Japan and participated in the occupation of Veracruz. During the First World War, MacArthur commanded troops at the Marne and the Argonne Forest, receiving two Croix de Guerre, a silver star, a Distinguished Service Cross, and promotion to brigadier general. After the war, he returned to West Point, where he served as superintendent of the academy and then went on to become the army's chief of staff. In 1935, MacArthur began his fifth tour in the Pacific, as field marshal of the newly created Philippine Army. With the outbreak of the Second World War, MacArthur returned to the U.S. Army, where he rose to the rank of four-star general and became commander of U.S. troops in the Far East. After being forced to retreat from the Philippines, leaving thousands of American and Filipino troops behind, MacArthur led the campaign that eventually retook control of the eastern Pacific from Japan. By the end of the war, MacArthur had won a Medal of Honor and risen to the rank of five-star general. In 1945 he became the Supreme Commander for the Allied Powers in Japan, presiding over the occupation of the defeated country. With the outbreak of war in Korea, the general was again called upon to defend American interests, a call he readily accepted.

On July 13, American military leaders in the Pacific met in MacArthur's occupation headquarters in the imposing Dai Ichi Building in Tokyo. There, MacArthur held court, smoke pouring from his pipe as he laid out his strategic vision for intervention in Korea. He insisted that the United States strike a decisive blow in Korea and, in doing so, smash the Communist offensive around the Pacific Rim. The goal must be to destroy the Korean People's Army, not simply to restore the Thirty-Eighth Parallel. The North Korean attack was a thinly veiled Soviet move to gain influence in the Far East: Stalin did not want a full-blown war, but he was happy to support Kim's move on the peninsula. The United States, MacArthur argued, should send two armies to Korea along with all its ships in the Pacific and a large contingent of aircraft. His plan was to "isolate the battlefield" using American warplanes, armed with nuclear weapons if necessary, to cut DPRK forces off from Soviet and Chinese support. Then American troops would stage an amphibious landing at Inchon, flanking North Korean troops. Finally, UN forces from the south would sweep northward while the troops at Inchon would sweep south, crushing the North Koreans caught in between. But Washington must not underestimate North Korean troops. They were fierce fighters who would not be defeated easily.[34]

Some civilian U.S. officials were hesitant, however, favoring a more measured approach to the crisis. Political leaders in Washington continued to pursue a Europe-first strategy and were reluctant to devote so much manpower to the Pacific theater of the Cold War. If MacArthur's forces became bogged down in Korea, Western defenses in Europe would languish. Furthermore, the plan for an amphibious landing was risky, and administration officials were understandably reluctant to give MacArthur control of atomic weapons. An angry MacArthur recognized the same line of reasoning that he believed had plagued him in World War II: by saving its troops for Europe, Washington was forcing him to fight with limited forces in the Pacific. This would not be the last disagreement between MacArthur and Truman over the question of limiting the war.[35]

For the moment, however, the first American troops sent to halt the North Koreans had their hands full. Fresh from their relatively comfortable occupation duties in Japan, the army units that formed the vanguard of the American intervention had been told that they were embarking on a police action that was likely to take only a few weeks. Their commanders hoped that the DPRK would be cowed by the mere presence of American forces—that when the North Koreans discovered they were fighting U.S. forces, they "would turn around and go back." The American confrontation with KPA forces on July 5, on a highway twenty-two miles south of Seoul, would belie this assumption. Task Force Smith was made up of several hundred soldiers commanded by thirty-four-year-old lieutenant colonel Charles B. Smith. They had no heavy armor and few weapons capable of stopping North Korean tanks. They were, according to MacArthur, "an arrogant display of strength, sent ahead into Korea to give the Communists pause." The Americans sighted the first tank columns at 7:30 a.m. Forty-six minutes later, American artillery began firing at the oncoming force. As the North Korean T-34 tanks continued, the Americans fired rockets, which failed to penetrate their armor. Although the United States had developed rockets that could pierce the tanks' armor, these had not been supplied to the troops. The Americans harassed the oncoming columns, but they could not stop them. By early afternoon, Colonel Smith ordered his forces— bloodied, short on ammunition, and overwhelmed by the strength of their opponents—to withdraw.[36]

The Americans were not prepared for the force they confronted. Far from the ragtag, poorly armed soldiers they had expected to meet, the North Korean army was seasoned, committed, and well equipped. One in three had fought with Mao's forces in China; now they were fighting to reunify their nation. For many North Korean soldiers, the war had begun as an anticolonial struggle to expel the Japanese, had turned into a war to bring communism to China, and was now focused on destroying a pro-Western puppet regime in Seoul. Unlike their American counterparts, KPA troops had a clear vision of what they were fighting for and were willing to die to achieve it. Now they had U.S. and South Korean forces on their heels.[37] North Korean forces employed a variation of Soviet deep-battle tactics: an advance contingent of troops would engage enemy forces in a frontal attack, tying them down while auxiliary units rushed around the enemy's flanks to attack from the rear. Generally, this amounted to setting up roadblocks and ambushes against enemy columns. These techniques proved devastatingly effective against UN troops, which were usually restricted to moving along roads rather than across Korea's rugged terrain. Using camouflage and attacking by night to avoid American aircraft, the KPA was able to inflict heavy casualties on UN and ROK forces.[38]

The opening days witnessed not only the chaos of this retreat but also the brutality that would characterize the conflict. Rhee's evacuation of Seoul triggered the execution of between one hundred thousand and two hundred thousand political prisoners in South Korea—lest they join the ranks of the advancing Communist forces.[39] In July, Western journalists reported the massacre of perhaps seven thousand people in a village outside Taejon. Victims were shot or hacked to death with swords before being thrown into six mass graves. On July 2, U.S. Army intelligence reported that South Korean police were rounding up "all Communists and executing them on the outskirts of the city." CIA sources warned that police appeared to be "executing Communist suspects in Suwon and Taejon, in an effort both to eliminate a potential 5th column and to take revenge for reported northern executions in Seoul." Prisoners were forced to the edge of earthen ditches and then shot in the head so that their bodies would fall into the waiting graves. Publicly, U.S. officials tried to suppress news of the massacres or shift blame onto Communist forces.[40]

When American troops working with the ROK air force reported decomposing corpses floating in the water off Jinhae-gu in August, they were told that these were captured Communist spies. "Ammunition was scarce," a U.S. Air Force colonel remembered; "the spies had been taken out onto water and, with hands bound behind their backs, shoved overboard." Many U.S. officers were appalled by the ROK's treatment of prisoners. "They were skeletons," one American wrote upon seeing a group scheduled for execution, "and they cringed like dogs. They were manacled with chains . . . compelled to crouch in the classical Oriental attitude of subjection." Moreover, the South Koreans did not try to hide these acts from UN forces: they were taking place in the shadow of U.S. Army headquarters in Pusan and had been "going on for months. Nobody had said a word."[41]

In the pandemonium of the early weeks of the war, U.S. forces would also be drawn into the slaughter. On July 26, troops from the U.S. Seventh Cavalry Regiment and hundreds of South Korean refugees met at the village of No Gun Ri, around one hundred miles southeast of Seoul. Both groups, soldiers and civilians, were fleeing the advance of North Korean forces. "We just annihilated them," remembered one former machine gunner. Fearing the presence of North Korean infiltrators among the refugees, U.S. commanders had issued the following orders: "No refugees to cross the front line. Fire everyone trying to cross lines. Use discretion in case of women and children." On only their third day at the front, terrified U.S. soldiers from the occupation forces in Japan confronted what they feared might be an attack from Communist guerrillas. As the group of refugees from nearby villages approached U.S. positions, witnesses reported that American warplanes, which may have been suspicious of North Korean guerrillas, began strafing the civilians. The refugees took cover in a culvert beneath a nearby railroad bridge. The Associated Press team that broke the story in 1999 reported that American soldiers "directed refugees into the bridge underpasses—each 80 feet long, 23 feet wide, 30 feet high—and after dark opened fire on them from nearby machine-gun positions." For the next three nights, U.S. gunners continued to fire on the survivors beneath the bridge. "People pulled dead bodies around them for protection," remembered one survivor. When North Korean forces took the position, they reported finding four hundred bodies at the site.[42]

Massacres such as this one were disturbingly common: nearly six years later, South Korea's Truth and Reconciliation Commission would uncover evidence suggesting 1,222 incidents of mass killing during the war.[43] As the war swept down, and then back up, the peninsula, it took a horrific toll on the civilians caught in its path. The residents of Cheongwon watched for over a week as a stream of trucks, four in the morning and three in the afternoon, loaded with people slated for execution arrived in the village. Later estimates of those killed at the village reached as high as seven thousand. South Korean soldiers sent to root out Communists near the village of Hampyeong instead attacked a group of peasants. "They told us to light our cigarettes," one survivor recalled. "Then they began shooting their rifles and machine guns. After a while an officer called out, 'Any of you who are still alive can stand up and go home now.' Those who did were shot again." In the nearby village of Naju, South Korean police hunting suspected Communists disguised themselves as KPA troops and then killed ninety-seven villagers who welcomed them with Communist flags.[44] North Korean forces were responsible for their share of massacres as well—which were, not surprisingly, better reported in the American press. In the early weeks of the war, DPRK troops earned a reputation for the summary execution of American and South Korean prisoners. Reports of slain U.S. servicemen, their hands bound, outraged the American public. In a report presented on September 18, General MacArthur drew attention to the DPRK's brutal treatment of prisoners while lauding the ROK's treatment of POWs as "perfect."[45]

Korean civilians suffered terribly in the first phase of the war. The residents of Seoul watched as North Korean forces seized the city, began throwing up posters of Kim Il-sung and Stalin, and launched a hunt for reactionaries. Many citizens cheered the arrival of the Communist forces and praised the liberation of their city. Others mobbed the roads leading out of the city, fleeing the advancing DPRK armies. Refugees heading south battled starvation in the countryside as they struggled to avoid North Korean troop columns and sporadic attacks from American aircraft hunting for targets in Communist-controlled territory. Tens of thousands of those who made it to refugee camps faced squalid conditions and the threat of smallpox, typhoid, and cholera. An estimated two million refugees would move into UN-controlled territory, straining food stores and medical supplies and adding to the challenges faced by the struggling UN forces.[46]

By the end of July, American and South Korean troops had been pushed back to only a foothold around Pusan, in the far south of the peninsula. UN forces would have to hold on to the hills along the Nakdong River or be driven from Korea entirely. "There will be no more retreating," their commander told them. "There are no lines behind which we can retreat. This is not going to be a Dunkirk or Bataan. A retreat to Pusan would result in one of the greatest butcheries in history." But as the last American troops crossed the river, the North Koreans remained tight on their heels. U.S. forces set up a defensive line on the high ground along the half-mile-wide river and prepared for the North Koreans to attack. The Americans were in a far stronger position than in earlier weeks. Their forces were concentrated behind strong natural defenses, where their superior firepower could be used more effectively against the DPRK. Further, the stabilization of the battlefront allowed American warplanes to be put to greater use attacking North Korean columns moving southward. All the while, men, weapons, and supplies disembarked at the port of Pusan to reinforce UN defenses. By the beginning of August, UN forces on the peninsula outnumbered those of North Korea. If Pusan was to be the UN expedition's last stand, it would at least be a strong one. For the next six weeks, Pyongyang's forces hurled themselves at the UN lines in a series of massive nighttime assaults aimed at smashing through the Pusan perimeter before the United States could mobilize its full resources. Some of the fiercest clashes occurred at a bend of the river called the Nakdong Bulge, where North Korean troops came close to overrunning UN positions. While the fighting raged along the river, UN and DPRK tanks fought a weeklong battle in the steep valley (dubbed the Bowling Alley) to the north of Taegu. North Korean T-34s and American Pershing battle tanks traded armor-piercing shells throughout the valley. But UN defenses held and staged a successful counterattack that brought the battle for the valley to an end on August 24. The Battle of the Pusan Perimeter continued until mid-September.[47] UN forces had stabilized the perimeter and prevented wholesale disaster. MacArthur now began planning his next move.

THE SUMMER OF 1950 FUNDAMENTALLY TRANSFORMED the Cold War struggle. Faced with the threats of Communist China and a nuclearized Soviet Union, American leaders resolved to throw their military resources into interventions in the postcolonial world. Breaking with George Kennan's visions of containment as a patient political and economic struggle, the United States adopted a central Cold War strategy that would henceforth be a militarized endeavor.

Moscow and Beijing had also demonstrated their commitment to supporting left-wing revolutionaries. Working with Beijing, Stalin could project greater influence into North Korea without deploying the Soviet Army in peripheral areas such as Korea. Likewise, the Sino-Soviet partnership allowed Mao to increase Beijing's support for revolutionary movements throughout East Asia. Finally, the Korean intervention showcased what was to become an enduring dynamic of the Cold War: areas of seemingly marginal strategic significance could become major geopolitical flashpoints.

REHEARSING FOR WORLD WAR III

1 9 5 0 – 1 9 5 4

The Western armies managed to stop the North Korean advance from nearly driving them off the peninsula. If America and its allies hoped to reverse their fortunes, they would need to mount a dramatic counterattack. And according to General MacArthur, the stakes could hardly have been higher. The general insisted that the world was witnessing a concerted Communist offensive in Asia. "It is plainly apparent that here in Asia is where the Communist conspirators have elected to make their play for global conquest," he told a group of American military leaders. "The test is not in Berlin or Vienna, in London, Paris, or Washington. It is here and now—it is along the Naktong River in South Korea . . . we here fight Europe's war with arms, while there it is still confined to words. If we lose the war to Communism in Asia, the fate of Europe will be gravely jeopardized. Win it and Europe will probably be saved from war and stay free. Make the wrong decision here—the fatal decision of inertia— and we will be done. I can almost hear the ticking of the second hand of destiny. We must act now or we will die."

MacArthur had been eyeing the Port of Inchon since the early days of the war. He hoped to avoid a prolonged push northward that would force American troops to engage with large numbers of DPRK infantry in pitched battles over the length of the rugged peninsula. A spectacular amphibious landing behind North Korean lines, in contrast, would allow U.S. forces to concentrate their firepower in one quick punch that would take advantage of their technological superiority. Inchon, the primary port of Seoul, lay some 25 miles west of the capital and 150 miles north of the Pusan battlefront. Though it seemed the obvious choice, Inchon presented a daunting array of challenges. The approach to the harbor ran through narrow channels guarded by high ground suitable for gun emplacements and was subject to strong currents. Fourteen-foot-tall seawalls stretched along the coast, further deterring a landing by hostile troops. The harbor itself had one of the largest tidal ranges in the world: at low tide, UN troops would have to trudge through at least a thousand yards of sludge under enemy fire. The water would be only deep enough for landing craft at two times in the near future: September 15 and October 11. MacArthur rejected the latter date at a meeting with his top officers in late August. He refused to allow the North Koreans to continue their assault on Pusan for another seven weeks. The landing, he insisted, must take place on the September date, three weeks away.[1]

INCHON

At daybreak on September 15, a battalion of U.S. Marines, the spearhead of the invasion, landed on Wolmi Island in the middle of Inchon's harbor. Amphibious forces could not bypass Wolmi, as it commanded a strategic position with a view over much of the surrounding harbor, but the severe tides forced American troops to land on the island ten hours before the main force could assault the seawall that protected Inchon. U.S. Marines managed to take the island in around ninety minutes, but in doing so, they surrendered the element of surprise. For the next nine hours, American gunships and aircraft pounded North Korean defenses in Inchon. With rain clouds rolling over the city, the first marines scrambled over Inchon's seawall at 5:33 p.m. and advanced into the city streets. "As the pall over Inchon thickened," one reporter recalled, "the air became choked with fumes and cinders." By 1:30 a.m., U.S. forces had surrounded the city. The Inchon landing had been a startling success, giving UN forces a beachhead within striking distance of Seoul.[2]

The UN counterattack unleashed a second wave of destruction on the densely populated peninsula. U.S. warships had leveled much of the city of Inchon in their attack. Some of the landing troops marveled that any of the city's buildings remained standing. One later seemed surprised that there were "quite a number of citizens still alive. They came stumbling from the ruins . . . numbers of them quite clearly driven into a sort of numbed dementia by the night of destruction." Like their South Korean counterparts, the North Koreans began massacring political prisoners as they prepared to retreat. In the wake of the Inchon landing, DPRK officials emptied Seoul's West Gate Prison, sending thousands of South Korean captives to the North and executing those who could not be moved. U.S. sources would later estimate that around a thousand were slaughtered. Reports of other atrocities filtered in as UN forces advanced on North Korean–held territory, with total estimates numbering in the area of thirty thousand killed.[3]

MacArthur insisted that Seoul be retaken by September 25—the three-month anniversary of the start of the war. This would require a punishing frontal assault on the city and its nearly twenty thousand defenders, rather than a flanking maneuver that would likely prove less destructive. North Korean forces, overextended by their push to breach the Pusan perimeter in the South, could do little to resist MacArthur's drive toward Seoul. On September 20, American troops began crossing the Han River in force and advancing into the hills that guarded the western approaches to the city. On September 22, UN forces engaged with North Korean defenders on the outskirts of Seoul. After four days of heavy fighting, DPRK forces broke and

American units took the western gates of the city.[4] Under the cover of morning mist, UN columns pushed into the more heavily populated quarters of Seoul and toward the city's gasworks, railroad yards, and military barracks. Fires from gasoline and oil reserves that had been set ablaze sent pillars of black smoke into the sky as U.S. Navy and Marine Corsairs made bombing runs against North Korean lines.[5]

As scheduled, MacArthur declared victory in Seoul on September 25. The *New York Times* announced that the city's fall was "a stunning blow to Communist prestige throughout the Far East and an enormous lift to the prestige of the Americans who were able to bring a victorious force across thousands of miles of water." Seoul, the paper declared, was the "first capital to be freed from Communist rule anywhere in the world." In fact, heavy fighting continued in many parts of the city between UN troops and stiff pockets of North Korean resistance.[6] In an effort to limit their own casualties, U.S. forces poured heavy fire into the city, with devastating results for its residents. "Telephone and power lines festooned the streets or hung from shattered poles which resembled grotesque Christmas trees," one reporter wrote. "A tiny figure . . . stumbled down the street. Her face, arms, and legs were burned and almost eaten away by the fragments of an American white phosphorous shell. She was blind, but somehow alive." As American forces advanced, they made the most of their advantages in firepower. "Villages were destroyed to flush out single snipers," historian Callum MacDonald wrote. "Few people," one British reporter noted, "had suffered so terrible a liberation."[7]

"If the city had been liberated," another reporter observed, "the remaining North Korean defenders did not know it." By September 26, American tanks had penetrated to Seoul's main boulevard, where they engaged in street fighting against North Korean tanks, barricades, and snipers. So heavy was the rate of fire that American tank crews had to be relieved as their vehicles became choked with fumes. Block by block, U.S. troops pushed deeper into the burning city as civilian casualties poured into hospitals.[8] "Three months ago," wrote a reporter for *Time*, "Mapo [Boulevard] was a bustling, cheerful sycamore-lined thoroughfare with a doubletrack trolley, grocery, wine and tea shops and a sprinkling of residences. This morning Mapo wore a different look. The burned and blackened remains of the boulevard's shops and homes sent clouds of acrid smoke billowing over the city. Buildings still ablaze showered sparks and ashes high into the air to cascade down on red-eyed, soot-faced marines."[9]

For nine days, UN forces used a crushing combination of U.S. Marine artillery, air strikes, and tanks to support ground forces struggling to retake Seoul. This, the Second Battle of Seoul, would be tremendously costly. The Americans lost some 3,500 troops; the North Koreans suffered 14,000 casualties, with another 7,000 taken prisoner. Both DPRK and ROK forces executed civilians as Seoul's districts changed hands. Critics would argue that the cost was too high: in their rush to take the city by September 25, UN forces had waged a frontal assault on the city rather than enveloping it and forcing the surrender of the DPRK garrison. Moreover, American troops had employed their massive firepower to clear the city's defenders, amplifying the carnage of the battle.[10]

EXPANDING THE WAR

MacArthur's spectacular victory turned the tide of the war. The Inchon landing and the fall of Seoul severed the main supply line between North Korea and DPRK units in the South. UN forces began a sweeping offensive designed to crush the retreating North Korean army. But American leaders now faced a critical choice: whether to restore the Thirty-Eighth Parallel as the boundary between North and South Korea and claim a victory for international law, or to press the offensive in a bid to roll back communism in Korea and reunify the peninsula under the leadership of the pro-Western regime in Seoul. Had American political and military leaders chosen the former, Korea would likely be remembered as a triumph for the Western alliance: a moment when the United States used its military power, backed by the legal authority of the United Nations, to halt the advance of communism and restore the ROK. Instead, the Americans chose to turn their gaze to the north.

Certainly, the Truman administration faced tremendous pressure to expand the aims of the war. Until Inchon, U.S. leaders had been preoccupied with surviving the North Korean onslaught—not with the question of what to do in the event of a North Korean retreat. MacArthur's victory at Inchon accomplished one of the most stunning military reversals in modern warfare and brought into sight the prospect not only of survival but of a larger and more meaningful victory. Militarily, it made little sense to allow Kim Il-sung—the aggressor according to most Americans—to regroup and prepare for another potential attack on the ROK. "Troops could not be expected," Dean Acheson would famously remark, "to march up to a surveyor's line and stop." Indeed, MacArthur insisted that he be allowed to pursue retreating KPA troops into North Korea. Further, there would be political costs to halting the offensive: one Gallup poll taken in the wake of Inchon found that some 64 percent of Americans favored expanding UN operations north of the Thirty-Eighth Parallel. The Republican Party, still chastising Truman for the loss of China, would surely exploit any sign of Democratic weakness in Korea. Indeed, it would have been difficult for Truman and his advisors to stand in the way of the strong tide running in favor of invading North Korea. Acheson confidently proclaimed that Korea would be "a stage to prove what Western Democracy can do to help the underprivileged countries of the world."[11]

But the president had already secretly decided to expand the war into the north. On September 11, Truman signed off on NSC-81, a document that outlined American policy for the next stage in the war. The United States, working together with the United Nations, should seek the "complete independence and unity of Korea" so long as doing so would not risk a war with China or the USSR. Though they did not believe Moscow and Beijing would intervene in the South, leaders in Washington expected the Communist powers to defend North Korea. American and UN military forces should proceed north of the Thirty-Eighth Parallel only if they could do so without provoking a major Soviet or Chinese response. The war in Korea should not be allowed to expand into a global conflict. Although NSC-81's tone was one of caution, its underlying message was that U.S. forces should escalate the war if they could do so without provoking a wider war. However, this threshold would be harder to recognize than Truman or MacArthur realized.[12]

As North Korean forces retreated, MacArthur prepared to push forward. His new orders, transmitted on September 27, were to destroy the KPA and reunify Korea under Rhee's leadership while keeping a watchful eye for Soviet or Chinese intervention. "Unless and until the enemy capitulates," MacArthur announced, "I regard all of Korea open for our military operations." On October 1, the general demanded the surrender of North Korean forces. He did not receive an answer. U.S. Army patrols crossed the Thirty-Eighth Parallel on October 7 in advance of the main force, which began moving into North Korea two days later.[13]

What MacArthur, Truman, and Acheson all failed to understand, however, was that by crossing the Thirty-Eighth Parallel, they effectively forced Beijing to intervene. Mao and his lieutenants had been watching events in Korea with increasing concern. They had given their blessing to Kim in the lead-up to the DPRK attack on the South—one hundred thousand North Koreans had fought with the CCP in the Chinese Civil War; why should Koreans die to liberate China and then be prevented from fighting to liberate Korea? But Mao worried about the potential impact of the war on the newly formed PRC. The war provided a justification for the United States to ramp up its support for Chiang's regime in Taiwan, dramatically increase U.S. troop deployments in East Asia, and threaten the CCP's vision for a wider socialist revolution in the region. Further, Mao understood that the fighting in Korea could easily spread to threaten China itself. At the same time, Beijing recognized that, if the PRC could stand up to "U.S. imperialist aggression" in Korea, it would represent a significant boost to the regime's domestic legitimacy and international prestige. For Mao, involvement in Korea represented a high-risk gamble that, if successful, would be a critical step in pushing Washington's influence out of East Asia and remaking the region in Beijing's image.[14]

In August, Mao had warned his comrades that an American victory in Korea would embolden the Western imperialists: it could be a prelude to U.S. attacks on Manchuria, a Nationalist assault across the Taiwan Straits, and potentially a French offensive in Indochina. China must prepare to intervene to support the North Koreans. Suspecting a coming American attack at Inchon, Beijing had begun sending units to Manchuria in preparation to enter the war and warned Kim not to forget that "you are fighting the chief imperialist. Be prepared for the worst." When MacArthur's forces landed at Inchon and seized Seoul, Kim began begging Mao to intervene. Chinese commanders estimated that intervention would cost the PRC at least 60,000 killed and 140,000 wounded in the first year. But the Korean battlefield presented certain advantages to the Chinese. Beijing's forces could offset Western firepower by waging a type of "jigsaw warfare" along confused, uneven, and constantly shifting battle lines. Chinese forces would focus on enveloping and destroying American units as part of a strategy designed to inflict horrific casualties on Western forces and drain the American public's enthusiasm for the war.[15]

There was one last chance for diplomacy, however. On September 29, a Dutch diplomat informed the State Department that Beijing was considering intervention in Korea. The following day, Premier Zhou Enlai announced that "the Chinese people absolutely will not tolerate foreign aggression[;] nor will they supinely tolerate seeing their neighbors being savaged by foreigners." On October 2, Zhou warned the Indian ambassador to the PRC that a U.S. incursion into North Korea would prompt Chinese intervention. Acheson dismissed the warning as a bluff. American leaders underestimated the threat from the PRC. Only months out from its victory in the civil war, Beijing was thought to be preoccupied with internal challenges and the issue of Taiwan. Further, if the PRC was indeed Moscow's puppet (as many in Washington wrongly believed), the United States must stand resolute.[16]

Undeterred by rumors of Chinese intervention, American forces pressed forward. In the aftermath of Inchon, President Truman decided that the time had come to meet MacArthur face-to-face. MacArthur had already turned down two requests to visit Washington, but the upcoming congressional elections and the drama of the war itself pushed the president to go to the general on October 15. Wake Island was chosen as the meeting site, a far longer trip for Truman than for MacArthur—a fact that bothered some of Truman's aides. "When does the king go to the prince?" asked the president's appointment secretary. "While General MacArthur had many attributes of a foreign sovereign," Dean Acheson quipped, "and was quite as difficult as any, it did not seem wise to recognize him as one." Secretary of Defense George Marshall declined to make the trip, in part because of his distaste for MacArthur. The strongest objection came from the hero of Inchon himself. MacArthur resented being called away from the war for what he viewed to be clearly political reasons.[17]

The general's contempt showed when the two met. MacArthur broke protocol by failing to salute the president, a snub that Truman apparently failed to notice. Truman expressed concern over what appeared to be Chinese preparations to intervene in Korea, but MacArthur dismissed the danger. If the PRC had intervened in the initial months of the war, he explained, "it would have been decisive. We are no longer fearful of their intervention." If Chinese troops tried to take Pyongyang, he told the president, "it would be the greatest slaughter in the history of mankind." Some of the general's comments suggest that he was in fact hoping for the chance to fight Mao's armies. In August, he had told Gen. Matthew Ridgway, who at the time was serving on the Pentagon staff in Washington, that he welcomed Beijing's entry to the war because it would give him the opportunity to "deliver such a crushing defeat that it would be one of the decisive battles of the world—a disaster so great it would rock Asia and perhaps turn back Communism. . . . I pray nightly that they will. I would get down on my knees." Ridgway later said, "Whether this vision of himself as the swordsman who would slay the Communist dragon was what prompted his eventual reckless drive to the borders of Manchuria no one of course can now divine. But I suspect that it did add luster to his dream of victory." In any case, MacArthur's October message for Truman was unequivocal: the war was "won in Korea." Pyongyang would fall within a week, and the entire affair would be wrapped up by the end of the year. When the meeting adjourned, Truman announced, "I've never had a more satisfactory conference since I've been president." Neither man knew it, but the heyday of America's war in Korea was about to pass.[18]

Four days later, Pyongyang fell to ROK forces. "The besieged capital of North Korea," wrote one American reporter, "looks from the air like an empty citadel where death is king . . . a blackened community of the dead, a charred ghost town from which all the living have fled before a sudden plague." On the ground, however, it was a different story. UN troops met cheering crowds waving South Korean flags as they entered the battered city. "At one intersection we slowed down to pass a sandbag barricade," wrote another journalist. "The crowds lining the street surged out around us, offered us sesame cookies and handshakes." Surely, many of these same citizens would greet Communist forces with North Korean flags when they returned six weeks later. For the time being, however, Western observers were thrilled to enter "the first Communist capital to be liberated by the forces of the free world." They found a city festooned with Communist and Soviet propaganda. The walls of public buildings and houses were plastered with pictures of Stalin and Lenin. Kim's office was "[r]ich with gaudy rugs and expensive furniture . . . dominated by an enormous mahogany desk which is flanked on the left by a foot-high plaster bust of Kim, on the right by a bust of Stalin."[19]

Kim and the DPRK government had retreated to the North as UN troops advanced. South Korean and American soldiers trudged through Kim's abandoned offices in the old residence of the Japanese governor and took souvenir snapshots of the city's nearly empty streets. "We thought the war was over," remembered one South Korean officer. "The North Koreans were now completely wiped out, throwing away their weapons as we met them." But while American officials predicted an exemplary occupation of the North, a demonstration of the virtues of Western democracy, the reality was far different. Assailed by guerrilla resistance, U.S. forces firebombed whole valleys and villages; captured guerrillas were surrendered to ROK troops for brutal interrogation; and air force planes strafed farmers working in their fields. Perhaps deadliest of all were the South Korean security forces. ROK counterintelligence officers, tasked with rooting out and eliminating members of the Workers' Party, sent an estimated 150,000 people to be executed or pressed into forced labor. North Koreans would later claim that 15,000 people were massacred in Pyongyang.[20]

CHINA ENTERS THE WAR

Even as American and South Korean soldiers celebrated their victory in the North Korean capital, Chinese troop columns were marching toward the Yalu River and the border between China and North Korea. Some 250,000 Chinese soldiers marched for eighteen nights under cover of darkness and hid beneath camouflage during the day to avoid detection from UN reconnaissance planes. Beijing's commander, Peng Dehuai, ordered his troops to take favorable positions and wait for UN forces to close in. Chinese units were to set a series of traps in the path of the advancing UN troops, encircle the enemy, and eliminate them.[21]

Peng was a veteran Communist commander who had fought with Mao and Lin Biao in the Jiangxi Soviet and the Long March. During the last years of the Chinese Civil War, he had commanded the Northwest Field Army and played a pivotal role in the fighting around Shaanxi and the CCP's retreat from Yan'an. Peng had been born into a humble peasant family in Hunan and enlisted in the GMD army at sixteen. He had a "bluff, lusty face" and enjoyed the reputation of being a tenacious fighter. "Peng met the enemy head-on in frontal assaults," Harrison Salisbury explained, "and fought with such fury that again and again he wiped them out. Peng did not believe a battle well fought unless he managed to replenish—and more than replenish—any losses by seizure of enemy guns and converting prisoners of war to new and loyal recruits to the Red Army." Now Peng led the Chinese People's Volunteer Army south of the Yalu to lay a massive ambush for UN forces.[22]

North Korean forces had anticipated an American landing at Inchon and had prepared to execute "the great strategic retreat" in the likely event that their forces were turned back from Pusan. Moreover, rather than mounting a stiff defense at the Thirty-Eighth Parallel, KPA forces had continued retreating, drawing MacArthur's troops farther north and begging Beijing to intervene. A captured North Korean notebook observed that UN troops "were not fully aware of the power of our forces, they pushed their infantry far forward . . . to the Yalu River. This indicated that they underestimated us. All these conditions were favorable to lure them near." Another captured North Korean explained that the withdrawal had been planned: "We withdrew because we knew that UN troops would follow us up [to the Yalu River], and that they would spread their troops thinly all over the vast area. Now, the time has come for us to envelop these troops and annihilate them."[23] The Chinese followed suit, with Peng employing a strategy of "purposely showing ourselves to be weak, increasing the arrogance of the enemies, letting them run amuck, and then luring them into our areas."[24]

UN troops would be dispersed as they drove forward, and their supply lines would be stretched. The strongest Chinese units would focus on the more vulnerable UN contingents while Beijing's less effective troops engaged with the enemy's best troops. By doing this, Peng hoped he could knock his adversary off balance, deal a devastating blow to two or three American or ROK divisions, and rout the UN forces. Chinese soldiers would be hard-pressed in this offensive, however. The bitter cold combined with the difficulty of moving supplies past UN air patrols to frontline troops to present the greatest threat to Chinese troops: malnutrition. "For all the heroic rhetoric of the [Chinese] political officers," historian Allan Millett explains, "Chinese soldiers often attacked in search of their next meal."[25]

South Korean forces first encountered Chinese troops in late October. Two days later, American forces made contact with the Chinese. By November 1, reports of heavy attacks from unidentified troops began to filter in to the UN command. Chinese forces bloodied ROK and American units but then appeared to withdraw. One British soldier described an encounter with troops that were "unlike any enemy I had seen before. . . . They wore thick padded clothing, which made them look like little Michelin men. I turned one body over with my foot, and saw that he wore a peaked cap with a red-star badge. These soldiers were Chinese." Captured Chinese prisoners were interrogated, but they gave no clear picture of what was happening. By early November, American leaders recognized that Beijing's forces were operating in North Korea, but the full scope of the intervention was not yet clear. UN and ROK units continued their race to the Yalu River.[26]

On November 23, American troops, unaware of the thousands of Chinese soldiers surrounding them, savored a special Thanksgiving dinner of turkey, mashed potatoes, cranberry sauce, and pumpkin pie. While the Americans feasted, the Chinese subsisted on a small ration of millet. The following day, MacArthur launched what was intended to be the final offensive of the Korean War—an assault that would seize the Yalu and bring American soldiers home by Christmas. As MacArthur's troops pushed north, however, the CIA warned of "large, coordinated and well-organized guerrilla forces in the rear area," and UN pilots reported columns of Communist soldiers "swarming all over the countryside."[27] Beijing sprang its trap as American and South Korean forces slept on November 25. American troops awoke to bugles and the crackle of gunfire as Chinese forces stormed their positions. The surprise attack threw MacArthur's lines into disarray. UN forces, embarking on what they thought would be the last major operations of the war, were now driven back by the onslaught from battle-hardened PRC troops willing to suffer massive casualties in order to drive off the foreign invaders.[28]

"We face an entirely new war," MacArthur reported to the Joint Chiefs of Staff on November 28 as his forces retreated. Beijing had entered the conflict, and the United States now was effectively at war with China in Korea. The general explained that he lacked the resources necessary "to meet this undeclared war by the Chinese."[29] Beijing's intervention set off a frantic discussion in Washington about how to respond. In a conversation with the president and the National Security Council, Acheson laid out the principal issues that confronted the United States: MacArthur must withdraw from North Korea. "We can't defeat the Chinese in Korea," Acheson explained; "they can put in more than we can." Similarly, UN forces must be extremely careful not to allow the war to expand into Manchuria. If this were to happen, it would risk setting off a wider war. He warned that the United States was now "much closer to the danger of a general war." "We must consider Korea not in isolation," he argued, "but in the world-wide problem of confronting the Soviet Union as an antagonist."[30] The CIA also warned of the threat of a general war. Beijing was almost certainly acting with the knowledge and blessing of Moscow, the Agency explained, and both Communist powers must recognize—or perhaps even hope for—the potential of the situation in Korea expanding into a wider war. A wider war in Korea would divert U.S. military forces to an "indecisive theater" of the Cold War, where they would be subject to "attrition and containment." Ultimately, the Agency warned, "Soviet rulers have resolved to pursue aggressively their world-wide attack on the power position of the United States . . . regardless of the possibility that global war may result." The United States should expect further "direct or indirect Soviet aggression in Europe and Asia," and prepare for the "possibility" that the Kremlin "may already have decided to precipitate [a] global war."[31]

The White House remained adamant that the Chinese Communist offensive must be stopped. "We will take whatever steps are necessary to meet the military situation. . . . That includes every weapon that we have," President Truman announced in a press conference on November 30. When asked if that meant the atomic bomb, the president replied, "There has always been active consideration of its use. I don't want to see it used. It is a terrible weapon, and it should not be used on innocent men, women, and children." The White House quickly backpedaled, stating several hours later that, though it considered atomic weapons as an option whenever American troops were in combat, it had no immediate intention of using them. Though it was hardly necessary to do so, Truman seems to have been reminding Moscow and Beijing that Washington still had the bomb.[32]

On the ground, the UN retreat set off another wave of atrocities as South Korean forces rushed to butcher as many suspected Communists as possible before the Chinese and North Korean troops could liberate them. South Korean security services had crossed into North Korea behind UN troops in an attempt to purge the area of Communists. "With bulldozers we will dig huge excavations and trenches," President Rhee told one reporter, "and fill them with Communists." The State Department worried about finding some means to rein in the South Koreans in order to prevent a "bloodbath." Likewise, British officials concluded that the ROK was working to "hunt out and destroy communists and collaborators" throughout the North and, in doing so, running the risk of creating an international scandal.

As Chinese troops moved south, the pace of the killings accelerated. Hundreds of men, women, and children were killed and dumped into mass graves as the ROK and UN armies retreated. Before abandoning Pyongyang, one American witnessed South Korean officers ordering the summary execution of hundreds of DPRK prisoners. "To one side several North Koreans hung like rag dolls from stout posts driven into the ground. These men had been executed and left to hang in the sun. The message to the prisoners sitting on the ground was obvious."[33] In Sinchon, some fifty miles southeast of Pyongyang, ROK troops forced some four hundred women and children into a warehouse where they were interrogated in regard to the hiding places of their sons and husbands. They were refused food and water and, after begging for the latter, were thrown human excrement. Days later, the building was soaked with gasoline and set ablaze.[34]

American forces were responsible for their own form of slaughter, albeit a far less personal one. With UN forces reeling from the Chinese assault, MacArthur ordered the air force "to destroy every means of communication and every installation and factories and cities and villages. This destruction is to start at the Manchurian border and to progress south." The general hoped to unleash a wave of aerial destruction that would incinerate the Communist forces in their tracks. But this was only the latest campaign in the ongoing air war over Korea, a war that would continue throughout the conflict. Although they faced challenges from Chinese MiGs, some of which were piloted by Soviet personnel, UN aircraft would control the skies throughout most of the war. They used this aerial supremacy to rain munitions down upon North Korean forces, railways, river dams, and population centers for the three years the war lasted. Among the most horrific weapons in the UN arsenal was napalm: the sticky, incendiary jelly manufactured by Dow Chemical and used for fire-bombing. A Hungarian reporter described the effect of the bombing campaign: "Everything which moved in North Korea was a military target." There "were no more cities in North Korea." By the end of the war, U.S. aircraft had dropped over 32,000 tons of napalm on Korea along with 635,000 tons of conventional bombs. Eighteen of North Korea's twenty-two largest cities suffered at least 50 percent destruction—75 percent of Pyongyang was destroyed, 80 percent of Hamhung was leveled.[35]

But this brutal bombing campaign could not stop the Chinese and North Korean advance. Hiding beneath camouflage by day and moving by night, Communist infantry evaded American aircraft and continued their assault on UN lines. Some of the fiercest fighting of the war took place around Chosin Reservoir, a man-made lake surrounded by rugged mountains in the heart of North Korea. "The country around Chosin was never intended for military operations," the U.S. Marine commander in the area would recall in an interview. "Even Genghis Khan wouldn't tackle it." While Chinese infantry were able to move through the mountains, the UN's motorized troops were forced to move along the few roads cut into the terrain. The only path in and out of the region—for UN troops—ran through the town of Hagaru-ri, at the south of the lake, connecting the area with the port of Hungnam. Here was a chance for Mao's armies to deal a crushing blow to the Western intervention in Korea by surrounding the isolated American forces and inflicting massive casualties that might convince leaders in Washington to withdraw. Making matters worse, a cold front had moved in from the north in the days before the Chinese assault, bringing subzero temperatures and turning the area into a sprawling, snow-covered trap. On December 1, UN forces began a fighting retreat from the reservoir, attempting to blast their way through the frozen mountain passes as Chinese infantry attacked them from the surrounding heights. Ten days later, the battered remains of the UN forces reached the port of Hungnam, where landing craft were waiting to evacuate them. U.S. Marines took 4,418 combat casualties, with thousands more suffering from frostbite. Chinese losses in the campaign numbered more than 37,000—a testament to both the ferocity of fighting and the willingness of Beijing's units to accept massive casualties. Although the marines' valiant retreat prevented what could easily have been an even larger disaster, the fact remained that U.S. forces had been trounced by a lightly armed peasant army.[36]

MACARTHUR'S DISMISSAL

With UN forces in retreat, General MacArthur pushed Truman to remove the military restrictions that, in the general's view, had prevented a victory on the peninsula. On December 7, the general told the army chief of staff that, without significant reinforcements, he considered the UN position in Korea untenable. The time had come, he insisted, for the United Nations to commit its "full power" to meeting the "Communist threat." UN forces should be authorized to conduct air strikes against China and to set up a naval blockade of the PRC. Furthermore, Nationalist forces from Taiwan should be brought to Korea to meet Beijing's troops—a move that would transform Korea into a proxy war between Mao and Chiang. If he was not allowed to expand the war to China, MacArthur warned, the UN position in Korea would be lost. If Korea truly was a test of American resolve in the Cold War, a critical campaign in the global struggle between Washington and Moscow, the United States should unleash its full power on the peninsula and the surrounding region.[37]

Still, Truman remained reluctant. A wider conflict with China could be disastrous for the United States, the president's advisors had warned since the latter days of November. The fighting in the first months of the war had shown that American armed forces were unprepared for major combat. Furthermore, if Washington launched an attack on China, it would strain international support for the intervention in Korea: America's allies had agreed to an effort to restore the Thirty-Eighth Parallel, not to a war with the PRC. Worst of all, an attack on China would commit U.S. forces to the Pacific theater, leaving Western Europe open to a possible Soviet attack. Acheson again stressed that the United States must take a global view: "We should never lose sight of the fact that we were facing the Soviet Union all around the world." Moscow would welcome an American attack on Manchuria as a pretext for a wider war. "If we allowed the Russians now to trap us inside their perimeter," he warned, "we would run the risk of being sucked into a bottomless pit. There would be no end to it, and it would bleed us dry." Washington must "draw a line" and stick to it, he told the president. The restoration of the Thirty-Eighth Parallel as a Cold War boundary came back into focus as the goal of the UN intervention.[38]

On December 23, Gen. Walton Walker, commander of the U.S. Eighth Army, was killed when his jeep collided with a South Korean truck. His replacement, Matthew Ridgway, immediately set to work strengthening the forces under his command and preparing for a war of heavy attrition. However, even as Ridgway rebuilt the Eighth Army, the Chinese offensive was slowing. Like the North Korean and UN forces before them, the Chinese found that, as they drove deeper into the peninsula, their lines of supply grew longer. Under constant threat from UN air strikes, these lines became increasingly vulnerable as Beijing's forces moved south. By mid-February, Ridgway's forces had halted the Chinese offensive at a line south of Seoul and regained control of Inchon. On February 21, the Eighth Army began Operation Killer, designed to inflict heavy casualties on Communist forces and clear a path to the Han River and Seoul. Heavy rains flooded rivers, turned roads to mud, and risked setting off mudslides in the path of UN forces. Nevertheless, Ridgway proceeded with the assault. During the next two weeks, American and South Korean forces pushed the Chinese back, inflicting an estimated ten thousand casualties and suffering twenty-five hundred of their own. After Killer's success, Ridgway launched Operation Ripper, designed to flank

Seoul and capture the city without a costly frontal assault, and to establish a defensive line roughly along the Thirty-Eighth Parallel. Following on Ripper's success, Ridgway launched Operations Rugged and Dauntless, driving thirty miles into North Korea and establishing a defensive line against Chinese counterattacks.[39]

While the Truman administration backed away from its visions of rollback in Korea, General MacArthur remained convinced that the peninsula was the battlefield upon which the United States must strike a decisive blow against communism. On December 24, with Chinese forces poised to cross the Thirty-Eighth Parallel, MacArthur had issued a request for authority to use nuclear weapons to seal off Manchuria's border with North Korea to block Chinese operations on the peninsula. "I would have dropped between 30 and 50 atomic bombs," he explained. Then MacArthur added that he would have "spread behind us—from the Sea of Japan to the Yellow Sea—a belt of radioactive cobalt" with a half-life of 60 to 120 years.[40] Even more troubling, as far as the White House was concerned, were the general's public statements. In mid-February, MacArthur dismissed the notion of restoring the Thirty-Eighth Parallel through positional warfare as "wholly unrealistic and illusory." Rather, he announced, "we must materially reduce the existing superiority of our Chinese Communist enemy engaging with impunity in undeclared war against us, with the unprecedented military advantage of sanctuary protection . . . against our counterattack upon Chinese soil." At the end of the month, he warned Americans that Communist moves in Asia threatened "the heart of Europe and America" and must be "decisively defeated." One week later, he announced that the "continuation of existing limitation upon our freedom of counter-offensive action" prevented a major UN attack northward. "Vital decisions have yet to be made—decisions far beyond the scope of the authority vested in me as the military commander," he explained, which would determine whether the war turned into a victory or a stalemate. The Thirty-Eighth Parallel had no natural defenses, he added the following week, and would require massive amounts of manpower to defend. The only things that could prevent such a stalemate would be Truman's decision to send more troops to Korea and the removal of "the limitations on strategic bombing of Chinese bases in Manchuria." These decisions, he added, "must not ignore the heavy cost in allied blood which a protracted and indecisive campaign would entail."[41]

The biggest shock, however, came on March 24. MacArthur explained that, while China's "great numerical potential" had challenged UN forces, Western "methods of mass destruction" had leveled the playing field. No amount of "bravery, however fanatical, or the most gross indifference to human loss" could overcome this UN advantage in firepower. "The enemy therefore must by now be painfully aware," MacArthur then added, "that a decision of the United Nations to depart from its tolerant effort to contain the war to the area of Korea through expansion of our military operations to his coastal areas and interior bases would doom Red China to the risk of imminent military collapse." However, the general announced, should Beijing choose to recognize these realities and be willing to accept a peaceful solution to the conflict, "I stand ready . . . to confer in the field with the commander in chief of enemy forces." MacArthur had issued both a threat to China and an offer of a truce without authorization from Washington.[42]

The British ambassador to the United States expressed growing reservations about the UN commander—reservations shared by many in the Western alliance: "Our principal difficulty is General MacArthur. He seems to want a war with China. We do not." Finally, on April 5, Republican congressman Joe Martin read a letter from MacArthur to the House of Representatives:

It seems strangely difficult for some to realize that here in Asia[,] where the Communist conspirators have elected to make their play for global conquest, and we have joined the issue here raised on the battlefield, that here we fight Europe's war with arms while the diplomats there still fight it with words; that if we lose this war to Communism in Asia the fall of Europe is inevitable; win it and Europe most probably would avoid war and yet preserve freedom. . . . [W]e must win. There is no substitute for victory.

"This looks like the last straw," Truman wrote in his diary after hearing MacArthur's remarks. "Rank insubordination." The following Monday, April 9, the White House and the Joint Chiefs agreed to dismiss the UN commander. The next day, the news was relayed to MacArthur's headquarters in Tokyo: the commander of UN forces in Korea was out of a job and would be replaced by Matthew Ridgway.[43] MacArthur's repeated insubordinations and efforts to pressure the White House into using atomic weapons had challenged one of the most fundamental provisions of the U.S. Constitution: civilian command over the armed forces. It is no great exaggeration to say that, in firing MacArthur, Truman had acted to defend the constitutional system on which his country was founded and prevented the rise of what some historians have called an American Caesar. As Truman later wrote, "I fired him because he wouldn't respect the authority of the President. I didn't fire him because he was a dumb son of a bitch, although he was, but that's not against the law for generals. If it was, half to three-quarters of them would be in jail."[44]

MacArthur's dismissal also confirmed Truman's determination to limit the war to the Korean Peninsula. The White House strongly opposed the prospect of transforming the conflict into a larger war in Asia, let alone a global war against communism. This determination to limit the war was not inevitable, however. If UN troops faced the prospect of imminent expulsion from Korea—a Dunkirk scenario—it is conceivable that the Truman administration would have been forced to drop atomic bombs in order to save them. The political and international implications of total defeat in Korea might well have been too disastrous for the White House to resist a nuclear strike on Chinese forces. Yet perhaps the most important factor in Truman's decisions not to launch a nuclear attack on the PRC and to dismiss MacArthur was the changing situation on the ground in Korea.

STALEMATE

MacArthur's dismissal, coupled with Truman's retreat from the brink of nuclear war, signaled the beginning of the next phase in the conflict. The period of dramatic assaults and retreats along the peninsula had come to an end—the rest of the war would be a static conflict of attrition. The first six months of the war had taught the bloody lesson to both UN and Communist forces that it was not possible to maintain offensives far past the Thirty-Eighth Parallel. As UN forces were pushed south, they drew closer to their supply bases around Pusan, and their forces became more concentrated. Meanwhile, the Communist lines were stretched and increasingly vulnerable to American air strikes. Conversely, as UN troops pushed northward, they confronted Chinese forces that were better supplied and equipped to harass the allied advance. The war had become a stalemate. Barring a major American attack on Manchuria or the entry of the Soviet Union, it was likely to remain that way. It remained a limited war in terms of geography, the weapons employed, and the revised aims of the intervention, but not, ultimately, in its casualties.

Although the dramatic offensives and retreats were no more, the bloodshed continued. A complex network of trenches, tunnels, foxholes, and bunkers appeared along the hills that marked the front lines between UN and Communist forces. In the winter months, the opposing armies suffered through bitter cold, frozen equipment, and frostbite. The summer brought suffocating heat, clouds of insects, and disease that spread through the trenches. American air strikes pounded the hardened Communist fortifications by day; by night,

Communist troops launched human-wave attacks on the UN lines. Thousands died in the fighting over hills and tactical positions, but the larger strategic balance remained the same. When Peng complained to Mao of "massive unnecessary casualties," his concerns were brushed aside. The chairman told his general to expect a long war of attrition. As Mao later told Stalin, "The enemy will not leave Korea without being eliminated in great masses." Mao was willing to make maximum use of his tremendous advantages in manpower by accepting massive casualties. China, he wrote, had already suffered "more than 100,000 casualties . . . and is expecting another 300,000 this year and next." He was prepared to exhaust the Americans on the blood-soaked hills of Korea.[45]

It would take two more years for the two sides to negotiate a final armistice. Gen. Mark Wayne Clark, who had succeeded Ridgway as commander of UN forces in 1952, signed the armistice on July 27, 1953, with a heavy heart. "I had grave misgivings that some day my countrymen would be forced to pay a far higher price in blood than it would have cost if the decision had been made to defeat the Communists in Korea," he later wrote.[46]

THE PEOPLE OF KOREA EMERGED FROM THE WAR TO find their country devastated and split in half by one of the most dangerous borders in the Cold War world. Most of the nation's major cities had been reduced to smoking ruins, and dozens of villages had been wiped off the map. The war had claimed more than three million lives, many of them civilians massacred in successive waves of political repression. The once-arbitrary border between North and South Korea had been transformed into the most enduring frontier of the Cold War. The peninsula now lay under the iron grip of two rival dictators who presided over highly militarized, superpower-backed regimes. The two Koreas would henceforth exist in a perpetual state of war. Washington had sacrificed victory by expanding the war in an attempt to roll back communism in Korea, falling into the PRC's trap. Had Truman and MacArthur halted at the Thirty-Eighth Parallel, the war would be remembered as a triumph for international law, the United Nations, and the Western alliance. Instead, Washington settled for the not-insignificant achievement of restoring the Cold War frontier that bisected Korea. The Thirty-Eighth Parallel became a heavily fortified barricade against further Communist expansion in the northern Pacific.

Beijing had secured a significant, if costly, victory. Chinese troops had stood up to the Western alliance and survived the onslaught. After two and a half years of brutal warfare, China had fought the Western imperial powers to a standstill. This achievement added to Mao's growing prestige, and Beijing emerged from the war as a Great Power in East Asia with significantly larger influence in world affairs.[47] But the real winners were Kim Il-sung and Syngman Rhee. The conflict had helped to consolidate two brutal dictatorships, a Communist regime in Pyongyang and an authoritarian regime in Seoul. Kim strengthened the foundations for a totalitarian dynasty that would survive into the twenty-first century. For his part, Rhee proved adept at manipulating the superpower struggle to his advantage. As historian Gregg Brazinsky points out, the war left Rhee's regime with "its territory more secure, a military establishment that could not have been imagined prior to the conflict, and far greater control over society."[48] Rhee would not be the last unpopular anticommunist dictator the United States would back during the Cold War.

The military lessons of Korea were also mixed. Washington's decision to intervene had demonstrated that the superpowers would indeed be willing to go to war to defend seemingly peripheral regions in the developing world. In this regard, Korea helped to confirm the message of NSC-68: the United States must be prepared to fight the expansion of communism anywhere in the world. Still, there was a threshold of destruction that American leaders were not willing to cross. The United States chose not to launch nuclear attacks in the pursuit of victory in the developing world. Superpower interventions in the Third World would be limited at least in this regard. The war also demonstrated the power of Mao's strategy of protracted guerrilla warfare, and the tactic of envelopment and annihilation when employed against a superpower army. Maoist guerrillas now appeared as a fearsome new presence in the Third World and the broader landscape of international affairs. The Chinese willingness to accept massive casualties in a bid to exhaust the will of the Western powers was, in itself, enough to give American policymakers pause.

Indeed, the rising power of communism in East Asia highlighted Washington's need to develop an effective strategy for waging limited war and contesting Maoist rebellions in the Third World. If the United States hoped to defend the world from the scourge of communism, it had to develop the means to wage small, bloody wars on the distant frontiers of the Cold War world.[49] Not everyone in Washington shared this perspective, though. For many, the war for Korea also showcased the potential of American firepower. When used in the right conditions, American firepower suggested the possibility of offsetting the willingness of the Communist powers to accept massive casualties. This strategy carried a heavy price, however. The expenditure of staggering amounts of firepower dramatically increased the civilian death toll.

Ultimately, the war in Korea served as a testament to the terrifying impact of so-called limited war on civilians. Heavy bombing raids, urban warfare, and brutal massacres ravaged the peninsula. And as Allan Millett writes, "the middle ground of Korean politics had disappeared forever on June 25, 1950. Winning or losing had become life or death."[50] After his dismissal, MacArthur told the U.S. Congress that the destruction he saw was unparalleled: "I have seen . . . as much blood and disaster as any living man, and it just curdled my stomach. After I looked at that wreckage and those thousands of women and children and everything, I vomited." An Australian journalist traveling through North Korea observed, "Not even the smallest hamlet had been spared. . . . . Villages could be recognized only as level black patches . . . [and] whole towns had been moved into primitive cave shelters."[51]

Truman's intervention established a new, militarized frontier between the Communist bloc and the Western alliance along the Pacific Rim—a complement to Central Europe's Iron Curtain. But Korea would not be the last casualty in the battle for East Asia. Much of the same nightmarish violence witnessed on the peninsula would be repeated in the war that was already under way in Southeast Asia.

FRENCH INDOCHINA AND THE DEATH OF COLONIALISM

1945–1954

The third great clash in the battle for East Asia broke out in Indochina amid the crumbling edifice of the French Empire. Like China and Korea, Indochina had fallen under the control of imperial Japan during the Second World War. Though relatively short-lived, the Japanese occupation weakened many institutions of French colonial rule, exposed the vulnerability of Western control, and exacerbated existing social divisions inside Indochina. In short order, the occupation served as a rallying point for hundreds of resistance cells, many of which came under the control of Communist leaders. When French colonial authorities returned following Japan's defeat, the anti-Japanese resistance directed its energies toward throwing off the yoke of Western imperialism. Mao's victories in China and his example of guerrilla warfare inspired Vietnamese forces to wage a similar struggle. Yet the battle for Indochina, like the battle for Korea, played out in the midst of the superpower struggle. In the space of two generations, Indochina would become the bloodiest battleground of the post-1945 era. Desperate to recover their doomed empire, French leaders would play upon Washington's Cold War fears to pull the United

States deeper into involvement in yet another Communist revolution along the Pacific Rim. These pressures, combined with rising fears of a general Communist offensive in the East following Mao's victory in China, convinced the United States to enter the fray. Through a succession of vicious wars, Indochina was to become the graveyard of French imperialism, the greatest challenge to American power in the Third World, and the site of the most violent confrontation between the U.S. military and the forces of communism. As in Korea, none of this seemed plausible at the close of World War II.

THE FRENCH INDOCHINA WAR

At 7:00 in the evening on March 9, 1945, the Vichy French governor-general of Indochina, Jean Decoux, received a visit from the Japanese ambassador, Shunichi Matsumoto, at his offices in Saigon. The ambassador presented Decoux with an ultimatum: in an effort to defend against an imminent American assault on Indochina, the Japanese Empire demanded that all French security forces in the colony be placed under Japanese control. At 9:15 p.m., Japanese forces arrested Decoux and began seizing French colonial offices throughout the city. French forces put up a brief resistance, and a number managed to escape to neighboring China, but the Japanese victory was never in any real doubt. As the Japanese consolidated control over the colony and prepared for the expected Allied attack, Vietnamese nationalists sensed their opportunity. "Thus the French imperialist wolf was finally devoured by the Japanese fascist hyena," Ho Chi Minh later told American intelligence officers.[1]

Born in 1890, Ho was a veteran revolutionary who had journeyed to Versailles in 1919 to call upon President Woodrow Wilson to uphold the American leader's appeals for self-determination in Vietnam. His slight frame, hollow cheeks, and searching eyes belied a fiery political will. Ho was the leader of the most powerful rebel group, the Viet Minh. Although he had spent much of his time as a political activist in exile, Ho would win the "race" to seize the mantle of revolutionary leadership as the bonds of empire began to slip free. Espousing a blend of anticolonial nationalism and revolutionary socialism, the Viet Minh rejected French colonialism, the Japanese occupation, and the peasant-landlord rural politics in Vietnam. During the five months of direct Japanese control (March–August 1945), Viet Minh fighters and the United States became allies. Agents from the Office of Strategic Services worked with the Viet Minh to coordinate resistance activities and rescue downed American pilots. Ho, assigned the name OSS Agent 19, struck them as "an awfully sweet guy."[2]

Even as Ho organized his forces to challenge the Japanese, a larger tragedy gripped Vietnam in the form of a severe famine that had grown over 1944 and peaked in the spring of 1945. Between 1943 and 1945, the price of rice increased 1,400 percent as falling production and speculation made the staple increasingly hard to find. Any efforts to ship in rice surpluses from Cochinchina, in the South, were hampered by the ongoing war. As the famine grew worse in the countryside, some villagers had begun eating rice husks, roots, bark, and clover. Others took to the roads in search of food, and stories of cannibalism spread across the land. One survivor described the suffering in verse:

Along all highways famished bodies moaned,
lying curled up in sun, in dust and filth. . . .
And day by day, toward cities, toward Hanoi
more corpses, yet more corpses dragged themselves,
bringing the trail of flies, the stench of smells,
then crumbled down along some street or lane.

The Viet Minh responded to the famine by demanding the distribution of government food stores and the suspension of taxes on grain. Throughout the region, cadres encouraged villagers to seize grain storehouses and threatened local officials who refused to cooperate. All the while, the group continued to gain new recruits. By acting as a relief agency and providing a structure for organization at the local level, the Viet Minh was able to dramatically increase its standing in Vietnamese society. Hanoi's casualty estimates of the famine ranged from one to two million (between 10 and 20 percent of the total population) and soon became a rallying cry for the Viet Minh, who blamed both the Japanese and the French colonial authorities for creating the disaster.[3]

Japan's defeat ended the occupation, but the battle for Vietnam was just beginning. Even as the Viet Minh celebrated their independence from Japan, France (backed by the United States) prepared to restore its lost empire in Indochina. This decision came with reservations on the part of the Americans. As Franklin Roosevelt had explained to Stalin in 1943, the United States was no champion of the French Empire: "[A]fter 100 years of French rule in Indochina, the inhabitants were worse off than they had been before." Following Japan's surrender, however, Washington tilted in favor of supporting French claims. The nascent Cold War with the Soviet Union, the need to secure French participation in the Western Cold War alliance (what would become the North Atlantic Treaty Organization, or NATO), and concerns about the growing power of the Communist Party within France itself would all push the Truman administration toward the restoration of French rule in Indochina.[4]

On August 29, 1945, Ho Chi Minh entered Hanoi. The ancient capital of the medieval Dai Viet dynasty, Hanoi had been transformed into a modern city by the French—electric streetcars rattled along its tree-lined boulevards and in between its shimmering lakes. The streets teemed with thousands of recently arrived peasants, who had come to the city from the countryside in search of a new life in postwar Vietnam. Ho and his comrades arrived in Hanoi amid a flood of optimism. Japan had surrendered two weeks before, the French Empire was in ruins, and Vietnam stood on the brink of independence. Four days earlier, Emperor Bao Dai, a virtually powerless figurehead subject to the whims of both the French and Japanese rulers, had abdicated, and proclaimed his support for Ho as the next leader of the nation. On September 2, Ho addressed a crowd of thousands in Ba Dinh Square. "All men are created equal," he intoned, borrowing the words of Thomas Jefferson. "They are endowed by their Creator with certain inalienable rights; among these are Life, Liberty, and the pursuit of Happiness. . . . All the peoples on the earth are equal from birth, all the peoples have the right to live and to be happy and free." As the festivities continued, the crowd watched as a small airplane circled the square. When it made a pass low enough that those on the ground could see the American flag on its wings, the crowd broke out in cheers.[5]

While the Vietnamese celebrated their independence in Ba Dinh Square, French authorities had moved to restore their power in Indochina. In late August, French colonial officials had begun parachuting into Tonkin, Annam, Cochinchina, and Cambodia while a military column prepared to reenter Tonkin from China. The following month, British troops arrived in Saigon to accept the surrender of Japanese forces and liberate imprisoned French forces—who were subsequently rearmed. News of the events in Saigon sparked a general strike in Hanoi on September 17. "If only there was a way to stop the inevitable onslaught," Ho wrote. In March 1946, twelve hundred French troops arrived in Hanoi under the command of Gen. Jacques-Philippe Leclerc. While jubilant French colonists took to the streets to celebrate their return, Viet Minh leaders prepared for war. "They are weak," Ho told his colleagues. "Colonialism is dying. The white man is finished in Asia."[6]

The long-anticipated confrontation arrived in late 1946. On November 22, violent skirmishes broke out between French security forces and Viet Minh troops in the port city of Haiphong, killing 240 Vietnamese and 7 Frenchmen. Two days later, French officials decided to "teach a hard lesson to those who have so treacherously attacked us." Just after 10:00 in the morning, French ships and planes began shelling the city. Large sections of Haiphong's Vietnamese quarter were destroyed, and estimates of civilian casualties ranged from the hundreds into the thousands. The final countdown to full-scale war had begun. At 8:00 in the evening on December 19, lights flickered out along Hanoi's streets as an explosion rocked the city. Viet Minh agents had attacked the city's power plant, sending a signal for the general offensive to begin. In the following days, the fighting spread to other cities throughout the country. As Ho had told one American journalist, the conflict would be "a war between an elephant and a tiger. If the tiger ever stands still the elephant will crush him with his mighty tusks. But the tiger does not stand still. He lurks in the jungle by day and emerges only at night. He will leap upon the back of the elephant, tearing huge chunks from his hide, and then he will leap back into the dark jungle. And slowly the elephant will bleed to death. That will be the war of Indochina." He was more direct with French officials: "If we have to fight, we will fight," he warned. "You will kill ten of us, and we will kill one of you, and in the end it is you who will be exhausted."[7]

As fighting raged on the streets of Hanoi, Viet Minh radio called for a people's war of national liberation. The group would follow a strategy based on Mao's three-stage model: defensive war, equilibrium, and final offensive, with a special emphasis on the growing influence of the Communist world in international affairs. Vietnamese revolutionaries recognized that their struggle was linked to currents in the Cold War.

Viet Minh fighters began a strategic withdrawal from the cities with the aim of reconsolidating their forces in guerrilla units in the countryside. Although French troops were able to kill a considerable number of guerrillas in the initial months of the war, the Viet Minh leadership remained intact. As the rebels' recruitment efforts began to bear fruit, their ranks swelled.[8] The principal architect of the Viet Minh strategy was Vo Nguyen Giap. Born in 1911 in the small village of An Xa, Giap was a promising student with a keen interest in history.

He attended the University of Hanoi, graduating with a degree in politics and economics, and then took a position as a schoolteacher. He joined the Communist Party in 1931 and then fled to China during the Second World War, eventually settling in Yan'an. There, in the stronghold of the Chinese Communist Party, Giap would learn the art of guerrilla war from Mao's commanders.[9]

Over the next seven years, Giap waged the war of the Vietnamese tiger against the French elephant in Indochina. Viet Minh forces would rely on guerrilla tactics as part of a larger strategy of attrition against the French. By avoiding open battles, using the cover of local terrain, laying ambushes, and striking at enemy forces where they were weak, Giap's guerrillas sought to exhaust French resolve. Conversely, French commanders worked to draw the rebels into set-piece battles, engineering a series of pincer movements designed to trap and destroy the Viet Minh. At the same time, French officials scrambled to expand popular support for the friendly regime in Saigon under Emperor Bao Dai. To the French, this was *la guerre sale*, "the dirty war," a frustrating, indecisive battle against a largely unseen foe. French forces controlled cities and major towns, but the surrounding countryside remained in the hands of the Viet Minh. "In outlying areas," writes Duong Van Mai Elliott, "the *pourriture*, or rotting from within[,] would begin. . . . Military posts in these areas would become isolated. At night, the self-defense militiamen would become prisoners in their own reinforced posts, afraid to go out on patrol. Outside, the Viet Minh, masters of the night, would come and go as they pleased."[10]

Having completed their withdrawal from the cities, the Viet Minh continued building their strength over the course of 1947. In January 1948, the party announced the start of the equilibrium stage of its struggle. The Viet Minh would now begin a counteroffensive against the colonial army. "If the enemy attacks us from above, we will attack him from below. If he attacks us in the North, we will respond in Central or South Vietnam, or in Cambodia and Laos. If the enemy penetrates one of our territorial bases, we will immediately strike hard at his belly and back . . . cut off his legs [and] destroy his roads." It was a strategy of guerrilla war designed to sap French strength over a protracted struggle. As rebel attacks increased, the Viet Minh were able to seize new territory and recover areas lost in the previous year.

In 1950, General Giap launched a campaign to establish control over the northern border regions with the aim of opening new supply lines between Viet Minh bases and the newly established People's Republic of China. Bolstered by this aid from China, the general calculated that the time had come to launch a final offensive in 1951. Viet Minh forces would engage French troops in open battle along the edge of the Red River Delta and then move to retake Hanoi. On January 13, twenty-one Viet Minh battalions attacked the French garrison at Vinh Yen. For four days, the French troops weathered the rebel onslaught as Giap employed human-wave attacks designed to overwhelm the defenses. Then, on January 17, Vietnamese forces were repulsed after suffering heavy casualties. In March, Giap would again try to win a set-piece battle against French units, in Mao Khe. For a second time, Viet Minh forces failed to achieve a breakthrough. Giap's third attempt to crush French forces in a conventional battle came at Ninh Binh, in May. The fighting raged for over a week, but the French were able to withstand the attack and inflict massive losses on the Viet Minh. The staggering losses incurred in these attacks convinced Giap to revert to guerrilla tactics and ensured that the war would continue.[11]

DIEN BIEN PHU

It was now France's turn to seek a way to end the bloody stalemate in Indochina that was draining French resources and creating increasing political controversy back home. In May 1953, Paris replaced Gen. Raoul Salan with Henri Navarre as the top military officer in Indochina. Revered as a brilliant strategist, Navarre arrived in Saigon charged with turning the tide of what many in France feared was a losing war. He hoped to retake the initiative in the conflict with the Viet Minh through a surge in the number of French troops while, at the same time, building up pro-Western Vietnamese forces. "We can conquer only by attacking," he proclaimed.[12] As part of this offensive strategy, Navarre would employ a system of "hedgehogs," fortified outposts occupying strategic locations in hostile territory. He hoped to project French military power into Central Vietnam and into North-west Vietnam in defense of Laos. He later admitted that the system "constituted a mediocre solution [but it] appeared as the only possible one. It would not prevent light enemy detachments from roaming through the countryside, but, leaving in our hands essential points, would prevent an [outright] invasion." The general determined that the isolated outpost of Dien Bien Phu, located in the far northwestern corner of the country, would provide the best location in the area for an air base. The French base dominated the mountain passes to Laos in the west and China in the north. The base itself sat at the bottom of a valley surrounded by rugged highlands. Home to ethnic Tai minori-ties, the valley formed an important link in the opium trade routes through the region that helped fund the Viet Minh. An airstrip, built in 1939, had served anti-Japanese resistance activities and now func-tioned as a *base aéro-terrestre* for French counterinsurgency operations against the Viet Minh. Limestone mountains ringed the valley, their peaks overlooking the French fortifications and the neighboring vil-lage below. The surrounding heights were a sufficient distance from the airstrip so as to prevent the installation of enemy artillery in any but the most vulnerable positions on the hills facing the base. Navarre wrote that the "batteries would be in view of the [French] observation posts. . . . They would, therefore, be silenced by our counter-battery fire or by our bombers." Dien Bien Phu, the general insisted, would be a "deep stab into the enemy's rear areas." The fortress formed the center of the French defense of Northwest Vietnam and "must be held at all costs." "Victory," Navarre bragged to his staff, "is a woman who gives herself to those who know how to take her."[13]

General Giap reacted cautiously to the news of Navarre's decision to occupy Dien Bien Phu. "This is an operation that works to our advantage," he proclaimed, but he was wary of a potential trap. Giap had learned the painful lessons of frontal assaults on French positions in 1951, and he was not eager to repeat his mistakes. Furthermore, an attack on the French base presented monumental challenges. A three-hundred-mile march across forbidding terrain lay between Dien Bien Phu and his army in Laos. Equipment, food, men, ammunition, and supplies would all have to be moved vast distances (often on foot) over difficult terrain under constant threat from attack by French aircraft. But if Viet Minh forces could be placed in position, they would be able to encircle the isolated base and lay siege to the garrison inside. At the end of 1953, the two sides prepared for a showdown at Dien Bien Phu. As French troops under the command of Col. Christian de Castries prepared eight strongholds across the floor of the valley— allegedly named after Castries's mistresses: Anne-Marie, Béatrice, Claudine, Dominique, Eliane, Françoise, Gabrielle, and Huguette— Giap's soldiers moved into position on the surrounding heights. Giap's forces toiled through February and into March 1954, reinforcing artillery positions and digging a network of trenches around the French defenses.[14]

At 5:00 on the evening of March 13, 1954, the Viet Minh attacked. As artillery shells screamed down around them, the defenders at strongpoint Béatrice watched enemy soldiers rise from trenches a mere two hundred meters from their lines. Ninety minutes later the Viet Minh scored a direct hit on Béatrice's command bunker, killing most of the men inside. By 9:00 p.m., all the officers at Béatrice had been killed. Just after midnight, the strongpoint fell to the attackers. Meanwhile, French troops at Gabrielle, the northernmost strongpoint, withstood the initial assault, but their defenses began to crumble under the punishing artillery barrage. On the morning of the fifteenth, following a failed counterattack, Gabrielle fell to Giap's forces. Two days later, the Viet Minh took Anne-Marie to the northwest, closing the circle around the remaining French defenders in the valley. With the fall of the three outlying posts, the French position became increasingly untenable. Giap's antiaircraft batteries were now free to harass the airstrip, which would soon be destroyed by a Viet Minh commando unit, adding to the difficulty of resupplying the garrison. French forces were trapped inside a shrinking defensive perimeter and subject to devastating artillery fire from the surrounding heights.[15]

Over the next seven weeks, French and Viet Minh soldiers fought over the ruined ground of the valley floor. As the Viet Minh slowly tightened the lines around the garrison, French officers scrambled to gain control of airdropped supplies. Monsoon rains often shrouded the battlefield, preventing effective use of French aircraft and compounding the misery of the men fighting below. Despite launching a series of valiant counterattacks, the French saw their perimeter continue to contract. By the first of May, the battle lines cut through the French strongpoints at Huguette, Dominique, Eliane, and Françoise. On May 7, Giap ordered a final assault. Twenty-five thousand Viet Minh charged against the remaining 3,000 French defenders, overwhelming them. As Giap's troops closed in, the French commander radioed his superiors in Hanoi to report that the battle was lost. At 5:30 in the evening, as Viet Minh troops seized the command bunker, a French sergeant radioed, "In five minutes, everything will be blowing up here. The Viets are only a few meters away. Greetings to everybody." Ten minutes later, Vietnamese soldiers raised the red Viet Minh flag over the bunker. A total of 2,242 French soldiers had been killed, and nearly 12,000 had been taken prisoner. Estimates of Viet Minh casualties topped 20,000.[16] Giap would reflect that the victory at Dien Bien Phu "had a far-reaching influence in the world. . . . [T]he news of the victories won by our army and people . . . have greatly inspired the progressive people the world over."[17]

Dien Bien Phu sounded the death knell of the French Empire in Indochina. One day after Giap's guns fell silent, diplomats from the United States, the Soviet Union, the People's Republic of China, the

United Kingdom, France, and the Viet Minh took up the question of Indochina at the 1954 Geneva Conference, convened to resolve the conflicts in Korea and Indochina. Exhausted, bloodied, and humiliated, French leaders were ready to put an end to their nightmare in Indochina. Although they still controlled much of Indochina, the defeat at Dien Bien Phu proved to be the last straw. The Soviets and the Chinese also pushed for the war to end. Moscow needed time to consolidate the regime after Stalin's death in 1953, and Beijing was ready for peace after the brutal fighting in Korea. Both Communist powers, moreover, feared the prospect of U.S. intervention in Indochina. The Geneva Accords called for the temporary division of Vietnam along the Seventeenth Parallel. In the North, Ho's Democratic Republic of Vietnam (DRV) would assume power. In the South, the Bao Dai government would retain authority. The two Vietnams were to be reunified through a general election to be held in July 1956. This partial victory for the DRV was the result of Ho's caution: better to consolidate the DRV gains and prepare for future reunification than to press for total victory and invite retaliation. Indeed, despite the defeat at Dien Bien Phu, nearly half a million French troops remained in Indochina. More worrisome was the fact that another, even greater power waited in the wings. The United States had taken a keen interest in the French war out of a desire both to contain Communist expansion and to strengthen France as a Cold War ally. By the end of the conflict, Washington was funding 80 percent of the French war effort and American pilots were flying support missions for French forces. The Americans feared that the same fires of revolutionary communism that had overwhelmed China and nearly taken Korea now threatened Southeast Asia. But President Eisenhower was reluctant to use U.S. military forces to save French colonialism and wary of provoking Chinese military intervention in the conflict. He therefore pulled back from the brink of intervention at Dien Bien Phu, a move that might have included a tactical nuclear strike on Giap's forces. Nevertheless, American leaders were preparing to step into France's role in the region and provide a bulwark against the further spread of communism. While the DRV celebrated its victory at Geneva, the seeds of another conflict took root.[18]

SINO-SOVIET SPLIT

As the representatives from Hanoi, Beijing, Moscow, Pyongyang, Seoul, Paris, London, and Washington sat down to sign the Geneva Accords on the morning of July 21, 1954, Communist forces in Asia could list a remarkable set of achievements. Seven years before, Mao's troops had been written off by both Moscow and Washington, Korea sat divided and largely ignored, and Viet Minh forces struggled against an overwhelmingly superior French Army. But in the intervening years, East Asia had been transformed. Mao's Communists had seized control of the world's most populous nation; Beijing's and Pyongyang's armies had fought the United States to a standstill in Korea; and the Viet Minh were about to oust the French from Indochina and establish their own state in North Vietnam. Meanwhile, Western forces appeared to be in retreat. Chiang and the GMD nursed their wounds on their fortress island of Taiwan. The United States had refused to intervene in China and Indochina and had been bloodied in Korea, and French forces had surrendered at Dien Bien Phu. By most accounts, 1954 should have been a year of celebration for the forces of left-wing revolution around the developing world. Yet deep fissures in the Communist world were set to tear apart the seemingly ascendant Sino-Soviet alliance and, in doing so, transform the Cold War yet again.

While leaders in Hanoi hoped to continue their unfinished struggle to create a united, Communist Vietnam, Chinese and Soviet leaders were ready to sacrifice the Viet Minh's aspirations for the sake of their own larger policy goals. For Moscow and Beijing, the Geneva Conference had offered an opportunity to gain added recognition from the Western powers and to consolidate the significant achievements of the East Asian offensive in China, Korea, and Southeast Asia. While Soviet leaders had little interest in Indochina, Mao and his comrades were convinced that the complete liberation of Vietnam would entail a long struggle. Worse, the escalation of a war in Southeast Asia would give an opening to Washington to stage a military intervention in Indochina. "We've already lost too many men in Korea," Chinese premier Zhou Enlai told Nikita Khrushchev in the lead-up to the Geneva Conference. "We're in no condition to get involved in another war at this time." At Geneva, Soviet and Chinese leaders placed their own national interests above the goal of continuing the Communist offensive in Southeast Asia. The Sino-Soviet Alliance, then, served to restrain the more bellicose factions among the Vietnamese Communists.[19]

Yet this lull in fighting would last only as long as the alliance between the two Communist giants. And for all their triumphs, Beijing and Moscow could not overcome bitter differences rooted in both political and ideological concerns. Also, Mao Zedong would never forget Stalin's lukewarm support during the Chinese Civil War. The Communists' battlefield victories provided an immediate salve to these tensions, but resentments festered. Chinese leaders also remained skeptical of the Soviet model's applicability to societies in the developing world. Over the course of the 1950s, a budding competition between the two Communist powers emerged for the leadership of the revolutionary movement in the Third World.[20]

Most observers in Washington seemed oblivious to the tensions between Beijing and Moscow. "Every act of communism in Asia has its inception in and takes meaning and direction from the Kremlin," a 1954 CIA report insisted. The leaders of the CCP were nothing more than "puppets of world communism, i.e. of Moscow; they are entirely satisfied to be puppets." Mao was, according to the report, "100 per cent puppet. . . . He will never change his present relationship with the USSR." The same could be said for the entire leadership of the Chinese Communist Party: "The CCP will do exactly what the world revolutionary leadership, Moscow, tells them." China would remain politically subservient, economically dependent, and militarily attached to the USSR. China would "never, under the CCP, make a heavy industry that will assure her independence." The United States should not waste its time seeking to find points of disagreement between Moscow and Beijing, the paper argued. "There will be no split in the forseeable [*sic*] future."[21] This myth of a Communist monolith would prove difficult to shake. Indeed, another fifteen years would pass before U.S. leaders found the means to exploit the growing rift between Moscow and Beijing.

Meanwhile, the decade after Geneva transformed Sino-Soviet relations. Beijing and Moscow could hide their differences while war raged in Korea and Indochina, but peace brought new challenges. Although Stalin's death in 1953 left Mao as the reigning patriarch of the global Communist movement, the Kremlin had no intention of surrendering leadership to Beijing. An even larger point of contention appeared in February 1956, when Stalin's successor, Nikita Khrushchev, delivered his now-famous "secret speech" to the Twentieth Congress of the Communist Party in Moscow. In the address, Khrushchev denounced the repression of the Stalinist era, repudiated Stalin's cult of personality, and set in motion a sweeping campaign to transform the institutions of the Soviet state. The speech shocked Chinese leaders, who accused Khrushchev of rejecting Leninism and Stalinism in favor of a new "revisionism" that threatened to derail the Communist project. Communist parties in China, North Korea, and North Vietnam had each constructed a cult of personality and used the Stalinist model as the basis for their organizations. While Khrushchev had targeted his address at the Soviet party, its implications spread far beyond the borders of the USSR. Khrushchev's policy of peaceful coexistence with the Western powers, which was announced that same year and appeared to call for accommodation with the capitalist world, only made matters worse.[22]

Mao and his comrades balked at what they saw as Khrushchev's moderate Cold War policies. The Kremlin's calls for Chinese caution during the Taiwan Strait Crisis in 1958 further irritated Chinese leaders, as did the Soviet refusal to share nuclear weapons technology with the PRC. For a time, Mao's decision to launch the Great Leap Forward masked the growing animosity between the Communist powers. A sweeping land reform campaign, the Great Leap envisioned the mass collectivization of agriculture drawing upon the nation's massive labor resources. In the space of a generation, Mao hoped to catapult China's economy ahead of that of Great Britain. The results were catastrophic. Poorly planned reforms combined with brutal repression to generate massive famines that, according to historian Frank Dikötter, led to as many as 45 million "unnecessary deaths." Enormous projects to build canals and dams and to fell millions of acres of trees ravaged the countryside. Government forces executed an estimated 2.5 million people who resisted the reforms, leading one historian to place the Great Leap Forward alongside the Nazi Holocaust, the Soviet Great Terror under Stalin, and the Cambodian genocide.[23]

Four years and tens of millions of deaths later, Beijing abandoned the disastrous Great Leap Forward only to find itself embroiled in a border war with India in October 1962. While Chinese and Indian troops skirmished along the frontier, U.S. and Soviet leaders locked horns over Soviet missiles in Cuba. Khrushchev's decision to remove the missiles from Cuba at the end of the 1962 Cuban Missile Crisis gave Beijing new ammunition in its propaganda war against Moscow. The Kremlin, Chinese leaders argued, had abandoned the heroic Cubans to the depredations of U.S. imperial power. Khrushchev's refusal to back Beijing in the 1962 Sino-Indian War added yet another line to Mao's list of grievances.[24] Alone, none of these issues would have caused the split between the Communist powers. Put together, however, they ripped apart the Sino-Soviet axis and opened a new stage in the wars of containment.[25]

PART II

THE INDO-ASIAN

BLOODBATHS AND THE

FALL OF THIRD WORLD

COMMUNISM

1964 – 1979

THE SEVEN YEARS BETWEEN 1954 AND 1961 WITNESSED A sharp drop in the overall level of global violence. Yearly war deaths, which had peaked in 1950 at nearly six hundred thousand, fell to less than fifty thousand in 1955. But the second half of the decade was marked by numerous crises and one pivotal anticolonial war. In November 1956, Soviet troops stormed into Hungary to crush a rebellion against the Soviet puppet regime in Budapest. This rebellion, the first major revolt in a Soviet satellite country, might have been a major propaganda coup for the Western bloc, but the world's attention was fixed not on Eastern Europe but on the Middle East. There, British, French, and Israeli forces staged the last great military expedition of the colonial era when they attacked Gamal Abdel Nasser's Egypt in a failed bid to wrest control of the Suez Canal from the nationalist leader. The Suez Crisis signaled the end of the colonial era and prompted the United States to assume Britain's role as the key Western power in the region. Two years later, in 1958, U.S. forces mounted their first military intervention in the Middle East when U.S. Marines entered Lebanon to shore up the faltering Maronite Christian regime in Beirut. That same year, an artillery duel between China and Taiwan brought the two nations to the brink of open war. While dramatic, none of these events generated the massive casualties seen during the wars in China, Korea, and French Indochina.

The largest conflict of the late 1950s, the Algerian War of Independence, became emblematic of the global struggle for decolonization. Between 1954 and 1962, French military forces fought a bloody war against Algerian revolutionaries in a doomed bid to preserve French colonialism in North Africa. Some half a million people were killed in the brutal colonial war that resulted in the final death of French imperialism. In the process, the Algerian fighters became international celebrities and postcolonial issues assumed a more prominent role in international politics. As the 1960s began, the victories of the Algerian revolution, the proliferation of new nation-states in Africa, and the success of the Non-Aligned Movement pushed postcolonial nations into the spotlight in international forums such as the United Nations. Third World revolutionaries assumed ever more visible roles as guerrilla leaders such as Che Guevara, Ho Chi Minh, and Yasser Arafat became household names. At the same time, Washington, Moscow, and Beijing all moved to expand their influence in the Third World.

As the forces of revolution surged forward, the comparative lull in global violence came to an end and the Cold War entered a new era. Throughout the 1960s and '70s, the changing balance of power among the United States, the Soviet Union, and China fueled a new round of deadly wars along the shores of the South China Sea and the Indian Ocean. Deteriorating relations between Moscow and Beijing helped generate competition for influence in the postcolonial world after Chinese leaders began attacking Soviet premier Nikita Khrushchev for his failure to provide sufficient support for wars of national liberation. Khrushchev responded by trumpeting the Kremlin's support for Third World revolutionaries and beefing up foreign aid to progressive states in the developing world. Likewise, Soviet social scientists focused their energies on revamping their socialist

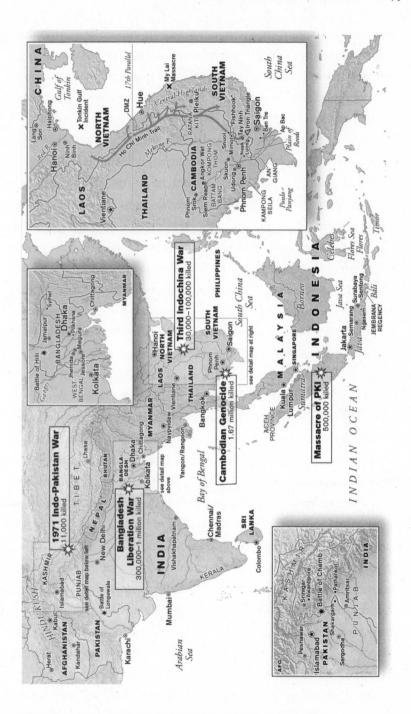

The Indo-Asian Bloodbaths of the Middle Cold War, 1960–1979

development models in the hope of staging modernization projects in postcolonial countries. If Moscow's experience of rapid, state-based industrialization could be replicated in the developing nations of Asia and Africa, the Soviet system and claims to world leadership would be vindicated.[1]

Meanwhile, Mao and his comrades stressed the symbolic importance of the Chinese Revolution for fighters throughout Africa and Asia in a bid to seize the mantle of leadership from Khrushchev. The growing rift between Beijing and Moscow fostered fierce competition in the developing world. Bruised by his showdown with the United States during the Cuban Missile Crisis, Khrushchev faced the need to restore Moscow's credibility with Third World allies by taking a more activist Soviet stance in the postcolonial world. Meanwhile, Chinese leaders hoped to put the disastrous experience of the Great Leap Forward behind them and to bolster their claims to the leadership of the Third World revolutionary project. As the new decade of the 1960s began, both Beijing and Moscow jockeyed to bolster their standing in the non-Western world. Both would find ideal opportunities to do so in Southeast Asia, which perched on the brink of a new round of revolutionary violence. In January 1961, Khrushchev announced the Kremlin's support for wars of national liberation. The Soviet leader praised revolutionaries in Algeria, Cuba, and Vietnam and promised to aid movements struggling against the forces of colonialism and oppression.

American leaders saw the full transcript of Khrushchev's address on January 18, 1961, only two days before John F. Kennedy's inauguration. Despite warnings from U.S. intelligence officials that Khrushchev was merely responding to Chinese criticisms, the incoming administration took the premier's words at face value. Kennedy and his advisors feared that the signals out of Moscow and Beijing represented the beginning of a new Communist offensive in the Third World. Responding in his inaugural address, Kennedy called upon Americans to "pay any price" to "assure the survival and the success of liberty" throughout the world. He continued: "To those people in the huts and villages of half the globe . . . we pledge our best efforts to help them help themselves." Kennedy's words marked the beginning of a new American campaign to win the Cold War in the Third World.[2]

In the coming months, the United States launched a series of initiatives to contest left-wing revolutions around the world. U.S. military forces would act as military advisors to local forces waging counterinsurgencies in a frontal assault on liberation fighters around the Third World. At the same time, American social scientists, engineers, and economists staged development projects designed to modernize traditional societies and ameliorate the poverty, inequality, and hardship that served as recruiting tools for Communist parties. In this way, U.S. officials would spread what one historian has called "the right kind of revolution." They would deploy American military, scientific, and economic power to foster the development of modern, prosperous, and pro-Western states throughout the Third World. A 1962 paper titled "U.S. Overseas Internal Defense Policy" laid out a more detailed schematic for this campaign. The paper argued that the war against Communist revolutionaries must "be joined in the villages which normally represent the critical social and political organizational level." In this type of conflict, a battle for the hearts and minds of the developing world, "the *ultimate and decisive target is the people* [emphasis in original]. Society itself is at war and the resources, motives and targets of the struggle are found almost wholly within the population." Using this rationale, the United States embarked upon a series of counterinsurgencies concentrated in Southeast Asia.[3]

Cold War rivalries shaped local violence in multiple ways. The Sino-Soviet competition for influence in the Third World had already begun fueling a number of conflicts in Southeast Asia. Communist leaders in Hanoi, partially restrained by Chinese and Soviet support for the Geneva Accords, recognized an opportunity to renew their battle to liberate South Vietnam as the tentative alliance between

Moscow and Beijing collapsed. Communist forces in neighboring Cambodia used the escalating war in Vietnam to launch their own bid for power. To the south, the Indonesian Communist Party (PKI) used increased support from Beijing to expand its influence in the region's largest country. Meanwhile, increased U.S. support to right-wing military forces in South Vietnam and Indonesia spurred leaders in Saigon and Jakarta to crack down on moderates and left-wing movements. And in less than a decade, an unlikely spirit of coopera-tion between Beijing and Washington, spurred on by deadly border clashes between Chinese and Soviet soldiers, would swing U.S. and Chinese support behind Pakistani forces waging genocide in Ban-gladesh. As a result, through the middle decades of the Cold War, societies in the developing world sat at the center of a three-way competition between the Great Powers. The societies around the monsoon lands of South and Southeast Asia were about to enter the bloodiest stage of the Cold War. The Indo-Asian bloodbaths would tear the Communist world apart at the same time as ethnic and sec-tarian warfare resurged in the postcolonial world.

MAKING A QUAGMIRE IN VIETNAM

1961 – 1965

Vietnam was a country divided at the Seventeenth Parallel. In the South, Western influence still reigned. The streets of Saigon, named for French military leaders, lined by ornate colonial façades and shaded by lush trees, bustled with activity. Cafés served cognac, escargots, and crêpes suzette while stylish boutiques sold the latest bikinis, jewelry, and perfumes from Paris. While the downtown still teemed with French soldiers and European businessmen, Vietnamese and Chinese districts that ringed the posh center city overflowed with native Saigonese and recent refugees from the countryside. In these quarters, the smells of incense and cooking *pho* hung in the damp air. This "great tropical metropolis," one American reporter warned, "lies under the ominous shadow of Communist victory and entrenchment" in the distant North. The Viet Minh, driven by "fanatical dedication and zeal, iron discipline and terrifying efficiency," were plotting to retake South Vietnam. Communist cadres moved through the Vietnamese neighborhoods, spreading Hanoi's influence in the so-called wild south. Meanwhile, the denizens of Saigon carried on amid the corruption of the city and the crumbling edifice of European colonial power.[1]

Seven hundred miles to the north lay the city of Hanoi. Ho Chi Minh's forces took the former seat of the French colonial adminis-tration of Tonkin on October 9, 1954, as the French Expeditionary Corps abandoned the city. The monsoon rains that had shrouded the French withdrawal broke as the Communist columns reached the capital. Thousands of Hanoi's citizens poured into the streets to greet the Viet Minh soldiers. Clad in the green uniforms of the People's Democratic Republic of Vietnam, Communist troops entered the city in Soviet trucks, in jeeps, on bicycles, and on foot. Welcoming the Communists, residents unfurled banners emblazoned with slogans such as "Long Live President Ho." Crowds cheered as Viet Minh sol-diers brandished their weapons and towed American-made artillery pieces captured at Dien Bien Phu around Hoan Kiem Lake, in the center of the city. As power passed from the hands of the French to the Communists, some eight hundred thousand people, many of them Vietnamese Catholics, fled to the South. At the same time, one hun-dred thousand Vietnamese from the South moved to North Vietnam. However, another ten thousand revolutionaries remained in South Vietnam covertly.[2]

At the beginning of the next decade, new leaders in Washington and Moscow chose to throw their resources toward a new campaign to wage the Cold War in the developing world. While Khrushchev voiced his support for wars of national liberation in the Third World, Kennedy expanded U.S. Special Forces capabilities and launched a series of development programs designed to turn back the tide of Communist revolutions in the postcolonial world. Here, along the shores of the South China Sea, the United States would wage its larg-est intervention of the Cold War. But the Vietnam Wars, the deadliest series of conflicts of the post-1945 era, would ultimately prove to be little more than a sideshow in geopolitical terms. By the time the Vietnam Wars drew to a close in the late 1970s, the strategic land-scapes of the Cold War and the postcolonial world had fundamentally changed. This transformation was less the result of the bloody fighting between Hanoi and Saigon than of developments taking place on Vietnam's periphery and beyond, in places such as Indonesia, Cambodia, and Bangladesh. Nevertheless, Washington's intervention in Vietnam's civil war constituted the central battlefield of the Indo-Asian bloodbaths.

THE TWO VIETNAMS

The French Indochina War and the Geneva Accords had left two radicalized regimes to rule over a divided Vietnam. While the Communist regime in Hanoi consolidated its hold over the country, launching a bloody socialist revolution that led to the execution of thousands of the regime's enemies, the pro-Western government in Saigon suffered from many of the same problems that had plagued the Chinese Nationalists and Rhee's regime in South Korea. Corruption, incompetence, unpopularity, and authoritarianism plagued the Saigon leadership. The lull in conflict that lasted for half a dozen years after 1954 set the stage for a new round of Cold War violence, fueled in no small part by the competition between Moscow and Beijing. But local forces held the initiative. Neither Saigon nor Hanoi viewed the division of the country as a permanent solution to Vietnam's problems. Both hoped for eventual reunification through peaceful or, if necessary, violent means.

Washington threw its support behind Saigon. Though the Eisenhower administration had refrained from direct intervention to save French colonialism, it now hoped to direct American resources (financial, military, technological, and moral) toward building a Saigon regime that could withstand the revolutionary tides sweeping through the Far East. As Eisenhower told reporters in the midst of the Dien Bien Phu battle, the United States must defend Southeast Asia from the further spread of communism. If Indochina were to fall, the president explained, the United States and its allies would confront "the 'falling domino' principle": "You have a row of dominoes set up, you knock over the first one, and what will happen to the last one is the certainty that it will go over very quickly. So you could have a beginning of a disintegration that would have the most profound influences. . . . Asia, after all, has already lost some 450 million of its peoples to the Communist dictatorship, and we simply can't afford greater losses."

The fall of South Vietnam threatened the "island defensive chain" of Japan, Taiwan, and the Philippines and presented a threat to Australia and New Zealand, Eisenhower warned. Where the French had failed, the Americans were determined to succeed. "We must work with these people," the president argued, "and then they themselves will soon find out that we are their friends and that they can't live without us." Secretary of State John Foster Dulles wrote that it was pointless to "mourn the past." The United States must now "seize the future opportunity to prevent the loss of northern Vietnam from leading to the extension of communism throughout Southeast Asia and the Southwest Pacific."[3]

The Americans chose to build their anticommunist bastion in South Vietnam on the shoulders of one man: Ngo Dinh Diem. Born into an educated family in 1901, Diem was a devout Catholic (in a country that was overwhelmingly Buddhist), with a deep affinity for Confucianism. He proved to be a bright student and entertained thoughts of joining the priesthood but instead chose to study law in Hanoi. During the 1940s, Diem had hoped to raise a Third Force in Vietnam, a middle alternative between French colonialism and Viet Minh communism, and he became a prominent voice calling for greater Vietnamese autonomy from France. He was captured by Viet Minh cadres in 1946, brought to his only face-to-face meeting with Ho Chi Minh, and offered a position in the revolution. Diem declined, citing the Viet Minh's execution of his older brother, Khoi, some months before. Though unsuccessful, Diem's activities in the 1940s ensured that he was one of a shrinking number of Vietnamese leaders who remained, for the most part, untainted by collaboration with the Japanese, French, or Viet Minh.

After learning of a Viet Minh order for his assassination in 1950, Diem left the country for Japan. He would be gone for four years, during which time he would travel to California; Washington, DC; the Vatican; Paris; and New York and would meet with American academics, U.S. and French officials, Secretary of State Dean Acheson, and Pope Pius XII. He eventually settled in New Jersey and began giving public talks promoting greater U.S. involvement in Vietnam. Diem caught the attention of a number of conservative groups around the United States and of government officials eager to find Cold War allies in the developing world. As his lecture circuit continued, Diem came to the attention of American leaders. His criticisms of the Viet Minh, the fact that he was relatively free from the taint of collaboration with the French and Japanese, and his calls for modernization made him an increasingly attractive candidate for the role of a pro-American leader in post-France South Vietnam. Meanwhile, Diem's brother Ngo Dinh Nhu worked to build a base of political support inside Vietnam, forging alliances between various local factions and political networks.[4]

When the French garrison at Dien Bien Phu collapsed in the spring of 1954, Diem and his American supporters recognized that their chance had arrived. Emperor Bao Dai understood that France's moment in Indochina had passed and America's was now beginning— by choosing Diem as premier of the Republic of Vietnam, Bao Dai signaled his desire to expand his relationship with the United States. French officials were dismayed by the emperor's decision, however. Diem, they warned, had an "almost total lack of professional competence" and was "too narrow, too rigid, [and] too unworldly . . . to have any chance of creating an effective government." Prime Minister Pierre Mendès-France put it more simply: "Diem is a fanatic."[5]

Fanatic or not, Diem faced a daunting task: Vietnam was literally a country divided. As the creation of a collapsing French colonialism and with a relatively short life expectancy, the Republic of Vietnam (RVN) had little historical claim to existence. Few observers expected

Ho and the Communists to have a great deal of trouble winning the Geneva Conference–mandated elections in 1956 to reunify the nation. Leaders in both Saigon and Washington refused to sign onto or participate in the plebiscite, a move that would undercut any RVN claims to popular legitimacy. Division existed in the upper echelons of the government as well. Diem's troubled relationship with Emperor Bao Dai dated back to the 1940s, and the two would not gladly share the reins of power. The most pressing problems, however, came from divisions within South Vietnamese society. "Vietnam's wild south," historian Jessica Chapman writes, had "responded to the dislocations caused by French colonial rule and Japanese occupation by balkanizing into competing armed administrative units." Throughout much of the countryside, Communist insurgents moved more or less freely, sowing discontent and revolutionary unrest. Aside from the Communists, rival religious sects, the Cao Dai and the Hoa Hao, commanded private armies that contested RVN control in the Mekong Delta. In the cities, the Binh Xuyen, an organized crime syndicate descended from pirates who had roamed the mangrove swamps of the Saigon River, ran prostitution rings, casinos, extortion rackets, and opium dens while exercising a considerable degree of control over the national police. American diplomats compared the situation to the "city of Chicago placing its police force in [the] hands of [the] Al Capone gang during [the] latter's heyday." Diem, the CIA's station chief lamented, "only controlled the space of his [own] palace grounds."[6]

These domestic tensions came to a head in the spring of 1955. In March, the Cao Dai, Hoa Hao, and Binh Xuyen joined under the United Front of Nationalist Forces in a bid to contest the growing power of the Saigon government. Recognizing this threat, Diem moved to crush these rival forces and consolidate his own power. After sporadic violence broke out in Saigon, Diem announced the removal of the Binh Xuyen's police chief. The following day, a full-scale conflict broke out between Binh Xuyen forces and the Vietnamese National Army. The so-called Battle of Saigon raged for two days as government paratroops assaulted Binh Xuyen positions and the defenders launched mortar attacks on Diem's palace. At dawn on April 30, rebel forces began a retreat from Saigon, regrouping in the swamps south of the capital. In the coming months, government forces would finish mopping up the resistance as Diem emerged in firm control of the Saigon government. His victory also eliminated most of the remaining reservations from the U.S. government—which had considered abandoning Diem prior to the showdown with the sects. "As this crisis develops," one State Department official observed, "we are being forced to take a more and more unequivocal and strong stand for Diem." On the heels of this victory, Diem announced that he would hold national elections to determine Saigon's next head of state and that he had no intention of participating in the scheduled 1956 elections to reunify North and South Vietnam. The national elections, held in October 1955, were fraught with corruption. Diem won with a suspiciously high 98 percent of the total votes, defeating Bao Dai and claiming the position as head of state. At the same time, Diem dismissed North Vietnam and Communist rebels in South Vietnam as puppets of Moscow and Beijing and, in July, launched his "Denounce the Communists Campaign." In the coming years, some twenty-five thousand suspected subversives would be rounded up and thrown in Diem's prisons. By the end of 1955, Diem had emerged, against long odds, atop the regime in Saigon. In doing so, he had dramatically increased his prestige in the eyes of U.S. officials—he had become, in the words of *Life* magazine, America's "Miracle Man in Vietnam."[7]

U.S. leaders now looked to South Vietnam as a cornerstone in their larger defense of Southeast Asia against the spread of communism. And although he had consolidated his domestic position, Diem still faced the monumental challenge of building South Vietnam into a stable, prosperous nation capable of withstanding subversion from the Communist North. Among Diem's most vocal champions was Michigan State University political scientist Wesley Fishel, who would head the Michigan State University Vietnam Advisory Group, a partnership between the university, the U.S. Department of State, and the Saigon government to provide state building and modernization assistance. Fishel argued that the Saigon government would have to "stimulate a rapid development of national consciousness and engender strong support" among the population. This would be no small feat; ravaged by years of colonialism, occupation, and war, South Vietnam was a nation in which a conservative elite controlled massive tracts of land. One-quarter of 1 percent of the population owned 40 percent of the land cultivated for rice in South Vietnam. It would require a revolutionary modernization program to give South Vietnamese peasants a stake in the survival of Diem's regime. For leaders in Washington, South Vietnam would become nothing less than a "test case" for America's ability to combat "wars of national liberation." Between 1955 and 1961, the United States would channel some $1.65 billion in aid to the RVN. Rural community development projects sat at the center of these modernization schemes. In 1959, the regime launched an ambitious initiative to create "Agrovilles" throughout the countryside. Peasants were resettled inside these planned communities, which were touted as centers of rural development. At the same time, the Agrovilles were designed to be more easily defended against Communist infiltration. Three years later, the Kennedy administration chose to adopt the Strategic Hamlet Program. The project was designed to resettle some fifteen million villagers, placing them inside government-controlled settlements. Journalist Bernard Fall described the project as "the most mammoth example of 'social engineering' in the non-communist world." Inside these fortified communities, peasants were subject to increased state surveillance; the areas outside the strategic hamlets would become free-fire zones. Though ambitious, these community development projects uprooted peasants, often forcing them to abandon their homes and build new ones inside government communities, taking them away from ancestral lands and farther from the rice paddies where they worked. In practice, Diem's

Agrovilles and Kennedy's Strategic Hamlets alienated much of the rural population.[8]

North of the Seventeenth Parallel, Hanoi was also implementing crash efforts to build a modern state. As in the South, land reform sat at the center of these programs. The party was intent on extending its control over the 80 percent of the population that lived in the countryside. Leaders in Hanoi aimed to break the power of rural landlords while increasing the dependence of local villagers on the central party. The campaign soon generated a reign of terror throughout the countryside as villagers denounced their neighbors and staged sporadic uprisings against heightened government control. By 1956, violent opposition to the state's land reform campaign had coalesced into a widespread wave of rebellions that had to be put down with military force. Thousands died as a result of the disastrous land reform campaign. In August, Ho Chi Minh issued an official acknowledgment of the campaign's mistakes, but the damage was done. The ruling clique in Hanoi that had launched the land reform efforts (namely, Truong Chinh, Ho Chi Minh, Pham Van Dong, and Vo Nguyen Giap) had suffered a major blow and now launched a "rectification" campaign designed to correct these previous "errors." This campaign produced a major shift in power in Hanoi, away from Ho and Giap and toward new elements in the party. The principal victors in this realignment were Le Duc Tho, leader of the rectification campaign, and Le Duan. Together, these two men would emerge as the most powerful leaders in North Vietnam.[9]

Born into a humble family in 1907, Le Duan was a founding member of the Indochina Communist Party. He spent most of the 1930s in a French prison. After being released in 1937, he climbed the ranks of the party hierarchy before being sent back to prison from 1940 to 1945. His second release came in time for the Viet Minh's August 1945 revolution against French colonial rule, allowing him to serve as the party's secretary of the Regional Committee of South Vietnam and later head of the Central Office for South Vietnam (COSVN) in the war against the French. After the French defeat, Le Duan stayed in South Vietnam to take charge of the clandestine efforts to organize the Communist resistance. There, he wrote his 1956 manifesto, *The Path to Revolution in the South.* The work, argues historian Lien-Hang Nguyen, represented Le Duan's attempts to "simultaneously outflank any competitors in the South and state his campaign in the North." Its publication came in the depths of the party's struggles with the failed land reform and presented an appealing alternative: rather than focusing its energy on the difficult task of development in the North, Hanoi could place priority on completing the revolution in the South. Le Duan's southern revolution could allow the party to direct attention away from North Vietnam's domestic troubles and toward the goal of reunifying Vietnam. Le Duan's influence would grow steadily over the next four years until, in September 1960, he became general secretary of the Politburo and effectively took control of the party.[10]

In the years leading up to Le Duan's ascension, Hanoi's leadership was split between the so-called North Firsters, who sought to advance the socialist revolution in North Vietnam, and the South Firsters, who placed priority on liberating Vietnam south of the Seventeenth Parallel. A campaign of political agitation had continued after 1954, involving thousands of Viet Minh cadres that had stayed in the South after the Geneva agreements. The Diem regime's widespread political oppression also generated popular support for the Communists among significant segments of the population. By 1959, the push toward revolution in the South had become so strong, and the plight of the southern insurgency in the face of Saigon's repression so dire, that the Politburo issued Resolution 15, authorizing an armed struggle to liberate the South. Hanoi began deploying 4,600 volunteer troops in the South and expanding the network of supply routes through Laos and Cambodia that would come to be known as the Ho Chi Minh Trail. Hanoi remained cautious, favoring incremental escalation rather than a full-blown invasion that might incite the United States to intervene in order to save its client. In 1960, Hanoi announced the formation of the National Front for the Liberation of South Vietnam (later NLF). While officially classified as a broad coalition of rebel groups, in practice the NLF functioned largely as an appendage of the Communist Party. Much of the organization's membership was made up of southern revolutionaries, but its leadership answered, more often than not, to Hanoi.[11]

As aid began flowing in from the North in late 1959 and through 1960, the southern insurgency escalated. Communist cadres worked to incite rural uprisings throughout the countryside. Fortified government hamlets were one of their principal targets. Revolutionary forces attacked village officials and government agents, eliminating the "tyrants and traitors" of the "puppet" regime in Saigon. As fighting between rebel and government forces intensified, the Communist cadres sought to develop liberated zones throughout South Vietnam to serve as "leopard spot" bases. As the North Vietnamese Army's official history explains, "In the mountains, where the military struggle would play the primary role, we would annihilate enemy troops in order to widen our liberated areas, build bases, and expand our armed forces. In the rural lowlands the military and political struggles would play coequal roles. . . . In urban areas the political struggle would be preeminent."

Communist forces would build bases of military strength in remote regions, cultivate ties with villagers in order to allow movement through populated zones, and construct networks of political agents in urban areas where the Diem regime's influence remained strongest. Meanwhile, North Vietnam would serve as a massive rear base, channeling support and reserve forces to the war in the South. By the end of 1961, Communist ranks there had swelled to one hundred thousand guerrillas.[12]

THE MAKING OF A QUAGMIRE

Even as the fighting in South Vietnam intensified, the superpowers turned their attention toward the broader conflict in the developing world. In early January 1961, Nikita Khrushchev reaffirmed his support for the concept of peaceful coexistence: a war between the United States and Soviet Union would be disastrous, "millions would die." Local wars were also to be treated carefully, so that they would not set off a larger conflict between the superpowers. Moscow would continue to support "wars of national liberation," however. These conflicts were "inevitable as long as imperialism exists," and the combatants would receive aid from the Soviet Union. CIA analysts judged this to mean that the Kremlin would "pursue a more aggressive program in all 'colonial' areas." Peaceful coexistence between the superpowers did not mean an end to conflict in the Third World. Indeed, the absence of conflict across the East-West divide might translate to an intensification of conflict in the developing world. But the Soviet premier was not alone in his turn to the Global South.[13]

That same month, a new leader stepped into the White House, one who would bring a new determination to win the Cold War in the Third World. The youngest man ever elected president of the United States, John Fitzgerald Kennedy brought an air of vigor to the Oval Office. In his inaugural address, he pledged to "pay any price, bear any burden, meet any hardship, support any friend, oppose any foe to assure the survival and the success of liberty." As part of this effort, the new president would reach out to the developing world. "To those new states whom we welcome to the ranks of the free, we pledge our word that one form of colonial control shall not have passed away merely to be replaced by a far more iron tyranny." He also warned these nations of the dangers of seeking support from the Communist bloc: "[R]emember that, in the past, those who foolishly sought power by riding the back of the tiger ended up inside."[14] Even as Khrushchev declared his support for wars of national liberation, Kennedy prepared to defend the Third World against the further spread of Communist influence. To do this, the Kennedy administration would deploy a new strategy in the Cold War struggle: counterinsurgency. If Communist revolutionaries depended on the support of the people, U.S. forces and their allies would win the "hearts and minds" of the population and deprive the insurgents of this base of support. It would not take long for the White House to discover the ideal testing ground for its new strategy of fighting the Cold War in the Third World.

Eight days after his inauguration, Kennedy sat down to review a report from counterinsurgency expert Gen. Edward Lansdale, who had recently returned from Vietnam. The general's report was troubling: the current situation in South Vietnam appeared untenable. The pro-Western Diem regime was waging a dangerous battle against a mounting Communist insurgency aimed at toppling the Saigon government and reunifying the country under Hanoi's rule. "The U.S. should recognize that Vietnam is in a critical condition and should treat it as a combat area of the cold war," Lansdale argued. Kennedy took the sobering news to heart. For "the first time," he told the general, he appreciated "the danger and urgency of the problem in Viet-Nam."[15] "It was a shock to me to look over maps of the estimated situation with U.S. and Vietnamese intelligence personnel," Edward Lansdale had explained to Secretary of Defense Robert McNamara, and see that the Communist forces "had been able to infiltrate the most productive area of South Vietnam and gain control of nearly all of it except for narrow corridors protected by military actions." Lansdale joined an ever-louder chorus of voices warning the White House about the deteriorating situation in Vietnam. "The situation gets steadily worse almost week by week," journalist Theodore White told Kennedy. "Guerillas now control almost all the Southern delta—so much that I could find no American who would drive me outside Saigon in his car even by day without military convoy. . . . What perplexes the hell out of me is that the Commies, on their side, seem able to find people willing to die for their cause."[16]

As the guerrilla war in South Vietnam intensified, the Cold War superpowers deepened their involvement, and a disturbingly familiar pattern reappeared in Vietnam: as had been the case in China and Korea, the United States opted to back a repressive anticommunist regime with a narrow base of popular support while the USSR supported indigenous Communist forces that, while ruthless, commanded a broader popular following and had a far more efficient power structure. As in China and Korea, the coming struggle in Vietnam was to result in massive bloodshed. But if patterns reminiscent of China and Korea were discernible in Vietnam, so, too, was a new dynamic in America's Cold War in the developing world: the resolve to bring U.S. social science expertise to bear on the challenge of staging modernization in Southeast Asia. Guerrilla warfare, Deputy National Security Advisor Walt Rostow told an audience at Fort Bragg, was "a product of that revolutionary [modernizing] process and the Communist effort and intent to exploit it." Communist forces that sought to exploit the instability created by modernization were nothing more than "scavengers of the modernization process." Rostow and his allies in the Kennedy administration hoped to use modernization, backed by military operations, to redirect the forces of revolution in the developing world away from Communist influence.[17] Kennedy's advisors were convinced that South Vietnam was worth saving. In November 1961, McNamara and Secretary of State Dean Rusk argued that the "loss of South Viet-Nam to Communism would involve the transfer of a nation of 20 million people from the free world to the Communist bloc. The loss of South Viet-Nam would make pointless any further discussion about the importance of Southeast Asia to the free world; we would have to face the near certainty that the remainder of Southeast Asia and Indonesia would move to a complete accommodation with Communism, if not formal incorporation with the Communist bloc."[18]

Vietnam gave the incoming administration a chance to bolster its credibility after setbacks in Cuba and Laos, at the 1961 Vienna summit between Kennedy and Khrushchev, and in Europe after the erection of the Berlin Wall in 1961. The Vietnamese battlefield would provide the Kennedy administration with an opportunity to flex its muscle on the front lines of the global struggle against communism in the Third World, the "principal battleground [between] the forces of freedom and Communism," according to the president's advisors. In this contest, guerrilla warfare represented "an international disease" that the United States must eradicate. Combined with its efforts to stage modernization, Washington would employ an array of new counterinsurgency operations designed to blunt the military capabilities of Communist insurgents. Rostow pushed Kennedy to employ American helicopters and Green Berets, army Special Forces troops charged with providing counterinsurgency training and assistance to the South Vietnamese. "In Knute Rockne's old phrase," he argued, "we are not saving them for the junior prom." In response to a sharp escalation in NLF operations over 1961, the president sent Rostow and Gen. Maxwell Taylor, the president's military representative and future chairman of the Joint Chiefs of Staff, to South Vietnam to assess the situation in October. Not surprisingly, their findings were sobering. The Diem regime was largely incompetent; it lacked popular support and seemed unable to meet the challenges it faced. Saigon was gripped by a "deep and pervasive crisis of confidence and a serious loss of national morale." Government forces had adopted a "defensive outlook," reacting to crisis rather than taking action to improve the security of the state. The United States, Rostow and Taylor argued, should increase its commitments to South Vietnam. They recommended that Washington send an additional eight thousand advisors to the country to boost the fighting capabilities of the South Vietnamese Army and allow the regime to go on the offensive against the insurgency. Their report promoted a "limited partnership" between Washington and Saigon. The U.S. Military Assistance Advisory Group (MAAG) should be transformed into "something nearer—but not quite—an operational headquarters in a theater of war," Taylor told the president. "The U.S. should become a limited partner in the war, avoiding formalized advice on the one hand, trying to run the war, on the other."[19]

Kennedy was reluctant to fully implement Taylor's recommendations. He told historian Arthur Schlesinger Jr., "The troops will march in; the bands will play; the crowds will cheer; and in four days everyone will have forgotten. Then we will be told we have to send in more troops. It's like taking a drink. The effect wears off, and you have to take another." Vietnam was a country thousands of miles away about which most Americans cared little. Washington had already sent millions of dollars in aid to Saigon, with little sign of improvement. Nevertheless, the president could not simply abandon the regime, effectively handing yet another victory to the Communists in East Asia. Rather, Kennedy chose to waffle: Washington would increase aid to Saigon and continue its support of anticommunist forces in neighboring Laos, but it would not seek a major escalation of the conflict; at the same time, Kennedy would bring pressure on Diem to introduce liberal reforms aimed at increasing the regime's base of popular support. The Kennedy administration stayed on the fence—Washington would neither make the commitments necessary to win the war in Vietnam nor cut its losses and withdraw.[20]

Under Kennedy, the indecisive conflict in South Vietnam intensified. The number of NLF forces in South Vietnam increased from four thousand in 1960 to twenty-five thousand in 1963. As NLF ranks grew, NLF tactics evolved from simple hit-and-run attacks to better-coordinated raids by larger units. "Self-defense forces" laid booby traps, dug tunnels, and collected taxes while People's Army of Vietnam (PAVN) units coordinated the flow of infiltrators into South Vietnam. As the ranks of the insurgency grew, so did the complex of supply routes that made up the Ho Chi Minh Trail. For the duration of the war, Hanoi directed a steady flow of supplies and cadres by foot, cart, and bicycle along the trail, a grueling journey that took an average of two months. Of those who set out on the trail, an average of 1.7 percent died from fatigue or disease, with malaria taking the greatest toll. In response, the beefed-up U.S. military presence in Vietnam sought to implement a "special war" strategy. U.S. military advisors would provide training and tactical support to Army of the Republic of Vietnam (ARVN) units that would bear the brunt of the fighting. In 1962, American forces began providing helicopter and air support to South Vietnamese troops battling the Communist insurgents. By the end of the year, eleven thousand U.S. advisors were operating in the RVN. While the introduction of larger numbers of advisors and U.S. helicopter support significantly enhanced ARVN mobility and fighting power, South Vietnamese leaders increasingly refused to commit their troops without this American support. Making matters worse, the Americans struggled with the strategic dimensions of their mission: to a troubling degree, U.S. commanders seemed to be searching for a way to win the last major war in Asia. In particular, American advisors were keen to prepare the ARVN for a Korea-style invasion of conventional PAVN units across the Seventeenth Parallel. However, "the real threat," one ARVN officer complained, "[existed] at the village level in the form of . . . highly disciplined guerrilla units where cumbersome conventional units could not operate effectively. The French had already proved this to us. We wondered why we had to repeat the mistake for the Americans."[21]

As 1962 came to a close, the United States found itself quietly slipping into a rapidly escalating guerrilla war in Vietnam. The Diem government remained inefficient and unpopular, the American-backed Strategic Hamlet Program had alienated peasants throughout the countryside, and U.S. military advisors were playing an ever-expanding role in combat against a Communist insurgency that showed no signs of breaking. Hanoi was also hard at work. Over the summer of 1962, North Vietnamese leaders secured assurances from Mao that Beijing would intervene to defend the regime against a U.S.–South Vietnamese invasion. Likewise, China would expand its aid programs to North Vietnam, offsetting the U.S. escalation.[22]

In the first days of 1963, both Washington and Saigon received an alarming indication of just how dire the situation had become. For some time, American officers had lamented that NLF insurgents

favored guerrilla attacks and generally refused conventional engagements with ARVN troops. If only the NLF would "stand and fight,"
they argued, South Vietnamese soldiers could decimate their ranks.
But on January 2, 1963, at the village of Ap Bac, some forty miles
southwest of Saigon in the Mekong Delta, the Americans would be
proven wrong. One week earlier, NLF forces had infiltrated the area
and created a "liberated zone" from which to harass government
forces. In what the regime expected would be a fairly routine operation, a force of 2,000 ARVN troops supported by American advisors
and helicopter gunships responded with an assault designed to drive
the guerrillas out of the area. Some 350 NLF fighters watched the
preparations from fortified positions in the village—their commanders had resolved to test their growing strength against the ARVN
soldiers on terrain that they deemed advantageous.[23]

At 7:00 a.m., as a thick fog hung around the trees and the thatched
roofs of the village, American helicopters dropped to the ground and
released the South Vietnamese infantry riding inside. Forty-five minutes later, as the vanguard of the ARVN force closed to within thirty
meters of the NLF lines, the guerrillas opened fire. The battle raged
for the next fourteen hours as ARVN and American forces tried to
dislodge the Communist defenders. While infantry tried to flank the
guerrillas, M113 assault vehicles attacked their lines, and artillery
pounded their positions; American fighter-bombers and gunships
joined the bombardment while helicopters flew reinforcements to the
battlefield. At 10:00 p.m., under the cover of darkness, NLF commanders pulled their forces out, staging a successful retreat to their
bases in the Plain of Reeds. The NLF had suffered eighteen killed and
thirty-nine wounded. Eighty ARVN soldiers had died in the fight
along with three Americans. The attackers suffered another one hundred wounded and lost five helicopters. Lt. Col. John Paul Vann, the
American advisor to the ARVN commander at Ap Bac, expressed his
frustration at the catastrophe. "It was a miserable damn performance,"
he fumed in the wake of the battle. "These people won't listen. They

make the same goddamn mistakes over and over again in the same way."[24] The Battle of Ap Bac sounded a wake-up call for the Kennedy administration. The NLF had been outmanned and outgunned at Ap Bac. Heavily armed South Vietnamese troops, supported by American aircraft, had thrown thousands of rounds of ammunition at the guerrillas in a conventional fight and had still managed to lose. The battle served as a sobering indication of deep problems in Saigon's war effort and a warning that the situation in South Vietnam was about to get worse.

On the morning of June 11, 1963, several hundred Buddhist protestors accompanied by a light blue Austin Westminster sedan filed along the busy streets of Saigon. They stopped at a congested intersection and formed a protective cordon while a seventy-six-year-old monk named Thich Quang Duc stepped out of the sedan and sat down in the middle of the street. Another monk doused the man with gasoline and, as an assembling crowd watched, the elderly monk struck a match, setting himself ablaze. Thich Quang Duc's self-immolation, a stunning act of resistance that would come to symbolize the unfolding disaster in South Vietnam, was in protest of the Saigon regime's recent crackdown on Buddhists throughout the country. On the heels of the military catastrophe at Ap Bac, Diem, a Catholic ruler of a predominantly Buddhist nation, had chosen to ramp up enforcement of a little-observed law decreeing that the RVN flag must always be larger and flown higher than other flags. In May 1963, the deputy chief of security in the city of Hue had demanded that Buddhist flags be taken down in accordance with that law. Local religious leaders refused, sparking a confrontation with police that left nine dead, including two children. The unrest in Hue soon escalated into a nationwide uprising, to which Thich Quang Duc's martyrdom marked a dramatic crescendo. Diem declared martial law and dismissed the protestors as pawns of the NLF, while Madame Nhu, the celibate president's sister-in-law and the de facto First Lady of South Vietnam, told reporters that she "would clap hands at seeing another monk barbecue show." In the end, some fourteen hundred people would be killed in clashes between protestors and state security forces.[25]

While Diem and Madame Nhu remained unmoved by the bloodshed, the same could not be said of leaders in Washington. In tandem with the humiliation of ARVN forces at Ap Bac, the Buddhist uprising seemed to suggest that the situation in South Vietnam was spiraling out of control. Over the sweltering summer months of 1963, officials in the Kennedy administration argued over how to proceed. By late August, rumors of anti-Diem plots in the South Vietnamese military raised the prospect of a coup. The U.S. ambassador to South Vietnam, Henry Cabot Lodge, warned against blocking the coup. "First, it seems at least an even bet that the next government would not bungle and stumble as much as the present one has," he wrote. "Secondly, it is extremely unwise in the long range for us to pour cold water on attempts at a coup, particularly when they are just in their beginning states."[26] President Kennedy remained torn. While Diem was floundering, there was no good reason to believe that a new government would be more effective. "We're up to our hips in mud out there," he lamented. Grudgingly, however, the president was coming to accept the prospect of toppling Diem. In October, ARVN commanders notified State Department officials in Saigon of their plans to stage a coup against the regime and gauged Washington's feelings about such a move. Lodge transmitted the news to the White House and, on October 9, received an affirmative response. "While we do not wish to stimulate [a] coup," the response read, "we also do not wish to leave [the] impression that [the] U.S. would thwart a change of government or deny economic and military assistance to a new regime if it appeared capable of increasing [the] effectiveness of [the RVN] military effort." The Kennedy administration had given the conspirators a green light.[27]

The coup began early on the afternoon of November 1, 1963. ARVN troops surrounded the police headquarters and other government buildings in Saigon as Diem and his brother Nhu fled to a security bunker in the garden of the Gia Long Palace. Late that afternoon, as the leaders of the coup threatened to bomb the palace if the Ngo brothers continued to refuse to surrender, Diem placed a frantic call to Ambassador Lodge. "I admire your courage and your great contributions to your country," Lodge told Diem. "Now I am worried about your physical safety." The ambassador urged Diem to surrender, but the president insisted that he was "trying to reestablish order." A few hours later, the Ngo brothers fled the palace in a small Citroën car to the Cholon quarter of the city, where they took refuge in a Catholic church. The next morning, Diem contacted the coup's leaders and announced that he was prepared to surrender. Diem and Nhu were arrested by a military convoy and placed, with their hands tied, in the back of an M113 armored personnel carrier. As the convoy made its way back to the Joint General Staff headquarters, officers inside the armored vehicle shot Diem and Nhu at close range. Twenty days later, another assassin would cut down President Kennedy in Dallas. In the space of three weeks, two of the three principal leaders in the Vietnam War exited the scene. The lone survivor, Le Duan, was about to take action.[28]

CHOOSING WAR

As Americans reeled from the shock of Kennedy's assassination and generals in Saigon celebrated their victory over Diem, leaders in Hanoi recognized a historic opportunity. In late November 1963, the Central Committee of the North Vietnamese Communist Party convened its Ninth Plenum to consider how to respond to the rapidly changing situation in its struggle with Saigon. The result, Resolution 9, signaled a pivotal decision to intensify the party's war to reunite North and South Vietnam and lean toward China. Hanoi's decision clashed with Soviet policies that sought a relaxation of tensions with the United States. Had they been forced to rely solely on the Kremlin's support, North Vietnamese leaders would likely have been restrained. Soviet leaders insisted that any aggressive moves by Hanoi threatened to invite a U.S. escalation in the South and a rise in Cold War tensions. But the Sino-Soviet split created new openings for Hanoi. While Moscow was reluctant to endorse Hanoi's war plans, Beijing was more forthcoming. By supporting Resolution 9, Mao and his comrades in the PRC recognized an opening to strengthen relations with Hanoi, score a victory in their political clash with the Soviets, and take the offensive against U.S. power in Southeast Asia. Accordingly, Beijing increased its military and economic aid to Hanoi and praised the Vietnamese Communists for furthering the cause of world revolution.[29]

Increasing aid from Beijing, coupled with PRC propaganda attacks, pressured Moscow to expand its commitments to Hanoi lest the Soviets be seen as having abandoned their fellow revolutionaries in Southeast Asia. Khrushchev's ouster in 1964 opened the door to closer relations between Hanoi and the new collective leadership in the Kremlin—Leonid Brezhnev would in the coming years emerge as the key leader in the Kremlin. "Under Khrushchev," a CIA report noted, "the Soviets had sharply disagreed with . . . Hanoi and Peking" and warned of the potential for a direct confrontation with the United States. "Khrushchev's tactics had the effect of forcing the North Vietnamese into Peking's arms," the report argued. "The North Vietnamese, who probably were never too happy about being forced to rely solely on Peking, appear to have been more than willing to have the opportunity of getting more freedom of maneuver and a better bargaining position."[30] By playing Moscow and Beijing off each other, Hanoi had leveraged the Sino-Soviet split to secure critical military aid from both Communist powers.

In December, General Secretary Le Duan told party leaders that he planned to launch a general offensive against the Saigon regime in the coming year. Rather than following a patient application of Mao's three-stage theory of guerrilla war, Hanoi would "go for broke" in an effort to bypass the difficult equilibrium phase of the struggle.

A general military offensive, the secretary explained, would incite mass uprisings in South Vietnamese cities. As protestors poured onto the streets, they would overwhelm the Saigon regime, pushing it over the brink. He hoped to introduce this dramatic innovation to Mao's theory, accelerating the pace and expanding the intensity of the southern revolution. The post-coup upheaval in Saigon reinforced Le Duan's confidence that his General Offensive–General Uprising strategy could achieve a knockout blow to the RVN regime before the United States could intervene in force. Hanoi would increase the flow of supplies and troops, including main-force units of the PAVN, into South Vietnam in preparation for launching a mass offensive in the Central Highlands in 1964.[31]

Even as Le Duan chose to escalate the war in the South, a new leader in Washington deliberated over his nation's future in Vietnam: Lyndon Johnson. The Texas native was a large man with a booming personality to match. Johnson had been a strong presence in the U.S. Senate and had, throughout his career, focused on domestic rather than foreign policy. More than anything, he hoped to pass new civil rights legislation and make social reform the centerpiece of his "Great Society" programs, a substantial extension of New Deal social policies. Nevertheless, he recognized that his political credibility and his ability to pass domestic reforms hinged on waging an effective foreign policy. He was determined to continue his predecessor's policies in Vietnam, choosing to keep all Kennedy's top foreign policy advisors and continue supporting the Saigon regime. He would not accept a reversal in Southeast Asia. As he later told one biographer, "I knew that Harry Truman and Dean Acheson had lost their effectiveness from the day that the Communists took over in China. I believed that the loss of China had played a large role in the rise of Joe McCarthy. And I knew that all these problems, taken together, were chickenshit compared to what might happen if we lost Vietnam." His message to South Vietnamese leaders, his own generals, and the U.S. embassy in Saigon was clear: "Lyndon Johnson is not going down as the president who lost Vietnam. Don't you forget that." Johnson was soon to find, however, that it was easier to reject defeat than to devise a winning strategy.[32]

On August 2, 1964, three North Vietnamese torpedo boats attacked the USS *Maddox*, an American warship operating in the Gulf of Tonkin. The American ship returned fire on the North Vietnamese boats while four U.S. warplanes launched from a nearby aircraft carrier gave pursuit. Two days later, the *Maddox* reported a second attack that later turned out to be false, the result of bad weather in the area. While U.S. officials claimed that the alleged attacks were unprovoked, the *Maddox* had in fact been assisting South Vietnamese commandos conducting raids on North Vietnamese installations in the area. As historian John Prados explains, the "missions were unilaterally controlled by the U.S., using boats procured and maintained by the U.S. Navy, attacking targets selected by the CIA, in an operation paid for by the United States." Shortly before midnight on August 4, President Johnson delivered a televised address to the nation to announce the attacks and to explain that U.S. forces were now engaging in retaliatory strikes. "[T]his new act of aggression, aimed directly at our own forces, again brings home to all of us in the United States the importance of the struggle for peace and security in southeast Asia," he told the nation. "Aggression by terror against the peaceful villagers of South Viet-Nam has now been joined by open aggression on the high seas against the United States of America." Three days later, Congress passed the Gulf of Tonkin Resolution by a vote of 414–0 in the House and 88–2 in the Senate, authorizing the White House to take "all necessary measures to repel any armed attack against the forces of the United States and to prevent further aggression." Congress had effectively given the president a blank check to wage an undeclared war in Vietnam.[33]

The Gulf of Tonkin incident provided Johnson with the pretext to retaliate against Hanoi, an action that U.S. officials had been discussing for some time. Johnson's precarious political position played a central role in shaping his hawkish approach to Vietnam during the first year of his presidency. He had ascended to office due to Kennedy's assassination and felt obliged to continue his predecessor's policies in Southeast Asia. Moreover, Johnson faced a bruising battle for the White House in 1964, with Republican presidential nominee Barry Goldwater, godfather of modern American conservatism and a zealous Cold Warrior. With his landslide victory in the November election, however, Johnson no longer had any reason to doubt his political mandate. Nevertheless, over the winter of 1964–65, the president began to expand American involvement in Southeast Asia. In short, as historian Frederick Logevall explains, Johnson "chose war" in Vietnam.[34] The American escalation would be incremental: Johnson and his advisors sought to ease the nation into the war and limit its impact on the American economy. Likewise, they hoped to avoid any action that would invite retaliation from Moscow or Beijing. By slowly ratcheting up American involvement, Johnson quietly took the decisive steps in leading the United States into another bloody war in Asia. Nineteen sixty-four, then, witnessed the pivotal decisions in both Washington and Hanoi to escalate the war for South Vietnam.

In the early morning hours of February 7, 1965, NLF fighters launched an attack on a U.S. helicopter base at Pleiku, in the Central Highlands. The guerrillas killed 8 Americans and wounded another 126; ten aircraft were destroyed. The attack on Pleiku was part of a wider wave of NLF operations launched at the end of the cease-fire celebrating Tet, the Vietnamese Lunar New Year. Certainly, the fact that so many Americans had been killed gave Pleiku special significance. More important, however, was the American response. The attack became the provocation that the White House used to launch a full-scale war in Vietnam. As National Security Advisor McGeorge Bundy, who was visiting South Vietnam at the time of the attack, quipped, "Pleikus are streetcars—if you miss one, another will come along soon." Johnson, however, decided not to wait. American forces unleashed an initial wave of reprisals on North Vietnam in retaliation for Pleiku, sending a total of 132 warplanes in a punishing assault. It was only the beginning. Six days later, Johnson opened Operation Rolling Thunder, a massive strategic bombing campaign against North Vietnam. Washington hoped that an expanded air war would drain Hanoi's ability to sustain the insurgency in the South. Rolling Thunder would "set a higher price" for guerrilla operations, Bundy insisted, and "increase our ability to deter such adventures." Moreover, Bundy hoped that the campaign would have a "substantial depressing effect upon the morale of Viet Cong cadres in South Vietnam." In this latter respect, Rolling Thunder would fail. As a captured guerrilla told his interrogators, news of the devastation in the North "pushed us to fight harder so the South would soon be entirely liberated and the North would be spared further destruction."[35]

The bombing campaign would last for three and a half years. In all, the United States dropped some 643,000 tons of bombs on North Vietnam as part of Rolling Thunder. American fighter-bombers (F-105 Thunderchiefs, F-4 Phantoms, and A-4 Skyhawks) carried out the majority of attacks. The effects were devastating: as historian Mark Clodfelter writes, the campaign destroyed 65 percent of North Vietnam's petroleum facilities, nearly 60 percent of its bridges, 9,821 vehicles, and almost 2,000 rail cars. Despite its massive display of American airpower, in strategic terms, Rolling Thunder proved largely ineffective. For every $1.00 of damage inflicted on the North, Washington spent $6.60. More than 1,000 Americans would be killed or captured as part of the campaign. Though Rolling Thunder targeted Hanoi's transportation capacity, the guerrilla infiltration from the North continued, and in some cases even increased. Indeed, Le Duan and his comrades used the American bombing campaign to pressure Moscow and Beijing to increase the flow of aid to Hanoi. Although the Johnson administration tried to limit the scale of civilian destruction, Rolling Thunder would kill some 52,000 civilians.[36]

Although few Americans realized it, their nation had entered what would be the bloodiest conflict of the Cold War era. Driven by the logic of NSC-68, Truman, Eisenhower, Kennedy, and Johnson had gradually escalated American commitments in Indochina. Johnson's decision to go to war in Vietnam represented the culmination of years of existing policy. Over the next decade, Southeast Asia served as the focus of U.S. counterrevolutionary efforts to stop the spread of communism. Ironically, though, events elsewhere were about to transform the strategic landscape of the region and the wider Cold War. Indeed, many of the greatest geostrategic transformations of the middle Cold War took place outside Vietnam. While the fighting in South Vietnam took center stage, a series of bloodbaths broke out around the Indian Ocean basin that would help reshape Great Power relations in the coming decade. As the war in Vietnam raged, the Sino-Soviet split tore the Communist world apart and helped spark a series of massacres in the developing world. The most violent stage of the Cold War had begun.

THE MASSACRE OF THE INDONESIAN PKI

1 9 6 5

Even as the United States ramped up its military mission in South Vietnam, a nightmare was taking shape in Indonesia. A sprawling Southeast Asian archipelago of more than seventeen thousand is-. lands, Indonesia boasted the world's fifth-largest population, divided into some three hundred ethnic groups speaking more than seven hundred different languages. The archipelago traversed the key strategic waterway linking the Indian and Pacific Oceans, and its constituent islands contained a wealth of natural resources. The largest Muslim-majority nation in the world, Indonesia was also home to the world's third-largest Communist Party—after the Chinese and Soviet Communist Parties. Washington, Moscow, and Beijing all understood that the island nation represented a great prize in the struggle for influence in Southeast Asia and the wider Third World. Since the start of the Cold War, in the words of historian Bradley Simpson, U.S. officials had seen Indonesia as the linchpin of America's containment strategy in the region. Into the mid-1960s, both the Kennedy and Johnson administrations considered Indonesia of greater strategic significance than even Vietnam. "More is involved in Indonesia," Secretary of State Dean Rusk would observe in 1964, "than is at stake in Vietnam."[1] Indonesia also emerged as one of the most hotly contested nations in the Sino-Soviet competition for influence in the Third World. Further, its proximity to Vietnam placed it in the shadow of the escalating war.

From mid-October 1965 through mid-1966, Indonesian military forces, paramilitary groups, student organizations, and gangs of Muslim youth perpetrated one of the most concentrated campaigns of mass political violence in contemporary world history, massacring some five hundred thousand civilians suspected of supporting the Indonesian Communist Party (PKI). This horrific violence established a brutal military regime aligned with the United States and transformed the strategic landscape of the Cold War in East Asia and the wider Third World. It also served as a harbinger of the collapse of the Communist movement in the Third World and the rise of a new set of revolutionary fighters who embraced the forces of religion and ethnicity thought by many to have all but disappeared from the Cold War world.

The events of late 1965 in Indonesia "significantly altered the regional balance of power [in Asia] and substantially reduced America's real stake in Vietnam," Secretary of Defense Robert McNamara would later write. "The largest and most populous nation in Southeast Asia had reversed course," he noted, dealing a devastating blow to China's influence in the region.[2] The reversal of which McNamara spoke entailed nothing less than the wholesale massacre of the world's third-largest Communist Party.

SUKARNO'S INDONESIA

Since gaining independence from the Netherlands in 1949, Indonesia had been ruled by Sukarno, an ardent nationalist and champion of Third World solidarity.* Born to a minor aristocrat in East Java in

---

* Many Javanese follow a mononymic system. Therefore, "Sukarno" represents his full name.

1901, Sukarno studied engineering at the Bandung Institute of Technology and worked as an architect. He began his political career as a young man, working with anticolonial activists and being arrested in 1929. Over the 1930s, Sukarno emerged as a prominent nationalist working to push the Dutch out of Indonesia. Yet Indonesia's liberation from European imperialism would take an unexpected form. When Japan invaded the archipelago in 1942, Sukarno recognized an opportunity to weaken Dutch authority. He agreed to cooperate with the Japanese occupation forces while simultaneously pushing his vision of Indonesian national identity. As in French Indochina, Japan's defeat in 1945 forced the end of the Japanese occupation but raised the prospect of European colonialism's return. As Dutch officials scrambled to reestablish control of Indonesia, Sukarno and his fellow nationalist leaders confronted the prospect of going to war to fight for their independence. Sukarno remained hesitant. Japanese forces still occupied the islands, and Dutch forces would not abandon their colony without a fight. Frustrated with their leader's lack of resolve, nationalist elements kidnapped Sukarno and forced their captive to issue a call for liberation. On the morning of August 17, 1945, Sukarno stepped out onto the front porch of his house in Central Jakarta to declare Indonesian independence.

In the following weeks, Indonesian independence fighters launched attacks on Europeans and on Western assets, leading to a series of bloody incidents. In October, British troops occupied major cities in the country and began preparations for the return of Dutch imperial forces. The following month, a major skirmish between British and Indonesian forces erupted in Surabaya while sporadic clashes broke out elsewhere. Through 1946, British officials hoping to withdraw their troops hurried to hand control back over to the Dutch. Under the auspices of the Netherlands Indies Civil Administration, Dutch officials moved to reestablish their authority over the islands while nationalist guerrilla forces organized to wage a liberation war. Fierce fighting killed thousands over the next three years. Dutch forces held the major cities, but the countryside belonged to the rebels. Meanwhile, international opinion turned against Dutch efforts to regain control of Indonesia. In early 1949, the U.S. government threatened to suspend Marshall Plan aid to the Netherlands if Amsterdam refused to grant sovereignty to Indonesia. In the face of mounting pressure, the Dutch relented and gave the archipelago independence at the end of the year.

President Sukarno next set to work building the apparatus of the new Indonesian state. Few polities on earth rivaled Indonesia's ethnic, cultural, and linguistic diversity, making the leader's task all the more challenging. To meet this challenge, Sukarno proclaimed the nationalist ideology of Pancasila. Indonesians, he argued, were united by five core principles: religion, a sense of humanity, the unity of Indonesia, democracy, and social justice. Clashes between rival factions in Indonesian politics, together with a string of U.S.-backed rebellions, derailed the country's initial attempts at parliamentary democracy. When rebels created a separatist government in Sumatra in 1958, U.S. officials saw a chance to challenge Sukarno's hold on power. The CIA set up a short-lived covert program to aid the rebels. After the Indonesian military shot down a CIA B-26 and captured its American pilot, Washington chose to shut down the covert program and expand its aid program to the Indonesian armed forces. Meanwhile, Sukarno worked to consolidate power in his own hands. In 1957 he had announced a new policy of Guided Democracy. Three years later, he proposed the political philosophy of Nasakom, which looked to nationalism, religion, and communism as the cornerstones of the Indonesian state. In practice, Guided Democracy created a trilateral power structure, with Sukarno at the top and the army and the PKI representing competing, subsidiary legs.

This tenuous balance might have held had it not been for an array of international challenges. Even as he mapped out the structure of the state, Sukarno pushed to transform Indonesia's standing in world affairs. Sukarno had risen to international prominence in 1955, when

he hosted the Bandung Conference, which brought together prominent Third World leaders such as Egypt's Gamal Abdel Nasser and
India's Jawaharlal Nehru in a show of Afro-Asian solidarity. Sukarno,
Nehru, and Nasser crafted Third World nonalignment as a deliberate
rejection of Cold War influence: the postcolonial nations of the world
would follow their own path, not the courses laid out by Moscow
and Washington. At the same time, Sukarno pushed to expand the
borders of Indonesia itself. In 1960, he staged a diplomatic and military offensive to establish dominion over the western half of New
Guinea. Three years later, Sukarno launched a military campaign
against British and Malaysian forces in a bid to block the creation of
the Malaysian state. Sukarno's policies increased Jakarta's visibility in
global affairs, but they also drew the attention of outside powers. In
the years following the Bandung Conference, Sukarno made a series
of well-publicized trips to Beijing, Moscow, and Washington, DC,
and hosted Chinese, Soviet, and American emissaries in Jakarta. U.S.
officials viewed Sukarno's activities with growing concern. Indonesia
was one of the largest nations in the developing world and arguably
the most strategically important state in Southeast Asia.

As the United States escalated its military activities in South Vietnam, Sukarno denounced American intervention, moved closer to
Beijing and Moscow, continued his undeclared war against Malaysia,
and encouraged the growth of the PKI. Under Guided Democracy,
he sought to play rival factions inside Indonesia off one another and
thereby defend his position as the central figure in Indonesian politics.
Outside Sukarno, the PKI and the military represented the country's
most powerful political factions. For its part, the Indonesian military
remained a force to be reckoned with. In the years following 1949,
the armed forces amassed extensive political, social, and economic
power over Indonesian society. Viewing themselves as guardians of
the nation, army officers maintained significant financial interests
and remained willing to interfere in the civilian arena. A doctrine

proclaimed in April 1965 explained that the military's sphere of interest included "the ideological, political, social, economic, cultural, and religious fields." Sukarno cultivated the PKI (which sought greater political power in addition to closer relations with Beijing) as a bulwark against the military's political influence. In doing so, though, he polarized politics in Indonesia and threatened the army's position.[3] So long as he maintained this fragile balancing act, his grip on power remained firm. American officials increasingly saw Sukarno as a nuisance who was potentially soft on communism. Nevertheless, as the U.S. undersecretary of state for political affairs, Averell Harriman, argued in 1964, Washington would continue to deal with the troublesome leader "unless, of course, some of our friends wished to try to overthrow him." The army was not likely to move, however, without some sort of provocation. British officials, who nursed their own resentments over Sukarno's undeclared war against Malaysia and vehement anticolonialism, suggested in November 1964 that "there might be much to be said for encouraging a premature PKI coup [against the government] during Sukarno's lifetime." Such a coup would provide the pretext for the army to crush the Communists.[4]

The PKI remained a major force in Indonesian society and politics throughout the early 1960s. The party claimed a membership of 3.5 million along with 23 million affiliated persons, many of whom were workers, peasants, teachers, and low-level government bureaucrats who rallied to the PKI's calls for mass education and greater political mobilization of Indonesian society.[5] The PKI also provided a foothold for Chinese influence in Southeast Asia's largest country. Beijing's power over the PKI was substantial but not controlling. "Peking indirectly holds the P.K.I.'s purse strings," *New York Times* reporter Neil Sheehan wrote in 1965. "It is an open secret that most of the party's operating funds are extorted from the large and wealthy Chinese business community [in Indonesia]."[6] While Beijing bankrolled the PKI, Moscow provided aid and training to the Indonesian

Air Force and Navy, and Washington expanded its ties to the Indonesian Army. As such, Indonesia represented a three-way battlefield among U.S., Soviet, and Chinese political forces.

In 1963, the PKI launched "Unilateral Action," a quasi-Maoist campaign designed to mobilize Indonesian peasants in a bid to force the implementation of land reform programs. The program's biggest achievement may have been to antagonize large landowners in Indonesia, many of whom were Muslim religious leaders and aristocrats. The party's rapid growth and its increased militancy won enemies in the military and among Muslim organizations. Reports of sporadic attacks by unnamed assailants on PKI offices and clashes with the military circulated through the spring and summer of 1965. As the PKI gained strength through the first half of the 1960s, the party's opponents began to mobilize, driving two of the PKI's rivals, the Indonesian National Party (PNI) and the Nahdlatul Ulama (NU), to the right. The growth of the PKI, then, fueled an increasing polarization of Indonesian society as the army, the PNI, and the NU grew increasingly wary of a Communist takeover. The PKI's call for the creation of a people's militia, coupled with CIA black propaganda (aimed at smearing the PKI and spreading disinformation) about Chinese arms shipments to the Communists, exacerbated these fears.[7] So, too, did Sukarno's statements about his plan to "drive all Indonesian politics to the left" and eradicate "reactionary" elements in the army.[8]

Indonesia's leftward drift worried U.S. officials who already feared Communist advances in South Vietnam. A National Intelligence Estimate issued by U.S. agencies in 1964 explained that Sukarno maintained an iron grip over Indonesian politics and was using his power to wage a dangerous undeclared war against Malaysia, to strengthen the PKI, and to build closer ties with Communist China. "The road ahead for Indonesia is a troubled one of domestic deterioration, external aggression, and overall Communist profit," the report warned.[9] Jakarta's decision to withdraw from the United Nations in protest of Malaysia's ascension to a seat on the Security Council in January

1965 raised further concerns. In a letter to British prime minister Harold Wilson, President Lyndon Johnson worried that "Indonesia seems to be moving rapidly toward more aggressive policies externally and toward communist domination at home." Though the president stressed the need for diplomacy to woo Sukarno away from this leftward drift, he was adamant that some action must be taken. "I feel strongly," he continued, "that we cannot let Indonesia continue along its present path without exhausting every possible measure to turn it from catastrophe."[10]

The situation grew worse over the following month, when PKI-led unions launched a campaign aimed at taking over American-owned plantations in Indonesia in response to Washington's stepped-up bombing campaign in Vietnam. The party had also coordinated a number of attacks on U.S. Information Service offices and libraries in Jakarta and other cities and organized demonstrations against the screening of American films as part of a wider anti-Western movement. By seizing American estates, the Communists launched a direct assault on U.S. property throughout the country.[11] The CIA suspected that Sukarno hoped to capitalize on the embattled U.S. position in Southeast Asia. His goal, the Agency predicted, was to split influence in the region between Indonesia and China. He would "continue his dalliance with Peiping" in what the Agency considered ill-conceived hopes of managing Chinese influence in the coming years. Although the threat of a Communist takeover did not appear imminent, the Agency explained, "there is sufficient chance of such developments over the next year or two to warrant especial US intelligence and planning attention."[12] Intelligence operations had already begun. In a partially redacted NSC memo from February 1965, the State Department reported that it had been working with an unnamed party on a clandestine aid program in Indonesia designed to strengthen pro-Western elements, counter the PKI, and reduce Beijing's influence in the country. U.S. officials developed a plan for "black letter operations, media operations, including possibly black radio, and political action within existing Indonesian organizations and institutions," all designed to paint the PKI as "ambitious, dangerous," and an "instrument of Chinese neo-imperialism." The aid program would also provide "covert assistance to individuals and organizations capable of and prepared to take obstructive action against the PKI."[13]

Anti-Sukarno sentiment was mounting in Indonesia. In late April, U.S. ambassador Howard Jones told Washington that he had heard rumors of an impending coup against Sukarno. He warned that "important civil and military elements" in the country were considering an action in May or June, when Sukarno left the country. The ambassador warned that any hint of U.S. involvement could be "the kiss of death" to the coup and its participants. A month later, Jones followed up, reporting that the plans were "maturing slowly" and had been postponed.[14] Not that Washington would have been upset to see Sukarno go. The U.S. consul general in Jakarta, Francis Galbraith, warned that the Indonesian government had become "deeply hostile" to U.S. foreign policy. "If [the Indonesian virus] is allowed to spread unchecked in [the Afro-Asian] world," he argued, "it could be [a] particularly insidious front runner for international communism." Perhaps the greatest threat, he continued, was that Sukarno's vision, which blended religious, nationalist, and Communist elements, might serve as a stalking horse for Chinese ambitions and was sure to have a greater appeal in the Islamic Middle East. But there was still a chance to prevent this. "We believe," Galbraith wrote, "that [the] US should begin energetically though quietly to tool up for [an] effective counter-propaganda effort and other counter-actions against Sukarno's policies."[15]

Through the steamy summer months of 1965, Sukarno continued to provoke Washington. In late July, he announced his intention to build a nuclear bomb in the near future. U.S. officials doubted Indonesia's ability to accomplish such a feat on its own but noted the possibility of Chinese involvement. Beijing might consider aiding the development of Indonesian nuclear weapons or might be planning a test of one of its own bombs on Indonesian soil. Neither scenario would please Washington.[16] Sukarno's August 1965 proclamation of an anti-imperialist "Beijing–Pyongyang–Hanoi–Phnom Penh–Jakarta Axis" further inflamed U.S. fears about Indonesia's drift toward the Chinese camp.[17] U.S. officials kept a wary eye on the situation during the summer of 1965. Washington's new ambassador in Jakarta, Marshall Green, wrote that Sukarno was "attempting to move all forces in Indo[nesian] society to [the] left or, more explicitly, to policy orientation similar to that [of the] PKI." In the process, he continued, Indonesia had become "an almost completely closed society." Public officials, radio, press, and television subjected the population to a "steady propaganda diet," vilifying the United States and echoing anti-American rhetoric emanating from "Peiping, Pyongyang, Hanoi and Moscow."[18] In a meeting of top-level foreign policy advisors in late August, Undersecretary of State George Ball worried about the implications of Sukarno's actions. "Isn't Indonesia as important as all Indochina?" he asked. "Wasn't it inexorably going Communist?" He then asked if the CIA was in a position to do anything about the situation. National Security Advisor McGeorge Bundy told Ball that it was not, and the meeting adjourned.[19]

On September 1, 1965, less than a month before the Indonesian political system would be overturned, U.S. intelligence agencies distributed a special estimate on the possibility and implications of a Communist takeover in Indonesia. They explained that Sukarno's recent actions had brought Jakarta's foreign policy into "close harmony with that of the Communist states of Asia." The longer Sukarno remained in power, the more likely a Communist "takeover" became. "If Sukarno lives," the report explained, "it is probable that in two or three years the Indonesian state will be sufficiently controlled by the Communists to be termed a Communist state." However, if he died or became incapacitated in the near future, "the PKI drive to power would probably be slowed for a time." The stakes in a "large, populous, rich in resources, and strategically situated" state such as

Indonesia were high. Beijing and Hanoi would both "be encouraged in their struggle with the US in Vietnam, while the confidence of Laos, Thailand, and South Vietnam would be undermined." Indonesia would be in a position to exert greater influence into South Asia as well. A Communist takeover in Jakarta would pose "a potential threat to the Western position in Southeast Asia and to important world sea and air lanes." Malaysia and the Philippines would face particular dangers. At the same time, a Communist Indonesia "would become the object of more intense Sino-Soviet rivalry" as both Moscow and Beijing competed to win greater influence in Jakarta. Moreover, a Communist takeover in Jakarta was sure to have a "heavy impact on world politics. It would be seen as a major change in the international balance of political forces and would inject new life into the thesis that communism is the wave of the future."[20] U.S. officials hoping for a miracle that could reverse Jakarta's drift toward Beijing were about to get their wish.

THE SEPTEMBER 30 COUP

Ninety minutes past midnight on October 1, 1965, seven squads of armed men left Halim Air Base on the outskirts of Jakarta. The trucks carrying them rumbled through the deserted streets of the capital and took positions outside the residences of seven of the Indonesian Army's top generals. At 4:00 a.m., the men sprang into action, forcing their way into the homes, overwhelming security guards, and insisting that the generals had been summoned for a meeting with Sukarno. The kidnappers managed to capture three of their targets and kill three others, along with two bystanders. Gen. Abdul Haris Nasution managed to escape, although his five-year-old daughter was mortally wounded. The attackers returned to the air base with their three captives and the bodies of the three slain generals. Soon after, the prisoners were beaten, stabbed, and shot. The executioners then threw the six corpses down an unused well, which they then sealed.[21]

The operation's engineers were a shadowy group calling itself the September 30 Movement. Its leadership included the commander of the presidential guard, an army colonel, a major from the air force, and two members of the Special Bureau of the PKI. At 7:15 a.m., Indonesian radio broadcast a statement from the movement announcing the arrest of several generals and warning of more actions to come. The movement took control of Jakarta's radio station and moved approximately one thousand troops into Merdeka Square, in the center of the capital. Representatives also visited the presidential palace to inform Sukarno of the operation and place the president under their "protection," but they were unable to locate him.[22]

The group's precise motivations have remained a matter of historical controversy. The leaders of the September 30 Movement claimed that they had launched the operation to preempt a military coup against Sukarno. However, what would become the official Indonesian version of events argued that the PKI had staged a coup aimed at seizing control of the state. This theory gained support after state authorities forced confessions from the movement's leaders. Two leading Indonesian scholars at Cornell University, Benedict Anderson and Ruth McVey, argued that the so-called coup was in fact an internal army affair aimed at eliminating complacent top brass. Others speculated that Sukarno himself masterminded the operation as part of his campaign to move Indonesian politics to the left. Yet another theory argues that conservative military leaders engineered the operation that simultaneously removed more moderate generals at the head of the army and provided a pretext for an assault on the PKI. Likewise, the full scope of U.S. involvement in the affair remains unclear. The execution of the key participants and the continued classification of U.S. documents have ensured that the full story remains hotly contested,[23] but the events that followed did little to support the Indonesian government's account.

Six of the army's top generals lay dead at the bottom of a well. The seventh, Nasution, was deeply traumatized. Curiously, however, the September 30 Movement made no attempt to capture the army officer most likely to lead the counterattack, Major General Suharto. Nor did the movement take steps to neutralize the army's elite Para-Commando Regiment (RPKAD), which would spearhead the campaign. Forty-four-year-old Suharto led the Army Strategic Reserve Command (Kostrad) and often stood in for higher-ranking brass when they were traveling. After the September 30 plotters returned to Halim Air Base, Suharto began to regroup, calling on RPKAD commander Sarwo Edhie Wibowo to assemble his forces and retake Jakarta's radio station on the night of October 1, and then ordering the troops assembled in Merdeka Square to disperse. The next day, RPKAD forces pushed their way into Halim, giving Suharto control over most of the area around Jakarta.[24] While his soldiers took positions around the capital, Suharto and his comrades launched a propaganda campaign against the September 30 Movement, dubbing the group "Gestapu," a play on words (from the Indonesian name for the movement) designed to evoke Nazi connotations. The culprits, according to Sukarno, were the PKI and elements of the Indonesian Air Force. The discovery of the generals' bodies and the spectacle of their state funeral (over which Suharto himself presided) on October 5, 1965, provided more fodder for the army's propaganda campaign. The army issued radio broadcasts and newspaper stories praising the generals as "heroes of the Revolution" and spreading false rumors that female PKI members had sexually mutilated the corpses.[25]

State Department officials appear to have been caught off guard by the developments in Jakarta. On October 2, George Ball, acting secretary of state, noted that Suharto seemed to be in control and that the situation "doesn't look too bad." Secretary of State Dean Rusk even suggested that the upheaval in Indonesia "could work out advantageously" for the United States.[26] As Ball told James Reston of the *New York Times* two days later, "This is a critical time for the Army. . . . If the army does move they have [the] strength to wipe up [the] earth with PKI and if they don't they may not have another chance."[27] Writing from Jakarta, Ambassador Green recommended that Washington take this opportunity to "extend our contact with the military" in Indonesia and to signal to Nasution and Suharto "our desire to be of assistance where we can," provided that U.S. involvement remained covert. The "most needed immediate assistance we can give [the] army," he argued, would be to help "[s]pread the story of PKI's guilt, treachery and brutality."[28] These efforts were already under way. American radio stations had begun broadcasting "material pointing [the] finger at PKI and playing up [the] brutality of September 30 rebels . . . from Radio Djakarta and Indo press."[29]

Meanwhile, journalists and observers suggested that the U.S. government had played at least an indirect role in the coup. Late in October, columnist Andrew Tully reported that it was common knowledge in Washington that "CIA agents forced the Reds' hand." Over the last several years, Tully wrote, the Agency had promised U.S. support "for any movement designed to undermine the partnership between Sukarno and communism," channeling some fifteen million dollars to Indonesian Army officers through Swiss bank accounts. These efforts to build the Indonesian Army, Tully insisted, forced the PKI into launching a premature coup that ultimately failed. "And so," he explained, "the U.S. won the first round in its underworld battle with Peking."[30]

MASSACRE OF THE PKI

While the army's propaganda fueled growing outrage against the PKI, Suharto consolidated his military forces. In the coming days, Suharto forced a severely compromised Sukarno (who would officially remain president until 1967) to name him head of Indonesia's armed forces and ordered Sarwo Edhie's RPKAD troops to prepare for an attack on the PKI in Central Java. On October 19, RPKAD units made a show of force in the city of Semarang in northwest Java. Sarwo Edhie's soldiers rounded up one thousand suspected subversives and incited

Muslim youth affiliated with the NU to vandalize PKI and Chinese-owned buildings in the city. These actions would become a pattern in other areas as the RPKAD carried out a campaign to destroy the PKI's infrastructure. PKI branches put up resistance in some villages, cutting telephone lines, blocking roads, and attacking anticommunists, but they were generally overwhelmed by the better-armed soldiers. Nevertheless, RPKAD forces were still severely outnumbered. Realizing the enormity of his task, Sarwo Edhie decided to enlist the help of youth, religious organizations, and nationalist groups in late October. "We gave them two or three days' training," he recalled, "then sent them out to kill the communists." RPKAD forces began organizing anticommunist youth into a "home guard" armed with "bamboo spears, farm implements, swords, daggers, slingshots, and bows and arrows." Muslim youth wrapped scarves emblazoned with "God is great" across their foreheads while nationalists sported red-and-white colors. These vigilante gangs abducted suspected Communists, interrogated them, and then staged summary executions of those found guilty.[31]

Though most of the killing took place in rural areas, news of the slaughter made its way back to the U.S. embassy in Jakarta. Muslim groups in Aceh had "apparently put all but [a] few PKI out of action," embassy officials wrote in late October. "Atjehnese have decapitated PKI and placed their heads on stakes along the road. Bodies of PKI victims reportedly thrown into rivers or sea as Atjehnese refuse to 'contaminate Atjeh soil.'" The army was working with youth organizations in a "systematic drive to destroy [the] PKI in northern Sumatra with wholesale killings reported," a November cable read. Local police estimated that anticommunist groups working with the "blessing of the Army" were killing between fifty and one hundred PKI members every night in East and Central Java. Meanwhile, a missionary working in Surabaya reported the massacre of nearly four thousand people in nearby areas in early November. As news of atrocities poured into Jakarta, embassy officials realized that they were witnessing a nationwide massacre of the Indonesian left. A long-standing "tradition of blood feuds" helped fuel the violence, officials concluded in February 1966; "many of the killings that are taking place under a political cover are actually motivated by personal and clan vendettas."[32]

Far from sparking outrage in Washington, reports of the army's role in coordinating the massacre of thousands of Indonesian civilians encouraged U.S. officials to expand military aid packages. "We should try to fortify their confidence that Indonesia can be saved from chaos, and that [the] Army is the main instrument for saving it," Rusk argued. "We should get across that Indonesia and Army have real friends who are ready to help." He went on to suggest that the United States could provide weapons and equipment to help the army "deal with the PKI." Indeed, the secretary of state suggested, Suharto's campaign against the left might give Washington an opportunity to eliminate Moscow and Beijing's influence from the army.[33] On October 30, officials in the State Department and the Pentagon resolved to establish a "covert plan of assistance in which [the] DOD would work [*less than 1 line of source text not declassified*] to insure [*sic*] the minimum risk of exposure." In particular, the army needed tactical "short-range communications equipment to support sustained operations against PKI guerrilla[s]."[34] State Department officials concluded, "In the life and death struggle which has finally been joined with the PKI, the Army deserves our support." Though Indonesia would likely remain leery of the United States, a November 3 report argued, Washington now had an opportunity to undermine Jakarta's relationships with Moscow and Beijing.[35]

While Washington rushed to establish a closer relationship with the Indonesian Army, Suharto's forces continued to direct the wholesale massacre of Indonesian civilians. Having ravaged large areas of Java and Sumatra through October and November, the RPKAD began moving into Bali in early December. Although violence had already broken out on the island, the largest massacres coincided with the soldiers' arrival. RPKAD troops played a key role in providing logistical support to civilians who performed most of the killing. Suharto's forces gave weapons and ammunition to anticommunist groups, aided in communications, and used army trucks to transport alleged PKI members. A local historian described "a river of blood in which several thousands were killed in [the regency of] Jembrana alone." Entire villages participated in the killing. "One man would stab a victim while another would hit him on the head with a rock," a witness recalled. Other victims were shot. Some were tortured before they were killed. The executioners threw thousands of corpses into the sea or into mass graves. While local hatreds fueled the slaughter, one scholar concluded, Suharto's military forces provided the pretext, coordination, and logistical support that made it possible.[36]

The number of those killed remains a mystery. RPKAD commander Sarwo Edhie claimed that three million people had been killed under his watch. The most systematic attempt to count the dead suggested that one million people had been killed. But the most common figure cited by scholars is five hundred thousand. The nature of the killings reinforced their obscurity. The killers carried out their gruesome work in small groups, under the cover of darkness. While the army orchestrated many of the massacres, local people seem to have been responsible for most of the actual killing. They used simple weapons such as knives and clubs. Victims were killed near their homes, and their bodies were left nearby. The archipelago contained no shortage of potential grave sites. The killers dumped bodies into the country's abundant rivers, in lush forests, in limestone caves, and in remote fields. Indonesia's humid, tropical climate ensured that corpses decomposed rapidly. Unlike other states that had sponsored mass killing, such as Nazi Germany and Democratic Kampuchea, Indonesia kept few records. What surviving documents there are make for macabre reading. In East Java, gangs of Muslim youth working with army engineers brought suspected PKI members to prepared holes outside the village of Sentong. Victims were led to the graves, choked, and then beaten to death with iron rods. The executioners then decapitated the bodies, filled in the graves, and planted banana trees on the fresh earth. Other reports told of victims being hacked apart or dragged to death behind jeeps. The killers often raped female victims before executing them. In the village of Ngasem, Muslim youth captured a teacher and paraded him through the streets before cutting off his head and placing it on a stake planted alongside an intersection.[37]

Continued reports of the atrocities did nothing to deter U.S. support for the Indonesian Army. Ambassador Green alerted Washington on November 18 that the army was slaughtering the PKI. "RPKAD is not taking prisoners," he wrote in November. "I gather this means they are shooting the PKI on sight."[38] Nevertheless, Green voiced support for a proposal to send financial aid to KAP-Gestapu, the "army-inspired but civilian-staffed action group," he wrote, that "is still carrying [the] burden of current repressive efforts targeted against PKI."[39] Moreover, at least one U.S. official helped Suharto's forces hunt down PKI members. On December 17, 1965, a political officer in the U.S. embassy in Jakarta, Robert Martens, transmitted a list of PKI political leaders to Indonesian military authorities. He sent another list in March 1966 and a third in August. In all, Martens later reported, the cables contained the names of thousands of people. It is a near certainty that it was anticommunist forces that slaughtered many of them.[40] Ambassador Green argued in December that the new order in Indonesia "will be infinitely more *healthy* and more promising than what we had before Oct. 1 [emphasis added]." Green's cable contained no hint of irony.[41] The following day, the Australian embassy in Jakarta estimated that Indonesia had experienced approximately "1,500 assassinations per day since September 30th."[42]

THE MASSACRE OF THE PKI PROVED TO BE ONE OF THE pivotal events of the middle Cold War. "It is hard to overestimate the potential significance of the army's apparent victory over Sukarno," argued Robert Komer, a key member of Johnson's national security staff.[43] "Of all China's recent reverses abroad," a 1966 CIA report noted, "probably the most serious has been the elimination of pro-Communist elements" in Indonesia. The loss of the PKI, "the largest Communist party supporting Peking in the Sino-Soviet dispute," represented a "major diplomatic debacle" for the Chinese. The CIA predicted that "Communists abroad sympathetic to Peking may begin to have second thoughts about too close identification with the Chinese."[44] The PKI's destruction, historian Odd Arne Westad has argued, was "perhaps the greatest setback for communism in the Third World in the 1960s."[45] The Indonesian killings occurred at a critical juncture in the Cold War as the U.S. war in Vietnam was escalating and the PRC was heading into the social turmoil and political purges of the Cultural Revolution. The massacres, moreover, ended Sukarno's leftward drift and placed his pro-Western military regime in power over the largest country in Southeast Asia and the most populous country in the Muslim world. The massacre, in the words of one scholar, led to the "reorganization of social forces and reintegration of Indonesia into the capitalist world economy."[46] That the new order in Indonesia was built on the graves of perhaps half a million civilians barely registered. "No one cared," one State Department official later wrote, "as long as they were Communists, that they were being butchered."[47]

In July 1966, *Time* magazine praised the purge of the PKI and Sukarno's demise as the "West's best news for years in Asia." Certainly, the most hardened U.S. officials could celebrate the grisly annihilation of the world's largest nongoverning Communist Party. The new regime removed Sukarno from power and placed him under house arrest, where he remained until his death from kidney failure in 1970. In the coming years, the Suharto regime would emerge as a model for a new breed of pro-Western authoritarian regimes that served to shore up American defenses along the hotly contested Cold War borderlands of southern Asia. But the massacre of the PKI also served as a turning point in the politics of warfare during the Cold War. Prior to 1965, the greatest battles of the era focused on clashes between political ideologies. Although the Indonesian killings touched on these same disputes, they also pulled religious groups into the killing fields in unprecedented numbers. While the struggle between Communist and noncommunist factions lay at the heart of the Indonesian killings, the army's mobilization of civilian death squads made up of Muslim youth from the NU served as a harbinger of sectarian violence in the postcolonial world. In the following decades, religious zeal and ethnic rivalries would supplant secular political ideology as a driving force in many of the bloodiest episodes of the late Cold War. Ignoring these troubling dimensions of violence, pro-Western forces around the world hailed the turn of events in Indonesia as a major victory in the struggle for Southeast Asia.[48]

THE TET OFFENSIVE AND
USSURI RIVER CLASHES

1 9 6 7 – 1 9 6 9

With Suharto firmly in control of Indonesia, U.S. officials could breathe a sigh of relief. The largest and most strategically important country in Southeast Asia lay securely inside the Western camp. The massacre of the PKI dramatically decreased the geostrategic dangers of the war in Vietnam. Even if Hanoi won, Southeast Asia's greatest prize, Indonesia, was in the hands of a staunchly anticommunist military regime. But this stunning reversal came too late to avert the escalation of the U.S. war in Vietnam. Also, ironically, the destruction of the PKI raised the stakes in Vietnam for both Moscow and Beijing. Vietnam supplanted Indonesia, in the words of historian Bradley Simpson, as the focus of the Communist states' competition to demonstrate "their credibility as revolutionary powers" in Southeast Asia.[1] Although Suharto's rise might have helped convince the superpowers that the war in Vietnam was no longer a priority, American, Soviet, and Chinese leaders had already committed to turning that nation into a Cold War battlefield. Tragically, as Vietnam became the site of the largest superpower intervention of the post-1945 era, changing events in Asia were set to alter the superpower struggle for the Third World in ways that few could have predicted.

The twenty months between January 1968 and September 1969 fundamentally transformed the dynamics of the Cold War. In that time, Hanoi launched the most decisive military campaign of the Vietnam War, which devastated American hopes of winning the conflict. Yet, even as Washington's plans collapsed, the Sino-Soviet split reached a violent crescendo as Soviet and Chinese troops clashed along their Far Eastern border. The disintegration of the American war effort in Vietnam thus coincided with an escalation of the Sino-Soviet split that brought Moscow and Beijing to the brink of nuclear war. As Sino-Soviet relations reached their nadir, the prospect of diplomatic reconciliation between Washington and Beijing came into view. Should a U.S.-Chinese rapprochement occur, it would shake the very foundations of the Cold War struggle. As in 1949, Mao and his comrades held it in their power to redirect the course of superpower competition.

SEARCH AND DESTROY

Following their Cold War victory in Indonesia, U.S. officials embarked on a series of escalations in their war for Vietnam. As American bombers pounded targets in the North, American troops intensified their efforts to win the ground war in the South. The man who would bear the brunt of the responsibility for crafting American strategy in the war was Gen. William Westmoreland. A native of South Carolina and graduate of West Point, Westmoreland assumed command of the U.S. Military Assistance Command, Vietnam (MACV), in June 1964. Many American officials supported an oil spot counterinsurgency strategy—American and ARVN forces would hold strategic enclaves from which they would slowly expand their influence. Westmoreland rejected this strategy. It was too passive, and all but surrendered the South Vietnamese countryside to the NLF. Moreover, "it put American troops in the unfortunate position of defending static positions," Westmoreland argued. Instead, the general favored a strategy of attrition that combined pacification efforts with search-and-destroy missions. ARVN units would take responsibility for the former, as they were better equipped to interact with the local population. This would leave U.S. forces available for offensive operations designed to destroy the NLF's military capacity. Because the Communist guerrillas avoided large-unit engagements, particularly with American troops, U.S. forces would conduct search-and-destroy missions designed to hunt down and eliminate NLF units. Gen. William DePuy, commander of the army's First Infantry Division, explained: "The game in the jungle is to send in a small force as bait, let the enemy attack, and be able to react with a larger force in reserve nearby." One journalist described the war in the Vietnamese countryside as essentially "a game of hide-and-seek."[2]

Over time, search-and-destroy operations came to play a central role in Westmoreland's strategy. U.S. forces launched the largest such operation of the war, Cedar Falls, in early 1967, against the so-called Iron Triangle. An NLF stronghold located twenty-five miles north of Saigon, the area was home to a sprawling complex of camouflaged bases and underground tunnels. First built during the French War, the Iron Triangle represented a strategic nexus for the insurgency and a critical target for the Americans. For nearly three weeks in January, U.S. forces pounded the region with B-52 strikes while thirty thousand troops combed through the area and military bulldozers leveled large stretches of countryside. In the course of the operation, American and ARVN troops drove thousands of peasants from their homes to new Strategic Hamlets under government control. While Washington initially claimed success, NLF cadres filtered back into the area only days after the American withdrawal. One journalist compared American tactics to a sledgehammer hitting a floating cork: "Somehow the cork refused to stay down."[3]

The broader logic of search-and-destroy missions hinged on the hope of finding a crossover point in the war against the Vietnamese Communists. If U.S. and ARVN forces could kill guerrillas faster than they could be replaced, leaders in Hanoi would have no choice but to abandon the revolution in the South. The war in Vietnam could be managed through metrics, with businesslike efficiency. Ultimately, success in the war would be measured in the number of NLF killed; progress would be charted in body counts. Secretary of Defense Robert McNamara, former president of Ford Motor Company, emerged as one of the strongest advocates of this technocratic gospel. This numbers-driven approach to war was deeply flawed. First, raw statistics were a poor indicator of progress in fighting the war. As one journalist observed in 1966, the numbers "are meaningless in themselves. . . . Statistically, the war has been won several times already." Nor, for that matter, did body counts provide a means for gauging the allegiance of the South Vietnamese peasantry to the Saigon regime or for measuring any decrease in the will of Hanoi or the NLF to continue the struggle. In short, body counts were not a metric for determining the progress of the U.S. military's real goal in South Vietnam: pacification. Furthermore, the Pentagon's statistical focus provided a strong incentive for field commanders to inflate their estimates of enemies killed. With commendations, promotions, and other rewards hinging on a unit's ability to rack up impressive numbers, the urge to exaggerate NLF casualties proved difficult to resist.[4]

The most troubling problem with the U.S. counterinsurgency strategy, however, concerned its propensity to encourage indiscriminate violence against Vietnamese civilians. "They would set up a competition," one veteran remembered. "The company that came in with the biggest body count would be given in-country R and R or an extra case of beer. Now if you're telling a nineteen-year-old kid it's okay to waste people and he will be *rewarded* for it, what do you think *that* does to his psyche?" In other instances, units that had failed to achieve their quota simply executed their prisoners in order to increase their body counts. The Pentagon's practice of designating "free-fire" zones only compounded the indiscriminate slaughter. In these areas, "everyone, men, women, children, could be considered [a fair target]," one soldier explained. "[Y]ou could not be held responsible for firing on innocent civilians since by definition there were none there." Later, a congressional investigation estimated that, by 1968, no fewer than three hundred thousand South Vietnamese civilians had been killed or wounded in free-fire zones. The ultimate result was to create, in journalist Nick Turse's characterization, a "system of suffering" on an industrial scale.[5]

The brutal realities of this system converged on Son My village (which included the hamlet of My Lai) on March 16, 1968. Units from the U.S. Army's Twenty-Third Infantry Division had begun a sweep of the area in an effort to locate and destroy a suspected NLF stronghold. The soldiers were airlifted into the village by helicopter with orders to ferret out guerrillas suspected of taking refuge among the population. U.S. troops began forcing the villagers out of their homes and herding them into the village commons, killing a number in the process. As the roundup continued, the sporadic violence escalated into a general massacre. One soldier recalled receiving orders to "kill everything that breathed." The killing continued for four hours. While some soldiers slaughtered old men and children, others raped women and girls, burned homes, and mutilated the dead for trophies. A group of 50 villagers, mainly women and children, were gunned down in an irrigation ditch. "The people in the ditch kept trying to get out and some of them made it to the top," one soldier who witnessed the atrocities remembered, "but before they could get away they were shot, too." A two-year-old boy who tried to crawl out of the ditch was thrown back in and shot. The official account of the massacre reported 128 "Viet Cong" killed in the operation. Later estimates placed the death toll at over 500, the majority of whom were women and children. The 1968 My Lai Massacre would gain a place in popular memory as a horrific indictment of America's war in Vietnam, a chilling example of all that went wrong in the conflict. Far too often, however, My Lai is presented as an aberration, an isolated case. If My Lai was an aberration, it was because the case became so widely known. In truth, civilian massacres in South Vietnam were shockingly commonplace. Ronald Ridenhour, a GI who played a central role in exposing the massacre, explained, "[T]his was an operation, not an aberration."[6]

Indeed, My Lai was only one of hundreds of reported massacres in South Vietnam, some of which surpassed the killing in Son My. For seven months in 1967, an elite unit of the American 101st Airborne Division named Tiger Force waged a campaign of terror through the Central Highlands of Vietnam. The ostensible purpose was to locate guerrilla supply routes and force local villagers to relocate to Strategic Hamlets. In a prize-winning series of stories, reporters from the *Toledo Blade* estimated that Tiger Force butchered hundreds of unarmed civilians during the period. Many were shot or stabbed; others were killed when soldiers threw grenades into bunkers crowded with women and children. The soldiers tortured prisoners and mutilated dead bodies. Members of the unit began cutting off the ears of corpses, affixing them to shoelaces, and wearing them as necklaces. "There was a period when just about everyone had a necklace of ears," one medic recalled. "We would go into villages and just shoot everybody. We didn't need an excuse. If they were there, they were dead." Reports of sexual assault, decapitations, and the murder of civilians for sport added to the list of atrocities. "Remember, out in the jungle, there were no police officers. No judges. No law and order," another member explained. "Whenever somebody felt like doing something, they did it. There was no one to stop them." But Tiger Force was not a "rogue" unit, its former members insisted: "[W]hile they're saying this was a ruthless band ravaging the countryside, we were under orders to do it." Indeed, at the end of the campaign, in late November, the unit's members received commendations for their actions and Tiger Force was reassigned to a base near Cambodia. Yet the actions of Tiger Force were hardly unique: "I've seen atrocities in Vietnam that make Tiger Force look like Sunday school," a former sergeant remembered. "Everybody I killed, I killed to survive. They make Tiger Force out to be an atrocity. Well, that's almost a compliment. Because nobody will understand the evil I've seen."[7]

In late 1968, American commanders launched an operation dubbed Speedy Express, designed to destroy Communist forces in the Mekong Delta. While B-52s dropped thousands of tons of bombs, F-4 Phantoms rained down napalm and helicopter gunships sprayed suspected guerrilla positions with machine-gun fire. The navy ran swift boats along the river as Navy SEALs and thousands of infantry searched the delta, using night-vision equipment to set ambushes around the clock. Anyone who ran from U.S. forces or aircraft was considered hostile and a viable target. The attacks took a heavy toll on civilians. One air force captain tasked with damage assessments counted sixty-two bodies after one raid: "In my report I described them as so many women between fifteen and twenty-five and so many children—usually in their mothers' arms or very close to them—and so many old people." The Pentagon recorded the dead as Viet Cong. In some areas, an army commander remembered, "the countryside looked like the Verdun battlefields." An anonymous sergeant who witnessed Speedy Express penned a letter to General Westmoreland decrying the slaughter. "My information about killing is worse than shooting prisoners one time, it is about nobody giving a damn about the Vietnamese," the sergeant wrote. "If I am only 10% right . . . [the killing amounted to] a My Lay [sic] each month for a year." In all, the Pentagon counted nearly 11,000 enemy killed in the operation. U.S. forces captured only 748 weapons, leading many observers to conclude that most of the casualties were in fact civilians. Nevertheless, the U.S. military considered the operation a success.[8]

The ground war in Vietnam entailed a sickening level of violence against civilians. As one Newsweek reporter wrote, "My Lai was a shock to everyone except the people in Vietnam." In 1971, former naval officer (and, in 2004, Democratic presidential candidate) John Kerry told Congress that American soldiers had "raped, cut off heads, taped wires from portable telephones to human genitals and turned up the power, cut off limbs, blown up bodies, randomly shot at civilians, razed villages in a fashion reminiscent of Genghis Khan, shot cattle and dogs for fun, poisoned food stocks and generally ravaged the countryside of South Vietnam."[9] Ultimately, these war atrocities were tied to a pervasive problem in Washington's strategy: the inability to measure progress in the war effort. In a conflict with no clear battlefront, American military and political leaders struggled to define, let alone gauge, meaningful success. Victory appeared to be always just out of reach.

The bloody and inconclusive war had begun to take its toll on political leaders on all sides. By the end of 1967, some twenty thousand Americans had been killed in Vietnam; the Vietnamese themselves, both civilians and combatants, had suffered far more casualties. While some Americans—such as Robert Komer, head of the American pacification program in South Vietnam—still insisted that progress was being made and that a successful end was in sight, others had become deeply skeptical. In private, Vice President Hubert Humphrey worried that Washington was "throwing lives and money down a corrupt rat hole" by supporting the regime in Saigon. Furthermore, America's international prestige was also suffering a blow. "The picture of the world's greatest superpower killing or seriously injuring 1,000 noncombatants a week, while trying to pound a tiny, backward nation into submission on an issue whose merits are hotly disputed," Robert McNamara noted, "is not a pretty one." In November, an increasingly despondent McNamara wrote to the president to express his severe concerns about the war. He doubted that any further escalation of troop levels would produce significant progress in the war. Further, it would increase the scope of the violence, driving the number of American casualties up to the level suffered in Korea. "Nor is there any reason to believe that the steady progress we are likely to make, the continued infliction of grievous casualties, or the heavy punishment of air bombardment will suffice to break the will of the North Vietnamese and the Viet Cong to continue to fight," he worried. "Nothing can be expected to break this will other than the conviction that they cannot succeed. This conviction will not be created unless and until they come to the conclusion that the US is prepared to remain in Vietnam for whatever period of time is necessary to assure the independent choice of the South Vietnamese people." But the American people lacked the will to continue the war. They were "frustrated" by the slow rate of progress and afraid of further escalation. They did not, McNamara argued, "give the appearance of having the will to persist."[10]

McNamara joined a growing number of Americans who had become disillusioned with the conflict. Through 1967, a clear majority of Americans still supported the war in Vietnam, but a vocal section of the population had turned against it. In late October, seventy-five thousand antiwar demonstrators converged on Washington, DC, to demand an end to the American intervention. Protestors waved placards bearing photographs of Ho Chi Minh and Che Guevara (the Argentine guerrilla commander and a key figure in the Cuban Revolution, killed two weeks before in Bolivia) and emblazoned with the slogan "Support Our GI's, Bring Them Home Now!" The demonstrators organized a massive rally in front of the Lincoln Memorial and surrounded the Pentagon, engaging in sporadic clashes with police. President Johnson's attorney general, Nicholas Katzenbach, would later reflect that the march on the Pentagon was "the moment that the fever broke in the whole anti-war movement." In November, Johnson's former national security advisor, McGeorge Bundy, warned, "Public discontent with the war is now wide and deep. One of the few things that helps us right now is public distaste for the violent doves—but I think people are really getting fed up with the endlessness of the fighting." In response to the growing unrest, President Johnson directed the FBI and the CIA to increase surveillance of antiwar groups. While the FBI's COINTELPRO, a covert and at times illegal counterintelligence program that had been used to spy on civil rights groups, devoted greater resources to the protestors, the CIA developed a series of domestic surveillance programs that would later be consolidated into Operation CHAOS.[11]

But Johnson was not the only leader cracking down on domestic dissent. In Hanoi, Le Duan was also feeling political pressure from the ongoing conflict. The failure of the general bid to win the war through escalation, to say nothing of its triggering American intervention, helped sow dissension in the ranks of DRV leadership. Whereas Le Duan and his supporters favored large-unit operations aimed at total victory, Ho and Giap pushed for a strategy of protracted war and negotiations. Tensions from the Sino-Soviet split were also bound up in the drama unfolding in Hanoi. Le Duan understood that in order to fight the Americans, North Vietnam would need aid from both Beijing and Moscow. But while the Soviets had deeper pockets, the Kremlin pressed Hanoi to open peace negotiations with Saigon and Washington. Meanwhile, the Chinese controlled cross-border aid shipments and voiced greater enthusiasm for Hanoi's war. Since 1963, Hanoi had sought a delicate balance between the feuding Communist powers. Further complicating Le Duan's position, factions within the ranks of the Vietnamese Communist Party had begun to call for greater democracy and government transparency. In 1967, notable party dissident Hoang Minh Chinh published a two-hundred-page manifesto, "Dogmatism in Vietnam," which blasted the party for its lack of democracy. The party leadership reacted by denouncing Chinh as a traitor and launching a series of purges against suspected dissidents in the ranks of the party, the officer corps, the medical community, academia, and the intelligentsia and against journalists and artists. In what became known as the Revisionist Anti-Party Affair, hundreds of mid- and upper-level leaders in Hanoi were rounded up and thrown in prison. While Ho and Giap, both national heroes, were too prominent to be arrested, Le Duan was able to purge a significant number of their supporters. The purges sent a signal to Beijing that despite receiving increased Soviet aid, North Vietnam had no intention of scaling back its war efforts. In one fell swoop, Le Duan managed to reinforce his hold on power in Hanoi, marginalize Ho and Giap, secure North Vietnam's position vis-à-vis the Sino-Soviet split, and clear the way for another general offensive in the coming year.[12]

THE TET OFFENSIVE

Just before 3:00 on the morning of January 31, 1968, a squad of nineteen NLF guerrillas detonated a charge outside the U.S. embassy in Saigon, blowing a three-foot hole in the wall surrounding the compound. Communist fighters stormed onto the grounds and began a six-hour firefight with the marine guards inside. The embassy attack marked the most spectacular operation in a nationwide offensive launched by the Communists at the end of the celebrations for the Vietnamese Lunar New Year, Tet. More than eighty thousand troops attacked most of South Vietnam's large cities and three-quarters of the nation's provincial capitals. They struck at the heart of American and RVN power: in the densely populated strongholds that were supposedly safe from Communist infiltration. Communist soldiers swept in from the countryside, linking up with clandestine forces and propaganda teams in the cities. Once inside, the insurgents sought to incite a general insurrection among the population against government forces. As American troops reestablished control of the U.S. embassy, fighting raged through the Cholon district of Saigon. Communist forces made their largest gains in the ancient imperial capital of Hue, which they managed to occupy for almost a month. Hue's nineteenth-century citadel was transformed into a Communist fortress. U.S. forces launched a devastating counterassault to retake the city, with aircraft bombing and strafing Communist positions while infantry waged bitter street battles in crowded neighborhoods. Of the

17,000 houses in the city, nearly 10,000 were destroyed. "Nothing I saw during the Korean War, or in the Vietnam War so far," an American correspondent remarked, "has been as terrible, in terms of destruction and despair, as what I saw in Hue." After retaking the city, American and South Vietnamese troops made a series of grisly discoveries beneath the ruined streets: Communist forces had massacred between 2,800 and 5,700 civilians and dumped their bodies in mass graves. Accused of being counterrevolutionaries, many of the victims were buried with their hands bound; some had been tortured; some had been buried alive.[13]

Planning for the Tet Offensive had begun in Hanoi in 1967. The purges of General Giap's staff in the Revisionist Anti-Party Affair placed Le Duan in a position to gamble on a spectacular campaign in early 1968 that might turn the tide of the war. Following the secretary's General Offensive–General Uprising formula, the Tet attacks were intended to spark a series of urban insurrections throughout South Vietnam that would sweep away the Saigon regime. In this respect, Tet represented a dismal failure for Communist forces. In every city and town, NLF and PAVN units were beaten back by U.S. and ARVN forces wielding massive firepower. The southern insurgency in particular was decimated by the counterattack; the NLF would suffer some fifty thousand casualties, losing nearly 80 percent of its strength. The offensive had exposed clandestine cadres who had rushed to join the fray—they were now easy targets for South Vietnamese security forces. In military terms, Le Duan's general offensive had been a catastrophe. The NLF had been devastated, suffering losses from which it would never recover. Henceforth, regular PAVN units would do the majority of the fighting in the South, and the political leadership in Hanoi would be calling the shots.[14]

In political terms, however, it was a different story. Eleven hundred Americans had been killed in the offensive, along with 12,500 civilians. The fact that Communist forces were able to mount such a damaging assault belied earlier statements from the White House and the Pentagon that an end to the conflict was in sight. "What the hell is going on?" CBS anchorman Walter Cronkite fumed. "I thought we were winning the war!" Many Americans who watched news broadcasts of the carnage in Vietnam agreed. A photograph of the Saigon police chief summarily executing an NLF prisoner on the street now joined the image of Thich Quang Duc's 1963 self-immolation as an iconic visual representation of the chaos and destruction in Southeast Asia. "It became necessary to destroy the town to save it," a U.S. Army major told an Associated Press correspondent in the wake of the bombing of the village of Ben Tre. To many observers, the statement increasingly appeared to be an appropriate metaphor for the larger American war effort in Vietnam. While the White House was despondent, General Westmoreland insisted that Tet had been a military defeat for the NLF: Communist forces were on the run, and the United States should take the offensive. In late February, Westmoreland and Earl Wheeler, chairman of the Joint Chiefs of Staff, requested an additional 206,000 troops for a war that the United States was supposed to have already won. "To say that we are closer to victory today is to believe, in the face of the evidence, the optimists who have been wrong in the past," Cronkite told television viewers on February 27. "To say that we are mired in stalemate seems the only reasonable, yet unsatisfactory conclusion." Eleven days later, the *New York Times* broke the story of the Pentagon's request for 206,000 more troops, sparking a public outcry. Although the White House had already decided to decline Westmoreland's request, the damage was done. Seventy-eight percent of Americans now believed that the United States was not making progress in the war; Johnson's approval rating had bottomed out at 26 percent.[15]

The time had come for the Americans to clean house. In March, Westmoreland was fired by way of promotion to army chief of staff. His replacement, Creighton Abrams, represented a stark contrast to Westmoreland. While his predecessor had seemed "the very model of a modern major general," appearing in a neatly pressed uniform and maintaining meticulously cordial relations with journalists, Abrams was a gruff soldier who had served as a tank commander under Gen. George Patton in World War II. Westmoreland had graduated at the top of his class from West Point; Abrams graduated the same year, only in the middle. "Chances are if he was in civilian clothes, sitting on a park bench, a cop would tell him to move along," one reporter quipped of Abrams.

With the change in leadership came a significant shift in strategy. Body counts were out, and pacification was in; enemy-centric search-and-destroy missions fell out of favor while population-centric counterinsurgency tactics of "clear and hold" gained ground. Abrams implemented the Accelerated Pacification Campaign, designed to increase the government's presence in the countryside and achieve a greater degree of integration between American troops, ARVN units, and various government security forces. As part of this effort, special attention would be given to training ARVN soldiers in the hope of giving them a more pronounced role in the conflict. While these efforts bore fruit, giving Saigon a greater presence in rural areas, they also came at a heavy price: the twelve months following the 1968 Tet Offensive would be the bloodiest of the war.[16]

No small amount of that blood would come from the Phoenix Program. Developed by the CIA and implemented in 1967, it would form another element of the new pacification strategy in Vietnam. Phoenix teams consisted of Provisional Reconnaissance Units, propaganda specialists, Communist defectors, and Navy SEAL commandos. Operating in small squads of six to twelve men, the teams ran clandestine operations designed to hunt down and arrest suspected Communist political cadres. Suspects were subject to interrogation and routine torture, with thousands being killed before or after arrest. While U.S. troops and ARVN units attacked the Communist military forces, Phoenix targeted civilians, the political infrastructure of the insurgency. The program soon earned the reputation of an assassination outfit, a characterization that many operatives rejected.

The U.S. military calculated that the Phoenix resulted in the "violent deaths" of more than twenty-six thousand Vietnamese. Beyond the slaughter of thousands of potentially innocent civilians, the Phoenix's critics argued that it may have actually helped the Communists by compounding the alienation of local villagers caught up in its net. Proponents of the program, however, have held it up as an example of a successful counterinsurgency strategy that proved effective at undermining the political infrastructure of the Communist insurgency.[17]

Ultimately, neither Le Duan's Tet Offensive nor Abrams's Accelerated Pacification Campaign managed to achieve its goal of delivering a knockout blow to the other side. In fact, the Tet Offensive and the twelve months that followed demonstrated that the war was indeed a bloody stalemate. While the Communists lacked the firepower to completely overrun U.S. and ARVN positions, Washington and Saigon lacked the commitment and coordination to reestablish firm control of the countryside. Neither side was able to achieve a decisive victory.[18] However, the very fact that the war was stalemated on the ground would lead to a changing of the political tides in the United States.

For the first time, a majority of Americans began to fear that the war in Vietnam was unwinnable. After five bloody years of direct American involvement, and two decades of substantial U.S. assistance, the anticommunist forces appeared no closer to victory. On March 26, President Johnson convened a meeting of the "Wise Men" (senior statesmen, including former secretary of state Dean Acheson, former chairman of the Joint Chiefs of Staff Gen. Omar Bradley, former army chief of staff Gen. Matthew Ridgway, and former ambassador to South Vietnam Henry Cabot Lodge Jr.) to discuss the situation in Vietnam. While some members of the group believed that a continued push by the military could achieve substantial progress in the war, the majority determined that the cause was essentially lost. As Acheson argued, the United States could "no longer do the job we set out to do in the time we have left and we must begin to take steps to disengage." The conclusion was demoralizing. "The establishment bastards have bailed out," a despondent Lyndon Johnson fumed. Though frustrated, the president took the Wise Men's recommendations to heart. Five days later, in a historic televised address, Johnson announced that he would henceforth limit the bombing of North Vietnam in an effort to begin peace negotiations aimed at ending the war. At the close of the broadcast, he told the nation, "I shall not seek, and I will not accept, the nomination of my party for another term as your president." The man who had won the 1964 election in a landslide, his political capital drained by the war, was stepping down.[19]

If 1968 was the bloodiest year of war in Vietnam, it was also one of the most violent years in the United States. On April 4, the most prominent figure of the American civil rights movement, Martin Luther King Jr., was gunned down by a white supremacist in Memphis, Tennessee. King's assassination set off a wave of violent protests in dozens of cities across the country that resulted in millions of dollars of damage and left scores dead or injured. In June, Robert F. Kennedy, Democratic presidential candidate and younger brother of John F. Kennedy, was assassinated by a deranged Palestinian at a political rally in Los Angeles. In August, the proceedings of the Democratic National Convention in Chicago were overshadowed by battles between city police and antiwar protestors on the streets that left hundreds injured. These spectacles, added to the rising crime rates throughout the country, led many Americans to long for a return to an earlier era. Indeed, to a large number of Americans, it appeared as if the United States might be on the brink of its own revolution.

One man in particular would capitalize on these fears of a coming anarchy and on the Democratic Party's disarray: Richard Nixon. Born into a working-class family in Yorba Linda, California, Nixon rose to national prominence as a zealous anticommunist in the darkest days of the late-1940s Red Scare. He had served as vice president under Eisenhower and as the Republican candidate for president in 1960. To voters who were dismayed by the violence on the nation's streets and appalled by the behavior of antiwar activists, Nixon appeared as a force of stability and a reminder of less complicated times. Like the majority of his countrymen, Nixon wanted an end to the Vietnam War, but he did not want the United States to lose. His campaign issued the vague promise of "Peace with Honor," which would secure America's exit from the disastrous war without admitting defeat. Though Nixon-the-candidate spoke of a secret plan to end the war, Nixon-the-president would choose to expand it. Instead of peace, Nixon brought an intensification of the violence in Southeast Asia. He also assembled a new foreign policy team, headed by Harvard government professor Henry Kissinger. Kissinger fancied himself a diplomatic mastermind, a modern-day American Machiavelli. Recent evidence also suggests that, conspiring together, Nixon and Kissinger worked to ensure that Johnson's peace initiatives in the last months of his presidency would go nowhere. In a move that bordered on treason, the Nixon campaign sent messages to leaders in Saigon assuring them that South Vietnam would receive a better deal with Nixon in the White House. Nixon urged Nguyen Van Thieu, who had been elected president of South Vietnam in 1967, to stonewall at the negotiating table, guaranteeing that the war would continue and opening a clear path for the Republican candidate to the White House. Having sabotaged Johnson's peace negotiations, Nixon and Kissinger sought to achieve victory in Vietnam where their predecessor had found only frustration and stalemate.[20]

Nixon's plan to end the war had three main components: Vietnamization, the president's so-called Madman Theory, and linkage. The first of these, Vietnamization, aimed at shifting the burden of fighting the ground war onto the ARVN. By combining an intensified training program with an even greater focus on pacification operations, the Nixon administration hoped to gradually pull American units out and replace them with South Vietnamese forces. With the second component, Madman Theory, Nixon hoped to convince leaders in Hanoi, Moscow, and Beijing that he might be reckless enough to launch a nuclear strike against North Vietnam if the Communist powers refused to negotiate. "I want the North Vietnamese to believe I've reached the point where I might do *anything* to stop the war," he told his chief of staff, H. R. Haldeman. "We'll just slip the word to them that, 'for God's sake, you know Nixon is obsessed about Communism. We can't restrain him when he's angry—and he has his hand on the nuclear button'—and Ho Chi Minh himself will be in Paris in two days begging for peace."

The third dimension of his strategy, linkage, represented a diplomatic campaign aimed at convincing the Soviet Union to bring pressure on Hanoi to come to the negotiating table. Linkage would tie peace negotiations in Vietnam to diplomatic issues in the Middle East, China, Europe, and Latin America and negotiations over trade and nuclear arms. In effect, this could function as a global quid pro quo between the superpowers: if Moscow worked with Washington in Vietnam, the Americans might help the Soviets with trade issues or with tensions in the Middle East.[21] Events along the Sino-Soviet border were about to present the Nixon administration with the perfect opportunity to try this new approach.

THE SINO-SOVIET BORDER WAR

While Vietnam occupied the world's attention, a different and arguably more far-reaching drama was unfolding inside the Communist bloc. Mao's China had moved into a phase of sustained domestic turmoil with the onset of the Cultural Revolution in 1966. The failures of the Great Leap Forward, growing pressures from the Sino-Soviet split, and a sense that the revolution had lost its energy prompted leaders in Beijing to launch a sweeping program designed to reinvigorate Chinese political society. Chinese leaders expanded Mao's cult of personality and called on increasingly radical groups of youth to help revitalize Chinese society by attacking old ideas, old culture, old customs, old habits. Student radicals organized into groups of Red

Guards swept across the country burning books, destroying historic relics, and staging protests. Thousands of officials and intellectuals were purged, tortured, and in many cases killed. While this revolutionary zeal gripped Chinese society, Beijing retreated from global affairs, dramatically reducing relations with capitals around the world. The staggering setback of the slaughter of the PKI in Indonesia, the escalating violence in Vietnam, and the ongoing rift with Moscow helped convince Beijing to concentrate its energies at home.

The worldwide Communist movement, already suffering from the Sino-Soviet rift, received another shock over the night of August 20–21, 1968, when Warsaw Pact forces invaded Czechoslovakia. The Soviet-led intervention crushed the so-called Prague Spring, a local movement that had introduced sweeping liberal reforms into the socialist system in Czechoslovakia. Fearing that the events in Prague threatened the Warsaw Pact, Soviet leaders sent military forces to crush the movement and arrest its leaders. While the Warsaw Pact's military operations were successful, the invasion rattled much of the Communist world. By crushing the reformists in Prague, the Kremlin had sent a signal to fellow Communists around the world that it would tolerate no dissent. In the long run, the invasion of Czechoslovakia dealt a severe blow to Moscow's credibility. In November, Leonid Brezhnev would formalize this policy when he announced what came to be known as the Brezhnev Doctrine: the Soviet Union would claim the right to intervene in fellow socialist countries in order to prevent their governments from abandoning communism.

Beijing blasted the invasion of Czechoslovakia as a "barefaced . . . specimen of fascist power politics played by the Soviet revisionist clique of renegades." Moscow, the *Peking Review* argued, "has brazenly resorted to direct armed aggression . . . and is trying to create puppets with the help of guns. It is exactly what Hitler did in the past . . . and the U.S. imperialism of today is doing in its aggression against Vietnam." In the wake of the Prague Spring and the declaration of the Brezhnev Doctrine, leaders in Beijing had good reason to fear their Soviet counterparts.[22] As Sino-Soviet tensions escalated, Beijing launched a series of provocations along the border with the Soviet Union.

Just before 9:00 on the morning of March 2, 1969, a group of thirty Chinese soldiers landed on a small, uninhabited island rising from the waters of the Ussuri River. Zhenbao Island—called Damansky Island by the Russians—was less than a third of a square mile of land in the Ussuri River, which demarcated the boundary between Northeast China and the Soviet Union. For years, Beijing had disputed the international boundary, insisting that it had been established on the basis of unequal negotiations in the nineteenth century between the Russian Empire and the Qing dynasty. Moscow brushed aside Beijing's complaints and maintained a small contingent of border guards in the area. Beginning in late 1968, the area became a site of periodic nonlethal scuffles between Soviet and Chinese troops. On March 9, Soviet guards sighted the Chinese soldiers and dispatched four vehicles to confront them. At 9:17, according to a Chinese report, the Soviet guards opened fire, triggering a general exchange that drew in Chinese reinforcements and left nearly sixty Soviets dead.[23] A Soviet report maintained that Chinese forces fired the first shots, a claim with which CIA analysts would later agree. The incursion by a well-armed group of Chinese soldiers, Moscow argued, represented a deliberate provocation. Military equipment, telephones, and telephone lines near the area suggested that the Chinese had staged an ambush against the border guards. Soviet analysts surmised that Beijing had provoked the incident in an attempt to whip up domestic support for the regime in the run-up to the Ninth National Congress of the Chinese Communist Party in April.[24]

Two weeks later, Moscow launched a reprisal operation against Chinese positions on Zhenbao. At just past 8:00 on the morning of March 15, Soviet commanders attacked the Chinese with six armored vehicles and some thirty soldiers. The Chinese had laid antitank mines, which slowed the Soviets. A second attack came at 9:40 a.m., followed by artillery fire and more attacks through the afternoon. Beijing's official statements claimed that Chinese forces had inflicted significant casualties and destroyed several Soviet vehicles.[25] With the apparent escalation in fighting, Mao called on the Chinese people to mobilize militia forces throughout the country. "[W]hen the war breaks out," he announced, "they will supplement the field army."[26]

Tensions remained high over the course of the summer, with both sides maintaining troops along the border. Fighting broke out again in mid-August, along the border in Xinjiang, when Soviet troops launched a punitive raid that slaughtered a Chinese border patrol.[27] Several days later, William Stearman, a special assistant to the State Department for North Vietnam, sat down to lunch in the Hotel America in Washington, DC, with Boris Davydov, second secretary of the Soviet embassy. Stearman was shocked by the direction the conversation took. "Davydov asked point blank what the US would do if the Soviet Union attacked and destroyed China's nuclear installations," Stearman told his superiors. "He assured me that he was completely serious." The Soviet diplomat explained that such a strike would set back China's nuclear program, which had become weaponized in 1964, for decades and would likely undercut the "Mao clique" in Beijing, opening an opportunity for "dissident senior officers and Party cadres" to seize power. A startled Stearman told Davydov that he was in no position to offer a definitive response, but he was sure that any such attack would be a matter of "considerable concern as no one could predict the consequences." In any event, the United States had no wish to become involved in a war between the USSR and the PRC. Davydov replied that a surprise attack carried little risk of a wider war because the destruction of Chinese nuclear facilities would severely weaken Mao's position. As far as the Kremlin was concerned, the recent attacks on Zhenbao represented "the last straw . . . and the Chinese had to be shown that they couldn't get away with these acts."[28]

Davydov's inquiry touched off a flurry of activity in Washington.

State Department analysts considered the likelihood of a Soviet attack low, as Moscow could "not be assured of destroying [the] entire Chinese inventory of nuclear weapons." Further, an attack on the PRC could easily trigger a "protracted, possibly all-out war."[29] Nevertheless, National Security Council staffer William Hyland suggested that such a clash might benefit the United States. "As many have pointed out," he wrote in late August, "a Sino-Soviet war, for a limited period and if limited in scope, is by no means a disaster for the US. It might just be the way to an early Vietnam settlement. It might also be a 'solution' to the China nuclear problem." Rather than seeking strict neutrality, Hyland suggested, Washington should consider its own national interests. Kissinger considered this analysis "1st rate."[30] But State Department academic consultants worried about the dangers of a larger clash. A Soviet attack on China, they warned, was likely to bolster Chinese nationalism, strengthen Mao's position, and risk "destabilizing" both Asia and Western Europe.[31]

State Department intelligence concluded in September that a war between Moscow and Beijing would amount to a "Communist Nightmare." Communist parties outside China and the USSR had referred to a potential conflict between the two Great Powers as a "colossal disaster." Rather than rallying to Moscow or Beijing, analysts noted, fellow Communist states around the world had looked with dismay upon a conflict that resembled nothing so much as a clash "characteristic of traditional great powers." Compounding the debacle, the war scare had resulted in a diffusion of authority from both Moscow and Beijing to myriad Communist parties outside their borders.[32]

In this context of mounting tensions, Mao had issued a call for general mobilization on August 28. The order called for an end to factionalism and for unity in the face of external threats from "class enemies in China . . . U.S. imperialists and the Soviet revisionists . . . and Indian reactionaries." The greatest danger came from Soviet forces "carrying out armed provocations on our border." Now was the time for "unity between the army and the people," he insisted. "All activities to divide our own strength should be opposed."[33] Chinese military leaders warned that "Soviet revisionists have made China their main enemy, imposing a more serious threat to our security than the U.S. imperialists." In this new geopolitical situation, Washington and Beijing shared a common adversary in Moscow. The war scare also helped convince Chinese leaders to rein in the Cultural Revolution. Although the end of the movement was still years away, its most radical phase was drawing to a close. Beijing also began to consider ending its brief period of isolation and reengaging the wider world. With relations with the Communist bloc at a low point, Chinese leaders turned to look across the Pacific to the United States. As Foreign Minister Chen Yi envisioned in September 1969, "It is necessary for us to utilize the contradiction between the United States and the Soviet Union in a strategic sense, and pursue a breakthrough in Sino-American relations."[34]

THE MONTHS BETWEEN JANUARY 1968 AND SEPTEMBER 1969 represented a Cold War watershed. Both Washington and Moscow received crushing setbacks. The 1968 Tet Offensive devastated the U.S. war effort in Vietnam and threw the centerpiece of Washington's containment strategy into crisis. Ever greater numbers of Americans began to accept the likelihood of defeat in Vietnam. But the Kremlin received its own blow. The clashes along the Ussuri River served as perhaps the final and most violent break in the Sino-Soviet split. Far from combining forces at the head of a worldwide socialist revolution, Moscow and Beijing perched at the brink of a full-scale, fratricidal war that might easily escalate into a nuclear conflict. By the autumn of 1969, leaders in both Washington and Beijing had begun to consider the prospect of rapprochement. Even as the Vietnam War entered its bloodiest phase, geopolitical transformations in the wider world threatened to make the fighting in Southeast Asia largely irrelevant. If Mao and his comrades chose to make common cause with Nixon and Kissinger, the strategic landscape of the Cold War would change entirely. The Americans might lose the battle in Vietnam but win the war for the wider Third World. Before that could happen, however, another massacre would take place.

SELECTIVE GENOCIDE
IN BANGLADESH

1 9 7 1

The path to U.S.-Chinese rapprochement in the early 1970s was rid-
dled with pitfalls. Washington had refused to recognize Mao's regime
after 1949, and both governments had staked much of their foreign
policy in the intervening decades on the need to battle one another's
influence. American and Chinese armies fought a bloody war against
each other in Korea, and Beijing was one of Hanoi's principal backers
against Washington and Saigon in the ongoing Vietnam War. Leaders in both Beijing and Washington, moreover, faced intense domestic
challenges. While Mao fought to rein in the excesses of the Cultural
Revolution, Nixon struggled to stem the tide of political and social
protests sweeping across college campuses and cities in the United
States. Put simply: neither leader could afford to extend an olive
branch across the Pacific only to be rejected. If rapprochement were
to be achieved, therefore, Nixon and Mao would need a third party
to serve as liaison. This search for an intermediary, combined with
his determination to gain the upper hand in the superpower struggle,
would lead Nixon to throw his support behind a Third World government that was in the midst of carrying out a wholesale massacre of

its own population. Washington's larger Cold War priorities led the White House—not for the first or last time—to back a pro-Western regime responsible for genocidal policies. Nixon's opening to China, then, would be purchased, in no small part, with the blood of hundreds of thousands of civilians. And as had been the case in Indonesia, these killings took on a disturbing ethno-religious character.

The best candidate for the delicate role of emissary between Nixon and Mao was the state of Pakistan. Pakistan enjoyed a unique position between both the United States and China. A U.S. ally in the Cold War, it also maintained a bitter relationship with one of China's principal rivals, India. Since the 1950s, Pakistan had served as an important player in Washington's bid to contain Soviet influence in South Asia and the Middle East. Warm relations between Moscow and India served as an added force pushing U.S. and Pakistani leaders closer together. Further, while serving as vice president under Dwight Eisenhower, Nixon had developed an affinity for Islamabad and a special contempt for New Delhi. While he considered Pakistani leaders straightforward and "frank," he found their Indian counterparts arrogant and condescending. But the years following the 1965 India-Pakistan War had witnessed strained relations between Washington and Islamabad, a result of U.S. frustration with Pakistan for having started the war. Nixon entered office determined to revive the alliance. While the United States sought an ally in the struggle against Moscow, Pakistani leaders hoped that Washington would serve as a patron in their regional struggle against India. From the birth of the U.S.-Pakistani alliance, then, leaders in Washington and Islamabad maintained very different goals.[1]

But Islamabad had its own problems. Pakistan had emerged in 1947 from one of the great massacres of the twentieth century as the British Empire in India collapsed along ethnic and sectarian lines into two states, India and Pakistan. The former would be a Hindu-majority state and the latter a Muslim-majority state. Partition (1947) set off the largest migration in human history as some ten million people rushed to relocate. Meanwhile, massive riots broke out across the country, killing hundreds of thousands. Pakistan was born as a divided state, its eastern and western sections separated by nearly a thousand miles of Indian territory. One Pakistani leader called the nation a "geographic monstrosity." More than just territory separated the two Pakistans. While an arid, mountainous landscape covered West Pakistan, the East was lush, tropical, and flat. The East was home to an ethnic-Bengali majority (which was itself split between a Muslim majority and Hindu minority) while the West was divided among Punjabis, Pashtuns, Sindhis, and a number of smaller groups. Urdu was the most widely spoken language in West Pakistan, while the majority of East Pakistanis spoke Bengali, a language they shared with millions more Bengalis across the border, in the Indian province of West Bengal. East Pakistan also held the majority of Pakistan's population, with some seventy-five million people to the West's fifty-five million. But it was the leaders of West Pakistan who held the reins of political and military power.

This imbalance remained a constant source of tension between the two parts of Pakistan. When Pakistan's founder, Mohammad Ali Jinnah, announced that Urdu would be the official state language, Bengali leaders opted to break away from the dominant party in West Pakistan, the Muslim League, and found their own political party, the Awami Muslim League, in 1949. The Awami League quickly grew to become the largest political organization in East Pakistan and the key opposition party in Pakistan. At the head of the party sat Sheikh Mujibar Rahman. A fifty-year-old Bengali with heavy glasses and a thick black mustache, Mujib, as his followers knew him, rose to the top of the nationalist movement in East Pakistan. Under his leadership, the Awami League advanced a proposal for autonomy in 1966. The proposal called for self-government in the two halves of the country, with cooperation on defense and international affairs. While the majority in the East embraced the proposal, West Pakistani leaders rejected it and arrested Mujib. Even as the nationalist movement built momentum in the East, political ferment gripped the country. In 1969, in the face of growing opposition to his leadership, President Ayub Khan of the Muslim League resigned, placing Gen. Yahya Khan in power. Yahya created a military government, declared martial law, and began preparations for national elections to be held in 1970. The two most prominent challengers to succeed Ayub Khan in the elections would be Mujib's Awami League and the Pakistan People's Party (PPP), led by opposition leader Zulfikar Ali Bhutto. The PPP put forward a center-left platform that called for an end to military rule, greater democracy, and socialist economic policies. With only weeks remaining before the general elections, catastrophe struck.

On the night of November 12, 1970, a massive cyclone tore through the low-lying coastal regions of East Pakistan. One-hundred-twenty-mile-per-hour winds blasted twenty-foot waves across the shores of one of the most densely populated regions of the world. During the best of times, the residents of the flat littoral waged a battle against the sea, maintaining dikes designed to keep the waters at bay. They now stood helpless in the path of one of the worst storms of the century. After the storm had passed, scores of coastal islands lay submerged and cut off from contact with state authorities; hundreds of thousands of their inhabitants were missing, carried out to sea by the receding tides. The surging waters had swept bodies into the trees, where many remained. Government officials estimated that as many as half a million people may have been killed, making the Bhola Cyclone one of the worst natural disasters in recorded history. Journalists flying overhead could smell the stench of death as survivors combed through the flooded ruins searching for the dead. Thousands of crushed cattle lay strewn across the sodden fields. Salt water clogged miles of rice paddies, devastating the harvest upon which the local population depended. Those who had managed to survive the cyclone now faced the threat of famine, cholera, typhoid, and dysentery.[2] As the waters receded, the desperate survivors looked to

officials in Islamabad for relief. The cyclone highlighted the dispari-
ties between the two halves of the country, but it was merely the first
wave of an even greater storm set to sweep through East Pakistan.
The events of the coming months would transform South Asia and
the wider Cold War world.[3]

A nation already gripped by political unrest now faced a catastrophe of historic proportions. The government's response only made
matters worse. President Yahya Khan made a brief stopover in Dhaka
on his return from China two days after the storm. Apparently inebri-
ated from in-flight refreshments, he stumbled through a brief speech
at the airport in which he remarked that the situation "didn't look so
bad." This, in addition to an aerial tour of some of the devastation,
marked the totality of the president's first visit to the disaster-stricken
area. The East Pakistan press blasted the government's response, complaining about the lack of West Pakistani military personnel to help
with rescue operations and accusing the president of failing to respond
to the disaster. In an impassioned speech, Mujib railed that West Pakistani leaders "are guilty of almost cold-blooded murder." The staff
at the U.S. consulate in Dhaka was perplexed by Islamabad's "display
of indifference" to the disaster. The consul general, Archer Blood,
blamed the government's lack of response on the growing animosity
between East and West Pakistan. "Yahya had been offered a golden
opportunity to bring the two wings closer in the mutual enterprise of
disaster relief," he later wrote, "but had muffed the chance."[4]

The United States joined an international relief effort, sending
aid, along with helicopters to assist its distribution. But as National
Security Advisor Henry Kissinger calculated, Washington's relief effort might prove problematic. Islamabad was clearly bungling its response to the disaster. "A highly visible appearance that the U.S. was
injecting its independent management," Kissinger argued, "would
carry the implication that President Yahya's government in West Pakistan could not or would not effectively manage this situation in

East Pakistan." With the national elections approaching, Kissinger worried that U.S. aid might undermine Yahya's political position. In what was only a hint of the callousness to come, the national security advisor placed a higher premium on supporting the military government in Islamabad than in saving lives in East Pakistan.[5]

Given the scope of the disaster, many observers expected Yahya to postpone the national elections until the following year. But the general was convinced that the elections would produce a split vote between the competing parties and a divided Parliament that would leave him in control of a new civilian government. On December 7, 1970, Pakistanis crowded around television sets to watch live coverage of the election returns. The results stunned them. Boosted by ongoing resentment over Islamabad's response to the cyclone, the Awami League captured 160 of East Pakistan's 162 open seats in the National Assembly, but it did not win a single seat in West Pakistan, where Bhutto's PPP captured 81 seats. Beyond the Awami League's crushing victory, the election exposed the gaping political divide between East and West Pakistan. State Department intelligence analysts warned that with "an absolute majority, the Awami League may be tempted to press too hard for more autonomy than the West Pakistanis are prepared to accept." A showdown between East Pakistanis seeking autonomy and West Pakistanis desperate to hold the country together appeared increasingly likely. Leaders in Islamabad feared that, if seated with a majority in the National Assembly, Mujib and the Awami League would legally secede from Pakistan or reduce the power of the military. Unwilling to hand over power, Yahya attempted to broker a compromise with Mujib and Bhutto. Talks achieved little, however, as Mujib and the Awami League demanded that the regime acknowledge their electoral victory and suspend the ongoing state of martial law in effect since Yahya's seizure of power in 1969. With negotiations deadlocked, West Pakistani military leaders began drawing up plans to intervene in the East in order to crush the Awami League.[6]

OPERATION SEARCHLIGHT: THE INVASION OF
EAST PAKISTAN

In the late hours of March 25, 1971, army units launched their assault. Rolling through ramshackle barricades thrown up on the streets of Dhaka by Bengali students, the military struck first at local security forces. The barracks of the East Pakistan Rifles, East Pakistan's primary border protection force, which had revolted from the West Pakistani military, were surrounded, and members of the units systematically slaughtered. Another contingent of troops surrounded the Tanti and Sakhari Bazaars and began razing houses with the residents still inside. The military staged another attack, setting fire to the offices of the Bengali daily *Ittefaq*, roasting forty people who remained inside. Pakistani troops deployed artillery and heavy machine guns against Dhaka's civilian population, with brutal results. Archer Blood spent the night on the roof of his residence watching tracer bullets flicker over the city and listening to machine-gun fire. Thirty-seven-year-old Sydney Schanberg, a reporter for the *New York Times*, reported seeing massive fires on the campus of Dhaka University from the Intercontinental Hotel as the sound of constant, heavy gunfire rattled through the city. A UN official witnessing the massacres reported more conservative but still horrifying estimates of five thousand to seven thousand civilians killed. "There were innumerable fires," he wrote in a secret report, "and almost all the quarters . . . of the poorest people were intentionally burned down by the Army. No living thing could be found in these burned quarters afterwards." The following morning, the city was quiet. Army vehicles moved through the streets, and government-controlled radio announced that the Awami League had been outlawed. The regime had branded Mujib a traitor and imposed a curfew throughout the city. The rebel-controlled radio reported that at least three hundred thousand people were killed in the first forty-eight hours.[7]

Simon Dring, a reporter for the *Daily Telegraph*, had seen first-hand the Pakistan Army roll into Dhaka in American-built M-24 tanks. The first casualties, he explained, were those people who tried to set up ramshackle barricades of automobiles, furniture, and tree stumps in the streets. The university, he reported, had been turned into a grisly killing zone: bodies floating in the lake, corpses smoldering in the burned-out residence halls, and students shot down on the lawns. The thirty dead bodies that remained inside Iqbal Hall, Dring wrote, "could never have accounted for all the blood in the corridors." Meanwhile, army units surrounded Sheikh Mujib's house, arrested the leader, beat his bodyguards, ransacked the property, and shot down the Bengali flag flying outside. The following day, at noon, troops converged on the old quarter of the city and began pouring fire into the "sprawling maze of narrow, winding streets." Soldiers with gasoline cans began dousing buildings with petroleum as other units took up firing positions. "Those who tried to escape were shot," Dring wrote. "Those who stayed were burnt alive." Their work completed, the soldiers moved on to other neighborhoods to repeat the process.[8]

Similar reports surfaced from elsewhere in the city. On the morning of March 26—as Bangladeshi Independence was declared— Pakistani troops attacked civilians waiting at the old city's dock at Sadarghat. After setting up a machine gun on the roof of the terminal, the soldiers opened fire on the crowd. Witnesses who visited the scene recalled pools of dried blood on the terminal floor, corpses dragged "into buses and burned," and bodies floating in the river. Army units also attacked the Hindu temple complex of Ramna Kalibari, located in the center of the Ramna Race Course. Pakistani forces massacred scores of civilians found inside and then set fire to the pile of machine-gunned bodies before demolishing the ancient temple.[9]

Over the following days, Archer Blood and his staff watched as the army tightened its grip on the city, set up military checkpoints at key intersections, and laid dragnets for suspected dissidents. Reports of the army's assault on Dhaka University were particularly troubling. The urban campus had become a rallying point for student supporters of the Awami League. Blood wrote that military units had attacked the university with the plan "to take no prisoners and to kill all students present at the dorms." Students in one dormitory were shot in the rooms or "mowed down when they came out of the building in groups." Meanwhile, soldiers set the women's dormitory on fire and machine-gunned the girls who tried to escape. Following rains on the night of March 29, Blood reported seeing evidence of mass graves outside Iqbal and Rokeya Halls. The "stench was terrible," he later wrote. Military leaders also targeted members of the university faculty, who were hunted down and shot in their homes. The heads of the philosophy, statistics, history, and English departments were all murdered in what U.S. consulate staff speculated had been a "preplanned purge." Bengali intellectuals viewed the attack on the university, Blood cabled Washington, as a campaign designed to "erase all traces of current 'trouble making' generation." Another army unit demolished the Central Shahid Minar, a monument to the martyrs of the 1952 Bengali-language movement. One of the American officers at the consulate watched the military hauling truckloads of prisoners to the East Pakistan Rifles camp at Peelkhana to be shot.[10]

On March 28, Blood cabled the State Department in Washington with a grisly description of the events he and his staff were watching. "Here in Dacca," he wrote, "we are mute and horrified witnesses to a reign of terror by the [Pakistani] military." The regime appeared to be in the process of hunting down and murdering Awami League supporters, university faculty, and student leaders. Meanwhile, non-Bengali Muslims backed by the military were staging raids into Dhaka's slums, "murdering Bengalis and Hindus," and setting off an exodus of refugees from the capital. "Full horror of [Pakistani] military atrocities will come to light sooner or later," Blood warned his superiors. He argued that there was little reason for Washington to continue "pretending to believe" Islamabad's denials. At the very least, he pleaded, the U.S. government should bring private pressure on Pakistan to end the slaughter.[11]

It was becoming increasingly evident that the Pakistani military had launched a nationwide campaign of terror. Refugees fleeing East Pakistan's second-largest city, Chittagong, reported similar attacks there by the military. The army, they claimed, had torched large sections of the city's slums, leaving nothing but the smoking ruins of thousands of bamboo huts. A student who had fled the city reported counting four hundred bodies floating in one section of the river. "They seemed to be enjoying killing and destroying everything," a Danish witness noted.[12] "Each day," a British witness reported, "I could see fresh groups of bodies piled up on the pavements. . . . There were men, women, even babies with bayonet and gunshot wounds. Some appeared to have been crushed."[13] Scott Butcher, a political officer in the U.S. consulate in Dhaka, remembered seeing "bodies rotting in the fields." He saw one rotting corpse "in a main street, obviously left there as an example." Another official, traveling in the countryside, reported visiting Hindu villages where people had been lined up and shot by the hundreds. The army had burned mills, destroyed entire rice crops, and left the survivors to starve. Many of those who were able fled, joining a torrent of refugees moving west toward India.[14]

In the face of this onslaught, there was little the Awami League could do. In the longer term, though, Awami League leaders were certain that East Pakistan could be liberated from Islamabad's control. With Mujib arrested, the acting Awami League leadership declared independence and begged the world community for assistance. On April 11, the prime minister of the provisional government of Bangladesh, Tajuddin Ahmad, broadcast a message to the people of the newly created country over the Free Bengal Radio Station, calling for their support in a liberation struggle. Although Yahya had "ordered his Army to commit genocide," Ahmad announced, the Bengali people were resisting. In the process, a "new Bengali Nation has been born amidst the ruins of the battlefield." Though the military's crackdown had been brutal, most of the country lay outside the army's control and open to foreign journalists. The new prime minister asked the outside world for weapons and aid to continue the liberation struggle, looking in particular for support from the Soviet Union and India. The "massacre of 75 million people and the attempt to suppress their struggle for freedom is now an international issue of major dimensions which threatens the conscience as much as the peace of the region," Ahmad intoned. "The battle will not be long because our strength multiplies daily as our plight gets wider recognition in the world," the prime minister insisted. "But we can expect much blood to be shed by these butchers and much wanton destruction and pillage before they are wiped out by the liberation army."[15]

THE U.S. RESPONSE

As reports of the atrocities in East Pakistan streamed into the White House, officials in the Nixon administration debated their response. Pakistan had stood as an important U.S. ally in South Asia since the 1950s, when Islamabad had joined the Baghdad Pact, an alliance of Southwest Asian states stretching along the southern borders of the USSR from the Dardanelles to the Himalayas.[16] While Indian leaders such as Jawaharlal Nehru celebrated Cold War nonalignment, Pakistan's government served as a pro-American bastion in the region. But Nixon had even more ambitious plans for his South Asian ally. In a private meeting during a visit to Islamabad in early August 1969, Nixon asked Yahya to act as Washington's go-between in setting up a clandestine channel to Beijing. After two decades of hostility with the Communist nation, Nixon was eager to establish relations with the People's Republic of China. By reaching out to China, he hoped to exploit the widening rift between Moscow and Beijing, turning the world's most populous nation into a potential ally in the Cold War. To do this, however, he would need a secret channel to the PRC—a channel that Yahya might be able to provide. The Pakistani leader was only too happy to accept this opportunity to strengthen the bonds between his nation and the United States. The following day, an enthusiastic Nixon told his chief of staff that Yahya struck him as "a real leader, very intelligent, and with great insight into Russia-China relations."[17]

The mounting bloodshed in East Pakistan complicated Nixon's plans. Why, increasing numbers of observers asked, did the White House refuse to condemn the atrocities? While the Nixon administration might discount newspaper stories from correspondents watching the violence in Dhaka, grisly reports from U.S. Foreign Service officers were not so easy to dismiss. Archer Blood's telegrams in particular created a headache for a White House that preferred to ignore the slaughter being carried out by its ally in South Asia. In a March 29 conversation, Nixon and Kissinger each expressed his support for Yahya's success in crushing the Awami League. "The use of power against seeming odds pays off," Kissinger argued. "[H]ell," Nixon replied, "when you look over the history of nations 30,000 well-disciplined people can take 75 million any time. Look what the Spanish did when they came in and took the Incas and all the rest. Look what the British did when they took India. . . . But anyway, I wish him well. I just . . . I mean it's better not to have it come apart than to have to come apart." In a conversation with Nixon the following day, Kissinger ridiculed Blood in a display of machismo that might have been comical had it not been so monstrous: "That consul in Dacca doesn't have the strongest nerves." Nixon was convinced that Washington should maintain its distance: "The main thing is to keep cool and not do anything. There's nothing in it for us either way."[18]

Unlike Nixon and Kissinger, Blood and his staff in Dhaka refused to watch in silence while a U.S. ally butchered thousands of its unarmed citizens. On April 6, 1971, Blood sent a cable to Washington that shook the foreign policy establishment. Signed by twenty-nine members of the consulate staff, the so-called Blood Telegram was a scathing condemnation of Washington's silence over the ongoing brutality in East Pakistan:

Our government has failed to denounce the suppression of democracy. Our government has failed to denounce atrocities. Our government has failed to take forceful measures to protect its citizens while at the same time bending over backwards to placate the [West Pakistani] dominated government and to lessen likely and deservedly negative international public relations impact against them. Our government has evidenced what many will consider moral bankruptcy. . . . [W]e have chosen not to intervene, even morally, on the grounds that the Awami conflict, in which unfortunately the overworked term genocide is applicable, is purely [an] internal matter of a sovereign state. We, as professional public servants express our dissent with current policy and fervently hope that our true and lasting interests here can be defined and our policies redirected in order to salvage our nation's position as a moral leader of the free world.

Humanitarian interests aside, Blood noted, Islamabad was not likely to prevail in the current conflict. The probable outcome, he argued, would be the creation of an independent East Pakistan. "At the moment we possess the good will of the Awami League," he concluded. "We would be foolish to forfeit this asset by pursuing a rigid policy of one-sided support to the likely loser."[19]

Upon receiving the cable, a furious secretary of state William Rogers telephoned Kissinger "to talk about that goddamn message from our people in Dacca." Kissinger worried that the cable would probably be leaked to Democratic senator and likely 1972 presidential candidate Edward "Ted" Kennedy.[20] Rogers fired back a sharply worded cable to Dhaka denying the charges that Washington had not taken steps to protect U.S. citizens in East Pakistan and explaining that its lack of an official response to the crackdown was motivated by a desire to avoid any action that might put Americans in harm's way. Moreover, he wrote, the State Department viewed the fighting in East Pakistan as "an internal matter of the Pakistan Government." In a further attempt to wash his hands of the matter, Rogers added that Washington had received reports of atrocities on both sides, though even he was not so bold as to "equate the two."[21] Blood and his staff shot back a scathing reply. The situation in East Pakistan, Blood insisted, should not be treated as a legitimate government restoring order over rebellious citizens because Islamabad had little legitimate authority. "How many votes did Yahya obtain?" Blood demanded. "We do not see [the] issue as [a] distinctly internal one. Aside from international moral obligations to condemn genocide (of Pakistani Hindus, although by Websters [sic] Definition [the] term likewise seems applicable to Awami League followers who [are] being hunted down with vengeance)," he wrote, the conflict had "definite colonial versus anti-colonial aspects."[22]

Although the White House might dismiss the cables coming from Dhaka as the hysterics of weak-nerved bureaucrats, Blood and his staff were not the only officials worried about the likely outcome of the fighting in East Pakistan. CIA analysts made it clear that Islamabad had very little hope of restoring control over the eastern half of the country. While the military had arrested most of the Awami League's top leadership, most of the rank-and-file members remained at large. Furthermore, many of the East Pakistan Rifles had escaped and melted into the surrounding countryside. The army controlled only the two largest cities, Dhaka and Chittagong. "The prospects are poor that the 30,000-odd West Pakistani troops can substantially improve their position," U.S. analysts noted, "much less reassert control over 75 million rebellious Bengalis. . . . The refusal of Pakistan's military leaders to honor [the 1970 elections] and their attempt to terrorize the Bengalis into submission have almost certainly ended any general desire in East Bengal to see the Pakistani union continue." To make matters worse, the report continued, Islamabad could not seal the border with India, and New Delhi had likely already begun sending aid to Bengali guerrilla fighters. Fearing that a prolonged guerrilla conflict could generate a more radical leadership in East Pakistan, India might be tempted to stage a full-scale military intervention that would almost certainly overwhelm West Pakistani forces in East Pakistan. National Security Council staff reached similar conclusions. Although the Pakistani military might manage to hold on to power through repressive measures for months or even years, a mid-April report stated, "it is our assessment that Pakistan as a unitary state cannot survive."[23]

While the White House stalled, voices inside and outside the U.S. government continued to call for action. As Nixon and Kissinger feared, Ted Kennedy did indeed choose to pursue the question of the slaughter in East Pakistan. In July, Kennedy excoriated the Nixon administration for its efforts to "whitewash one of the greatest nightmares in modern times." In August, Kennedy visited Bangladeshi refugee camps in East India. What he saw appalled him. "Nothing is more clear, or more easily documented, than the systematic campaign of terror—and its genocidal consequences—launched by the Pakistani army on the night of March 25th," he reported. "All of this has been officially sanctioned, ordered and implemented under martial law from Islamabad. America's heavy support of Islamabad is nothing short of complicity in the human and political tragedy of East Bengal."[24]

That complicity included actively arming the government that perpetrated the massacre of civilians in East Pakistan. On April 10, the *New York Times* reported that Washington was still sending spare military parts and ammunition to Islamabad. "There is growing evidence," the paper reported, "that the Pakistani Army has been using American tanks, jet aircraft and other equipment in its attempt to crush the movement for autonomy."[25] Though it had delayed shipments of arms to Islamabad, the flow of ammunition and spare parts (necessary to maintain Pakistan's substantial stores of American military hardware) continued. Much as Nixon and Kissinger might have liked to deny it, they maintained leverage over Yahya that might be used to rein in the crackdown. Yet, instead of pressuring Islamabad to ease its repression, they lamented the growing criticism of their policies. The "Dacca consulate is in open rebellion," Kissinger complained. A widening chorus of critics both within and outside Washington were now calling for the United States to begin aiding the Bengalis. Nixon shared Kissinger's frustration. "The people who bitch about Vietnam bitch about it because we intervened in what they say is a civil war," he fumed. "Now some of those same bastards . . . want us to intervene here—both civil wars." Many of those same voices also called for a suspension of U.S. aid to West Pakistan, Kissinger added. "For us to cut off aid would infuriate the West Pakistanis."[26]

Still, State Department officials doubted that the Pakistan Army could "substantially improve its position, much less reassert control over the Bengalis." Moreover, even if it were able to do so, Islamabad would not be in a position to create anything resembling a representative government in East Pakistan. If, on the other hand, East Pakistan managed to secure independence quickly, it would likely enjoy a moderate political leadership. However, they warned, a prolonged struggle would likely radicalize leaders in the East.[27] In any case, it increasingly appeared that "the breakup of Pakistan is inevitable."[28] On April 28, 1971, Kissinger sent his recommendation to the president. While unqualified support for West Pakistan would encourage Islamabad to "drag out the present situation and increase the political and economic costs to them and to us," cutting off aid would tilt the balance in favor of East Pakistan. Instead, he argued, the United States should pursue a middle path aimed at helping West Pakistani leaders achieve some sort of negotiated settlement. Shipments of spare military parts would continue, but new weapons systems would be embargoed so as to avoid angering Congress. Nixon agreed with Kissinger's reasoning and added a handwritten note: "*To all hands. Don't* squeeze Yahya at this time [emphasis in original]."[29]

Nixon and Kissinger's refusal to bring pressure on Yahya stemmed from a number of factors. Certainly, their view of Pakistan as a Cold War ally was critical. Why, they asked, should Washington criticize a pro-U.S. government in order to help India, a state that leaned toward the USSR, and left-wing Bangladeshi rebels who were likely to align with New Delhi? As Kissinger told Nixon, the Indians were "sons-of-bitches, who never have lifted a finger for us, why should we get involved in the morass of East Pakistan? All the more so, I quite agree with the point, if East Pakistan becomes independent, it is going to become a cesspool. It's going [to] be 100 million people, they have the lowest standard of living in Asia."[30] However, no concern was more pressing than the White House's central diplomatic gambit of 1971: preparations for an opening to the People's Republic of China. Deteriorating relations between Beijing and Moscow—culminating in the Ussuri River Clash of 1969—presented a clear opportunity for Nixon to accomplish his long-standing goal of opening relations with China.

For the people of Bangladesh, the timing could not possibly have been worse. Pakistan's critical assistance in Nixon and Kissinger's efforts to set up a back channel to China guaranteed that the White House would withhold condemnation of the crackdown in Bangladesh. Certainly, Nixon and Kissinger had a high tolerance for their allies' human rights abuses. But if ever there was a time for the White House to turn a blind eye to a Third World massacre, this was it. The ongoing disaster of the war in Vietnam, the geopolitical stakes involved in the opening to China, and the prospect of strengthening Washington's alliance with Pakistan presented the Nixon White House with an easy choice. Bangladesh would become a casualty of Nixon and Kissinger's Cold War strategy.

THE INDIA-PAKISTAN WAR

1971

While Nixon and Kissinger struggled to downplay the nightmare in East Pakistan, the atrocities created a far more immediate set of problems for neighboring states. The killings touched off an exodus of refugees, who fled across the border into India, pulling the world's second-most-populous state toward the brink of war with its neighbor to the west. As a conflict between South Asia's two largest nations approached, both Beijing and Washington backed Pakistan and sought to defend a regime that was busy slaughtering hundreds of thousands of civilians. More than any previous conflict, the India-Pakistan War of 1971, which created Bangladesh, would showcase the unraveling of the Cold War paradigm of conflicts between Communist and pro-Western forces and the rise of a new ethno-religious politics of violence in the Third World. The issue at stake in East Pakistan was not whether a Communist Party would seize control of a Third World country. Rather, conflicts over ethnic and religious identity had begun to eclipse East-West ideological disputes. Nevertheless, as violence escalated in South Asia, both Cold War superpowers maintained a strong interest in supporting their respective allies. And again, the Sino-Soviet split would place Beijing in a position to tilt the balance. Before the end of the 1971, the killings in East Pakistan would spark a regional war that, in turn, threatened to ignite a broader international conflict. Like Korea and Vietnam, East Pakistan seemed a strange place to fight a war that raised the prospect of a direct superpower confrontation. But its location along the contested borderlands of Cold War Asia magnified the geopolitical significance of the impoverished South Asian country.

Most immediately, however, the killings in East Pakistan created severe dangers for another postcolonial power: India. India's prime minister, Indira Gandhi, was an imposing figure. Fifty-one years old, with arched eyebrows and black hair streaked with gray, Gandhi was India's first female head of state. She and her advisors had been initially wary but encouraged by the conflict brewing in Pakistan. On the one hand, they hoped that an Awami League electoral victory might generate a Pakistani government that would be friendlier to India. Unlike West Pakistani officials, who harbored deep resentments toward India stretching back to the violent experiences of the 1947 Partition and more recent territorial disputes, East Pakistani leaders maintained better relations with New Delhi. However, the Gandhi administration was not eager to see the creation of an independent Bangladesh. Such a move was likely to introduce a measure of instability to the region. Moreover, an independent Bangladesh might encourage the Maoist rebellion across the border in the Indian province of West Bengal, which was home to millions of Bengalis who shared a language with the Bengali majority in East Pakistan. Although Yahya and his colleagues in Islamabad accused Gandhi of secretly aiding the rebellion in East Pakistan, the Indian government was far more interested in gradual reform there than in full revolution. Reports of the violence from Operation Searchlight raised concerns in New Delhi, but many believed that the crackdown was little more than a temporary measure. Surely, Indian leaders assumed, Islamabad realized that it could not use its soldiers to permanently repress the secessionist movement in East Pakistan. Furthermore, Indian intervention carried significant dangers. Gandhi was wary of meddling in what much of the international community was likely to view as an internal Pakistani matter. Her administration warned that "interference in events internal to Pakistan will not earn us either understanding or good-will from the majority of nation-states." It was therefore in New Delhi's interest to avoid allowing the question of intervention in East Pakistan to become a matter of public debate in India.[1]

However, events in East Pakistan were spinning out of control. In early March 1971—following the Awami League's electoral victory but several weeks before Operation Searchlight began—Gandhi had commissioned a study of the possibility of recognizing an independent Bangladesh. If the leaders of East Pakistan did choose to secede, an independent Bangladesh would be in desperate need of food, medical aid, and military support. But official intervention, Indian officials predicted, would almost certainly prompt a military response from West Pakistan. New Delhi urged officials in the Nixon administration to restrain Yahya from cracking down, which was sure to result in catastrophe, but Pakistan was already mobilizing. On March 19, Gandhi's advisors warned the prime minister that "2½ Divisions of Pak Army is poised to decimate East [Pakistan]." As the violence escalated and the flow of refugees across the border into India increased, pressure mounted on New Delhi to respond. While many Indians recoiled at Pakistan's human rights abuses, Gandhi's administration understood that the flood of refugees might pour across the border to spread famine, devastation, and the threat of revolution into India. Pakistan's atrocities were creating very real security concerns for New Delhi. Indian military leaders disagreed as to the best course of action. Some called for a quick intervention, going so far as to suggest that Yahya's regime would prefer being defeated in a conventional war with India to the likely humiliation of being beaten by the poorly armed Bengalis. But the chief of the Indian Army, Gen. Sam Manekshaw, urged caution. With the monsoon rains imminent, an invasion force was likely to become mired in the extensive marshes of East

Pakistan. Better to wait until fall, he argued, when the rains would have ended, the roads dried out, and the mountain passes to China blocked by snow, rendering a possible Chinese intervention far more difficult. "If you still want me to go ahead, I will," he told Gandhi. "But I guarantee you a one-hundred percent defeat." He later added, "Give me another six months and I guarantee you a hundred percent success." The prime minister chose to wait.[2]

"THIS IS GENOCIDE"

As the slaughter in East Pakistan continued, reports of the atrocities spread around the world. Anthony Mascarenhas, a Karachi-based journalist traveling with Pakistani soldiers through East Pakistan, wrote a shocking exposé in June. Knowing that he could never publish the story in Pakistan, he arranged to have the report published in London's *Sunday Times*. "THIS IS GENOCIDE," he wrote, "conducted with amazing casualness." Pakistani forces were in the midst of a systematic massacre of the Hindu population in both the cities and the countryside. Regular soldiers and paramilitaries engaged in "kill and burn" missions that ravaged local communities. Mascarenhas saw bodies of slain Bengalis sprawled in the fields, the decapitated heads of students on the roofs of university buildings, and cowering prisoners begging for their lives. He watched "truck loads of other human targets and those who had the humanity to try to help them hauled off 'for disposal.' " In the face of the onslaught, he wrote, Dhaka's Hindu populations "have vanished." The Pakistani major in command of the group that Mascarenhas was traveling with insisted that "we are only killing the Hindu men," but the bodies of women and children told a different story.[3]

Accusations of genocide, issued by journalists, political leaders, and U.S. State Department officers, accumulated over the summer of 1971. Political killings were one thing, but evidence that the Pakistan Army was targeting Hindus evoked the specter of ethnic violence.

While the ongoing slaughter took its toll, the shadow of famine and disease loomed. Most vulnerable were the millions of refugees created by the violence, many of whom had crossed from East Pakistan into India. "They are now massed, like a human chain," *New York Times* reporter Sydney Schanberg wrote in June, "in schools, public buildings and open fields along India's 1350-mile border with East Pakistan." The refugees had filled local hospitals, driven up the price of food, and overwhelmed sanitation systems. "Dysentery is rife," Schanberg reported. "Cholera and smallpox have broken out." Bodies had been left along the roads by those too fearful of the epidemic to move them—vultures, crows, and dogs fought over the remains. Schanberg visited one clinic with twenty beds trying to serve more than a hundred patients. "The sounds of the epidemic—coughing, vomiting, groaning and weeping—echo through the small brick building and across the lawn," he told readers. Rumors suggested that an even direr situation existed across the border in East Pakistan. With the arrival of the monsoon rains, the refugees' plight threatened to grow worse. Beyond the immediate humanitarian concerns, New Delhi worried about the potential for political unrest. Tensions between the refugees and local residents had already appeared, and the potential for intercommunal strife between Hindus and Muslims remained a threat. Many Indian leaders feared that the refugee camps might become hotbeds for rebel groups and secessionist movements.[4]

Pressure on the Gandhi administration to intervene continued to mount throughout the summer of 1971. Schanberg reported that India, an impoverished country whose residents subsisted on a per capita income equivalent to eighty dollars per year, could not possibly bear the burden of feeding and caring for more than three million refugees. Further, the hordes of destitute refugees had created tensions with local Indian citizens. The refugees had driven food prices up and pushed wages down. This discord could easily develop into intercommunal violence. In particular, Indian leaders worried that the Muslim-led assault on the Hindus of East Pakistan might incite

India's Hindu majority to launch reprisals against the nearly sixty million Muslims living inside India. Ultimately, no amount of aid would solve the problem. "The ulcer lies in East Pakistan," Schanberg wrote, where the "army's pogrom is continuing."[5]

On May 13, 1971, Prime Minister Gandhi sent a message to the White House explaining India's dilemma. The "carnage" in East Pakistan had created a massive refugee problem, which in turn had developed into a security threat to India. The refugees had entered the most "overcrowded" and politically unstable part of India, and there was now a possibility that the situation would become "explosive." "The influx of refugees," she announced, "thus constitutes a grave security risk which no responsible government can allow to develop." Gandhi argued that the crisis represented a premeditated policy of ethnic cleansing. "Pakistan is trying to solve its internal problems by cutting down the size of its population in East [Pakistan] and changing its communal composition through an organised and selective programme of eviction." This policy had the added benefit for Islamabad, she insisted, of sowing ethnic and religious tension in India.[6]

As the threat of war loomed, the Nixon administration urged restraint from New Delhi and Islamabad. State Department officials warned that Pakistani and Indian troops were massing along the borders. An estimated 3.4 million refugees had crossed the border, and millions more might follow. The Indian Border Security Force had established training camps for some ten thousand East Pakistani guerrillas. Meanwhile, Indian warplanes patrolled overhead. If the situation continued, either New Delhi or Islamabad might choose to launch a preemptive strike against the other. Further, should a war break out, there remained a distinct possibility of a "secondary escalation" in which China and the USSR might intervene in support of Pakistan and India, respectively.[7] New Delhi's ambassador, Lakshmi Jha, warned Henry Kissinger that the situation in the Indian province of West Bengal was "very explosive" and that New Delhi needed to find some way of getting the refugees to return. But a defiant

Kissinger challenged the ambassador, insisting that "you can't go to war over refugees." One scenario raised by some in New Delhi, the ambassador replied, involved arming the refugees and sending them back into East Pakistan to participate in guerrilla operations. Regardless, if the situation continued, it risked plunging the whole of South Asia into conflict. "I can tell you now," Kissinger threatened, "that we would deplore this matter getting totally out of hand."[8] In their private exchanges, Nixon and Kissinger expressed frustration with New Delhi. "The Indians need—what they really need is a"—the president fumed—"a mass famine." "They're such bastards," Kissinger cut in. "They are the most aggressive goddamn people around there."[9]

While Nixon and Kissinger blew off steam, the Pakistan Army continued its slaughter in East Pakistan. Reports of rape, starvation, and massacres continued to seep out of the country. Soldiers in the village of Haluaghat called all the young men in for blood donations. "The young men lay down on makeshift cots, needles were inserted into their veins," *Newsweek* reported, "and then slowly the blood was drained from their bodies until they died." A Bengali journalist told of his journey home, passing "through a dozen villages which had been burned and deserted, with bodies everywhere being eaten by crows. The smell! The horror!"[10]

Despite the mounting death toll in East Pakistan, the White House remained determined to use Islamabad as a back channel to Beijing. Nixon's opening to China remained the administration's top priority. In May, Kissinger complained to the U.S. ambassador to Pakistan that the "entire liberal community" in the United States had turned against Pakistan. The U.S. ambassador to Delhi, who supported U.S. consul general Archer Blood's position, "seems to have gone berserk," he fumed. Meanwhile, reports from Dhaka were "exaggerating the amount of killing and bloodshed there." The bottom line, Kissinger argued, was that the back channel to Beijing must be kept open. "Yahya must be kept afloat for six more months," he insisted. Nixon and Kissinger would stand behind Islamabad and ensure that the

flow of U.S. arms to Pakistan continued. Kissinger even took a macabre delight in Pakistan's arrangements for the secret diplomacy with
China in the midst of the ongoing slaughter in Bangladesh. "Yahya
hasn't had such fun since the last Hindu massacre!" he told his staff.[11]

GUERRILLA WAR

By the time summer arrived in Dhaka, life in the capital seemed almost as if it might be returning to normal. Rubble had been cleared
away, traffic filled the streets, and the city's residents went about their
business. After darkness fell, though, and the lights flickered out,
a different picture emerged. The residents of Dhaka awoke to the
nightly crackle of gunfire and suffered through "frequent blackouts."
Meanwhile, a secret rebel radio station broadcast celebratory reports
of the victories of the "liberation army." The countryside also told a
different story. Western journalists could not help but draw parallels
between the guerrilla wars in Vietnam and East Pakistan. The Pakistan Army held the cities and the major roads, but guerrillas prowled
through the hinterland, dynamiting bridges and attacking electrical
stations. "Even the lush, rice-growing terrain of the Ganges River
delta," a *New York Times* correspondent wrote, "is similar to that of
the Mekong River delta in Vietnam."[12]

In the weeks following the March crackdown, Indian leaders had
authorized their army and units of the Border Security Force to begin organizing and training an army of exiles from East Pakistan.
Dubbed the Mukti Bahini, or Liberation Army, the rebels were former soldiers from the East Bengal Regiment, survivors from the East
Pakistan Rifles, fugitive police officers, and student volunteers. Many
had no military training whatsoever; even fewer had received training
in guerrilla operations. To prepare the ragtag units for a prolonged
guerrilla war, Indian forces built an estimated fifty-nine training
camps. As their numbers grew, Indian advisors began training a select
group of rebels in underwater commando operations. Other rebels

received technical training, instruction in guerrilla operations and in the use of small arms, mortars, and rockets. Mukti Bahini fighters received obsolete weapons, however, and were forced to buy more modern equipment on the West Bengal arms market. By the end of June, Indian officers had trained some thirty thousand resistance fighters. This number would double by November.

Though the Mukti Bahini's initial operations were largely ineffective, Indian aid helped build the army into a more formidable guerrilla force. Also, the arrival of the monsoon rains in June transformed the battlefield in Bangladesh to the rebels' advantage. Heavy rains washed out dirt roads and created quagmires that trapped Pakistani armor. The soggy ground slowed supply routes and cut communications links between urban headquarters and large portions of the countryside. The guerrillas took advantage of the Pakistan Army's limited mobility and disrupted communications to launch sabotage campaigns against bridges, gas and electric stations, and communications networks. Mukti Bahini frogmen, meanwhile, attacked ships in the Port of Chittagong. In mid-October, the Indian Army began providing increased artillery support for the rebels, adding a deadly new dimension to their guerrilla war.[13]

Pakistani military leaders faced the daunting task of destroying an insurgency that enjoyed both popular support and the backing of a large neighboring power. New Delhi could supply the guerrillas along a three-thousand-mile border that was impossible to seal. Nevertheless, Pakistani commanders launched a multistage campaign to establish control of major towns and cities; push the Mukti Bahini back from the border; open road, rail, and river links; and then fan out to secure the remaining countryside. To do this, Pakistani commanders hoped to use a single division of troops supported by one squadron of 1950s-era F-86 jets. All these goals, moreover, were to be accomplished by May 15, a plan that, in retrospect, seemed hopelessly optimistic. "We became like a foreign army in a hostile land," the commander of the Pakistani forces reported. "The Bengalis used to call us the 'Army of Occupation.' Mukti Bahini had the support not only of local Bengalis, but of the whole of the Indian economic, political, and military set-up, in addition," he claimed somewhat dubiously, "to advisors from Russia."[14]

In September, the CIA issued a report on the situation in Bangladesh. Pakistani forces numbered some eighty thousand men who controlled urban centers and some of the countryside during the day. But after darkness fell, tens of thousands of Mukti Bahini guerrillas, supported by New Delhi, took the offensive. A loose coalition of resistance fighters combined sabotage operations, attacks on transportation, and political assassinations with cross-border raids that took a steady toll on Pakistani troops. CIA analysts drew parallels between the Mukti Bahini camps in India and the Algerian National Liberation Front (FLN) bases in Tunisia. Schools in East Pakistan stood empty, and economic activity had slowed to approximately one-third of pre-March levels. CIA analysts guessed that at least two hundred thousand people had been killed. Meanwhile, the massacres and ongoing guerrilla war had generated "one of the largest and most rapid population transfers in modern times." More than eight million refugees had fled into India at a rate that had peaked at one hundred thousand people per day. Likewise, between 80 and 90 percent of the refugees, the report continued, were Hindus—a clear indication that Pakistani authorities had targeted the Hindu population. This massive displacement imperiled the stability of all the states in the region. "In many respects," the report warned, "the refugee problem is the principal threat to peace in the subcontinent." As the crisis continued, the risk of famine grew. Analysts doubted that an acceptable political solution was possible. With the Pakistan Army having thrown down the gauntlet, it was unlikely that a compromise could be reached between East and West Pakistan. Mukti Bahini rebels were likely to prevent moderates from serving in any elected assembly, and any such body established by the military was "likely to be more shadow than substance." The report noted that "Bengal will remain a serious problem for India, Pakistan and the world at large. Gravely overcrowded, devoid of natural resources, wracked with violence, its people will probably become even more prone to extremism and acts of desperation than they now are."[15] The situation, it seemed obvious, could not continue much longer.

THE DRIFT TOWARD WAR

Indian leaders had already said as much. In mid-June, Swaran Singh, India's foreign minister, laid out what amounted to a case for war: "We in India have been at the receiving end of the results of the reign of terror and killings that has gone on in East Bengal since March 25." Islamabad's actions, by creating the refugee crisis, endangered the "economic, social and political fabric of our society and our state. These actions threaten to engulf our region in a conflict." New Delhi, he announced, "cannot sit idly by if the edifice of our political stability and economic well-being is threatened." The leadership in Islamabad, he told reporters, had created the crisis that now could possibly "destroy the prospect of peace and progress for our children." India would not allow the status quo to continue indefinitely. "To any responsible Government, this would be an intolerable situation."[16]

By early October, the CIA reported that New Delhi and Islamabad had each massed some two hundred thousand troops along India's northwestern border. The forces were on a state of alert, and the possibility of miscalculation sparking a major war remained high. India, CIA director Richard Helms warned, might choose to invade East Pakistan in a bid to end the refugee crisis, which now comprised some nine million displaced people. Meanwhile, rumors were spreading through the Pakistani leadership that Yahya was planning a preemptive strike in the coming weeks. As the monsoon rains ceased and waters receded, the Mukti Bahini had launched a new series of assaults. Helms warned that the Indians might send up to one hundred thousand guerrillas across the frontier in the next two months in a bid to establish a liberated zone—an act that "would almost certainly send the Pakistanis to war."[17]

Washington's ambassador to India, Kenneth Keating, expressed his concerns to Minister Singh about reports of increased guerrilla activity and urged New Delhi to take measures to close the border to further incursions. Washington was concerned, Keating explained, that continued hostilities might lead to a full-scale war. But Singh protested that Pakistan's ongoing "military repression" remained the root cause of tensions in Bangladesh. Some 33,000 refugees per day continued to surge across the border, adding to the 9.5 million already inside India. Of these millions, only 45,000 military defectors and embittered youth had turned to insurgent violence. In other words, he insisted, less than 1 percent of the refugees had turned to attacking their oppressors. New Delhi did not have the ability to exert complete control over the situation. "We cannot stop [the] refugee influx into India nor [the] return of some for whatever purpose into East Pakistan," he told Keating. "We cannot shoot people down coming or going. . . . India cannot prevent [the] movement of such people and does not have heart to attempt to do so." Further, it was not India that bore the responsibility for the present situation but the United States. "History will demonstrate [that the] US has greatest responsibility in [the] present situation since [its] support for [Islamabad] has contributed to hardening and continuation of [Pakistan's] military policy of repression." He also insisted that India had no plans to attack Pakistan. However, if the Pakistani military initiated hostilities, India "will defend itself with every means available"—a threat that did not yet include nuclear weapons, which New Delhi would acquire in 1974.[18]

State Department officers in the Dhaka consulate warned that the guerrilla war continued to escalate. Major urban areas remained secure, but the rebels had perfected tactics of ambushes and hit-and-run attacks. The guerrillas appeared to have nearly total control of some districts, moving freely and establishing their own administrative offices. In particular, the Mukti Bahini had taken to attacking Razakars, East Pakistani paramilitary volunteers who had earned a reputation for brutality. Meanwhile, Pakistani authorities had failed to build popular support. Ongoing atrocities only bolstered widespread resentment against Islamabad. State Department officers attributed increased rebel strength to Indian support. The slow attrition of Pakistani troops—officials estimated ten to twelve killed per day—represented a steady drain on the military: "[T]hese figures over [an] extended period of time could create [a] serious morale problem among troops far from home, living among unfriendly people and in [a] difficult and wearing climate."[19]

As tensions continued to mount, Prime Minister Gandhi made an official visit to Washington in November 1971, where she had a private meeting with the president in the Oval Office. On its face, the meeting between the two heads of state was awkward but cordial. Nixon stressed the view that a war in South Asia would run counter to all interests, while Gandhi expressed her concern over U.S. military support for Islamabad and revisited the problems that the refugee crisis had created. The conversation might have seemed banal had it not been focused on the suffering and death of hundreds of thousands of people.[20] But afterward, in private conversation, both Nixon and Kissinger unleashed a string of venomous and sexist attacks on the prime minister. The two men agreed that Gandhi was "a bitch." Kissinger used the invective three times in the nine-minute conversation. "We really slobbered over the old witch," Nixon ranted. "I dropped stilettos all over her." Kissinger observed that "the Indians are bastards anyway," before blaming New Delhi for starting a war—apparently untroubled by the continuing slaughter in Bangladesh.[21]

Meanwhile, reports continued to stream in from U.S. officials outlining ongoing Pakistani brutalities in Bangladesh. A mid-November report from the deputy director of the U.S. Agency for International Development noted that Pakistani military commanders in Bangladesh operated nearly independently from political leaders in Islamabad, following or ignoring orders as they wished. Military rule functioned "behind the façade of a civilian governor" and was "progressively and seriously alienating the Bengali population." There remained little reason to believe that commanders would move to create a genuinely representative civilian government in Dhaka. The military had handpicked the candidates for upcoming elections, 70 percent of whom were running unopposed. Meanwhile, attacks on Hindus continued. The army carried out "terror raids against the population and villages" while "local vigilantes" and guerrillas devastated any semblance of public order. In the midst of the chaos, the population had fled the countryside to seek refuge in the cities.[22]

On November 22, 1971, Washington received reports of a major incursion into Bangladesh by Indian infantry, armor, and aircraft in the Jessore sector. Kissinger suggested that India might be trying to establish a guerrilla sanctuary in East Bangladesh that could be used as a launching pad for further operations. The State Department speculated that the incident might also be an attempt by New Delhi to force Yahya to make further political concessions or to provoke Islamabad into launching an attack on India that would give Gandhi a pretext for full-scale war.[23] Kissinger was convinced that India would win, and he worried about the geopolitical impact of such a victory. Washington did not want "one power to dominate in the area," he noted, "and the defeat of Pakistan would certainly strengthen the Soviet position."[24] Nixon blamed New Delhi for the crisis but was convinced that India would "win without any question." He insisted, "Pakistan eventually will disintegrate. So it is very much in our interest to get the damn thing cooled if we can."[25] But the drift toward war now seemed irreversible. On November 30, the White House received information suggesting that Pakistan was planning to launch a preemptive strike on India.[26]

"A HELLUVA WAY TO START A WAR"

At 5:09 on the evening of December 3, 1971, twelve Pakistani F-86 Sabre warplanes took off from Peshawar airfield. Islamabad launched twenty more aircraft on missions against Indian airfields and radar stations in the Punjab, Srinagar, Awantipora, Amritsar, and Pathankot. Pakistan sent only 32 of its 278 warplanes in the first salvo of the 1971 India-Pakistan War.[27] Officials in Washington were confused. "I'm surprised that the Paks attacked at such a low level," the chairman of the Joint Chiefs of Staff remarked. "These aren't significant airfields," a puzzled Kissinger added. "That's a helluva way to start a war."[28] Despite the fact that Pakistan had launched the attack and despite the thousands slaughtered in Bangladesh, the White House's sympathies still lay with Yahya. "Pakistan thing makes your heart sick," Nixon told Kissinger. "For them to be done so by the Indians and after we have warned the bitch."[29] Kissinger lamented what he saw as "Indian-Soviet collusion, raping a friend of ours." Ultimately, he warned, "if the Soviets get away with this in the Subcontinent, we have seen the dress rehearsal for a Middle Eastern war."[30]

A CIA report published the day of the attack argued that the Kremlin's policy of backing India stemmed from a desire to gain an advantage in the Sino-Soviet battle for the Third World. "The Soviets see in India's 550 million people a counterweight to the 750 million Chinese and are anxious to make sure that these two potentially powerful countries do not join forces against the USSR," analysts wrote. The report speculated that news of Nixon's plans to visit China increased the Kremlin's anxieties: "On the subcontinent, the Soviets were able to exploit India's own concern over US moves toward China, as well as New Delhi's present need for great-power support, to nail the Indians to the close relationship with the USSR." Soviet leaders, the report argued, hoped that the war with Pakistan would block any potential rapprochement between India and China. Further, Pakistan's likely defeat would deal a blow to Beijing's reputation as "the defender of the small- and medium-sized nations and show the rest of the world that the Chinese are the real 'paper tigers.'"[31]

Shortly after midnight, Prime Minister Gandhi broadcast a public message announcing that her country was under attack. "Today," she told the nation, "the war in Bangla Desh has become a war on India." Since March, she explained, India had worked to find a peaceful solution to the "annihilation of an entire people" in Bangladesh "whose only crime was to vote for democracy." But the world had ignored their plight. "So today," she intoned, "we fight not merely for territorial integrity but for the basic ideals which have given strength to this country and on which alone we can progress to a better future."[32] The next day, Yahya made a statement to the people of Pakistan claiming that India had struck the first blow. "India's latest and serious aggression against us is her biggest and final onslaught on us," he announced. "The time has now come for us to inflict [a] crushing blow on the enemy. Rise like one man for your survival and honour and stand like an iron-wall against the enemy. You are on the side of righteousness and justice. Strike the forces of falsehood like a Godly curse, inspired by the spirit of faith and firm determination."[33] While New Delhi invoked the causes of democracy and human rights, Islamabad appealed to god and justice.

With the failure of Pakistan's preemptive strike, Indian forces stood poised to launch their long-planned counterattack. Their initial thrust came not by air or land but by sea. Shortly after the outbreak of the war, an Indian warship operating out of Visakhapatnam picked up unidentified sonar echoes outside the harbor. The warship deployed depth charges, and one hour later, an explosion was heard. Divers would discover the wreckage of the Pakistani submarine *Ghazi* at the bottom of the sea. New Delhi held its air force back until midnight, when it launched retaliatory strikes against Pakistani airfields in Bangladesh and in Islamabad, Sargodha, and Karachi. In contrast to Pakistan's tentative assault, India unleashed a massive attack, suffering heavy losses but destroying nearly half of Pakistan's air force in Bangladesh. The Indian Navy, meanwhile, assembled a squadron of missile boats to launch an attack on Pakistani oil facilities at Karachi. On the evening of December 4, Indian Air Force jets attacked Karachi, hitting some of their targets. Early the next morning, under cover of darkness, missile boats approached Karachi harbor and fired their full armaments before the Pakistani defenders had a chance to react. The same morning, a Pakistani submarine managed to sink the Indian frigate *Khukri*, but New Delhi had scored a dramatic success. The attack depleted Islamabad's petroleum reserves, robbing Pakistani heavy armor of desperately needed fuel.[34]

In the village of Sudih, some twelve miles inside the border of East Pakistan, a group of Indian tanks and infantry crushed two companies of Pakistani defenders after a fifteen-hour battle. The "bodies of 22 Pakistani soldiers lie sprawled in the trenches of their bunkers," Sydney Schanberg wrote. "Two lay sprawled in a bamboo clump where a shell had hit them, an unbroken hand mirror and shaving gear strewn around them." As Pakistani forces retreated through the village, the Indians attacked them with their artillery, flatting many of the mud huts and setting blazes throughout the area.[35]

New Delhi's initial gains came as a result of careful preparation. In the weeks leading up to the start of the war, Indian forces had taken strategic positions near the border with Bangladesh. Small-scale incursions during November 21–25 allowed Indian forces to further prepare the field for their full-scale invasion planned for December 6. Pakistan's feeble preemptive strike presented a gift to New Delhi, allowing Indian leaders to blame Pakistan for starting the war and giving justification for the invasion of Bangladesh. As a result, Indian military forces moved their invasion one day earlier, to December 5. Once inside Bangladesh, Indian troops overwhelmed Pakistani defenses. Pakistani forces were outmanned, outgunned, and forced to contend with a hostile population, Mukti Bahini guerrillas, and

Indian regulars. Making matters worse, the Indian Air Force established control of the skies while the Indian Navy controlled the sea.[36]

Islamabad believed that its best hope in a war against India lay in a strategy of deterrence. Aware that East Pakistan was all but indefensible, Pakistani leaders planned to concentrate their attacks in the West, along the contested borders of Kashmir. While Pakistani forces in the West took the offensive, troops in East Pakistan would focus on defense. In the event of a prolonged war, Islamabad would seek Chinese intervention in the Himalayas. Indian operations naturally inverted this strategy, focusing on the defense of the western frontier while pressing the offensive in East Pakistan. While Indian forces in the East enjoyed a clear advantage, Pakistani leaders hoped that gains in the West might be used to trade territory after the war had ended. Islamabad also hoped to convince U.S. and European leaders that the danger of a South Asia crisis sparking a larger conflict was great enough to necessitate outside diplomatic intervention before India could bring the full weight of its military and demographic superiority to bear. For Pakistan, military victory hinged on the ability to make quick territorial gains in the West while its soldiers stymied the advance of Indian forces in the East.[37]

Pakistani forces managed to make some gains in the western theater in Kashmir and the Punjab. In the south, a regiment of Chinese-made T-59 tanks supported by four thousand infantry and a squadron of American-made Sherman tanks penetrated some sixteen kilometers into India in a thrust toward Longewala. They diverted the Twelfth Indian Infantry Division from attacking the Karachi rail line and disrupted lines of supply. The Indians managed to halt this advance, however, with the use of British-made Hunter fighter-bombers, which destroyed twenty-five Pakistani tanks before Indian ground troops arrived to mop up what remained of the column. In the northern sector, Pakistani commanders unleashed a massive assault on the Indian salient around Chamb, forcing the Indian defenders to fall back on December 6. The Pakistanis, who had forced their way through after "bloody hand-to-hand combat" during the night, found a ghost town surrounded by battle-torn land. The hillsides were "blackened" by heavy shelling; the grass burned. "Not a soul is left in the neat and solid-looking one-story stone or stucco houses," a reporter wrote. The following day, Pakistani troops pressed their advantage, crossing the Tawi River and forcing the Indian brigade to continue its retreat.[38]

Hundreds died on both sides in the fierce fighting over the shallow river. "Today, the broad, dusty plain was littered with wrecked tanks, jeeps, and trucks and the bodies of several dozen Pakistanis," one reporter wrote. "They came at us in a great mass, yelling and screaming," an Indian sergeant told another journalist while a transistor radio in his foxhole played sitar music. The defenders had so far been able to hold the line. Surrounding villages had been evacuated, but cattle still grazed in the fields, untroubled by the sounds of gunfire and warplanes screaming overhead.[39] To the south, Indian forces mounted a large counterattack on the heavily fortified Shakargarh bulge. Minefields slowed the Indian advance and gave Islamabad time to reinforce the sector with two tank regiments of U.S.-made Pattons. In this, the largest tank battle of the war, Indian forces eventually captured 750 square kilometers of territory. Both sides suffered heavy losses in some of the heaviest fighting of the war.[40]

While Indian troops struggled to halt the Pakistani offensive in the West, their counterparts in the East poured across the border into Bangladesh. In a series of coordinated assaults, Mukti Bahini guerrillas and Border Security Forces engaged with Pakistani troops while regular Indian Army units moved to encircle the defenders. At the same time, Indian forces used helicopters to airlift soldiers into positions behind Pakistani lines in preparation for an assault on Dhaka. Pakistani forces planned to stage a series of strategic withdrawals, slowing the Indian thrusts and falling back to strongpoints. Though Pakistani planners hoped that this strategy would conserve their forces while depleting Indian units, in practice it systematically removed Pakistani forces from key battlefields as they holed up in their fortresses in places such as Sylhet and Jamalpur. In other cases, Indian commanders managed to cut off Pakistani forces and stymie Islamabad's operations through sound planning. Indian units drove into Bangladesh, capturing Jhenaidah and Megura and blocking the road to Jessore. The commander of Pakistan's 107 Brigade chose to withdraw, giving up most of the district without a fight. Heavier fighting took place at Hilli, but the Indians' superior numbers and firepower eventually forced Pakistani units back.[41]

"LOOKING DOWN THE GUN BARREL"

On December 8, Sydney Schanberg entered the recently liberated Jessore District. Most of the young women remained in hiding, fearful of assaults from Pakistani soldiers. But other residents celebrated the Indian victory, waving newly made Bangladeshi flags amid the lingering scars of battle. Retreating Pakistani forces had destroyed roads and bridges and abandoned burned-out vehicles, bedding, and sundry possessions. "A letter from a boy in West Pakistan to his soldier-father tells him to 'crush India,'" Schanberg wrote. Closer to the front, reporters found the bodies of two Bengali civilians lying in a field, "being gnawed on by dogs," a disturbing indication of the violence that followed the battle. "The evidence is growing that the Pakistanis are slaughtering Bengalis as they retreat and that the Mukti Bahini and other Bengalis are, in turn, taking vengeance on the Pakistanis and their civilian collaborators." Indian officers reported finding Pakistani soldiers' mutilated bodies—victims of a continuing cycle of violence and retribution. Meanwhile, a flood of Bangladeshi refugees followed one or two miles behind advancing Indian forces, returning to their homes.[42]

Pakistani leaders, well aware that they were outmanned and outgunned, looked to outside intervention for salvation. If their forces in the West could make quick gains and their units in the East could hold out, a UN-brokered cease-fire (pushed through by the United

States and China) or a Chinese intervention against India might be their best hope. Pakistani leaders tried to play upon Cold War anxieties to draw Washington into the conflict. Yahya warned Nixon that, with the military situation deteriorating rapidly, it seemed doubtful that Pakistani troops in East Pakistan could hold out. "If India should succeed in its objective, the loss of East Pakistan with a population of 70 million people dominated by Russia will also be a threat to the security of South Asia. It will bring under Soviet domination the region of Assam, Burma, Thailand and Malaysia," he wrote. "The far-reaching consequences of such a development to the future of Asia need no comment."[43]

American officials desperately wanted to help Islamabad, but the Nixon administration's influence was limited. The White House was particularly worried about the impact of the war on the global balance of power. The "Russians are playing for big stakes here," Kissinger warned the president. "When all the baloney—all the *New York Times* editorials are said and done if the Soviets and Indians get away with this, the Chinese and the United States will be standing there with eggs on our face."[44] Furthermore, the crisis in South Asia would likely impact the recent rapprochement between Washington and Beijing. As Kissinger told the president, "China would be watching closely to see what friendship with the United States really meant." Further, the war could be a "dry run" for Soviet policies toward the Middle East.[45] To forestall an Indian victory, Nixon was willing to increase the stakes and risk an even larger war. "I think we've got to tell [China] that some movement on their part we think toward the Indian border could be very significant. . . . [D]amnit, I am convinced," he told Kissinger, "that if the Chinese start moving[,] the Indians will be petrified. They will be petrified." But the White House was playing a dangerous game: major Chinese troop movements toward the Indian border risked provoking a Soviet response that could, in turn, spark a larger superpower confrontation.[46]

With Pakistani forces collapsing in the East, Kissinger worried that India might seize Kashmir and transform West Pakistan into "a vassal state." "The question is," he argued, "when an American ally is being raped, whether or not the U.S. should participate in enforcing a blockade of our ally." Although it violated the U.S. arms embargo in place since the 1965 India-Pakistan War, Kissinger suggested authorizing Jordan to send American-made fighter jets to Islamabad to defend the country. But Kissinger's aides explained that the administration could not legally authorize Amman to do anything that Washington itself could not.[47] Kissinger now feared the worst. New Delhi planned to dismember West Pakistan, he told the president, and annex Kashmir. Should this happen, he warned, Chinese leaders would conclude that the United States was too weak to protect its allies. Beijing would then lose interest in aligning with Washington. "So I think this," he told Nixon, "unfortunately, has turned into a big watershed." The United States had not done enough to "scare off the Indians." The only option, Kissinger argued, was to "convince the Indians the thing is going to escalate. And to convince the Russians that they are going to pay an enormous price." This, Nixon replied, would require an aggressive move by China. "As I look at this thing," he told Kissinger, "the Chinese have got to move to that damn border. The Indians have got to get a little scared." Kissinger added that the United States could arrange the transfer of Jordanian warplanes to Pakistan and send an aircraft carrier task force into the Bay of Bengal.[48]

While the Nixon administration scrambled to formulate a response, Indian forces in Bangladesh drove forward. The sodden ground, crisscrossed by waterways, did as much to slow the Indian advance as the Pakistani defenders. The attackers faced the challenge of seizing ground and then bringing up bridging equipment to traverse the rivers before moving forward. By December 10, Indian troop columns had reached the banks of the Meghna River, across which lay the approaches to Dhaka. Meanwhile, columns driving through Jessore were approaching the Padma River, guarding the southern approaches to the capital.[49] "The war in the East has reached its final stages," Kissinger noted. Indian forces were encircling Dhaka and "preparing for the final assault." The commander of Pakistani forces in the East had called for an armistice, a transfer of power to elected officials, and the evacuation of his forces. In the West, Indian defenders had weathered Islamabad's assault while Indian air strikes had heavily depleted Pakistan's petroleum reserves. Some analysts predicted that Islamabad would run out of fuel in two weeks. Meanwhile, India's naval blockade, anchored by the aircraft carrier INS *Vikrant*, had choked any resupply efforts to Pakistani forces in the East.[50]

"We can't let these goddamn sanctimonious Indians get away with this," Nixon raved. "Here they are raping and murdering. They talk about West Pakistan. These Indians are pretty vicious."[51] Indian forces were charging through Bangladesh as Pakistani forces fell into a disorganized retreat. Kissinger reported large tank battles raging in Kashmir and warned that a Soviet missile cruiser and cruise missile submarine might be heading toward the Bay of Bengal.[52]

With tensions rising, Nixon and Kissinger's anxieties began to take apocalyptic tones. Nixon wanted to press Moscow on its support for New Delhi, which the White House sought to brand as the aggressor. "It's a typical Nixon plan," Kissinger told the president. "I mean it's bold . . . at least we're coming off like men." Upon learning that Beijing had requested an urgent meeting with American officials, Nixon and Kissinger concluded that China was poised to take military action. Both men worried about the potential for the conflict to escalate into a nuclear confrontation between the United States and the Soviet Union in what Kissinger called "the final showdown." If the Soviets moved against the Chinese and India defeated Pakistan, he warned, "we may be looking down the gun barrel." With the balance of power in South Asia transformed, he continued, a "ghastly war" would break out in the Middle East, Europe would fall under Moscow's influence, and the United States would be left only with parts of Latin America.

"[Y]ou'll be alone," Kissinger told the president. "We've been alone before," Nixon replied.[53] Tensions ebbed several hours later, following Moscow's assurance that Gandhi had promised not to launch a full invasion of West Pakistan. Kissinger took the opportunity to stroke Nixon's ego once again: "What you did this morning [in engaging in brinksmanship with Moscow] Mr. President was a heroic act." To which the president replied, "I had to do it."[54]

While Nixon and Kissinger planned Armageddon, the USS *Enterprise* steamed toward the Bay of Bengal and Indian forces closed in on Dhaka. Inside the capital, residents prepared for the onslaught. Officials had begun rationing food and gasoline, but tea remained plentiful. Double-decker passenger buses and garbage trucks crawled through the city beneath a camouflage coat of mud amid a sea of rickshaws, cars, and the occasional cow. Workers dug air raid trenches and picked through the rubble left by Indian bombing raids that had killed scores of civilians. Stable hands at the Ramna Race Course exercised horses whose nerves had become frazzled by the warplanes attacking the nearby airport.[55] By December 14, Indian columns had advanced to within seven miles of the capital, where they battled with the Pakistani rearguard forces scrambling to retreat across the Lakhya River. Indian warplanes streaked across the skies overhead, bombing government buildings, as artillery pounded away at the collapsing defenses. Inside the city, wounded soldiers flooded hospitals and the Red Cross established a neutral zone in the Intercontinental Hotel.[56]

As the Indians closed in, Gen. Amir Abdullah Khan Niazi, commander of Pakistani forces in Bangladesh, telephoned the U.S. consulate. Though his forces remained intact, he considered the situation hopeless and now sought to arrange a cease-fire. Provided Indian commanders guaranteed their safety and the safety of those who had worked with the regime, Niazi was prepared to order his troops to stand down.[57] The U.S. embassy in Islamabad confirmed that President Yahya saw no choice but to seek a cease-fire. Yahya judged the military situation in the East to be "irretrievable," and an armistice seemed the only means of preventing a "holocaust."[58] The official surrender ceremony was held on the Ramna Race Course's grassy field on December 16. Niazi and Lt. Gen. Jagjit Singh Aurora, head of India's Eastern Command, sat at a single table to sign the surrender, formally ending the war in the East. For troops on the outskirts of the capital, however, the war continued. Indian artillery in the rice paddies of Barpa shelled Pakistani positions as a crowd of locals looked on. Pakistani forces on the other side of the Lakhya River waited in their bunkers, ready for an assault. Even after the last guns fell silent, tensions remained high. Wary Pakistani soldiers kept a watchful eye for Mukti Bahini forces bent on retribution. Razakar paramilitary home guards were high on the target lists of those Bangladeshis seeking revenge.[59]

Two days later, the American press corps in Dhaka reported a grisly discovery. Scores of bodies had been found in a field outside the capital. The victims, their hands tied behind their backs, had been bayoneted, garroted, or shot. They were some of the estimated three hundred Bangladeshi intellectuals captured by Pakistani troops and guarded by Razakars. Pakistani security forces targeted doctors, teachers, professors, and writers in the last major assault on the Bangladeshi intelligentsia before the end of the war. Crowds attacked two of the men believed to be implicated in the killings, beat them to death, and threw their bodies into pits. Meanwhile, a group of armed Razakars had fortified a mosque and were shooting at mourners.[60] Elsewhere, groups of looters tore through the city as guerrillas took revenge on Pakistani soldiers and suspected collaborators unlucky enough to be caught. Bihari Muslims who had helped the Pakistani authorities faced particular dangers from their vengeful countrymen.[61]

A different sort of destruction was under way in Islamabad. Angry crowds in West Pakistan's capital poured out into the streets to denounce Yahya. With the blame for the humiliating defeat falling on his office, Yahya chose to resign. Zulfikar Bhutto, leader of the center-left Pakistan People's Party, immediately assumed the reins of power and set about consolidating his regime. The new president placed Yahya under house arrest and freed Mujib, who returned to Dhaka to cheering crowds. Among Bhutto's first tasks was to compose a letter to Nixon, decrying the massacre of Pakistani allies under way in Bangladesh. "The news from Dacca is grim," he wrote. Reports spoke of "inhuman atrocities and mass murders of innocent people" in the capital and throughout East Pakistan. Bhutto pleaded with Nixon to bring pressure on New Delhi to prevent a "blood-bath."[62] But the White House had not moved to quell the massacre of Bangladeshis by the Pakistan Army, and it was just as reticent in its response to the reprisal killings.

EAST PAKISTAN OCCUPIED A UNIQUELY TRAGIC ROLE IN the history of the Cold War. The nation that would become Bangladesh found itself in possibly the worst possible place at the worst possible time: a victim of mass violence just as the secrecy-obsessed Nixon administration moved toward rapprochement with China. As a former member of the Mukti Bahini would recall, the "Cold War played a direct role in the creation of Bangladesh, but our liberation war was a sideshow of a sideshow of the main show, which was the Cold War." The Cold War in the developing world was often incredibly violent, but to the superpowers, "it was nothing more than a chess game" of power politics, and Pakistan was a "pawn in the arsenal of the State Department's imperial maneuvering."[63] Another former student activist and freedom fighter argued, "Though USA congress, senate, media and people in general, condemned Pakistani atrocities and supported Bangladesh liberation war, Nixon and Kissinger supported Pakistan. If Nixon and Kissinger hadn't supported Yahya Khan, the Bangladesh genocide would have been avoided or at least minimized."[64]

Ultimately, for the White House, the stakes and implications of the South Asia crisis reached beyond India, Pakistan, and Bangladesh. Nixon's efforts to enlist Chinese assistance in threatening India represented the first truly significant instance of tentative cooperation between Washington and Beijing following the final rupture in Sino-Soviet relations. Nixon and Mao would use the Pakistani back channel to achieve a public rapprochement in 1972 that would, in turn, help bring Washington and Beijing into alignment with each other against Moscow. Conversely, the 1971 India-Pakistan War would become yet another bitter chapter in the deadly rivalry between the two South Asian states, each of which would develop nuclear weapons in the years to come.

The episode also witnessed the birth of a new coalition of U.S., Chinese, and Pakistani forces. Although it suffered a defeat in the 1971 India-Pakistan War, this nascent partnership would evolve over the coming decade and reach maturity during the Soviet-Afghan War in the 1980s, when Islamabad would play a central role in shaping the character of the Afghan resistance and its affiliated transnational jihadist movement. This unlikely alliance of an authoritarian Islamic regime, the world's most populous Communist state, and a liberal-democratic superpower to support Islamic rebels marked a tectonic shift in the politics of postcolonial revolution. In the Cold War's final decade, the United States and its allies would be the largest sponsors of guerrilla movements in the postcolonial world.

The liberation of Bangladesh and the 1971 India-Pakistan War was a critical chapter in the story of the collapse of the Communist revolutionary project in the Third World and the rise of what would become a new conglomeration of revolutionary forces. At the same time, the Pakistani genocide in Bangladesh served as yet another harbinger of the resurgence of ethno-religious violence in the postcolonial world as the tide of Communist revolution receded.

THE FALL OF PHNOM PENH AND SAIGON

1975–1979

Even as the events in South Asia and Nixon's opening to China redrew the geopolitical landscape of the Cold War in the Third World, Washington, Hanoi, and Saigon continued fighting the war in Vietnam. Far from reining in the slaughter in the Cold War's killing fields, the turning points of 1968, 1969, and 1971 set the stage for a final round of mass violence in Indochina. While they renegotiated their relationship with Beijing, Nixon and Kissinger fought to end the Vietnam War on favorable terms. To do this, they chose to expand the war across South Vietnam's border into Cambodia. The U.S. invasion would help turn the tide in Cambodia's ongoing civil war and fuel the rise of one of the most murderous regimes of the twentieth century. Together with the massacre of the PKI in Indonesia, the Ussuri River clashes, and the genocide in Bangladesh, the Cambodian Civil War and the events that followed destroyed the Third World Communist project and fundamentally transformed the wars of containment.

"A KINGDOM OF TECHNICOLOR BLUE SKIES"

Cambodia, one American reporter wrote, "is a kingdom of Technicolor blue skies, and vivid rice paddies, of fantastic ancient stone temples tucked away in great rain forests and of saffron-robed Buddhist priests chanting each evening in a farewell to the hot tropical sun and greeting the languorous purple twilight."[1] Upon colonizing Cambodia in 1867, the French incorporated it into their Indochinese empire as a center for rice production. But as in China, Korea, and Vietnam, Japan's rise and the Pacific War destroyed the edifice of colonial power in Cambodia. On the morning of March 9, 1945, Japanese troops launched an armed takeover of the Vichy French regime in Cambodia. The operation, coordinated with the seizure of Vietnam, toppled the shell of French colonial rule and brought the nation under direct Japanese control. In Cambodia, the Japanese found a largely compliant population and an accommodating ruler: Prince Norodom Sihanouk. Born into the Kampuchean royal family, Sihanouk was an affable young ruler who had studied music, literature, and drama in Saigon before being chosen by Vichy authorities in 1941 as the successor to King Sisowath Monivong. Sihanouk had seemed an ideal choice for the Vichy official: a man whom they might easily control and who was unlikely to challenge his colonial masters. This same quality, however, meant that the prince would serve his new Japanese masters just as eagerly. Two days after the coup, Sihanouk declared an end to more than eighty years of French colonial rule and renamed the kingdom Kampuchea. The prince would play along with the Japanese fiction of ending Western colonial rule without mentioning that it was being replaced by Tokyo's dominion. The leader of a weak nation pressed between more powerful neighbors, Sihanouk was prepared to bend to the prevailing winds.[2]

Japan's formal control of Cambodia was short-lived. The detonation of American atomic bombs above Hiroshima and Nagasaki in

August 1945 brought the Pacific War to a close and signaled the end of Japanese rule in Cambodia. With the collapse of Tokyo's empire, Sihanouk announced that he had been opposed to Japan's armies all along. French colonial authorities, eager to reestablish order in post-1945 Cambodia, were content to keep the ever-agreeable prince in power. Under Sihanouk's leadership, Cambodia avoided the worst of the fighting between France and the Viet Minh in neighboring Indochina; the prince would neither welcome nor contest the belligerents' incursions into his territory. His goal was to keep his small nation out of the conflict next door. In 1953, at the tail end of losing the war in Indochina, the French granted Cambodia independence.

But Cambodia's real struggle was just beginning. Cambodian civil society encompassed a range of political groups that remained, on the whole, underrepresented in the postindependence government. While Sihanouk had refrained from open resistance to French colonial rule, Issarak resistance fighters had carried out a low-level insurgency in Cambodia's forests and countryside. In the cities, the Krom Pracheachon organization fielded left-wing political candidates and functioned as the legal front for Cambodian Communists; the Communist Workers Party of Kampuchea, meanwhile, remained underground. At the other end of the political spectrum, the Khmer Serei mounted sporadic operations against Sihanouk's regime at the same time that it fought against the Communists. Conservative elements in the country denounced communism and socialism and called for closer ties with Western powers. Sihanouk hoped to keep all these groups in check while maintaining the privileges he had enjoyed under colonial rule. What little power the National Assembly held was further circumscribed by the fraudulent 1955 national elections, in which Sihanouk's Sangkum Party won every seat. This tenuous balance would soon be upset, however.

In late February 1963, high school students and police clashed in the provincial capital of Siem Reap, located just outside the ancient temple complex of Angkor Wat. Tensions between students and police had been mounting for some months, but the refusal of local authorities to investigate the killing of one of the protestors sparked a confrontation. A crowd of a thousand students surrounded police headquarters, destroying portraits of Sihanouk and denouncing his political party. Several students were killed when police retaliated, prompting Phnom Penh to send in troops to restore order. Wary of angering Beijing and Hanoi, Sihanouk refrained from blaming the Communists for the disturbance and instead identified a group of thirty-four alleged subversives that included a number of members of the National Assembly. This denunciation triggered a witch hunt in Phnom Penh that drove a large number of intellectuals from the capital. Among them were the leaders of the Khmer Rouge, a secretive Communist organization whose cautious leaders were at pains to keep their identities concealed. While Sihanouk strengthened his grip on power in the capital, the Khmer Rouge built a base of power in the eastern forests of Cambodia under the protection of Vietnamese Communists operating in the area.[3]

The commander of this shadowy movement was a man named Saloth Sar—but the world would come to know him by his nom de guerre, Pol Pot. Sar was born in a fishing village in Kampong Thom Province in 1925, the eighth of nine children. He was, by most accounts, an unremarkable youth, and there was little to suggest he would grow up to become one of the greatest monsters of the twentieth century. His older sister became one of King Monivong's concubines, giving Sar entry to the palace. He attended lycée in Phnom Penh before leaving to attend technical school in Paris in 1949. In the French capital, Sar fell in with the Cercle Marxiste, a group of left-wing Cambodian students, and soon his political activities overshadowed his studies. He was taken with the writings of both Stalin and Mao, and his admiration for iconoclastic socialism increased after a trip to Tito's Yugoslavia. Marxism's appeal for young Sar lay in its promise of revolution. It was during this time in Paris that he met Ieng Sary, a fellow student radical who would become Sar's brother-in-law and second in command of the Khmer Rouge. While their dreams of leading a Communist movement in their native land germinated, Sar's technical studies languished. After failing his exams in three successive years, he was dismissed from the university and returned to Cambodia.[4]

Back in his native country, Sar found the Communist movement at a critical juncture. France was only months away from granting Cambodia its independence; across the eastern border, the Viet Minh were on the brink of victory against French colonial forces. Local radicals were being pulled in a number of directions. For many in the resistance, national independence had been the prime goal. With France pulling out, the need for revolution seemed minimal. Other radicals now turned to Sihanouk as the principal enemy. Meanwhile, the presence of the Vietnamese revolution exerted a strong pull on left-wing politics inside Cambodia. As 1953 opened, and Sar made his return, fighting continued between Issarak rebels and French forces. Sar's hopes of earning quick promotion through the ranks of the Communist Party leadership were disappointed, however. The Communist cell he joined was under Vietnamese control, and Sar was assigned to menial tasks rather than the leadership roles to which he felt entitled in light of his overseas experience. This treatment fueled his resentment toward the Vietnamese and his conviction that the Cambodian revolutionaries must strive for "self-reliance, indepen-dence and mastery. The Khmers should do everything on their own," he told one of his comrades.[5]

Rung by rung, Sar climbed the ranks, and soon came to the atten-tion of Tou Samouth, leader of the Khmer wing of the Indochinese Communist Party. Sar became Samouth's assistant, which placed him in a position of considerable power within the semiclandestine orga-nization. As the conflict between the Communists and the central government intensified, Sihanouk cracked down on the party cadre, allowing Sar and his comrades from Paris to move up in the organi-zation. Ensconced within the party leadership, Sar was able to gradually build power amid the changing political currents in Cambodia. By 1962, the power balance in the country had reached a tipping point. In January, Sihanouk launched a full-scale assault on the legal left-wing party in Cambodia. He arrested twelve members of the party leadership and promised to have them executed. The removal of the sanctioned leftists in the country left the secret Communist Party as the principal left-wing opposition group in Cambodia. Seven months later, in July, Samouth was arrested by government forces and taken to Defense Minister Lon Nol's house, where he was tortured and executed.[6]

Samouth's murder left Sar in control of the Communist Party, which was fast becoming more powerful. Sihanouk's continued attacks on the left drove many underground and into the ranks of the Khmer Rouge. As the left abandoned Cambodia's cities, the locus of the revolutionary struggle moved to the forests. This flight from the cities would play a key role in shaping the nature of the Khmer Rouge revolution after its victory a dozen years later.[7] Following the student uprising in Siem Reap, Sar became "Brother Number One." Ieng Sary and Son Sen, Sar's comrades during his time in Paris, formed a controlling majority of the central committee that oversaw the party. Together, they made up the shadowy Angkar, the Communist organization that would constitute the nucleus of the Khmer Rouge. Though Sar and his comrades found refuge with the Vietnamese for the next eight years, this protection did not breed affinity. The Cambodian leaders nurtured festering resentments against Vietnamese forces in the country that would break out after the Khmer Rouge's rise to power.[8]

KEEPING SIHANOUK FROM COMMITTING SUICIDE

Even as Communist leaders regrouped in the forests, Sihanouk moved to counterbalance his domestic crackdown on the left in the realm of diplomacy. On November 5, 1963, the prince threatened to reject aid from the United States, which had been sending economic and military assistance to Cambodia since 1955. Sihanouk suspected, correctly, that Washington had had a hand in the coup that toppled South Vietnamese president Ngo Dinh Diem on November 1 and resulted in his murder. If Diem's fate was the fruit of friendship with the United States, the prince judged that he could do without. Radio broadcasts from the U.S.-backed Khmer Serei forces (an anticommunist, antimonarchist opposition group operating along the border with South Vietnam) compounded Sihanouk's fears. American leaders were concerned by what they perceived to be the prince's threats in response to the coup in Saigon. The U.S. ambassador in Phnom Penh warned that Sihanouk "has created crisis where one did not exist and in [the] process may be opening up Pandora's box which could serve (1) to create very internal opposition he fears . . . and (2) to pave way for Communist regime and his own eventual elimination." The prince's "rigid diet cure" and exhaustion, the ambassador added, had "left him in highly nervous and overwrought state of mind." Sihanouk's rejection of U.S. aid was only the beginning of the fallout from the Diem coup, however.[9]

Washington's efforts to repair the relationship with Phnom Penh were hampered both by President Kennedy's assassination later that month and by Sihanouk's unwillingness to change course. "Despite inevitable appearance of yielding to pressure," NSC staffer Robert Komer wrote, "our problem remains that of keeping Sihanouk from committing suicide." The situation deteriorated further in early December, following the arrest and execution of Khmer Serei representative Preap In. The twenty-six-year-old man had returned to Cambodia after receiving guarantees of his safety from the regime. Instead of receiving amnesty, however, he was arrested by police, thrown into an iron cage, and subjected to a show trial. Refusing to confess to being a traitor, he was sentenced to execution before a firing squad. Sihanouk ordered that the young man's execution be filmed and broadcast in movie theaters for the next month, as an example to the population.

However, this brutal display of force only increased the alienation that many Cambodians felt toward the regime.[10]

Whether he realized it or not, Sihanouk's position was growing ever more precarious. His clumsy attempts at neutrality won him more enemies than friends, while his oppression of domestic political opponents drove any challengers to the regime underground. The deterioration of relations with Washington continued during the ensuing months, until May 1965, when Sihanouk chose to make a final break in diplomatic relations with the United States. The move came in response to a *Newsweek* article that accused the prince of keeping concubines and described the queen of being "money mad" and operating a "string of bordellos at the edge of the city." Characteristically, the prince's fateful decision was more emotional than practical: the result of personal offense rather than shrewd geopolitical calculation. By severing relations with Washington, the prince removed one of the few remaining barriers to the Vietnamese Communists. Initially, this strategy made sense: because the regime chose to tolerate PAVN units—who were operating inside its borders by 1964—Hanoi would have little reason to interfere with Cambodian affairs. In the long term, however, this appeasement strategy would prove disastrous. By accommodating Vietnamese Communists in a bid to keep his country out of the war next door, Sihanouk brought the conflict into Cambodia.[11]

All the while, the prince sought to counterbalance his international strategy of appeasing Hanoi by tightening the screws on domestic opposition. Since the late 1950s, Phnom Penh's security forces had waged a vicious campaign against leftists. The regime targeted journalists in particular. In 1959, government agents assassinated the editor of the left-wing paper *Pracheachon*. The following year, police arrested Khieu Samphan, editor of the Communist paper *L'Observateur*. The government's campaign against Communists operating in the forests was less successful. Opposition forces were difficult to locate and often found sanctuary with Vietnamese units that the regime dared not attack. While brutal, Phnom Penh's crackdown was ultimately ineffective. The prince appointed the conservative, pro-Western Lon Nol, now his deputy prime minister, to lead the crack-down on the Cambodian left. Born in 1913, Lon Nol made his name in the army and entered politics in the 1940s. Sihanouk, who believed that Lon Nol would be a loyal and easily controlled subordinate, had made him army chief of staff after independence in 1955. Eschewing mainstream Cambodian Buddhism, Lon Nol embraced astrology and mysticism. He was, according to journalist Elizabeth Becker, a "religious reactionary, a firm devotee of the occult and a practicing mystic who carried around the battered talismans given him in his youth by his village wiseman."[12]

Lon Nol, with the prince's encouragement, ran for and won the post of prime minister in 1966. Sihanouk then announced that he was forming a "countergovernment" of leftists. Once again, the prince sought to offset competing political factions within Cambodia and neutralize all opposition to his leadership. However, Lon Nol nurtured a political ambition that Sihanouk failed to recognize. As the prime minister began appointing a cabinet composed of individuals who were not under the prince's thumb, Sihanouk threw himself into his hobbies. He used government funds to publish the salacious magazine *Pseng-Pseng* and, after 1965, devoted much of his time to producing and directing films. In the next four years, he would write, direct, produce, and often star in a series of nine movies. The films were a garish, poorly executed celebration of the Cambodian elite through which Sihanouk's monarchy showcased the lives of the privileged to a nation whose economy was slipping into a state of decline. In retrospect, they appear as a dramatic representation of the degree to which Sihanouk had fallen out of touch with reality. In November 1969, the prince staged an international film festival in Phnom Penh to screen his masterpiece, *Crepuscule*. The film won the festival's grand prize—no others were allowed to compete—and Sihanouk took home a solid-gold trophy minted at the national bank.[13]

THE CIVIL WAR BEGINS

While the prince awarded prizes to himself, a civil war raged in Cambodia. Fighting had erupted some two years before in Battambang Province, in the northwest. Festering peasant resentment over forced sales of rice by corrupt local officials broke out into open rebellion in February 1967, when antigovernment demonstrators killed three local officials. Violence escalated when Phnom Penh refused to accept protestors' demands that it remove the garrison in the town of Pailin. In April, peasants killed two government soldiers and stole a cache of weapons. More attacks followed, prompting Sihanouk to send in paratroopers to crush the uprising. By the end of the month, Lon Nol's savage pacification campaign had killed hundreds. Government forces bombed suspected rebel positions, and stories about trucks full of severed heads being sent back to Phnom Penh circulated in the capital. While Communist leaders recognized the Samlaut Uprising in Battambang Province as a golden opportunity, they were unable to take advantage of it. The peasant revolt had been too sudden and the government response too brutal. Sihanouk accused three members of Parliament, Hou Youn, Khieu Samphan, and Hu Nim, of sparking the rebellion, and demanded that they appear before a tribunal. Recognizing the likelihood of their execution, Hou Youn and Khieu Samphan fled the capital to Communist sanctuaries in the jungle; Hu Nim later followed. After their disappearance, the ministers became known as the "Three Ghosts." Many Cambodians suspected that the three had been executed; some whispered that the ministers had been dissolved in sulfuric acid or crushed by bulldozers. Only later would the former ministers resurface as members of the resistance. The government's campaign of reprisals against left-wing leaders continued in the following months, as droves of intellectuals abandoned the cities to take refuge in the forests, where they, too, came under the control of the Communists.[14]

While Sihanouk's regime saw this exodus as evidence that its power had been restored, the nation inched closer to civil war. Having pulled its last supporters out of Phnom Penh, the Khmer Rouge transferred its headquarters to the remote highlands in the northeast. As government troops fanned out into the countryside, the Communists prepared to launch their armed struggle from the mountain forests of Ratanakiri Province. Communist cadres would begin arming peasants, arguing that the local tribes were "like dry straw in the rice fields—which need only a spark to set it on fire." There, in the malarial jungles of the northeast, the party reshaped its ideology. As a matter of necessity, the Cambodians emphasized self-reliance and the "purity" of their revolution: Hanoi was preoccupied with its own war, and Beijing backed Sihanouk. Theirs would be the perfect Communist revolution.[15]

At the same time, the rising tide of violence in Vietnam spilled over the border into Cambodia. In 1967, the U.S. military launched Operation Salem House, in which small teams of Americans and ARVN soldiers would infiltrate across the border in search of Vietnamese Communist sanctuaries. As the scope, size, and number of these missions increased—and the operation was renamed Daniel Boone—the frontier between the two nations became a war zone. A September 1967 report from a State Department legal advisor warned that military operations in Cambodia were a slippery slope: once U.S. forces were authorized to launch large attacks in the country, the pressure for escalation would be considerable. "We should be fully aware now of where the end of this road is likely to lead and not begin to go down it unless we are prepared to travel to the end," the report argued.[16]

With violence escalating across the Indochinese battlefield, the Cambodian Communists chose to launch their uprising. On January 18, 1968, Communist forces staged an attack at dawn on an army post in Bay Damran. In the following weeks, the Communists and tribal peoples in the surrounding areas conducted a series of similar strikes. The attackers seized weapons, burned government buildings, and killed state security forces. The operations carried more symbolic importance than strategic significance. Rather than seriously challenging state control, they served to announce the beginning of a new phase in the revolution. By the end of winter, some ten thousand peasants had flocked to the insurgency—now rebranded as the Khmer Rouge. Sihanouk recognized that the uprising threatened to make a mockery out of any notion that the regime controlled these remote areas. Phnom Penh was determined to crush the insurgency before it could take root and field a more significant challenge. To this end, the prince recalled Lon Nol (who had resigned during the fallout from the Three Ghosts' escape) to put down the rebellion. Government aircraft began attacking Communist-controlled villages, cutting off food supplies to rebel-held areas, and forcing peasants into government-run strategic hamlets. In April, Lon Nol's soldiers captured the Communists' Northwest Zone headquarters and drove the surviving forces in Battambang back to Pailin. The insurgency also struggled in the north and east, as the government hardened its defenses. The Communists fared better in the remote northeast; there, the dense rain forests provided an ideal environment for the guerrillas and prevented government forces from coordinating an effective pacification campaign.[17]

The Khmer Rouge's relationship with outside supporters presented another challenge: although the party stressed self-reliance, a successful resistance required outside support. Likewise, the fate of the revolution in Cambodia was ultimately tied to the fate of the revolution in South Vietnam. Hanoi and Beijing also faced a dilemma in this regard. On the one hand, they felt compelled to support their revolutionary comrades in Cambodia. However, they also understood that support for the rebels threatened to alienate Sihanouk's regime, drive Phnom Penh closer to the United States, and lead to a crackdown against Vietnamese forces operating in the country. Zhou Enlai encouraged Hanoi to behave cautiously. The Cambodian revolutionaries must be made to understand, Zhou argued, that Vietnam represented the first battle in the larger struggle to liberate Indochina. "If the whole of Indochina joins the efforts to drive the US out of Vietnam, then the Laotian and Cambodian revolutions will be successful," he told members of the Vietnamese Politburo. Ideally, the Cambodians would "join efforts to fight the Americans first and then fight the reactionary forces in Cambodia."[18]

"THE NIXON DOCTRINE IN ITS PUREST FORM"

The mounting insurgency infuriated Sihanouk, who blamed the Communists for inciting rebellion among local villagers. The prince justified the counterinsurgency (which took a larger toll on peasants than on Communist cadres) as entirely necessary. "I do not care if I am sent to hell," he thundered. "I will submit the pertinent documents to the devil himself." The prince announced that the country was in a state of "total war" and escalated his campaign of repression against those leftists who remained within reach of his government forces. Already convinced that the Khmer Rouge was being led by Khieu Samphan, Sihanouk now publicly suggested that Hanoi and Beijing might be supporting the rebellion. As the rebel ranks swelled, Saloth Sar remained in the shadows: the mysterious Brother Number One. In the coming years, he would change his name to Pol Pot.[19]

The rising unrest throughout the country threw light on the inability of the Cambodian military to maintain full control over its territory in the face of threats from domestic insurgence and Vietnamese Communists. In response, Sihanouk once again pivoted in an effort to return the balance of power to his favor. In late 1967, the prince began sending signals to the Washington that he might be open to reconsidering his relationship with the United States. Former First Lady Jacqueline Kennedy paid a visit to the ruins at Angkor Wat in November. In January 1968, as Hanoi prepared to launch the Tet Offensive in South Vietnam, the U.S. ambassador to India, Chester Bowles, traveled to Phnom Penh. Both Washington and Phnom

Aerial view of Hiroshima after the atomic bomb blast, August 1945. (Truman Library)

Winston Churchill, Harry Truman, and Joseph Stalin shake hands at Potsdam, July 1945. (National Archives and Records Administration)

Mao Zedong addresses his followers, December 1944.
(National Archives and Records Administration)

U.S. ambassador Patrick Hurley and Col. I. V. Yeaton meet with CCP leaders Mao
Zedong and Zhou Enlai in Yan'an, August 1945. (National Archives and Records
Administration)

S. Marines patrolling amid ruined buildings on Wolmi Island in Inchon Harbor, South
Korea, September 15, 1950. (National Archives and Records Administration)

U.S. Marines storming the seawalls at Inchon Harbor, South Korea, September 15, 1950 (National Archives and Records Administration)

A Korean woman searches through ruins in Seoul, South Korea, November 1950. (National Archives and Records Administration)

UN Forces crossing the Thirty-Eighth Parallel, 1950.
(National Archives and Records Administration)

U.S. Marines guarding captured North Koreans, 1950.
(National Archives and Records Administration)

U.S. Marines move forward after close-air support flushes out Communist forces from their hillside entrenchments. Billows of smoke rise skyward from the target area. Hagaru-North Korea, December 26, 1950. (National Archives and Records Administration)

U.S. soldiers traverse mountains north of Seoul, South Korea, January 31, 1951. (National Archives and Records Administration)

U.S. Marines guarding captured Chinese troops, Hoengsong, South Korea, March 2, 1951. (National Archives and Records Administration)

President Richard Nixon shakes hands with Indonesia's president, Suharto, 1970. (National Archives and Records Administration)

Napalm bombs explode south of Saigon, South Vietnam, 1965. (National Archives and Records Administration)

Black smoke floats over Saigon, South Vietnam, during the Tet Offensive, 1968. (National Archives and Records Administration)

U.S. soldiers wait for the helicopter that will evacuate their fallen comrade, Long Khanh, South Vietnam, 1966. (National Archives and Records Administration)

U.S. soldiers burn a suspected guerrilla camp in My Tho, South Vietnam, April 1968. (National Archives and Records Administration)

CONFIDENTIAL   084

PAGE 01   DACCA 01138   061008Z

21
ACTION NEA-08

INFO OCT-01   SS-20   AID-12   USIE-00   NSC-10   NSCE-00   CIAE-00

INR-07   SSO-00   RSR-01   RSC-01   /060 W
                                             092431
P 060730Z APR 71
FM AMCONSUL DACCA
TO SECSTATE WASHDC PRIORITY 3124
AMEMBASSY ISLAMABAD
INFO AMCONSUL KARACHI
AMCONSUL LAHORE

C O N F I D E N T I A L DACCA 1138
LIMDIS
SUBJ: DISSENT FROM U.S. POLICY TOWARD EAST PAKISTAN

JOINT STATE/AID/USIS MESSAGE

1. AWARE OF THE TASK FORCE PROPOSALS ON "OPENESS" IN
THE FOREIGN SERVICE, AND WITH THE CONVICTION THAT U.S.
POLICY RELATED TO RECENT DEVELOPMENTS IN EAST PAKISTAN
SERVES NEITHER OUR MORAL INTERESTS BROADLY DEFINED NOR
OUR NATIONAL INTERESTS NARROWLY DEFINED, NUMEROUS OFFICERS
OF AMCONGEN DACCA, USAID DACCA AND USIS DACCA CONSIDER
IT THEIR DUTY TO REGISTER STRONG DISSENT WITH FUNDAMENTAL
ASPECTS OF THIS POLICY. OUR GOVERNMENT HAS FAILED TO
DENOUNCE THE SUPPRESSION OF DEMOCRACY. OUR GOVERNMENT
HAS FAILED TO DENOUNCE ATROCITIES. OUR GOVERNMENT HAS
FAILED TO TAKE FORCEFUL MEASURES TO PROTECT ITS CITIZENS
WHILE AT THE SAME TIME BENDING OVER BACKWARDS TO PLACATE
THE WEST PAK DOMINATED GOVERNMENT AND TO LESSEN LIKELY
AND DESERVEDLY NEGATIVE INTERNATIONAL PUBLIC RELATIONS
IMPACT AGAINST THEM. OUR GOVERNMENT HAS EVIDENCED WHAT
MANY WILL CONSIDER MORAL BANKRUPTCY, IRONICALLY AT A
TIME WHEN THE USSR SENT PRESIDENT YAHYA A MESSAGE DEFEND-
ING DEMOCRACY, COMDEMNING ARREST OF LEADER OF DEMOCRATI-
CALLY ELECTED MAJORITY PARTY (INCIDENTALLY PRO-WEST) AND
CALLING FOR END TO REPRESSIVE MEASURES AND BLOODSHED.
IN OUR MOST RECENT POLICY PAPER FOR PAKISTAN, OUR IN-
TERESTS IN PAKISTAN WERE DEFINED AS PRIMARILY HUMAN.

CONFIDENTIAL

The so-called Blood Telegram, written by Archer Blood and the staff of the U.S. consula
in Dhaka, East Pakistan, in protest of the Nixon administration's refusal to denounce
Pakistani government atrocities, April 6, 1971. (National Security Archive, George
Washington University)

**The National Security Archive has asked that the following citation be includ
with the above photo of the Blood Telegram:**

An aerial view of Muslim-occupied West Beirut and the Mediterranean shoreline. Buildings throughout the city had been damaged by shelling during the ongoing confrontation between Israeli forces and the Palestine Liberation Organization, April 1983. (National Archives and Records Administration)

An aerial view of the Beirut stadium that had been used as a PLO munitions dump, September 1982. (National Archives and Records Administration)

Two U.S. ships, the USS *Wisconsin* and the USS *Tripoli*, patrol the Gulf of Oman during the Iran-Iraq War, October 1987. (National Archives and Records Administration)

An Afghan Mujahideen with a shoulder-fired, surface-to-air missile, August 1988. (National Archives and Records Administration)

Soviet infantry and combat vehicles in Afghanistan, August 1988.
(National Archives and Records Administration)

President Ronald Reagan meeting with Afghan Mujahideen leaders in the Oval Office,
February 1982. (National Archives and Records Administration)

Helicopter-tank operation in Afghanistan. (Courtesy of *Soviet Military Power*, 1984;
National Archives and Records Administration)

fghan Mujahideen return to a village destroyed by Soviet troops, March 1986. (National Archives and Records Administration)

A Khmer Rouge soldier waves his pistol and orders store owners to abandon their shops n Phnom Penh, Cambodia, on April 17, 1975, as the capital fell to Communist forces. A rge portion of the city's population was reportedly forced to evacuate. (Photo from a West German television film; AP Photo/Christoph Froehder)

Iraqi soldiers in foxholes near their pontoon bridge crossing over the Karun River during an air attack on October 17, 1980, in Basra, Iraq. (AP Photo)

Penh shared an interest in keeping the conflict in Vietnam out of Cambodia, but they had different views on how this goal should be accomplished. Sihanouk wondered what the United States was doing in Vietnam at all when the Soviet Union and the People's Republic of China seemed to be the larger threats. Bowles was more concerned with obtaining the prince's blessing for limited U.S. incursions into Cambodia, to root out Vietnamese Communist forces along the border. While neither side achieved all its goals, Bowles left feeling that the meeting had been a success. "I am fully conscious of mercurial and unpredictable characteristics of the Prince," Bowles wrote. "In any dealings with Cambodia we must expect sudden switches and caustic and unfair criticism. However, we should not let Sihanouk's intemperate and sometimes childish outbursts deter us from the main business at hand: to keep Cambodia neutral, to keep the Viet Cong and NVA out of its territory and, with an eye to the future, to improve our own relations with this small but important country."

To this end, Sihanouk would accept limited strikes by U.S. forces in pursuit of Vietnamese Communists. A critical point of contention seemed to be the question of B-52 bombing runs on Cambodian territory. The commander of U.S. forces in South Vietnam, Gen. William Westmoreland, pushed for Cambodia to be opened up to heavy bombing raids by the United States. While the Bowles mission was an important first step in the restoration of U.S.-Cambodian relations, the meeting would mark a critical turning point in what came later.[20]

In March 1969, President Richard Nixon launched a massive bombing campaign against Vietnamese Communists in Cambodia, code-named Operation Menu. National Security Advisor Henry Kissinger explained that some four divisions of Vietnamese Communist troops were operating out of Cambodia. The Vietnamese, according to Kissinger, had forced Cambodian officials and most of the population out of these areas. He reasoned that Operation Menu did not represent a violation of Cambodian neutrality—such neutrality did not exist in the border regions because they had fallen under control of the Vietnamese Communists. Moreover, Kissinger claimed that Sihanouk had acquiesced to Operation Menu. The prince had told Bowles, Kissinger claimed, that he wanted the United States to "force the Viet Cong to leave Cambodia." To do this, Sihanouk would allow U.S. forces to engage in "hot pursuit" of Vietnamese cadres: "In unpopulated areas, where there are not Cambodians, in such cases I would shut my eyes," Sihanouk said. The Nixon administration seemed to have interpreted these signals as a green light for expanding the war across the Cambodian frontier.[21]

But the effects on the ground were not as clean as the White House hoped. As leaders in both Washington and Phnom Penh were well aware, Cambodians did indeed live in the areas that the United States was bombing. According to a report from the Joint Chiefs, the area designated "Breakfast," as part of the morbidly named Operation Menu, contained an estimated 1,000 Cambodian peasants; "Lunch" had another 200 civilians; some 300 civilians lived in the "Snack" area; 700 peasants lived in the "Dinner" zone; "Dessert" contained another 120 civilians. While the report estimated that civilian casualties would be minimal, it warned that this projection was "tenuous at best." Nixon and Kissinger, aware that the public was likely to be outraged by news of the attacks on Cambodia, sought to keep the operation secret. The White House informed only a small number of officials and directed the bombing runs by diverting B-52s charged with attacking targets in Vietnam.[22]

While American bombs pounded the northeast, the political situation in Phnom Penh was changing rapidly. The Cambodian economy was in a poor state, and Sihanouk's regime was doing little to fix it. While the prince's aides called on him to put "an end once and for all to the improvisations, fantasies, and prestige spending," Sihanouk had other ideas. In early 1969, he opened a string of casinos in an effort to generate government revenue from the thriving gambling operations throughout the country. The spectacle of Cambodians gambling away their meager savings as the prince celebrated his film

Crepuscule and war raged in the countryside came to symbolize the regime's decadence in its waning months. To many of his conservative critics, Sihanouk seemed powerless to arrest the nation's descent into chaos. In July, the prince tried to bluff the National Assembly by announcing his resignation as premier—if his critics on the right were unhappy with his handling of the economy, they were welcome to try their own solutions. Sihanouk seems to have hoped that this move would absolve him of responsibility for the nation's troubles and silence his detractors. This time, however, the prince's gambit failed. The National Assembly elected Lon Nol as prime minister and Prince Sisowath Sirik Matak as his deputy. Both men proved to be strong conservative opponents of the prince. Sihanouk's influence languished in the following months, and in January 1970, he left Cambodia for medical treatment.[23]

With the prince abroad, Prime Minister Lon Nol and Sirik Matak launched a coup d'état against Sihanouk. On March 8, the military staged demonstrations against the Vietnamese presence in the country. Four days later, the assembly denounced Sihanouk's "pro-communist Vietnam" policies while Lon Nol demanded that all Vietnamese troops evacuate Cambodia by dawn on March 15. The plotters stationed tanks outside key government buildings in the capital, cut off outside communication, and arrested the few officials still loyal to Sihanouk. While whispers of CIA involvement circulated through the streets of Phnom Penh, the new regime declared the creation of the Khmer Republic. As its first act, the regime pledged to drive the Vietnamese from Cambodian soil.[24] All participants recognized that the war in Indochina was likely to broaden. Privately, Beijing expressed hopes that Sihanouk would join forces with the Communists and Vietnamese guerrillas in a united front. Lon Nol would feel pressure to attack North Vietnam, China would support Hanoi, and fighting had already broken out in Laos. In this way, Chinese premier Zhou Enlai told North Vietnamese officials, "Indochina will become a battlefield."[25]

As Cambodian and Vietnamese units clashed around Communist sanctuaries, Lon Nol called for outside assistance in reasserting control over his country. South Vietnamese forces were the first to take advantage of the situation. Saigon began launching air strikes and limited infantry incursions as early as March 20. Officials in Washington recognized an opportunity to partner with the new regime in Phnom Penh against their shared enemy. The prospect of expanding B-52 bombing runs in direct support of Cambodian government units proved particularly enticing to U.S. military planners. By mid-April, the Royal Cambodian Army began receiving U.S. military aid while American helicopter gunships flew sorties against Communist positions.[26] On April 28, President Nixon decided to authorize a joint U.S.–South Vietnamese invasion of Cambodia against the recommendations of his secretaries of state and defense. Nixon intended to destroy the Vietnamese Communist headquarters, the Central Office for South Vietnam (COSVN), which was reputed to be in the "Fishhook" region of Cambodia. Two days later, the president announced to the nation and the world that the invasion of Cambodia—which, he was careful to point out, was "not an invasion of Cambodia"—was designed to protect the phased withdrawal of U.S. forces in the region by dealing a decisive blow to the Communist ability to operate in South Vietnam. "A majority of the American people want to end this war rather than to have it drag on interminably," Nixon said. "The action I have taken tonight will serve that purpose."[27]

The news of the invasion sparked a national wave of protest that culminated in the shooting of four students by members of the Ohio National Guard on the campus of Kent State University. As tempers flared throughout the United States, American and ARVN forces crashed through the forests of eastern Cambodia in search of the COSVN. As they did so, they cleared landing zones for helicopters, destroyed plantations, and leveled villages. On May 3, American troops destroyed the town of Snuol (home to some two thousand people) after twenty-four hours of shelling. When the dust settled, seven bodies were found, four of which were civilians. The towns of Mimot and Sre Khtum were also destroyed, along with dozens of smaller hamlets. Thousands of refugees fled the advancing forces. The COSVN and large concentrations of Vietnamese Communist fighters were nowhere to be found, however. American officials seemed unable to grasp the reality that the COSVN was a highly mobile, "multiunit element" that could easily escape advancing enemy forces. U.S. and ARVN units could not locate the COSVN because it did not represent any fixed location. As their headquarters melted away into the jungles, so, too, did Communist fighters. The invasion drove Vietnamese and Khmer Rouge insurgents away from the frontier and deeper into Cambodia.[28]

As fighting intensified, the regime's wrath fell on Vietnamese civilians inside Cambodia. Phnom Penh announced a curfew for the 120,000 Vietnamese in the capital. Elsewhere, local authorities rounded up ethnic Vietnamese and forced them into holding centers surrounded by barbed wire. In short order, reports of small massacres in the countryside surfaced. On April 10, government soldiers slaughtered 89 civilians in the town of Prasaut. Lon Nol's security forces moved into the large Catholic Vietnamese settlement in Chrui Changwar, outside Phnom Penh, at the end of April and forced 800 workers onto barges waiting on the Bassac River. The next day, dozens of corpses with bound hands floated past the ferry at Neak Luong, outside the capital. Lon Nol had arrested 30,000 Vietnamese in an attempt to root out potential subversives; the regime deported some 190,000 more to South Vietnam. Lon Nol's pogrom quickly soured relations between Phnom Penh and Saigon and sparked reprisals against Cambodian civilians by ARVN units along the border.[29]

The chaos of spring 1970 opened new doors for the Communists. The first came from Sihanouk himself. He was now a prince without a kingdom—deposed, living in exile, and eager for a chance to regain influence inside Cambodia. Sihanouk resorted to a characteristic tactic: switching sides in a play to reposition himself in power. On March 23, the prince issued a radio broadcast from Beijing to proclaim the creation of an umbrella resistance organization, the National United Front of Kampuchea (FUNK). He called on all Cambodians to "uphold the banner of revolt" and to "engage in guerrilla warfare in the jungle against our enemies"—the Lon Nol regime. Suddenly resurfacing, the Three Ghosts, Hou Youn, Khieu Samphan, and Hu Nim, declared their support for the FUNK while the Khmer Rouge suspended all denunciations of Sihanouk. In a supreme irony, Cambodia's playboy monarch was poised to become the figurehead of the Khmer Rouge. On the ground, the clash between Hanoi's and Phnom Penh's forces resulted in increased cooperation between Khmer Rouge and North Vietnamese forces. Although Khmer Rouge leaders still sought to maintain distance and autonomy from their Vietnamese comrades, the fighting allowed them to expand the scope of their operations.[30]

Lon Nol was now determined to regain the upper hand. In August, he launched Operation Chenla I, a large offensive designed to recapture a sizable chunk of territory that had been lost to the North Vietnamese. Government forces targeted Route 7, the road that linked Phnom Penh with the town of Skuon, in the east. After an indecisive campaign that left the military depleted, Lon Nol declared victory and held celebrations in the capital. Evidence of the government's victory, however, was harder to find in the countryside, where fierce Vietnamese counterattacks strained Cambodian defenses. On January 21, 1971, the fiction of Lon Nol's victory became impossible to maintain as Vietnamese sappers slipped into Pochentong International Airport, outside Phnom Penh, and destroyed nearly all of the republic's air force. Several weeks later, Lon Nol suffered a stroke that left him partially paralyzed and raised the prospect that the regime was about to fall. The general returned in March, however, with a renewed determination to prosecute the war. He announced a new offensive, Chenla II, which was designed to reestablish road links with the northern city of Kompong Thom, along Route 6. When the military brass objected, citing the need to recoup their losses from Chenla I, Lon Nol ignored them.[31]

To lead the operation, Lon Nol chose one of the more colorful figures in the Cambodian Army, Col. Um Savuth. "He was an astonishing personality," journalist William Shawcross wrote, "a thin, twisted man who walked with a long white cane, drove his jeep at terrifying speeds, and was nearly always drunk." The colonel was best known for once having placed a cat on his head and ordering a subordinate to shoot it off. The shot missed and instead hit Um Savuth in the skull, leaving him partially paralyzed. Afterward, to manage the pain, the colonel maintained a near-constant state of inebriation. Chenla II commenced in August 1971, under heavy monsoon rains. Um Savuth chose to keep his troops on the road rather than sending them into the muddy countryside. Government forces failed to secure their flanks, but they were able to reach Kompong Thom on October 11 with little fighting. The commander of U.S. forces in South Vietnam complained that the Cambodians had "opened a front forty miles long and two feet wide." In Phnom Penh, however, Lon Nol celebrated yet another great victory. At the end of the month, the North Vietnamese counterattacked, smashing into government forces along the road to Kompong Thom. Lon Nol's troops fled or were killed in the rout. Much of their equipment and heavy weapons were abandoned.[32]

The defeat was a disaster for the regime. Some three thousand troops had been killed, and thousands more had fled. Chenla II was the Khmer Republic's last major offensive; government forces were now clearly on the defensive. In Phnom Penh, Lon Nol had little credibility left—many Cambodians assumed that the regime was merely marking time until its inevitable collapse. While older citizens worried about the fate of their nation, thousands of young Cambodians abandoned the cities and towns to join the Khmer Rouge in the surrounding forests. Despite the alarming situation on the ground, American leaders were resolved to continue their support for Lon

Nol. In November, President Nixon told reporters, "Cambodia is the Nixon Doctrine in its purest form." Unlike in Vietnam and Korea, he assured his audience, Americans would not be doing the fighting inside Cambodia. "We hope not to make that mistake again if we can avoid it." Meanwhile, a war that would continue for three more years and claim the lives of half a million Cambodians dragged on.[33]

While the residents of Phnom Penh worried about the future, Khmer Rouge leaders had high hopes. For the time being, however, they faced a brutal American bombing campaign. B-52 strikes carpeted large sections of eastern Cambodia, pummeling strips of the countryside a half-mile wide by two miles long. "It was as if an enormous scythe had swept through the jungle, felling the giant teak and *go* trees like grass in its way, shredding them into billions of shattered splinters," a Vietnamese guerrilla recalled. "It was not just that things were destroyed; in some awesome way, they had ceased to exist." The raids terrorized the local peasants caught in their path. Those who survived were "completely disoriented," one villager recalled, adding, "They couldn't even hold down a meal." Though it failed to destroy COSVN and the headquarters of the Khmer Rouge, the bombing campaign set off a mass exodus from the Cambodian countryside. A flood of refugees abandoned their hamlets and villages and settled in ramshackle shelters surrounding the cities. By 1975, the population of Phnom Penh had ballooned to 2.5 million from a prewar size of 650,000. Thousands more fled into the forests, where many fell under the control of the Khmer Rouge. As journalist Philip Short wrote, "the B-52s placed a millstone round the government's neck by inundating the cities with a demoralized detritus of human misery . . . and gave the Khmer Rouges a propaganda windfall which they exploited to the hilt." It was Lon Nol and his American allies, cadres told terrified villagers, who had inflicted this devastation on Cambodia; the Khmer Rouge promised to liberate the nation from the tyrannical regime and drive out the "imperialists."[34]

In reality, North Vietnamese troops did most of the fighting between 1970 and 1973, while the Khmer Rouge used the opportunity to build up their forces. Khmer Rouge leaders trained soldiers and officers and outfitted their growing army with captured American weapons. The rebels used the proceeds from rubber plantations under their control to buy medical supplies and gasoline from corrupt government officials. All the while, Communist leaders emphasized the "independence and sovereignty" of their movement while downplaying the role that Hanoi's forces had in shielding Cambodia's nascent insurgency. As the movement grew, Cambodian Communists and refugees who had spent the 1960s in North Vietnam began to filter back into the country in the hope of aiding the revolution. Khmer Rouge cadres greeted these "returnees" with distrust—their loyalties were in doubt after their having spent so much time among the Vietnamese. While they were generally barred from leadership positions, many returnees were put to work instructing new recruits with the technical and political skills that they had acquired during their time in North Vietnam.[35]

As fighting tore through the countryside, the residents of Phnom Penh carried on much as they had before the war, albeit under what one observer described as an "eerie blend of normalcy and hopelessness." Motorcars and bicycles jostled with pedestrians for space on the crowded, tree-lined boulevards. Café-goers sipped French wine, cognac, or ice-cold Angkor beer, while brothels southeast of the city ran a busy trade. The wealthier residents of the city enjoyed the luxury of the Cercle Sportif country club or escaped the heat by spending time at swimming pools; those looking for other distractions frequented opium dens. Crowded markets sold crafts amid the fragrance of street vendors cooking rice bowls seasoned with fermented fish sauce over smoking charcoal braziers. This calm was interrupted in March 1972, when PAVN units staged their first major attack on the capital. Moving their artillery within range of the city, PAVN forces launched a major assault over the night of March 21–22. Between one hundred and two hundred shells hit the capital, killing scores of residents.

Refugee slums on the outskirts bore the brunt of the barrage. As rounds rained down on outlying neighborhoods, a squad of commandos destroyed a government radio station, slitting the throats of the colonel in charge along with his French wife and son.[36]

While the war inched closer to Phnom Penh, Khmer Rouge cadres led a severe existence. The party leadership maintained a sequestered, heavily guarded forest camp of thatched-roof huts. Pol Pot and his comrades slept on woven bamboo mats and adhered to a rigid set of security measures. This suspicion and secrecy emanated from the leadership down through the rank-and-file. Civilian life inside Khmer Rouge–controlled zones was generally orderly. The party maintained a loose administration that allowed peasants to continue to observe customary holidays and religious festivals. Aware that most villagers had little understanding of or affinity for Marxism, cadres employed Sihanouk's symbolic leadership of the movement as a means of encouraging popular support. The party held village assemblies twice a month, however, leading the population in revolutionary songs and celebrating the revolution. Guerrillas were forbidden from stealing from the local population and were ordered to provide rudimentary health care when possible. On the whole, Communist rule at the village level remained fairly moderate during the civil war. The party's prohibitions on extramarital affairs, bottled beer, and manufactured cigarettes, along with basic efforts to redistribute wealth, gave only the subtlest hints of the massive transformation to come.[37]

AFTER TET

For most of the world, the fighting in Cambodia was merely a sideshow of the larger war in Vietnam. In the aftermath of the Tet Offensive, increasing numbers of Americans had begun to ask what all the fighting was ultimately for. Richard Nixon began pulling troops out of Vietnam in July 1969 and, in the same month, announced what would become known as the Nixon Doctrine. An extension of the president's Vietnamization scheme, the doctrine called for states in the developing world to shoulder a greater burden of fighting against Communist aggression. Washington would continue nuclear deterrence in order to defend vital interests and would provide financial and military aid to anticommunist regimes in the periphery, but the United States would not send in combat troops. Local powers would act as regional proxies, fielding police forces bankrolled by the United States. Although this new containment strategy would have far-reaching implications for other embattled nations in the Third World, it came too late for South Vietnam. And the question remained as to what, precisely, the Nixon administration intended for its beleaguered Southeast Asian ally.[38]

While policymakers in Washington scrambled to get ARVN units up to speed, leaders in Hanoi plotted another stab at victory. Over the course of 1971, Le Duan drew up plans to stage a third General Offensive–General Uprising designed to topple the Saigon regime. PAVN units had defeated a limited ARVN incursion into Laos earlier in the year and, in doing so, had exposed the continuing problems with Nixon's Vietnamization programs. Likewise, Nixon and Kissinger's diplomatic overtures to the USSR and China made it clear that Washington was seeking a way out of the war. But Le Duan had no desire to have his comrades in Moscow and Beijing pressuring him to make concessions at the negotiating table. The party leadership planned to try once again for a knockout blow against the Saigon regime. As historian Lien-Hang Nguyen writes, "if the ARVN collapsed, the United States would have no choice but to settle on Hanoi's terms." On March 30, 1972, PAVN forces launched a nationwide attack on ARVN positions. Thousands of PAVN troops swept into South Vietnam alongside tanks and heavy weaponry. Dubbed the Easter Offensive by Americans, the campaign witnessed a massive North Vietnamese assault across the Seventeenth Parallel into South Vietnam combined with attacks from Communist units in Cambodia and Laos against Saigon and the Central Highlands. In the first weeks of the offensive, Le Duan and his comrades in Hanoi came to believe that their gambit was working and that victory lay within reach.[39]

The Easter Offensive dampened the mood in Washington. As had been the case with the 1968 Tet Offensive, the ability of Communist forces to mount such a massive assault belied any optimism about the American war effort. Nevertheless, Nixon resolved to strike back against the Communist attack, refusing to allow what he called a "little shit-ass country" to humiliate his administration. Under Operation Linebacker, the president ordered a new round of B-52 strikes against North Vietnam and sent American aircraft to attack PAVN units moving through the south. "The bastards have never been bombed like they're going to be bombed this time," he swore. While the bombing slowed the North Vietnamese offensive, ARVN units on the ground performed better than expected, which led some in Washington to conclude that the expanded Vietnamization's training programs were having a positive effect. Though U.S. and South Vietnamese forces had managed to turn back the assault by autumn, they were not able to turn the tide of the war. Leaders in Hanoi, Saigon, and Washington all understood that ARVN forces could not hold out against the Communists forever. The uneasy stalemate on the battlefield returned.[40]

The White House seemed to be making more progress in Paris, however, where ongoing peace talks were nearing a breakthrough. In the fall of 1972, Kissinger and Le Duc Tho agreed, in principle, to a settlement that would entail a full withdrawal of U.S. troops and the creation of a tripartite electoral commission made up of representatives from Nguyen Van Thieu's regime in Saigon, the National Liberation Front (NLF), and neutral parties. Thieu rejected the agreements, though, insisting that acceptance would be tantamount to suicide. Further attempts by American negotiators to adjust the settlement led Hanoi to reject the agreement altogether, which resulted in diplomatic stalemate. Enraged by North Vietnamese intransigence, Nixon and Kissinger ordered a renewed bombing campaign against North Vietnam, the heaviest yet, code-named Linebacker II. For twelve days, B-52s pummeled North Vietnamese targets, until Hanoi finally agreed to resume negotiations. The final peace agreements, reached in January 1973, provided for a full withdrawal of American forces from South Vietnam and left the Thieu regime in power in Saigon, but also allowed NLF and PAVN units to remain in South Vietnam. Although Thieu officially accepted the accords, he privately outlined his policy of Four Noes: "no neutrality, no coalition government, no concession of territory to North Vietnam, and no Communist activity in South Vietnam."[41]

The Paris Peace Accords reflected the realities that had been clear to a majority of Americans in 1968: the United States could neither achieve victory in Vietnam nor maintain combat troops in the country indefinitely. For four years, in a futile effort to change this reality, Nixon and Kissinger had continued a war that cost an additional twenty thousand American lives and killed hundreds of thousands of Vietnamese. It seems that neither man was willing to accept the inevitable reality that the United States had been defeated in Southeast Asia. Ultimately, the differences between the 1969 proposals for an end to the war and the agreement reached in 1973 were negligible. Historian Larry Berman argues that "we can only conclude that many tens of thousands died for very little."[42]

While their precise intentions in signing the Paris Peace Accords remain unclear, Nixon and Kissinger appear to have favored different options. Kissinger called for a "decent interval" solution: the United States would provide enough aid to the Thieu regime to prevent its collapse for a decent interval of time following U.S. withdrawal. When South Vietnam eventually fell, according to this plan, Washington would be able to claim that it had left a viable regime in Saigon and that it was incompetent local leaders—or Nixon's successor in the White House—rather than the Nixon administration that had caused that regime's collapse. This particularly Machiavellian solution was designed not to ensure the survival of South Vietnam but to absolve the Nixon administration of any responsibility for losing the war. In contrast to Kissinger, Nixon proposed an alternative solution aimed at perpetuating a permanent stalemate in Vietnam. The president would withdraw American combat troops but leave on the table the option of B-52 air strikes. Washington would defend Saigon by carrying out retaliatory bombing campaigns against North Vietnam if Le Duan persisted in his efforts to undermine the regime in Saigon. While Kissinger's decent interval strategy would amount to the betrayal of an American ally, Nixon's stalemate strategy would prolong the brutal and indiscriminate bombing campaign against North Vietnam. Ultimately, however, neither man would enjoy the final word.[43]

North Vietnamese leaders appeared to follow a more measured strategy that ultimately won the day. In a conversation with Zhou Enlai, Le Duan offered his assessment of the war: Washington's "objective was not only to turn South Vietnam into their colony, but also to realize their global strategy in Vietnam. . . . [T]hey wished to control the South, then attack the North of Vietnam, thus damaging the defense system of socialism in Southeast Asia and threatening the national independence movement in the world."[44] The Vietnam War would have lasting global implications, but not in ways that either Washington or Hanoi anticipated.

VICTORIES

The wars in Indochina changed dramatically following the signing of the January 1973 Paris Peace Accords among Washington, Hanoi, and Saigon. With the conclusion of the U.S. military intervention in Vietnam, the Nixon administration was able to focus its regional forces on Cambodia. At the same time, Hanoi pulled its troops out of that country, leaving the battlefield to government forces and the Khmer Rouge. The American withdrawal from South Vietnam led, paradoxically, to a dramatic escalation in U.S. bombing strikes in

Cambodia. Whereas in the entirety of 1972, B-52s dropped 37,000 tons of explosives on Cambodia, in a mere three months in the spring of 1973, they dropped 95,000 tons. While the flow of refugees into Phnom Penh increased, this savage aerial campaign did little to hurt Communist forces. As one U.S. Air Force history warned, "the enemy remains steadfast while Lon Nol's troops continue to decline in effectiveness." Khmer Rouge leaders blamed the Vietnamese for the escalation in American attacks. The Khmer Rouge's erstwhile comrades in arms had made their own peace with the United States, leaving the Cambodians to carry on the battle by themselves. Making matters worse, war-weary leaders in Hanoi sought to pressure the Khmer Rouge to open negotiations with the Lon Nol government by withholding aid to the Cambodian Communists. "Hanoi has dropped us," Khieu Samphan complained. This sense of abandonment and betrayal only served to intensify Khmer Rouge resentment toward the Vietnamese.[45]

The combined devastation of American bombing and Khmer Rouge offensives pushed the Lon Nol government to its breaking point. Although the B-52 raids slowed the Communist advance, they created a massive refugee problem for the government. The population's flight from the countryside led to a sharp drop in food production at the same time that refugees strained supplies in the cities. Desperate residents stripped the bark from Phnom Penh's trees for use as fuel while malnutrition increased. All the while, the Khmer Rouge tightened its control of the Mekong River and the roads into the capital. The regime was now almost entirely dependent on aid from the United States. Rice speculators throughout the city hoarded the increasingly precious commodity while the population starved and the regime cracked down in an attempt to forestall its downfall. As the siege continued, however, few doubted the Khmer Republic's coming collapse.[46] Washington suspended its bombing operations in August 1973, after pouring into Cambodia three times the tonnage of bombs it had dropped on Japan in World War II. In March 1974,

Khmer Rouge forces captured the city of Udong and forced twenty thousand of its inhabitants into the countryside. The Communists executed those they identified as "class enemies" and forced the rest into labor. Lon Nol managed to retake the city in July, but the government's predicament was dire. The garrison at Kampong Seila, besieged for nine months, began resorting to cannibalism. In August, Richard Nixon, one of the Khmer Republic's last major international supporters, resigned amid the Watergate scandal (the result of a 1972 burglary against the Democratic National Committee headquarters and its subsequent cover-up). As 1974 drew to a close, the stage was set for the Khmer Rouge's final offensive against Phnom Penh.[47]

On New Year's Day 1975, the Khmer Rouge began the offensive that was to give them control of Cambodia. Government troops at Udong staged a valiant defense that held the northern line through January. The Communists fared better in the south, however, where their forces managed to cut off river convoys to the capital by mining the Mekong and sinking old vessels to block the channel. Khmer Rouge troops overran Udong in late February while Washington's special envoy to Vietnam warned that the situation in Cambodia was likely to "end in [a] massacre" and pleaded that "any means of avoiding a bloodbath should be urgently sought." In early March, Pol Pot moved his headquarters forward to within twenty miles of Phnom Penh while foreign embassies began evacuating nonessential personnel. Communist soldiers seized the strategic ferry at Neak Luong on April 1, bringing the Khmer Rouge to the gates of the capital. As the republic entered its final days, order inside the city began to break down. While upper-class Cambodians fled with as much of their wealth as they could carry, the majority of the population waited anxiously. Hospitals rationed their dwindling medical supplies while the desperate efforts to airlift rice into the city came under attack from Communist artillery. While thousands starved on the streets, posh restaurants continued to serve French wines to their patrons. On April 12, the U.S. ambassador and his remaining staff boarded a helicopter bound for a U.S. naval ship waiting offshore—a similar scene would be repeated two weeks later in Saigon.[48]

Even as Lon Nol's regime teetered on the brink of collapse, North Vietnamese forces launched their final offensive against the Saigon regime. If observers in Washington, Saigon, and other cities around the world were surprised, it was only because the assault had not come sooner. Over the winter of 1974–75, PAVN forces steadily drove ARVN units back. On April 27, Communist troops reached the outskirts of Saigon. Thousands of South Vietnamese loyalists searched for a means of escape as PAVN forces drove toward the capital. Photographers captured dramatic images of American helicopters evacuating diplomats and South Vietnamese sympathizers from the roof of the U.S. embassy compound in Saigon. On April 30, just hours after the last American personnel had evacuated, North Vietnamese tanks crashed the gates of the embassy compound. Ironically, Thieu's presidency survived Nixon's, but it was hardly the decent interval scenario that some U.S. officials may have wanted. Prior to Nixon's resignation, the U.S. Congress had moved to reassert its authority over the White House's power to wage war with the passage of the 1973 War Powers Resolution.

In the final weeks of the 1975 North Vietnamese offensive, Nixon's successor, Gerald Ford, pleaded with Congress to authorize an additional $722 million in aid to Saigon to shore up remaining ARVN forces. Congressional leaders refused, however. Since 1965, the United States had spent $111 billion in defense of South Vietnam—the notion that one last infusion of aid might prevent Saigon's collapse was thus considered ludicrous. Instead, Congress approved $300 million to aid the evacuation of South Vietnamese refugees. Those who stayed behind suffered a far worse fate than the refugees. Following the fall of Saigon, sixty-five thousand southerners would be executed and another two hundred thousand sent to reeducation camps.[49]

Meanwhile, Americans were left to wonder what had gone wrong. In hindsight, it appears that Vietnamese Communists had been willing to accept extraordinary casualties to achieve their goals. Washington never came close to reaching the anticipated "crossover point" in which U.S. forces inflicted a level of damage on North Vietnam that would have led Le Duan to abandon the struggle to reunite the two Vietnams under Communist rule. As the CIA's station chief in Saigon argued, "even if we Americans had by our criteria 'won' the Vietnamese war, it is unlikely the Vietnamese would have credited us with the victory. . . . [T]hey would have treated their reverses more as a temporary setback than a defeat . . . then would have geared down once again to prolonged guerrilla struggle."[50] Le Duc Tho told Kissinger, "If our generation cannot win, then our sons and nephews will continue. We will sacrifice everything, but we will not again have slavery. This is our iron will. We have been fighting for 25 years, the French and you. You wanted to quench our spirit with bombs and shells. But they cannot force us to submit."[51]

AMERICA'S BITTER DEFEAT IN SOUTH VIETNAM CAST A long shadow over U.S. foreign policy. In the coming generations, American presidents would grapple with the so-called Vietnam Syndrome, a public and official resistance to sending U.S. troops into combat for fear of repeating the wrenching experience of the Vietnam War. Many Americans both inside and outside government wondered whether their nation's golden age had come to an end and whether U.S. military forces could fight effectively in future conflicts. Ironically, however, Washington's geopolitical position emerged from the Vietnamese debacle remarkably intact. Although few if any policymakers realized it at the time, following the war the United States moved into a position vis-à-vis the Soviet Union that was, in many respects, stronger than that which it had enjoyed a decade before. The geopolitical stakes in Vietnam, which had appeared so high to the Kennedy, Johnson, and Nixon administrations, turned out to be far lower than expected. In truth, Suharto's victory in Indonesia would prove far more decisive in the Cold War struggle for influence in Southeast Asia.

But no issue was more critical than the ongoing Sino-Soviet split. The growing cleavages within the Communist world would, by the end of the 1970s, all but wipe out Communist gains of the previous decades and place the United States in a position to capitalize on the disarray. Cambodia, the small, largely forgotten casualty of the war in Vietnam, was about to enter one of the deadliest chapters in twentieth-century history. Over the next four years, the small nation would lose nearly a quarter of its population and help ignite a new round of fighting between Communist powers in Southeast Asia that would, in turn, tear the Communist Third World apart.

THE CAMBODIAN NIGHTMARE

1975–1979

As dawn came to Phnom Penh on April 17, 1975, white sheets fluttered from windows throughout the city. Government leaders had ordered their forces to stand down, and the capital was now open to the Communist Khmer Rouge. Clad in black and wearing checked scarves, victorious Communist troops marched into the city. To the capital's residents, the soldiers seemed strange—most came from the countryside, and few had ever seen a city as large as Phnom Penh. To the victors, the city appeared as a den of corruption and vice, the ultimate symbol of the regime's depravity and the ruinous effects of foreign influence. Few soldiers smiled as they took control of strategic locations throughout the capital. Groups of Khmer Rouge entered the city's hospitals, which were overflowing with wounded from the months-long siege. With little hint of mercy, the soldiers ordered patients and attendants to leave; some insisted that the evacuation was necessary to avoid imminent B-52 strikes. Men, women, and children with horrific injuries formed a gruesome procession down the staircases and out into the streets. Throughout the city, Communist soldiers pounded on the doors of homes and ordered those inside to leave immediately. They were to abandon their possessions and take only the clothes on their backs and what food they could carry. The roads out of the city were soon choked with some two million people. What few provisions the Communists gave them along the way were insufficient; the water ran out first. Bodies of the fallen were left along the sides of the road as thousands of refugees marched past. Foreigners took refuge first in the Hotel Phnom and then in the French embassy. The party forced all nonnationals out of the country within two weeks. Year Zero had begun.[1]

It was here in Cambodia—or Democratic Kampuchea, as the Khmer Rouge would rename the country—that the Cold War era's darkest chapter would play out. For most Americans, the fall of Saigon was a tragedy; the fall of Phnom Penh and the butchery that followed barely registered. The regime's extreme isolation was partly responsible for this. Khmer Rouge leaders did everything in their power to close their state off from foreign influence and eradicate its vestiges. But by 1975, many Americans both inside and outside the halls of power were eager to forget their painful involvement in Southeast Asia. Moving on was not so easy for those living in the region. Democratic Kampuchea sat at the center of a perfect storm in geopolitics. Centuries of hostility between Vietnam and Cambodia, the experience of French colonialism, and Japanese occupation during World War II formed a troubled foundation for Cambodian independence. Though its leader, Prince Norodom Sihanouk, had sought neutrality, the nation could not escape the tides of war sweeping through neighboring Vietnam. Hanoi, Saigon, Beijing, and Washington all helped turn Cambodia into a secondary battlefield of the Vietnam Wars.

Yet it was the Cambodians themselves who would perform most of the killing. The vicious logic of revolutionary communism would reach its apogee and begin its decline in Democratic Kampuchea as the Khmer Rouge erased the distinction between theory and practice, between utopian Marxist fantasy and cruel reality. The Khmer Rouge would link its unyielding vison of Communist revolution with a xenophobic ethnic nationalism.[2] Together, these two prongs drove a reign of terror that killed nearly a quarter of the nation's population. Compounding the tragedy, Cambodia sat at the point where America's violent Cold War interventionism collapsed into indifference and disillusionment. The Nixon administration had pummeled much of the countryside with American bombs with little regard for what happened after. The nation of Cambodia was a casualty of both the Khmer Rouge genocide and the global Cold War. The collision of the two forces, global and local, would help transform the country into a cemetery and drive the final nail into the coffin of Third World Communist solidarity.

PEACE

When Khmer Rouge forces entered Phnom Penh on the morning of April 17, 1975, a small group of foreign correspondents remained. As the Communist troops combed through the city, searching for foreigners and hunting former government officials, the journalists (who had been confined to the French embassy) agreed to embargo their dispatches until all nonnationals had made it out of the country. Among them was *New York Times* reporter Sydney Schanberg. The city had fallen, he wrote, to an army of peasant soldiers, "darker skinned than their city brethren, with gold in their front teeth. To them the city is a curiosity, an *oddity*, a carnival, where you visit but do not live." The Khmer Rouge forced a "mammoth and grueling exodus" from the capital in a bid to stage a total peasant revolution. Communist forces rolled through the city streets waving weapons and ordering citizens to evacuate over loudspeakers. Terrified refugees took to the roads "like a human carpet." "A once-throbbing city became an echo chamber of silent streets lined with abandoned cars and gaping, empty shops," Schanberg wrote. "Streetlights burned eerily for a population that was no longer there."[3]

The effort to empty the cities took a brutal toll. Many individuals who refused to abandon their homes were summarily shot. One witness reported seeing "two piles of bodies in civilian clothes, as if two whole families had been killed, babies and all. Two pieces of cardboard stuck out of the pile, and someone had scrawled in charcoal: For refusing to leave as they were told." Along the roads, scores of the wounded, the elderly, and the very young perished as a result of exhaustion, malnourishment, and dehydration. It would take some of the evacuees weeks to reach their destinations. As the refugees plodded away from the capital, Khmer Rouge cadres called on them to reveal their occupations. Some of the skilled workers were taken away and sent back for service in Phnom Penh. Many of those who admitted that they had worked for the military or government were taken back to the city and shot. Not all Phnom Penh's residents were evacuated. The Khmer Rouge rounded up government officials, military commanders, and police and executed them in large numbers. Historian Ben Kiernan places the immediate death toll at twenty thousand, half of whom died in the evacuation. Khmer Rouge forces followed a similar procedure in other cities and towns throughout Cambodia, evacuating all the country's principal population centers in the following weeks.[4]

Upon hearing the news of the government's surrender on April 17, the residents of Battambang, in the northwest, cheered. Peace had come, they hoped, and the Khmer Rouge would force food prices back down. Later that evening, when radios announced the evacuation of Phnom Penh, the mood darkened. "Would the same thing happen to us?" one student wondered. After taking Battambang, Khmer Rouge officers ordered all Lon Nol's troops to assemble, with their weapons, in front of the prefecture on April 18. In the following days, the party sent in trucks to collect these troops to be sent for retraining. After leaving Battambang, Khmer Rouge officers stopped the convoy and ordered all passengers out of the vehicles. Soon, witnesses heard the sound of Chinese AK-47s. On April 24, Communist cadres speaking over loudspeakers gave all remaining civilians three hours to evacuate Battambang. "Anyone caught in the city after that would be killed," one man remembered. "Even the dogs would be shot." The roads north of the city were littered with rotting bodies. Farther along, the evacuees found the corpses of hundreds of army officers with their hands tied behind their backs.[5]

The refugees faced a foreign landscape. Much of the country-side had been bombed, and many of the villages were unwelcoming. Once-critical aspects of their lives in the cities (wealth, education, social status) no longer counted in postrevolutionary Cambodia. The lucky ones had family in their ancestral villages who took them in. Those who did not struggled to scrape together enough food to continue. In some places, the Khmer Rouge forced evacuees to build entirely new villages.

While the cadres reshaped the face of the Cambodian country-side, party leaders set up their new government in the nearly deserted capital of Phnom Penh. Although they were disappointed by the absence of large stores of military hardware, the destruction in the capital reinforced their determination to rebuild Cambodia as a utopian Marxist state. It was a state in which the deposed monarch, Prince Sihanouk, would have little influence. Having seized Phnom Penh, Khmer Rouge leaders had little use for the prince, who would spend much of his time outside the country. The real power in Cambodia now lay in the hands of Angkar (the organization) and its supreme leaders, Pol Pot, Ieng Sary, and Khieu Samphan.[6]

Pol Pot's arrival in the capital was a closely guarded secret. He and the Khmer Rouge leadership were taken to the old French rail station, which had been transformed into a fortress. Inside the walls of this colonial building, the party leaders laid down the foundations of the new state. When night came, they placed sleeping mats across the floors. The evacuation had been necessary, they later argued, in order to neutralize any foreign spies operating in the capital. In this goal the move had been brutally effective: a CIA official in Saigon later lamented that the evacuation had "left American espionage networks throughout the country broken and useless." More than this, the party's decision to empty the cities served "to preserve the political position of cadres and combatants," a Central Committee study reported, "to avoid a solution of peaceful evolution which could corrode [the revolution] from within; to fight corruption, degradation and debauchery; to get the urban population to take part in [agricultural] production; [and] to remove Sihanouk's support base." In one fell swoop, students and intellectuals had been "extricated from the filth of imperialist and colonialist culture," the document continued, while "the system of private property and material goods [was] swept away." Pol Pot intended to transform the nation into an agrarian powerhouse. "Agriculture is the key both to nation-building and national defence," he announced. This total socialist revolution was to take place, moreover, with scant foreign assistance. Outside aid would corrupt the purity of the Khmer Rouge's revolution and undermine Cambodia's independence.[7] While Mao Zedong advised Pol Pot to find his own course rather than copy the Chinese model, the Khmer Rouge were already well on their way toward crafting their vision of a new state.[8]

One month later, Pol Pot and the party leaders emerged to present their plan for building the new Democratic Kampuchea. Party officials from across the country converged on the athletic stadium north of Phnom Penh for a five-day meeting starting on May 20, 1975. Here, Angkar delivered its vision for the revolutionary state. It was a telling indication of that state's nature that most of those in attendance did not ultimately survive the Communists' four years in power. One account of the meeting delineated eight main points of Pol Pot's program:

1. Evacuate people from all towns.
2. Abolish all markets.
3. Abolish Lon Nol regime currency and withhold the revolutionary currency that had been printed.
4. Defrock all Buddhist monks and put them to work growing rice.

5. Execute all leaders of the Lon Nol regime, beginning with the top leaders.
6. Establish high-level cooperatives throughout the country, with communal eating.
7. Expel the entire Vietnamese minority population.
8. Dispatch troops to the borders, particularly the Vietnamese border.

Others remembered these points as well as blanket hostility toward "money, schools, and hospitals." The Khmer Rouge outlined a stark vision for the country: an antiurban, anti-Buddhist, xenophobic, anticapitalist society. The political apparatus would also take extreme measures to root out and destroy any individuals who opposed its vision for Democratic Kampuchea. Even more chilling, the party announced the division of the population into two groups. Individuals who had lived in Khmer Rouge–controlled areas prior to the fall of Phnom Penh were entitled to full rights. Those who did not were "candidates" for this status. The beleaguered evacuees from the capital and other major cities would have to prove themselves worthy of membership in the new Democratic Kampuchea.[9]

The party divided Cambodia into seven zones: the Northwest, North, Northeast, East, Southwest, West, and Center. These were holdovers from the civil war during which the Khmer Rouge had forced peasants into defensive cooperatives. Movement across these zones was strictly policed, and the harvest placed under party control. Within this administrative system, outsiders were viewed with hostility, Cambodia's borders were fortified, and booby-trapped buffer zones were established. From 1975 onward, the party transformed this wartime necessity into the structure of state control in Democratic Kampuchea. Khmer Rouge secretaries within each zone held formidable power, exercising control over both the security apparatus and the local economy. While they functioned as integral parts of the larger party structure, Khmer Rouge leadership within the zones exercised some autonomy from the party center in Phnom Penh. In the coming years, Pol Pot and his comrades in the capital would endeavor to extend as much control over the zones as possible.[10]

Those in the countryside lived a severe life. Villagers, many of whom were already struggling from the effects of the civil war and the American bombing campaign, were now saddled with the added burden of feeding and housing refugees from the cities. These "old people" were in a better position than the "new people," who had to adapt to a completely new form of existence. The Khmer Rouge authorities divided the population into groups of ten to fifteen families headed by a chief. Each family was given a plot of land in the forest, which it had to clear in order to begin cultivating maize, cassava, and yams. The party nationalized most of the rice paddies. The refugees from Cambodia's cities had few if any farming tools, a fact that exacerbated the difficulty of the labor. Workers toiled long hours building dikes, plowing fields, and clearing forests. Unexploded ordinance from the war made the work all the more dangerous. Despite these efforts, food remained in short supply. "On the road to Phnom Srok," reported one witness, "there were tens of thousands of people from Phnom Penh, all gaunt and lifeless, marching in columns several kilometers long." The party reduced rice rations in many areas to 180 grams (approximately 230 calories) every two days. Disease spread quickly through the population due to malnourishment and poor sanitation.[11]

Khmer Rouge goals were nothing less than utopian. A document drafted in the spring of 1976 revealed that the party planned to more than double the average harvest to three metric tons of rice per hectare. The party center had chosen to launch its own Great Leap Forward, in a blatant, though unacknowledged, attempt to emulate China's example, while expecting to avoid the disastrous results. The document made it clear, moreover, that these changes should be carried out with brutal efficiency by granting the leadership the "Authority to Smash (People) Inside and Outside the Ranks" of the party.[12] A report published several months later referenced the "Super Great

Leap Forward," in which the party aimed to dramatically increase food production and to undermine popular resistance to its plans. Citing one example, the report discussed complaints against the use of "No. 1 fertilizer [human excrement]. They say people have never used excrement before, and now the revolution uses it to make fertilizer. . . . But if we go down personally and explain cause and effect to them, they will understand." The party would combine these efforts with an ongoing campaign to eradicate "any remnants that are not proletarian, and not collective, or are still private."[13]

Pol Pot and his comrades turned Cambodia, in the words of one journalist, into a "slave state." Under the Khmer Rouge, the country was transformed into a massive labor camp; one survivor described it as a "prison without walls." The ultimate purpose was to create an entirely new Cambodia, to realize a complete revolution in Khmer society. The three goals of peasant revolution, agrarian development, and national defense formed integral and mutually reinforcing aspects of the Khmer Rouge's program. The Khmer Rouge pursued these goals ruthlessly, slaughtering any and all who stood in their way. The party first sought to destroy Cambodia's "feudal" elite, which Pol Pot and his comrades argued had oppressed the nation for centuries. Markets, private property, and currency were all eradicated; the cities were emptied; and the nation was transformed into a society of peasants. In this same vein, the party sought to banish foreign influence from Cambodia. Sihanouk's attempts at development had been disastrous, and economic autarky seemed the best path for the nation. The Khmer Rouge's second goal was to "build" Cambodia into a prosperous nation. In contrast to Sihanouk and Lon Nol's industrial modernization projects, the Khmer Rouge focused on agrarian development through collective agriculture. The party worked to reshape the population into an agrarian machine. "The characteristics of peasants," Pol Pot wrote, "are often negligence, lack of zeal and lack of self-confidence. They know only how to work by following orders." Every aspect of daily life must, in theory, come under the Khmer Rouge's control—diet, agricultural work, sleeping and waking, and even marriage became the domain of the party. By channeling its power into every dimension of peasant life, the Khmer Rouge sought to remake the nation into a productive instrument of party control.[14]

The third goal in the Khmer Rouge's plan called for the defense of the nation. Cambodia was a comparatively weak state flanked by more powerful neighbors, Thailand and Vietnam. French colonialism and the recent American war had only served to inflame the party's desire for independence. The party's alliance with Hanoi had forced the people to tolerate the intrusive Vietnamese presence on Cambodian soil. Lon Nol's alliance with Washington had brought the devastating B-52 strikes. Added to this mixture was the deep-seated xenophobia of Pol Pot and his comrades. The years of taking orders from Hanoi's agents in Cambodia had exacted a toll on the Khmer Rouge. In the wake of the Khmer Rouge's overwhelming victory over the Lon Nol regime, it was time for Cambodia to claim its independence and rebuild itself as a great nation.[15] Khmer Rouge leaders believed they had good reason to be optimistic in this regard. An official report from 1976, for example, noted that Cambodia enjoyed certain advantages: "Compared to other countries, we have very many more qualities," the report argued. "First, they have no hay. Second, they have no grass. In other countries, they use hay in various other ways, not to feed cows."[16]

"AN INDENTURED AGRARIAN STATE"

Ultimately, the party center sought to achieve this total revolution at a rapid pace. Another document from 1976 insisted that "socialism must be built, as rapidly as possible, taking us from a backward agriculture to a modern one in five to ten years, and from an agricultural base to an industrial one in fifteen to twenty years." This was necessary, party leaders explained, in order to defend the country from the "enemies" to the east and west: "[T]hey will persist with a vengeance and penetrate our territory, if we are weak."[17]

The Khmer Rouge created what Kiernan calls "an indentured agrarian state." While many peasants supported the revolution in its early stages, Pol Pot's clique of intellectuals led it. And when famine began in the coming years, most of peasantry's support disappeared. The nation became "a gigantic workshop." Brutal discipline forced the population throughout the country into arduous labor in fields and rice paddies. No wages were paid, and no leisure was permitted. The party forced the majority of the population into "thatch huts or barrack-style houses," separated from their families and often from their spouses. Meals were strictly regimented as part of the party's effort to exercise total control over daily existence. Far from being a revolution led by and for the peasantry, Kiernan writes, the system created by the Khmer Rouge deprived Cambodians of "three of the most cherished features of their lifestyle: land, family, and religion."[18]

Restrictions extended to every level. The Khmer Rouge viewed Western medicine with suspicion; some cadres believed that wearing eyeglasses or having light skin or uncalloused hands indicated that an individual was a capitalist. The party prohibited the use of language that suggested hierarchy, historian David Chandler wrote, and introduced a "syrupy politeness on commands. People taken off to be killed . . . were asked to 'help us collect fruit' or to 'come with us for further study.'" It was not uncommon for villagers to simply disappear without warning; nor was it unusual for Cambodians to discover the bodies of victims dumped in the forests. Under the Pol Pot regime, the rhyme "Angkar kills but never explains" became popular. As the workers toiled long hours in the fields, they were forced to sing choruses of revolutionary songs. Doing so, cadres explained, would lift their spirits. After completing their work, Cambodians returned to their dwellings, where they ate gruel with meager rations of rice. Meanwhile, the leaders of Democratic Kampuchea directed a steady stream of indoctrination through political meetings and party-controlled radio broadcasts touting the virtues of the revolution. To guard against dissent, the party enlisted young men and women to conduct surveillance against villagers and to report any signs of opposition. A crushing blow to national morale arrived in 1976, when the party sent much of the rice harvest to China in exchange for military aid.[19]

Leaders in the United States had known of Khmer Rouge atrocities even before the fall of Phnom Penh. A paper from February 1975 blamed much of the brutality on Vietnamese cadres inside Cambodia who subjected the local population to "a rigid Stalinist pattern, pressganging the people and killing and terrorizing peasants and monks." And the Cambodian Communists were perhaps even worse. The paper reported that their campaign of terror against the population was "perhaps unparalleled since the Nazi era." U.S. officials cited reports that the Khmer Rouge had killed thousands, including children, using knives, bayonets, and firearms, and dumped the bodies in mass graves in the forest. "The evidence is clear that a large-scale blood bath . . . would surely be the Communists' policy following a Communist victory."[20] But even as they watched their predictions come true, leaders in Washington had little remaining credibility in the wake of the Vietnam War and the Watergate scandal. As Kissinger lamented, "We have reached a point where if people run extermination camps, unless you have international inspection it is not recognized by the liberal community [in the United States]."[21] In 1976, the CIA concluded that the Khmer Rouge government had become "the most extreme of the world's totalitarian regimes." The forced evacuation of Cambodia's cities had been carried out with "unprecedented cruelty," resulting in hundreds of thousands of deaths, "including almost the entire educated stratum." The Khmer Rouge had taken a different course than other successful Communist revolutions, orchestrating the "complete abolition of private ownership and the departure from a money economy," and refusing to align with Beijing or Moscow. The extreme secrecy surrounding the party leadership was perhaps the most conspicuous feature of the revolution. The result, the CIA concluded, amounted to the creation of a "unique 'Cambodian model.' "[22]

Citing a State Department report from Thailand in May 1975, President Gerald Ford's national security advisor, Brent Scowcroft, noted that Cambodia was "under the control of a xenophobic collective leadership dedicated to attaining a radical change in the social, political, and economic makeup of the country in the shortest time possible." The regime was executing teachers, students, and former soldiers who had served under Lon Nol. Anyone, for that matter, "who shows any sign of being educated also risks arrest or execution." In many cases, the families of the accused also fell victim to the executioners. The killers typically beat the victims to death using "hoe handles or other blunt instruments." The regime appeared to be on a quest to eradicate all knowledge as it burned books, destroyed libraries, and closed down schools. Khmer Rouge leaders also targeted organized religion, casting Buddhist monks out of their pagodas and using the buildings for grain storage. Widespread malaria, dysentery, and cholera plagued those who managed to escape the regime's direct wrath. "In several areas," Scowcroft continued, "the family unit is being destroyed with children permanently separated from their parents and husbands and wives placed in separate work groups." In an effort to carry out a total revolution, Pol Pot and his comrades sought to eradicate the structure of the Cambodian family.[23] The regime found children especially useful. "Only children can purely serve the revolution and eliminate reactionism," a Khmer Rouge official claimed, "since they are young, obedient, loyal, and active." The regime deliberately staged executions in front of children as both a warning and an example. For the party, young people represented a blank slate: they were relatively naïve, compliant, and less attached to the social order of prerevolutionary Cambodia. Children served as ideal spies and informants.[24]

However, none of this precluded a rapprochement between the

Khmer Rouge and Washington—at least as far as U.S. policymakers were concerned. Officials in the Ford administration worried about the potential for Hanoi to expand Vietnam's influence. To block Hanoi's bid for regional power, the Ford administration hoped to reconcile with the Khmer Rouge and support a greater Chinese presence in Southeast Asia. "Our strategy is to get the Chinese into Laos and Cambodia as a barrier to the Vietnamese. I asked the Chinese to take over in Laos," Secretary of State Henry Kissinger told Thailand's foreign minister in late 1975. "You should also tell the Cambodians that we will be friends with them. They are murderous thugs, but we won't let that stand in our way. We are prepared to improve relations with them." He then added, "Tell them the latter part, but don't tell them what I said before."[25] President Jimmy Carter's administration would follow a similar course. As Carter's national security advisor, Zbigniew Brzezinski, remembered, "I encouraged the Chinese to support Pol Pot. Pol Pot was an abomination. We could never support him, but China could."[26] Having chosen to focus on the Cold War geopolitical struggle, American leaders were willing to overlook local atrocities in pursuit of global priorities.

THE KILLING FIELDS

Meanwhile, the slaughter in Cambodia continued. If there was an epicenter of the Khmer Rouge nightmare, it was the notorious prison known as Tuol Sleng. The facility occupied the former Tuol Svay Prey High School, in southwest Phnom Penh. Tuol Sleng, designated S-21 in official party correspondence, represented the inner sanctum of Democratic Kampuchea. While Democratic Kampuchea was closed to the world, S-21 was shut off from the wider nation. Its mission consisted of incarcerating and investigating inmates, passing sentences, and carrying out counterintelligence operations against suspected enemies. In practice, S-21 served as a torture and execution center. Those who ran the facility had no interest in rehabilitation and no inmates were granted release. Rather, all prisoners were slated for execution after months of brutal interrogation. More than fourteen thousand Cambodians would be tortured and killed in Tuol Sleng during its three and a half years of operation. S-21's commandant, Kang Keck Ieu (aka Duch), was a former mathematics teacher from Kompong Thom who had fallen in with the Khmer Rouge during Sihanouk's reign. As the chief of security in Sector 33, Duch personally beat prisoners during interrogations. By October 1975, he had been placed in charge of Tuol Sleng. By all accounts, he was a man obsessed with conspiracies and fears of internal subversion. Tuol Sleng's staff was divided into three main units, tasked with interrogation, documentation, and defense. Discipline for both guards and interrogators at S-21 was strict, and the hours long. Among their other duties, guards were instructed not to speak with prisoners or learn their names, and to prevent the inmates from committing suicide.[27]

Prisoners were segregated by gender and importance. The most important captives received limited special treatment. Those important enough to require prolonged interrogation were shackled to the floor in cinder-block cells six feet long and two and a half feet wide. Less important inmates were chained to the floor in classrooms, with their ankle irons connected by long poles. Women and children were generally kept for only brief periods before being executed; men deemed to possess important information suffered longer interrogations. Interrogators deprived subjects of sleep, beat them with electric cords, and forced them to eat excrement. Their goal was to extract suitable confessions from the victims before they were killed. In his zealous quest to root out and destroy the enemies of the revolution, Duch kept meticulous records. Medical notebooks found at the facility suggest that staff performed experiments on prisoners. Some inmates were apparently bled to death; reports of vivisections on anesthetized captives for instructional purposes in other parts of the country give us reason to believe that similar operations may have been performed at Tuol Sleng. A substantial number of prisoners died from starvation, disease, or injuries suffered during interrogation before S-21's administrators were able to execute them.[28]

Initially, the staff at S-21 buried their victims in an impromptu cemetery on the grounds of the prison. Soon, as the death toll mounted, more room was required. The Khmer Rouge designated a new killing field at Choeung Ek, nine miles southwest of Phnom Penh. The party sent its most hardened cadres to work at Choeung Ek: "men who were able to do anything." Daily executions on the grounds ranged from a few dozen into the hundreds. Witnesses later remembered the stench of bodies, excrement, and urine that hung in the air. Once every few weeks, several trucks would arrive at Tuol Sleng. Doomed prisoners were loaded onto the vehicles one at a time. Upon arrival at the killing fields, guards shoved the victims, still bound and blindfolded, off the trucks and onto the ground. After referencing their names against lists, executioners separated the victims into small groups before leading them to shallow prepared ditches. "They were ordered to kneel down at the edge of the hole," one of the executioners remembered. "Their hands were tied behind them. They were beaten on the neck with an iron ox-cart axle, sometimes with one blow, sometimes with two." The ghastly scene repeated itself night after night beneath electric lights that illuminated the grounds.[29]

THE DECLINE AND FALL OF DEMOCRATIC KAMPUCHEA

In pursuit of total revolution, the Khmer Rouge overturned centuries of Cambodian history. It destroyed political and social structures throughout the country and transformed the nation into a forced labor camp in an effort to build Democratic Kampuchea into an agrarian powerhouse. The party's goals were as ambitious as they were unrealistic. Ultimately, the Cambodian people would pay the price for the Khmer Rouge's fantasies.

The hunger that followed the evacuation of the cities grew worse in the coming months and years. The shortfall in the rice crop was exacerbated by Pol Pot's decision to continue exporting grain as a critical source of revenue. Revolutionary defense required a strong military, and a strong military did not come cheaply. However, the heart of the problem rested on a cruel irony: despite its centralized planning and punishing work regime, Democratic Kampuchea's system of collective farms and slave labor was not as productive as the prerevolutionary order. The party took the most able-bodied Cambodians away from the crops to dig ditches and build irrigation works. Those who remained, virtual slaves, worked only hard enough to avoid punishment. Famine and disease, which plagued one-third to one-half of the nation, made matters worse. So, too, did the tendency of local party officials to exaggerate the size of their yields in order to avoid punishment at the hands of the regime. By some estimates, Democratic Kampuchea was only 60 percent as productive as prerevolutionary Cambodia.

As famine set in throughout the countryside, Pol Pot refused to question the party's policies. "There are people in charge," he announced, "who question the stance of the independence-mastery and self-reliance." If the party solves this problem, "we will be able to advance." The problem, according to party leaders, lay not in the Khmer Rouge sociopolitical model but, rather, in its implementation. The time had come for the Khmer Rouge to clean house.[30]

Over the course of 1976 and 1977, the Khmer Rouge devoured a large number of its top officials in a sweeping series of purges. The increasingly isolated and paranoid Khmer Rouge ruling clique feared that it was surrounded by conspirators. The first purge, sparked by economic troubles, focused on the Northern Zone and its head. Koy Thuon, minister of commerce, was the former chief of the Northern Zone, a relative moderate within the party, and a known philanderer. The party came to focus on him as the source of its economic problems. A series of bombings in February 1976 in Siem Reap, a city formerly under Koy Thuon's control, compounded these suspicions. Theories explaining the explosions ranged from attacks from U.S.

fighter-bombers, Thai warplanes, Vietnamese jets, or even Cambodian aircraft seeking to eliminate suspected mutineers in the city. In April, two grenades exploded outside the Royal Palace in Phnom Penh, further escalating concerns of a possible rebellion. Soon afterward, Koy Thuon disappeared. The party later claimed that he had been placed under house arrest. He was accused of allowing "petty bourgeois" elements to "infiltrate" Democratic Kampuchea and thereby undermine the development of a strong Communist economy. The following January, Khmer Rouge leaders increased the charges to espionage for the CIA and hauled Koy Thuon off to S-21. By April 1977, 112 officials from the Northern Zone were incarcerated with him.[31]

While the Khmer Rouge manufactured imagined enemies at home, it created real ones abroad. After 1975, the uneasy partnership between the Cambodian revolutionaries and Hanoi quickly deteriorated. In the weeks following the fall of Phnom Penh, Khmer Rouge forces had attacked islands in the Gulf of Thailand that had been disputed with Vietnam. On Poulo Panjang, Cambodian soldiers massacred several hundred Vietnamese civilians and destroyed their villages. A Vietnamese counterattack retook the island, but it was too late to save the local inhabitants. While Cambodian marines fought for control of the territorial islands, Pol Pot issued orders to expel ethnic Vietnamese from the country and fortified Cambodia's borders with its western neighbor. Although Hanoi and Phnom Penh soon papered over their differences, these early clashes were merely a hint of greater troubles to come. Sporadic skirmishes increased in 1977 and reached a symbolic crescendo in late April, when Khmer Rouge forces launched a series of raids against the Vietnamese province of An Giang. Marauding Cambodian soldiers slaughtered scores of villagers in a brutal display of the Khmer Rouge's animosity toward its former patrons. Hanoi responded by launching retaliatory air strikes and mobilizing its forces along the border. Relations between the two countries worsened over the summer.[32]

On September 24, 1977, Phnom Penh launched another major

attack, this time against Tay Ninh Province in Vietnam, massacring hundreds of civilians and laying waste to villages along the border. A Hungarian journalist based in Hanoi who visited the villages two days later described a macabre scene. "In house after house bloated, rotting bodies of men[,] women and children lay strewn about. Some were beheaded, some had their bellies ripped open, some were missing limbs, others eyes." The carnage along the border seemed to confirm the worst rumors about the holocaust unfolding inside Democratic Kampuchea. Months later, the area still lay in ruins: a landscape of charred buildings, abandoned rice paddies, and "hundreds of graves."[33] As his troops battled the Vietnamese, Pol Pot told leaders in Beijing that the Soviet Union, Vietnam, and Cuba were working together to attack Kampuchea. In addition to invasion plans, Pol Pot insisted, "They are also preparing to assassinate our leadership with high-accuracy guns and poison." Hanoi hoped to take over all of Southeast Asia, he warned, and the peoples of Cambodia and Laos looked to Beijing for support in their efforts to resist.[34]

Hanoi responded by launching an incursion into Cambodia designed to push Khmer Rouge troops back from the border and exact revenge. Vietnamese columns struck into Cambodia and then quickly retreated. The Cambodian units that pursued them were slaughtered by another force of Vietnamese troops lying in wait. In December, Hanoi launched a second and larger invasion composed of infantry divisions, T-54 tanks, artillery, and armored personnel carriers. The vastly superior Vietnamese units butchered Cambodian forces and pushed deep into the country. With the situation on the battlefield appearing increasingly grim, the Khmer Rouge turned to the realm of diplomacy. On December 31, 1977, Phnom Penh radio announced the invasion as the start of a massive propaganda campaign against Hanoi. Having made a convincing show of military force, Vietnamese leaders elected to withdraw, hoping that Phnom Penh was now chastened. They would be disappointed.[35]

While Pol Pot and his comrades heralded the Vietnamese withdrawal as a major victory, the party leadership recognized that its forces had been overwhelmed on the battlefield. This failure sparked a second major round of purges, which focused on the Eastern Zone. The party had found its scapegoat for the nation's poor economic performance in Koy Thuon; now it needed someone to blame for the setbacks in the border war. That person became So Phim, head of the Eastern Zone. The Vietnamese victories, Pol Pot concluded, had come as a result of Phim's treachery: he had "opened the way" to the invaders. Sensing the danger, Phim warned his officers in March 1978 to be on guard. The party had arrested a number of loyal officials. By mid-April, more than four hundred Eastern Zone cadres had been arrested and taken to S-21. In May, Phnom Penh radio called on the nation to "purify our armed forces, our Party, and the masses of the people." Phim still had faith in Pol Pot, however; he concluded that the spate of arrests must be the result of some mistake. As the purge continued, Phim sent envoys to Phnom Penh, all of whom were arrested. On May 25, the party sent a military force to attack the Eastern Zone and capture Phim. Still believing that the party had made some sort of mistake, Phim tried to arrange a meeting with Pol Pot. In answer, the party sent two boatloads of marines. The troops failed to capture Phim, but one managed to shoot him in the stomach. As government forces closed in, aircraft dropped leaflets proclaiming Phim a traitor. He was finally cornered at sunset on June 3. Knowing that the end had come, Phim shot himself. Soldiers then murdered his wife and children.[36]

Although it shifted blame away from the party center, the purge weakened the Khmer Rouge's military forces in the east. Instead of a realistic military strategy, the party indulged in fantasies of miraculous victory. In May 1978, Pol Pot called on the population to prepare for the wholesale destruction of Vietnam:

One of us must kill thirty Vietnamese. . . . Using these figures, one Cambodian soldier is equal to 30 Vietnamese soldiers. . . .

We should have two million troops for 60 million Vietnamese. However, two million troops would be more than enough to fight the Vietnamese, because Vietnam has only 50 million inhabitants. . . . We need only 2 million troops to crush the 50 million Vietnamese, and we would still have six million people left. We must formulate our combat line in this manner, in order to win victory. . . . We absolutely must implement the slogan of one against thirty.[37]

As the purges continued across the border, leaders in Hanoi decided that the time had come to deal with Democratic Kampuchea. In February 1978, they began building a Cambodian resistance organization that would aid in the fight against the Khmer Rouge and form the nucleus of a new regime in Phnom Penh. Most of the Cambodians who had trained in Hanoi in the 1950s and '60s had returned to Cambodia and were murdered in the purges. Hanoi gathered those who had remained in Vietnam, along with escapees from Democratic Kampuchea. By the end of the spring, the Vietnamese had built a network of secret camps, many of which occupied former American bases. In April, Hanoi commissioned the First Brigade of the Cambodian exile army, the Kampuchean United Front for National Salvation.[38]

As tensions between Vietnam and Cambodia mounted, Hanoi ramped up its rhetoric. In September, Vietnamese prime minister Pham Van Dong delivered a speech denouncing the regime in Phnom Penh. "They have turned the whole of Kampuchea into a hell on earth," he announced, "a gigantic concentration camp, in which all elementary human rights, all ordinary activities of a society, all activities of family life, and all cultural and religious activities, are abolished." Khmer Rouge policies amounted to "genocide" against the Cambodian people. But Pol Pot and Ieng Sary were supported by Beijing, which viewed the Khmer Rouge as "suitable instruments for carrying out its great-nation expansionist scheme" and hegemonic ambitions in Southeast Asia. The clashes along the Vietnamese border were part of Beijing's strategy to undermine Hanoi, as was the systematic destruction of villages and the massacre of Vietnamese villagers.[39] Beijing, in turn, claimed that Hanoi harbored hegemonic ambitions in Southeast Asia "in close coordination" with the Soviet Union. Beyond attacking Cambodia in a bid to "annex" that nation, Beijing said, Vietnamese forces were making incursions across the border into China and killing a number of Chinese citizens along the frontier. Hanoi had also "brutally persecuted and expelled" thousands of ethnic Chinese from Vietnam.[40]

In mid-December, the CIA warned that after Hanoi's failed efforts to reach a "modus vivendi with the present regime in Phnom Penh" and after months of costly border clashes, Vietnamese forces were poised to attack. Considering the weakness of the Khmer Rouge and Beijing's limited control over the situation, a report predicted, "the prognosis for the Pol Pot regime is not good." Vietnamese troops "could easily be in Phnom Penh in a matter of days, if not hours." The Chinese hoped to prevent an open war with Hanoi, but they were also determined to "resist further Vietnamese expansion in the region" and to block an increase in Soviet influence in Southeast Asia. The signing of the November 1978 Treaty of Friendship and Cooperation between Hanoi and Moscow exacerbated Beijing's concerns. The PRC's credibility as a Great Power in Southeast Asia was now on the line. Rising tensions were threatening to spark a war that could have "larger consequences outside the realm of Southeast Asia." If clashes between Vietnam and Cambodia drew China into a conflict with Hanoi, the CIA report warned, Soviet leaders might feel the need to provoke "some sort of military confrontation on the Sino-Soviet border." The risk of a larger war now came into view.[41]

On December 21, 1978, Hanoi launched its invasion. Vietnamese forces stormed into the northeastern highlands toward Stung Treng. Four days later, Hanoi's main invasion force crashed across the border into Cambodia. In all, the invasion was made up of fourteen

Vietnamese divisions with heavy armor and air support. Using the "open lotus" tactic employed in the 1975 fall of Saigon, Hanoi's units penetrated deep into Cambodian territory, flowing around defensive fortifications to attack Khmer Rouge command posts. They then "blossomed out" and attacked entrenched units from the rear. The assault overwhelmed Pol Pot's troops. But this was not simply a display of force or a punitive raid. Rather, the Vietnamese were intent on toppling the regime in Phnom Penh. While Hanoi denied reports of the invasion, arguing that the units fighting in Cambodia were members of the Salvation Front, Vietnamese forces drove deeper into the country. Hanoi installed a puppet regime in the "liberated" territory, under the name the People's Republic of Kampuchea (PRK) and headed by Heng Samrin. Refugees from the Khmer Rouge terror filled the PRK's ranks. The fall of the Khmer Rouge and the death of any semblance of a pan-Asian Communist movement had arrived.[42]

THE THIRD INDOCHINA WAR

On January 7, 1979, Vietnamese units entered Phnom Penh. Khmer Rouge defenses had crumbled before Hanoi's onslaught, and Cambodia now lay open to the invaders. The Khmer Rouge leadership had fled Phnom Penh, along with thousands of their followers. An eerie silence hung in the air throughout a city that had once been home to millions. The capital's streets were littered with rusted-out cars, abandoned appliances, broken televisions and typewriters, and worthless paper currency. The only signs of life appeared around a few factories and barracks ringed by barbed wire. Several hundred workers, hopeful that the violence was now really over, remained to welcome the victors. The staff of S-21, who also remained, were not so happy to see the Vietnamese. Two Vietnamese journalists, having noticed the stench of rotting corpses, discovered the prison. Inside, they found the bodies of fourteen recently executed prisoners. Some were chained to beds with their throats slit, the blood on the floor still wet. In room after room, they found shackles, tiny prison cells, and Tuol Sleng's archive, which the staff had failed to destroy. As Vietnamese authorities burned the bodies and began to comb through the documents, the horrors of S-21 began to emerge. The wider world was slow to accept the reports emanating from occupied Phnom Penh. To many in the international community, Hanoi's invasion bore the mark of a heavy-handed attempt to exert Vietnamese authority in the wider region. Rumors of Khmer Rouge atrocities seemed so outlandish that they were initially dismissed as propaganda.[43]

The People's Republic of China (PRC) was among the nations that viewed the Vietnamese invasion with concern. Beijing was growing increasingly worried about Hanoi's willingness to assert itself in the region. Sometime in late November or early December, China's leadership appears to have resolved to attack Vietnam. The war in Cambodia appeared to confirm the PRC's worst fears. In the next months, Chinese leaders began making their case for war against Vietnam. On February 12, 1979, Beijing's representative to the United Nations, Chen Chu, delivered a statement to the Vietnamese embassy in China and the UN Security Council detailing a list of grievances against Vietnam. Under cover of darkness or dense fog, Hanoi's forces had infiltrated across China's border, set land mines and roadblocks, and launched artillery attacks on Chinese positions along the frontier. Vietnamese troops had attacked villagers, border guards, and houses in a series of "rabid provocations" that had left scores dead. "The Vietnamese authorities must stop their military provocations against China," Chen warned; "otherwise they must be held responsible for all the consequences arising therefrom."[44] Hanoi responded by accusing Chinese forces of more than two thousand incursions between 1974 and 1977 as part of a long history of "dark schemes" and encroachment into Vietnam. Beijing's provocations increased dramatically, Vietnamese officials charged, over the course of 1978 and the early months of 1979. These raids, along with artillery barrages, had killed scores of Vietnamese. Indications that the Chinese were massing large troop formations along the border suggested that even larger clashes were about to come. In pursuing these "hostile designs" and "big-nation expansionist ambitions," Hanoi warned, Beijing was risking "peace and stability in Southeast Asia and in the world."[45]

On February 17, 1979, some six weeks after the fall of Phnom Penh, hundreds of heavy guns of the Chinese People's Liberation Army (PLA) unleashed a punishing barrage against Vietnamese forces along the border. "It is the consistent position of the Chinese government and the people that we will not attack unless we are attacked," Beijing's official Xinhua News Agency announced. "If we are attacked we will certainly counterattack. . . . We do not want a single inch of Vietnamese territory, but neither will we tolerate wanton incursions into Chinese territory." Following these opening volleys, 85,000 Chinese soldiers swarmed across the forested hills along the border at twenty-six different points. The "human wave" attacks that had proved so successful against the Americans in Korea now collapsed into bloody chaos amid the tangle of tunnels and defense bunkers built by the Vietnamese along the frontier. Hidden Vietnamese machine guns directed a spray of fire toward the advancing Chinese ranks as they stumbled through minefields and fell victim to booby traps. After the heavy losses of their initial thrust, PLA commanders adopted a more methodical approach, advancing slowly behind heavy armor and seizing four provincial capitals. The Chinese began their assault on the last capital along the border, Lang Son, on February 27. For the better part of a week, PLA troops fought vicious street battles through the city. When the guns fell silent, much of the capital had been leveled and dead bodies lay strewn amid the wreckage. After overwhelming the Vietnamese defenders, Beijing sent in demolition teams to complete the destruction. PLA units destroyed schools, hospitals, government buildings, and bridges throughout the region in an effort to "teach Vietnam a lesson," destroy Hanoi's defenses along the border, and force Vietnamese troops out of Cambodia.[46]

On March 6, Beijing declared victory and began withdrawing its forces. However, the PRC's losses (between ten thousand and twenty thousand killed) were at odds with this triumphal façade. Like the French and the Americans before them, the Chinese had received in Vietnam more than they bargained for. Hanoi also declared victory, though its thousands of casualties and the devastation in the northern provinces cast a shadow on this supposed triumph. Ultimately, there was no winner in the Third Indochina War—aside from, perhaps, those Cambodians who were saved from the Khmer Rouge.

In addition to the thousands killed, the war destroyed the last pretenses of pan-Asian Communist solidarity. Hanoi and Beijing were more fearful of one another than of the United States. Chinese leaders worried about Soviet ambitions as well. The following month, Beijing's foreign minister, Huang Hua, warned UN secretary-general Kurt Waldheim that the world situation had grown increasingly tense. Washington had adopted a "defensive position while the Soviet Union . . . assumed an offensive posture." Western leaders had naïvely placed their faith in superpower détente while Moscow had increased its power. The Soviets had "succeeded in lulling Europe . . . ; this super power had increased its activity at the flanks." While Cuban forces (allied with the Soviet Union) fought in Africa, the Kremlin had its eyes on "Western Asia: Yemen, Afghanistan and Iran." Like-wise, Moscow was working through Hanoi to destabilize Southeast Asia in the hope of turning Indochina into a "Soviet military base." He explained that the "Vietnamese were the Cubans of Asia but rather more dangerous." The recent round of fighting in Southeast Asia was the result of increased Soviet aggression around the world. Ultimately, Huang warned, the Kremlin hoped to push into the Persian Gulf and Southeast Asia before linking these two thrusts in the Strait of Malacca.[47] There was no longer any doubt that Beijing recognized Moscow as the greatest threat to its interests. This transformation had fundamentally altered the dynamics of conflict in the Cold War world.

In April, CIA analysts painted a picture of Communist forces in disarray. The "Vietnamese are the big losers," the report argued. "They are accepted as aggressors in Kampuchea; 'hegemonists' throughout Indochina. . . . [Most local Southeast Asian nations regard] them as [the] principal threat to individual and regional stability." As Hanoi's main supporters, the Soviets also appeared as a threat: "[T]hey suffer in Asian eyes both from close identification with Vietnam and failing to provide sufficient aid to their Vietnamese ally." Moreover, "Chinese charges of Soviet 'hegemonism' appear credible." The war with Hanoi had paid some dividends to Beijing. China had proved that it was no "paper tiger" and had shown itself willing to use force against Vietnam.[48]

With the Soviets, Chinese, Vietnamese, and Khmer Rouge at one another's throats, the Americans emerged as the big winners. Less than a decade after its humiliating defeat in Vietnam, the United States found itself in a surprisingly strong geostrategic position in Asia.

THE SERIES OF COMMUNIST VICTORIES IN EAST ASIA had come to an end. The wave of mass violence that swept through the Indian Ocean rim between 1965 and 1979 killed more than six million people.[49] The Indo-Asian bloodbaths of the middle Cold War also demolished global Communist solidarity. The Sino-Soviet split fueled much of the period's violence, just as that same violence exacerbated the rift between Beijing and Moscow. Beijing's growing animosity toward the Kremlin, the massacre of the PKI in Indonesia, the Sino-Soviet border clashes of 1969, and the PRC's inability to control Hanoi helped convince Chinese leaders to seek rapprochement with Washington. Beginning with the Bangladesh Liberation War of 1971 and carrying through to the Sino-Vietnamese War of 1979, leaders in both Washington and Beijing forged an unlikely partnership in a struggle against the Soviet Union and its allies. The wars in Indonesia, Vietnam, Bangladesh, and Cambodia tore the Communist world apart and laid waste to the Third World Communist project.

For a new generation of revolutionaries, secular radicalism had lost much of its appeal. As the Chinese, Cambodians, and Vietnamese buried their dead, a new constellation of revolutionary forces rose in the west, over the Iranian Plateau, across the plains of Mesopotamia, and along the shores of the Mediterranean. The Cold War era's third great wave of killing had already begun.

PART III

THE GREAT SECTARIAN
REVOLT OF THE LATE
COLD WAR

1975 – 1990

THE FINAL DECADE OF THE COLD WAR WITNESSED A striking shift in the trail of revolutionary war from East and Southeast Asia into new regions. The collapse of the Portuguese Empire in Mozambique and Angola and the Kremlin's decision to commit significant resources to Marxist regimes in Somalia and Ethiopia helped inflame a series of wars in sub-Saharan Africa in the mid-1970s. In 1977, Moscow launched a massive military operation to save the Marxist government in Ethiopia, sending some $1 billion in aid to Addis Ababa. In the south, Cuban military forces aided the Angolan government against U.S.- and Chinese-backed rebels and South African troops in a vicious civil war.[1] Across the Atlantic, the United States threw its support behind pro-Western forces in a series of brutal guerrilla wars in Central America. Throughout the late 1970s and '80s, U.S. leaders backed repressive right-wing regimes in El Salvador and Guatemala and ran a covert guerrilla war against the Marxist regime in Nicaragua.[2] In this way, the 1980s became the bloodiest decade of the Cold War in both Latin America and Africa.

The decade's largest wars, the late Cold War's most pivotal and most destructive conflicts, though, are those that broke out along the

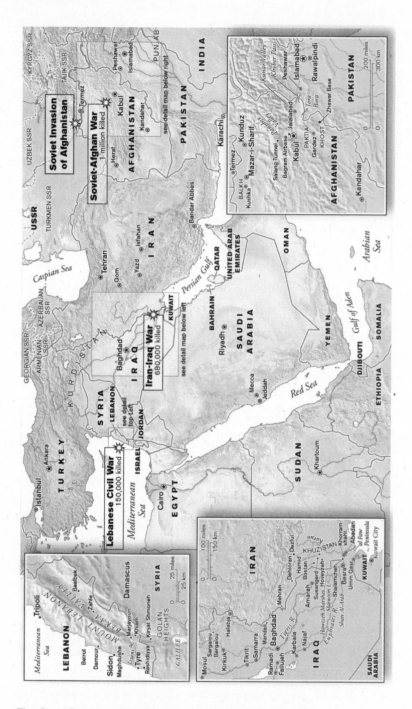

The Great Sectarian Revolts of the Late Cold War, 1975–1990

contested frontiers of Southwest Asia, in the central Islamic world. The figures who would gain prominence on these Middle Eastern battlefields, the Ayatollah Khomeini, Saddam Hussein, and Osama bin Laden, would cast long shadows over international politics in the post–Cold War era. This third wave of conflict departed from the earlier paradigm of left-wing guerrillas fighting pro-Western governments. Rather than Communist revolutionaries, a new breed of radicals driven by religious and ethnic politics seized the vanguard. Blazing a trail that was "neither East nor West," this next generation of fighters rejected both Washington and Moscow's influence. Marxist doctrine held little appeal for these fighters. The failures of secular revolutionary movements and governments had led many young revolutionaries to turn toward deeper ethnic and sectarian affiliations. Far from a resurgence of ancient religious fury, this next wave of revolutionary zeal forged a new politics of warfare. A great sectarian revolt, it drew upon existing ethnic and religious identities to create new visions of postcolonial revolution. And like earlier postcolonial revolutionaries, this new generation was not monolithic. The sectarian warriors of the late Cold War fought as much against one another as against outside forces.[3]

Three vicious conflicts raged through the decade. Where East and Southeast Asia had served as the key theaters of the first and second waves of post-1945 violence, the Middle East emerged as last major battlefield of the Cold War age. The Lebanese Civil War, which began in 1975, served as a harbinger of broader changes. As rival sectarian militias transformed the small republic into a dystopian battlefield, neighboring states and outside powers launched interventions. If Lebanon signaled the rise of a new force in revolutionary politics from the Middle East, the 1979 Iranian Revolution sounded the loudest call. As the world watched, theocratic revolutionaries who seemed more fit for the fifteenth century than the twentieth seized power in one of the region's largest and most powerful states. This revolution's shock waves helped set off a vicious war between Iran and Iraq along the ancient frontiers of the Shia and Sunni worlds. But the era's bloodiest conflict broke out in neighboring Afghanistan, where the Soviet Union staged its largest intervention of the Cold War, in defense of a failing Marxist regime battling Islamic guerrillas. For most of a decade, the Afghan Mujahideen waged a deadly jihad against Soviet troops that helped to bring the Communist giant to its knees. Together, these three conflicts shifted the focus decisively away from the Marxist paradigm of revolutionary violence and toward ethno-religious modes of conflict. This great sectarian revolt signaled the rise of a new revolutionary politics in world affairs that would come to dominate the conflicts of the early twenty-first century.

Leaders in both Washington and Moscow recognized these changes, but they did not fully appreciate their implications. As the CIA warned in 1981, the recent wave of resurgent Islamic nationalism had destabilized the Middle East and now threatened U.S. strategic interests.[4] But officials in the White House and the Kremlin remained fixed in their Cold War mind-sets. If ethno-religious fighters destabilized existing regimes, American and Soviet officials worried, their Cold War adversaries were likely to benefit. U.S. national security advisor Zbigniew Brzezinski warned in late 1978, "An arc of crisis stretches along the shores of the Indian Ocean, with fragile social and political structures in a region of vital importance to us threatened with fragmentation. The resulting political chaos could well be filled by elements hostile to our values and sympathetic to our adversaries." But Brzezinski underestimated the power of these new players. "There was this idea that the Islamic forces could be used against the Soviet Union," State Department officer Henry Precht later explained. "The theory was, there was an arc of crisis, and so an arc of Islam could be mobilized to contain the Soviets. It was a Brzezinski concept."[5] This rationale would drive the Carter administration's paradoxical decision to establish an aid program for Islamic fighters in Afghanistan at the same time that the White House agonized over the fallout from the Islamic revolution in Iran.

While the sectarian resurgence created problems in Washington, it represented a more immediate threat to the sclerotic Brezhnev regime in Moscow. Soviet leaders worried that the waves of Islamic radicalism sweeping through Iran and Afghanistan might spill over the border to the large Muslim populations living inside the Soviet Union. U.S., Indian, and British officials speculated in mid-1979 that Soviet leaders were justifiably concerned that the Islamic "virus might spread to the Soviet Moslem population." Resurgent Islamic fundamentalism also threatened the young Marxist regime in Kabul, which began pleading with the Kremlin to intervene in Afghanistan. Though they were loath to see a Communist regime on their own border collapse, Soviet leaders worried about the prospect of staging a military intervention in the fractious nation.[6] In the end, Cold War priorities pushed both superpowers to join the fray in ill-conceived attempts to respond to the great sectarian revolt. U.S. leaders denounced Iranian fundamentalists at the same time that they channeled aid and weapons to Afghan jihadists. Soviet leaders, meanwhile, charged into a conflict that bore striking similarities to the American war in Vietnam. By the time the smoke cleared, nearly three million people lay dead and a new mode of revolutionary violence had risen from the Cold War's ashes.[7]

THE LEBANESE CIVIL WAR

1975 – 1978

The Cold War world's final wave of mass violence appeared in an unlikely place. Nestled on the shores of the sparkling Mediterranean, Beirut had often been called the Paris of the Middle East. Lebanon's capital had served as a sort of free city in the Middle East in the 1950s, '60s, and early 1970s. Lauded for its tolerance, diversity, and relatively open society, Lebanon was seen by many outsiders as a model of a functioning, multisectarian republic—an oasis in an otherwise troubled region. Probably the most Westernized city in the Arab world, Beirut was a playground for wealthy Arabs and European expats, who frequented its posh boutiques and sandy beaches by day and danced in its bustling nightclubs into the early hours of the morning. Though the regime was pro-Western, Lebanese democracy allowed a wide range of groups to operate inside the state's borders. Beirut was a haven for intellectuals, political activists, refugees, Palestinian guerrilla fighters, and wealthy Arabs on holiday. The city was also a key theater of operations for a variety of intelligence agencies: American, Soviet, Egyptian, Palestinian, and Israeli.

In many ways, Lebanon embodied the tensions faced by developing states during the Cold War. Born out of European imperialism, the country remained subject to the changing dynamics of the superpower struggle, the regional disruptions of the Arab-Israeli conflict, and the forces of revolution and modernization in the Arab world.[1] Throughout the first half of the Cold War, Lebanon survived as a moderate state—with the help of U.S. Marines, who spearheaded Washington's first military intervention in the region in 1958—sandwiched between its larger, superpower-armed neighbors, Israel and Syria.[2] While conservative elements within Lebanon looked toward Europe and the United States, left-wing forces inside the country pushed for closer association with progressive states such as Syria, Egypt, and the Soviet Union. Meanwhile, Beirut grew into a modern metropolis flowing with international capital and linked into global networks of culture, communication, and transportation. Outside this cosmopolitan center, though, the Lebanese countryside remained poor and its population deeply religious. Thus, Lebanon was pulled between the international and the regional, the modern and the traditional, the capitalist and the socialist, and the secular and the religious elements found in many Third World countries in the Cold War age. It was perhaps natural, then—if no less tragic— that the centrifugal forces of sectarianism and communal violence would descend on this small republic. As the Cold War's ideological moorings gave way to a resurgence of ethnic and religious conflict, Lebanon fell into a fifteen-year state of civil war.

Beginning in 1975, sectarian tensions among Lebanese Christians, Muslims, rival warlords, and Palestinian guerrilla fighters transformed central Beirut (along with much of the rest of the country) into a war zone. By the early 1980s, a no-man's-land of vacant streets shrouded by overgrown vegetation and burned-out buildings known as the Green Line separated Muslim West Beirut from Christian East Beirut. Snipers from rival militias perched in abandoned high-rises along the boundary, listening to transistor radios, smoking French cigarettes, and exchanging sporadic fire with their adversaries on the other side. To the south, fighters from the Palestine Liberation

Organization (PLO) had transformed the refugee camps in the Fakhani District of West Beirut into virtual fortresses, complete with tanks, artillery, and thousands of well-armed guerrillas. Steel shutters covered the shops along Hamra Street (once the most fashionable shopping strip in the Middle East), and the area teemed with armed men moving between ramshackle stalls hawking shoes, T-shirts, frozen chicken, and canned fruit juice.[3]

The Lebanese Civil War served as a harbinger for a new type of conflict that became increasingly common in the 1980s, '90s, and 2000s, as a new constellation of revolutionary forces eclipsed the Cold War paradigm. Fueled by ethnic strife, tribal politics, and religious disputes rather than clashes between Marxism and liberal capitalism, these new wars were low-intensity conflicts, fought by insurgents, paramilitaries, international peacekeepers, guerrillas, and conventional armies. The war in Lebanon also conjured the specter of a postcolonial world filled with weak and failing states. The Lebanese case showed that civil-administrative structures created under European imperialism might collapse into anarchy as internal and external pressures increased. These failed states could become breeding grounds for new and frightening varieties of warfare. Lebanon, and the capital of Beirut in particular, presented a dystopian vision of ethno-religious warfare in the post–Cold War order where civilians were targets and cities became battlefields.

THE SWITZERLAND OF THE MIDDLE EAST

A longtime ally of the United States, Lebanon was known in the early 1970s as a sort of Switzerland of the Middle East: a culturally diverse society with an open political and financial system, home to regional banks and a haven for tourists and Foreign Service officers in the Cold War Middle East. Yet this shining exterior masked deep tensions in Lebanese society. Lebanon had been cobbled together by the French imperial authorities during the early decades of the twentieth century. The French had connected the Mount Lebanon region (which had for centuries been the refuge of minority groups such as Maronite Christians and Druze) with the primarily Muslim coastal cities of Beirut, Sidon, Tyre, and Tripoli. The imperial authorities had also attached the Beqaa Valley, a rich strip of land with a Muslim-majority population oriented toward Syria, in an effort to establish a viable state that would be administered by the pro-French Maronites of Mount Lebanon. The end result was a confessional state governed by the 1943 National Pact, an agreement that divided power among the various religious communities proportionally.

Based on the 1932 census, the pact fixed parliamentary representation at a ratio of six Christian ministers to every five Muslim and guaranteed that the office of the president would be held by a Maronite Christian, the office of prime minister by a Sunni Muslim, the office of president of the National Assembly by a Shia Muslim, the office of deputy speaker of the Parliament by a Greek Orthodox Christian, and that of the chief of the General Staff by a Druze. In effect, this arrangement ensured that Lebanon's political system would be dominated by its Christian population. This domination would be challenged in the coming decades by Muslim groups seeking to gain a greater share of political power.

In 1958, a civil war broke out in the country, leading the United States to mount its first military intervention in the Middle East. While the U.S. intervention ensured the survival of the Lebanese political system, it did nothing to address the deep tensions that remained in the country. Lebanon's non-Christian minorities continued to call for a new census, one that would show that the Christian plurality of the 1930s had been eclipsed by higher Muslim birthrates, and for a revision of the National Pact to allow greater Muslim representation in Lebanese politics. But Lebanon's Christians resisted any change to the status quo.

Despite these tensions, Lebanon flourished during the early decades of the Cold War. This was what some called the "Lebanese

Paradox"—the deeply divided society was also among the most prosperous in the Middle East, a shining example of a cosmopolitan, multisectarian republic in a region that was fast gaining a reputation for being a hotbed of conflict and a stronghold for authoritarian rulers. Beirut, the "playground of the Arab World," perched on an outcrop of land along the Mediterranean, grew beyond the older French quarters as its banks attracted funds from across the region and its beaches and boutiques attracted tourists. But growth had its dark side. The flood of rural peoples to the capital created a "poverty belt" around the outer districts of the city, which included smaller villages in the process of being absorbed as suburbs and the Palestinian refugee camps of Tal al-Za'atar, Sabra, Shatila, and Burj al-Barajneh, created after the 1948 Arab-Israeli War to house the thousands of Palestinian refugees who poured into Lebanon. By the early 1970s, 40 percent of Beirut's population lived inside this belt, packed into high-density neighborhoods with poor sanitation, insufficient water supply, and stolen electricity. It was among the denizens of these depressed neighborhoods on the outskirts of the city that the increasingly extreme political messages of political parties on both the left and the right gained traction.[4]

Added to this volatile mix in the late 1960s and early '70s was the presence of Palestinian guerrilla fighters, led by Yasser Arafat's Palestine Liberation Organization. Energized in the wake of the 1967 Arab-Israeli War, Palestinian guerrillas became active in Jordan, Syria, and Lebanon. In September 1970, the Hashemite regime in Amman cracked down on the guerrillas, expelling them from Jordan and leaving Lebanon as the prime theater for PLO operations against Israel. With its headquarters now in Beirut, the PLO brought Lebanon firmly into the crosshairs of the Israeli military, which was intent on crushing the power of the Palestinian guerrillas. There began a cycle of Palestinian attacks and Israeli reprisals that undermined the authority of the Lebanese government; inflamed tensions among Beirut, Israel, and the United States; and generated an ever-mounting Lebanese body count. Meanwhile, within Lebanon, the predominantly Sunni PLO augmented the political power of Lebanon's non-Christian majority. Although Arafat's Fatah, the largest and most influential guerrilla group within the PLO, strove to remain aloof from the internal affairs of Arab host states, other groups, such as the Popular Front for the Liberation of Palestine (PFLP), called for a wider revolution in the Arab world and worked to challenge the authority of more moderate regimes. Such actions had led to the expulsion of the Palestinian guerrillas from Jordan in 1970. Now many observers called for a similar crackdown in Lebanon.[5]

Fearing that these increasing pressures might indeed lead to efforts by conservative Lebanese leaders to restrict the guerrillas' activities, Arafat's PLO began to move toward alignment with the left-wing Lebanese National Movement (Al-Harakat al-Wataniyya al-Lubnaniyya, or LNM), led by Druze chieftain Kamal Jumblatt. A fixture in Lebanese politics, Jumblatt remained a vocal proponent of efforts to revise his country's system of confessional representation. In addition to his left-wing Arab nationalist political message, Jumblatt was among those Lebanese pushing for greater support for the Palestinian guerrillas. With the aid of the PFLP and good relations with the PLO, Jumblatt and his allies emerged as a major force in Lebanese politics during the early 1970s. In 1969, Jumblatt created the LNM as a counterforce to a number of right-wing Christian militias that had formed in Lebanon.[6]

Against the progressive-revolutionary politics of the LNM and the PLO stood the forces of Lebanon's conservative Christian community. The most prominent was the Phalange Party, which had been created as a quasi-Fascist group in the 1930s by Pierre Gemayel. Hailing from a prominent Maronite family from Mount Lebanon, Gemayel formed the Phalangists into a powerful, highly organized defender of Christian interests and one of the principal adversaries of the PLO in Lebanon. Heavily armed, Gemayel's Phalange would be one of the principal combatants in the civil war, fighting to preserve Christian dominance in Lebanon. Aligned with the Phalange was Camille

Chamoun's National Liberal Party (NLP) and its armed wing, the Tigers. A pro-Western former president of the republic, Chamoun had helped spark the 1958 civil war in Lebanon and in that same year invited U.S. military intervention to preserve the state.[7]

The years leading up to the 1975 civil war saw the rise of a series of rival militias in Lebanon, each representing factions of a religious-ethnic community. The LNM and PLO sought to overturn the Christian-dominated status quo while the Phalange and the NLP fought to preserve it. The militias grew into a sort of Lebanese Mafia controlled by sectarian warlords with extensive ties to political leadership at the local and national levels, financed by networks of businesses, and protected by gangs of street soldiers. State security forces struggled to maintain order but were, on the whole, outmanned and outgunned by the paramilitary organizations operating in Lebanon. The division of the Lebanese military along sectarian lines compounded matters. To compel Christian soldiers to take action against the Phalange—or Muslim soldiers to move against the PLO or LNM—could risk a larger mutiny in the military. By the mid-1970s, Lebanese society sat on the brink of civil war.

This descent into chaos was not inevitable. Indeed, 1975 appeared to be an auspicious year for peace in the region. The 1973 Arab-Israeli War had prompted a resumption in international efforts to reach a comprehensive settlement to the region's longest-running conflict. Egypt and Israel, the two principal combatants in the conflict, appeared to be moving toward accommodation, and Anwar el-Sadat, Egypt's president since 1970, was in the process of pulling the largest nation in the Arab world away from alignment with the Soviet Union and toward the United States. In fact, 1975 would serve as a milestone in U.S.–Middle East relations, the beginning of a turbulent new era that would simultaneously witness the ascendency of Washington's influence and the emergence of a new set of challengers to American supremacy. The first signal of this new set of challenges would come with the disintegration of Lebanon in 1975.

THE DEATH OF THIRD WORLD COMMUNISM

The sectarian violence that broke out in Lebanon confounded observers around the world. That quarreling religious communities inside a prosperous, modern state could fall into a vicious civil war flew in the face of prevailing Cold War logic. Many assumed that late-twentieth-century wars were fought over political ideology, not religious faith. And 1975 should have been a banner year for the secular revolutionaries. Progressive forces around the world that supported the cause of Palestinian liberation began the year rejoicing that Yasser Arafat, leader of the secular PLO, had delivered a triumphal speech on the floor of the UN General Assembly to thundering applause in late 1974. In January 1975, North Vietnamese forces launched a military campaign that would bring them final victory in April with the fall of Saigon. That same month, Cambodian Communists seized control of Phnom Penh, creating the new socialist state of Democratic Kampuchea. In June and November, Mozambique and Angola gained independence from Portugal, driving the final nail into the coffin of the Portuguese Empire and ending an era of European imperialism that had lasted some five hundred years. Nineteen seventy-five, then, marked the high tide of a movement of secular left-wing forces sweeping through the Third World. But even as the revolutionaries celebrated, events in the Middle East and Central Asia suggested that that revolutionary tide had begun to recede.

Between 1975 and 1979, secular revolutionaries around the postcolonial world suffered a series of devastating blows as an array of actors moved against them. Geopolitical transformations in the Cold War, the increasingly acrimonious Sino-Soviet split, and the emergence of a new set of religious revolutionaries combined to slow the series of left-wing victories and open the door to a resurgence of ethnic and religious conflict around the developing world. By the end of the decade, left-wing forces found themselves embattled and the world they had sought to create in turmoil.

No force was more disruptive than the growing rift between Moscow and Beijing. By the mid-1970s, that cleavage was being felt in the developing world. While Soviet and Chinese leaders hurled insults at one another and their troops patrolled the border along the Ussuri River, left-wing parties in the Third World were left to choose between the two Communist powers. Meanwhile, China itself had emerged from the depths of the Cultural Revolution. With the death of Mao Zedong in 1976, a new cadre rose to power in Beijing led by Deng Xiaoping. After coming to power, Deng launched a sweeping campaign of reforms that transformed the PRC's financial system into a de facto market economy under the control of a nominally Communist government. Combined with Beijing's antagonism toward Moscow and its Cold War tilt toward Washington, these transformations shocked left-wing forces around the world.

The second great defection of the 1970s came from Cairo. Under Gamal Abdel Nasser, Egypt had carried the flag of Arab revolution and had hosted the largest Soviet military deployment in the developing world. But following Egypt's crushing defeat in the 1967 war with Israel, Yasser Arafat and the Palestine Liberation Organization emerged as the new vanguard. Nasser's successor, Anwar el-Sadat, was determined to change course in the Arab-Israeli conflict and the Cold War. After launching a surprise attack on Israeli military forces in the occupied Sinai in October 1973, Sadat managed to force a new round of negotiations in the Arab-Israeli peace process. In 1975, Sadat signed the Sinai Interim Agreement, which effectively returned the peninsula to Egyptian control in exchange for a de facto strategic alliance among Egypt, the United States, and Israel. For all intents and purposes, Sadat had switched sides in the Cold War, dealing yet another blow to the global cause of left-wing revolution.

Meanwhile, any lingering doubts about the solidarity of the global Marxist project were destroyed in 1979, when two of the most celebrated revolutionary states in the Third World, China and Vietnam, went to war against each other following Hanoi's invasion of Cambodia. Four of communism's greatest twentieth-century revolutionary states, the Soviet Union, China, Vietnam, and Cambodia, had fallen into fratricidal war. The 1965 massacre of the Indonesian PKI and the Cambodian genocide dealt similar blows to the champions of Marxist revolution in the developing world. Together, these Indo-Asian bloodbaths dashed dreams of international Communist solidarity and left future revolutionaries to look for new sources of inspiration. The legions of warriors that rushed to late–Cold War battlefields in Lebanon, Iraq, Iran, and Afghanistan fought under the flag of religious resurgence, not socialist revolution. In the last decade of the Cold War, a new ethno-religious radicalism would rise from the ashes of the Third World Communist project. The war in Lebanon presaged these transformations.

THE WAR BEGINS

The shots that pushed Lebanon into open conflict were fired on April 13, 1975, as Pierre Gemayel was attending the consecration of a new church in the predominantly Christian suburb of Ain al-Rummaneh southeast of Beirut. A car carrying half a dozen armed members of the Palestinian guerrilla group the Democratic Front for the Liberation of Palestine (DFLP) passed by and refused to be diverted by Gemayel's bodyguards. It is not clear who fired the first shots, but one Palestinian and three Phalangists were killed. Sometime later, Gemayel's men ambushed a busload of Palestinian guerrillas returning home after a celebration, killing twenty-seven. The shootings ignited street battles between Palestinians and Phalangists in several districts of the city as militiamen deployed the stockpiles of weapons amassed over previous years. The following day, merchants kept their shops shuttered while militiamen threw up barricades to control access to Christian and Palestinian quarters of the city. As the war in the streets escalated, Lebanese authorities demanded that Gemayel hand over the Phalangists responsible for attacking the

Palestinians. The fighting soon spread to the cities of Tripoli, Sidon, and Tyre, to the north and south of the capital.[8]

Sporadic fighting continued into the summer of 1975, leaving some eight hundred killed by the end of June. Authorities advised Beirut's residents to remain indoors and off the dangerous streets. Armed men in masks manned barricades blocking the main routes into the city. Those brave enough to travel were subject to searches and passport checks at the many roadblocks that sprouted up throughout the city. Snipers patrolled rooftops around Beirut while cars of armed men careened through the streets.[9] A hasty truce brought an end to the fighting in July but did nothing to resolve underlying tensions. By September, violence had resumed. Residents of the provincial capital of Zahlé awoke each morning to find new bodies of the slain, many with their hands bound, in alleys, orchards, and fields outside the city. Gunfights, looting, bombings, revenge killings, and kidnappings had become common occurrences. Violence in the northern port city of Tripoli, sparked by a traffic accident, claimed thirty-one lives in the first week of September; water and electricity had been cut off after pipelines leading into Tripoli were bombed.[10] As the death toll mounted, this pattern of periodic violence coalesced into what many recognized as a civil war. In the following weeks, heavy fighting resumed in the capital.

In late October, one of the most iconic battles of the war began in the heart of Beirut's blossoming downtown. On October 24, members of the secular pan-Arabist al-Mourabitoun militia entered the Rizk Tower, a twenty-eight-story high-rise with commanding views over the Christian quarter of the city. Once inside, the gunmen established snipers' nests and rocket positions that could threaten the Maronite neighborhood of Achrafieh. In response, Phalangist soldiers seized three of the Beirut's largest downtown hotels: the Holiday Inn, the St. George's, and the Phoenicia. For the next two weeks, the two sides exchanged fire between the towers. Structures designed as luxurious Western hotels became fortresses in a ferocious battle for control over the ancient city of Beirut. Two truces allowed the frightened guests and staff of the buildings to collect their belongings and evacuate. By early November, burned-out vehicles and barricades rendered the surrounding streets all but impassable. On November 4, Prime Minister Rashid Karami negotiated an indecisive cease-fire that allowed for the evacuation of the hotels, the return of the militiamen to their respective enclaves, the razing of the remaining barricades, and the establishment of joint gendarme-PLO patrols to police the cease-fire.[11]

The Battle of the Hotels transformed one of Beirut's most modern multiplexes, a nonsectarian port of entry for the wider world, into a war zone. In the wake of the battle, Beirut split into sectarian cantons ruled by rival militias running protection rackets and guarding their territory. In between these areas, PLO fighters and gendarmes patrolled a demilitarized buffer zone—the so-called Green Line running down the Damascus Road and separating Muslim West Beirut from the Christian neighborhoods in the east. Radio Lebanon gave the city's residents updates on navigating the battle-torn streets, directing them away from dangerous intersections and toward safe routes and announcing which facilities were open for the day.[12]

With remarkable speed, the Paris of the Middle East had fallen into a state of brutal violence. Wealthy Christians living in the hills outside the city made a sport of launching mortars at the Palestinian refugee camps below, Maronite militiamen carved crosses into the chests of their victims, and left-wing militias carried out vicious reprisals. Meanwhile, Beirut became a center for the international arms trade as rival armies clambered for the most sophisticated weapons. Eastern European gunrunners established a strong presence in the city while Lebanese entrepreneurs fanned out into Africa to procure weapons from rebel groups in Biafra and Ghana. Soviet weapons captured by the Israelis in the 1967 war eventually found their way into Lebanon and the hands of the militias. As the conflict continued, the global flow of arms ensured that the combatants enjoyed ready access to weapons. All the while, Western pop music blared on radios on both sides of the Green Line.[13]

THE MIDDLE EAST'S NEW BATTLEFIELD

After months of fighting, Beirut's residents had become accustomed to violence. But they were unprepared for what came on the morning of December 6, 1975. Enraged over the killing of four of their comrades, Phalangist militiamen threw up barricades along several of Beirut's major highways. Armed men demanded that drivers produce their official identity cards, which marked individuals by religion. Many of those identified as Muslim were dragged from their cars and executed, an act that set off a wave of panic throughout the city. By 2:00 p.m., state radio was declaring the city streets unsafe and warning residents to remain indoors. Cars careened through dangerous neighborhoods, pulling violent U-turns and dodging potentially deadly roadblocks. Meanwhile, reports of summary executions spread through the capital. Sporadic gunfire and grenade explosions echoed against Beirut's concrete-and-glass high-rises. Some estimates placed the day's toll of massacred Muslims at higher than three hundred.[14]

Black Saturday (as December 6 came to be known) and the events that followed would pull another combatant into the conflict: the PLO. Up to the end of 1975, Yasser Arafat and the PLO had tried to keep out of the fighting. While the growth of Palestinian influence in Lebanon had helped push the country toward civil war, Arafat and his comrades in Fatah had sought to maintain a policy of noninterference in the internal affairs of their host states. Certainly, the PLO had established a considerable base of power inside Lebanon and in Beirut in particular. Since the late 1960s, Palestinian leaders such as George Habash, commander of the PFLP, had called for the transformation of Beirut into an "Arab Hanoi." In this scheme, Lebanon would serve as a rear base for a Palestinian national liberation movement designed to regain control of former Arab territory in Israel/

Palestine. The 1970 civil war in Jordan that forced the PLO out of that kingdom had left Lebanon as the last sanctuary for Palestinian guerrillas seeking to launch operations against Israel. In the five years that followed, Palestinian revolutionaries built a formidable presence inside Lebanon. But for the Palestinian fighters, the real battle lay to the south, along the frontier with Israel and in the international arena, where they hoped to secure a larger role in the U.S.-led Arab-Israeli peace process. The rising tide of sectarian violence in Lebanon—to say nothing of the Maronite pledges to drive the Palestinians out of the country—could not but draw the predominantly Muslim Palestinian population into the fray.

In the wake of the Black Saturday killings, Lebanese Muslim militias launched a retaliatory offensive against Beirut's downtown hotel complex that nearly overwhelmed the Christian forces inside. Amid the fighting, downtown shops and banks suffered widespread looting as the capital spiraled further downward into a general war. In response to this latest round of fighting, Maronite militias began what would be a long campaign of "sectarian cleansing," expelling Muslims from Christian neighborhoods in Beirut and outlying towns and furthering the fragmentation of the nation into religious enclaves. On January 3, 1976, Christian forces laid siege to the Palestinian camps of Tal al-Za'atar, Jisr al-Basha, and Dbayeh, as well as the slums of Karantina in northeast Beirut. Maronite leaders hoped to draw the PLO into a showdown that would force the Lebanese government to increase restrictions on the guerrillas. Arafat sensed the trap and remained reluctant to walk into it. Cut off from the camps and facing a state of virtual siege in its headquarters in West Beirut, however, the PLO had little choice but to launch a counterattack. On January 6, Arafat and his lieutenants agreed to a plan designed to break the siege: one force of PLO-LNM fighters would attack from West Beirut and drive toward Tal al-Za'atar while defenders within the camp broke out to meet them; meanwhile, a third group of guerrillas would land boats on the beaches near Karantina and link up with Palestinian troops to the south, in the neighborhood of Naba'a. Internal divisions and the lack of a unified command doomed the attacks, however. Its offensive having failed, the PLO found itself embroiled in a set of indecisive battles around the capital.[15]

Fatah units now joined the battle in force, launching attacks around Zahlé, in the west, and the Christian coastal town of Damour, twelve miles south of Beirut. These assaults came too late to save the besieged camp at Dbayeh, however, which was overrun and emptied by Christian militias on January 14. Four days later, Phalangist militia along with army units stormed the coastal slums of Karantina, home to some thirty thousand poor Muslims. A contingent of Palestinian fighters entrenched in a furniture factory resisted the attackers for three days before being killed. Christian forces poured into Karantina and began laying waste to the shanties in their path. Images of militiamen guzzling champagne over corpses and of women and children being expelled at gunpoint soon hit the international press. At least 150 people were killed—some estimates placed the death toll much higher—and tens of thousands of survivors were forced out of the Christian-controlled zones. On January 23, Palestinian forces seized Damour, killing scores of Maronites inside and forcing thousands of survivors out of the area. As these reciprocal rounds of ethnic cleansing signaled, the war was taking a gruesome turn. Both sides were using military force to create ethnically homogenous bases of power.[16]

The bloodletting in Karantina and Damour threw the rift between Christian and Muslim forces into sharp relief. In the weeks that followed, a group of Muslim soldiers in the Lebanese Army mutinied and formed the Lebanese Arab Army (LAA), which linked up with Jumblatt's left-wing LNM. Jumblatt recognized a historic opportunity and approached the PLO to form an alliance against the Christian militias. With some reluctance, Arafat and his comrades agreed. The resulting coalition of Lebanese Muslim and Palestinian fighters, dubbed the Joint Forces, was now the strongest army in Lebanon.

From his presidential palace in Damascus, the forty-five-year-old president of Syria, Hafez al-Assad, had watched the fighting in Lebanon with concern. In the wake of the 1970 war in Jordan, Assad had seized power, bringing an era of unprecedented stability to his country. Yet he replaced the revolving-door leadership in Damascus with his own brand of authoritarian rule. Hailing from a remote mountain region in northwestern Syria, he was the grandson of a fearsome Alawite chieftain nicknamed al-Wahhish, the "wild beast." The Alawites are a mystical sect of Shi'ites and a small minority in predominantly Sunni Syria, making up less than 15 percent of the state's population. Assad had developed a reputation for being both clever and ruthless. He had risen through the ranks of the air force, where he joined other officers in the Syrian socialist Ba'ath Party, which was poised to seize control of the government. By 1971, he had eliminated his rivals and assumed uncontested rule of the state. Soon after seizing power, Assad emerged as one of the key players in regional politics. Even Kissinger had found him a formidable adversary during the post-1973 Arab-Israeli peace process.[17]

Assad understood that the war in Lebanon presented a grave threat to his country. An LNM-LAA-PLO military victory threatened to destabilize the region at a critical juncture in the Arab-Israeli peace process. With Maronite forces crushed, the PLO would assume preeminent power in Lebanon, and Arafat and his guerrillas, freed from Lebanese constraints, would create a revolutionary government in Beirut and intensify their war against Israel. Should this happen, Israeli forces were sure to respond with attacks against a Palestinian-controlled Lebanon. If Arafat and the PLO gained the upper hand, Syria would be forced to live with a radical new state along its western flank. If the Israeli counterattack succeeded, it would transform Lebanon into a conservative Christian state that would threaten the regime in Damascus. Either outcome translated into a severe blow to Syrian influence in the region. It was therefore in Syria's best interest, Assad concluded, to restore the delicate balance of power between Muslims and Christians in Lebanon. On March 27, as the Joint Forces' offensive slashed through the mountains of Lebanon, Jumblatt made the journey to Damascus to meet with Assad. The Druze leader listened to Assad's demands but remained steadfast. The LNM and PLO were no puppets of Damascus.[18]

Unable to impose his will upon his supposed allies, Assad chose to betray them. On May 31, 1976, a Syrian column forced its way into Lebanon. But a subtler intervention had begun in January, when Damascus had ordered units from the Syrian PLA, along with the Syrian-controlled Palestinian guerrilla group Saiqa, into Beirut. In March, the Joint Forces staged an assault on the presidential palace in Baabda that nearly overwhelmed its defenses, which were bolstered by Syrian-backed units from Saiqa and the Palestine Liberation Army (PLA). Soon after, the Joint Forces captured the hotel district and the heavily contested Holiday Inn tower. This victory completed what would become known as the Green Line between Muslim West and the Christian East Beirut, the front line of the civil war. At the end of the month, Fatah units launched a major assault in the mountains above the capital. Palestinian fighters overran a series of Christian villages, putting them in a position to threaten Gemayel's hometown of Bikfaya. With their success in the so-called Mountain War, the Joint Forces seemed perched on the brink of victory.[19]

The curious spectacle of Syrian Ba'athists fighting in support of conservative Maronite militias against Palestinian guerrillas and progressive Lebanese forces was indicative of the chaotic nature of a war in which all parties would fight against one another at some point. Though both Saiqa and the PLA were composed of Palestinians, the organizations functioned as adjuncts of the Syrian government, which allowed Assad to manipulate the Palestinian issue—they were, in effect, rivals of Arafat and the PLO. This was only a half-measure, however, as Assad soon discovered. In late May, he chose to intervene with Syrian Army units. But Syrian soldiers were in for a nasty surprise: battle-hardened PLO and LNM defenders in Beirut, Tripoli, Sidon, and Mount Lebanon inflicted punishing casualties upon the attackers. Syria's intervention would be no easy task, but having crossed into Lebanon, Assad was now committed to a bloody war on forbidding terrain. As Henry Kissinger would observe, Syria faced the opposite of the American predicament in Vietnam: Assad's forces controlled the countryside (most notably the fertile Beqaa Valley) while the cities remained battlegrounds among the PLO, Lebanese militias, and Syrian soldiers.[20]

Assad's gamble carried regional and international repercussions as well. Both the United States and Israel worried about the fallout from the invasion. For Israeli leaders, Assad's move threatened to give their most intractable rival in the region control over their northern neighbor. A minority within the Israeli government called for an interventionist policy of supporting the two largest non-Muslim minorities in Lebanon, the Maronites and the Druze, in the hope of creating mini-states that would be allied with Israel. But there was little enthusiasm in the wider Israeli cabinet for a direct intervention in Lebanon. Still, Israeli officials balked at the prospect of allowing Syria to establish control over Lebanon. Ultimately, leaders in Prime Minister Yitzhak Rabin's government in Jerusalem were willing to allow Syria to send its troops, rather than Israeli soldiers, into Lebanon in order to rescue the Maronites and reinstate the status quo. If Syrian forces mauled the PLO in the process, all the better. However, the Israeli government would not accept Syrian domination of the country. Rather, Syrian forces had to refrain from crossing a series of "red lines," which ran along the approaches to South Lebanon and the border with Israel, or risk Israeli retaliation. These included prohibitions on surface-to-air missiles inside Lebanon.[21]

American officials found themselves in an even more complicated position. Recent months had witnessed the completion of a critical phase in the Arab-Israeli peace process whereby Egypt and Israel signed onto the 1975 Sinai II Accords, engineered largely by U.S. secretary of state Henry Kissinger. The accords placed the two nations on a path toward a peace treaty and positioned the United States as the key arbiter in this process. In exchange for peace, Egypt and Israel would receive $2 billion and $3 billion, respectively, in annual U.S. aid. This allocation made them the two largest recipients of U.S. foreign aid. In geopolitical terms, Sinai II removed Egypt from the Arab-Israeli conflict and made the largest state in the Arab world a major American ally. As a result, Cairo defected from the Soviet orbit and moved into alignment with the United States. The war in Lebanon, however, threatened to throw the entire region into disarray, jeopardize the peace process, and risk a showdown with the Soviet Union. In the event of an Israeli invasion, State Department officials predicted, it would take only three to four days for Israel to reach the outskirts of Damascus, at which point Assad would call for Soviet intervention. Moscow could send an airborne division of seven thousand to eight thousand troops to Syria in a matter of days, which would then lead to the question of the United States sending marines into the region from ships in the Mediterranean. Hence, in the space of a week, an Israeli invasion could spark a confrontation between the superpowers. American goals therefore came to focus on containing the conflict in Lebanon and preventing the war from sparking a larger conflagration.[22]

Yet, if Assad's assault remained contained to Lebanon north of the red line, Syrian operations in Lebanon might accomplish Washington's goals of returning the country to the prewar status quo and devastating the PLO. As an added bonus, Syrian intervention had soured Syria's relationship with the Soviet Union. Assad's war with the PLO pitted two of Moscow's most important allies in the region against one another. As Kissinger told President Ford on April 13, 1976, "I think over the long run the Lebanese developments will help. I think Arafat will lose his influence in favor of Saiqa. This will remove the PLO's veto over the actions of Syria. The danger is that Assad may be overthrown." On April 15, the secretary of state described Syria's role in Lebanon as "constructive." Under Kissinger's guidance, Washington had made a startling about-face on Assad's intervention. Kissinger's definition of "constructive" intervention would take on ominous overtones in early August.[23]

Although Syrian troops failed to bring an immediate end to the conflict, their intervention did relieve some pressure on Christian forces. The Phalangists used this opportunity to attack the besieged Palestinian refugee camp of Tal al-Za'atar on June 22, 1976—home to fifty thousand to sixty thousand refugees and the last holdout of Muslim control in East Beirut. Crushing the camp would, for all intents and purposes, complete the ethnic cleansing of the eastern suburbs. While Christian leaders claimed that the Palestinians had transformed the camp into a military fortress, the PLO insisted that it was still full of civilians. As Maronite artillery pounded the camp from the west, Syrian forces cut off supply routes to the east. Arafat was determined to make a stand in the camp, regardless of the price in blood. Tal al-Za'atar would be the PLO's Stalingrad, and it would send a message to the world. The camp's defenders would become martyrs to the Palestinian cause. The Phalangists were more than happy to give Arafat the slaughter he expected. As famine conditions took hold of the camp, attempts by the Red Cross to evacuate civilians were rebuffed. By mid-July, the camp's water supply had dwindled to a single working tap, salt water became the only means of sterilization, and doctors working in the camp were forced to resort to amputations to treat cases of gangrene and tetanus. After fifty-two days of bombardment, the camp fell to the attackers. Christian forces then moved in for an orgy of violence and looting. As a flood of unarmed refugees from the camp made their way to the crossing into West Beirut, they came under fire from Maronite militia. Between one thousand and two thousand men, women, children, and the elderly were shot or butchered by Christian forces as they fled the camp. Any survivors or wounded who remained inside the camp were buried alive by bulldozers that leveled the area soon after. No fewer than three thousand Palestinians, mostly civilians, were killed during the siege and fall of Tal al-Za'atar.[24]

The massacre at Tal al-Za'atar marked the violent climax of the first phase of the war. In the wake of the camp's fall, fighting between the PLO and the Syrians continued. One group of Palestinian guerrillas staged a suicidal attack on the Semiramis Hotel in Damascus. They managed to take several hostages before Syrian soldiers forced their way back into the building. The Assad regime then chose to make a public display of hanging the three prisoners—a warning to future militants. Meanwhile, Syrian forces in Lebanon continued their assault on Palestinian lines. Though they suffered heavy casualties, Assad's forces managed to push the PLO defenders back. The combatants were exhausted, however. On October 15, Arafat and Assad agreed to attend a summit in Riyadh, Saudi Arabia, and accepted a truce the following day. In Riyadh, the member states of the Arab League agreed to the creation of the Arab Deterrent Force (ADF) to serve as peacekeepers in Lebanon. Though the ADF was ostensibly a multilateral peacekeeping force, twenty-five thousand of its thirty thousand troops were Syrian soldiers. The Arab League now officially sanctioned Syria's military presence in Lebanon.[25] The message was clear: the broader Arab community had no desire to enter the Lebanese morass. If Assad wanted to bear that burden, he was welcome to do so. Lebanon was now a fractured state, broken up into Muslim, Christian, and Palestinian cantons, and simmering with ethnic resentments.

THE SOUTH LEBANON WAR

Even as the sectarian conflict raged in Beirut and on Mount Lebanon, the war between Israel and the PLO continued. Although the majority of the guerrillas had suspended overseas attacks, splinter groups of Palestinian fighters continued to wage what the United States and

Israel denounced as "international terrorism" operations. On June 27, 1976, a group of Palestinian and German guerrillas from a splinter faction of the PFLP hijacked an Air France flight from Tel Aviv to Paris after it made a stop in Athens. The gunmen redirected the airliner to Entebbe, in Uganda, and then forced the passengers into one of the airport terminals. Idi Amin's regime cooperated with the hijackers, and Ugandan soldiers were soon providing security for the group. After allowing the non-Israeli passengers to leave, the gunmen issued demands for the release of several dozen prisoners being held in Israel, Kenya, Switzerland, Germany, and France. While the Israeli cabinet deliberated over negotiating with the guerrillas, the Israel Defense Forces (IDF) laid plans for a daring rescue mission. On July 1, Prime Minister Yitzhak Rabin authorized the operation, which would depart two days later. Four C-130 cargo planes would make the eight-thousand-kilometer journey to Uganda along with a 150-man task force. Using the radar echo of a British transport plane to mask its identity, the first Israeli plane landed at 11:00 p.m. The lead commando unit, wearing black face paint and dressed in Ugandan army uniforms, stormed the terminal, killing several of the guerrillas and a dozen Ugandan soldiers. In less than a minute, the IDF commandos had taken control of the terminal and the hostages inside it. Three of the hostages were killed in the firefight along with one Israeli soldier, Yonatan Netanyahu, brother of future prime minister Benjamin Netanyahu. A fourth hostage, who had been hospitalized prior to the raid, was later killed in retaliation for the operation. At 12:41 a.m., the C-130s were in the air, along with the freed hostages and the Israeli commandos, on their way back to Israel.[26]

Although the Entebbe Raid seized headlines and became an instant legend in the annals of counterterrorism operations, the focus of Israel's war with the PLO had shifted to South Lebanon. While the north and west, the areas above Israel's declared red line, fell under the shadow of the Syrian occupation, the south remained a wild no-man's-land of Palestinian commandos, rogue Christian warlords, and frequent Israeli military strikes. PLO fighters had pulled back south of the red line after the creation of the ADF. In the south, the guerrillas enjoyed freedom of movement and close proximity to targets in Israel. But the influx of Palestinian commandos angered Christians and Shi'ites in the south. Among the former were Christian soldiers who had deserted the Lebanese Army after it began to break apart in 1976. Eager to bring these rogue soldiers back under government control, the Lebanese General Staff sent Maj. Saad Haddad to the south with orders to reassemble the forces. A Greek Catholic from Marjayoun, Haddad quickly built a following that he formed into the Free Lebanon Army (FLA). Largely cut off from the central government in Beirut, Haddad's forces were able to operate with considerable autonomy. Israeli leaders recognized Haddad and his soldiers as potential allies in the war against the PLO and soon began providing weapons and supplies to the FLA. By using Haddad's forces to harry the Palestinians, Israel could relieve pressure on its northern flank. By the fall of 1976, South Lebanon had become a battlefield between Palestinian fighters and Haddad's Christian army.[27] With Israeli assistance, Haddad established a "fiefdom" in South Lebanon. Under Haddad's and Israel's patronage, the area was transformed into a lawless borderland: Israeli-registered cars passed signs in Hebrew as they traversed new roads cut along invasion routes, shopkeepers stocked Israeli beer, and an Israeli-backed warlord (Haddad) held power.[28]

Israel was poised to take an even harder line against Lebanon and the PLO. On May 17, 1977, the political tides in Israel shifted. The Labor Party, which had been in power for almost thirty years, was defeated in national elections by the right-wing Likud Party. At the head of Likud sat sixty-three-year-old Menachem Begin. Begin's appearance—slight, balding, with a face partially hidden by thick eyeglasses—masked a fearsome political leader. Born in Russia in 1913, he had lost both parents and a brother in the Holocaust. The horrors of Nazi Europe nurtured an intense strain of Zionism in the young man. After being sent to Palestine in 1942, he chose to join the Irgun, an underground militant Jewish organization. Following the end of World War II, the Irgun, now under Begin's command, began a bloody guerrilla war against the British imperial authorities in Palestine. The organization gained infamy in 1946, when it bombed the King David Hotel in Jerusalem, killing ninety-one Arabs, British, and Jews. After Israel declared independence in 1948, Begin emerged as a leading right-wing politician. As the head of Likud, he promoted an expansionist policy in favor of creating a "Greater Israel" that would include Judea and Samaria (ancient territories now designated as the Palestinian-controlled lands along the West Bank of the Jordan River) and parts of the Kingdom of Jordan on the East Bank. "The right of the Jewish people to the Land of Israel is eternal," Likud's manifesto explained. "Judea and Samaria shall therefore not be relinquished to foreign rule; between the sea and the Jordan [River], there will be Jewish sovereignty alone." Any Israeli withdrawal from this territory or the creation of a Palestinian state would "endanger the existence of the State of Israel." This stance amounted to an unequivocal rejection of a Palestinian state.[29]

Paradoxically, it would be Begin, the hard-line Likud leader, who would take the biggest strides toward peace with Israel's largest and most powerful neighbor, Egypt. Since the 1973 war, the Arab-Israeli peace process had been advancing by fits and starts. Nixon's secretary of state, Henry Kissinger, had negotiated the Sinai II Accords on the eve of the Lebanese Civil War, and the new president, Jimmy Carter, hoped to achieve similar success. Begin's electoral victory in 1977 stalled the process. With the former commander of the Irgun in power in Israel, the prospects for peace looked bleak. In the midst of the deadlock, Egyptian president Anwar el-Sadat took a bold gamble. On November 9, 1977, he announced his willingness to go to Israel and speak on the floor of the Israeli Knesset in Jerusalem in order to make the case for peace. It was an unprecedented offer of enormous symbolic significance: no major Arab head of state had paid an official visit to Jerusalem since Israel's birth in 1948. In response,

Begin invited Sadat to the Knesset, and ten days later, the Egyptian president appeared. The move not only marked the resumption of the political process that would eventually lead to the signing of a peace treaty between Egypt and Israel in 1979 but also transformed the structures of geopolitical power in the Middle East. Although the rapprochement between Egypt and Israel effectively removed Cairo from the regional conflict—as well as playing an important role in Sadat's 1981 assassination—it did nothing to address the PLO's grievances. Coupled with Begin's rejection of the Palestinian right to self-determination, Egypt's departure all but guaranteed the resumption of hostilities between Israel and the PLO.

On March 11, 1978, Fatah guerrillas struck at the very heart of Israel. A group of eleven guerrillas commanded by Dalal Mughrabi, a nineteen-year-old woman whose family had fled Jaffa, landed in two Zodiac inflatable boats on a beach fifteen miles south of Haifa. There, they encountered and gunned down an American photographer, Gail Rubin, before moving up to the coastal highway above the beach. The guerrillas managed to stop and hijack a tour bus full of Israelis and headed for Tel Aviv. As the bus sped down the highway, the Palestinians fired their weapons and tossed grenades at passing cars. Israeli police stormed the bus after it crashed into a barricade. Dozens of passengers were killed in the firefight—in all, thirty-five Israelis and nine Palestinians died in what came to be known as the Coastal Road Massacre. Israeli commentators lamented it as the worst terrorist attack in their nation's history. The PLO claimed responsibility for the operation, citing the need to continue its armed struggle against Israel. The Palestinian fighters refused to be ignored or forgotten. If there would not be peace, there would be war.[30]

That war came three days later, when Israel sent twenty-five thousand troops across the border into Lebanon to root out and destroy the suspected perpetrators. Operation Litani, the IDF's name for the invasion, was designed, in Begin's words, "to root out the evil weed of the PLO." In order to keep its own casualties down, the IDF relied on heavy armor and artillery to blast away any potential resistance. The result, predictably, was heavy civilian casualties. While the IDF shelled towns and villages, Haddad's soldiers terrorized the population. In one of the grisliest episodes of the invasion, Christian forces aligned with the Israelis rounded up dozens of Shi'ite men, women, and children; forced them into a mosque in the village of Khiam; and massacred them with machine guns. Faced with the threats of marauding Christian warlords and the Israeli bombardment, tens of thousands of refugees took to the roads. By some estimates, the invasion killed two thousand Lebanese and Palestinians, nearly all of them civilians, and created a quarter million refugees. Many of these would move north, to the ring of shantytowns that surrounded Beirut. This exodus from South Lebanon would help energize the growing Shi'ite minority in Lebanon, which would rise to the forefront of national politics in the years to come. In the meantime, the Israelis had created a "security belt" along the border, controlled by Haddad's forces and peacekeepers from the UN Interim Force in Lebanon (UNIFIL). But they had not seriously weakened the PLO. The majority of its fighters had moved north along with the refugees. "So why did Israel invade?" asked British journalist Robert Fisk. The "real meaning of this bloody little adventure," he explained, would only become clear four years later.[31]

ALTHOUGH FEW OBSERVERS RECOGNIZED IT AT THE time, the civil war in Lebanon was a prologue to a larger series of upheavals that was about to grip Southwest Asia. The changing contours of the Arab-Israeli conflict and the shifting geopolitical balance in the Middle East had unleashed a new power struggle for leadership among the major Arab states. At the same time, the ongoing collapse of Third World communism on the battlefields of Southeast Asia was sapping the appeal of left-wing political forces around much of the postcolonial world. As time would tell, sectarian violence of the sort taking place in Lebanon and the specter of state collapse would become increasingly familiar. Both these forces would complicate the continuing superpower struggle for influence in the Cold War borderlands of southern Asia. Indeed, the world community was about to receive an even greater shock, in the form of a theocratic revolution across the southern frontiers of the Soviet Union, in Iran.

THE IRANIAN REVOLUTION

1978–1979

As the 1970s drew to a close, the forces of sectarian revolution gained a second foothold in the Middle East in the Imperial State of Iran. If the Lebanese Civil War hinted at the coming transformation in Third World politics, the revolution in Iran thundered the arrival of a new era. It was not the sort of revolution that was supposed to happen in the late 1970s. For as long as nearly anyone could remember, revolutionaries had been Marxists, anarchists, or nationalists. They were driven by dreams of overthrowing conservative regimes and leading their nations toward new, quasi-utopian futures. They were, almost without fail, secular. But it had become clear that the revolution unfolding in Iran was not following that script. What began in 1978 as a broad-based movement in opposition to Shah Mohammed Reza Pahlavi's monarchical rule had grown into something drastically different. As the world watched, a fearsome new force seized power in Tehran, in the form of a revolutionary theocratic regime led by the Ayatollah Ruhollah Khomeini. To many in the West, the revolution in Iran seemed like a scene from the fifteenth century rather than the twentieth. As one member of President Jimmy Carter's national security staff wrote, "the notion of a popular revolution leading to the establishment of a theocratic state seemed so unlikely as to be absurd."[1] But as observers around the world would soon learn, the Iranian Revolution was a thoroughly modern phenomenon. The forces of political Islam, long submerged beneath the currents of secular nationalism and Marxism, were about to surge once again to the surface.

Even more than Lebanon, Iran occupied a central position along the outer frontiers of the Cold War. Along with Saudi Arabia, Iran served as one of Washington's "twin pillars" in the Middle East, a bastion of pro-Western power in an otherwise troublesome region. Guarding the southern frontier of the Soviet Union, Iran stood as a bulwark against Communist expansion. Since 1953, the Shah had served as a key U.S. security partner. This relationship had grown stronger under the Nixon administration, which began sending top-shelf weapons systems and massive infusions of U.S. economic aid to Tehran. The regime used U.S. security aid to repress domestic opposition and tighten its brutal hold over Iranian society.[2] But no amount of American guns or cash could save the Shah from the coming storm. In the thirteen months between January 1978 and February 1979, a popular revolution would sweep the Shah from power and transform Washington's key partner in the region into one of its bitterest enemies.

THE MAKING OF THE SHAH'S REGIME

Tehran sits on a plain in the north-central part of Iran, beneath a ridge of snow-capped mountains that separate the city from the waters of the Caspian Sea. Designated the capital of Iran by the Qajar dynasty in 1795 and rebuilt by Reza Shah in the 1920s, the city experienced steady growth through the twentieth century. By the 1970s, with Reza Shah's son Mohammed Reza ruling the country, Tehran had blossomed into a bustling metropolis just coming to terms with wealth from rising oil prices. Dozens of gray high-rises pierced the skyline, their concrete walls sheltering offices and apartments. Automobiles careened through the congested streets below, forcing motorcycles to dodge pedestrians on the crowded sidewalks. The din from the traffic drifted into elegant restaurants serving European cuisine. The city's elite enjoyed evenings at the opera or the ballet, while the less affluent took in American films at one of Tehran's cinemas. Such distractions remained out of reach for the residents of the sprawling labyrinth of tenements that ringed the southern edges of the city, however. Thousands of Iranians had abandoned the countryside to crowd into the growing cities. Outside the capital, amid the arid hills, many Iranians lived in houses made of baked clay. A majority of the population remained illiterate and impoverished. Iranian society was changing rapidly, however. Although wealth remained concentrated in the hands of the few, the nation's oil industry, government reforms and education programs, a ballooning economy, and a large, secular middle class were fast transforming the country.[3]

Ninety miles to the south, across the dry central plateau, the ancient city of Qom rose out of the desert. After describing its "blue tiled domes and golden minarets twinkling in the light," a British visitor wrote, "I often thought this was what our own European cities must have looked like in the Middle Ages." As one drew nearer, however, slums appeared on the outskirts, their streets lined by steel-shuttered shops. The heart of the city was an oasis of green trees, turquoise mosques, seminaries, and public squares. Though only a two-hour trip by car, Qom seemed a world away from the busy streets of the capital. While Iran's seat of political power lay in Tehran, Qom was the center of Shia religious authority in the nation. Whereas Tehran was the Shah's city, Qom belonged to the clerics. While few observers foresaw it, the tension between the two cities was about to produce a revolution that would transform international affairs in the coming decades.[4]

Things might have been very different. In the early 1950s, Iran appeared to be heading away from the Shah's authoritarianism and toward democracy. Tehran was home to one of the postcolonial world's brightest luminaries: Prime Minister Mohammed Mossadegh. For the last several years, Mossadegh had been engaged in a bitter stand-off with the British-owned Anglo-Iranian Oil Company (AIOC), which controlled the majority of Iran's oil industry. The prime minister was convinced that, in order to develop Iran's economy and bring the nation into the modern world, the government needed to establish control over its own natural resources. The revenue from Iran's oil industry, he concluded, would fund the modernization of the country. The British had no intention of liquidating their assets, however. In the wake of failed negotiations in 1951, Mossadegh nationalized the AIOC. While it proved popular on the streets of Tehran, the prime minister's move angered British leaders and raised concerns in Washington that Iran might be drifting toward the Soviet orbit. By 1953, tensions had reached a boiling point. The new Eisenhower administration resolved to take decisive action, authorizing CIA agents to launch a coup against the regime in Tehran.

Kermit Roosevelt, a thirty-seven-year-old CIA political officer and grandson of President Theodore Roosevelt, took point in the operation aimed at overthrowing Iran's first democratically elected leader. Working alongside British intelligence, Roosevelt and his fellow CIA officers manufactured a crisis by disseminating false propaganda attacks against religious and opposition leaders in order to give the impression that the regime was cracking down on dissent and by inciting antigovernment protests in the capital. Meanwhile, CIA officers coordinated with conservative officers in the Iranian military to launch a coup against Mossadegh. On August 19, 1953, four days after a failed first attempt, CIA-backed military officers arrested the prime minister. The officers then returned the Shah, who had fled to Baghdad to wait out the results of the coup, to power in Tehran. Having toppled Mossadegh, Washington and London restructured Iran's oil industry, splitting it up among five American, one British, and one French company. For Roosevelt and his bosses in the Eisenhower administration, the coup seemed almost too good to be true. The

United States had removed a troublesome government for the cost of a few million dollars without putting any American lives at risk. It was quite a bargain—or so it seemed at the time.[5]

Indeed, it appeared that Eisenhower and the CIA had purchased a valuable friend in a heavily contested region. For the next quarter century, the Shah functioned as a pro-American bastion in the Middle East. Under Richard Nixon, Iran emerged alongside Saudi Arabia as one of America's "twin pillars" in the Middle East: reliable, wealthy, pro-Western allies upon which Washington hoped to build a wider regional policy. During these years, U.S. officials deployed an array of reassuring metaphors for Iran's lack of domestic turmoil— Iran was an "island," an "oasis," and a "pillar" of political stability. While states such as Egypt, Syria, and Iraq leaned toward the Soviet Union and maintained hostile relations with Israel, the Shah's regime could be counted on to back American power in the region. Perhaps even more important, the Shah, along with the Saudi monarchy, helped guarantee a ready supply of cheap petroleum into the global market. In return, the United States furnished the Shah's army with some of the world's most advanced military technology. By the mid-1970s, Washington and Tehran were engaged in arms deals worth an estimated $50 billion. The Nixon and Ford administrations gave the regime access to state-of-the-art military equipment, including F-14 and F-16 fighter planes and Airborne Warning and Control System (AWACS) electronic surveillance aircraft. Perched atop enormous reserves of crude oil and boasting a formidable army outfitted with advanced American weapons systems, the Shah seemed to be in an almost unassailable position.[6]

If this was not enough, the regime also held an iron grip on Iran's domestic political scene. The Shah tolerated no dissent and kept a watchful eye on his citizens. To do this, the regime created a secret police service, Sazman-i Etela'at va Amniyat-i Keshvar, more commonly known as SAVAK, which employed some sixty thousand agents throughout the country. Some observers estimated that, at its height, the service involved one in three Iranian males as either an agent or an informant. Iranian citizens lived in fear of the agency, which was infamous for employing an array of vicious torture techniques. Stories of prisoners being beaten, burned with cigarettes, and electrocuted were only the tamest reports from SAVAK's interrogation rooms. Inside one police installation, a Western journalist discovered a machine that used a deli meat slicer to shave off prisoners' hands. In another cell, the reporter found a pile of arms. A third cell contained human remains floating in acid. As the guardians of Washington's client in the region, some SAVAK agents received training in the United States. SAVAK also maintained extensive ties to the Israeli intelligence service, the Mossad, which included training and joint operations that had taken place since the Iranian organization's creation in the late 1950s.[7]

While the Shah's blanket of political repression fell across the country, there was one center of power that the regime could not afford to crush: the Shia clergy. Based in the holy city of Qom, in the desiccated stretches of north-central Iran, the Shia religious leadership occupied a central place in Iranian society. The rise of the Pahlavi dynasty did little to change this. While the Shah could strike against secular political groups, the elite clergy remained largely untouched. The result was the creation of a sort of dual authority in Iran: one religious in the form of the Shia clergy, and one secular in the form of the Shah's regime. Beneath the edifice of state power lay a sprawling network of religious authority that extended into every corner of Iranian society. Peasants and tribal groups in the countryside, urban workers, the shop owners of the country's bazaars, military conscripts— all were linked to the structure of religious power emanating out of Qom. While the majority of Iran's Islamic leadership came to accept the Shah's rule, a handful of clerics still resented the Shah's heavy-handed assertion of secular authority. For the time being, however, the Shah reigned supreme.[8]

In January 1963, the regime entered its tenth year of iron-fisted rule in Iran. Mossadegh remained under house arrest, SAVAK's repression had scattered domestic opposition groups, and Tehran's relationship with the United States was strong. Iron-fisted autocracy was not enough for the Shah, however. He wished to transform his country into a modern, industrialized powerhouse in the Middle East. To this end, he launched an ambitious new development program dubbed the "White Revolution" to modernize Iranian society. At its heart, the program contained a sweeping land reform campaign designed to break up the power of the old aristocracy and redistribute property to Iran's peasantry. In addition, the Shah proposed industrial reforms, women's suffrage, and literacy programs. While officials in Washington found much to praise in the White Revolution, a wide variety of groups in Iran objected. Elites opposed land reform that would break up their estates; the clerics opposed giving greater political power to women and the regime's efforts to interfere with religious schools; and liberals argued that the program did nothing to address the country's oppressive political atmosphere.[9]

The most prominent voice of protest against the White Revolution came from one of the country's clerics, Ruhollah Musavi Khomeini. At sixty years of age, the sharp-eyed religious scholar cut an imposing figure. Known as one of the more radical clerics in Qom, he had become a rising star by the early 1960s. Khomeini feared that, if successful, the Shah's reforms would weaken the power of the clergy in Iranian society. He warned his fellow clerics that the Shah's plans were "threatening the foundation of Islam," and he insisted that the religious leadership was "duty-bound to resist him." Though it opposed open resistance, the religious establishment chose to boycott the national referendum on the White Revolution, scheduled for January 26, 1963. The regime responded with a public relations blitz. Two days before the referendum, the Shah and a military retinue journeyed to Qom to address a crowd of supporters, many of whom were bused in from Tehran. After extolling the virtues of his land reforms, the Shah looked up from his prepared speech. "Black [i.e., clerical] reaction understands nothing," he told the crowd; "its brain has not moved for a thousand years." Conservative clergy who opposed his reforms were "stupid men" who "don't want to see this country develop." Two days later, Iranians voted to approve the White Revolution's measures and the regime declared a triumphal success. But the struggle with the clerics was only just beginning.[10]

In further protest against the Shah's reforms, the clergy announced that it would not join in the celebration of Nowruz, the Iranian New Year, on March 21, 1963. The Shah's "tyrannical regime," Khomeini thundered, had violated "the sanctity of Islamic laws." Khomeini now came under close scrutiny by state security forces. The cleric and the Shah were on a collision course. On June 3, Khomeini denounced the Shah in a widely publicized address as a "wretched, miserable man," and called upon the leader to abandon the White Revolution. Government agents in the crowd recorded the speech and relayed it to the authorities. Two days later, in the predawn hours of June 5, SAVAK agents raided Khomeini's home. He was absent, but officers were able to trace him to his son's house, where he surrendered peacefully. As news of the arrest circulated through Qom, thousands of protestors poured onto the streets. The Shah responded by declaring martial law, but it was not enough to quell the violence. The following day, army tanks parked in front of government buildings as thousands of demonstrators assembled throughout the country. Soldiers were ordered to fire on protestors who threatened the regime. A CIA report on the incident noted that the troops "performed well and showed no hesitancy in firing on the mobs when necessary." While exact figures do not exist, police records indicate no fewer than 380 killed or wounded. Khomeini was imprisoned for ten months before being released in April 1964. Arrest and incarceration had not cowed the cleric, however. Khomeini seized headlines again in October by denouncing the regime's decision to extend diplomatic immunity to American military personnel working in Iran. "They can no longer call us reactionary," he told his comrades. "The point is that we are fighting against America. All the world's freedom-fighters will support us on this issue. We must use it as a weapon to attack the regime so that the whole nation will realise that this Shah is an American agent and this is an American plot."

It was the last straw. One week later, SAVAK agents arrested Khomeini and drove him directly to Tehran's airport, where they placed him on a plane to Turkey. He would spend the next fourteen years in exile.[11]

"THINKING THE UNTHINKABLE"

Having banished Khomeini, the Shah appeared to have regained the upper hand. Though certainly a nuisance, the so-called Black Reactionaries were not considered by the regime to be a serious threat. The Shah, like his patrons in Washington, was convinced that the greater danger came from Communist agents and secular revolutionaries. While SAVAK occupied itself with cracking down on dissent and chasing left-wing guerrillas with ties to the Palestine Liberation Organization, the White Revolution continued with uneven results. The regime's land reform program sputtered and was eventually terminated in 1971. Traditional elites maintained their opposition to the reforms, while those who benefited from the new polices—primarily wealthy businessmen—felt little loyalty to the regime. Larger transformations were afoot, however. Sparked by the 1973 Arab oil embargo, petroleum prices had skyrocketed. As revenue from Iran's oil industry soared, cash poured into the country. While this deluge seemed positive, it unleashed dangerous economic instability. Rampant inflation and financial volatility accompanied rising petroleum prices and threw Iran's economy into turmoil. The rising cost of living coupled with regressive income taxes choked the working class and fueled dangerous resentments among a wide cross-section of Iranian society. By 1975, the nation found itself at the beginning of a mounting economic crisis. While the Shah's hold on power was still strong, the currents of change were pulling Iran in a new direction.

On the afternoon of January 7, 1978, the Tehran newspaper *Ettela'at* published an article accusing Khomeini of collusion with British colonialists against the regime. The cleric, it charged, was a paid agent of British oil interests intent on undermining the Shah's modernization plans. Though hackneyed, the article set off a furor in Qom. During his exile, Khomeini had widened his following through published writings and recorded sermons that were smuggled into Iran. Even as the Shah maintained his grip on power in Tehran, Khomeini's influence spread through the country. Seminary students interpreted the attack on Khomeini as an attack on the clergy and, more broadly, on Islam. They resolved to stage a series of protests against the article and the regime. Tensions mounted over the next two days, culminating in a riot in which protestors, armed with stones and iron bars, rampaged through the streets of Qom, destroying shops and storming a police station. After their warnings to the crowd went unheeded, police opened fire, killing at least five students. The so-called Qom massacre became a rallying point for opposition forces throughout the country. The massacre cast the regime in a violent struggle against the clergy and the more than nine thousand mosques and religious institutions it controlled. From this massive, nationwide power base, a religious revolution was set to burst forth.[12]

While Khomeini, living in Paris, praised the protestors, religious leaders inside Iran urged caution and implored the students to observe the Arba'een, the traditional forty-day-period of mourning, in the hope of allowing tempers to cool. The U.S. ambassador in Tehran, William Sullivan, warned that the Shia movement was among the best organized in the country. While officials in the Pahlavi regime dismissed the clerics as ignorant, backward, or "crypto communists," Sullivan argued that Khomeini's supporters should not be underestimated. "The Islamic establishment is neither as weak nor as ignorant as the Shah's [government] and some western observers would portray it," he wrote. "It has a far better grip on the emotions of the people and on the money of the Bazaar than any other groups." It was, moreover, resistant to Communist control. Khomeini's movement would be equally resistant, however, to Western influence.[13]

Following the end of the mourning period, on February 18, demonstrators again took to the streets in cities across the country. Protests turned violent in Tabriz, where crowds clashed with soldiers and police, who killed thirteen and left hundreds wounded. Observers in the American consulate noted that the demonstrators appeared to be well coordinated. Banks and government buildings were ransacked along with cinemas and the local Pepsi-Cola plant. The "mob," they reported, "and the whole disaffected class of people from whom the mob spring have once again become a potent weapon to use against the regime."[14] Rather than cooling the protestors' rage, the mourning periods fueled resentments and gave space for added coordination. At the end of March, protests erupted yet again, with violence in Tehran, Isfahan, and Yazd. Dozens of protestors were killed when police opened fire on the crowds. Following the next Arba'een, clashes returned to Qom, where the Shah's security forces killed more demonstrators. The clashes subsided in June as tempers cooled and the demonstrators came to recognize that the forty-day cycles had given the regime a tactical advantage in its ability to make preparations. No one could have prepared for what came next, however. On August 19, 1978, flames engulfed the Rex Cinema in Abadan. Three hundred seventy people perished in the inferno. While both the regime and the opposition flung recriminations at one another, investigations later suggested that Islamic militants had locked the emergency exits. For many Iranians, however, the fire was the last straw. In the days following the catastrophe, the ranks of protestors swelled, and the regime was forced to place ten cities under martial law. The opposition had grown from a movement of discontented seminary students to encompass a broad section of Iranian society.[15]

The Shah scrambled to defuse the mounting demonstrations by calling for greater democratization, granting amnesty to hundreds of political prisoners, and forming a new government. But it was too late to dam the torrent of opposition. The Eid al-Fitr celebrations, in early September, brought tens of thousands onto the streets in cities throughout the country, alongside demonstrators calling for the Shah's abdication. By September 7, the crowds in Tehran had grown to half a million. In desperation, the Shah placed the capital under martial law. The battle commenced the following morning. Helicopter gunships swooped over the shantytowns in the south while protestors threw up barricades throughout the city. Jaleh Square sat at the epicenter of the clashes as thousands of students, surrounded by government tanks and commandos, staged a sit-down protest. After failed attempts to disperse the crowds, security forces opened fire. Once the smoke cleared, the regime announced eighty-seven killed. Demonstrators claimed that more than four thousand had been slaughtered. In the words of one scholar, September 8, or Black Friday, as it soon came to be known, "placed a sea of blood between the Shah and the people . . . and left the country with two simple choices: a drastic revolution or a military counterrevolution."[16] Iranian journalists warned U.S. officials not to dismiss Khomeini as irrational or a puppet of foreign interests—the Ayatollah had more "influence over the masses than the Shah." As xenophobia and suspicion of outsiders grew, the United States was in a "no-win situation." The creation of an Islamic state, Iranian journalists insisted, was now "guaranteed."[17]

Another Arba'een followed the Black Friday massacre. While government forces prepared for the worst, opposition leaders turned their attention to a less confrontational form of rebellion: general strikes. The day after the Black Friday killings, workers at the Tehran oil refinery walked out. By the beginning of October, observers counted thirty-six active strikes. By November, businesses and facilities across the country had shut down. Journalists, airline workers, and customs officials struck alongside rail workers and laborers at power plants.

Even bankers staged intermittent strikes. From exile, Khomeini cheered the workers on: "From now on, it is time for all of us to close our businesses, not forever but for the short time it will take to overthrow the ruling oppressors! Do not hurry to re-open shops and factories." On November 4, students battled with police at the gates of Tehran University. Once again, the regime claimed that only a handful were killed while rumors spread through the streets of thousands dead. Protestors responded by torching buildings in the capital. The Shah tried to calm the protests even as he formed a military government and unleashed state security forces on the demonstrators. "I cannot but approve the revolution of the nation of Iran," he announced in a televised speech. Promising to enact a new constitution, he told viewers, "I have heard the message of your revolution, nation of Iran."[18]

On the heels of the clashes at Tehran University, Ambassador Sullivan sent a cable to his superiors titled "Thinking the Unthinkable." There was a very real possibility, he wrote, that the Shah might not survive—it was time to consider reaching out to Khomeini. The ambassador received no reply. Meanwhile, CIA analysts warned that Khomeini's influence "is now so strong that neither other clerics nor civilian opposition leaders will take actions he opposes." The State Department's intelligence office gave an even bleaker assessment: the regime could not survive in its current form. If the Shah hoped to arrest Iran's "descent into chaos," he must either accept the role of constitutional monarch or abdicate. Although short-term repression was inevitable, in the long run, a crackdown "will lead to even greater violence and risks the total collapse of authority and the radicalization of Iranian politics."[19] But what might come next remained a matter of open debate. The CIA warned, "No single group or coalition gives any promise of a genuinely democratic government should it come to power. . . . [I]t would lack the power to impose its will, it would be inexperienced and dependent on the same bureaucracy that has failed the Shah, and it would be a constant target for other ambitious elements, including the military." In December 1978, the

Agency reported that, although they lacked the resources to stage a coup themselves, Iranian Communists "could make rapid gains" if the government collapsed.[20]

As the Shah's regime sped toward collapse, a power struggle was under way inside the Carter administration. Secretary of State Cyrus Vance was fighting a losing battle for the administration's foreign policy against National Security Advisor Zbigniew Brzezinski. A skilled bureaucratic infighter, Brzezinski, the Democratic Party's answer to Henry Kissinger, had gained the upper hand. While Vance and the State Department advocated moderation, Brzezinski and the NSC pushed for a hard-line approach. The Shah, Brzezinski was convinced, should unleash the full force of his military upon the protestors and crush the opposition. This analysis ran at odds with reports from observers in Tehran such as Ambassador Sullivan. The Shah himself had expressed doubt that further use of force would prove effective against the demonstrations. "After watching his troops kill over ten thousand of his own people in the streets of Iran's cities," scholar James Bill wrote, "the shah determined that violent tactics were doomed to fail." Brzezinski had no use for such indecision, however. Having been outmaneuvered in Washington, Vance, Sullivan, and the State Department were forced to watch as "Brzezinski and his staff arrogantly shaped a policy that placed America on the losing side in a revolution."[21]

Unsatisfied with Sullivan's reports from Tehran, Brzezinski chose to dispatch his own emissary for a second opinion: air force general Robert "Dutch" Huyser. Not surprisingly, the general's views conflicted with those of the ambassador. Where Sullivan saw a military on the brink of collapse, Huyser saw a force that was strong enough to restore order. While the ambassador argued that Khomeini enjoyed wide support, the general estimated that only 10 to 20 percent of Iranians backed the Ayatollah. Also, Huyser was more concerned about the potential for the Soviets to take advantage of the situation: "[I]f Iran became an Islamic Republic," he warned, "it would eventually end up in the Communist camp." Although Huyser and Sullivan had a cordial working relationship, Huyser's presence in Iran sent a clear signal that Carter did not fully support his ambassador. "While Sullivan was the best informed American official concerning the Iranian situation," Iranian dissidents later complained, "his views were ignored in Washington because they were bad news (*akhbar-i bad*) and therefore unacceptable." Spending most of his time with the Shah's military forces, Huyser had not even managed to meet opposition leaders. To many Iranians, the Huyser mission seemed yet another indication of Washington's unwavering support for the Shah. Carter's public pronouncements made the situation worse. "We have historic friendships with Iran," the president announced in late October. "I think they are a great stabilizing force in their part of the world." As late as December 12, 1978, Carter announced his expectation that the monarch would maintain power in Tehran: "The shah has our support and he also has our confidence." Behind closed doors, however, U.S. officials warned that he had "only a marginal chance of surviving."[22]

As December began, the Shah's reign entered its final weeks. Thousands of demonstrators took to the streets to commemorate the Shia holy days of Tasu'a and Ashura on December 10–11. While opposition leaders feared that a harsh military crackdown would create a bloodbath, the Shah chose not to unleash the army on the protestors. Scholars disagree as to why he made that choice. James Bill suggests that a massive crackdown would likely have led the army to disintegrate. Historian Said Arjomand, however, argues that the military was probably the stablest institution in Iran. In contrast to military forces in other revolutions, the Shah's forces did not unravel: they remained intact and loyal to the monarchy until well after the leader's departure. Surely, Arjomand argues, the military would have moved mercilessly against protestors if so ordered. Historian Charles Kurzman suggests that the answer lies in the person of the Shah himself. Although he built a ruthless regime, the Shah had proved indecisive at key moments in Iranian history, such as with Mossade-gh's challenge in the early 1950s and the Khomeinist revolt in 1963. Added to this, the Shah was well aware that his life was drawing to an end as the growing cancer in his body took its toll. Kurzman also argues that the Shah's strategy was somewhat more nuanced than often acknowledged. The regime sought to provide both carrots and sticks to protestors. If the demonstrations ceased, dissidents could expect reforms. If they remained on the streets, they could expect more violence of the type routinely seen over the course of 1978. Finally, the Shah would have recognized that repression had its limits: there were simply too many protestors, and too much of the country was in a state of upheaval.[23]

"A PERSONALITY CULT WAS IN THE MAKING"

Tears formed in the corners of the Shah's eyes as he delivered his last address in his home country near the imperial pavilion of Tehran's Mehrabad Airport on January 16, 1979. Clad in a suit and overcoat against the winter cold, the ruler addressed a small group of government officials and military leaders. "I hope the Government will be able to make amends for the past and also succeed in laying the foundation for the future," he told the group. Two members of the palace guard bent to kiss his shoes before he boarded a plane to Egypt for an "extended vacation." The news of the Shah's departure sent a shock wave through Tehran as joyful throngs crowded the streets, weeping and throwing flowers at soldiers. Two weeks later, on the morning of February 1, 1979, the seventy-eight-year-old Khomeini stepped off an Air France jet and onto Iranian territory. "Our final victory will come when all foreigners are out of the country," he told the cheering crowd in the terminal. "I beg God to cut off the hands of all evil foreigners and all their helpers." Millions more packed along the streets as the Ayatollah traveled through Tehran. State censors blocked the broadcast of Khomeini's arrival, airing a picture of the Shah instead.[24]

"A personality cult was in the making," Khomeini's biographer wrote; "overnight Khomeini had been transformed into a semi-divine figure." Four days later, he appeared for his first public address. "This is not an ordinary government," he told the audience. "It is a government based on the *shari'a*. . . . Revolt against God's government is a revolt against God. Revolt against God is blasphemy." The Ayatollah's statement was one of the first clear indications of his intention to create a theocratic state in Iran. But moderates within the revolution (liberals, middle-class professionals, and the left) paid little heed to Khomeini's words. Instead, the nation focused on the rapid disintegration of the Shah's regime. Robbed of the monarch, the edifice of government power quickly crumbled. On February 8, a large group of members of the air force declared their allegiance to Khomeini, prompting the Shah's imperial guard to attack the rebels. The clashes quickly escalated to a general conflict between remaining loyalists in the military and revolutionaries who feared that the military might launch a coup to restore the old regime. In a last-ditch effort to regain control of the situation, Prime Minister Shapour Bakhtiar declared a dusk-to-dawn curfew. In response, Khomeini commanded his followers to challenge the government order and called for a jihad against loyalist military units. The following morning, the military brass decided to stand down "in order to prevent further disorder and bloodshed." Government troops were ordered back to their bases, and any serious hope of restoring the regime vanished.[25]

Still rooted in a Cold War mind-set, American officials worried about the potential for Communist forces to benefit from the revolution. In mid-January, the CIA had warned that "radical elements" were increasingly active among the revolutionaries. Although conservative religious forces were dominant, the left could become a greater threat in the future. State Department officers also worried about links between the left-wing Iranian Mujahideen-e-Khalq and Palestinian revolutionaries. Other reports suggested that, given Khomeini's personal aversion to Marxism, the revolution was not likely to take a leftward turn. Indeed, the revolution was going in a very different direction. Khomeini had ordered the arrest of all senior officials in the Pahlavi regime, and rumors of mass executions began to circulate. For every publicized execution, dozens of other former officials were reportedly rounded up and shot. Meanwhile, Khomeini had ramped up his anti-American rhetoric. "Dissolution, chaos, and violence are hallmarks of today's politics in Iran," Sullivan wrote.[26]

With the institutions of the old regime in ruins, the victorious opposition set about building the new state. But one final obstacle remained to Khomeini's goal of creating an Islamic state in Iran: his secular allies within the revolution. While the clerics rightfully claimed a central place in the revolutionary regime, moderate, secular elements were well represented, at least initially. In the months following the Shah's departure, however, Khomeini and his supporters moved steadily to consolidate his hold on the reins of power. While the Interim Government of Iran under Mehdi Bazargan held official power, Khomeini's Council of the Islamic Revolution functioned as a sort of "parallel" government, passing its own laws, extending control over the courts, and fielding a military force in the Revolutionary Guard. The weak and divided moderate forces within the revolution had little chance against the Khomeinists' coordinated campaign to seize power.[27] All the while, Khomeini continued his insistence that Iran become an Islamic republic. In June, the Ayatollah blasted his secular critics among the intelligentsia. "Those who did not participate in this movement have no right to advance any claims," he argued. "It was the mosques that created this Revolution, the mosques that brought this movement into being." Khomeini continued to enjoy overwhelming popular support. A national referendum held in March (which was boycotted by some of its opponents) showed 98 percent of voters in favor of creating an Islamic republic. Bazargan later claimed that the "clergy supplanted us and succeeded in taking over the country." The secular political parties "went to sleep after the revolution." The years of repression under the Shah had left Iran's secular opposition severely weakened. By the end of the Shah's reign, the clergy represented the only organized voice of opposition strong enough to consolidate control over the new regime.[28]

The revolution's religious turn took many by surprise. Analysts in the State Department, the CIA, and academia all failed to foresee the revolution's turn toward theocracy. Ambassador Sullivan's "Thinking the Unthinkable" telegram of November 1978 had predicted that Khomeini would play a symbolic, "Gandhi-like" role in revolutionary Iran. The following month, James Bill predicted that Iran's clergy "would never participate directly in the formal government structure." While analysts recognized the power of the clergy, the concept of a theocratic revolution in the depths of the Cold War seemed too far-fetched to merit serious consideration. As late as March 1979, CIA director Stansfield Turner worried that "leftists" would use the revolution to seize power in Tehran. But the drama in Iran would prove Khomeini's doubters wrong. By the spring of 1979, the CIA began to realize that Khomeini was not slipping into a passive role. Rather, it appeared that the Ayatollah would continue to exert considerable, and perhaps even decisive, influence over the state.[29] "Lacking any political channels," former NSC staffer Gary Sick later wrote, "people turned to the only popular institution not totally dominated by the shah's system—the mosques." With the collapse of the old regime, the path was virtually open for the ayatollahs to seize control.[30] The final blow to the secular elements in the revolution came in the form of an international incident that seized the world's attention.

HOSTAGE CRISIS

The U.S. embassy in Tehran sat on a sprawling, twenty-seven-acre campus ringed by brick walls separating the compound from the teeming city around it. Shaded by pine trees, the campus contained a chancery, the ambassador's residence, staff buildings, tennis courts, and a swimming pool. Like many American embassies during the

Cold War, it was the local face of American power in the country. For Iranian revolutionaries, the compound was an imperialist salient in the heart of the capital, an enemy stronghold that for decades had supported the Shah's hated regime. As the revolutionary tide surged, demonstrators sprayed anti-American graffiti on the embassy's outside walls while sporadic rocks and gunshots forced the staff to put up sandbags and bulletproof plastic panels on the windows. The compound was about to become a pivotal battleground in the ongoing Iranian Revolution. In the last weeks of October 1979, a group of Islamist students devised a plan to seize the embassy: they would do so under the banner of the Ayatollah in a bid to shift power away from Bazargan's government and toward the clerics. If successful, the seizure would compromise Bazargan's authority. He could come to the rescue of the American diplomats, but doing so would lend credence to accusations that the prime minister, who had just been photographed shaking hands with Zbigniew Brzezinski, was an imperialist lackey. Conversely, he could do nothing, but inaction would make his government appear weak. For Bazargan, it was a no-win situation.[31]

On the morning of November 4, 1979, an unusually large crowd of protestors convened in front of the embassy. U.S. embassy officials—which now consisted of a skeleton staff led by chargé d'affaires Bruce Laingen after the departure and retirement of Ambassador Sullivan earlier in the year—were not overly concerned and set about holding meetings, filing memoranda, and conducting their normal daily operations. By late morning, however, the crowd had grown larger, and a number of staffers became concerned. Soon, the first students began scaling the embassy walls. As officials barred their doors and began frantically shredding sensitive documents, the protestors outside shouted through bullhorns. "We do not wish to harm you," one announced. "We only wish to set-in." Iranian students with bolt cutters began attacking the locks on the lower windows. Within a matter of hours, the demonstrators controlled the embassy and had taken dozens of its staff hostage. Blindfolded and with their hands bound, the hostages were paraded before photographers. While the students had initially intended a short-term, symbolic occupation of the embassy, they were emboldened by their success and by word that they had gained Khomeini's support. Just as important, it seemed clear that government forces would not intervene. In exchange for the hostages, the students demanded the return of the Shah (who had been admitted to the United States on October 22 to seek medical treatment), to face trial. The capture of the embassy, the so-called Den of Spies, had turned into a major coup for the Islamist elements of the revolution.[32]

Officials in the Carter administration scrambled to find some way to address the crisis. As initial hopes for a quick resolution faded, Brzezinski directed members of the NSC staff to devise a range of diplomatic and military responses. It would be necessary, they decided, to open direct communications with Khomeini and the clerical leadership. But the return of the ailing Shah to face trial in a revolutionary court was out of the question. Meanwhile, the aircraft carrier USS *Midway*, steaming through the Indian Ocean, could be used to launch retaliatory strikes if the hostages were harmed. The holy city of Qom and Iranian oil fields sat at the top of the potential target list. Officials from the PLO also offered to serve as liaisons between Washington and Tehran, in the hope of securing the hostages' release. For the time being, however, the two sides were in a deadlock: the United States would not extradite the Shah, and the revolutionaries in Iran had no reason to free their prisoners.[33] Making matters worse, the students who had seized the compound had captured a large cache of classified State Department documents that embassy staff had not had time to burn. Although many of the documents had been shredded, the Iranians gathered a team of students and disabled war veterans to reassemble these. Over the next six years, the Iranians would compile three thousand pages of documents that they would publish in the eighty-five-volume "Documents from the US Espionage Den" series. In time, some of the most sensitive communiqués on U.S.-Iranian relations would sell on the streets of Tehran for a few coins.[34]

The American hostages were now pawns in a power struggle within the Iranian Revolution. The capture of the embassy fanned the flames of radicalism and empowered the Khomeinists to cast moderate leaders in the provisional government as U.S. lackeys. Impotent in the face of the crisis and under increasing attack, Prime Minister Bazargan resigned on November 6. During what would become months in captivity, the hostages received stern treatment. Troublemakers were blindfolded, handcuffed, and sometimes kept in solitary confinement. Ranking officials and the handful of CIA officers in the Tehran station were subjected to interrogation and, initially, beatings. On the whole, however, their confinement was not unduly harsh by Iranian standards. Indeed, a number of the hostage-takers who had been prisoners of the American-trained SAVAK had endured far worse. For their part, the American hostages rightfully saw their captivity as an egregious violation of diplomatic norms. As the revolution veered toward greater radicalism, the "guests of the ayatollah" became a potent symbol of resistance against American power.[35]

The hostage crisis represented an equally powerful symbolic humiliation for the Carter administration. The American news media seized upon the plight of the captives, airing nightly television broadcasts that served as unwelcome reminders of Carter's inability to secure their release. By early 1980, the more hawkish members of the administration were calling for a rescue operation. Secretary of State Vance opposed any military operation to liberate the hostages, insisting that it was likely to cause significant bloodshed and further strengthen Khomeini's hand. On April 11, while Vance was on vacation in Florida, Carter met with top officials to consider a rescue mission. Brzezinski argued that it was time "to lance the boil" in Tehran and redeem the nation's honor. The hawks won the day, and preparations for Operation Eagle Claw began. Learning of the operation, a horrified Vance proffered his letter of resignation. On the evening of April 24, eight Sea Stallion helicopters from the USS *Nimitz* in the Arabian Sea and six C-130 aircraft met at a remote airstrip

275 miles southeast of Tehran. The helicopters would carry teams of Delta Force commandos to the U.S. embassy in Tehran for an assault on the compound. "When we went into that Embassy," the commando's leader explained, "it was our aim to kill all Iranian guards." If Iranian reinforcements arrived, the rescue team was to radio for C-130s armed with 105-millimeter cannons to "hose down the streets." It was a risky operation that would most likely have generated heavy casualties on both sides. Before the assault, however, three helicopters broke down and one crashed into a C-130. The ensuing carnage left eight Americans dead and forced the operation's commanders to abort the mission. The following day, as Iranian forces picked through the wreckage and the regime declared yet another victory over the United States, the hostage-takers moved their captives to more secure locations throughout Tehran, to prevent any further rescue attempts.[36]

The Eagle Claw disaster was only the most dramatic manifestation of larger changes taking place in Washington's orientation toward the Middle East. On October 1, 1979, Jimmy Carter had announced the creation of the Rapid Deployment Joint Task Force (RDF). Drawing on the 82nd and 101st Airborne Divisions, the 7th Marine Amphibious Brigade, the 24th Mechanized Division, the 6th Cavalry Brigade, Army Ranger and Special Forces units, air force Tactical Fighter Wings, a force of B-52s, and three aircraft carrier battle groups, the RDF fielded an impressive, multiservice combat force designed to give the United States the capacity to stage military interventions in the region to protect access to vital oil supplies.[37] In light of the growing range of upheavals in the Middle East, the RDF's role was soon expanded. In 1981, the Reagan administration would announce its intention to transform the RDF into a theater-level command. Two years later, U.S. Central Command (CENTCOM) came into being. Focusing on the Middle East, North Africa, and Central Asia—in short, the heartlands of the Islamic world—CENTCOM would become the most active American military command of the post–Cold War era.

The revolution in Iran was causing problems for leaders in Moscow as well. U.S. analysts warned that, although the resurgence of political Islam created short-term problems for Washington, events such as the Iranian Revolution posed graver long-term dangers for the USSR. Soviet leaders feared that the "virus" of Islamic fundamentalism might spread to their own Muslim population. In response to Khomeini's criticisms of Moscow, Soviet forces had begun jamming radio signals emanating from Iran. In August, the CIA concluded that relations between Moscow and Tehran were "cool at best" and not likely to improve. Khomeini's antipathy toward the Soviets, born in part from the Iranian leader's deep suspicion toward atheist Marxism, frustrated the Kremlin's efforts to expand its influence in Iran in the wake of the revolution. "While Moscow takes some consolation in the fact that the US has fared no better," the Agency noted, "the Soviets in recent weeks have probably concluded that neither can they make progress as long as Khomeini and his supporters remain in power." By September 1979, Soviet leaders had begun issuing open criticism of the "theocratic" regime in Tehran. By "stirring up religious fanaticism and anticommunist hysteria," argued the Moscow daily *Izvestia*, mouthpiece of the Soviet government, Tehran was doing nothing to help the Iranian people. Even worse, Soviet leaders worried that the ayatollahs were taking steps to export their revolution to other states in the region.[38]

In October, the CIA warned that Khomeini and his comrades were "encouraging and in some cases assisting Shia dissidents in neighboring states." Iraq represented the "most explosive" potential target for Iranian leaders hoping to export their revolution. Fifty-five percent of Iraq's population was Shia, the country housed the holy shrines in Najaf and Karbala, and the two nations had been rivals for centuries. Iraqi leaders remained highly sensitive to Iranian "meddling with its Shia community." Iranian statements had also inflamed Shia dissidents in Bahrain and Kuwait. Khomeini's calls for the Afghans to "take a lesson from Iran" and "kick out" the pro-Soviet government there had raised concerns across the border. Analysts explained that the "tribal insurgency" in Afghanistan had taken cues from the revolution in neighboring Iran. Although Iran was unlikely to "pursue an activist foreign policy," CIA analysts concluded, the "messianic, Pan-Islamic radicalism of the Iranian clergy will continue to strain relations between Iran and [its neighbors] and to stimulate efforts by Arab states to organize a coordinated response." Iraq, in particular, was likely to "play the role of protector of the Gulf," using the Iranian Revolution as a pretext for increasing its regional influence.[39]

IRAN'S UNTHINKABLE REVOLUTION SHOOK THE FOUN- dations of the Cold War in the Third World and set in motion a wave of dislocations that would transform the Middle East. Khomeini would soon join the ranks of Mao Zedong and Ho Chi Minh as one of the foremost postcolonial revolutionaries of the Cold War age. Like the Chinese and Vietnamese Revolutions before it, the Iranian Revolution helped fuel a series of wars in neighboring states and prompted a buildup of U.S. and Soviet military commitments to a new theater of war along the Cold War borderlands. Tehran would emerge as the focus of the third and last great wave of revolutionary violence in the Cold War era. President Carter's response to the Iranian Revolution and the events that followed set the stage for a massive increase in the U.S. military presence in the region. But the United States would not be the first superpower to intervene in the great sectarian revolt of the late Cold War. Soviet leaders had already launched their own war in neighboring Afghanistan.

THE SOVIET INTERVENTION
IN AFGHANISTAN

1978 – 1979

As Moscow feared, the political drama unfolding in Tehran reverberated across the surrounding region. In less than a year, three of
the four states that shared a border with Iran would be at war. For
the men who sat in the Kremlin, none of Iran's neighbors appeared
more troublesome than Afghanistan. Whereas the events in Iran reversed the tide of secular revolution, Afghanistan's story seemed more
in line with prevailing Marxist narratives. There, a 1978 revolution
had brought a Communist Party into power. The new regime opened
the door to a dramatic increase in Soviet influence in the region. But
appearances could be deceiving. Even as Communist leaders consolidated control in the Afghan capital, Islamic rebels gained strength
in the countryside. By the end of 1979, the regime faced a mounting
insurgency. Leaders in Moscow, for their part, hoped to defend the
Marxist regime in Kabul and use it as a bulwark against the Islamic
radicalism radiating out of Tehran. But as rebellion spread through
the hinterlands, the People's Democratic Party of Afghanistan (PDPA)
grew increasingly embattled.

During the second half of 1979, Moscow, Washington, and Islamabad went to war in Afghanistan. A sense of mutual insecurity—heightened by the Iranian Revolution—drove leaders in all three capitals to intervene in local Afghan power struggles. While the Soviets worked to build the regime in Kabul into a bulwark against U.S. and militant Islamic influence, the Americans and Pakistanis set up a pipeline of aid to the Mujahideen, Afghan guerrilla fighters struggling against the Soviet Army. None of the major players could have predicted the outcome of their decisions. In the closing years of the Cold War, Afghanistan would become the last great battlefield of the superpower struggle. The Soviets staged their largest intervention of the Cold War in a bid to save the PDPA regime in Kabul. The United States responded by bankrolling a rebellion that would grow into a jihad against the Soviets. America's allies in this program, the Pakistani, Chinese, and Saudi governments, used the conflict in Afghanistan as a means of increasing their regional influence. In the process, Pakistan would emerge as a major player in the Islamic world and restore a measure of pride lost during the 1971 defeat in Bangladesh. The war in Afghanistan helped launch a global jihadist movement whose fury would reverberate long into the next century. The battle for Afghanistan transformed the Cold War and the world that followed.

THE GRAVEYARD OF EMPIRES

Insurgencies were nothing new in Afghanistan. Indeed, ungoverned spaces (rather than tight state control) were the norm in the country.

The so-called graveyard of empires occupies the eastern reaches of the Hindu Kush Mountains at the convergence of South and Central Asia, the Middle East, and China. A dry land made more formidable by scorching summer heat and icy winter winds, Afghanistan is made up of craggy mountains, verdant valleys, and deep, cold rivers. Although the nation is majority Sunni Muslim, it is split along ethnic and tribal lines, with Pashtuns and Tajiks representing the largest ethnic group. Afghanistan's daunting geography, crisscrossed by forbidding mountain ridges, has bolstered these divisions.

Like so many states throughout the Third World, Afghanistan's modern borders were laid out by European imperial authorities. For centuries, the land was home to the ancient Silk Road connecting China in the East, India in the South, and Persia and Europe in the West. Its high rocky passes guard the main overland approaches to India, making it the historical frontier between the Russian and British Empires in the nineteenth and early twentieth centuries. Throughout the nineteenth century, the British and Russian Empires had staged a rivalry for influence in Afghanistan. The so-called Great Game ensured that the nation remained a buffer state between the Russian Empire and British colonial interests in India. Generations of foreign interference combined with Afghanistan's imposing terrain to create a nation in which a comparatively weak central government ruled over a conglomeration of largely isolated and autonomous "village-states."[1] For most Afghans, tribal ties were more important than connections to the distant government in Kabul. Power struggles and policy debates in the capital had little impact on the residents of dusty villages tucked into the country's remote valleys.

Though many Afghans were uninterested in the outside world, the outside world remained interested in them. The Cold War renewed Afghanistan's geopolitical significance as a buffer state perched along the southern frontier of the Soviet Union. During the 1950s, as Dwight Eisenhower developed his Northern Tier Strategy, which sought allies in the Middle East and Central Asia who would form a bulwark against Soviet expansion, Afghanistan appeared as a potential prize to both Washington and Moscow. By the late 1950s, Nikita Khrushchev feared that the United States might seek to transform the nation into an American military base, a forward position in Washington's bid to "encircle" the USSR.[2]

While Afghanistan was hardly a central theater of the Cold War struggle in the early 1960s, those in the Kremlin remained eager to bolster their influence there. After the founding of the People's Democratic Party of Afghanistan in 1965, Soviet leaders worked to strengthen ties with Afghan Communists. In 1973, the PDPA helped Prime Minister Mohammad Daoud Khan stage a bloodless coup against King Zahir Shah, which eliminated the monarchy and made Afghanistan a republic. Over the next five years, Daoud worked to build the fractious country into a stronger, more modern state. Pakistani leaders supported rebel groups inside Afghanistan as part of a low-level conflict between the two nations, while a rift that had begun between the Parcham and Khalq wings of the PDPA in the 1960s continued as a source of tension. Convinced that Afghanistan needed to modernize before it could become socialist, the Parcham faction advocated gradual reforms. In contrast, the more radical Khalq faction sought an immediate—and if necessary, violent—socialist revolution in Afghanistan.

In the summer of 1975, a ragtag collection of tribal leaders staged a nationwide uprising against Daoud's regime. The rebellion was poorly coordinated, and its leaders were enamored of notions of heroic, left-wing guerrilla warfare. As a result, the rebels lacked support from the clergy and the majority of the peasants. They made easy targets for government troops who moved in to crush the insurgents. State forces arrested hundreds of youths and dozens of intellectuals, many of whom were imprisoned and executed without trial. The only region where the rebels managed to make gains was the northeast. Daoud's brutal response restored order at the same time that it taught the insurgents a valuable set of lessons: the support of the clergy would be instrumental to any successful rebellion, and the rebels would have to work closely with the peasantry and the military. Still, the hundreds of leaders killed in the subsequent crackdown would be sorely missed in the coming decade, when another, more successful, rebellion would be launched.[3]

While he worked to manage internal disputes (banning the Parcham and Khalq in 1976), Daoud tried to improve Kabul's ties with powerful players on the international stage. In 1974, he visited Moscow, where he secured a half-billion-dollar aid package from Soviet leaders eager to foster good relations with their neighbor. He also reached out to the Shah in Iran, from whom he received the promise of $2 billion in aid. In a move that troubled leaders in the Kremlin, Daoud scheduled a trip to Washington in September 1978. The planned visit was the most worrisome event in a series of actions that Moscow interpreted as a potential drift toward the United States. During another visit to Moscow the following year, the Afghan leader stormed out of a meeting with Brezhnev. To the Kremlin, it appeared as if Iran and the CIA were pulling Daoud into the Western camp. Daoud's defection would risk turning Afghanistan into yet another Western base along the Soviet Union's vulnerable southern frontier.[4]

In mid-April 1978, with tensions rising, a prominent Afghan Communist leader, Mir Akbar Khaibar, was assassinated. Rumors spread through the country that the murder had been ordered by the regime as the beginning of a widespread crackdown against the PDPA. Antiregime demonstrations erupted throughout the country in response to the killing. The following week, security forces arrested seven leading Communists; this was followed by a purge of hundreds of pro-Communist government employees. On April 27, Communist military officers launched a coup against the regime that killed Daoud and much of his family. Three days later, military commanders handed the reins of government to Nur Muhammad Taraki, leader of the Khalq faction of the PDPA, who announced the creation of the Democratic Republic of Afghanistan. The Saur Revolution, as the coup came to be known, brought a Marxist regime to power in Kabul and set the stage for a struggle that was to last into the next century.[5]

THE PATH TO SOCIALISM

The Saur Revolution presented Moscow with a dilemma. Although the KGB had probably been aware of the coming coup, its execution was haphazard and premature. The revolution brought to power a regime controlled by a divided Communist Party led by squabbling, inexperienced leaders in an underdeveloped country riven by tribal disputes—hardly an auspicious foundation upon which to build a socialist utopia. Nevertheless, Afghanistan's strategic importance seemed indisputable, and the Kremlin was not inclined to ignore a fellow Marxist regime that had just seized control of a country that shared a long border with the Soviet Union. In a meeting with the Soviet ambassador to Kabul, Taraki insisted that "Afghanistan, following Marxism-Leninism, will set off on the path of building socialism and will belong to the socialist camp." However, he added, it would be necessary to announce these goals to the Afghan people somewhat "later," so as not to spark resistance. Still, Soviet officials were troubled by the enduring split in the PDPA between the Parcham and the Khalq.[6] Nevertheless, Moscow prepared to send large amounts of development aid to Afghanistan. In July, a delegation from the USSR Academy of Sciences arrived in Kabul. Taraki greeted the delegation warmly. He explained that Moscow was working to help the PDPA "make the dreams of the Afghan people come true; to develop realistic plans and implement them in practice."[7]

U.S. officials saw trouble on the horizon. Infighting between the Afghan Communists threatened the new regime as it worked to consolidate its power. "In the longer run," the State Department predicted, "the Afghan tribes, stirred by traditional religious leaders, could create disorder in the countryside for the 'godless communists' in Kabul."[8] The U.S. ambassador in Kabul, Adolph Dubs, warned that the new government was "overwhelmingly dependent on the Soviet Union." Taraki and the PDPA were "ideologically inspired" by the Soviets and increasingly dependent on Moscow for financial and technical assistance. The new leadership in Kabul hoped to implement a Soviet model of development centered on the collectivization of agriculture. The Marxist leadership "represents a minority of the Afghan population," the ambassador stated, and "there is considerable opposition to the regime inside Afghanistan in the middle class, the clergy, and the tribes." In light of this opposition, there was a very real possibility of "assassinations, terrorist acts, and guerrilla warfare in the mountainous tribal areas" of the country. In the interim, Moscow would seek to encourage development in Afghanistan while establishing a "Soviet dominated regime." Considering the importance of the Persian Gulf for Western security interests, the ambassador argued, "it is incumbent upon us to do everything we can to shore up Iran and Pakistan against the new threat to their security posed by the Soviet-backed regime in Afghanistan."[9]

A November 1978 speech by Afghan deputy prime minister Hafizullah Amin did little to ease U.S. suspicions. In an address that Ambassador Dubs called "obsequious and effusive," Amin proclaimed the Saur Revolution as a "continuation of the path of the Great October Revolution" that had brought the Bolsheviks to power in Moscow. The speech "clearly identifies the Afghan revolutionary movement with that of its northern neighbor," Dubs wrote. In doing so, government leaders had "clearly offended many Afghans by openly declaring their state to be socialist, and by appearing to toady to the Soviets." Commenting on a reception at the Soviet embassy, complete with an "unending supply of vodka," Dubs speculated that the regime's fears of tribal unrest and rebellion might be driving Kabul into Moscow's arms. "Concerned by continued disturbances in the tribal areas and by alleged evidence that anti-[government] elements are being assisted from the outside, the new regime may acutely feel that it is threatened and that it must, therefore, rely on the Soviet Union as its ultimate protector." Dubs could have had no idea that he would, in the space of a few months, become a casualty of this very unrest.[10]

Much of the population's anger with Kabul stemmed from the regime's development programs. The PDPA's modernization schemes aimed at breaking traditional and tribal structures of authority in a bid to centralize power in Kabul. Regional rivals would be eliminated, and Afghanistan's historically diffuse political authority would be replaced by a strong, modern state led by the Communist Party. National literacy campaigns and ideologically based school curriculum reforms would create a population committed to the PDPA's Marxist vision. The new regime simultaneously brought Pashtun leaders into positions of power. "It was the most-Pashtun . . . government Afghanistan had ever had," notes political scientist Barnett Rubin. Between July and December 1978, the regime rolled out a broad series of reforms, including land reform, the creation of agricultural cooperatives, new regulations for rural mortgages, and revisions to marriage statutes. These changes aimed to overthrow traditional networks of social and economic power and replace them with state-controlled mechanisms. The regime coupled these efforts at political transformation with a sweeping campaign of repression. Starting with the April coup, dozens of former officials were thrown in jail or executed. The regime then moved against Islamists, Maoists, and Parchamists whom it considered potential political rivals. Students, teachers, army officers, and minorities came next.[11]

Yet opposition to the PDPA's programs continued to mount through the beginning of 1979. A secret U.S. memorandum reported that the "localized tribal fighting" that had begun in the wake of the Saur Revolution "has since grown into a countrywide insurgency." Struggling government forces were increasingly dependent on Soviet aid and military advisors. Should the situation grow worse, it was "conceivable" that Kabul might request direct Soviet intervention in the coming year. Moscow would be reluctant to intervene directly, however, for fear of being "bogged down indefinitely trying to shore up a discredited regime." Meanwhile, antigovernment fighters "operate with impunity in over half the country" and had managed to overrun a handful of government positions. Although they lacked central leadership, tribal insurgents were well versed in guerrilla warfare and able to subsist in the countryside indefinitely. "Faced with the hostility of the great majority of the traditionally independent population," the memo predicted, "the regime . . . has no better than an even chance to complete its second year in power."[12] Though it was more prevalent in the countryside, the increasingly violent resistance had even reached the streets of the capital.

ROUSING THE MASSES

Sometime around 8:30 on the morning of February 14, 1979, an armed man dressed as a police officer stopped the car carrying U.S. ambassador Adolph Dubs at an intersection in Kabul. Four men forced their way into the car and then ordered the driver to proceed to the Kabul Hotel. The kidnappers hustled Dubs through the crowded lobby and up to a room on the second floor. Officials from the U.S. embassy rushed to the hotel, where they met Afghan police arriving on the scene. Police officers established contact with the gunmen at 9:15 and initiated a series of sporadic negotiations while snipers and an assault team took positions outside. U.S. officials urged the police and Soviet officials on the scene to exercise restraint. It was clear, however, that the police intended to storm the room. Negotiations continued for several hours, during which time Bruce Flatin, a political counselor in the U.S. embassy, was able to communicate with Dubs through the door's keyhole. Flatin became alarmed, however, when Afghan police told him to instruct Dubs to wait ten minutes and then head to the bathroom or fall to the floor. Fearing an assault, Flatin pleaded for caution, but the police insisted that they had received orders to attack. Shortly before 12:50 p.m., police began moving civilians away from the scene. Soon thereafter, "heavy gunfire" erupted in the room, hallway, and across the street. Some forty seconds later, it was over. U.S. officials moving through clouds of cordite smoke made their way into the room to find a lifeless Dubs slumped beside a wardrobe with bullet holes above his right eye, in his chest, and in his wrist. The police were beating one of the kidnappers who had been captured in the initial stage of the standoff, while the blood-soaked bodies of the other gunmen were carted off.[13]

Dubs's killing set off a flurry of activity in Washington. Much of the anger was directed at Soviet officials who, the Americans argued, had been more interested in eliminating the kidnappers than saving the ambassador. The *New York Times* suggested that the ambassador's death threatened to strain relations between Moscow and Washington. The simultaneous U.S. decision to evacuate nonessential personnel from Tehran owing to mounting violence in the Iranian Revolution contributed to a mood of growing tension in the region.[14] For the time being, however, Afghan and Soviet officials had bigger problems than an angry White House. In the weeks following Dubs's death, fighting between Afghan forces and rebels intensified. Some of the fiercest battles were taking place between government troops and the Peshawar-based Afghan National Liberation Front, which had called for a jihad against the regime. Rebel fighters in Kunar, Paktia, and Herat Provinces had attacked government troops and forced Kabul to send reinforcements to the areas. Fighting was expected to intensify as the Afghan New Year and the anniversary of the Saur Revolution approached.[15]

The bloodiest fighting broke out in the western city of Herat. On the morning of March 15, 1979, the area's peasants, upset over the local impact of Kabul's land reforms, began congregating around the city's mosques. Religious leaders inflamed the growing crowd, which soon began attacking symbols of the state and seizing government buildings. The demonstrators were joined by elements of the army's Seventeenth Division, which staged a mutiny against the central government. In short order, the rebels gained control of the city, which they were to hold for the next week. Lacking any clear leader, the rebellion degenerated into a state of near anarchy as looters roamed through the ancient bazaar and mobs massacred Soviet advisors in the city. Widely varied estimates place the number of Soviet personnel killed at anywhere from a handful to two hundred. From its epicenter in Herat, the revolt soon spread to the surrounding countryside. On March 20, government forces brandishing Qurans and green flags entered the city while warplanes bombarded the suburbs. In the brutal campaign to retake Herat, somewhere between five thousand and twenty-five thousand people were killed.[16]

In the midst of the rebellion, Taraki pleaded with Soviet premier Alexei Kosygin to send Soviet troops to put down the uprising. Taraki argued that Iran and Pakistan had incited the rebels. Moscow could send soldiers from the Central Asian Republics, Tajiks and Uzbeks, in Afghan uniforms. "No one will recognize them," Taraki insisted. Kosygin refused. "Two hours later the whole world will know about this," he argued. "Everyone will begin to shout that the Soviet Union's intervention in Afghanistan has begun." The USSR might be able to airlift weapons and tanks, but Taraki was unsure whether the regime could marshal enough Afghan officers to drive them.[17] Three days later, as government troops battled with rebel forces in Herat, Brezhnev told Taraki that Moscow would not intervene militarily in Afghanistan. "This would only play in[to] the hands of the enemies," he warned, "yours and ours." Rather, the Kremlin would continue to support Taraki's regime as it took steps to unify the PDPA and expand its base. At the same time, he insisted, Kabul should work to break the power of the "reactionary clergy" and "split their ranks."[18] Meanwhile, on the ground, Afghan patrols, supported by Soviet military advisors, worked to crush the power of the rebels.

The town of Kerala rests at the foot of the Hindu Kush Mountains, some twelve miles northwest of the ancient mule trail that snakes through the Raghani Pass connecting Pakistan to Afghanistan. In 1979 it was home to some five thousand Pashtun inhabitants who worked in the surrounding wheat fields. Like many peasants in the area, the residents of Kerala were sympathetic to the antigovernment insurgents hiding out in the surrounding hills—a fact that did not escape Afghan military patrols. On April 20, a contingent of two hundred government troops, along with twenty Soviet advisors, entered the town. The soldiers demanded that all the men inside assemble for a meeting and sent the town's women to the mosque. While tanks and armored personnel carriers blocked the town's exits, government troops demanded that the town's male population renounce support for the rebels and swear allegiance to Kabul. The villagers refused. At some point, the soldiers appear to have decided to make an example of Kerala. "They forced all the men to line up in crouching positions in the field just outside the town and then opened up with their machine guns from behind," one survivor told reporters. "Then they spread out through the town gunning down all the remaining men they could find." Minutes later, as the town's women screamed, an army bulldozer began plowing the bodies, some still clinging to life, into a mass grave in a nearby field. Survivors estimated that some 1,170 men and boys, the majority of the town's male population, were slaughtered.[19]

The regime's bloody counterinsurgency campaign did little to quell the rebellion. In June, the U.S. embassy reported that insurrection remained rampant. The regime maintained a modicum of order in the large cities, but the countryside belonged to the guerrillas. "At the present time," the report warned, "the government . . . probably rules less than one-half of this country." The guerrillas had also managed to disrupt the regime's control over the nation's sparse system of roads. "Rebel forces have been able to seize short sections of highway and hold them for three-to-five hours." But the regime was likely to retain control of Kabul, the embassy explained, as long as the rebels remained disorganized and cut off from substantial outside aid. The capital remained "an oasis of relative calm," disrupted only by the frequent departure of helicopter gunships, the presence of security personnel on high alert, and occasional nighttime firefights.

The rebels, or Mujahideen—translated literally as "holy warriors" but used to refer to both religious and secular fighters in the Afghan insurgency—comprised a broad range of groups. Some resented the regime's "cultural imperialism" and "increasing Pushtunization," while others mainly opposed the PDPA's land reform program. Still other rebels were "traditionalists" intent on defending Islamic society against the regime's social reform programs. "Many of these rebels seem to share some convictions in common," the U.S. embassy report continued, "such as universally held perception that they are defending Islam and [that the Khalq officials] are godless infidels who have sold out Afghanistan to Russian imperialism." For the time being, though, the military and police forces remained loyal to Kabul. "As long as the majority of Afghan troops and pilots can stomach the slaughter of their own people," the report concluded, the regime could probably survive. "The rebels still do not look like winners, but as Afghan history has so often illustrated, things can change quickly here."[20]

Soviet leaders were growing increasingly frustrated with the situation in Afghanistan, which they blamed on counterrevolutionaries and "reactionary circles of Muslim religion." The rebels, one Soviet diplomat noted, "make use of the conservative and reactionary traditions of Islam" to mobilize resistance against the regime. Iranian, Pakistani, and Chinese support for the rebels made matters worse. A "Maoist clique" within the Mujahideen had received training in China that it was now using to stage "diversion and terrorist actions" against the regime.[21] In May, the Soviet Politburo authorized a fifty-three-million-ruble military aid package to Kabul that included artillery, ninety armored personnel carriers, nearly fifty thousand machine guns, a thousand grenade throwers, and almost seven hundred aviation bombs; it also authorized another fifty thousand rubles in medical equipment. Moscow remained reluctant, however, to send helicopters and planes with Soviet crews to fight in Afghanistan for fear of driving up support for the Mujahideen and drawing criticism in the international sphere.[22] In June, the Soviets again urged Taraki and the PDPA to unify their party leadership in an effort to bridge internal divisions and stabilize the political situation in Afghanistan. At the same time, Moscow warned Kabul to guard against dangerous rumors that the PDPA was cracking down on Muslims in Afghanistan. "Both domestic and foreign Muslim reactionaries are playing on this," they warned, in an attempt "to rouse the masses of believers against the PDPA." Kabul should reach out to Muslim leaders and encourage them to throw their support behind the revolution at the same time that the regime worked to allay popular fears that socialism represented a threat to Islam in Afghanistan.[23]

Unbeknownst to the Politburo, its main adversary had just decided to join the fight. On July 3, Carter authorized a limited CIA propaganda and psychological warfare campaign in support of the Afghan rebels. The president also gave the go-ahead to provide them with nonmilitary aid through third-party governments—most notably, Pakistan. The initial allocation of half a million dollars was exhausted in six weeks. By late August, Pakistani leaders were calling on Washington to begin sending military aid to the insurgents. Carter had taken a first step in what would become a massive covert operation to provide aid to the Islamic militants in Afghanistan some six months before the Soviet invasion.[24]

Beyond destabilizing the regime in Kabul, U.S. aid to the Mujahideen served to strengthen ties with Pakistan. In the wake of the recent revolution in Iran and Afghanistan's drift toward Moscow, Washington's relationship with Islamabad had come to seem more important. To Carter and other American officials, Pakistan now appeared as one of Washington's few allies in a region that was turning increasingly hostile to U.S. interests. The White House also encouraged its European allies and Beijing to coordinate with Islamabad as a means of counterbalancing Soviet power in Southwest Asia. In the wake of the Iranian Revolution, Washington would partner with Islamabad.[25] But aid to the Mujahideen came at a cost. In November, the U.S. embassy in Kabul offered a gloomy, and prescient, conclusion about Afghanistan's future: "[A]nimosities are by now so deep that long-term domestic and perhaps regional instability is probably a certainty. By the same token, an insurgent 'victory' would bring about its own brand of instability and bloodshed, and would probably be marked by economic, social, and political disruptions and anarchy for years to come. The ultimate victims of the ongoing struggle will be the Afghan people."[26]

STORM 333

Soviet officials were losing patience with a regime in Kabul that seemed to refuse to unify its ranks. In early September, the KGB outlined a plan to remove Hafizullah Amin, serving as the minister of national defense, whom it judged to be the primary source of the regime's problems. Kabul's military repression, a KGB report argued, was undermining the regime's authority and alienating the population. But Amin had other plans. On September 14, 1979, he arrived at the presidential palace with his bodyguard, Sayed Daoud Tarun, in tow. As the two ascended the staircase, a gunfight erupted between Tarun and Taraki's guards. Tarun was cut down, but Amin managed to escape to the Ministry of Defense. He then ordered troops to surround the palace and arrest Taraki. Amin's forces moved out through the capital, arresting Taraki's supporters in what was now obviously a coup d'état. Observers later speculated that the gunfight on the palace steps was in fact a deliberate provocation designed to give Amin an excuse to launch the coup. Several weeks later, Amin ordered his former colleague's execution. Guards used a pillow to suffocate Taraki while he was still in his dressing gown. The regime then reported that he had died of a "brief and serious illness." Taraki's murder incensed leaders in the Kremlin. "What a bastard," fumed Brezhnev, "to murder the man with whom he made the revolution." Moscow's comparatively moderate ally in Kabul had been slain by a brutal leader who seemed intent on driving the country into a full-scale civil war. Soviet officials now began to seriously consider moving against Amin.[27]

The Kremlin watched as the insurgency continued to mount. In October, units from the Seventh Infantry Division outside Kabul mutinied. The regime controlled only about 20 percent of the country. While Soviet leaders still worried about the dangers of a military intervention, the alternative prospect of watching the PDPA regime slowly implode might be worse. As the KGB gathered members of an alternate Afghan government in Moscow, to be led by exiled Parcham leader Babrak Karmal, the Politburo held meetings to determine the best course of action. If the Kremlin decided to remove Amin, Moscow already had the troops in place to do it. In April, Soviet officials had sent Spetsnaz special forces troops and the so-called Muslim Battalion, made up of soldiers from the Central Asian Republics of the Soviet Union, in the hope that they would be better able to relate to the Afghan population, to Afghanistan. On December 10, Defense Minister Dmitry Ustinov relayed orders from the Politburo to the military to prepare to send seventy-five thousand to eighty thousand troops across the border. Two days later, KGB chairman Yuri Andropov told the Politburo that Amin may have been recruited by the CIA to create a "New Great Ottoman Empire" on the southern flanks of the USSR. That same day, NATO decided to deploy Pershing II intermediate-range ballistic missiles in Europe.[28]

On December 24, 1979, in the face of significant protest from Soviet officials, Ustinov signed a directive authorizing the deployment of Soviet combat troops in Afghanistan. In light of the "military-political situation in the Middle East," the directive announced, Moscow would move its forces into Afghanistan to give "international aid to the friendly Afghan people and also create favorable conditions to interdict possible anti-Afghan nations from neighboring countries." But the directive was merely a formality. The Soviet intervention in Afghanistan was already under way.[29]

Beginning on December 10 and continuing until the end of the month, the Kremlin began moving Soviet forces into Afghanistan. Soviet paratroopers, Spetsnaz, and the Muslim Battalion were charged with seizing critical objectives in Kabul, such as communications facilities, while Moscow concentrated forces for the main thrust of the invasion across the border. On December 25, the Soviet Fortieth Army began moving over a pontoon bridge constructed across the Amu Darya River into Afghanistan. Meanwhile, bases in Uzbekistan and the then-named Belorussia launched a massive airlift of troops to the Bagram Airfield, outside Kabul. While troop columns from the Tenth Motorized Rifle Division proceeded south through the Hindu Kush, the airlifted forces would secure the capital. Plans to eliminate Amin were already under way. On December 13, one of the president's Soviet cooks slipped poison into his cola. The attempt succeeded only in sickening Amin's nephew, who was evacuated to Moscow for medical treatment. The next attempt was set for December 27. Code-named Storm 333, the plan called for Spetsnaz and KGB units to stage a direct assault on Amin's residence in the Tajbeg Palace, outside Kabul.[30]

At 6:20 p.m. that same day, Soviet forces crept up to three Afghan tanks guarding the palace. Snipers killed the Afghan sentries while Soviet soldiers seized the unmanned tanks. At 7:15, the lead units fired two red flares—the signal for the attack to begin. Antiaircraft guns fired on the palace to create a diversion while units from the Muslim Battalion advanced in infantry fighting vehicles. Palace guards directed a hail of gunfire at the advancing force, but the Soviets pressed on. After reaching the doors, the Soviet troops stormed into the building and, amid the screams of women and children, began shooting out the lights. Witnesses recalled seeing a confused Amin, connected to IVs and suffering from a second botched KGB poisoning, roaming the corridors. The Soviet doctors treating him, unaware that their countrymen had poisoned him, took the president to the bar and removed the tubes from his arms. As the assault continued, Soviet forces fought their way deeper into the palace. After the gunfire subsided, Amin's body was identified. He had been killed in the bar alongside his five-year-old son. Ten Soviet troops had been killed, along with an estimated 250 Afghan defenders. Though bloody, the battle at the palace was only the beginning.[31]

"A REGIONAL CRISIS"

Officials in Washington watched the Soviet takeover of the country with alarm. On December 26, 1979, the CIA briefed senior officials from the State Department, the White House, the Pentagon, and the National Security Council on the situation in Afghanistan. More than two hundred Soviet cargo planes had landed at the Kabul airport the previous day, bringing with them substantial numbers of combat troops. "The greatest risk that we face is a quick, effective Soviet operation to pacify Afghanistan," the assembled officials concluded. "Our objective, then, should be to make the operation as costly as possible for the Soviets."[32] CIA analysts suggested that the Soviets would have their hands full in Afghanistan: "The Communist revolutionaries have tried to overturn tradition rather than adapt it, to eliminate local autonomy, to destroy the elite class by confiscating its land, and to undermine the authority of the Muslim religious establishment. These actions have aroused the resistance of the fiercely independent Afghans. The present no-win situation—persistent insurgency and fragile Communist control of urban areas—is expected to continue."

Ultimately, political power in Afghanistan would remain dispersed. The Communists would hold power in the cities, but tribal authorities would control the countryside. "Afghanistan will not be ruled very much differently than it was in the past," the report concluded.[33]

Carter's national security advisor, Zbigniew Brzezinski, offered a more alarmist appraisal. The United States was "now facing *a regional crisis* [emphasis in original]" he told the president in a secret memorandum. "Both Iran and Afghanistan are in turmoil, and Pakistan is both unstable internally and extremely apprehensive externally." By sending its troops into Afghanistan, Moscow had moved one step closer in its "age-long dream" of having bases on the Indian Ocean. The fall of the Shah in Iran had led to the "collapse of the balance of power in Southwest Asia, and it could produce [a] Soviet presence right down to the edge of the Arabian and Oman Gulfs." Moscow's intervention posed "an extremely grave challenge" to the United States. While he noted that there was a chance Afghanistan "could become a Soviet Vietnam," Brzezinski remained skeptical. The Mujahideen lacked the unified leadership, external support, and foreign sanctuaries that the Viet Cong had enjoyed. Nevertheless, he stressed that the Mujahideen should receive support. "This means more money as well as arms shipment to the rebels and some technical advice." Brzezinski suggested that Pakistan and China could serve as facilitators in supporting the guerrillas. He also suggested reaching out to "Islamic countries" to launch a "propaganda campaign and . . . a covert action campaign to help the rebels." In three pages, written two days after the Soviet invasion, Brzezinski had outlined what would become the largest CIA covert operation of the Cold War.[34]

On December 28, Secretary of State Cyrus Vance wrote a widely circulated telegram warning U.S. embassies around the world of the evolving situation in Afghanistan. Moscow had launched a "massive Soviet airlift" that had already moved more than a division of troops into the capital. News of the coup against Amin circulated amid reports of fighting between Soviet and Afghan forces near the Radio Kabul Building and outside Amin's residence. Soon after, Soviet soldiers appeared posted at key intersections and outside government buildings throughout Kabul. Meanwhile, Soviet radio transmitters had announced that Babrak Karmal had succeeded Amin as the president of the Revolutionary Council. Indications of a buildup of "at least five divisions" at the Afghan borders "suggests that the Soviets have additional military objectives beyond the change of government in Kabul."[35] That same day, Carter told British prime minister Margaret Thatcher that "Moscow had changed a buffer nation into a puppet nation under Soviet direction. This would have profound strategic consequences for the stability of the entire region."[36]

The following week, Carter delivered his reaction to the Soviet intervention in a nationally televised address. The president opened with a reference to the shared "outrage" over the ongoing hostage crisis in Iran before turning to "another very serious development which threatens the maintenance of the peace in Southwest Asia." Moscow's aggressive moves in Afghanistan risked destabilizing the entire region. "A Soviet-occupied Afghanistan threatens both Iran and Pakistan and is a stepping-stone to possible control over much of the world's oil supplies," he told the nation. Because of this, Carter announced, he would be issuing an embargo on grain exports to the USSR and increasing economic and military aid to Pakistan. In talking points on the speech, the White House stressed that the Kremlin's invasion "places the Soviets within fighter range of the Persian Gulf—our oil lifeline." The following month, January 1980, U.S. officials would announce their intention to boycott the 1980 Moscow Summer Olympics if Soviet forces did not withdraw from Afghanistan.[37] Meanwhile, the CIA warned that the Soviets had demonstrated the ability to "exploit their superiority in conventional forces to achieve objectives in peripheral land areas . . . with relative impunity." Officials ordered new military estimates on potential Soviet attacks against Iran, Pakistan, and the Balkans.[38] Administration officials feared that Moscow's moves in Afghanistan were the start of a campaign, launched in the wake of the Iranian Revolution, designed to bring Soviet forces to the shores of the Persian Gulf. Driven by these anxieties, the Carter White House embarked on a dramatic expansion of U.S. power in the Middle East.

On the evening of January 23, 1980, Carter appeared before Congress to deliver his annual State of the Union address. "The 1980s have been born in turmoil, strife, and change," he announced to the nation and the world. "At this time in Iran, fifty Americans are still held captive, innocent victims of terrorism and anarchy. Also at this moment, massive Soviet troops are attempting to subjugate the fiercely independent and deeply religious people of Afghanistan. These two acts—one of international terrorism and one of military aggression— present a serious challenge to the United States of America and indeed to all the nations of the world."

By linking the hostage crisis in Iran and the Soviet invasion of Afghanistan, Carter signaled the White House's view that Southwest Asia was in the midst of a regional crisis. The president also called upon Iranian leaders to recognize that the "real danger to their nation lies in the north, in the Soviet Union and from its troops now in Afghanistan." Nevertheless, Washington was determined to defend its assets in the region. "Let our position be absolutely clear," Carter announced. "An attempt by any outside force to gain control of the Persian Gulf region will be regarded as an assault on the vital interests of the United States of America, and such an assault will be repelled by any means necessary, including military force." The president's pledge would come to be known as the Carter Doctrine, an announcement to the world that the United States considered the Persian Gulf and the surrounding territories to fall within its security perimeter.[39]

The Defense Intelligence Agency echoed these dire assessments in a heavily redacted report written the following month. If it managed to establish a secure position in Afghanistan, the agency argued, the USSR would take a "major step toward overland access to the Indian Ocean and to domination of the Asian sub-continent, which in turn would place the Soviets in a position for drawing the oil-producing countries of the Persian Gulf into their orbit of power." From their base in Kabul, the report warned, Soviet forces could destabilize the entire region. "Given the continued dependence on Middle East oil by the US and its allies," the authors concluded, "the Soviet occupation of Afghanistan translates into a direct threat to the West."[40]

Yet U.S. fears were exaggerated. In truth, the Soviet intervention in Afghanistan was relatively small. As former CIA officer Bruce Riedel later wrote, the Soviet Fortieth Army, reconstituted in 1979 for the purpose of the Afghan operation, initially consisted of approximately 80,000 men. At its peak, Soviet forces in Afghanistan numbered 110,000 split into three motorized rifle divisions, one airborne division, four infantry brigades, two airborne brigades, six hundred tanks, eighteen hundred armored vehicles, and five hundred aircraft.

"For a country the size of Texas or France," he noted, "that was a small force." In comparison, Moscow had sent 500,000 men to put down the 1968 uprising in Czechoslovakia. The Kremlin had chosen to fight the war on a shoestring budget. Moscow devoted an average of 2.5 percent of the USSR's yearly military expenditures to the war in Afghanistan. The CIA, meanwhile, estimated that the Soviets had never committed more than 3 percent of their total military forces to Afghanistan. By devoting such meager resources to the conflict, Riedel argued, Moscow effectively chose to cede the countryside to the Mujahideen.[41] This was not a force fit to pacify Afghanistan, let alone conquer the entire region.

SOVIET TACTICS AND STRATEGY

During the opening phase of the war, Soviet commanders focused on the deployment of the Fortieth Army. The first Soviet armored vehicles crossed the Amu Darya River near Termez as twilight fell on Christmas Day 1979. The main body of the invasion continued crossing throughout the night, taking control of the area around Kunduz before turning south toward Kabul on the evening of the twenty-seventh. That same night, a Soviet Motorized Rifle division south of Kushka crossed into Afghanistan and advanced on the city of Herat. This western thrust of the invasion continued south to Farah, before proceeding southeast to Kandahar, where it would link up with divisions pushing south from Kabul in a giant encirclement linking the northern, eastern, and western sectors of the country, while notably maintaining a distance from the Pakistan border regions in the south.

The bulk of the Soviet Fortieth Army had entered Afghanistan as of mid-January. Early on, Soviet commanders committed over a third of their strength to the tasks of securing key government and military facilities and maintaining lines of communication and transportation. Soviet garrisons were concentrated in large population centers and devoted much of their energy to defending major roads, escorting convoys, and securing airfields. The Soviets did not expect to encounter heavy resistance. They wrongly assumed that their deployment would "sober up" the Mujahideen and allow Afghan government troops to handle the bulk of the combat operations. Instead, Soviet garrisons encountered heavy resistance and found themselves working alongside Afghan forces that were, according to the Soviet General Staff, "weak and ineffective." Almost immediately, the Fortieth Army found itself engaged in heavy combat with rebel formations.[42]

During the first weeks of the war, the Mujahideen launched large-scale, conventional attacks on Soviet forces. While such tactics had been successful against the Afghan Army, Soviet troops represented far tougher adversaries. After suffering heavy losses, rebel commanders quickly reverted to guerrilla tactics, splitting their forces into units of twenty to one hundred men and adopting hit-and-run tactics against heavily armed Soviet garrisons. The rebels also pulled back into the mountains, which provided rugged terrain better suited to guerrilla tactics. By fighting in areas that were impassable for Soviet tanks and infantry fighting vehicles, the Mujahideen could negate many of the Fortieth Army's technological advantages. The Mujahideen proved particularly adept at setting ambushes for Soviet patrols and launching surprise raids. The insurgents generally avoided engagements with superior forces. When pressed, the rebels retreated. When forced to fight, either in defense of critical bases or in the case of encirclement, the Mujahideen engaged in close-quarters combat with Soviet troops, thereby preventing Soviet artillery and aircraft from supporting soldiers on the ground. In response, Soviet commanders decided to concentrate on eliminating the rebel's regional strongholds.[43]

These large-scale operations comprised the second and bloodiest stage of the war, lasting from 1980 to 1985. Soviet commanders continued to focus on holding cities and roads while pacifying the surrounding countryside. In retaliation for frequent ambushes along the roads, Soviet forces razed neighboring villages. In time, the highways were lined with the shells of burned-out vehicles and ruined buildings. Soviet commanders also planted hundreds of thousands of mines throughout the country in an effort to protect their garrisons and interdict Mujahideen supply routes. Many of the explosives were plastic "butterfly mines," scattered by aircraft across large swaths of territory.[44]

The increasing violence sparked opposition among the population. In February 1980, the Karmal regime began cracking down on political dissent in the capital. Political activists encouraged shopkeepers to shutter their stalls and distributed antigovernment leaflets denouncing the regime and calling on the Soviets to leave the country. On February 21, state security forces arrested two hundred suspected members of the underground in a bid to crush the movement. As night fell, cries of "Allahu Akbar" rang out through the streets in a show of defiance against the authorities. The next morning, crowds formed in Kabul's old quarter and began marching toward the city center. They were met by government troops along the Salang Watt thoroughfare, who used loudspeakers to order the procession to disperse and fired warning shots into the air. After the crowds refused to disband, some of the troops opened fire. The demonstrators then fled into the warren of surrounding streets, some taking refuge in mosques, others looting shops. Demonstrators swarmed through other sections of the city as well. In an apparent mutiny, police officers in the Khushal Maina neighborhood came out in support of the protestors. Soviet troops appeared around midday in armored vehicles while helicopters swooped overhead. Sporadic clashes continued until nightfall, when security forces restored order. Though estimates of the dead ran as high as two thousand, the real number, according to one eyewitness, was probably closer to four hundred. The uprising marked the beginning of increased state repression and urban resistance in the capital. "Not a night passed without shops being looted or houses searched [by government forces] and their inhabitants molested or insulted and their valuables taken," remembered one resident.[45]

THE MUJAHIDEEN

Initial resistance to the Soviet occupation was largely spontaneous. For centuries, Afghans had found themselves caught between intrusive foreign empires, and fierce independence had long ago become ingrained in their national culture. When the Soviets arrived at the end of 1979, the Mujahideen were made up of mostly local volunteers operating in unorganized bands. Led by tribal and village leaders and fighting with colonial-era rifles, stolen government guns, muskets, and swords, they staged raids on government garrisons to steal weapons and loot supplies. Many of these materials ended up in bazaars throughout the country as the rebels sold off their spoils to provide for their families back home. But the Soviet occupation transformed this unorganized, local resistance by internationalizing the war. Leaders in neighboring countries (particularly Pakistan) worried about creeping Soviet influence on their frontiers. Likewise, governments in the region and farther afield, such as in the United States, Egypt, China, and Saudi Arabia, worried that the Soviet intervention was the first step in a campaign aimed at expanding Moscow's influence in the Middle East. The Soviet intervention opened the door for a variety of outside forces to enter Afghanistan through the auspices of providing aid to rebel fighters. This foreign aid transformed the Mujahideen into organized, well-armed, well-financed guerrilla groups. But it also connected the rebels to outside ideological influence, much of it Islamic in character.[46]

Throughout the Cold War, U.S. officials had toyed with the idea of using Islam as a means to mobilize the Muslim world against the Soviet Union. By choosing to invade a Muslim country, State Department officers recognized, the Kremlin risked angering Islamic communities around the world. In January 1980, only days after the Soviet intervention, the Egyptian government convened an emergency meeting to consider the best response to the invasion. Egyptian officials resolved to establish training facilities and financial aid for the Afghan Mujahideen and to convene an Islamic summit on developments in Afghanistan. Three weeks later, some ten thousand people participated in an anti-Soviet demonstration at the state-controlled Al-Azhar Mosque in Cairo, beneath a banner that read, "Soviets, Kabul Will Be Your Grave." Leaders from the Muslim Brotherhood addressed the crowd, and Islamic students called for Cairo to sever all ties with Moscow.[47]

While Muslim groups around the Arab world began organizing against the Soviet intervention, Afghanistan's neighbor, Pakistan, provided the principal staging ground for what was to become a global jihad against the Soviet occupation. And Pakistan's president, Muhammad Zia-ul-Haq, would be its mastermind. Zia would be the longest-serving head of state in Pakistan, ruling the country for over eleven years. His arched eyebrows sat atop a stern gaze made more severe by the carefully manicured mustache typical of many military officers trained in the British system. Born in the Punjab, Zia had served with the British Indian Army in Burma during World War II, before joining the Pakistani military in 1947. In 1967, he was posted in Jordan, where he worked training the Hashemite military forces. Zia rose to prominence in September 1970, when he led government forces against Palestinian guerrillas in the Jordanian Civil War— also known as Black September. The posting also kept him away from the disastrous 1971 India-Pakistan War, leaving him among the few military leaders untainted by the defeat. A new government in Islamabad, under Zulfikar Ali Bhutto, brought Zia back to Pakistan and raised him to the rank of major general. Five years later, Bhutto made Zia army chief of staff. In July 1977, Zia led a military coup against the increasingly unpopular Bhutto, arresting the prime minister and placing the military in control of Pakistan.

Once in power, Zia launched a sweeping campaign to bring Islam into the Pakistani state and military. He strengthened ties to the Islamic party Jami'at-e-Islami and institutionalized Islam within the military. Under Zia, the army's motto was changed to "Faith,

Obedience to God, and Struggle in the Path of Allah." Meanwhile, the number of Islamic schools in Pakistan ballooned from around nine hundred in 1971 to more than eight thousand by 1988. Zia also enlarged Pakistan's intelligence bureau, the Directorate for Inter-Services Intelligence (ISI), from around two thousand staff in 1978 to some forty thousand by 1988. By the end of his rule, ISI had grown into a massive and feared organization that penetrated all sectors of the Pakistani state and society. One ISI official would later describe the agency as "probably the most powerful and influential organization in the country." Zia would also guide the regime through what was about to become a massive covert war with Soviet forces in Afghanistan. The convergence of Zia's Islamization of the Pakistani state and Islamabad's central role in channeling international support to the Mujahideen would help transform the war and the larger region.[48]

For leaders in Islamabad, the Soviet push into Afghanistan seemed to represent a very real threat. If the Kremlin truly was seeking to expand its influence in South Asia and to create a beachhead on the Persian Gulf, Pakistan might represent the next logical target after Afghanistan. But if the Soviet Army was bogged down fighting a bloody and expensive war in Afghanistan, Moscow would be dissuaded from pushing southward into Pakistan. Zia understood, however, that too much aid to the Mujahideen might provoke the Kremlin into attacking Pakistan. He told ISI to make sure that the conflict in Afghanistan continued to "boil at the right temperature." A staff of several dozen officers and a few hundred junior military personnel dressed in plain-clothes ran the secret war out of an ISI office in Rawalpindi, directing arms shipments, setting up financial transactions, and coordinating contacts among U.S., British, and Saudi intelligence and Mujahideen commanders. Meanwhile, the ISI set up a total of seven camps in Pakistan that would train more than eighty thousand rebel fighters by the end of the war. The most dangerous jobs, however, went to the clandestine ISI military advisors who fought alongside Mujahideen inside Afghanistan. To provide Islamabad plausible deniability if they were killed or captured, these advisors wore no uniforms and carried no identity cards.[49]

But Zia's strategy reached beyond the immediate war. As journalist Steve Coll later argued, Pakistani officials were "fighting a different war than we were." Pakistan sat on the front line of the war against the Soviet Union, and the battle for Afghanistan carried enormous regional implications for Islamabad. In particular, Zia and his colleagues focused on what would happen after a Soviet withdrawal. "They feared that the vacuum that Afghanistan might become would be a staging ground for Indian mischief and Indian hostility toward Pakistan," Coll explained. India loomed as Islamabad's "existential rival" against which Pakistan had fought and lost three wars, most recently in 1971. Pakistani officials looked to promote militant Islamic groups in Afghanistan as a means of containing Indian influence in a post-Soviet Afghanistan.[50]

While the ISI coordinated the secret war in Afghanistan, the United States served as its quartermaster. By 1986, Washington was spending six hundred million dollars a year (an amount that Arab Gulf states matched) to support the war. Pakistan was quickly transformed into a "strategic hub of American policy" in the region. The massive influx of aid propped up Zia's regime but also helped create a thriving black market for illicit arms. Karachi served as the port of call for CIA small-arms shipments. Rampant corruption at the local and state level ensured that many of the weapons made their way into the city's bazaars, where they helped contribute to skyrocketing levels of crime. Those arms that made it into Mujahideen hands in Afghanistan were delivered on trucks that, once emptied, were loaded with Afghan heroin that made its way back into Pakistan. The war transformed Karachi into a city crawling with drug traffickers, ISI agents, Afghan rebels, and foreign intelligence officers.[51]

This CIA-ISI aid pipeline transformed Afghanistan as well. While U.S. and Arab governments bankrolled much of the war, ISI coordinated the distribution of aid to no fewer than seven competing

Mujahideen organizations. This arrangement left Pakistani officials in charge of deciding which rebel groups received weapons and, ultimately, gave ISI a hand in deciding how those weapons should be used. In practice, ISI sent nearly two-thirds of military aid to Islamic groups. Zia's Islamization of the Pakistani state and military bled into Afghanistan through the CIA-funded pipeline. Rebel leaders who refused Islamabad's directives could expect to see their aid packages cut. In short order, the pro-Pakistani, Islamic Mujahideen organizations became the best-armed, best-funded rebel groups in Afghanistan. Nationalist and secular forces found themselves competing against better-supplied Islamic rivals with deep ties to ISI. Furthermore, because Islamabad's goal was to create a Soviet quagmire in Afghanistan, ISI officials chose to reinforce the division of Mujahideen forces. Rather than create a unified command structure that would have allowed the rebels to control their own affairs and raised the prospect of fueling Pashtun nationalism, Pakistan continued to divvy supplies among rival Mujahideen groups. In addition to flooding the country with weapons, the CIA-ISI program promoted warlordism, Islamization, and division and increased Pakistani influence inside Afghanistan.[52]

CIA and ISI officials worked with the commanders of seven principal Mujahideen organizations through the Islamic Unity of Afghan Mujahideen, or as CIA officers called them, the Peshawar Seven. The seven rival guerrilla factions functioned as an uneasy coalition united by a shared desire to drive the Soviet Fortieth Army out of Afghanistan. Six of the seven groups were Pashtun—Pashtuns represented the demographic plurality in Afghanistan, making up some 40 percent of the total population—with the Jami'at-e-Islami serving as the only Tajik organization. Three commanders, in particular, would emerge as leaders in the movement: Gulbuddin Hekmatyar, Jalaluddin Haqqani, and Ahmad Shah Massoud. Each was affiliated with an Islamic party. Each, moreover, later emerged as a challenger for power in Afghanistan after the war ended.

Hekmatyar was the ISI's favorite. Born in 1947 in northern Afghanistan, he quickly distinguished himself as a talented youth. From 1970 to 1972, he pursued an engineering degree at Kabul University, before being arrested for the murder of a fellow student. After his release the following year, Hekmatyar joined the organization Muslim Youth, where he emerged as the rival of another student at Kabul, Ahmad Shah Massoud. Hekmatyar split away from the organization in 1975 to form the more radical Hezb-e Islami party. After the failed uprising in 1975, Hekmatyar and many of his supporters fled to Pakistan, where they established connections with the ISI. Following the Kremlin's invasion of Afghanistan, the Zia regime naturally looked to Hekmatyar and the Hezb-e Islami as allies in the war against the Fortieth Army. Hezb-e Islami claimed to have twenty-seven provincial organizations in Afghanistan, but its strength was concentrated in Paktia and Nangarhar Provinces. "He was a nasty guy," one CIA officer remembered. "In the late seventies he was a Pakistani agent and the Pakistanis used him as an instrument." U.S. officials, who had little understanding of Mujahideen politics, simply went along with Islamabad's recommendations. Journalist Peter Bergen explained that "Hekmatyar's party had the dubious distinctions of never winning a significant battle during the war, training a variety of militant Islamists from around the world, killing significant numbers of *mujahideen* from other parties, and taking a virulently anti-Western line." In 1982, State Department intelligence noted that Hekmatyar's forces had engaged in frequent "turf fights" with other rebel groups, so much so that rival Mujahideen had begun to coordinate "partly in self-defense against [Hekmatyar's] followers." Hekmatyar's priorities, in retrospect, seem to have focused less on fighting the Soviets than on being in a position to take power once they left.[53]

Ahmad Shah Massoud presented a stark contrast to Hekmatyar. Born in 1953 in the Panjshir Valley and raised in Kabul, the Tajik leader was perhaps the most effective Mujahideen military commander. He studied engineering at Kabul University, where he joined

Muslim Youth. When Hekmatyar split away from the organization to form the Hezb-e Islami in 1975, Massoud remained loyal to the more moderate Jami'at-e-Islami, led by Burhanuddin Rabbani. Moderate and pragmatic, Massoud led the military wing of the party, and his battlefield prowess quickly earned him an international reputation. While he was no darling of the Pakistani ISI, journalists seemed taken with the young commander. "Massoud has displayed such leadership and knowledge of guerrilla warfare," one foreign correspondent wrote, "that he has earned a reputation here in Afghanistan not unlike that of Che Guevara." Another commented, "I wouldn't be surprised if in all of Afghanistan, the Russians fear—I mean truly fear—only one man: Massoud. He represents the best hope for the country, the best hope of developing a movement that can restore Afghan independence."

An earnest and by all accounts mild-mannered man, Massoud usually appeared in a military jacket, combat trousers, and a traditional rounded Afghan cap. His forces controlled the sixty-mile-long Panjshir Valley, which commanded the approaches to two of the major passes through the Hindu Kush and was home to the largest concentration of Tajiks in Afghanistan. It also sat in a position to menace the Salang Tunnel, a treacherous 1.6-mile-long passage cut into the mountains through which the Soviets moved massive amounts of supplies. As a natural choke point, the tunnel and its surroundings became one of the war's most important strategic positions.

As the commander of the Mujahideen in the Panjshir, Massoud (nicknamed the Lion of Panjshir) became one of the most important Afghan leaders of the war. In organizing his troops, he instituted a new military structure that split his forces into separate military commands, with guerrilla garrisons, mobile commando units, and a special strike force. More than simply a military leader, he displayed uncommon political acumen, appointing economic, political, and religious committees in each of the districts he controlled. The committees collected taxes, distributed welfare, ran schools, and administered a judicial system. Unlike most other Mujahideen commanders, Massoud impressed reporters as moderate, democratic, and relatively pro-Western. His reputation would continue to grow as he survived multiple assassination attempts launched by the KGB, the ISI, and rival Mujahideen leaders. His luck would run out, however, on September 9, 2001—two days before the 9/11 attacks—when two suspected agents from Osama bin Laden's Al-Qaeda organization, posing as journalists, detonated a suicide bomb during an interview with the guerrilla commander.[54]

While Hekmatyar and Massoud were the most prominent Mujahideen commanders during the war, another, Jalaluddin Haqqani, would rise to prominence in the decades after. An ethnic Pashtun from Afghanistan's southeastern Paktia Province, Haqqani earned advanced degrees in religious studies at the Dar al-'Ulum Haqqaniyya madrasa outside Peshawar. While Hekmatyar and Massoud had engineering backgrounds, Haqqani was a religious scholar. Following the 1978 revolution, Haqqani, together with many of his former comrades from Haqqaniyya, formed what became known as the Haqqani network. Haqqani's forces controlled a significant stretch of the tribal highlands in the Loya Paktia region, along the border with Pakistan. This territory formed an ideal staging area for Pakistani aid—it was largely impervious to Soviet incursions and reasonably close to Kabul and Jalalabad. Working with the Haqqani network and Saudi contractors, ISI used CIA and Arab funds to build the formidable Zhawar base and supply depot in Khost. Approximately 20 percent of the total CIA and ISI aid sent into Afghanistan was allocated to Haqqani's forces operating out of Zhawar. There, Haqqani used his religious training, strategic position, and access to massive resources to fuse Islamic theology with the struggle against the Soviet occupation. His most notable success was in establishing lasting ties with Islamic patrons in the Arab world. Though these ties generated aid and supplies in the early 1980s, by the later years of the war, Haqqani was bringing in substantial numbers of Arab volunteers to join the jihad against the Soviet occupation. He was among the first and most successful Mujahideen to argue that support for the Afghan jihad was a religious obligation for all observant Muslims. Under his guidance, Afghanistan would become the training ground for a new generation of Arab Islamic fighters. Haqqani, together with the so-called Afghan Arabs, would play a critical role in globalizing the jihad.[55]

Though it was officially clandestine, Soviet leaders were well aware of the CIA-ISI aid pipeline. In October 1980, Soviet defense minister Ustinov issued a report outlining the "foreign interference" in Afghanistan. In the wake of the 1978 revolution, he reported, Washington; its NATO allies; and China, Pakistan, Iran, and several Arab states had "launched subversive actions" against the PDPA regime. "The USA and its allies," he wrote, "are training, equipping and sending into DRA territory armed formations of the Afghan counterrevolution . . . [which] had become the main factor destabilizing the situation in Afghanistan." American, Chinese, Pakistani, and Egyptian instructors were training more than sixty thousand Mujahideen at forty-two sites across Pakistan. Iran was operating some thirteen rebel training camps in its territory. Meanwhile, Washington was sending weapons to the rebels through third-party countries such as Egypt and Saudi Arabia. The CIA was particularly interested in using "religious movements and groups in the struggle against the spread of Communist influence," and the "Afghan section" in the U.S. consulate in Karachi was encouraging the disparate Mujahideen factions to form a single unified command.[56] Soviet intelligence warned that the CIA had begun infiltrating rebels trained in Texas and California in January 1980 and had completed the construction of a training camp in Sarab Rud, Pakistan, in March.[57]

IF KHOMEINI'S IRAN FORMED THE EPICENTER OF THE great sectarian revolt, Afghanistan constituted its largest battlefield. The war against the Soviet presence in Afghanistan would become the crucible out of which a new kind of revolutionary war would emerge. In hidden bases deep in the Hindu Kush Mountains, a new breed of insurgent would be born. This transformation was nurtured by a global network of support made possible by the unique geopolitical realities of the late Cold War. Although still in its nascent stages, the covert program to aid the Mujahideen consummated the shadowy partnership between the Mujahideen and U.S., Pakistani, Chinese, and Saudi intelligence services. For most of the next decade, Washington, Islamabad, Beijing, and Riyadh bankrolled a network of Islamic militants engaged in a brutal struggle against the Soviet Army. It was now clear that the Soviets faced a far tougher fight in Afghanistan than they had anticipated. As the winter of 1980 approached, all sides dug in for a long, brutal war.

THE MIDDLE EAST AT WAR

1980–1982

In the coming decade, the Middle East would supplant Southeast Asia as the most war-torn region of the world. The Middle Eastern battlefields of the late Cold War stretched across the southern flank of the Soviet Union from the jagged mountains of the Hindu Kush, across the arid Mesopotamian plains, and west to the Mediterranean cities of Beirut and Sidon. While the first two waves of mass violence in the East had focused on Communist revolutions, ethnic and religious warfare dominated the third and final wave of conflict. In Afghanistan, the Soviet Army found itself mired in a bloody war. Like earlier invaders, the Soviets found Afghanistan easy to conquer but nearly impossible to control. Meanwhile, across the Persian Plateau, the revolution in Tehran continued to send shock waves across the region. As the ayatollahs consolidated control in Iran, its historic rival, Iraq, prepared to launch an assault on the Shia regime. To the west, along the shores of the Mediterranean, Israeli leaders prepared to launch their own invasion of their northern neighbor, Lebanon, in a bid to remake the Levant. The climactic final decade of the Cold War ravaged societies across the Middle East and transformed the face of war in the late twentieth century.

Following the collapse of Third World communism in the 1970s, the combatants on the battlefields of the Middle East mostly abandoned the East-West framework of ideological conflict. "In the last five years," a 1981 CIA report noted, "the link between religion and nationalism has been growing stronger in the Islamic world." This resurgence was not monolithic or directed by any single authority. Rather, the pressures of rapid modernization and ongoing political turmoil had helped transform Islam into a "potent political force." According to the CIA report, throughout much of the region, "Islam is increasingly being linked to nationalism, and the resultant political currents are taking a decidedly anti-US direction." Washington's close association with modernization drove much of this anti-U.S. sentiment, which was reinforced by "US global strategies." U.S. military deployments in the region, a thirst for oil, and "US support for Israel—a constant reminder of Muslim military defeat and Western imperialism," helped fuel this animosity. As a result, pro-Western leaders in the region would need to be careful about identifying too openly with Washington. "One challenge for the US," the report argued, "will be to distinguish between the rhetoric designed for internal consumption and a leader's personal willingness to enter into a relationship with the US for certain purposes." Analysts also warned that the Kremlin was likely to seek greater influence in Muslim politics. Nevertheless, the Islamic resurgence "presents problems for Moscow" owing to the difficulty of finding a synthesis between Marxism and Islam.[1]

Ultimately, this sectarian resurgence raised dangers for both superpowers. But both Washington and Moscow were too deeply invested in the Cold War struggle to remain disengaged from the conflicts raging along the southern periphery of the Soviet Union. Containment's momentum pulled the superpowers deeper into the war zones of the Middle East. As the fighting intensified, both superpowers shifted their attention to the region. Moscow and Washington escalated their intervention in Afghanistan and kept a nervous eye on Lebanon and Mesopotamia.

"WAR OF THE MINES"

Having deployed the Fortieth Army during the first phase of the war in Afghanistan, Soviet commanders now faced the difficult task of combating a growing, internationally backed insurgency in a country known for its defiance to outside control. Reports from the city of Kandahar, in southern Afghanistan, described guerrilla influence as "pervasive." Three separate curfews kept Afghans off the streets in the evening. While Soviet forces had imposed a 10:00 p.m. curfew, guerrillas had vowed to fire on anyone moving after 9:00. To be safe, most residents elected to stay indoors after 7:00. Meanwhile, the rebels had forced several schools to close, shot three teachers, and intimidated local butchers who had been hoarding meat. Residents had been forced to scrounge for food and supplies. Petroleum was available only on the black market, and the price of both wood and bread had increased dramatically.[2]

During the second phase of the war, which lasted from March 1980 to April 1985, the Soviet General Staff focused on major combat operations aimed at destroying regional rebel strongholds. The Mujahideen had quickly abandoned the massed guerrilla assaults seen in the first weeks of the conflicts, reverting instead to more traditional hit-and-run operations launched from mountain hideouts. Afghanistan's more rugged regions restricted Soviet movement and prevented the use of heavy military vehicles. The Mujahideen would stand and fight, Soviet commanders found, only when defending a vital base or when they were encircled. With this in mind, Soviet forces concentrated on large operations designed, in the words of the Soviet General Staff, to "liquidate the Mujahideen's regional bases." Tanks and heavy armor were unable to operate effectively off-road and therefore were of limited use beyond their vital roles in guarding convoys. Likewise, fighter jets were unsuited for providing close air support. Helicopter gunships were more useful in mountain warfare and, when employed in close coordination with ground troops, could prove devastating. The real challenge, argued Russian officers, was "not military, but political." Karmal's government, Russian generals later wrote, "did not live up to expectations." Kabul could not project effective control over the fiercely independent tribal regions of the country; Afghan government forces remained ineffective; and poorly conceived government reforms failed to win the support of the population in the villages. Despite Moscow's best efforts, the Mujahideen held "all the main agricultural areas of the country" while Soviet control was limited to cities and the major roads that connected them.[3]

The key to the war, a CIA officer later explained, lay in controlling supply routes. The Soviets needed to establish control over the Panjshir Valley and the Paktia and Khost Provinces, along the Pakistani border. The Panjshir, controlled by Massoud, represented a critical supply conduit for the Soviets. Paktia and Khost, controlled by Haqqani, held the key to closing off the CIA-ISI pipeline to the Mujahideen.[4] The guerrillas, conversely, had to keep their supply lines open while disrupting shipments of Soviet armaments to the Fortieth Army. Each side, then, fought to cut the other's supply lines. Both the Soviets and the Mujahideen laid thousands of mines throughout the country. While the Mujahideen mined roads in an effort to stop convoys, Soviet troops laid mines around garrisons, to prevent rebel attacks. In time, the Soviets would dub the conflict the "war of the mines." Much of the fighting took place in the form of ambushes along major Soviet supply routes. A favorite Mujahideen tactic involved disabling the lead and rear vehicles in a convoy and attacking, from the surrounding heights, the forces trapped between. In response, Soviet troops sent pickets into the hills along key roads in an effort to flush out potential ambushes. Meanwhile, Moscow committed the majority of the Fortieth Army to escorting convoys and garrison duties. Of the 133 battalions stationed in Afghanistan, only 51 were consistently engaged in offensive operations against the rebels. Special

Forces commandos, airborne troops, and reconnaissance battalions, constituting about 20 percent of the total forces in Afghanistan, bore the brunt of the fighting on the Soviet side.[5]

With the main contingents of the Fortieth Army in place, Soviet commanders launched a series of large-scale offensives against suspected rebel bases in the first half of 1980. The first major sweep came in late February and focused on the sixty-mile-long Kunar Valley, along the border with Pakistan. The operation began with an aerial and artillery bombardment of the valley. Helicopters then swooped in to drop troops onto the surrounding ridges while tanks and armored vehicles thundered in. All told, some five thousand Soviet troops, along with tanks, helicopters, and warplanes, participated in the operation. Rebel fighters put up a determined defense, but there was little they could do in the face of such firepower. Soviet troops devastated the villages in which they encountered resistance, leveling buildings and slaughtering both Mujahideen and civilians. After clearing the valley and relieving a government garrison, the Soviets pulled back. Not long after, the rebels returned.[6] Refugees reported that as many as nine thousand families had fled the valley, with some survivors claiming that Soviet forces had used napalm and other chemical weapons.[7] It would be the first of four offensives in the valley that year.

The Soviets launched similar operations in other provinces in a bid to crush rebel sanctuaries, cut lines of supply, and eradicate the Mujahideen. In particular, the Soviets focused on the mountainous regions in the east. Home to some of the fiercest Mujahideen, the area formed a vital supply link to Pakistan. The Panjshir Valley, which lay within striking distance of vital Soviet supply lines running along the Salang Highway, soon emerged as a second trouble area. In frontal engagements, Soviet firepower made short work of the rebels. Heavy armor was impervious to Mujahideen rifles, and Soviet aircraft could strike at will against any target they found. Severely outgunned, rebel fighters quickly abandoned their preferred tactic of massed assaults on Soviet positions.[8] But not every operation went as planned. In March

1980, Mujahideen slaughtered an entire Soviet mechanized battalion. The rebels ambushed the Soviets while they were traveling along a road in Paktia. Their path blocked, Soviet troops remained sheltered inside their vehicles, firing at the rebels taking cover behind boulders on the surrounding hillsides. After the Soviets' ammunition ran out, the Mujahideen moved in, killing everyone they found. Soviet commanders had not yet adjusted their tactics (designed for a conventional war in Europe) to the circumstances they faced in Afghanistan. By relying on heavy armor and motorized rifle battalions, the Soviets remained bound to major roads snaking through gorges, ravines, and narrow passes that provided endless opportunities for Mujahideen ambushes.[9]

By the spring of 1981, Soviet commanders had concluded that their short-term intervention in Afghanistan had become a major war. And Afghanistan's political problems rendered the Fortieth Army's combat operations ineffective. "In our view at this time it is necessary," they wrote, "to evaluate the real state of affairs in the D[emocratic] R[epublic of] A[fghanistan], to mark out a political and military strategy, and the main thing—to demand the DRA leadership switch from assurances to decisive actions." The Karmal regime had shown itself to be largely ineffective. No small part of the problem lay in the rampant factionalism within the PDPA—namely, the efforts of the Parcham wing to dominate all positions of authority. Making matters worse, Soviet officers complained, government bureaucrats showed little real concern for the situation in the countryside. Most officials did not live in the regions they represented, did not visit their provincial districts, and had little knowledge of the economic and political challenges that their constituents faced. As a result, the general population outside the capital had little allegiance to the regime in Kabul. Kabul's land reform programs were ill-conceived and poorly implemented. Desertion was rampant in the Afghan Army, with some units losing nearly a third of their strength. At best, Kabul controlled less than two-thirds of the country's districts, and even there, rebel influence survived. These failures had hamstrung the Fortieth Army's military mission. As a result, Soviet commanders had begun to call for Karmal's removal and the reorganization of the Afghan government. A delay in this task would only preserve "the totalitarian power of one person" and undermine the ultimate goal of the intervention in preserving the gains of the 1978 revolution.[10]

Likewise, Karmal had never been able to establish amicable relations with the tribal authorities along the Iranian and Pakistani borders. These historically independent populations had taken on significant strategic importance as the Soviets worked to cut off the pipeline of foreign aid streaming into the country from Pakistan and Iran. As Soviet commanders warned, "Imperialism is waging an undeclared war in Afghanistan. Following an active policy of political and economic isolation of the DRA, the US, Pakistan, Egypt, and China are giving significant economic aid to the so-called Afghan refugees and are creating and training large contingents of rebel bands on Pakistani and Iranian territory who are then sent into Afghanistan to fight the legal government of the DRA."[11]

According to the CIA, Khomeini's regime in Tehran had become "the most vocal Third World supporter of the Afghan insurgency." Afghan insurgents had accompanied the one hundred thousand to three hundred thousand Afghan refugees who had moved across the border into Iran and were now receiving training from Iranian volunteers. Iranian officials coordinated Mujahideen propaganda, set up insurgent offices in Tehran, and brought guerrilla leaders as guests on diplomatic trips.[12]

China represented another key base of support for the Afghan rebels. Chinese leaders, the CIA explained, saw Moscow's intervention as a move that added "another link in the Soviet encirclement of China" and threatened Pakistan. In response, Beijing strengthened its relations with Islamabad and launched a program to provide aid to the Mujahideen. Zbigniew Brzezinski had reached out to Beijing and encouraged China to expand its support for the rebels. In the coming years, witnesses would report the "widespread use of Chinese-manufactured arms—supplied via Pakistan—in Afghanistan." The similarity between Chinese and Soviet arms, moreover, contributed to the goal of keeping the arms supply covert. China had also begun training Afghan fighters at camps inside China. By the end of the war in 1989, China had sent a reported four hundred million dollars in aid to the Mujahideen.[13]

A "COMPLETE BLITZ"

Faced with the task of fighting a protracted guerrilla war in rough terrain surrounded by a largely hostile population, Soviet troops took many of their frustrations out on local villagers. One British observer traveling on the road from Iran to Herat described a deserted village that had once been home to some five thousand people. "I didn't see more than ten inhabitants there," he wrote. Soviet aircraft had launched a "complete blitz," destroying nearly every building in the area and leaving the ground pockmarked with craters. The entire region was now deserted. The local vineyards had been "reduced to gray dust." "The town that I stayed in," he wrote, "looks like Hiroshima." Human rights observers working with Helsinki Watch and Asia Watch concluded that the Soviets, after failing to win the support of the rural population, had "turned their firepower on civilians." The Soviets had resorted to a policy of indiscriminate reprisals against noncombatants in the countryside. If a convoy came under attack, the Soviets "attack the nearest village." If a region was known to harbor Mujahideen, Soviet planes launched bombing raids. Aerial bombing devastated rural communities. Afghan villagers learned to guess the intentions of aircraft flying overhead by their altitude: high and fast meant the population was safe; low and slow signaled an attack. Fighter-bombers arrived first, bombing mosques, shops, and houses. Next came helicopter gunships, which targeted the villagers and livestock that survived the initial bombardment.[14] In a "war of logistics,"

Moscow aimed to destroy support for the rebels by devastating the rural population that supported them. Soviet forces systematically attacked granaries, destroyed crops, slaughtered livestock, and rounded up young men for conscription in a bid to depopulate troublesome regions. These operations drove millions of Afghans to become refugees and, in the process, deprived the Mujahideen of shelter and supplies, forcing the rebels deeper into the mountains.[15]

Most of the refugees fled across the border into Pakistan. By 1982, dozens of camps lined the border. Two and a half years into the war, nearly one in five Afghans had fled, making them the largest refugee population on the planet. The tent cities had begun to look less like temporary camps and more like permanent settlements—mud-and-stone huts were replacing white canvas tents; mosques; bazaars, schools, and clinics had sprouted up; green Islamic Mujahideen flags flapped in the wind that blew down the mountainsides. The camps buzzed with refugees, nomads, rebel fighters, and Pakistani tribesmen. The United Nations, World Food Programme, and outside countries spent around a million dollars per day on food and medical supplies for the nearly three million displaced Afghans. Meanwhile, the millions of sheep, goats, and camels that the refugees had brought with them picked local pastures clean.[16] Beyond humanitarian concerns, U.S. officials recognized the political value of support for the refugees. As the embassy staff in Islamabad wrote, "assistance to the refugees serves important U.S. interests in the region—including stability in Pakistan, assurance of continuity for [Pakistan's] role in giving haven to the refugees, and the viability of the resistance in Afghanistan."[17] The world's largest population of refugees—more than 2.5 million by some counts—was an appendage to the war across the border, providing safe haven, logistical support, and propaganda for the Mujahideen's struggle against the Soviet occupation.

The Soviets also struggled to maintain their supply lines. Moscow moved three-quarters of its equipment and supplies into Afghanistan along the Salang Highway, a short trek from Massoud's Mujahideen stronghold in the Panjshir Valley. The entrance to the hundred-mile-long valley is guarded by a steep gorge, which then opens up to fields of maize and wheat, vineyards, and apricot orchards. Forces in the valley were also close enough to threaten Bagram Air Base, the largest Soviet airfield in Afghanistan, and the Afghan capital, Kabul. Soviet commanders could not long tolerate the presence of so fierce a rebel warlord as Massoud at the doorstep of their most vital installations. In April 1980, the Soviets launched the first of an eventual nine offensives to pacify the Panjshir. Three Soviet battalions, along with around a thousand Afghan soldiers, swept into the valley, clearing minefields, repairing bridges, and taking rebel positions. Massoud's guerrillas retreated before the onslaught, laying ambushes and sabotaging roads. Soviet forces advanced to the end of the valley to declare victory. As the Soviets withdrew, however, bands of Mujahideen filtered back into the valley, launching sporadic attacks on the retreating Russians. This first sweep established a pattern the Soviets would follow throughout the war: after taking an area using massive force, they would declare victory and withdraw, leaving the rebels, most of whom had retreated in advance of the onslaught, to retake the area.[18]

In such a war, decisive victory was all but impossible. Still, this did not stop the Soviets from trying. In May 1982, Soviet commanders launched their largest operation yet: a fifth major assault on Massoud's forces in the Panjshir Valley. The sweep came in part in retaliation for a guerrilla attack on Bagram Air Base in April that destroyed twenty-three aircraft and helicopters. Some twelve thousand troops participated in the offensive alongside tanks, mobile artillery, and combat vehicles. The ground forces were supported by massive waves of helicopter gunships and warplanes. The assault began with aerial bombardments followed by helicopters that dropped troops on key positions. Before the attackers closed in, Massoud was able to evacuate his three thousand guerrillas to the surrounding heights. There, the Mujahideen set up firing positions on the Soviet forces below. A Western reporter claimed that Massoud's forces destroyed fifty vehicles and thirty-five aircraft in the first ten days of the offensives. Rebel attacks on the Salang Highway nearby destroyed another sixty vehicles and blocked the vital route. "The Russians can stay as long as they want," one rebel commander boasted. "There is nothing much they can do except drive their tanks up and down the valley. Their bombing does not bother us." But the sweep was more devastating for civilians. Soviet bombardments destroyed houses, fields, and irrigation systems; slaughtered livestock; and killed scores of civilians.[19] While Massoud and the Panjshir had become a symbol of the resistance, the Soviets' failure to destroy the guerrilla forces in the pivotal early years of the war boded ill for their broader efforts in Afghanistan.

Unable to dislodge Massoud's forces from the Panjshir, Soviet commanders brokered a truce with the guerrilla leader in 1983. Three years into the war, the Kremlin had come to see Massoud as not simply a rebel fighter but also a shrewd political leader. "I'm not an adversary of the Soviet Union or the Soviet people," he told Russian negotiators. Under the cease-fire, both sides agreed to refrain from major operations, giving the Soviets greater security for their convoys passing through the Salang Tunnel and Massoud's forces an opportunity to regroup and focus on disputes with rival Mujahideen groups. Massoud also put energy into building up a civil administration in the Panjshir Valley. The Kremlin's willingness to negotiate with a Mujahideen commander was novel, but it did not last. After two failed Soviet assassination attempts, Massoud allowed the truce to expire in March 1984 and resumed operations against the Salang Highway the following month. Soon after, the Soviets launched their seventh and largest assault on the Panjshir Valley. Anticipating the offensive, Massoud evacuated his troops and much of the civilian population. The Soviets launched a combined air and ground attack consisting of three squadrons of Tu-16 bombers, the 108th Motorized Rifle Division, and five thousand Afghan troops. On April 16, Massoud blew up three bridges and began launching attacks on supply convoys in a bid to disrupt Soviet preparations. Five days later, Mujahideen fighters staged an assault on Bagram. Soviet commanders responded by pummeling the Panjshir with heavy bombing raids and sending combat vehicles roaring up the valley behind heavy artillery barrages. Meanwhile, Mi-24 helicopters dropped elite units into positions to trap retreating guerrillas, forcing Massoud's fighters higher up into the mountains. After several weeks, Moscow declared victory. Massoud had survived, but the Soviets had established a permanent ground presence in the valley.[20]

After three years of fighting in Afghanistan, there was still no end in sight. Soviet forces won most of their engagements with the rebels, but the insurgency survived. The Mujahideen continued to fight with religious zeal, maintained a complex set of tribal allegiances, and fiercely resisted attempts at outside control. Making matters worse, Washington showed renewed determination to continue its support for the insurgency. Ronald Reagan, the hard-line conservative Republican presidential nominee, had won a resounding victory over Jimmy Carter in the 1980 election. The Reagan administration was determined to increase the pressure on the Soviets around the world, prompting some commentators to speak of the rise of a second Cold War under Reagan's leadership. Operations in Afghanistan would form the centerpiece of Reagan's Third World offensive against Moscow. The Reagan administration, working alongside the Pakistani ISI, had determined to dramatically increase the cost of Moscow's intervention in both blood and treasure. As the Reagan White House geared up to launch a multipronged offensive against Soviet power around the world, Afghanistan emerged as the most promising theater of operation. As one historian argues, "Among the numerous battles Reagan waged around the world, Afghanistan should be understood as the central front."[21]

"LIKE LIGHTNING ON THEIR HEADS"

Even as the Soviets struggled to put down the insurgency in Afghanistan, another conflict erupted in neighboring Iran.

The Iranian Revolution, which had helped spark the conflict in Afghanistan, continued to destabilize the wider region. On September 22, 1980, under the cover of darkness, squadrons of Iraqi jets screamed over the border in a surprise attack on ten Iranian airfields. Iraqi president Saddam Hussein hoped to destroy Iran's air force fleet as it sat on the tarmac in an operation modeled on Israel's 1967 strike against Egypt. The Iraqis achieved the element of surprise, but their bombs were less effective. Poor training and second-rate Soviet avionics ensured that most of their strikes fell wide of their targets. As clouds of smoke drifted over Iranian air bases and pilots scrambled to their jets, Iraqi infantry and armored divisions stormed across the border at eight different points. In the north, Iraqi troops pushed into Iranian Kurdistan to block any possible Iranian counterattack against the Kirkuk oil fields. Meanwhile, Iraqi forces in the central region seized the high ground along the Baghdad–Tehran road to block a counterattack against the Iraqi capital. The real objective of the offensive, however, lay to the south, along the contested Shatt al-Arab waterway (forming the border between the two countries in the south) and the Iranian coastal cities of Abadan and Khorramshahr. Here, the Iraqis planned to expand the Iraqi coastline with a conquest of the southern borderlands, which contained large numbers of Arabs, minorities in overwhelmingly Persian Iran. The assault transformed the ancient frontier between the Ottoman and Safavid Empires once more into a war zone and touched off a conflict that would drag on for nearly eight years.[22]

Saddam's motives for the invasion grew out of both ambitions and anxieties. Five years earlier, Iraq had signed an agreement with Iran that recognized shared control of the Shatt al-Arab waterway and renounced Baghdad's claims to the Arab province of Khuzestan. The agreement, which favored Tehran, embittered Saddam and much of the controlling Ba'ath Party leadership. As part of the agreement, Tehran agreed to cease its support to Kurdish rebels in Iraq, allowing Baghdad to reassert control over Kurdish territories in the north. But the 1979 revolution, the fall of the Shah, and the near disintegration of the Iranian military presented Saddam's regime with a new opportunity to deliver on its revanchist dreams. Iran's refusal to revisit the agreements meant that Baghdad would need to regain its former control of the waterway "with blood and weapons," he told his generals in the weeks before the invasion. "This is a historical chance. It means we're getting back the Shatt al-Arab and the lands along our border but it means something greater, it means that Iraq has moved from one stage to another." The Ba'athist leader planned to seize key areas along the frontier and present Tehran a fait accompli. If the Iranians chose to escalate, Saddam boasted, "We will retaliate immediately. It is just a single phone call for our decision [to launch a military assault] to reach them just like lightening [sic] on their heads."[23]

CIA analysts warned that a victory in the war against Iran would dramatically increase Baghdad's influence in the Arab world, at least in the short term. "Jordan, Saudi Arabia, the smaller Persian Gulf states, and perhaps even Syria and the Palestine Liberation Organization will pay greater deference to Iraq," a report argued, "but they also will try to circumscribe Iraqi power and exploit Iraqi ambitions for their own purposes." Meanwhile, an Iraqi victory would threaten Israeli and Egyptian leaders, raise the odds of "leftists" seizing power in Tehran, and open the door to increased Soviet influence in the region.[24] The best-case scenario for Washington and its allies, then, would be a limited Iraqi victory that undermined the power of Tehran's ayatollahs but left Iran intact as a counterbalance to Iraqi power in the Gulf.

Beyond presenting an opportunity for the assault, the revolution in Tehran raised dangers for Saddam's Sunni regime in Baghdad. Iraq's Shia majority had greeted the news of Khomeini's rise with enthusiasm. "Iran has been sinking in its own blood for an entire year," Saddam had told his advisors in February 1979. "We are not worried about the current state of Iran, but rather the unpredictable outcome of the different phases [of the revolution] in Iran."[25] In March 1979, prominent Iraqi Shia cleric Baqir al-Sadr sent a cable to Khomeini, congratulating the Ayatollah on his victory and expressing hope for more Islamic victories to come. When Iraqi authorities banned Sadr from traveling to Tehran two months later, a surge of demonstrations swept through the Iraqi Shia community. In response, the regime staged mass arrests of suspected organizers and threw Sadr in prison. The riots that followed gave Saddam and the regime an excuse to crush Iraq's leading Shia movement, Al-Da'wa, and execute hundreds of prisoners. The following April, authorities tortured and executed Sadr after a failed assassination attempt against Deputy Prime Minister Tariq Aziz. Saddam deported to Iran some thirty-five Shia Iraqis suspected of harboring hostility toward the Sunni-controlled state.[26]

As sectarian tensions rose throughout Iraq, the Ba'athist regime grew ever more suspicious of Iranian machinations. Khomeini and his followers made no secret of their desire to spread their revolution to the wider Islamic world. Neighboring Iraq and its Shia majority (some two-thirds of the population) sat at the top of Tehran's list. While Khomeini formed the vanguard of the Islamic revolution, Saddam was a contender for the leadership of the secular Arab nationalist revolution—a position vacated by Egypt's Anwar el-Sadat in the wake of the 1979 Egypt-Israel Peace Treaty. In the summer of 1980, Saddam and his regime looked eastward, to an increasingly radical Shia regime in Iran that had issued open calls for Islamic revolution and had given support to Shia dissidents inside Iraq. That same regime had alienated the majority of the world community by holding the American embassy staff hostage for the better part of a year even as its military teetered on the brink of disintegration. For Ba'athist officials in Baghdad, the time appeared ripe to launch a preemptive attack on Iran that would topple Khomeini's hostile regime, remove the source of revolutionary unrest among Iraq's domestic Shia, and reclaim the privileges Iraq lost in the 1975 Algiers Agreement signed with Iran. Furthermore, Saddam perceived a narrow window of time in which to move before Khomeini could consolidate full control in

Tehran, reconstitute his military forces, and restore Iran's diplomatic standing in the wider world community. By mid-1980, Iraqi military intelligence concluded that the political turmoil of the revolution and the break with the United States had gutted Iran's military capabilities: "[I]t is clear that, at present, Iran has no power to launch wide offensive operations against Iraq, or to defend itself on a large scale." By striking in September 1980, Saddam and his generals seized what they saw as a historic opportunity to transform the region. They could hardly have been more wrong.[27]

"THEY WILL FIGHT UNTIL THEY DIE"

For the Iranians, the invasion came as both a blessing and a curse. The small contingent of military forces along the border could do little to slow the Iraqi advance. As Iranian troops scrambled to redeploy to the front, it appeared as if Saddam's gambit had paid off. Nevertheless, Khomeini took a defiant stance to the outside world: "A thief has come, thrown a pebble and then fled back to his home." The mood in the capital was one of panic, however. The regime was well aware of the poor state of military preparations, and some leaders began planning for a war of guerrilla resistance against the victorious Iraqis. In the days following the initial assault, however, a different picture emerged. Saddam's air strikes had inflicted less damage than either side had expected. With considerable effort, Iranian ground crews managed to launch a total of 140 F-4 Phantoms, F-5 Tigers, F-14 Tomcats, and support aircraft in a punishing round of reprisals that did considerable damage to Iraqi airfields. The first days of the Iran-Iraq War showcased the contest between American and Soviet warplanes as Iraqi MiGs clashed with the American-made jets flown by the Iranians. In general, the Iranian aircrews proved superior, but Tehran's inability to secure replacement parts for its aircraft suggested that this would not long be the case.[28]

Saddam had also miscalculated the political impact of the invasion in Tehran. The Iraqi leader had gambled that the situation inside Iran in the wake of the revolution was chaotic and that Khomeini's leadership was weak. Moreover, Saddam expected the Arab population in Khuzestan to welcome the invasion and join forces with the invaders. The attack achieved the opposite, however. Faced with an external threat, Iranians throughout the country and from all walks of life put aside domestic divisions and rallied to support the regime. The national emergency created by the assault also allowed Khomeini and his supporters in the regime to further consolidate their authority. The clerics launched a campaign of censorship in the press, coupled with moves to crack down on dissent. At the same time, the Iraqi attack gave a new sense of urgency to the ranks of the regime's supporters. Thousands of volunteers flocked to Tehran's defense. Far from dividing Iran, Iraq's invasion united it and gave the Khomeinists even greater power.[29]

At the front, Saddam's offensive had stalled. As the southern thrust of the Iraqi advance moved toward Khorramshahr and the massive oil facility at Abadan, it began to encounter stiff resistance from Iranian defenders. Khomeini called upon Iranians to turn each town in the invaders' path into a "Stalingrad." While Iraqi guns pounded the two locations, Iranian police, marines, naval cadets, and militias organized a ragtag defense. As black smoke poured from burning oil tanks at Abadan—set aflame by air strikes—Iraqi armored divisions pushed into the city of Khorramshahr. Iranian snipers harried the advancing Iraqis as they fought their way past ruined warehouses on the outskirts of both cities. Both armies rained artillery shells down upon deserted neighborhoods as soldiers and armor battled among the smoking ruins. "You know these Iranian Revolutionary Guards and Iranian soldiers are crazy," an Iraqi told one reporter. "They will fight until they die." By October 7, the Iraqis had seized Khorramshahr's port. Aside from occasional sniper fire from Iranians hiding in the wreckage, the docks lay silent. Iraqi soldiers picked their way through piles of damaged cargo on the piers—rolls of toilet paper flapping in the breeze, vegetable shortening melting in the sun. The retreating Iranians had left obscene graffiti mocking the Iraqis and their leader, Saddam Hussein. By the time the Iraqis gained control of the city, street fighting had leveled much of the city and left some seven thousand casualties. Both sides began referring to the city as Khunistan, or "City of Blood."[30]

As soldiers mopped up the Iranian resistance in Khorramshahr, Iraqi forces pushed east toward Abadan (bordered by rivers in the north and east and the Persian Gulf in the south and west), throwing up pontoon bridges across the Karun River. Ten miles of palm groves separated the Iraqis south of Basra from Iran's massive oil complex at Abadan. Iranian helicopter gunships strafed the advancing troops as Iranian artillery, dug in around Abadan, shelled the invaders. Iraqi guns returned fire, sending columns of smoke up around the refinery that turned the sky brown. Inside the city, residents dug trenches in the streets in anticipation of the coming assault. While Iraqi guns maintained a nearly continuous stream of fire on the defenders, Iranian warplanes staged retaliatory strikes on enemy artillery positions. Although the Iraqis were able to encircle the island almost completely and advance to within a mile of the city, Iranian reinforcements landed at the southern tip of Abadan and bolstered its defenses. The Iranians managed to repel repeated Iraqi attempts to take the island until the third week of November, when heavy rains turned the approaches to Abadan into an impassable quagmire.[31]

With the Iraqi offensive halted, all parties had a chance to take stock. The invasion, which was supposed to have accomplished its goals within two weeks, had not gone according to plan. Even so, the capture of Khorramshahr was a significant victory. "No major city in the Middle East," one historian wrote, "had fallen since the 1967 war." The price in manpower and equipment had been high, however, and the Iraqis could no longer sustain their offensive. As Saddam's troops turned to preparing defensive positions, Iran's leaders prepared for a counterattack. With the invasion stalled, the Islamic regime seized the opportunity to further consolidate power and launch a nationwide mobilization. Individual mosques throughout the country were charged with fielding units composed of twenty-two men who would receive training as part of the home guard, which was reorganized as the Basij paramilitary militia, which would receive its marching orders from the newly created Revolutionary Guard, charged with defending Iran's Islamic institutions. The Iranians recognized that they would not be able to match the Iraqis tank for tank. As long as the regime remained isolated in the world community and cut off from American supplies of weapons, Tehran would face a disadvantage in mechanized war. Iranian commanders therefore turned to their country's massive demographic advantages—Iran had triple the population of Iraq—to counter their foe's war machines. Iran would wage a people's war against the invasion, symbolized most dramatically by the use of "human wave" assaults. The twenty-two-man Basij squads would rush forward in battle, each unit tasked with seizing a specific objective, and overwhelm the Iraqis with their masses. To negate Iraqi command of the air, the Iranians began launching night assaults. With their legions of Basij soldiers marching under the banner of the Ayatollah, and backed by units of the Revolutionary Guard, Tehran hoped to expel the Iraqi invaders.[32]

With the coming of spring 1981, the war resumed in its full ferocity. Iraqi commanders hurled their forces against Abadan in an effort to break the defenders. By midyear, some sixty thousand troops were besieging the island. But the defenders were bolstered by a more stable political situation in Tehran, where the clerics had consolidated control over the legislative, executive, and judicial branches of government. The revolutionary regime now set about integrating its political, religious, and military organs by launching an Islamic education campaign in its military ranks. Clerics called upon the Basij and Revolutionary Guard to view the war as a battle of Islamic forces against nonbelievers. Khomeini denounced the "infidel" Saddam as "a perpetrator of corruption." In a public address, he proclaimed to Iranians, "You are fighting to protect Islam and he is fighting to destroy

Islam. . . . There is no question of peace or compromise." Conversely, Saddam had strengthened his position in Baghdad. Iraqis now celebrated the dictator's birthday as a national holiday and praised him as "the greatest Arab hero since the fall of Baghdad to the Mongols in 1257" and "the savior of the nation from darkness, backwardness and disunity." The Iraqi leader proclaimed the war dead martyrs because they had perished in defense of Islam against "the Persian infidels." Fearing that Iraq's Shia majority might choose to support its coreligionists in Iran, Saddam focused on the ethnic divisions between Iraqi Arabs and Iranian Persians. As both sides amplified their rhetoric, the bloodbath continued. By the first anniversary of the war's outbreak, some 38,000 Iranians and 22,000 Iraqis had been killed.[33]

Iran launched a massive counteroffensive in the autumn of 1981. Iranian troops struck Iraqi positions around Abadan at midnight on September 26, in a move that pushed the invaders back to the Karun River. Having relieved the immediate pressure on its oil facilities in the south, Tehran turned its attention to northern Khuzestan. Iranian commanders had devised a set of tactics that would prove devastatingly effective against the Iraqis' superior firepower. The Iraqis, reconnaissance revealed, rarely prepared adequate defenses around their bivouacs and fought poorly at night. Iranian assaults would be led by hordes of Basij and Revolutionary Guard units aimed at overwhelming the comparatively weak Popular Army units that the Iraqis used to fill out their lines of more experienced combat troops. As gaps appeared in the Iraqi lines, the Iranians would rush in, before fanning out to encircle the remaining Iraqi troops at the front. In this way, Iranian forces scored victories at Susangerd and Bostan in late November that created a vulnerable Iraqi salient around Dezful. After building up its forces over the course of the winter, Tehran launched the three-pronged Fath ol-Mobin operation against Dezful at midnight on March 22, 1982. Iranian columns cut through the Iraqi forces before closing around several Iraqi brigades on March 30.[34]

Tehran's victories in the north and at Abadan left the city of

Khorramshahr as the last major chunk of Iranian territory still under Iraqi occupation. Both sides began preparations for the coming battle. Saddam placed considerable political value on holding the city and committed his forces to a defensive strategy. Iraqi engineers prepared a network of earthworks, bunkers connected by underground passages, and minefields, and began razing buildings and clearing vegetation to create fire zones. Baghdad sought to transform Khorramshahr into a fortress defended by 150,000 Iraqi troops. On April 30, the Iranians launched another offensive, spearheaded by 35,000 Revolutionary Guards attacking Iraqi positions along the Baghdad–Basra road. The second phase of the operation began on May 1, when Iranian forces crossed the Karun River. Five days later, another Iranian force struck near Hoveyzeh and Hamid. Human-wave attacks slowly overwhelmed the Iraqi troops, who clung in vain to their prepared defensive positions. On May 9, Iranian troops seized control of the road running through Hamid, cutting supply lines and forcing the Iraqis to abandon their defenses and pull back to a ring around Khorramshahr. The city had become a trap for Saddam's troops. Short of supplies and ammunition, and outnumbered by a factor of two to one, the Iraqis could do little to stop the flood of Iranian troops. After ten days of savage fighting, Iranian troops cut Baghdad's supply line into the city. By May 23, the remaining Iraqi defenders had fallen back to their last redoubt inside Khorramshahr. As Saddam's forces began to collapse, 30 to 40 percent managed to escape across the Shatt al-Arab. Another twelve thousand were caught inside the city and taken prisoner. The fighting transformed the port city, in the words of one reporter, into "a wasteland of rubble, minefields and abandoned trenches. Virtually no building has escaped destruction. There is no life in the ruins."[35]

"A GRAND HISTORIC BATTLE"

With the liberation of Khorramshahr at the end of May 1982, Tehran expelled the Iraqis from all but a narrow strip of its territory. The Iraqis had suffered significant casualties, and another forty thousand of its troops had been taken prisoner. The war had also become a heavy burden on the Iraqi economy; by 1983, Baghdad carried twenty-five billion dollars in foreign debt. Blame for the defeats fell squarely on the shoulders of Saddam. The Iraqi leader had launched the war, served as its strategic engineer, and now carried the blame for recent setbacks. In June 1982, the Revolutionary Command Council (RCC), the military brass, and top Ba'ath officials held a meeting without the dictator to hammer out a cease-fire proposal. Baghdad proposed a truce in exchange for acceptance of the prewar status quo—a tacit admission that the war had been a mistake. Had Khomeini accepted the proposal, Saddam would likely have been pushed out of power. Tehran's rejection, however, gave the Iraqi leader an opening to reassert his control. Saddam stressed his personal role as the only leader who could deliver Iraq from its current predicament. At the same time, he cracked down on any hint of opposition, announcing that he had personally shot the minister of health for suggesting that he, Saddam, step down. He reorganized the RCC and the Ba'ath leadership, and also worked to reorganize the military, promoting officers loyal to the president and dumping enormous resources into rebuilding the organization's fighting capacity. The shift from offensive to defensive operations demanded a new strategy: Baghdad also increased spending on its chemical and biological weapons programs and its surface-to-surface missile force, in the hope of using both as deterrents against Khomeini's legions.[36]

While the summer of 1982 witnessed the reconsolidation of the regime in Baghdad, it also saw a hardening of attitudes in Tehran. The fighting had dispelled any U.S. hopes for the collapse of the Ayatollah's regime. Khomeini and his supporters had faced periodic internal challenges as the revolution solidified into a new regime. The most dangerous of these came from the left-wing People's Mujahideen, which had been fighting an urban guerrilla war against the clerical regime since 1981. Khomeini survived these internal challenges, however, at the same time that Iranian military forces turned back the Iraqi invasion. A 1982 CIA report concluded that the ruling clerics had institutionalized their power in Iran, "repressed internal opposition forces," and "Islamified" the military. The regime had maintained its support among Iran's "lower class" majority and launched a campaign to centralize economic planning and development.[37] Moreover, the CIA warned, Tehran was taking "full advantage of the impasse over [the Lebanese Civil War] to extend its influence in the Arab world and promote its hegemony in the Gulf." Iran had stepped into the role of "defender of Syria and the PLO" and had begun calling on the Gulf states to "return to the fold of Islam" and distance themselves from Washington.[38]

On the heels of its victory in Khorramshahr, Khomeini's regime faced a decision: whether to declare victory and seek an end to the war or to press its advantage and invade Iraq. The proponents of the former option could argue that Tehran had successfully defended its territory and, in the eyes of much of the international community, been the victim of Iraqi aggression—to continue the war would cast the regime as the aggressor and risk further alienating it from the wider world. Those calling for invasion could argue, conversely, that Iran had paid a heavy price in the war and now had an opportunity to destroy the hated Ba'athist regime and restore access to the Shia holy sites at Najaf and Karbala, to the south of Baghdad. While Khomeini understood the dangers of invading Iraq, he was loath to sue for peace—tens of thousands of Iranians had died in the fighting, and their sacrifice must be avenged. Sometime around June 20, 1982, the regime made the fateful decision to invade Iraq in a bid to destroy Saddam's regime.[39]

At 11:30 p.m. on the night of July 13, Iranian armed forces launched Operation Ramadan al-Mubarak. The previous day, Iranian state television had announced, "A grand historic battle is about to take place. The sons of Khomeini have gone to the Front, with the intention of marching to occupy Karbala." The offensive aimed at breaching Iraqi lines in the south and laying siege to Iraq's main port city of Basra. Tehran hoped that the Shia population there would rise up against the regime and welcome the invaders. Basra's defenses were formidable, however. Seven divisions occupied the city, which was ringed by a maze of extensive earthworks bristling with barbed wire and guarded by minefields and canals designed to slow the progress of attackers. Iraqi commanders had also positioned heavy armor along with helicopter gunships to guard the approaches to the city. Over the next month, the Iranians sent five human-wave assaults across the malarial marshes that lay between their front lines and the city. Led by Basij troops who had been sent ahead to clear mines, companies of Revolutionary Guard assaulted the city. Iraqi counterattacks focused on striking the Iranian flanks with mobile armor and gunships. After four weeks of fighting—during the height of which some observers estimated a thousand people were killed each day—Tehran halted its offensive. Iranian gains were meager: a strip of land twelve miles long and three miles wide. For this the Iranians had suffered a casualty ratio of three to one against the defenders.[40]

Iran's invasion helped resolve a dilemma for the superpowers. American officials had little affinity for either side. Baghdad was home to one of the more radical regimes in the Arab world, which also happened to be aligned with the Soviet Union. The regime in Tehran, for its part, was viciously anti-American—the hostage crisis was still fresh in the minds of most Americans—and had denounced the United States as the "great Satan." "In a perfect world," CIA analyst Bruce Riedel later wrote, "the United States would have liked to see the war either end quickly or go on indefinitely." However, Iran's offensive in the summer of 1982 raised the worst possible scenario: a victory for the ayatollahs. "Yes, the Iraqi regime was despicable," Riedel explained, "but still the feeling was that if Iran won the war, that would be the worst of everything—the Middle East as we knew it would soon be overrun by anti-Western fanatics. . . . It was a siege mentality. And yes, we were in that same bunker with Saddam

Hussein. Keeping Saddam going became an overriding policy objective of the United States in the region." Iran's invasion cast Ba'athist Iraq as a potential bulwark against the spread of Khomeini's revolution into the wider region.[41]

In the days leading up to Iran's attack, Reagan's national security advisor, William Clark, had warned the president that the invasion "will create shock waves throughout the Gulf and pose further dangers for U.S. interests in the Middle East, which are already threatened because of Lebanon." If successful, he claimed, the Iranian offensive could topple Saddam's regime and destabilize pro-American governments in Saudi Arabia, Jordan, and the Gulf. In this same vein, a declassified Reagan administration paper from mid-1982 advocated a "tilt toward Iraq" as the best option for dealing with the conflict in the region. The paper argued that the outcome of the war would impact U.S. access to Gulf oil and help decide Iran's strategic orientation in the larger Cold War struggle. Washington's policies, the paper continued, should seek to shield the Arab world from both Soviet influence and "radical forces (such as Iran)." At the same time, the United States should expand its military capabilities in the Middle East in the hope of deterring "overt Soviet aggression and, failing deterrence, to fight a conventional war limited to the region while denying the Soviets control of the Gulf." In light of these concerns, the paper concluded, U.S. officials should consider providing strategic intelligence to the regime in Baghdad in an effort to bolster its defenses against the Iranian invasion.[42]

While officials in Washington deliberated over a tilt toward Iraq, Moscow also began to reconsider its policies toward the belligerents. Like the United States, the USSR had initially sought to remain out of the war. Although Soviet leaders seized the opportunity to blame Washington for fomenting the crisis, they urged both sides to cease hostilities and move toward de-escalation. Indeed, news that its client in Baghdad had launched an invasion without first consulting the Kremlin did not come as a welcome surprise. Saddam's move aggravated an already strained relationship between Baghdad and Moscow brought on by Ba'athist repression of the Iraqi Communist Party (ICP) dating back to 1978. Rather than turn a blind eye to Baghdad's efforts to crush its domestic Communists, the Kremlin had authorized KGB operatives to open a clandestine aid channel to ICP agents operating a radio station in the northern Kurdish region. Relations between the two countries deteriorated further at the end of 1979, when Saddam denounced the Soviet intervention in Afghanistan. In early 1980, Moscow authorized the shipment of a thousand antitank rockets and thousands of submachine guns to the ICP. When Iraqi troops stormed across the Shatt al-Arab to attack Iran in September 1980, Soviet leaders were in no mood to lend their support. In retaliation for the attack, the Kremlin canceled all arms shipments to Iraq.[43]

By the summer of 1981, tensions between Moscow and Baghdad had begun to ease. With his offensive halted on the battlefields around Abadan, Dezful, and Khorramshahr, Saddam had a change of heart and endorsed the Soviet war in Afghanistan. The Kremlin reciprocated with a renewal of arms shipments to Baghdad. Iran's invasion of Iraq the following year created a new sense of urgency in the Kremlin. Frustrated as it might be with Saddam, the Politburo understood that the prospect of the Iranian Revolutionary Guard parading through Baghdad would be disastrous. A victory in Iraq would place Khomeini in a position to stir up Islamic revolutionaries throughout the Arab world, in Afghanistan, and inside the Soviet Union itself. In the summer of 1982, Moscow therefore increased its military support for Saddam's regime. Nevertheless, Soviet leaders were careful to limit the flow of arms so as not to give the Iraqis an overwhelming advantage against the Iranians. Neither the United States nor the Soviet Union wished to see a decisive victory in the war. As historian Christopher Andrew observed, both superpowers bought into Henry Kissinger's observation "What a pity they can't both lose!"[44]

This superpower ambivalence rankled Iraqi leaders. Saddam railed against Washington's duplicity. "America has two faces," he told his inner circle; "one face which is the one that it displays in front of us, but there is another face which aims at taming the Iranians though they do not want the Iranians to be defeated." Baghdad was convinced that Washington would abandon Iraq at the first indication of rapprochement with Tehran. While he was disappointed at the lack of full support from Moscow, Saddam recognized that the Kremlin was merely protecting its own interests by seeking an end to the Gulf conflict. In the eyes of the Iraqi regime, however, the USSR remained a "friendly country." Ultimately, transcripts of Saddam's secret conversations reveal that cooperation between parties in the Gulf conflict was born not of any genuine affinity, but rather of ruthless Realpolitik—a fact that would become clear in the coming decade.[45]

THE APPROACHING STORM

While the Soviet-Afghan and Iran-Iraq Wars escalated, the conflict in Lebanon dragged on. After five years of war and more than forty thousand deaths, the republic's citizens were accustomed to violence. Couples clad in gold lamé jumpsuits danced in multimillion-dollar nightclubs in East Beirut while snipers and militiamen armed with rocket-propelled grenades guarded the war-torn no-man's-land that bisected the capital. Shopkeepers who had been chased out of the downtown war zone threw up wooden stalls along the beach from which they continued to sell their wares. Sectarian militias roamed through lawless streets, toting firearms and rocket launchers, and engaging in sporadic clashes with their rivals. "Everyone," a Western reporter wrote in the spring of 1980, "from the hawkers in the street to the ministers of Government agree [sic] that a new and more vicious phase of the civil war is brewing."[46]

Amid this dystopian landscape, the Palestinian liberation movement—which had played a central role in sparking the war— found itself at a crossroads. The rapprochement between Egypt and Israel and the 1976 war with Syria had dealt serious blows to the

PLO's efforts to gain a seat in the peace process and a state in the West Bank and Gaza. However, the organization had gained unprecedented levels of international recognition by the end of the decade and emerged as a key player in Lebanon. The guerrillas had survived Operation Litani and now controlled large stretches of Lebanese territory. Shielded by UN peacekeepers in the south and the semifortified frontier between Christian and Muslim forces that began with the Green Line in Beirut, the PLO found itself in a position of relative security. With Lebanon split into sectarian enclaves, Palestinian leaders enjoyed control over a virtual mini-state stretching from West Beirut down into South Lebanon. Within this territory, Arafat and his comrades built the so-called Fakhani Republic, a virtual state-in-exile, with the structures of a formal government, in the Fakhani neighborhood of West Beirut, complete with a bureaucracy and financial infrastructure. At the same time, the organization began transforming its military units into a conventional force. Where the PLO had previously fielded primarily guerrilla units, the organization now began to acquire tanks, artillery, and combat brigades. On the international front, the Palestinians also increased the numbers of foreign military missions, sending advisors and trainers to revolutionary groups throughout the Third World. Among others, PLO officers worked with Nicaraguan Sandinistas, African National Congress guerrillas in South Africa, Iranian revolutionaries, and liberation fighters from Zimbabwe.[47]

This buildup did not escape the attention of Israeli policymakers, however, who still hoped to crush the Palestinian nationalists and their mini-state in Lebanon. On June 30, 1981, Prime Minister Begin and his Likud Party won another round of national elections in Israel. Begin's new cabinet included a larger number of hawks and made the notable addition of Ariel Sharon as defense minister. The white-haired, barrel-chested Sharon enjoyed a fearsome reputation as one of Israel's greatest generals. A decorated veteran of the 1948 and 1956 wars, Sharon had commanded Israel's first commando group, Unit

101, charged with launching reprisals against Palestinian villages in the wake of guerrilla attacks—including the infamous 1953 Qibya Massacre. He achieved greater notoriety during the 1967 Arab-Israeli War, when he commanded an armored division in the Sinai. In the mid-1970s, Sharon entered politics and became a strong proponent of building Israeli settlements in internationally recognized Palestinian territory.

Following Likud's victory in the 1981 parliamentary elections, Begin and Sharon moved to strike at the PLO. On July 10, 1981, Israeli jets attacked Palestinian targets in South Lebanon. Palestinian fighters responded with a barrage of rockets aimed at the town of Kiryat Shmona in the Galilee region of northern Israel. The escalation continued with Israeli air strikes against PLO positions in Damour, outside Beirut, and another, deadlier round of PLO rocket attacks that killed three Israelis. By July 16, Israeli warplanes were bombing bridges in the south and Palestinian bases in other parts of the country. The following day, Israeli planes struck several PLO buildings in Beirut in an apparent bid to kill Arafat. Although the chairman survived, the raid killed some three hundred people, mainly civilians. PLO spokesmen accused Begin of waging "a war of genocide against the Palestinians." As rockets continued to rain down on Galilee and the PLO remained defiant, Israeli leaders concluded that their current policies were ineffective.[48]

The Israelis were not the only players troubled by the war in Lebanon. Syria's president, Hafez al-Assad, had intervened in Lebanon in 1976 to impose his will on his smaller neighbor, expand Damascus's influence, and prevent the Lebanese chaos from creeping across the border into Syria. After years of fighting, however, none of these goals had been achieved. Syria's intervention created a substantial drain on the nation's finances. Moreover, as the violence and instability continued, a stream of refugees filtered into Syria, creating an added burden to the nation's slowing economy. Assad had also decided to reverse course in Lebanon, severing his embarrassing alliance with the conservative Maronites and patching over his relations with the Muslims and the PLO. Arafat remained a stubbornly independent force, however, and refused to submit to Damascus's will. The strains of the intervention had also helped to fan domestic troubles in Syria. Opposition to Assad's regime from the Syrian Muslim Brotherhood fed on economic and political resentments created by the Lebanese intervention. The Brotherhood's supporters railed against Assad's betrayal of the Palestinians at the same time that they suffered under rising inflation and economic upheaval. Predictably, domestic violence escalated in Syria from 1976 onward. A string of bombings and assassinations by the Brotherhood targeted prominent Alawites (members of the Shia sect to which Assad's family belonged) throughout the country, sending a message to Assad's regime. The bloodiest incident took place on June 16, 1979, when gunmen massacred dozens of Alawite cadets at the Aleppo Artillery School. In addition to the conflict in Lebanon, Assad now faced a war at home—one he intended to win, regardless of the cost. Over the next years, the spate of assassinations continued, punctuated by periodic urban uprisings and bloody retributions from the regime. Assad sent in his best troops to crush the Brotherhood. Commanded by his brother Rifaat, the Defense Companies was an elite, heavily armed praetorian guard charged with defending the regime. In June 1980, in retaliation for an attempt on Assad's life, Rifaat sent his soldiers into the Tadmor Prison, in Palmyra, where they systematically butchered some five hundred Muslim Brothers inside their cells. The following month, the regime massacred scores of young men in Aleppo.[49]

The final reckoning came in the old city of Hama, famous for its giant wooden waterwheels along the Orontes River. A stronghold of the Muslim Brotherhood, Hama had been in the regime's crosshairs for years. In the early morning hours of February 2, 1982, snipers ambushed a group of soldiers sent to arrest a Brotherhood leader. When government forces sent reinforcements, loudspeakers in mosques throughout the city raised the alarm, proclaiming a jihad against the attackers. Soon, Islamic guerrillas had overrun police and government buildings throughout the city and slaughtered dozens of Ba'athist officials. Assad now found his opportunity. In retaliation for the uprising, Rifaat's Defense Companies launched a murderous siege against Hama. Twelve thousand government troops surrounded the city in a bid to crush the Brotherhood once and for all. For the next three weeks, paratroopers engaged in bloody street fighting while tanks and artillery shelled guerrilla positions. In heavy fighting that left scores of civilians dead, the Brothers were slowly pushed back to the old quarters of the city. There, hidden in the labyrinth of narrow streets and ancient houses, they staged a desperate defense. Hundreds of Assad's troops died in the assault, along with uncounted numbers of civilians caught in the crossfire. At the end of the battle, government forces brought in bulldozers to raze the buildings that served as hiding places for the remaining defenders and their wounded. Thousands were crushed beneath the rubble. When the fighting was over, the regime simply built a new city—roads, shopping malls, hospitals, apartment buildings, schools—on top of the dead.[50] Rifaat later boasted that his forces had slaughtered thirty-eight thousand in Hama. Far from downplaying the numbers, the regime touted them. By transforming Hama into a massive cemetery, the regime chose to send a message to other would-be rebels. Assad would show no mercy toward challengers: it was a warning that would echo well into the next century. Assad had decimated the forces of Islamic resistance in Syria and secured his regime for decades to come.[51]

Hama would not be the only Levantine city to suffer a bloody siege that year. Since 1977, Menachem Begin had waged an indecisive war against the PLO in Lebanon. Air strikes, Christian proxies, and limited invasions had all failed to curb guerrilla operations from the north. By the start of his fifth year in office, Begin was determined to move away from tit-for-tat retaliation and take the offensive against the PLO. At the same time, he believed that Israel had a duty to defend non-Muslim minorities in the region, specifically, the

Christians in Lebanon. Begin envisioned the formation of a coalition of non-Muslim groups, led by Israel, that could serve as a geopolitical counterweight to the Muslim majority in the Middle East. The prime minister's diplomatic vision was backed up by Sharon's military design. This "big plan" entailed a full-scale invasion of Lebanon to achieve three key objectives: crush the PLO, place the Maronites firmly in control, and drive the Syrians out of Lebanon. It was a bold move designed to tilt the balance of power in the Middle East in Israel's favor. Much of the Israeli cabinet opposed Begin and Sharon's strategy, however. An invasion of Lebanon, they feared, would tarnish Israel's already suffering international image. To circumvent these objections, Sharon implemented a strategy of creeping escalation. Individual reprisals would gradually escalate into a cross-border offensive. Once IDF forces were inside Lebanon, objections from the Israeli cabinet would be insufficient to prevent a drive to Beirut. In preparation for the invasion, Sharon made a clandestine voyage in January 1982 to Beirut to meet with the young Phalangist commander Bashir Gemayel. The following month, Bashir paid a secret visit to Begin in Jerusalem.[52]

Bashir Gemayel was the brash, impulsive son of Maronite patriarch Pierre Gemayel. The youngest of six children, he was remembered by many as unremarkable aside from his tireless work ethic. Plagued by acne into his twenties, Bashir nonetheless maintained "a kind of puppy-dog openness" that, while charming, suggested "a certain bewilderment about the world," journalist Jonathan Randal wrote. In contrast to aging leaders such as his father, Jumblatt, and Camille Chamoun, Bashir appeared young and energetic—the hope of a new Lebanon. The thirty-four-year-old's boyish enthusiasm was only part of the story, however. Bashir had directed his Phalangist militia on vicious raids against Palestinians and Lebanese Muslims. However, his most notorious attacks targeted his Christian rivals. In 1978, Bashir sent one hundred of his men to attack the villa of Tony Franjieh, heir to the rival Maronite Franjieh clan. The Phalangists stormed into the home in the early hours of the morning, killing Franjieh, his wife and three-year-old daughter, and the family dog. Two years later, Bashir's men again attacked their Christian rivals. This time, the victims were Dany Chamoun's Tigers, a five-hundred-man militia commanded by the son of former president Camille Chamoun. During the so-called Day of the Long Knives (or the Safra Massacre), Bashir's forces battled with the Tigers in East Beirut near the hotel complex and seaside resorts. Scores of civilians were caught in the crossfire as the Phalangists massacred Chamoun's men. Some victims were thrown screaming out of high-rise hotel windows. Estimates of the dead ranged from ninety-four to five hundred men, women, and children.[53]

Begin and Sharon, along with their Mossad agents, were less interested in Bashir's bloody rise to power than in his potential to serve as the vassal prince of a new pro-Israeli, Christian state. To overcome objections within the cabinet, Begin and Sharon in late 1981 proposed two operations, Little Pines and Big Pines. The former entailed an invasion of South Lebanon halting at the Litani River; the latter was a plan to drive all the way to Beirut and open a corridor to the Maronite enclaves in the north. In reality, Sharon envisioned Little Pines as the first stage of the larger operation. Throughout the first half of 1982, he and Begin seized on every PLO provocation to build political support for their invasion and began sending signals to Washington of their intention to move into Lebanon. U.S. secretary of state Alexander Haig officially warned the Israelis against launching the invasion but privately gave a green light for a limited incursion into South Lebanon in the event that Israel was provoked. Sharon received his long-awaited pretext on the evening of June 3, 1982, when members of a renegade Palestinian guerrilla faction, the Abu Nidal Organization, shot the Israeli ambassador to London, Shlomo Argov, in the head. It was a thin justification for an invasion of Lebanon. Abu Nidal, the group's leader, had been expelled from the PLO in 1974 and given a death sentence by Arafat himself. But the Israeli government would not let such technicalities interfere with their pretext for invading a neighboring state. "They're all PLO," Begin quipped; "Abu Nidal. Abu Schmidal. We have to strike at the PLO."[54]

PEACE FOR GALILEE

On the morning of June 6, 1982, ninety thousand Israeli troops stormed across the Lebanese border along with eight hundred tanks and fifteen hundred armored personnel carriers. The Israeli juggernaut lurched into motion, backed by what one U.S. Foreign Service officer described as an American "hunting license" for Sharon. Still shrouding their larger vision for Lebanon, Begin and Sharon chose to name the invasion Operation Peace for Galilee, a moniker that would later draw ridicule from observers inside Israel and the wider international community. Henry Kissinger, now a private citizen, praised the invasion's "strategic rationale" in an editorial and explained that the prospect of the PLO moderating its behavior had always been a "mirage." Lebanese Maronites greeted the Israeli soldiers with rose water and rice as IDF tanks sped by, kicking up great plumes of dust. Even as Sharon and Begin repeated their promise not to move more than forty kilometers beyond the border, Israeli troops staged amphibious landings to the north at Sidon, some twenty-seven miles south of Beirut. Within twenty-four hours, the IDF had accomplished most of its goals as set out in Little Pines, but Begin and Sharon had no intention of stopping. They had entered Lebanon not to reinforce the so-called security belt in the south but to eviscerate the PLO and remake the Lebanese state. Their deception apparent, IDF units now charged northward toward Beirut as Israeli jets struck Syrian missile batteries in the Beqaa Valley. A jubilant Begin ordered Israeli commandos to find and assassinate Arafat. By June 13, an Israeli armored column was charging toward the presidential palace en route to link up with the Maronites in the north.[55]

The IDF sat at the gates of Beirut, peering down into a city devastated by seven years of civil war. Sharon seized control of the gendarmes' headquarters and established vehicle parks for his tanks. Maronite gawkers, curious about the new arrivals and hopeful that the Palestinians were on the verge of expulsion, filtered up from the city to greet the conquerors. As Sharon paused to complete the encirclement of the capital, Israeli forces battled with Palestinian defenders in refugee camps in the south. Hoping to minimize their own casualties, Israeli troops shelled Sidon with cluster bombs and phosphorous in an almost indiscriminate fashion. Residents dug a mass grave in the town's central square to accommodate all the bodies. Even then, a Western journalist wrote, the urban wreckage concealed uncounted corpses as the "sickly-sweet stench of death" wafted through the streets. At the Ain al-Hilweh refugee camp, outside Sidon, the IDF encountered some of the fiercest resistance of the war. Palestinian fighters, some only in their early teens, moved amid the densely packed buildings and shanties, armed with Kalashnikovs and rocket-propelled grenades (RPGs), in a desperate attempt to hold off the attackers. Unprepared for this type of urban combat, Israeli forces bombarded the camp for most of a week, using shells with aerial bursts to inflict the maximum amount of damage on the ramshackle dwellings. The camp's defenders died to the last man, holed up in a mosque that the IDF finally destroyed. No one knew how many civilians perished in the battle: "I regard all Palestinians, except the women, as potential terrorists," an Israeli officer told a reporter. IDF commanders refused to allow journalists into the area until a month later. "All that was left standing were a few cypresses and some radio antennae," one journalist recalled.[56]

In the days that followed, fighting raged through Beirut's southern suburbs as the IDF completed its encirclement of the capital. While PLO fighters staged a tenacious defense in some quarters, they were hopelessly outgunned by Israeli forces. As he surveyed the approaches to the city, Sharon prepared to do something no Israeli general had ever done before: capture a foreign capital. Previous governments had scrupulously avoided such actions for fear of becoming bogged down in a drawn-out conflict and alienating world opinion. Pictures of conquering Israeli forces subjugating civilians inside a neighboring metropolis would confirm the worst propaganda from the Arab world. Indeed, the cabinet in Jerusalem balked at the prospect of such an operation. But Sharon had little use for such reservations. He had come to kill and conquer. "The IDF's arrival in Beirut marked the transformation of Operation Peace for Galilee from a limited military action to protect Israeli citizens into a runaway war to conquer an Arab capital, and eventually a kind of Frankenstein's monster that would turn on its creators with terrible consequences still to be measured," two Israeli commentators later wrote.[57]

For the next seven weeks, Beirut was a city besieged. Israeli warplanes dived over PLO-controlled neighborhoods in an effort to intimidate the guerrillas and provoke them to expose their gun positions. Meanwhile, the IDF and Phalangists sent car bombs into the city to terrorize the defenders. The Israelis launched a concerted offensive on July 4—it was probably not a coincidence that they chose to do so while most leaders in Washington would be on vacation. The Palestinians and the Joint Forces responded to IDF incursions into the suburbs with artillery and rocket bombardments, which had the effect of blunting the offensive. The Israeli juggernaut rolled forward, however, as IDF units pushed to the edge of Beirut's Khalde Airport. After encountering heavier-than-expected resistance on the ground, Sharon launched a series of air raids against West Beirut that massacred hundreds of civilians. Strikes intended to kill PLO leaders in apartment buildings achieved little effect beyond killing noncombatants cowering inside. On August 1, the IDF launched a new assault on the airport, which resulted in a fifteen-hour battle before Israeli forces were able to establish control. Three days later, Sharon renewed his joint offensive, pushing toward the Shatila refugee camp, Beirut's port, the National Museum, Summerland Beach, and Tayyouneh. Around one hundred Israeli soldiers were killed in the fighting. The noose had tightened around West Beirut, but the Israelis had run up against a ring of strong concrete buildings crisscrossed by narrow streets and alleyways in which their heavy armor would be of little use. Any further ground advances would be made not over open ground but in vicious urban fighting against the dug-in Palestinian guerrillas. With their troops halted, the Israelis pounded West Beirut with artillery and air strikes, killing hundreds in the final days of the war. In a final blow, the Israeli Air Force flew two hundred sorties, killing an estimated five hundred people.[58]

Israel's bloody siege generated a firestorm of criticism in the international community. "What is Israel doing to itself?" the *New York Times* asked. The paper blasted Sharon as a "disastrous diplomat" whose style was "studied intransigence" toward Israel's own civilian government. "Israelis have dismissed as absurd any suggestion that a country meant to be the Athens of its region could become a Prussia." But the slaughter in Beirut told a different story. Grisly footage of wounded civilians aired on televisions across the world. "The military tactics employed by the Israeli army, in bombing and shelling Beirut, have no military or moral foundations," wrote the editors of the London *Times*. "It may be coincidence that Mr Begin and [Israeli foreign minister Yitzhak] Shamir are ex-terrorists; but the tactics they have instructed their armed forces to carry out in Beirut albeit against terrorists, have been tactics of terror too." A letter from a British parliamentarian printed the same day denounced Israeli tactics as "obscene barbarity." After viewing one broadcast, a furious Ronald Reagan phoned Begin to demand that the Israelis stop their artillery attacks against the civilian population. "I told him it had to stop or our entire future relationship was endangered," he later wrote. "I used the word 'Holocaust' deliberately and said the symbol of his country was becoming 'a picture of a seven month old baby with its arms blown off.'" The president continued to place pressure on Begin to cease the assault and work with American envoy Philip Habib in good faith. "Israeli air strikes, shelling and other military moves have stopped progress in negotiations," he wrote to the prime minister. "I find this incomprehensible." Reagan's harangue apparently worked. Following a final round of attacks, Begin called off Sharon and agreed to Habib's cease-fire plan.[59]

On August 21, American and French peacekeepers began the evacuation of 14,938 Palestinian and Syrian personnel from West Beirut by sea and overland to Syria. Arafat left for Tunisia on August 30 to tearful farewells from the PLO's supporters who remained. The Palestinians surrendered their heavy weapons to their Lebanese allies but kept their AK-47s. In the end, Arafat judged that transforming the capital into an Arab Stalingrad would be too costly. As it was, the war had been costly enough. The toll in the invasion ran as high as 19,085 Lebanese and Palestinians killed and another 30,000 wounded. Three hundred Israelis had been killed with another 1,500 wounded. The Syrians saw 400 killed and 1,400 wounded or captured. A Lebanese police report placed the casualties in Beirut alone at 5,675 dead and 29,506 wounded. Authorities estimated that 83.8 percent of these casualties were civilian. But the bloodshed was far from over.[60]

BY MID-1982, IT WAS CLEAR THAT THE AFTERSHOCKS OF the Iranian Revolution would continue to reverberate through the 1980s as a series of interconnected conflicts raged across the Cold War borderlands of the Middle East. As the fighting intensified, Iranian clerics, Iraqi officials, Afghan rebels, Lebanese militias, and Pakistani intelligence officers all sought to mobilize sectarian identities in pursuit of specific political agendas—fueling wars that increasingly pitted rival ethnic and religious groups against one another. Worried that the violence might upset the regional balance of power, leaders in both Washington and Moscow searched for ways to control these new forces. In the process, Southwest Asia emerged as a staging ground for new strategies of revolution and superpower intervention. While the White House consolidated the Rapid Deployment Joint Task Force into Central Command, the Kremlin expanded its military forces in the Soviet Southern Theater. As Soviet commanders continued their brutal efforts to crush the insurgency in Afghanistan, U.S. military and intelligence agencies laid plans that would lead them into even deeper involvement in the great sectarian revolt of the 1980s.

REAGAN'S WAR FOR THE MIDDLE EAST

1983 – 1987

The ongoing wars in the Middle East created multiple opportunities for outside interventions. Carter's reactions to the Iranian Revolution and the Soviet intervention in Afghanistan set the stage for more muscular responses under Reagan. Determined to roll back what they believed were Soviet advances in the Third World, officials in the Reagan administration launched a concerted offensive in the Middle East, Latin America, and Africa aimed at supporting rebel groups fighting against Marxist regimes. Afghanistan, which was quickly turning into a Soviet quagmire, proved to be the ideal staging ground for Reagan's program. But with new opportunities came new dangers. At the eastern edges of the Middle Eastern front, Israel's war in Lebanon would take a horrific turn that helped convince U.S. leaders to send troops into the midst of a civil war that had already raged for eight years. In Beirut, American troops encountered a frightening new force that was set to revolutionize the region. Meanwhile, the Reagan administration came to recognize Saddam Hussein's Iraq as a partner—albeit an unsavory one—in its struggle against Khomeini's Iran.

The Iranian Revolution and its aftershocks had destabilized the wider region and led both superpowers to revise their strategic plans for the Middle East. As a 1983 CIA report argued, the Iranian Revolution and the events that followed led both Washington and Moscow to "focus increased attention on the Persian Gulf region," to "enhance their capacity for military operations in the area, and to plan for the contingency of a Soviet-US confrontation over Persian Gulf oil." The "overall effect has been more to destabilize the region than to shift the balance sharply in favor of either superpower." While the United States had developed its Central Command, the Soviets had built up their Southern Theater of Military Operations, responsible for a zone stretching from Turkey through the Persian Gulf and into South Asia. Soviet commanders in the Southern Theater could call upon twenty-five active motorized divisions, seven hundred tactical aircraft and two hundred helicopters, and at least twenty warships. Moscow's ultimate goal, CIA analysts wrote, was to move the Gulf states "from a pro-Western to a pro-Soviet orientation." The Kremlin hoped to accomplish this objective without the use of military force, but Soviet leaders would consider intervention if Washington sent forces into Iran. Indigenous forces presented an added deterrent against superpower military action. In particular, the Iranians, driven by "revolutionary zeal," would resist any outside interventions and make any potential occupation "costly." While Moscow was unlikely to stage an invasion of the Gulf region, the report concluded, the turmoil of the previous four years had dramatically increased the danger of a superpower military confrontation in Southwest Asia.[1]

Many officials in Washington had come to see the central importance of the Middle East for the Cold War struggle in the 1980s. One alarmist report submitted to the director of national intelligence by a CIA officer in 1984 put it bluntly: "The future of the Soviet Union as a superpower, the East-West power balance, and the chance of a major US-Soviet conflict in the next two decades are likely to be determined, more than anywhere else, in the region south of Soviet borders stretching from India to the Eastern Mediterranean." The report continued: "The Southern Theater is by far the most important major region of the Third World to the Soviets, rivaling the strategic status of East Asia and even Europe in some ways." While they coveted the region's oil fields and access to strategic waterways, Soviet leaders also had reason to fear the power of Islam, which threatened to "undermine essential parts of the Soviet system at home if the Soviets do not eventually control it." Moscow had established preponderant military power in the region, far outstripping U.S. deployments. But a dissenting opinion from other analysts argued that the paper's claims were overblown. The rebuttal conceded that the region was the most troubling potential flashpoint for a U.S.-Soviet confrontation. However, the author argued, the report exaggerated Soviet opportunities in the region and downplayed the obstacles that Moscow faced. Indeed, the Kremlin had struggled to exert influence in the Arab world since Sadat's decision to expel Soviet advisors in 1972: the "Soviets have effectively been shut out of the Middle East since they 'lost' Egypt," the rebuttal argued, adding that "US policy has been exploiting these vulnerabilities with some success for the past ten years."[2]

Ultimately, both superpowers recognized the critical strategic importance of the Middle East and both now struggled to come to terms with the rapidly changing political movements in the region. As a lengthy 1984 CIA report noted, the "latest Islamic revival" in the Middle East had created new pressures on existing states in the region and raised the prospect of larger strategic implications. Drawing on "a set of social and religious values transcending national boundaries," this religious resurgence had developed an alarming "confrontational dimension." Analysts noted, "Ideological failures and a crisis of legitimacy continue to provide fertile ground for Islamic militancy." The "apogee" of this movement, the 1979 Iranian Revolution "sent waves of alarm through the leadership of neighboring states" and electrified both Sunni and Shia masses. Nevertheless, the report concluded, the resurgent fundamentalism had limited revolutionary potential.

Despite their ability to create problems in the region, Islamic militants were unlikely to topple governments in the near future.[3]

Increasingly in the mid-1980s, Washington and Moscow would find that their allies and adversaries alike had largely abandoned the Cold War ideological struggle of Marxism versus liberal capitalism and instead embraced ethnic and religious politics. The true scope of these transformations would take a generation to come into view.

ENGINEERING A BLOODBATH

U.S. officials watched the slaughter in Afghanistan with barely contained delight. While Carter had authorized aid to the Mujahideen as a quiet measure designed to make life more difficult for the Kremlin, the new president, Ronald Reagan, would enshrine support for rebel fighters such as the Mujahideen as one of the centerpieces of his foreign policy. Reagan and his advisors entered the White House in 1981 determined to pursue a more aggressive Cold War policy. Where his predecessors had worked toward détente with Moscow, Reagan sought confrontation. The new administration seemed determined not just to maintain U.S. power in the world but to win the Cold War with the Soviet Union. In the developing world, this drive to confront and defeat Soviet power took the form of rollback. Rather than simply containing the spread of communism, a policy that every president since Truman had followed, Reagan hoped to take the offensive, destabilizing pro-Soviet governments in the developing world and striking blows against Moscow's "evil empire." No battlefield seemed more promising than Afghanistan.

Although the Reagan administration stepped into the White House with the CIA-ISI pipeline already in place, the administration took a somewhat ad hoc approach to its operations in Afghanistan—this fact, combined with the covert nature of the aid program, meant that the story of Reagan's aid to the Mujahideen trickled out in bits and pieces over the 1980s. While the amount of U.S. aid to the Mujahideen was relatively modest, Reagan's team would have little trouble expanding the program. Among the most vocal cheerleaders for enlarging current operations was the new director of central intelligence, William Casey. The balding, sixty-seven-year-old native of Queens wore thick spectacles above heavy jowls. A veteran of the Office of Strategic Services, the CIA's World War II precursor, Casey hoped to resurrect the CIA as an active agency in the battle against the USSR. To this end, he advocated more aggressive Cold War policies in Europe, Central America, and Afghanistan. "The [Cold War's] primary battlefield," he later announced, "is not on the missile test range or at the arms control negotiating table but in the countryside of the Third World." The CIA's proxy war against the Soviet Union in Afghanistan, Operation Cyclone, provided the ideal opportunity for Casey and Reagan to take the fight to the Russians. In the early years, however, the Reagan White House remained skeptical of the prospects of a Mujahideen victory. In January 1982, the State Department gave a positive assessment of Mujahideen activities. Although they were outgunned and did not seem to have the offensive capabilities necessary to force a Soviet retreat, the rebels' accomplishments in the previous year had given Moscow cause for concern. The Mujahideen had stymied Kabul's efforts to exert control over the countryside, "put the regime increasingly on the defensive, brought about a crisis in the Afghan Army, and caused a breakdown in many areas of the economy." Though the rebels remained divided, their battlefield successes continued to mount. The Mujahideen exercised "de facto control" over 75 percent of the country. Rebel commanders collected taxes, set price controls, made laws, and served as judicial authorities. For the time being, the resistance was preventing the Soviets from turning control over to Afghan authorities.[4]

Aside from frequent references to the "freedom fighters" in Afghanistan, there seems to have been surprisingly few substantive policy discussions about Operation Cyclone in Reagan's first years in office. Part of this was due to the fact that the Carter administration had already laid the groundwork for the operation; Reagan's team simply continued authorizing aid to the rebels. The covert nature of the aid to the Mujahideen also necessitated a degree of discretion. Perhaps more than anything, however, the administration was reluctant to draw attention to the fact that aid to the Mujahideen required close coordination with Pakistan. While Pakistan's president, Zia, was a Cold War ally, his regime was on the verge of producing a nuclear weapon, making it a pariah in the international community. Islamabad's human rights record, its fraught relationship with India, and its increasingly strident Islamic rhetoric only made matters worse.[5] It would be several more years before Reagan decided to make the covert war in Afghanistan a priority.

The Kremlin, meanwhile, remained determined to save the Marxist regime in Kabul. From the beginning of the war, Soviet leaders had intended military operations to be in support of larger political goals. Alongside soldiers, Moscow sent legions of technicians, engineers, and economic advisors into Afghanistan. They rebuilt roads and bridges, built new hospitals and airports, and tried to bring the country's infrastructure into the twentieth century. Soviet volunteers worked with literacy programs and local universities to educate thousands of Afghan citizens. Like the Americans in South Vietnam, the Soviets hoped to transform Afghanistan into a showpiece for the benefits of Soviet modernization practices.[6] Soviet specialists built irrigation systems, dug natural gas wells, and erected factories in a largely altruistic bid to stage socioeconomic development in the Third World nation. And they did so with no small amount of confidence. "The Soviet leadership," one American scholar wrote, "can legitimately claim to have a developmental model [in the Soviet Central Asian Republics] that has managed to achieve one of the highest rates of literacy, the best health care system, and the highest general standard of living found anywhere in the Muslim world." If Soviet experts could achieve the same sort of success in Afghanistan, it would be a major boon to the Kremlin's model of state-based, socialist development.[7]

But any economic gains were more than offset by the war's destruction. Vicious fighting in the countryside, the flood of refugees, and deliberate attacks on urban and rural infrastructure devastated much of Afghanistan. Moreover, political chaos and economic upheaval created new opportunities for the resurgence of another industry: opium cultivation.[8] Meanwhile, human rights organizations attributed a litany of war crimes to Soviet forces and the Afghan government. The rural population in contested provinces often found itself in the middle of a war zone. Indiscriminate bombing by Soviet aircraft took perhaps the largest toll. Refugees streaming into Pakistan told harrowing tales of MiG warplanes bombing houses, fields, and orchards and strafing panicked villagers and livestock. Sometimes ground troops followed in the wake of the air raids. "The Russians bombed us," a shepherd from Kunduz told investigators. "Then the soldiers came, took all the women and old men, and killed them." Much of the killing appeared to be a reprisal for Mujahideen attacks. In April 1982, a unit of Soviet Special Forces massacred nearly two hundred people in Balkh Province after the mutilated remains of three Soviet soldiers were discovered. "The Soviet troops can't find the mujahedeen so they kill civilians," explained another soldier. "Our officers said we must go into a village and kill all the people and animals, sheep, horses, even dogs and cats." Refugees told stories of Soviet troops combing through villages, arresting suspected rebel sympathizers, staging brutal interrogations, and carrying out summary executions. "They took many people from their houses and killed them," claimed a former merchant. "They were bombed by jet fighters or thrown alive in wells and buried under the mud. They were thrown down from airplanes, and some were put under tanks alive, and the tanks crushed them. . . . Some of them were given electricity and killed that way. Some were cut into pieces alive."

Thousands more were maimed or killed by antipersonnel mines. While they were farther removed from the heaviest fighting, urban Afghans had to deal with the more frequent repression from the regime in Kabul. In particular, officers from the Afghan state intelligence agency, Khadamat-e Aetla'at-e Dawlati (KhAD), gained a fearsome reputation for widespread surveillance, conducting invasive house searches, torturing prisoners, and staging executions.[9]

But state authorities were not the sole purveyors of violence. Mujahideen fighters gained a fearsome reputation for skinning captured Soviet soldiers alive. Rebel fighters would often execute prisoners rather than deal with the burden of transporting and detaining them in their remote hideouts. One rumor attributed the massacre of a thousand captured Afghan soldiers to Massoud's men in the Panjshir Valley, an act that turned the river red with blood. Soviet bases around Afghanistan buzzed with tales of decapitation and dismemberment of prisoners. One particularly gruesome rumor told of the practice of skinning Russian prisoners and then surrounding their bodies with booby traps designed to maim any potential rescuers. Small wonder that many Soviet soldiers, faced with capture by the Mujahideen, instead chose to commit suicide. Some rebels, however, were happy to exchange Russian prisoners for ransom. But Afghan prisoners were less valuable and less likely to receive mercy.[10]

As the war dragged on, officials in the Reagan administration increasingly came to focus on the battle for Afghanistan. Reagan, like many ardent Cold Warriors, had long been convinced that Moscow's hand lay behind most of the world's troubles. "Let's not delude ourselves," he had announced while campaigning in 1980. "The Soviet Union underlies all the unrest that is going on. If they weren't engaged in this game of dominoes, there wouldn't be any hot spots in the world." Reagan entered office determined to launch what political scientist James M. Scott dubbed a "covert strategic offensive against the USSR." In March 1981, Casey proposed a plan for a CIA assistance program for rebel groups in Afghanistan, Angola, Cambodia, Cuba, Grenada, Iran, Laos, Libya, and Nicaragua. "We need to be backing these movements with money and political muscle," he argued. "*We need half a dozen Afghanistans* [emphasis in original]." Two years later, in January 1983, Reagan's advisors drafted a major policy paper, National Security Decision Directive (NSDD) 75, outlining a strategy to roll back Soviet influence around the world. The paper called upon the United States to "contain and over time reverse Soviet expansionism by competing on a sustained basis with the Soviet Union in all international arenas—particularly in the overall military balance and in geographical regions of priority concern to the United States." In the Third World, this would mean working to "weaken and, where possible, undermine the existing links between [Moscow's allies] and the Soviet Union. U.S. policy will include active efforts to encourage democratic movements and forces to bring about political change inside these countries." In Afghanistan, the U.S. aim should be "to keep maximum pressure on Moscow for withdrawal and to ensure that the Soviets' political, military, and other costs remain high while the occupation continues." Two years later, in January 1985, Casey told an audience in New York that Washington must support "freedom fighters resisting communist regimes." The following month, in his State of the Union address, the president told Congress and the nation that the United States "must not break faith with those who are risking their lives—on every continent from Afghanistan to Nicaragua—to defy Soviet-supported aggression." Several months later, conservative columnist Charles Krauthammer dubbed this policy the Reagan Doctrine.[11]

Having announced its doctrine, the White House worked to ramp up its support for the Mujahideen. In March 1985, Reagan's advisors drafted another policy paper, specifically on U.S. goals in Afghanistan, NSDD 166. Washington's goal was now to win the war in Afghanistan through its "program of covert action support to the Afghan resistance" and diplomatic strategy to isolate Moscow. "Our covert program," the report claimed, "will deny Afghanistan to the Soviets as a secure base from which to project power and influence into the region" and, in doing so, prevent the Kremlin from "exploit[ing the] possible post-Khomeini turmoil in Iran." U.S. support for the rebels would also "promote Soviet isolation in the Third and Islamic worlds" by driving home the idea "that the Soviet Union is an imperialist power which will subjugate Third World states militarily when it suits its interest to do so."[12] The White House was not alone in its desire to increase aid to the Mujahideen. Loud voices in Congress also called for greater commitment to the "freedom fighters" in Afghanistan. Most prominent among these was that of a rowdy, hard-drinking congressman from Texas, Charlie Wilson. Since first learning of the Afghan resistance struggle in 1980, Wilson had been pushing the House Appropriations Committee to increase its support for the Mujahideen. By 1984, Wilson was working with CIA officers to secure larger aid shipments for the rebels and taking trips to Afghan refugee camps in Pakistan.

Among those shipments was a weapon that would capture the imagination of millions of Americans: the FIM-92 surface-to-air missile, better known as the Stinger. Engineered as a shoulder-fired antiaircraft missile, the Stinger carried an advanced heat-seeking guidance system designed to home in on the heat of an aircraft's engines. In the wake of NSDD 166, voices in Washington had begun calling for the shipment of Stingers to the Mujahideen to help in warding off the devastating attacks by Soviet Mi-24 Hind helicopter gunships. The CIA, recognizing the potential dangers of supplying Islamic militants with high-tech, portable surface-to-air missiles, had been reluctant. The fact that the Stingers were produced by an American corporation and their distribution was tightly controlled only made matters worse. It would be impossible to maintain plausible deniability once Soviet helicopters started being shot down by missiles with "Made in America" stenciled on their sides. The State Department argued that it was worth the risk, and in 1986, the first Stingers were shipped to Gulbuddin Hekmatyar's guerrilla group. On September 26, 1986, a group of Mujahideen used Stinger missiles to down three Soviet helicopters outside Jalalabad, in eastern Afghanistan. According to some accounts, the CIA sent as many as twenty-five hundred missiles to the Mujahideen before the end of the war. In order to avoid the fearsome new weapon, Soviet aircrews were forced to take their craft up to 12,500 feet, an altitude at which ground support operations became far less effective. The CIA station chief in Islamabad, Milt Bearden, praised the introduction of the Stingers as the war's "most significant battlefield development." It would also be one of the most controversial. At the end of the war, the CIA launched a program to buy back the missiles from the Mujahideen, but by 1996, some six hundred Stingers remained unaccounted for. While reports that the Stinger single-handedly turned the tide of the war are probably over-blown, its symbolic value was considerable. Washington's willingness to send top-shelf military technology to the Mujahideen served as yet another indication that, six years into the war, victory in Afghanistan remained out of sight. And the new leadership in Moscow appeared ready for a change.[13]

"WE WERE BREATHING DEATH"

At the beginning of September 1982, Menachem Begin, Ariel Sharon, and Bashir Gemayel seemed to have secured a tremendous victory in Lebanon. They had driven the PLO out of the country, devastated the Syrian forces in the east, and were poised to remake Lebanon into a conservative, Maronite-controlled state. Lebanese presidential elections had taken place on August 23, even as Israeli guns were trained upon the capital and the expulsion of the PLO was under way. Gemayel's electoral victory, aided by Israeli pressure in territories under IDF occupation, surprised no one. Leaving nothing to chance, the delegates were escorted to voting stations by armed Phalangists. Upon hearing the electoral results, Mossad officers joined Maronite militiamen in celebration, discharging their rifles into the air. But Gemayel recognized that the time had come to pay his debts to the Israelis. "Begin and Sharon were not schooled by the Jesuits, as I was," he remarked, "and they are certainly not patrons of charity." One week later, Begin summoned Gemayel to a meeting at Nahariya, in northern Israel. After finishing their champagne toasts, the two leaders turned to business. Begin insisted that Gemayel pay a state visit to Jerusalem and sign a peace treaty before the end of the year. Gemayel was hesitant: "We are with you on a long haul on a genuine peace, not an artificial one." But he feared making a precipitous move that could compromise his efforts to consolidate his regime. Begin's irritation was palpable. "He treated me like a child!" Gemayel fumed afterward. None of the participants knew that it would be their last meeting.[14]

Ten minutes past four o'clock in the afternoon on September 14, 1982, a massive explosion shook the Phalangist headquarters in Achrafieh as President-elect Gemayel addressed a group of his followers. The bomb had been hidden by a member of the Syrian Social Nationalist Party. The blast killed Gemayel and twenty-six other officials. Upon hearing the news of Gemayel's assassination, Israeli leaders flew into a rage. Ignoring the cease-fire, IDF troops forced their way into West Beirut and attacked the PLO Research Center, looting its library and stealing twenty-five thousand volumes of material that documented Arab life in Palestine before the 1948 creation of Israel in addition to the activities of the PLO. "They have plundered our Palestinian cultural heritage," the institute's director told reporters. The goal, another Palestinian claimed, was "to obliterate all memory of Palestine, the country we have left behind." This, in a sense, "is what Sharon most wanted to take home from Beirut," reporter Thomas Friedman later wrote. "Palestinian? What's that?" read the graffiti left on the institute's walls after the Israeli soldiers had departed. Far worse violence was taking place to the south, however.[15]

On September 16, Sharon and the IDF sent Phalangist militiamen into the Palestinian camps in West Beirut under the pretext of hunting down PLO fighters who may have remained in hiding. The guerrillas had evacuated, however, and the civilians who remained were defenseless. Israeli officials had foreseen what would happen next: "One day the murders will start, and they will just go on and on without end." IDF chief of staff Rafael Eitan warned Sharon that the Christians were "thirsty for revenge. There could be torrents of blood." At 6:00 p.m., Phalangist fighters crossed through IDF lines to enter the Sabra and Shatila camps. Fifty minutes later, IDF radiomen monitored a transmission from a Christian officer asking his superior what to do with fifty captured women and children. "That's the last time you ask me," the Phalangist commander replied. "You know what to do." While Israeli forces looked on from one hundred yards away, the Phalangists raped, brutalized, and massacred hundreds of civilians. As darkness fell, the Israelis began firing up flares to aid the militiamen in their savage work. The rampage continued for thirty hours as Christian militia stomped infants to death, butchered children with knives, and executed unarmed civilians at gunpoint. "Do God's will," Phalangist leaders ordered their men as the slaughter continued.[16]

Observers remember the air being thick with swarms of flies and the stench of the dead. The streets of the Sabra camp were lined with piles of bodies. "We were *breathing* death," journalist Robert Fisk remembered, "inhaling the very putrescence of the bloated corpses around us." Fisk and his comrades picked their way through the ruins, retching periodically, and taking stock of the horrors that surrounded them. Children with their throats slit, women with torn dresses, and teenage boys who had been lined up against walls and shot. Other corpses had been hastily dumped into mass graves. Israeli officials placed the number of the dead at under eight hundred, while Palestinians and Phalangists estimated that more than three thousand had been killed. Fisk and others placed the number between one thousand and two thousand. More than the numbers, however, it was the manner of killings that sparked outrage. Even as Christian militia slaughtered the refugees, Washington's envoy to Israel, Morris Draper, warned Israeli leaders of the likelihood of an atrocity against the Palestinians. If the IDF remained in West Beirut, he predicted, "they will let the Lebanese go and kill the Palestinians in the camps."

SHARON: So, we'll kill them. They will not be left there. You are not going to save them. You are not going to save these groups of the international terrorism [*sic*].

DRAPER: We are not interested in saving any of these people.

SHARON: If you don't want the Lebanese to kill them, we will kill them.

It did not require a great cognitive leap to move from Sharon's logic of exterminating "terrorists" to the Phalangist justification for the killings at Sabra and Shatila. "Pregnant *women will give birth to terrorists*," a militiaman told an IDF witness to the massacre, "the *children* when they *grow up* will be *terrorists*." The U.S. government had guaranteed the refugees' protection as part of the Habib plan to evacuate the PLO from Beirut, and the IDF had pledged not to enter West Beirut. The war crimes at Sabra and Shatila had been predicted, but they had not been stopped.[17]

The political aftershocks from Sabra and Shatila shook governments in both Washington and Jerusalem. The Israeli cabinet issued a statement denouncing accusations of IDF responsibility for Sabra and Shatila as "blood libel," which "appalled" U.S. secretary of state George Shultz: "How could Begin and the cabinet issue such a statement? Were they all so dangerously ill informed? . . . Did they think we, let alone Israeli citizens, would believe simply anything, however outrageous?" The statement, Shultz later wrote, "suggested that either they were unhinged from reality or totally carried away with their momentarily commanding position."[18]

News of the massacre set off a wave of protests that swept through Israel. In late September, in an effort to defend its moral position, the Israeli government formed a committee of inquiry to look into the atrocity, to be led by Yitzhak Kahan, president of the Israeli Supreme

Court. While it was a remarkable feat for a nation at war to subject itself to such an investigation, many critics of Israeli foreign policy attacked the Kahan Commission as an attempt to whitewash Israel's role in the massacre. The commission, which released its report in February 1983, echoed the cabinet in dismissing any charges of direct IDF responsibility in the massacre as "libel." Likewise, it judged accusations of Israeli complicity in the slaughter due to "prior knowledge that a massacre would be perpetrated" as "unfounded." Sharon's conversations with Draper prove otherwise, however. Even so, the Kahan Report did find that Israeli forces bore "indirect responsibility" because they allowed Phalangists into the camps and then did nothing to stop the bloodshed. The commission found that the IDF decision to allow Christian militia into the camps "was taken without consideration of the danger—which [Israeli leaders] were obligated to foresee as probable—that the Phalangists would commit massacres and pogroms." Finally, the report found that Sharon bore "personal responsibility" for the atrocity and recommended his dismissal. In effect, the Kahan Commission watered down the IDF's responsibility, reducing it to negligence, and identified Sharon as a scapegoat.[19]

Although it mostly absolved the IDF of responsibility and did much to redeem Israel's international image, the report proved damning for Begin and Sharon. After initial refusals, Sharon resigned as defense minister. He remained in Begin's cabinet, however, and would, years later, become prime minister. Begin descended into a state of depression brought on by the death of his wife and the disastrous situation in Lebanon. On August 5, 1983, he, too, resigned. While the Israelis staggered away from the ruins of West Beirut, another power waited to take their place.

THE AMERICANS JOIN THE WAR

Officials in the Reagan administration shared the international community's revulsion at the Sabra and Shatila Massacre. This shock combined with a sense of responsibility for the killings—Habib had promised international protection for the refugees in return for the PLO's evacuation, and it was their departure that left the civilians vulnerable to the Phalangists and the IDF. Thus, when the Lebanese government asked Reagan to send peacekeepers to Beirut, he readily agreed. In late September 1982, twelve hundred U.S. Marines joined the Multi-National Force (MNF) alongside French, Italian, and a small contingent of British peacekeepers.

On paper, the MNF was to remain strictly neutral; the reality on the ground proved more complicated. Following Bashir Gemayel's assassination, his older brother, Amine, ascended to the presidency. Like Bashir, Amine represented the Phalangist minority and could hardly be seen as a neutral figure in Lebanese politics. This reality—which seems to have been lost on top officials in the Reagan administration—thrust the marines and the MNF into a dangerous position. Charged with supporting the Lebanese government, the MNF found itself pulled into the Lebanese Civil War. In November 1982, the MNF's role was expanded to provide noncombat support for government forces; by February 1983, U.S. Marines were prowling the streets of Christian East Beirut at Amine Gemayel's request. Put simply, by supporting the Gemayel regime, the MNF compromised its neutrality.[20]

While officials in Washington appeared oblivious to this dynamic, it was clear enough to rival militias in Beirut. In March, U.S. forces began coming under attack from hostile groups in the city. The real danger became clear only the following month, however, when a suicide bomber drove a truck filled with explosives up the front steps of the U.S. embassy building in Beirut. The blast killed sixty-three people, including seventeen Americans and the entire CIA station in Beirut. The station chief's severed hand was later discovered floating offshore, a gruesome testament to the force of the explosion. In response, the Reagan administration chose to throw American forces into the fray. In July, marines joined the Lebanese Armed Forces in an offensive against Druze militia fighting against the Phalangists in the Chouf Mountains, complete with a bombardment from the U.S. Sixth Fleet floating off the coast. That September, American ships shelled Syrian positions with five-inch guns. "Well, haven't we got anything bigger than a five-inch gun?" Reagan asked later. "We've got the [battleship] *New Jersey*," came the reply. "She can throw a shell as big as a Volkswagen twenty miles." Meanwhile, the marines in Beirut found themselves in what one journalist called a "peacekeeping hell." Prohibited from joining the combat, U.S. troops stationed at the airport crouched behind sandbags as snipers in the surrounding heights took potshots at their positions. The American peacekeepers, like the Syrians and Israelis who had entered Lebanon before them, had been sucked into a civil war that they did not fully understand.[21]

At 6:22 on the morning of October 23, 1983, a truck loaded with twelve thousand pounds of explosives careened past the guard post in front of the marine barracks in the Beirut Airport. The sentry on duty remembered only that the driver was smiling as he accelerated toward the barracks. Several seconds later, a massive explosion rocked the compound. Journalists sleeping ten miles away were awoken by the blast, which sent a mushroom cloud into the sky and left a crater thirty feet deep. As sirens began to wail throughout the city, another explosion destroyed the nine-story barracks housing the MNF's contingent of French paratroopers. The attacks killed 241 U.S. servicemen and 58 French troops. It was the deadliest single day for U.S. military personnel since the end of World War II. Aides woke President Reagan at 2:30 a.m. to tell him the news. As reports of the carnage and rescue operations trickled into the White House, a picture of the attack began to emerge. The bombers were apparently radical Shi'ite fighters attached to the same group, Islamic Jihad, that had staged the bombing of the U.S. embassy in April. "Having come to Beirut to protect the Lebanese," an American journalist later wrote, "the Marines now seemed to be the ones needing protection."[22]

The 1983 embassy and barracks bombings announced the

emergence of a formidable new player in the Lebanese Civil War: the Lebanese Shi'ite resistance. In the first years of the war, the Shia of Lebanon had remained largely on the sidelines. Poorest of the major minority groups in Lebanon, the Shia lacked the extensive political infrastructure of groups such as the Maronites, Sunnis, and Palestinians. Concentrated in South Lebanon, they had been caught in the crossfire between Haddad's Christian militia, PLO guerrillas, and the IDF. Increasing levels of violence, coupled with a gradual exodus of Shia from South Lebanon to the ring of slums around Beirut, had served to mobilize what was, by many estimates, Lebanon's largest minority group. Likewise, the Iranian Revolution provided a strong source of inspiration for Shi'ite activists throughout the wider region. Israel's invasions in 1978 and 1982 gave further impetus to Lebanon's Shia, who had at first welcomed the IDF but soon turned against the Israelis when it became clear that Sharon and Begin intended to stay. By the early 1980s, the Shia had become contestants in the struggle for power in Lebanon. Two main parties would emerge as leaders in the Shia political community: Amal and, somewhat later, Hezbollah.

Amal was the more conventional of the two. Founded in 1974 by Shi'ite imam Musa al-Sadr, the group claimed to represent the "deprived" and advocated for social justice in Lebanese society. Together with Amal's political operations, the group's leaders created an armed wing that would function as one of the key Shi'ite militias during the war. The movement received a significant symbolic boost when, during a visit to Libya in 1978, al-Sadr disappeared under mysterious circumstances. His disappearance endowed the leader with mythic importance—a national martyr among the Shia of Lebanon. Amal initially enjoyed a cooperative relationship with the secular PLO— Fatah guerrillas had trained the movement's fighters. Soon, however, Amal's leaders came to recognize the PLO as a dangerous presence in their midst. Gun-toting Palestinian guerrillas were often rude to local Shia villagers, and their presence invited frequent Israeli reprisals. It was one thing to support the Palestinian cause in spirit, but it was quite another to shelter guerrillas in the midst of an IDF invasion. Indeed, some one thousand Shia were killed in Israel's 1978 Operation Litani, which led many in the community to turn against the Palestinians. Amal's goals, ultimately, were to provide security and political representation for the Shia of southern Lebanon. To do this in the late 1970s and early '80s meant building a militia that could stand toe to toe with the various armed communities throughout the nation.[23]

While Amal occupied the mainstream of Shi'ite politics, Hezbollah represented more radical elements in the community. Hezbollah's origins are less clear. Founded by militant clerics in the early 1980s, it was, according to one scholar, "less an organization than a cabal." Israel's 1982 invasion of Lebanon catalyzed the movement. "When we entered Lebanon," Israeli prime minister Ehud Barak later recalled, "there was no Hezbollah. We were accepted with perfumed rice and flowers by the Shia in the south. It was our presence there that created Hezbollah." Prime Minister Yitzhak Rabin offered a more colorful metaphor: Israeli actions in southern Lebanon had let the Shia "genie out of the bottle." Both Iran and Syria sponsored the group, with the former playing the larger role. Indeed, many of Hezbollah's early communiqués echoed ideas circulating in Khomeini's Iran. A 1985 document lauded the Iranian Revolution and called on all Muslims throughout the world to turn to Islam as a means of "breaking the iron and oppression of tyrannical regimes." Combining Islamic revivalism with Third World revolutionary sentiment, the document divided the world between the wealthy, oppressive powers and the oppressed, downtrodden peoples of the developing world. Like the Iranians, Hezbollah rejected the influence of both Washington and Moscow: "The Soviets are not one iota different from the Americans in terms of political danger," wrote one author in Hezbollah's newspaper. While the USSR represented the greater ideological threat, the United States and its Israeli "spearhead" formed the more immediate military threat. By fighting the United States, "we are only exercising our legitimate right to defend our Islam and the dignity of our nation."[24]

While Hezbollah officially denied involvement with the 1983 bombings, a number of commentators insist that Islamic Jihad functioned as a front for the organization. Much of the confusion stems from the fact that Hezbollah had not yet coalesced as a unified movement in 1983. Rather, the group emerged out of the meeting of several Shia groups (including Amal) that fought for several years before organizing under a central command sometime around 1985. Further muddying the waters, Shia militants received extensive training and support from Iranian Revolutionary Guards at their base in Baalbek, in Lebanon's Beqaa Valley. This close association fed accusations that Hezbollah functioned as an Iranian proxy. The CIA places responsibility for the barracks bombing on Imad Fayez Mughniyeh. Like many members of Hezbollah, he had joined Fatah in his earlier years and then defected to the Shi'ite resistance in the run-up to Israel's 1982 invasion. Mughniyeh would later emerge as a central player in Hezbollah's armed activities. Adding to the CIA's suspicions, Hezbollah claimed responsibility for similar suicide attacks on Israeli forces around the same time. Former members of Hezbollah would later claim that the organization had indeed launched the embassy and barracks bombings and praise them as resistance operations against what they considered an "occupying force." Ultimately, the ongoing controversy sheds light on the mystifying situation inside Lebanon in which American peacekeepers found themselves.[25]

Deprived of a clear target against which to launch a reprisal for the marine barracks bombing, U.S. forces pulled back to ships along the coast. As the Reagan administration celebrated its easy victory over the Marxist government of the tiny Caribbean island of Grenada, American troops limped away from Lebanon. The president would identify many culprits for the embassy and barracks bombings, which he later described as "the source of my greatest regret and my greatest sorrow as president." He blamed the Lebanese Army for its unwillingness to end the war. He blamed the "depth of hatred and complexity of the problems" in the region. He blamed the religious fanaticism of the attackers. "I'm not sure how we could have anticipated the catastrophe at the marine barracks," Reagan later explained. Apparently, no one in the White House considered the lessons of eight years of a brutal civil war and the bloody examples of the Syrian and Israeli interventions to be of relevance to the American mission. Nor did Reagan seem to grasp the idea that by choosing to support Gemayel's forces and by shelling Druze positions, he had compromised the neutrality of the marines under his command. However, he was honest in his memoirs about the ineffectiveness of American efforts: "Our policy wasn't working." The American public had no appetite for a full-scale war in Lebanon, and as the White House had learned, "we couldn't remain in Lebanon and be in the war on a halfway basis." Reagan's adventure in Lebanon was over.[26]

CHANGING OF THE GUARD

For the Lebanese, however, the war continued. With Arafat's forces removed from the immediate picture, the Shia militias stepped in to take their place. While the PLO embodied a dream of secular liberation that transposed the examples of Mao, Frantz Fanon (the Martinican psychologist and theorist of the Algerian revolution), and Che Guevara into the Arab political experience, Hezbollah and Amal took their cues from Khomeini's revolution in Iran. CIA analysts argued that Iranian support had acted as a "major stimulant" for the growth of Shia fundamentalism in Lebanon. "The success of the Iranian revolution," a 1987 report claimed, "and the resulting wave of Islamic militancy throughout the Middle East fostered the spread of fundamentalism in Lebanon." The eclipse of the PLO and the rise of Hezbollah thus signaled a shift in the character of revolutionary politics in the Middle East. In this new environment, the sectarian nature of the conflict, visible from the earliest clashes in 1975, grew even more pronounced. Allegiances to religious communities fell into sharper relief as the Shia militias took center stage. As part of this process,

Hezbollah emerged as a powerful force in West Beirut. Posters announcing the group's presence began to appear on walls while sidewalk merchants peddled plastic effigies of Khomeini. Positions along the Green Line that were once home to PLO fighters now housed Hezbollah guerrillas—a literal changing of the guard that signaled the ascendance of a new power in Beirut and the wider region.[27]

In addition to suicide bombings, Shia fighters incorporated assassinations and kidnappings into their tactics. On January 18, 1984, militants claiming to belong to Islamic Jihad, an alleged Hezbollah front, gunned down the president of the American University of Beirut, Malcolm Kerr, on the university's pristine seaside campus. By murdering him, the gunmen killed a prominent symbol of American influence in the region. "We are responsible for the assassination of the president of AUB, who was a victim of the American military presence in Lebanon," Islamic Jihad announced. "We also vow that not a single American or French will remain on this soil." Kerr's tragic killing was part of a string of attacks against Westerners in Beirut launched by Hezbollah and affiliated groups. In the following weeks, militants kidnapped another professor, Frank Regier, and CNN bureau chief Jeremy Levin. On March 16, 1984, Islamic Jihad abducted the CIA station chief in Beirut, William Buckley. In June, the group announced that it had executed him, although U.S. officials concluded that Buckley had died of a heart attack. Meanwhile, militants had abducted another American, Rev. Benjamin Weir, while he was out walking with his wife. In May, U.S. officials warned of a plan to kidnap one hundred American citizens.[28]

While Western media focused on the hostages, the sectarian conflict in Lebanon dragged on. Following the IDF's gradual withdrawal from Beirut in 1983, a trickle of PLO fighters found their way back into Lebanon. By the end of 1984, their growing numbers had begun to alarm the Shia militias that had stepped into their place. Amal in particular began to edge toward open confrontation with the PLO. These tensions burst to the fore on May 19, 1985, when Palestinians clashed with Amal fighters in the Sabra refugee camp. The War of the Camps soon spread to Shatila and Burj al-Barajneh. Heavy fighting raged for the rest of the month between PLO guerrillas and Amal militiamen, leaving some six hundred dead and another two thousand wounded. While the PLO was forced out of Sabra, it retained a foothold in Shatila and managed to repel all the attacks against Burj al-Barajneh. Sporadic skirmishes occurred in September 1985 and March 1986, before full-scale conflict broke out once again in May. In this second round of fighting, the Palestinian defenders managed to rebuff Amal fighters equipped with Syrian T-54 tanks until another cease-fire was brokered, at the end of June. The third and bloodiest stage of fighting erupted in September, around the Rashidiya refugee camp, outside Tyre in South Lebanon. Within weeks, the fighting had spread to Beirut and Sidon. Palestinian units overran the village of Maghdusha, perched above the coastal highway, while Amal units supported by Syrian Special Forces laid siege to Rashidiya and Israeli warplanes bombed PLO positions. Clashes continued until mid-February 1987, when Syrian peacekeepers moved into West Beirut and a partial armistice was negotiated between Amal and the Palestinian leadership. Skirmishes continued into 1988, however. The War of the Camps left at least twenty-five hundred dead on both sides.[29]

The War of the Camps would significantly weaken Amal's influence. By attacking the Palestinians, by serving as a vehicle for Syrian influence, and by failing to win, Amal suffered major blows. In the wake of the clash with the Palestinians, tensions escalated between the two Shia militias, which had become rivals. Hezbollah leaders had objected to Amal's decision to attack the camps, and sent weapons to the PLO guerrillas. On February 17, 1988, militants abducted Lt. Col. William Higgins, head of the UN Observer Group in Lebanon, after a meeting with Amal leaders. While Hezbollah denied involvement, most outsiders blamed the group for Higgins's abduction. In response, Amal launched a sweeping manhunt with UN cooperation. The search for Higgins provided cover for Amal to begin a crackdown against Hezbollah in what the latter would dub the "war for domination." After retreating to its mountain strongholds around Iqlim al-Touffah, Hezbollah staged a counteroffensive in the southern suburbs of Beirut. Periodic fighting continued through the rest of the year, until January 1989, when Hezbollah forces overran pro-Amal villages in South Lebanon. In some of the fiercest fighting of the war, the rival militias battled for control of the region. A journalist wrote that "Corpses with heads chopped off or throats slit littered the bloody streets." One of Amal's senior clerics lamented that the "Shia community is committing mass suicide." A tentative truce was brokered later in the month, but fighting continued into 1990. As the civil war neared its end, Hezbollah emerged as the most dynamic political force in Lebanon.[30]

The Lebanese Civil War became the pivot of revolutionary violence in the latter half of the twentieth century as sectarian warfare eclipsed secular liberation struggles in the Third World. While the issue of the secular PLO dominated the first half of the war, the resurgence of political Islam took center stage after 1982. In this way, the fighting in Lebanon became a microcosm of global transformations in the late Cold War world. The small Mediterranean republic was the first to witness the communal violence, social fragmentation, and state collapse that would be characteristic of the post–Cold War order.

STALEMATE

Even as the war in Lebanon ground on, the bloody struggle between Iran and Iraq raged on the battlefields of Mesopotamia. On October 1, 1982, Iranian forces launched another offensive, aimed at capturing the heights above the town of Mandali. Seventy-two miles northeast of Baghdad, the town commanded the approaches to the Iraqi capital along with a key road to Kirkuk, in the north. The Iranians sent forty thousand Revolutionary Guards, regular soldiers, and an armored brigade against the Iraqi defenses. The Iraqi Second Army managed to blunt the initial assault and then stage a fighting retreat that took a heavy toll on advancing Revolutionary Guard units. After nearly a week of fighting, the depleted Iranian attack force had less than 20 square miles of territory to show for its efforts. With their offensive stalled outside Mandali, the Iranians launched another attack on Basra at the start of November. Revolutionary Guard units staging night assaults made significant gains against a slapdash Iraqi defense. After another week of combat, the Iranians had taken some 3,500 prisoners, 140 tanks, and 190 square miles of Iraqi territory. Late-fall rains then forced a halt in the fighting, which gave Baghdad time to rebuild its lines.[31]

The Iraqis had honed their tactics and substantially strengthened their defenses. While they had initially constructed a system of strongpoint defenses aimed at stopping armored assaults, they found that Iran's human-wave attacks could quickly isolate and smother individual fortresses. After Iran's first attack on Basra, Iraqi forces had adopted a system of earthworks composed of broad, raised sand embankments with prepared tank and artillery positions. Antiaircraft guns were repositioned to fire at ground targets so they could "hose down" waves of Revolutionary Guard and Basij. The Iraqis were able to build multiple defensive lines so that, if the first should fall, reserve positions were ready and waiting. Behind these fortifications, the Iraqis constructed a network of roads that gave them the ability to efficiently move mechanized reserves to positions where they were needed. Some of the larger Iraqi bunkers contained recreation areas with televisions and telephones, schoolrooms, clinics, and barbershops. In time, these fortifications ran almost the entire length of frontier between the two states.

While the Iraqis massed their firepower, the Iranians relied on manpower and zealous faith. Typical Revolutionary Guardsmen wore mismatched fatigues, tennis shoes, and scarves covered with Islamic slogans. Many were little more than boys with a meager three months of training. They were, one reporter observed, "an unsmiling lot, given to chanting at any opportunity." Rather than markings of rank, blue-and-gold insignias depicting a globe and an arm holding an AK-47 adorned their uniforms. Against Iraqi tanks, the Revolutionary Guard sent motorbikes and riders shouldering rocket-propelled grenades.[32]

By early 1983, the war had become a stalemate. Khomeini's regime was securely entrenched in Tehran and held the strategic initiative, while the Iraqis had built up their fortifications to withstand Iran's human-wave assaults. Iran's attacks along the frontier achieved negligible gains at substantial costs to both sides, but the balance of power remained static. Leaders in Washington and Moscow worried, however, about Baghdad's ability to hold the line. In June 1983, the Reagan administration agreed to sell sixty Hughes helicopters to Iraq. While officially designated for "agricultural use," these were to be converted for military purposes. Washington also began relaying satellite intelligence of Iranian troop movements to Baghdad through Saudi Arabia. Meanwhile, the Pentagon drew up plans for a military intervention in the event of an Iraqi collapse, which included strikes by A-10 ground attack jets against Iranian armor and bombing troops to drive Tehran's forces back against the border. In November 1983, Washington removed Iraq from its list of "nations that support international terrorism." The following month, the White House sent special envoy Donald Rumsfeld to Baghdad for his now-infamous handshake with Saddam. Moscow also agreed to the sale of two billion dollars' worth of warplanes, tanks, and missiles to the Iraqis. Both superpowers were now leaning toward Iraq in the hope of countering the rising threat from Iran and thereby restoring the balance of power in the Gulf.[33]

Both the Iraqis and the Iranians poured massive resources into breaking this stalemate. Tehran launched three offensives in February 1984. The first two, which targeted the Baghdad–Basra road near the Iranian border towns Mehran and Dehloran, were diversions designed to distract the Iraqis from their southern flanks. The main Iranian thrust, dubbed Operation Kheibar, aimed at Basra. Iranian columns attacked through the Hawizeh Marshes, a supposedly impregnable quagmire forty miles wide and thirty miles across made up of tiny reed-covered islands and floating vegetation surrounded by water between three and ten feet deep, which guarded the northern approaches to Basra. The Iraqis had stationed a sparse garrison along the wetlands in order to prevent guerrilla incursions, but they were unprepared for anything on the order of the Iranian assault. On the night of February 22, an Iranian flotilla set out through the marshes, seizing the island villages of Beida and Sabkha, some six miles west of the border. The Iraqis responded with artillery barrages and tank assaults, retaking the villages after a three-day battle. Afterward, the defenders bulldozed the three thousand Iranians killed into a mass grave along a sand embankment. Meanwhile, a second Iranian force launched human-wave attacks along the drier ground at the southern edge of the marshes, which the Iraqis countered with heavy armor and helicopter gunships. Iraqi engineers also flooded pockets of territory in an effort to halt the enemy advance. After heavy fighting, the Iraqis forced the invaders back across the marshes. Some estimates place the number of Iranian dead at 14,500, many of whom drowned in the retreat. A third prong of the Kheibar offensive targeted Iraqi oil facilities on Majnoon Island, at the western edge of the marshes. Following the Battle of Ghuzail, north of Basra, Iraqi commanders managed to muster enough troops to retake the southwestern quarter of Majnoon Island, which they were only barely able to defend against Iranian incursions. American intelligence estimated that 20,000 Iranians and 7,000 Iraqis were killed in the Kheibar offensive. By relying on their superior firepower, the Iraqi defenders had managed to hold the line in this, the First Battle of the Marshes.[34]

While Tehran struggled to break the stalemate with human-wave attacks along the frontier, Baghdad searched for new theaters of operation. Beginning on February 25, 1984—as Iranian columns pushed through the Hawizeh Marshes—Baghdad launched a series of aerial attacks on Iran's oil operations in the Persian Gulf. Over the next week, Iraqi jets hit seven ships and struck the oil terminal on Kharg Island, sixteen miles off Iran's coast. At the end of March, Baghdad rolled out its new French-manufactured Super Etendard warplanes, which carried antiship Exocet missiles. The Iraqis scored hits on Indian, Turkish, and Greek ships operating out of the Kharg installation. Tehran responded with its aging fleet of warplanes, which attacked Saudi and Kuwaiti tankers in May. In early June, Iraqi jets sank a Turkish tanker off Kharg. When the Iranians stepped up air patrols, Saudi Arabia set up its own defensive zone, which was patrolled by American-built F-15s. Iraqi aircraft staged another raid on Kharg late in the month. While neither side deployed the firepower to cut off petroleum exports, the conflict led to the militarization of the Persian Gulf. Leaders in capitals around the world who were dependent on Gulf oil kept a nervous watch on events lest they drive up international oil prices.[35]

Meanwhile, officials in Washington considered the wisdom of their tilt toward Iraq. On the one hand, a partnership with Iraq presented dangers for the United States, State Department officials explained. Having suffered under the weight of Iran's strategy of attrition, Baghdad had begun launching strikes in the Gulf, in a bid to transform "the strategic situation" of the war. Washington had to be careful not to enter into a position where the Ba'athists would be able to "force a level of U.S. support [to Iraq] we may not wish to provide (such as military protection of transport in the Gulf) or that we become identified with a regime whose longer-term political prospects remain uncertain."[36]

On the other hand, the threat of Iranian hegemony over the region remained troubling. "Iran is committed to a *revolutionary foreign policy* [emphasis in original]," the CIA warned, "which aims at propagating its radical interpretation of Shia Islam and the establishment of fundamentalist Islamic governments throughout the world."

The regime "has trumpeted the political significance of its Islamic revolution—not only for its Muslim neighbors, but for the world." These were new waters, the analysts explained—"we have little precedent to go on" in assessing the Ayatollah's likely behavior. Tehran hoped to transform the Gulf region by using "subversion, including terrorism" and by working with dissident groups to undermine governments such as those in Baghdad and Riyadh. The ultimate goal was to replace existing governments in the region with "radical Islamic regimes." Afghanistan had emerged as "another key target for exporting the revolution" as Tehran ramped up its aid to the Mujahideen. The Iranians were also taking advantage of the Lebanese Civil War to expand their influence in the Levant through relations with Shia militant groups. On the bright side, analysts noted, relations between Tehran and Moscow remained strained. Fearing Saddam's collapse and the rise of an Islamic fundamentalist regime in Baghdad, the Kremlin had increased aid to the Iraqis. "Nonetheless," the report noted, "the Soviets value Iran's anti-Americanism and do not want to push Iran back to the West." Moscow would continue to look for openings to improve its relations with Tehran.[37]

CIA analysts reported that all this had worked to transform the structure of power in Iraq. Under assault from Iran, which "espouses Saddam's overthrow as a religious duty," the regime in Baghdad had become dependent on "family and tribal ties" as well as "fear."[38] Nevertheless, CIA analysts noted, Baghdad had been especially effective at blocking Islamic "revivalist movements" in Iraq. Although Iraqi society had struggled with the same dislocations that had sparked fundamentalist revolutions in other Muslim countries, Saddam's regime had thus far managed to appease religious opposition with development aid at the same time that he crushed individual leaders who threatened his regime. Saddam's cult of personality had also succeeded in granting the leader an appeal to many segments of Iraqi society on a par with the "charisma that is commonly associated with religious prophets." In the long run, however, the regime had to achieve economic progress and win victories in the war if it hoped to forestall the "political and cultural disarray" that would "translate into more Islamic activity, especially among the disadvantaged Shias." Ultimately, analysts warned, the rise of a more robust fundamentalist movement in Iraq would threaten relations between Washington and Baghdad.[39]

For American policymakers, the defense of Iraq represented the least objectionable course of action. In a top-secret paper from 1984, State Department officers outlined a range of diplomatic and military options for dealing with the crisis in the Gulf. They noted that an Iraqi defeat "will probably lead to an Islamic fundamentalist, pro-Iranian regime in Baghdad. This is the outcome that would most destabilize the region and threaten our interests in the lower Gulf." An Iranian victory would be seen both as a defeat for the United States and a blow to American credibility in the region. Washington's failure to support Baghdad would lead other Gulf states, such as Saudi Arabia and Kuwait, to question whether the United States would come to their aid. An Iraqi defeat and its regional repercussions would inevitably impact foreign access to Gulf oil at the same time that it would dramatically increase Iranian influence throughout the Middle East.[40] If Saddam survived, the CIA noted, Iraq could act as a "magnet for Western economic investment and also as a buffer against Iran's attempts to export its revolution—thus furthering US objectives in the Persian Gulf."[41]

However, by supporting Saddam's regime in the war with Iran, Washington gained an unsavory ally that was threatening to pull the United States into a nasty war in the Gulf. The State Department reported that Iraqi forces were using chemical weapons "almost daily." Baghdad had acquired chemical weapons manufacturing equipment from Western firms and was now employing nerve agents on the battlefield.[42] U.S. military intelligence issued similar warnings. Facing a larger, more populous opponent intent on waging a war of attrition, Iraq had come to rely on a defensive strategy designed to extract the maximum toll on Iranian forces. "Torn between the need for man-power to reinvigorate Iraq's economy and perceived military require-ments," analysts noted, "it is unlikely that Hussein will dismantle his military machine to any great extent. This will leave Iraq with a large seasoned military force, one that likely will continue to develop its formidable conventional and chemical capability, and probably pursue nuclear weapons." The Pentagon, moreover, had no illusions about Saddam: the "ruthless but pragmatic" leader held complete control over the police and military and faced no significant internal challengers. The Ba'athists had hunted down and executed opponents and used brute force to crush Shia political movements. In the long term, analysts predicted, relations with Iraq would remain strained.[43]

Vicious fighting continued over the course of 1985, but the situa-tion on the ground changed little. In the embattled Iraqi port city of Basra, some ten miles from the front, frequent Iranian shellfire had brought much commercial life to a halt. The operators of the local fertilizer plant channeled their efforts into bagging sand to create bar-riers around important buildings, while the city's one million inhab-itants made do as best they could. Many business owners had closed up shop, covering their storefronts with steel shutters, as throngs of unemployed men offered shoeshines along the sidewalks. Rotting gar-bage cluttered the streets, and the military's presence remained con-spicuously high. The port, once vital to Iraq, was now largely derelict. Dozens of freighters sat rusting in the water, their holds empty. Food, at least, remained plentiful. Visitors noted the aroma of roast mutton wafting through the city and the stacks of flatbread and pastries for sale in stalls.[44] The impasse was about to be broken.

On February 10, 1986, as heavy rains washed over the al-Faw Pen-insula, at Iraq's far southern tip, thousands of Iranian troops stormed across the Shatt al-Arab waterway. Believing an attack unlikely, Bagh-dad had garrisoned al-Faw with the poorly trained units from the Popular Army. The Iranians quickly overran the Iraqi defenders, cap-turing the peninsula and advancing toward Basra. Iraqi commanders staged a series of counterattacks, all of which collapsed. As their vehicles sank into the sodden ground, the Iraqi defenders were forced to rely on infantry. Iraqi warplanes dealt negligible damage to the Iranian troop formations. In a last-ditch effort to halt the attackers, Saddam moved Special Forces and his elite Republican Guard units to the south. These forces, along with heavy artillery support and chemical weapons attacks, managed to halt the Iranian advance in the last week of February. But Iraqi attempts at a counteroffensive foundered. The Iraqis lost between eight thousand and ten thousand troops along with twenty to twenty-five aircraft. Saddam's Republican Guard had suffered a 30 percent casualty rate.

The al-Faw offensive ended the stalemate that had been in effect since 1983 and forced the Ba'athist regime to carry out an extensive reexamination of its strategies. Baghdad's defensive measures no longer appeared sufficient to stop Tehran's assaults, and Iraqi forces had been shown to be incapable of mounting effective counteroffensive operations. In the wake of the setback, Saddam's generals demanded that the regime release the military from political control. Officers must be promoted based on performance rather than loyalty to the regime. Following the battle, one historian writes, "the last vestiges of Saddam's Stalinist system were removed" from the military, measures to promote greater professionalization among the ranks were introduced, and the Republican Guard was expanded to six combat brigades.[45] Meanwhile, officials in Washington were embroiled in the largest political scandal since Watergate.

"WE WILL PAY THE PRICE"

If all had gone according to plan, it would have been a remarkable diplomatic feat. Beginning in the late summer of 1985, officials in the Reagan administration concocted a scheme designed to kill three birds with one magical stone. The plan began as an attempt to free a group of seven American hostages being held in Lebanon by Shia militia. Hostage-taking had become commonplace in Lebanon in the 1980s, as part of that nation's excruciating civil war. After repeated failed attempts to secure the release of these hostages, American officials sent feelers to Tehran in the hope that Khomeini's regime, the primary foreign sponsor of the Shia militias in Lebanon, might be able to lend assistance. Tehran had its own requests, however. The Islamic Republic was badly in need of replacement parts and ammunition for its American-made weapons. More pointedly, Iranian troops on the front lines desperately needed some means to counter the Iraqi advantage in heavy armor. In this same vein, the Iranians required surface-to-air missiles for defense against Iraqi air strikes. Officials in the Reagan administration recognized that they could use these military needs as diplomatic leverage with Iran in their efforts to secure the hostages in Lebanon. Cooperation between Washington and Tehran might also provide an opening for a rapprochement between the two regimes.

But there remained one significant obstacle to the shipment of American weapons to Tehran: the arms embargo on Iran in place since 1979. In order to clear this hurdle, officials in the Reagan administration devised a plan to transfer the weapons through Israel. While they were wary of the Islamic regime in Tehran, Israeli leaders believed that Iraq, with its ties to left-wing elements throughout the Arab world, represented the greater long-term threat to their country. Hence, Israeli officials agreed to a plan to transfer their own arms to Iran and then receive resupplies from the United States. In order to preserve the secrecy of these transfers, Reagan's NSC staff would oversee the operation. The NSC would then funnel the profits from these arms sales to right-wing Nicaraguan rebels, the Contras, fighting against the Marxist Sandinista regime in Managua. The transfer of these funds would, in turn, circumvent a congressional ban on military aid to the Contras that had been in place since 1984. In a nutshell, the Reagan administration would sell weapons to Iran via Israel in the hope of securing the release of American hostages in

Lebanon and then redirect the profits to guerrilla fighters in Nicaragua. The strangest element of the plan, ultimately, was the fact that anyone in the White House actually thought such a convoluted scheme would work, let alone remain secret. Perhaps the most notable voice of dissent came from Secretary of State George Shultz, who expressed doubt about the possibility of the scheme working and remaining secret. "I am very unenthusiastic about this," he wrote in December 1985. "Ultimately, the whole story will come out someday and we will pay the price."[46]

The entire operation began to collapse in the fall of 1986. On October 5, the Nicaraguan government shot down a CIA cargo plane carrying supplies to the Contras and captured the plane's sole survivor, Eugene Hasenfus, who admitted to working for the Agency. Four weeks later, on November 3, the Lebanese newspaper *Ash-Shiraa* published a report that brought the story to the world's attention. The paper revealed that the United States had sold weapons to Iran, against Washington's official position of neutrality in the Gulf conflict, and it named both former Reagan national security advisor Robert McFarlane and NSC staffer Oliver North as key liaisons in the transaction. As the White House scrambled to contain the damage, the mask of secrecy disintegrated. On November 13, the president appeared in a nationally televised address from the Oval Office in an effort to quash scandal. "The charge has been made that the United States has shipped weapons to Iran as ransom payment for the release of American hostages in Lebanon, that the United States undercut its allies and secretly violated American policy against trafficking with terrorists," he announced. "Those charges are utterly false." Rather, Reagan explained, he had authorized small shipments of "defensive weapons" in order to "convince Tehran that our negotiators were acting with my authority." The president's effort to skirt the issue failed, however, as the full extent of the operation became clear.[47] In Baghdad, Saddam offered his assessment. "This is nothing new," he told his inner circle.

"It is new in regards to their depravity, in the level of moral decay of the Americans and specifically their president."[48]

As furor over the scandal mounted, the White House and Congress set up separate commissions to investigate the affair. Investigations were hampered, however, by the fact that North and National Security Advisor John Poindexter had illegally destroyed key documents relating to the operation. As a result, the exact extent of Reagan's personal involvement was never made clear. In February 1987, the Presidential Commission delivered its findings, blaming Reagan for his lack of oversight and apparent ignorance of the details of the NSC's arms-for-hostages dealings. The congressional report, issued in November, criticized the White House for allowing private parties to conduct U.S. foreign affairs. Critics accused both reports of whitewashing the White House's involvement in conducting what amounted to an illegal secret war in Central America funded by illicit arms transfers to one of the nation's bitterest enemies. More than a dozen officials in the Reagan administration faced indictment for crimes related to the operation, but presidential pardons from Reagan's successor, George H. W. Bush (also accused of involvement), saved many from imprisonment. Lawrence Walsh, the independent counsel appointed to investigate the affair in 1986, accused the administration of working to "conceal President Reagan's willful disregard of constitutional restraints on his power. . . . Ronald Reagan's advisors succeeded in creating a firewall around him. He escaped meaningful interrogation until it was no longer of use, and he escaped prosecution altogether while subordinates suffered. . . . George Bush's misuse of the pardon power made the cover-up complete."[49]

THE TANKER WAR

Even as they circled the wagons in response to the Iran-Contra scandal, officials in the Reagan administration chose to increase America's naval deployments in the Persian Gulf. Tehran had stepped up its presence in the waterway in response to Iraq's attacks against Iranian oil operations. In November 1986, the Kuwaiti government had approached members of the Cooperation Council for the Arab States of the Gulf with a proposal for superpower intervention in order to protect neutral shipping. The following month, Kuwait reached an agreement with Moscow that would bring Soviet warships into the Gulf. "The idea of the Soviets playing a key maritime role in the gulf had no appeal to us," remembered Secretary of State George Shultz. In an effort to block the spread of Soviet influence into the region, Washington agreed to offer military protection to Kuwaiti shipping. In April 1987, the U.S. government agreed to register Kuwaiti tankers under the American flag, further extending naval protection. American policymakers understood that this move was likely to put U.S. ships in the crossfire between Iran and Iraq. "The ability of our forces to defend themselves, let alone others," Shultz noted, "had not been impressive in recent crises." As Washington expanded its military presence in the area, both sides moved toward confrontation. By the summer, Iran had trained twenty thousand Revolutionary Guardsmen to stage naval attacks in speedboats, placed Soviet-manufactured Silkworm antiship missiles along its coast, and mined Kuwait's harbor. The Iranians would not be the first ones to draw American blood, however.[50]

Just before eight o'clock in the evening on May 17, 1987, an American Airborne Warning and Control System (AWACS) surveillance plane flying off the Saudi coast spotted an Iraqi Mirage flying an attack run over the Persian Gulf. The crew of the USS *Stark*, a four-thousand-ton frigate recently stationed in the Gulf, picked up the Mirage's radar signature at seventy nautical miles from the ship. As the Iraqi plane approached, the Iraqi pilot targeted the *Stark* and fired a missile at the vessel. Oblivious to the approaching warhead, the ship's crew broadcast a warning to the Mirage as it drew closer. After launching a second missile, the Iraqi pilot broke away and set a return course to Basra. Soon after, a lookout on the *Stark's* deck sighted the first missile, which slammed into the ship's bow, igniting a blazing fire and killing twenty-eight crewmen. The second missile struck soon after, blowing a massive hole in the ship's side. It would take twelve hours for the crew to douse the flames. Thirty-seven servicemen had been killed. While they refused to allow American investigators to speak to the pilot, the Iraqis apologized for the accident and agreed to pay $27 million to the families of those killed in the attack.[51]

American naval forces now moved to take a more aggressive stance in the Gulf. By registering neutral vessels under the American flag, the U.S. government could claim the right of self-defense if any were attacked. But Washington was not prepared for the sort of conflict it was entering. Iranian vessels had laid some sixty mines across key shipping lanes. On July 22, 1987, a reflagged oil tanker, the *Bridgeton*, which was being escorted by two American warships, sailed into a mine. Though damaged, the *Bridgeton* remained afloat: oil tankers with double hulls had better protection against mines than did military vessels. As a result, the two American escorts took positions in the damaged tanker's wake to avoid impact with more mines. "They were being protected by the ship they were supposed to protect," historian Lawrence Freedman later quipped. While British ships were called in to aid in minesweeping operations, Washington increased its armada in the Gulf to forty-one ships. In September, American forces discovered mines during a search of the Iranian vessel *Al Fajr*. In retaliation for the search, Tehran launched an assault on a Saudi-Kuwaiti oil installation, attacked American helicopters, and fired Silkworm missiles at the supertanker *Sungari*. American forces responded on October 16 by striking the Rashadat oil platform, which the Iranians had been using as a military observation post. Fighting resumed the following April, when the USS *Samuel Roberts* struck an Iranian mine. U.S. forces retaliated by launching an attack on the Sassan platform and setting it ablaze, and with an assault on the Nasr platform, an active oil rig producing 150,000 barrels per day. Altogether, U.S. forces sank or crippled six Iranian ships.[52]

THE REAGAN ADMINISTRATION ACHIEVED A DECIDEDLY mixed record in its Middle Eastern interventions. Certainly, the 1983 marine barracks bombing in Beirut inflicted a grievous blow on American forces and tarnished Reagan's image at home and abroad. The Iran-Contra Affair also generated an embarrassing scandal that might, under different circumstances, have ended in Reagan's impeachment. Indeed, by the end of Reagan's time in office, most Americans probably hoped to stay very far away from the Lebanese quagmire. There were bright spots, however. Saddam Hussein's forces had blunted the Iranian offensive in Mesopotamia and appeared to be holding the line. And the U.S. Navy had established a fearsome presence in the Persian Gulf. Even more promising, the CIA and its Mujahideen allies had succeeded in bogging the Soviets down in a bloody counterinsurgency in Afghanistan. From a purely geopolitical standpoint, the United States and its allies appeared to be winning on the Middle Eastern battlefields of the late Cold War. In late 1986, CIA analysts argued that Soviet influence had largely been pushed out of the Arab world. The Iranian Revolution and the Soviet intervention in Afghanistan had strengthened the Kremlin's influence along the Northern Tier, for now, but Soviet leaders were sure to continue their efforts to extend control over the region. "The Middle East is the Soviet Union's most volatile borderland," the report noted. "Moscow regards the increased US military presence in the Middle East since the late 1970s as a major security concern and will devote considerable effort to counter it."[53]

Through the mid-1980s, the struggle for influence in the Middle East had confounded both Washington and Moscow. As the new generation of radicals turned away from the East-West ideological struggle, the superpowers confronted a perplexing dilemma.

CIA analysts argued that the resurgence in Islamic fundamentalism was driven by destruction of Nasser's Arab nationalism in the 1967 Arab-Israeli War, "the failure of secular ideologies to address political problems adequately," and the economic turmoil produced by the rise and fall of oil revenues. "Both Sunni and Shia fundamentalists have well-developed radical theologies that provide appealing alternatives to such 'failed' secular ideologies as nationalism, Marxist socialism, and Western capitalism." These fundamentalists threatened Washington's regional position because they scorned U.S. political and cultural influence as corrupt, materialistic, and exploitative, the report concluded. But U.S. losses would not lead to Soviet gains, as "fundamentalism is ideologically even more inconsistent with atheistic Soviet Communism."[54] The revolutionaries of the late Cold War embraced the concept of "neither East nor West," frustrating the designs of both superpowers.[55]

"YOU ARE CREATING A FRANKENSTEIN"

1988–1990

The end of the 1980s marked the end of an era. Millions around the world watched as the Berlin Wall, perhaps the most powerful symbol of the Cold War, fell in 1989. But Europe was not the only region in the midst of a transformation. Between 1988 and 1990, the wars in the Middle East each came to an end, their termination coinciding with the end of the Cold War between the United States and the Soviet Union. The end of the superpower struggle overshadowed the last stages of fighting in the Middle East, and as the world looked toward a new, post–Cold War order, the conflicts in Lebanon, Iran-Iraq, and Afghanistan were largely forgotten. But the end of the wars did not ultimately bring peace. The Middle Eastern wars of the 1980s ravaged local societies, radicalized political factions, created highly militarized states, and left bitter sectarian divisions. These troubling legacies would not long remain submerged.

By the end of 1987, CIA analysts had concluded that the "Islamic resurgence is likely to be the most powerful, widespread political force in the Arab world for the remainder of this century." Islamic revivalism stemmed in part from the "failure of various nationalist and socialist ideologies." By the 1970s, many Arabs had soured on "secular ideologies and institutions." Meanwhile, the Iranian Revolution and the supposed success of Islamic militants in forcing both Israel and the United States out of Lebanon seemed to demonstrate the power of religious revolutionaries to overcome secular governments. Increasing numbers of people in the region had come to blame outside powers for the clash between modernization and tradition, sectarian tensions, and the ongoing Palestinian problem. Because Islamic fundamentalists sought to push both U.S. and Soviet influence out of the region, Moscow had been unable to capitalize on these upheavals. Further, CIA analysts noted, the Kremlin "worried that the resurgence will spread among its Muslim minorities—some 45 million strong." Ultimately, the report argued, the Islamic resurgence created both dangers of further upheaval and anti-Americanism and opportunities for Washington to highlight "the incompatibilities between the Soviet Union and Islam."[1]

"LIKE DRINKING HEMLOCK"

The Iran-Iraq War was the first of the great Middle Eastern conflicts to come to an end. While American warships clashed with Iranian forces in the waters of the Persian Gulf over the course of 1987, the land war dragged on. The areas along Iraq's southern frontier continued to witness some of the heaviest fighting. In an effort to bolster their defenses, the Iraqis had flooded a large, shallow basin at the front, which became known as Fish Lake. A mere three feet deep, it was deep enough to slow infantry but too shallow for most boats. In addition to flooded marshes, the Iraqis maintained multiple lines of earthworks, bunkers, and gun positions, laced with barbed wire, each separated by a kilometer. If the first line fell, Iraqi forces could retreat to the second line and direct their fire on advancing Iranian infantry. Farther north, outside the Iraqi city of Amarah, Iraqi forces occupied a four-hundred-foot-tall ridge with commanding views of the marshes below. Western journalists described scenes reminiscent of First World War battlefields with winding trenches, barbed wire, sandbags, minefields, and field hospitals. Behind fifteen-foot-tall barriers, a network of roads allowed Iraqi commanders to rapidly bring reinforcements to embattled sectors. Soldiers at the front—some of whom had been fighting for the entire seven years of the war—carried AK-47s and gas masks. On the other side of no-man's-land, Iranian troops, many only teenagers, huddled in trenches and foxholes captured from the Iraqis. Toyota pickup trucks vastly outnumbered the tanks and armored transports.[2]

In late winter 1988, the Iraqis launched a ferocious assault on Iran's population centers and petroleum facilities. The so-called War of the Cities had begun three years before with bombing raids and occasional missile strikes aimed at demoralizing the civilian population. Since that time, each side had staged sporadic attacks on the other's cities. On February 29, 1988, Baghdad intensified its attacks, firing a barrage of Scud-B missiles at Tehran. In the next seven weeks, Baghdad launched an estimated 160 missiles aimed at the Iranian capital, in a brutal campaign that rocked the city.[3] Despite the damage, State Department analysts doubted the Scud attacks would have much effect on the war. The "basic nature of the war is unchanged," they noted. "Iraq can't win, but need not lose. Iran can win, but probably won't."[4]

After bombarding Tehran with long-range missiles, Baghdad launched a new campaign to retake the al-Faw Peninsula. On the night of April 16, 1988, Iraqi artillery opened up on Iranian positions on the northern edge of the peninsula. Using chemical weapons, the Iraqi guns pounded Iranian defenses while helicopters dropped commandos in the south. Iranian troops found themselves battling amid clouds of toxic gas and flanked by Iraqi forces to their rear. Facing collapse, the Iranians staged a harried retreat across the Shatt al-Arab, giving the Iraqis a stunning victory after some thirty-six hours of fighting. Baghdad had, for the first time in six years, retaken the offensive in the war. Ba'athist leaders judged correctly that American naval operations in the Gulf and contested parliamentary elections at home would distract Tehran from its land operations. State Department officials in Baghdad reported celebratory gunfire in the streets as news of the victory on al-Faw circulated. "The Iraqis won a crucial battle and the war will not be the same henceforward," they wrote. Though the events were kept out of the newspapers, the regime eagerly followed news of U.S.-Iranian clashes in the Gulf. "Iraqi officials are delighted at the bloody nose we have given the Iranians," the State Department noted. On May 23, Saddam's forces launched another assault along three points. Using chemical weapons and cluster bombs, Republican Guard units devastated Iranian defenders in Shalamche, east of Basra. By dropping mustard gas behind the front lines, the Iraqis prevented Iranian attempts to move up reinforcements.[5]

As Iraqi forces seized territory on land, the clashes in the Gulf erupted in tragedy. On the morning of July 3, 1988, Iran Air Flight 655 lifted off from Bandar Abbas on a regular flight to Dubai with 290 passengers and crew. Thousands of feet below, an American missile cruiser, the USS *Vincennes*, was sailing through the Strait of Hormuz. As the passenger jet closed to within forty kilometers of the *Vincennes*, the ship's captain, William C. Rogers III, sent a warning for the aircraft to change course. The ship's crew had mistaken the commercial aircraft for an F-14 fighter jet. As the airliner continued on its course, Rogers sent a second warning. Receiving no response, he launched two antiaircraft missiles that slammed into the jet's engines twenty-one seconds later. Sailors on the nearby frigate USS *Sides* claimed to have seen bodies falling from the sky. In the following days, Tehran invited international media to survey the wreckage and the row upon row of coffins on display at Bandar Abbas. Everyone on board the plane perished—including sixty-six children and an Iranian family of sixteen on their way to a wedding. Although it would never issue a formal apology for the incident, Washington eventually paid seventy million dollars to the airline and the victims' families.[6]

Facing crippling assaults from American ships in the Gulf and chemical attacks from Iraqi forces on land, Iranian leaders decided the time had come to seek peace. Though Khomeini had pledged never to accept a cease-fire with the reviled Ba'athists, eight years of war followed by the entry of the United States had driven the price of victory too high. In a letter to the Iranian people dated July 16, 1988, Khomeini explained his decision. Iran's generals anticipated that, due to the massive Western military aid it was receiving, Baghdad could not be defeated in the next five years. Moreover, Iran could not achieve its ultimate goals without the expulsion of U.S. forces from the Gulf—an unlikely prospect at best. Iraq's use of chemical weapons compounded Tehran's dilemma. "For all these reasons," Khomeini announced, "I am now inclined to agree to a full cease-fire. I trust you know that making this decision is like drinking hemlock for me." Iranian generals were convinced that Washington had virtually declared war on Tehran and that the United States was effectively running Iraq's war effort. Iranian leaders also feared that, due to the clashes in the Gulf, the Reagan administration was on the brink of a full-scale intervention in the war. Should this happen, it could bring about the fall of the regime and the end of Khomeini's revolution. On August 8, 1988, a UN-brokered cease-fire went into effect, bringing about an end to the open war between Iran and Iraq. But the truce would not stop the bloodshed in Mesopotamia.[7]

ANFAL

In the shadow of the Iran-Iraq War, another nightmare was already under way. If nothing else, the war with Iran had convinced Saddam of the need to consolidate his control over the Iraqi state. Potential sources of rebellion must be crushed. At the top of Saddam's list sat the Kurdish peoples of northern Iraq. The Kurds were an ancient population spread across the frontiers of Iraq, Iran, Syria, and Turkey. When the great European powers drew up the map of the post-

Ottoman Middle East after the First World War, the Kurds had been one of the peoples left stateless. Ever since, their national ambitions and tribal politics had been a concern for central governments in Baghdad, Tehran, Damascus, and Ankara. The Kurds of Iraq had staged three rebellions against the Ba'athist regime—in 1961–70, 1974–75, and 1983–85. During the war with Iran, the Kurdish areas in the north were exposed as a weak point in the Iraqi frontier. With the cessation of hostilities against Iran, Saddam found himself with an opportunity to put his legions of battle-hardened soldiers to a new task. Iraqi forces would wage a brutal campaign against the Kurds that butchered tens of thousands of men, women, and children.

To lead this operation, Saddam selected his cousin Ali Hassan al-Majid. "Chemical Ali," as he came to be known, marshaled the powers of the military, security services, and civilian government to carry out a vicious campaign of genocidal proportions that lasted from March 1987 to April 1989. Al-Majid pledged "to solve the Kurdish problem and slaughter the saboteurs." The party issued orders demarcating prohibited zones and commanding the army "to carry out random bombardments, using artillery, helicopters and aircraft, at all times of the day or night, in order to kill the largest number of persons present in these prohibited zones." Any individuals captured in these areas faced interrogation, and those between the ages of fifteen and seventy would be executed. In the meantime, al-Majid's forces launched chemical weapons attacks against Kurdish strongholds as well as civilian villages. Between April 21 and June 20, 1987, Iraqi forces razed more than seven hundred villages to create buffer zones around major roads and government installations designed to isolate Kurdish rebels. On October 17, 1987, Baghdad conducted a national census that gave the residents of the prohibited zones the option of abandoning their villages and moving into government-controlled areas or being designated as rebels.[8]

With the lines drawn, the Ba'athists prepared for a focused military campaign aimed at eradicating those Kurds who remained defiant. On the night of February 23, 1988, al-Majid's forces launched the Anfal campaign with an assault on the party headquarters of the Patriotic Union of Kurdistan at Sergalou-Bergalou. In a series of eight stages, Human Rights Watch reported, "Iraqi troops tore through rural Kurdistan with the motion of a gigantic windshield wiper." The assaults typically began with chemical attacks consisting of mustard and nerve gases designed to soften any potential resistance from Kurdish guerrillas. Civilian casualties, inevitable in such operations, were treated as acceptable. The largest such attack took place in the town of Halabja, where between three thousand and five thousand civilians were killed by chemical agents. After the clouds of poison gas drifted away, soldiers surrounded the area and razed all the buildings inside. Upon clearing the town, the military brought in demolition crews to level the area while truck convoys transported any survivors to concentration camps. While in September 1988 the regime released most of the women, children, and elderly being held in the camps, none of the captured men was set free. In at least two instances, the military staged summary executions of groups of men captured during the campaign. Human Rights Watch reported that "males from approximately fourteen to fifty were routinely killed en masse." The group estimated that no fewer than fifty thousand Kurds died during the Anfal campaign—that figure included thousands of women and children and, in many cases, entire families.[9]

American leaders were well aware that their ostensible allies in Baghdad were using chemical weapons in a genocidal campaign against the Kurds. In early September 1988, State Department intelligence warned that Iraqi government forces were using helicopters, warplanes, artillery, and armored vehicles against the Kurds. The Iraqis were "likely to feel little restraint in using chemical weapons" in the conflict. Indeed, analysts warned that the regime had already employed such chemical agents in its operations in August. The Ba'athists intended to force the Kurdish population away from its ancestral homelands in the mountains and onto the plains, "where they can be more easily controlled." This process would entail "considerable loss of life." A report from mid-September estimated that no fewer than five hundred Kurdish villages had been wiped off the map, noting that the real number was "probably considerably higher." One hundred thousand refugees had fled to Turkey, with another fifteen thousand moving into Iran.[10]

The White House and the State Department chose to look the other way, however. At the close of the Iran-Iraq War, a State Department paper from September 1988 reported that Iraq found itself as "the dominant power in the Persian Gulf, with a well-equipped battle-hardened army . . . and a new self-confidence bordering on arrogance." Freed from the burden of fighting Iran, Baghdad would take a more active stance in regional politics. "Saddam Hussein," the report warned, "is clever, ruthless and extremely ambitious." The Ba'athist regime was disciplined and relatively free of corruption—Iraq was, in the authors' words, "an Arab East Germany." The regime's human rights record was a cause for some concern and a "built-in-constraint" on closer relations between Washington and Baghdad. Though the two governments might not see eye to eye on the issues of human rights and chemical weapons, the report continued, they shared a number of interests: continued petroleum commerce, infrastructure development, and a desire to serve as a diplomatic "counterweight" to the influence of Libya and Syria. The Americans could use all the friends they could get in the Middle East, and with U.S.-Iranian relations in the gutter, the Reagan administration was in no hurry to alienate Saddam.[11]

Not all Americans were so ready to overlook the slaughter of the Kurds, however. On September 9, 1988, the U.S. Senate, in response to reports of Iraq's chemical attacks against the Kurds, unanimously passed the Prevention of Genocide Act. The bill would impose heavy sanctions on Iraq, cutting off five hundred million dollars in imports to the United States and two hundred million in U.S. exports to Iraq. If the Reagan administration sought to reestablish trade ties with

Iraq, it would have to certify that Baghdad "was *not* using chemical weapons against the Kurds and was *not* committing genocide." In effect, the legislation was designed to make it impossible for the White House to ignore the killing in northern Iraq. The bill, which had been passed quickly through the Senate, ran into trouble in the House of Representatives, however. Both the White House and American business interests opposed the legislation, citing inconclusive evidence of genocide and warning against sanctioning Iraq for a crime that, according to one *Washington Post* op-ed, "may never have taken place." Over the next weeks, the representatives opposed to the bill chipped away at its restrictions, eventually passing a largely neutered version on September 27. The next month, congressmen separated the genocide act from the tax bill to which it had been attached, and the measure died. The White House's Realpolitik, coupled with American business interests, had defeated any attempt to sanction Iraq for its actions. Even so, leaders in Washington were quickly losing any illusions they might have had about the Ba'athists.[12]

The feeling was mutual. Riding high on their recent victory over Iran and the apparent success of the Anfal campaign, Iraqi leaders were in no mood to kowtow to Washington. The U.S. ambassador in Baghdad, April Glaspie, noted a surge in "anti-American sentiment" following the Senate's condemnation of the regime's attacks on the Kurds. Glaspie warned that the principal tone of Saddam's public statements was one of "defiance and independence: we are not afraid of the U.S. and we do not need the United States." Ultimately, she wrote, if Saddam "perceives a choice between correct relations with the USA and public humiliation, he will not hesitate to let the relationship fall completely by the wayside." The Ba'athists were prone to a "neurotic penchant to suspect ulterior motives," she added, which fed the regime's fears that Washington would, sooner or later, tilt back toward Tehran.[13]

Unbeknownst to officials in Washington, their troubles in the Persian Gulf were just beginning. Though it resolved virtually none of the grievances between Baghdad and Tehran, the Gulf War left two powerful states in the region, each of which commanded massive, battle-hardened armies. Emboldened yet impoverished by the war with Iran, Saddam Hussein would soon turn his attention to his oil-rich Arab neighbors. Meanwhile, leaders in Tehran moved to reclaim the nation's influence by stationing Revolutionary Guard units around the region, supporting fellow Shia leaders in Syria and Lebanon, and launching a crash program to develop nuclear weapons. In the coming decades, the United States would stage two full-scale invasions of Iraq and become locked in a diplomatic standoff with Iran. In the process, U.S. Central Command (the successor to Carter's Rapid Deployment Joint Task Force) grew to become the most active military command in the post–Cold War era.

LEAVING AFGHANISTAN

While the Americans worried about their unsavory client in Baghdad, a new leader in the Kremlin (in power since 1985) struggled to find a way out of Afghanistan. At age fifty-four, Mikhail Gorbachev was the youngest man to take leadership of the Soviet Union since Stalin assumed power in the 1920s. The first Soviet leader born after the Bolshevik Revolution, Gorbachev represented a new generation. He was committed to reforming the Soviet political and economic system—not to achieve a revolution but, rather, to renew the vitality of the socialist state. Young and energetic, he breathed fresh air into the stale halls of the Kremlin. "In Gorbachev," U.S. secretary of state George Shultz noted, "we have an entirely different kind of leader in the Soviet Union than we have experienced before." As a young man, Gorbachev attended Moscow State University, where he studied law before returning to his hometown of Stavropol, where he quickly advanced up the ranks of the Communist Party. As an ambitious, principled, and hardworking young party member, he caught Leonid Brezhnev's eye. In 1978, the aging Brezhnev brought Gorbachev to

Moscow—the following year, Gorbachev joined the Politburo. There, he watched as first Brezhnev and then his successor, Yuri Andropov, and finally Konstantin Chernenko died in office. Gorbachev represented a departure from the generation of frail, decrepit leaders who had led the Soviet Union since the 1960s. Determined to revitalize the USSR, he launched a series of sweeping domestic reforms (glasnost and perestroika) that encouraged greater openness and transparency and proposed an economic restructuring of the Communist system. In foreign affairs, he sought to improve relations with the United States, scaling back the superpower competition and reducing nuclear arms. He also hoped to remove the Afghan lodestone that the USSR, for nearly six years, had carried around its neck.[14]

Even before he took power, Gorbachev understood that the Afghan intervention was draining the USSR's resources, demoralizing the nation's citizens, and hurting Moscow's standing abroad, and—most troubling for him—would hamper his efforts to overhaul the Soviet system. He, along with much of the Politburo, recognized that Moscow was not winning its long war in Afghanistan, a fact that was preventing efforts to implement broader reforms. Still, an abrupt withdrawal was out of the question. Such a move would be tantamount to admitting defeat and would deal a tremendous blow to the Kremlin's international credibility, throw Gorbachev's leadership into question, and devastate national morale. Instead, he sought a means of ending the war without accepting defeat. In October 1985, he met with President Karmal and warned the Afghan leader that the revolution was in trouble. Kabul had failed to build wide support among the Afghan people and had implemented its vision of socialist revolution too quickly. If it hoped to survive, Gorbachev told Karmal, the Afghan regime must slow its pace of reforms, seek accommodation with religious authorities, and win over the people. These needs were all the more urgent, he added, because Soviet forces would not remain in Afghanistan indefinitely. Gorbachev said he hoped to pull Soviet troops out of the country the following summer, leaving Afghan forces responsible for security. Upon hearing the news, a distraught Karmal pleaded with Gorbachev to reconsider: "If you leave now, next time you will have to send a million soldiers!"[15]

Although Gorbachev would not pull troops out the following summer, he was determined to end the war and get rid of Karmal. On November 13, 1986, he vented his frustrations to the Politburo. "We have been fighting in Afghanistan for already six years," he fumed. "If the approach is not changed, we will continue to fight for another twenty to thirty years." The military had failed to devise an effective strategy to win the war. "What, are we going to fight endlessly?" he fumed. It was time for decisive action. Gorbachev announced that he hoped to end the war "in the course of one year—at maximum two years." Moreover, Kabul's problems traced all the way to the top of the regime. "Karmal is walking like a pretzel," Gorbachev proclaimed, weaving and stumbling like a drunk man. The Kremlin had lost patience with the Afghan leader and now hoped for a change in leadership. Mohammad Najibullah, the newly elected general secretary of the PDPA, "needs our support," Gorbachev told his comrades. Najibullah understood Afghanistan's problems and would work toward "national reconciliation, strengthening the union with the peasantry, and consolidation of political leadership of the party and the country."[16]

The following month, Gorbachev told Najibullah that he had decided to pull Soviet troops out of Afghanistan and end the war. Beginning in January 1987, Soviet forces would cease offensive operations and engage the Mujahideen only in defense of Soviet positions.[17] But it would not be easy to end the bloodletting in Afghanistan, Gorbachev told the Politburo in February: "Now we're in, but how to get out racks one's brains." A quick withdrawal would raise doubts among Moscow's allies in the developing world. "They think this would be a blow to the authority of the Soviet Union in the national liberation movement," Gorbachev claimed. "And they tell us that imperialism will go on the offensive if you flee from Afghanistan." At the same time, withdrawal carried domestic political repercussions. "A million of our soldiers have been to Afghanistan," he explained. "And all in vain, it turns out." Some way must be found to withdraw Soviet forces while leaving Afghanistan a stable state with a regime that would not be hostile to the Soviet Union.[18] But rebel leaders and their international network of supporters had other plans.

While the Kremlin labored to draw down Soviet deployments in Afghanistan, the CIA and ISI continued pouring money and weapons into Afghanistan. By late 1986, they had recruited a new set of allies. From the beginning, elements in the Arab world had supported the Afghan struggle against the Soviet occupation. By the latter stages of the conflict, this support had grown into a transnational pipeline of volunteers from places such as Egypt, Algeria, and Saudi Arabia. The first Arab volunteers had arrived in Afghanistan escorting aid packages sent from wealthy oil states. By the second half of the decade, young Arab men were making the journey to participate in what they saw as a jihad against the Soviet occupation. Abdullah Azzam, a Palestinian professor and member of the Muslim Brotherhood, is credited with inspiring a flood of Arab volunteers to join the battle in Afghanistan. His booklet, *Defending the Land of the Muslims Is Each Man's Most Important Duty*, called upon Muslims everywhere to join the jihad. Somewhere between eight thousand and twenty-five thousand men answered. Although they contributed little to the armed strength of the Afghan Mujahideen, their experience of waging a jihad in Afghanistan was pivotal in establishing global networks of Islamic fighters that rose to prominence in the following decade.[19]

Foremost among these was the son of a Saudi billionaire, Osama bin Laden. Bin Laden had met Azzam while studying at King Abdulaziz University, in Jeddah, in the late 1970s. After leaving the university, he joined Azzam in Pakistan, where he helped facilitate the transfer of aid from the Arab world to the Mujahideen. Like many of the so-called Afghan Arabs, bin Laden worked with the Haqqani group in the mountains of Paktia. He found himself at the center of an emerging, global jihadist movement: CIA, Saudi, and ISI supply chains; zealous Islamic ideologies; and fearsome guerrilla fighters all met in the Haqqani camps along the Pakistani border. In late March 1986, Soviet commanders launched an attack on the Zhawar base, a Haqqani stronghold and critical stopping point for supplies moving across the border that the Mujahideen and the ISI were determined to defend. The Battle of Zhawar was the first major engagement in which large units of Arab fighters participated. Mujahideen fighters supported by Pakistani agents waged a desperate defense against Afghan and Soviet forces. The attackers managed to take the base for five hours on April 19 before being pushed back. Soviet engineers laid explosive charges that inflicted significant damage to the facilities, but they were unable to completely destroy the complex. Fearing a counterattack, government troops withdrew, and the Mujahideen were able to reclaim what was left of the camp. Both sides suffered significant casualties, but Kabul claimed victory in the engagement. In the wake of the battle, bin Laden threw his resources into rebuilding the base. In return for his efforts, the Haqqanis gave the young Saudi three caves along the edge of the camp, which bin Laden transformed into a comparatively luxurious multiroom accommodation. Following his reconstruction efforts at Zhawar, he established a training camp for Arab fighters at Jaji, north of Khost. While largely unknown to the outside world, the young Saudi was becoming an important figure along the Afghan-Pakistani frontier.[20]

While bin Laden's star was rising, Kabul's leader was about to fall. For some time, officials in the Kremlin had been losing patience with Babrak Karmal. The Afghan leader, they believed, had centralized power in his own hands and exacerbated the rifts inside the PDPA. Soviet leaders instead favored Najibullah, whom they had been grooming as Karmal's replacement. In March 1986, Gorbachev summoned Karmal to Moscow, where the Soviets encouraged him to abdicate. The Afghan leader remained stubborn, however, wrangling a return trip to Kabul, where he tried to block Najibullah's efforts to consolidate control over the Politburo and the Defense Council. Soviet leaders allowed him to remain as chairman of the Revolutionary Council until November, when he was finally pushed aside. For better or worse, Najibullah was now at the helm in Kabul, and Gorbachev was looking to get out of Afghanistan.[21]

While the Kremlin searched for an exit, officials in the Reagan administration worked to escalate the bloodshed. Milt Bearden arrived at the CIA station in Islamabad in August 1986. The forty-six-year-old CIA veteran was a large man with a broad nose and a charismatic swagger. He had become a close friend of William Casey's earlier in the decade, while stationed in Khartoum, and was the Director of Central Intelligence's choice to take over the Agency's operations in Afghanistan. "I want you to go out there and win," Casey had told Bearden. And there was little question about what victory would entail. "All of you guys out there, you try to recruit Soviets," Bearden boasted to other CIA station chiefs. "Me, I just kill them." Bearden combed the globe for pack mules he could use to send supplies across the border into Afghanistan, bringing in animals from as far away as China, Texas, and Djibouti. He also oversaw the deployment of the first Stinger missiles to Afghan rebels in September 1986. Bearden would coordinate the final escalation of the CIA's covert war in Afghanistan, oversee the end of the Soviet occupation, and witness the aftermath.[22] But the Soviets had no intention of going quietly.

The Kremlin believed that the key to accomplishing the withdrawal from Afghanistan lay in a campaign for national reconciliation. Gorbachev held a long discussion with Najibullah in July 1987 on the program's goals and current status. Both men agreed that a purely military solution to Afghanistan's problems was unlikely. National reconciliation aimed to expand the regime's base of support by bringing enough disaffected elements in the country back into the fold. Najibullah explained that some ten thousand reconciliation commissions were working with local communities and groups throughout the country. Kabul was making special efforts to broker deals with Mujahideen commanders, Najibullah noted, going so far as to recognize "a certain autonomy and independence of mid-level rebel chieftains on the territory which they control" in return for their recognition of the regime in Kabul. Likewise, the government was working to reintegrate refugees who had returned from Pakistan and Iran. Despite some initial success, the regime still faced daunting challenges. Critics of the national reconciliation campaign within the PDPA threatened to inflame the cleavages that had plagued the party since the 1970s. The regime also faced the task of bridging divides between Afghanistan's various ethnic communities and moving away from a government structure that privileged certain groups over others. All these efforts took place against the backdrop of a bloody and well-funded insurgency raging in the hinterlands. "Our country has become one of the main links of a policy of state terrorism being pursued by the US," Najibullah complained to Gorbachev.[23]

On November 19, 1987, Soviet commanders launched one of their largest offensives of the war, Operation Magistral, which was designed to blast open the road leading into Khost and relieve the besieged city. In an overwhelming display of force, ten thousand Soviet troops supported by another eight thousand Afghans were sent in to clear the rebels from the area. While armored vehicles pushed down the road, Soviet paratroopers dropped in along the surrounding heights to force the Mujahideen away from firing positions. In one of the war's most storied engagements, the company that had staged the 1979 assault on the Tajbeg Palace fought a ferocious battle with Mujahideen in defense of Hill 3234, along the road to Gardez. The Soviet company suffered heavy casualties (twenty-eight out of thirty-nine men) and nearly ran out of ammunition but managed to hold off the attack. Operation Magistral, like most other large operations during the war, ended in a Soviet victory followed by a withdrawal. In short order, rebel fighters moved back into the area where they were once again able to block the road to Khost. Magistral and the battle for Hill 3234 would come to symbolize both the heroism of many Soviet soldiers and the ultimate futility of the war itself.[24]

The Kremlin was indeed preparing to make good on its promise of pulling Soviet forces out of the country. During the Washington Summit in December, Gorbachev told Reagan that he hoped to withdraw all Soviet troops from Afghanistan within the next twelve months, if not sooner. But he noted that the "process should be tied to national reconciliation and the creation of a coalition government." He explained that the Kremlin wanted only to see a stable, neutral Afghanistan, and he assured Reagan that Moscow had no designs on bases in Afghan territory. In order to aid the withdrawal, he asked Reagan to cut off U.S. aid to the Mujahideen. Reagan deflected the request. The following day, Gorbachev pleaded with Vice President George Bush to suspend aid to the rebels. "If we were to begin to withdraw troops while American aid continued," he warned, "then this would lead to a bloody war in the country." The Soviets and Americans had common interests in Afghanistan—namely, seeing that the country did not fall into chaos after the Soviet withdrawal, and blocking the rise of a potentially dangerous Islamist regime. But Operation Cyclone, the CIA's covert aid program to the Mujahideen, was too successful for the Reagan administration simply to abandon it while Soviet boots remained in Afghanistan. Reagan's determination to use Afghanistan as a weapon against Moscow led Washington to drive a hard bargain and effectively rebuke Gorbachev's attempts at accommodation. Neither the prospect of hastening the Soviet withdrawal nor the threat of a coming anarchy in Afghanistan would move the White House.[25]

Soviet forces launched their last major combat offensive of the war on January 23, 1989. Operation Typhoon was a parting gift to Najibullah, who had requested that the Soviets make one last effort to crush Massoud's forces in the Panjshir Valley. Though many Soviet officers warned against the operation, which they saw as futile and needlessly destructive, the Kremlin acquiesced. After calling on the civilian population to evacuate, the Russians used their artillery and aircraft to pound the valley, smashing buildings and devastating roadside villages. Massoud and most of his fighters survived while Soviet soldiers were left to wonder at the ultimate purpose of the operation and the larger war. "Almost ten years of the war were reflected, as if in a mirror, in three days and three nights," one Soviet general later wrote; "political cynicism and military cruelty, the absolute defenselessness of some, and the pathological need to kill and destroy on the part of others. Ten years of bloodletting were absorbed into three awful days."[26]

Three weeks later, the last Soviet armored vehicle rolled across the Amu Darya Bridge, marking the end to the Soviet-Afghan War. Soviet officials reported nearly 15,000 of their troops killed during the nine-year conflict, with more than 50,000 wounded. Some reports claimed that casualties were even higher. Rough estimates of Mujahideen deaths started at 75,000 killed, with at least as many wounded. Estimates of total casualties ranged from 600,000 to 1.5 million killed and another 3 million wounded. Approximately 5 million Afghans had fled the country, and another 2 million were internally displaced.[27]

Although the war had ended for the USSR, Afghanistan's ordeal was only beginning. In a report written the previous spring, the CIA predicted that Najibullah's regime would not long survive the Soviet departure: "[W]e believe [the new regime] initially will be an unstable coalition of traditionalist and fundamentalist groups whose writ will not extend far beyond Kabul and the leaders' home areas." These new leaders of Afghanistan, the Agency warned, "will be Islamic— possibly strongly fundamentalist, but not as extreme as Iran. . . . We cannot be confident of the new government's orientation toward the West; at best it will be ambivalent, and at worst it may be actively hostile, especially toward the United States." There was also a possibility, analysts warned, "that no stable central government will develop in Kabul." Should this happen, they predicted, "Afghanistan could evolve into a Lebanon-like polity in which there is no effective central government and regional warlords battle each other and compete for hegemony in the capital."[28] As the spring thaw melted the snowy mountain passes and rival Mujahideen factions prepared for a new season of fighting, not just with Kabul but also with one another, it appeared that the CIA's dire predictions would come true. But with the Soviet departure, most of the outside world's attention had turned away from Afghanistan.

ARMS SMUGGLERS, PIRATES, WARLORDS, AND GUNMEN

There remained one last round of fighting before the Middle Eastern conflicts of the late Cold War finally came to an end.

After nearly fourteen years of war, the combatants in Lebanon had approached the point of exhaustion. Sectarian resentments continued to fester, however. In September 1988, outgoing president Amine Gemayel dismissed the serving prime minister, Selim Hoss, and appointed Gen. Michel Aoun to the office of prime minister—rather than passing to Hoss, a Sunni—so that Lebanon's head of state would remain a Maronite Christian. Aoun formed a military cabinet and announced the creation of his new government. Hoss rejected his dismissal and insisted that he remained the legitimate prime minister of Lebanon. After nearly fifteen years of civil war, Lebanon had two rival governments.[29] Aoun was determined to reunite Lebanon under his rule and push the Syrian forces out of the country. To do this, he declared a "war of liberation" against foreign forces inside Lebanon on March 14, 1989. Syrian units responded with a blockade against Aoun's territory and a ferocious artillery attack that destroyed 80 percent of Aoun's petroleum reserves. Aoun fired back with his army's guns, many of which had been acquired from the United States and Israel, and managed to inflict substantial damage against Syrian bases in the Beqaa Valley. As Syrian shells rained down on West Beirut, a flood of refugees abandoned the district, moving back toward South Lebanon, from whence many had come. Those that remained sheltered below ground as everyday life ground to a halt.[30]

In October, the surviving fifty-eight members of Lebanon's National Assembly—parliamentary elections had not been held since the beginning of the civil war in 1975—met in Taif, Saudi Arabia, with the support of Riyadh, Washington, and the Arab League. Their task was to revise the National Pact, which had formed the basis for sectarian power relations in Lebanon since 1943. The resulting Taif Agreement restructured political power to reflect the growth of the Muslim population and announced Lebanon as a state firmly rooted in the Arab world. However, in an acknowledgment of Maronites, the agreement stressed that Lebanon would remain the "final homeland for all its citizens." The document also called for the eventual abolition of the confessional system, but it did not establish a time line for doing so. The accords implicitly accepted Syrian influence in Lebanon, granting Damascus an official role in assisting Lebanese forces to establish the new government's authority and acknowledging the "special relationship" between the two nations. Finally, the Taif Agreement called for the disbanding and disarming of all sectarian militias, concentrating military power in the hands of the state. Although it signed on to the agreements, Hezbollah maintained its forces in South Lebanon, an act that it justified as necessary to continue its armed resistance against Israel's occupation.[31]

At the end of 1989, only one major force remained in opposition to the Taif Agreement: Michel Aoun. Many in the Christian population cheered as the general rejected Taif as a violation of Lebanese sovereignty and as a "repair to a rotten regime." International forces were coalescing against the general, however. In August 1990, Iraqi forces launched an invasion of Kuwait that sparked an immediate outcry around the world. As the United States built an international coalition to attack Iraq, Aoun lost one of his last remaining foreign supporters. Washington and Damascus found common ground in their opposition to the regime in Baghdad, and Assad found himself with a freer hand to deal with Lebanon. It would be the Syrians who finally crushed the general. On October 13, 1990, Syrian ground units moved en masse to attack Aoun's force as Syrian warplanes struck the presidential palace at Baabda. As the Syrians massacred the Lebanese defenders—the bodies of seventy-three soldiers who had been executed with a bullet in the skull were sent to one hospital—Aoun realized that his time had run out. The general ordered his troops to surrender and then fled Baabda to seek refuge in the French embassy, as Assad's forces seized the presidential palace. After a decade and a half, the civil war had come to an end.[32]

For fifteen years, Lebanon had appeared as a sort of Hobbesian nightmare, a war of all against all gripping the small country. As one historian noted, much of the most vicious fighting took place between rival militias within the same sect: Gemayel's Phalangists slaughtered Chamoun's Tigers; the PLO battled Saiqa; Amal and Hezbollah waged a brutal war against each other.[33] During this time, Lebanon's central government ceased to perform many of its basic functions. As the nation fractured into warring ethnic cantons, rival economic units emerged. Coupled with the rise of warlords and militia rule, illicit economies proliferated throughout Lebanon. By the early 1980s, Lebanon had become a leader in the global drug trade. Up to 40 percent of the cultivated land in the fertile Beqaa Valley was devoted to narcotics cultivation—mainly hashish and opium. Some estimates placed the market value on Lebanese-produced narcotics at $150 billion. Ports along the Mediterranean coast became havens for arms smugglers, drug traffickers, and pirates. The Lebanese black market flowed with everything from tax-free cigarettes to heroin, AK-47s to contraband livestock. This lawless atmosphere extended well into the major cities, where drivers were expected to pay "tolls" at rival militia checkpoints on major thoroughfares. The Lebanon of the 1980s became a potent example of the dangers of state marginalization—a land ruled by smugglers, pirates, warlords, and gunmen.[34]

WITH THE CONCLUSION OF THE WARS IN LEBANON, AF-ghanistan, and Iran-Iraq, the Cold War era's final stage of mass violence came to an end even as the Soviet Union itself teetered on the brink of collapse. The Middle Eastern wars of the 1980s ushered in a new type of conflict, one in which sectarianism replaced secular liberation as the primary vehicle of revolutionary politics in the developing world. Communal violence in Lebanon, the shock of the 1979 revolution in Iran, and the growing strength of the Afghan Mujahideen showcased the degree to which resurgent ethno-religious ideologies had eclipsed the Cold War politics of East versus West. The Middle Eastern conflicts of the late Cold War tilted the regional balance of power decisively in favor of the United States. From the late 1980s on, Washington stood unchallenged as the most influential outside power in the Middle East. But the price of this victory remained unclear. Over the course of the 1980s, U.S. leaders had mobilized the forces of militant Islam in their Cold War struggle against the Soviet Union. As U.S. officials understood, these groups were hardly friendly to American interests, and there was no reason to believe that they would hesitate to turn their fury against Washington after the Soviet departure. Even as the Soviet war in Afghanistan was coming to an end in 1989, Pakistani prime minister Benazir Bhutto cautioned George H. W. Bush about the dangers of Washington's support for militant Islam. "You are creating a Frankenstein," she warned.[35] Just how dangerous these forces would become would not be made apparent until the beginning of the next century.

"WE'RE GOING TO PUT THEIR HEADS ON STICKS"

On September 13, 2001, two days after Al-Qaeda militants crashed commercial jetliners into the World Trade Center, the Pentagon, and a field outside Shanksville, Pennsylvania, Cofer Black sat down for a meeting with President George W. Bush in the White House Situation Room. The fifty-one-year-old head of the CIA's Counterterrorism Center had spent the last two years preparing for war against the radical Islamic group Al-Qaeda. Black outlined a plan to launch a relentless assault against Al-Qaeda operatives around the world, with the goal of killing as many militants as possible. "When we're through with them," he told the president, "they'll have flies walking across their eyeballs." Black's gruesome words struck a chord with the president's national security advisors, many of whom had come of age during the Cold War, an era when sober diplomacy eclipsed violent military clashes. The United States was now embarking on a different type of war than the one that most remembered against the Soviet Union. It would be a conflict centered on special operations forces and targeted killings rather than issues such as nuclear diplomacy and economic rivalry. "We're going to kill them," Black explained later. "We're going to put their heads on sticks."[36]

To many of the architects of the so-called global war on terror, the fighting to come must have seemed very familiar. While men such as Secretary of State Colin Powell and Secretary of Defense Donald Rumsfeld spent the first decades of their careers preparing for a confrontation with the Soviet Union, the front lines of this new struggle against Al-Qaeda and similar groups were often manned by veterans of the Cold War's killing fields—sites of savage conflicts fought by mercenaries, guerrillas, and hard-faced soldiers, conflicts that killed hundreds of thousands in the far-flung corners of the world.

Greg Vogel (code-named "Spider") helped coordinate the CIA's war against Al-Qaeda and Taliban fighters in Afghanistan during the 2002 Operation Anaconda. A former marine who had served with CIA paramilitary groups in Central America, Vogel had also worked to train Afghan Mujahideen during the Soviet-Afghan War.[37] Another member of the CIA's paramilitary unit, Michael Vickers, stepped into key positions in the Pentagon to help design Washington's global war on terror. A veteran of the Grenada invasion, Vickers served as the "principal strategist" for the CIA's covert war against the Soviet Union in Afghanistan. During the Cold War, Vickers trained as a Green Beret to "parachute into enemy territory with a small nuclear weapon strapped to his leg," the *Washington Post* reported, "and then position it to halt the Red Army."[38] Far from a break from the earlier era of the superpower struggle, this new war was rooted firmly within it.

But Vogel and Vickers were not the only warriors who had come of age fighting on these distant battlegrounds. In the spring of 1989, a young street tough from Zarqa, Jordan, made his way to Afghanistan. Encouraged by his mother to join the jihad against the Soviets, Abu Musab al-Zarqawi arrived too late to do any fighting against the now-departed Soviet forces. Instead, he became a writer for a jihadist magazine. Ashamed of the tattoos acquired in his youth, he wore long sleeves among his fellow fighters. Zarqawi fought alongside Mujahideen groups in Paktia and Khost before returning to Jordan sometime in the early 1990s. Like other Arab veterans of the Afghan war, Zarqawi tried to bring the jihad home. Jordanian authorities caught wind of his activities, however, and imprisoned him throughout most of the 1990s. After the regime declared a general amnesty in 1999, Zarqawi mounted a failed attempt to bomb the Amman Radisson Hotel. He then fled to Pakistan and Afghanistan, where he connected with another jihadist who had come of age fighting Soviets in the mountains of Afghanistan, Osama bin Laden.[39] The Saudi militant had been busy in the years since the end of the war, establishing himself as one of the most prominent Islamic revolutionaries in the world. During the 1990s, he used his financial resources to build his organization, Al-Qaeda, into a major player in the world of militant Islam. He had also come to see the United States, the most important outside power in the Middle East and a key backer of regimes such as Saudi Arabia, Egypt, and Israel, as the principal obstacle to a broader Islamic revolution in the region. In an effort to drive U.S. influence out of the region, Al-Qaeda launched a series of attacks over the decade, including the 1998 bombings of the U.S. embassies in Dar es Salaam and Nairobi, and the 2000 attack on the USS *Cole*, off the coast of Aden. Bin Laden and his comrades moved from Afghanistan, to Saudi Arabia, and to Sudan before returning to Afghanistan in 1996.

To date, no researcher has produced documentation of direct links between Washington and bin Laden or, for that matter, Zarqawi. The weight of evidence suggests that the CIA and the future leaders of Al-Qaeda and ISIS were not in communication with one another during the Soviet occupation in Afghanistan. U.S. officials tended to leave direct contacts with the Mujahideen to their counterparts in the Pakistani ISI, and neither bin Laden nor Zarqawi would have been important enough then to command significant attention from Washington. Nevertheless, U.S. and Soviet operations in Afghanistan laid the groundwork for the rise of a global jihadist movement in the waning years of the Cold War. Likewise, the U.S. invasions of Iraq, spearheaded by the Reagan-era successor to Carter's Rapid Deployment Joint Task Force, Central Command, created the conditions for the rise of the Islamic State in Iraq and Syria (ISIS).

THE COLD WAR TURNED AFGHANISTAN, AND ULTI-mately the wider Middle East, into the epicenter of a growing global jihadist movement. The chaos that had engulfed Afghanistan after the Soviet departure helped to transform Afghanistan into an ideal breeding ground for Islamic revolutionary fighters. Al-Qaeda's leadership, ideology, and infrastructure had risen from the ashes of the Soviet war in Afghanistan. Zarqawi would build upon his background in Afghanistan to form a jihadist group inside American-occupied Iraq that, in time, would evolve into ISIS. With the ascension of Al-Qaeda's worldwide Islamic insurgency and America's war on terror after the September 11 attacks, figures such as bin Laden, Zarqawi, Vickers, and Vogel took commanding positions in a new global conflict. The shadow warriors of the superpower struggle now stepped into the light. Having sown the wind on the battlefields of the Cold War, the United States would now reap the whirlwind.

CONCLUSION

It is no exaggeration to say that the Cold War formed the crucible out of which a new system of radicalized Third World states emerged. The decades following 1945 brought an end to a five-hundred-year era of European colonial expansion. As the Great Powers of Europe retreated, two successor empires battled for control of the post-imperial world order. Neither the United States nor the Soviet Union sought to reconstruct the colonialism of the previous era, but both hoped that their respective sociopolitical systems would dominate the new age. The Cold War that their rivalry created generated violence throughout much of the world—nowhere more than Eurasia's southern tier. But even as the superpower struggle dominated world affairs, an array of regional challengers appeared in this Eurasian rimland to contest the Cold War paradigm with both words and arms. These local revolts—focused around but reaching far beyond Beijing, Hanoi, and Tehran—pulled the front lines of the Cold War into the developing world and, in doing so, fundamentally altered the landscape of international affairs as the twentieth century drew to a close.

The East Asian offensive tore through China, Korea, and Indochina between 1945 and 1954 and announced the stunning rise of the global Communist movement as a very real contender for world power in the wake of the Second World War. But the anchors of this movement, Moscow and Beijing, proved unable to hold their alliance together. During the second wave of mass violence, between 1961 and 1979, global communism collapsed. The series of wars in Vietnam, Indonesia, Cambodia, and Bangladesh that ravaged South and Southeast Asia laid waste to Communist solidarity in Asia and ended three decades of Marxist victories in Asia. But even as the Asian Communist revolution fell into ruin, a new breed of revolutionaries stepped forward to continue the battle for the Third World. The Cold

War's third wave of mass violence consumed the central Islamic world between 1975 and 1990, as ethno-religious warriors emerged as the new face of revolution in Lebanon, Iran, and Afghanistan.

Washington's decades-long war against communism crippled secular liberation movements throughout much of the Third World. In doing so, U.S. Cold War policies helped to destroy the principal alternative to ethnosectarian politics in much of the postcolonial world. American leaders believed that their battle against left-wing revolutionaries would leave liberal capitalism as the only viable political alternative. They were mistaken. By the last decades of the Cold War, a new generation of fighters chose to embrace ethnic and religious violence as a means of staging Third World revolution. Moreover, even after the Iranian Revolution, U.S. officials believed that they could harness the power of religious warriors such as the Mujahideen in the Cold War struggle against communism. Only after the end of the superpower struggle did American leaders realize that they had helped unleash a creature they could not now control.

Throughout the post-1945 era, the Americans courted authoritarians and religious forces as bulwarks against communism. In one case after another, U.S. leaders prioritized anticommunism over democracy in their Third World allies. At the same time, Soviet and Chinese Third World policies pulled postcolonial revolutionaries away from moderate socialism and toward more radical forms of Marxist thought. The East Asian offensive left a string of highly militarized Communist regimes and authoritarian dictatorships in places such as Beijing, Taipei, Pyongyang, Seoul, Hanoi, and Saigon. Likewise, the Indo-Asian bloodbaths bolstered military regimes in Hanoi, Saigon, Jakarta, Phnom Penh, and Islamabad as the Americans, Soviets, and Chinese poured resources into local conflicts. And the wars of the great sectarian revolt helped radicalize militant groups in Lebanon, Iran, and Afghanistan while simultaneously strengthening militarized regimes in Israel, Syria, Iraq, and Pakistan. In this way, U.S. and Soviet military, political, and financial support for conflicts raging throughout the postcolonial world helped destroy moderates and radicalize societies around the world.

The fallout from the ravaging of the Third World went largely overlooked in Washington and Moscow. As the superpower confrontation wound down, both Gorbachev and President George H. W. Bush envisioned a new, post–Cold War world. While Gorbachev hoped to see the integration of the Soviet Union into the global order, Bush had other ideas. On September 11, 1990—eleven years to the day before the 9/11 attacks—the president appeared before Congress to herald the dawn of the New World Order and call for united action against the recent Iraqi invasion of Kuwait. Though Bush spoke of cooperation between the United States and the Soviet Union, he outlined a vision of an American-dominated, liberal-capitalist international order. Bush's ideas resonated with most Americans for whom the lessons of the Cold War were clear. The free world and the Communist bloc had squared off in a head-to-head confrontation, and liberal capitalism had prevailed. History was marching inexorably toward an interconnected global order in which liberal-capitalist ideas would reign supreme. This idea, articulated most clearly by political theorist Francis Fukuyama, gained traction among Americans celebrating their ostensible victory in the Cold War. Americans both inside and outside government looked forward to a new era of American predominance, a unipolar world order in which the United States would stand as the unchallenged superpower.

But some scholars, such as Samuel Huntington and Bernard Lewis, warned of a coming "clash of civilizations" in which ideological struggles would be replaced by conflicts between so-called civilizations. Journalist Robert Kaplan warned of a "coming anarchy" bred of environmental collapse, disease, and resurgent tribalism. Meanwhile, historian John Lewis Gaddis suggested that the world might come to miss the "long peace" created by the Cold War's stalemate. Together, these thinkers argued that the Cold War had held back the tide of religious and ethnic strife. Now, with the superpower bulwarks removed, those violent forces were set to burst forth upon the world. Despite Huntington, Lewis, and Kaplan's dire warnings, the world experienced an overall decrease in the level of violence after 1990. Certain places, such as the former Yugoslavia, became more violent. But even Iraq, a nation that experienced two U.S. invasions, a decade of harsh sanctions, and years of brutal civil war, suffered more casualties on a yearly basis during the Iran-Iraq War than in the quarter century following 1990. Far from restraining conflict, the superpower confrontation actually fueled greater violence around the world. With the exceptions of Yugoslavia and sub-Saharan Africa, which was devastated by the Rwandan genocide and the horrifically violent and largely ignored Second Congo War, the post–Cold War world was a more peaceful place.

Indeed, for hundreds of millions of people in the Third World, the lessons of the preceding fifty years were not so straightforward, and the distinction between pre- and post-1990-era violence was not so clear. For societies across much of the non-Western world, the Cold War age was marked by vicious massacres and resurgent ethnic and sectarian strife. A half century of conflict radicalized societies throughout the postcolonial world and left an array of heavily militarized states and rebel groups across the globe. Moreover, American victories in the Cold War largely blocked secular, left-wing revolution as a viable path toward progress in the developing world. Despite these ostensible victories, Washington's image as a benevolent superpower had also been badly tarnished by episodes such as the Vietnam War, the Iran-Contra scandal, and decades of support for Third World authoritarian regimes. Likewise, the prospect of unchallenged American military, economic, and cultural domination held little appeal for large segments of the world. It was therefore hardly surprising that aspiring revolutionaries in the post–Cold War world rejected U.S. supremacy and looked elsewhere for political inspiration.

Nor was it a coincidence that most of the largest conflict zones after 1990 were Cold War–era battlefields. The most immediate challenge to Bush's New World Order came from Saddam Hussein's Iraq, which launched an invasion of Kuwait in 1990, prompting the first of two American invasions. Initially lauded as victories, America's wars neutralized Iraq's ability to counterbalance Iranian power and transformed Iraq into a haven for jihadist groups. Like Cold War–era presidents before him, George W. Bush bought into the myth of a monolithic enemy. Where the fiction of the Communist monolith had led Washington into misguided conflicts during the Cold War, the fear of coordination between Al-Qaeda and Baghdad steered the United States into a second, disastrous war in Iraq. And just as the notion of the Kremlin's total control over world communism often blinded U.S. leaders to tensions among Communist governments such as Moscow, Beijing, and Hanoi, the myth of a unified global jihadist movement masked deep rifts between revolutionary forces in the post–Cold War world. The ethnosectarian revolutionaries of the late Cold War emerged out of a common set of circumstances, but they pursued a very different set of goals.

Like Iraq, many twenty-first-century battlefields were places where the United States won significant Cold War victories. Washington's ostensible victory in Korea ushered in an era of high tension along the Thirty-Eighth Parallel that would last well into the next century as the Communist regime in North Korea maintained an iron grip on power, built nuclear weapons, and threatened a renewed war against Seoul. Likewise, the theocratic regime in Iran, itself a product of blowback from Cold War schemes, survived and focused on developing nuclear weapons and projecting its influence across the region by funding militant Shia groups such as Hezbollah. Meanwhile, neighboring Afghanistan slipped into a state of near anarchy after 1990 as rival warlords fielded weapons left over from the Soviet war to battle for control of the country. In 1994, a new rebel group led by former religious students calling themselves the Taliban was gaining ground in a series of offensives that would soon carry them to Kabul. In each case, Washington's Cold War victories laid the foundations for later foreign policy challenges. Huntington's "clash of civilizations" and Kaplan's "coming anarchy," then, were not the result of the Cold War's denouement but rather the fruits of the Cold War itself.

Paradoxically, the engineer of America's greatest defeat during the Cold War, Vietnam, became an important partner after 1990. Beginning in 1991, leaders in Washington and Hanoi pursued a rapprochement that would leave the two nations as unlikely allies in the face of the rising power of China. Beijing's post–Cold War policies suggested that the Communist giant viewed its Nixon-era rapprochement with Washington as a strategic convenience. After 1990, Beijing moved closer to post-Soviet Russia and continued its decades-long quest to expand its influence in world affairs, slowly extending its influence over the South China Sea, building its military capabilities, and sending advisors to countries across the developing world. Meanwhile, Washington's greatest Cold War victory, the supposed defeat of the Soviet Union, did not lead to a lasting rapprochement between Washington and Moscow. By late 1999, a former KGB operative controlled the Kremlin. Vladimir Putin seemed intent on restoring the glory of Moscow's empire, undermining NATO, and using Russia's formidable military to threaten the former Soviet republics of Georgia and Ukraine and expand Moscow's influence in the Middle East.

Ultimately, the chaos of the post–Cold War world dashed American hopes that the rest of the world would accept Washington's much-trumpeted victory in the superpower struggle. Rather, the violence and upheavals of the post–Cold War international order grew out of a different history, one rooted in southern Asia's liberation wars. The destructive dynamics that the superpower struggle helped unleash in the Third World outlived the Cold War and sowed the seeds for a new generation of conflicts in the twenty-first century. On balance, these conflicts have remained less bloody than their Cold War counterparts. Nevertheless, new rivalries among the United States, Russia, and China threaten to resurrect the proxy-style wars of an earlier era.

The half century after the end of World War II fundamentally transformed the world. For the United States, Europe, and Russia, the Cold War effectively defeated the Marxist revolutionary challenge and left capitalism as the reigning political-economic system. But events played out very differently in the Third World. There, the Cold War helped destroy European colonialism, creating dozens of independent states at the same time that it fueled mass violence that killed more than twenty million people and gutted the forces of moderate secular nationalism. Ultimately, both stories are critical to understanding the Cold War era and the twenty-first-century international order. The ferocious violence of the Cold War's killing fields was every bit as central to the making of the contemporary world as Europe's long peace.

ACKNOWLEDGMENTS

I began this book in Lexington, Kentucky, in 2012 and finished it six years later in New York. Along the way, I have been blessed to have incredible colleagues, students, and friends who supported my work at both the University of Kentucky and Columbia University in a myriad of ways. As a result, I have incurred countless debts.

I received generous financial support from the History Department and the Weatherhead East Asian Institute at Columbia University as well as from the History Department and College of Arts and Sciences at the University of Kentucky. The Tamiment Library at NYU, the Mershon Center at Ohio State, the History Department at Columbia University, the Clements Center at the University of Texas, and the Society for Historians of American Foreign Relations all gave me opportunities to share my thoughts about the book with informed audiences who offered invaluable criticisms.

I benefited from dozens of conversations with colleagues and students over the last six years, and it would be impossible to include everyone whose thoughts have shaped this book. However, my special thanks go to Charles Armstrong, Pierre Asselin, Nate Citino, Matthew Connelly, Nick Cullather, Chris Dietrich, Anne Foster, Frank Guridy, Aiyaz Husain, Daniel Immerwahr, Osamah Khalil, Mark Lawrence, Mitch Lerner, Doug Little, Lorenz Luthi, Edward Miller, Deborah Paredez, Kosal Path, Karen Petrone, Jeremy Popkin, Alexander Poster, Mark Selden, Jeremy Suri, Adam Tooze, and Odd Arne Westad.

A number of colleagues generously agreed to read portions of the book and offer comments. These include Roham Alvandi, Seth Anziska, Jeff Byrne, Susan Ferber, James Goode, George Herring, Ryan Irwin, Rashid Khalidi, Elisabeth Leake, Robert McMahon, Andrew Preston, Rob Rakove, Bradley Simpson, Ron Spector, and Salim

Yaqub. They saved me from a number of errors and have made this a much better book. Several anonymous peer reviewers also offered extremely helpful comments.

Since our time in Columbus, Ryan Irwin has been a constant intellectual companion, and our conversations have greatly enriched my work. My thanks also go to Mateo Farzaneh, Nuran Nabi, and Ali Ahmed Ziauddin, who took the time to speak with me about their experiences in some of the events discussed in this book. Andrew Mack also deserves special mention for allowing me to reproduce the *Human Security Report*'s graph that appears in my introduction. Many thanks also go to David Lindroth for his remarkable work designing the book's maps.

The students in my History 122 class at the University of Kentucky witnessed the formation of the first draft of this book in my lectures; the students in my UN3490 seminar at Columbia read pieces of the book in its near final form. I thank them for their thoughts, their insights, and their attention, and I hope that they learned as much from me as I did from them.

As I continue in my career, my recognition of the profound debt I owe to my mentors—Nick Cullather, Peter Hahn, and Robert McMahon—only deepens. George and Dottie Herring also deserve special mention in this regard, as does George's companionship in our explorations of the many distilleries scattered across the Bluegrass. I would also like to offer my sincerest thanks to John Gaddis, who saw parts of the manuscript and generously gave his blessing to the book's subtitle—recognizing it correctly as an homage to the enduring importance of his work.

My agent, John Wright, did as much as anyone to shape this book. For his great patience and his sage advice, he deserves my deepest gratitude. My editor at HarperCollins, Jonathan Jao, proved equally patient and wise. Tim Duggan was the first to see the potential in this book. Roger Labrie subjected the manuscript to an astonishingly thorough review. Jenna Dolan gave the manuscript another close read, correcting a number of mistakes. Sofia Groopman and Emily Taylor were enormously helpful in getting the final manuscript into shape.

My greatest thanks and love go to my family: to my parents, Tom and Connie; to my brother, Dan; to my in-laws Ba, Má, Dì Hai, Hùng, Hải, Hương, Hưng, Hạnh, Hiển, Hà Liên-Hằng (and their better halves); to my wife and best friend, Lien-Hang—to whom this book is dedicated—and finally, to the two most delightful people I have ever had the pleasure of meeting, Leila and Mia, who are growing up far too quickly.

NOTES

ABBREVIATIONS USED IN NOTES

CIA FOIA   Central Intelligence Agency documents obtained through the Freedom of Information Act Reading Room

CWIHP   Cold War International History Project, Woodrow Wilson Center

DIA   Defense Intelligence Agency (United States)

DNSA   Digital National Security Archive

DOS   Department of State

FRUS   *Foreign Relations of the United States* (series published by the U.S. Department of State)

INR   U.S. State Department Bureau of Intelligence and Research

NSA   National Security Archive at George Washington University

PPP   *Public Papers of the Presidents of the United States*

INTRODUCTION: A GEOGRAPHY OF COLD WAR–ERA VIOLENCE

1.   Walter LaFeber cites the number of twenty-one million deaths in his essay "An End to Which Cold War," in *The End of the Cold War: Its Meaning and Implications*, ed. Michael J. Hogan (New York: Cambridge University Press, 1992), 13. Other estimates, such as those of Matthew White (Necrometrics.com), cite higher numbers.

2.   Notable exceptions include Odd Arne Westad, *The Cold War: A World History* (New York: Basic Books, 2017) and *The Global Cold War* (New York: Cambridge University Press, 2005); Robert McMahon, ed., *The Cold War in the Third World* (New York: Oxford University Press, 2013); and Gabriel Kolko, *Confronting the Third World* (New York: Pantheon, 1988).

3.   A note on definitions is in order. I use the term *Third World* in the same sense as Alfred Sauvy: to refer to the non-Western nations of Asia, Latin America, and Africa—a sort of global Third Estate. For the purposes of style, I use the term interchangeably with the more precise *postcolonial world* and *developing world*. My use of the last term by no means implies my agreement with the tenets of Cold War–era development or modernization theory. The fullest treatment of John Lewis Gaddis's "long peace" thesis appears in *The Long Peace: Inquiries into the History of the Cold War* (New York: Oxford University Press, 1987). Chapter 4 of Gaddis's *The Cold War: A New History* (New York: Penguin Press, 2005) also expands on some of these ideas and investigates the ways in which Third World states were able to manipulate the superpowers.

4. See Greg Grandin, *Empire's Workshop* (New York: Henry Holt and Company, 2006), and Anne Applebaum, *Iron Curtain* (New York: Doubleday, 2012).

5. On Soviet attempts to block a hostile Western encirclement, see Vladimir Pechatnov, "The Soviet Union and the World, 1944–1953," in *The Cambridge History of the Cold War*, ed. Melvyn P. Leffler and Odd Arne Westad (New York: Cambridge University Press, 2010), 1:98, 1:100, 1:108; "Interview with Mr. Stassen and Stalin," April 9, 1947, Cold War International History Project, Woodrow Wilson Center, Washington, DC [hereafter CWIHP]; and Walter LaFeber, *America, Russia, and the Cold War* (New York: McGraw-Hill, 2002).

6. This brand of sectarian politics is a contemporary phenomenon: it is *not* a revival of age-old hatreds, as some commentators argue; nor is it a phenomenon unique to the Middle East or Islamic societies (as the following chapters will show). For the purposes of this study, I employ Ussama Makdisi's rough definition of sectarianism as "a deliberate mobilization of religious identities for political and social purposes." In Makdisi's words, sectarianism is "a process through which a kind of religious identity is politicized, even secularized, as part of an obvious struggle for power." Ussama Makdisi, "Moving Beyond Orientalist Fantasy, Sectarian Polemic, and Nationalist Denial," *International Journal of Middle East Studies* 40, no. 4 (Nov. 2008): 559–60; Ussama Makdisi, *Culture of Sectarianism* (Berkeley: University of California Press, 2000). For a broader review of the subject, see *Sectarianization: Mapping the New Politics of the Middle East*, ed. Nader Hashemi and Danny Postel (New York: Oxford University Press, 2017).

7. The task of establishing exact casualty figures is notoriously difficult. Many militaries keep accurate figures on their own dead, but few devote significant effort to tracking civilian deaths. Furthermore, warring governments and groups often have political motives either to downplay or to exaggerate body counts. A number of scholars have attempted to calculate twentieth-century war deaths, most notably R. J. Rummel and Matthew White, but their findings remain controversial. Rather than relying solely on their estimates, I have chosen to use figures cited by leading historians specializing in the specific wars discussed in this book. In general, these scholars cite a range and acknowledge the fundamentally disputed nature of these estimates. In no case do I use either the highest or lowest casualty estimates. Although we will never have exact figures, my interest in this study is on proportion. Ultimately, the debate over whether 2 million or 1.5 million people died in the Cambodian genocide, for instance, has little or no bearing on my larger arguments. For a more detailed discussion of these issues, see John Tirman, *The Deaths of Others* (New York: Oxford University Press, 2011), 318–22.

8. USAID, "U.S. Overseas Loans and Grants and Assistance from International Organizations," Sept. 30, 1992, usaid.gov.

9. CIA, "Soviet Foreign Aid to the Less Developed Countries," Feb. 9, 1966, CIA FOIA.

10. As one scholar explains, "Sectarianism . . . has been driven more by power politics and regime concerns than by ancient hatreds." Marc Lynch, *The New Arab Wars* (New York: PublicAffairs, 2016), 37.

11. I borrow the concept of a central nervous system in international history from Michael Geyer and Charles Bright's brilliant essay, "Global Violence and Nationalizing Wars in Eurasia and America: The Geopolitics of War in the Mid-Nineteenth Century," *Comparative Studies in Society and History* 38, no. 4 (Oct. 1996): 619–57.

12. For Reagan Doctrine aid numbers, see Ted Galen Carpenter, "Cato Institute Policy Analysis No. 74: U.S. Aid to Anti-Communist Rebels: The 'Reagan Doctrine' and Its Pitfalls," Policy Analysis, June 24, 1986, Cato Institute, https://object.cato.org/sites /cato.org/files/pubs/pdf/pa074.pdf.

13. See John Lewis Gaddis, *We Now Know* (New York: Oxford University Press, 1997), 283.

CHAPTER 1: THE IRON CURTAIN DESCENDS, 1945–1947

1. Max Hastings, *Inferno* (New York: Knopf, 2011), 600, 603; Antony Beevor, *Second World War* (New York: Little, Brown and Co., 2012), 737; David Reynolds, *From World War to Cold War* (New York: Oxford University Press, 2006), 250.

2. Tsuyoshi Hasegawa, *Racing the Enemy: Stalin, Truman, and the Surrender of Japan* (Cambridge, MA: Belknap, 2005), 179–81; Richard Rhodes, *The Making of the Atomic Bomb* (New York: Simon & Schuster, 1988), 715; "U.S. Strategic Bombing Survey," June 19, 1946, Truman's Papers, President's Secretary's File: "Atomic Bomb Hiroshima," Harry S. Truman Presidential Library and Museum [hereafter Truman Library], https://www.trumanlibrary.org/whistlestop/study_collections /bomb/large/documents/index.php?pagenumber=12&documentid=65&document date=1946-06-19.

3. Applebaum, *Iron Curtain*, xix

4. Gerard Daniel Cohen, *In War's Wake* (Oxford: New York, 2011), 4.

5. Beevor, *Second World War*, 768.

6. See Ronald Specter, *In the Ruins of Empire* (New York: Random House, 2007).

7. Max Hastings, *Winston's War* (New York: Knopf, 2010), 462–64; Frank Costigliola, *Roosevelt's Lost Alliances* (Princeton: Princeton University Press, 2012), 336.

8. Timothy Snyder, *Bloodlands* (New York: Basic Books, 2010), x, xiii, 415.

9. Hastings, *Inferno*, 22–23.

10. For a deeper discussion of these competing visions of world order, see Westad, *The Global Cold War.*

11. Marc Trachtenberg, *A Constructed Peace* (Princeton: Princeton University Press, 1999), 31, 35–36.

12. Vladislav Zubok, *A Failed Empire* (Chapel Hill: University of North Carolina Press, 2007), 36–37.

13. Joseph Stalin, Decree of the GOKO [State Defense Committee] No. 9168SS, June 21, 1945, trans. Gary Goldberg, CWIHP.

14. CC CPSU Politburo to Bagirov, "Measures to Organize a Separatist Movement in Southern Azerbaijan and Other Provinces of Northern Iran," July 7, 1945, trans. Gary Goldberg, CWIHP.

15. Bruce Kuniholm, *The Origins of the Cold War in the Near East* (Princeton: Princeton University, 1980), 274.

16. Jonathan Haslam, *Russia's Cold War* (New Haven, CT: Yale University Press, 2011), 48–49.

17. On the origins of the Azerbaijan crisis, see Louise Fawcett, *Iran and the Cold War: The Azerbaijan Crisis of 1946* (New York: Cambridge University Press, 1992).

18. Wallace Murray to SecState, Nov. 19, 1945, and Byrnes to Murray, Nov. 18, 1945, both in *Foreign Relations of the United States* [hereafter *FRUS*], Vol. 8: 1945 (Washington, DC: Government Printing Office, 1861–present), 433.

19. Loy Henderson, Memcon, Nov. 20, 1945, *FRUS*, Vol. 8: 1945, 435.

20. Averell Harriman to SecState, Dec. 11, 1944, *FRUS*, Vol. 5: 1944, 354–55; George Kennan to SecState, Nov. 7, 1944, *FRUS*, Vol. 5: 1944, 470.

21. Harry S. Truman, *Memoirs: Years of Trial and Hope* (New York: Doubleday, 1956), 2:96–97.

22. Zubok, *A Failed Empire*, 45.

23. Kuniholm, *Origins of the Cold War in the Near East*, 304.

24. John Lewis Gaddis, *George Kennan* (New York: Penguin Press, 2011); George Kennan to SecState, Telegram, Feb. 22, 1946, *FRUS*, Vol. 6: 1946, 709.

25. Winston Churchill, "The Sinews of Peace," Mar. 5, 1946, http://www.winstonchurchill.org/learn/speeches/speeches-of-winston-churchill/120-the-sinews-of-peace.

26. "Telegram from Nikolai Novikov, Soviet Ambassador to the US, to the Soviet Leadership," Sept. 27, 1946, CWIHP.

27. Vladislav Zubok and Constantine Pleshakov, *Inside the Kremlin's Cold War* (Cambridge, MA: Harvard University Press, 1996), 93.

28. Kuniholm, *Origins of the Cold War in the Near East*, 270–97.

29. 3E2IN Wilson to SecState, Aug. 12, 1946, *FRUS*, Vol. 7: 1946, 836–37.

30. Dean Acheson to Secretary of State, Aug. 15, 1946, *FRUS*, Vol. 7: 1946, 840–42.

31. JCS Memo, Aug. 23, 1946, *FRUS*, Vol. 7: 1946, 856–58.

32. NEA Memo, Oct. 21, 1946, *FRUS*, Vol. 7: 1946, 894–97.

33. Melvyn P. Leffler, *A Preponderance of Power: National Security, the Truman Administration, and the Cold War* (Stanford, CA: Stanford University Press, 1992), 113.

34. Quoted in Zubok and Pleshakov, *Inside the Kremlin's Cold War*, 93.

35. Zubok, *A Failed Empire*, 43, 46, 48.

36. See Lloyd Gardner, *Three Kings* (New York: The New Press, 2009), 66; "Attlee's opposition to the Chiefs of Staff's 'strategy of despair,'" Jan. 5, 1947, in *British Defence Policy Since 1945*, ed. Ritchie Ovendale (Manchester, UK: Manchester University Press, 1994).

37. Dean Acheson to SecState, Feb. 24, 1947, *FRUS*, Vol. 5: 1947, 44–45.

38. Quoted in Leffler, *A Preponderance of Power*, 143.

39. Minutes of the First Meeting of the Special Committee to Study Assistance to Greece and Turkey, Feb. 24, 1947, *FRUS*, Vol. 5: 1947, 45–47.

40. Minutes of a Meeting of the Secretaries of State, War, and Navy, Feb. 26, 1947, *FRUS*, Vol. 5: 1947, 56–57.

41. Quoted in Leffler, *A Preponderance of Power*, 143.

42. Memo by SecState to Truman, Feb. 27, 1947, *FRUS*, Vol. 5: 1947, 60–61.

43. Dean Acheson, *Present at the Creation* (New York: W. W. Norton, 1969), 219.

44. Leffler, *A Preponderance of Power*, 145.

45. Harry S. Truman, "Special Message to the Congress on Greece and Turkey: The Truman Doctrine," Mar. 12, 1947, Public Papers Harry S. Truman, 1945–53, Truman Library, p. 56, https://www.trumanlibrary.org/publicpapers/index.php?pid=2189.

46. X (George Kennan), "The Sources of Soviet Conduct," *Foreign Affairs*, July 17, 1947.

47. Walter Lippmann, *The Cold War* (New York: Harper, 1947), 21, 23.

48. Nicholas John Spykman, *The Geography of the Peace* (New York: Harcourt, Brace, and Company, 1944), 41, 43, 50–51. For a recent assessment of Spykman's work and influence, see Robert Kaplan, *The Revenge of Geography* (New York: Random House, 2012). My thanks to Ryan Irwin for bringing Spykman's work to my attention.

49. William Dalrymple, "The Great Divide," *The New Yorker*, June 29, 2015; Robert Trumbull, "Bands Organize Massacres in India," *New York Times*, Sept. 14, 1947. For more on Partition, see Nisad Hajari, *Midnight's Furies* (Boston: Houghton Mifflin Harcourt, 2015).

PART I: THE EAST ASIAN OFFENSIVE AND THE RISE OF THIRD WORLD COMMUNISM, 1945–1954

1. Hanson W. Baldwin, "Tense Lands in China's Shadow," *New York Times*, Dec. 24, 1950.

2. Fredrik Logevall, "Indochina Wars and the Cold War," in *Cambridge History of the Cold War*, ed. Leffler and Westad, 2:286.

3. CIA, "Sino-Soviet Military Agreement and Global War Plans," Dec. 13, 1951, CIA FOIA; CIA, "Reds Form Far Eastern Military Alliance," Nov. 16, 1951, CIA FOIA.

4. This is on the low side of available estimates. For the Chinese Civil War, Matthew White cites 2.5 million killed; see Necrometrics, http://necrometrics.com/20c1m.htm. Michael Lynch suggests 3.5 million but notes estimates of up to 6 million killed, *Chinese Civil War* (Oxford: Osprey, 2010). For the Korean War, Bruce Cumings cites a figure of 4 million killed, which includes 2 million civilian deaths: Cumings, *Korean War* (New York: Modern Library, 2010), 35. John Tirman cites figures around 3–3.5 million: Tirman, *Deaths of Others*, 92. For the French Indochina War, Michael Burleigh, *Small Wars, Faraway Places* (London: Macmillan, 2013), 243, cites a number of 290,000 killed.

CHAPTER 2: THE COLD WAR COMES TO CHINA, 1945–1946

1. Foster Hailey, "With the Chinese Communists," *New York Times*, Dec. 22, 1946.

2. For more on the evolving war strategies, see Diana Lary, *China's Civil War* (New York: Cambridge University Press, 2015); Harold Tanner, *Where Chiang Kai-Shek Lost China* (Bloomington: Indiana University Press, 2015); and Odd Arne Westad, *Decisive Encounters* (Stanford, CA: Stanford University Press, 2003).

3.   Theodore White and Annalee Jacoby, *Thunder Out of China* (London: Victor Gollancz, 1947), 50–51.

4.   Philip Short, *Mao: A Life* (London: Hodder & Stoughton, 1999), 353–56, 358.

5.   Gaddis, *We Now Know*, 58–59; Westad, *Decisive Encounters*, 29.

6.   Jay Taylor, *The Generalissimo* (Cambridge, MA: Belknap, 2009), 192.

7.   Gaddis, *We Now Know*, 58–59.

8.   Suzanne Pepper, *Civil War in China* (Berkeley: University of California Press, 1978), 7–8; Gerhard L. Weinberg, *A World at Arms* (New York: Cambridge University Press, 2005), 499–501.

9.   Lionel Chassin, *The Communist Conquest of China* (Cambridge, MA: Harvard University Press, 1965), 15, 18–19.

10. Pepper, *Civil War in China*, 8–10.

11. "Memorandum of Conversation Between Three Foreign Ministers," Dec. 19, 1945, *FRUS*, Vol. 7: 1945, 590.

12. Pepper, *Civil War in China*, 10–11.

13. Chen Jian, *Mao's China and the Cold War* (Chapel Hill: University of North Carolina Press, 2001), 24–28.

14. Ibid., 28.

15. Chassin, *Communist Conquest of China*, 23–25.

16. Interview with John Service, 1977, Courtesy of the Bancroft Library, University of California at Berkeley, Association for Diplomatic Studies and Training, www.loc.gov. https://adst.org/wp-content/uploads/2012/09/Service-John-S..pdf.

17. Ibid.; "Report by the Second Secretary of Embassy in China (Service), Oct. 9, 1944, *FRUS*, Vol. 6: 1944, 458.

18. Short, *Mao*, 402; Robertson to Secretary of State, Oct. 9, 1945, *FRUS*, Vol. 7: 1945, 578–79; Robertson to Secretary of State, Oct. 14, 1945, *FRUS*, Vol. 7: 1945, 579–80; Col. Ivan Yeaton, Memorandum, Apr. 16, 1946, *FRUS*, Vol. 9: 1946, 398; see also Ronald Spector, *In the Ruins of Empire* (New York: Random House, 2007), 69.

19. "Statement by the President: United States Policy Toward China," Dec. 15, 1945, Public Papers Harry S. Truman, Truman Library, https://trumanlibrary.org/public papers/index.php?pid=506.

20. Chassin, *Communist Conquest of China*, 54–55.

21. Wedemeyer to Eisenhower, Dec. 2, 1945, *FRUS*, Vol. 7: 1945, 751–52.

22. Leffler, *A Preponderance of Power*, 86–87.

23. Ibid., 127–28.

24. James Barron, "Henry Lieberman, a Times Editor, Dies at 78," *New York Times*, Mar. 16, 1995; Henry Lieberman, "Russians in China Greet Americans," *New York Times*, Jan. 24, 1946.

25. Tillman Durdin, "Russians in Manchuria Dash Hopes of Chinese," *New York Times*, Mar. 10, 1946; Harold Tanner, *The Battle for Manchuria and the Fate of China* (Bloomington: Indiana University Press, 2013), 15–16.

26. Albert Carr, "Manchuria: 'Richest Prize of the War,'" *New York Times*, Mar. 24, 1946.

27. Taylor, *Mao*, 341–46.

28. Edwin Pak-wah Leung, *Historical Dictionary of the Chinese Civil War* (Lanham, MD: Scarecrow Press, 2002), 69–71; Harrison Salisbury, *The Long March: The Untold Story* (New York: Harper & Row, 1985), 191–92.

29. Henry Lieberman, "Correspondent Tells of Battle All Around Him in Changchun," *New York Times*, Apr. 30, 1946.

30. Henry Lieberman, "Reds in Changchun Are Strong Force," *New York Times*, May 1, 1946.

31. Westad, *Decisive Encounters*, 40–45.

32. Chassin, *Communist Conquest of China*, 81–85.

33. Jonathan Spence, *The Search for Modern China* (New York: W. W. Norton, 1999), 464–66; Consul General to Secretary of State, Dec. 29, 1946, *FRUS*, Vol. 7: 1946, p. 1.

CHAPTER 3: THE COLD WAR'S FIRST BATTLEFIELD, 1946–1949

1. Benjamin Welles, "Cold Is Chinese Troops' Chief Foe on the Bleak Manchurian Battlelines," *New York Times*, Dec. 3, 1946.

2. Henry Lieberman, "War Near China's Grand Canal Increases the Peasants' Hardships," *New York Times*, Dec. 17, 1946.

3. Benjamin Welles, "American Colony at Peiping Fetes," *New York Times*, Dec. 25, 1946; Welles "Peiping's Defense Dented," *New York Times*, Dec. 27, 1946; Henry Lieberman, "Shanghai Is Arena in Inflation Chaos," *New York Times*, Nov. 25, 1946.

4. Short, *Mao*, 408–9.

5. John Leighton Stuart to SecState, Sept. 27, 1946, *FRUS*, Vol. 10: 1946, 122.

6. Steven Levine, *Anvil of Victory: The Communist Revolution in Manchuria, 1945–1948* (New York: Columbia University Press, 1987), 131–32.

7. George Marshall to Truman, Sept. 6, 1946, *FRUS*, Vol. 10: 1946, 73.

8. Leffler, *A Preponderance of Power*, 128; Notes of Meeting Between Marshall and Chiang, Aug. 16, 1946, *FRUS*, Vol. 10: 1946, 51–52.

9. Based on report from Nathaniel Peffer, Stuart to SecState, Oct. 17, 1946, *FRUS*, Vol. 10: 1946, 201.

10. Marshall and Stuart, Minutes, Dec. 18, 1946, *FRUS*, Vol. 10: 1946, 335.

11. Leffler, *A Preponderance of Power*, 128–29.

12. Taylor, *Generalissimo*, 359–65.

13. "Personal Statement by the Special Representative of the President (Marshall), January 7, 1947," Annex 13, 686–89, *United States Relations with China: With Special Reference to the Period 1944–1949* [hereafter *China White Paper*], Washington, DC: Office of Public Affairs, 1949.

14. Chassin, *Communist Conquest of China*, 105–7; "Memorandum Entitled 'Explanation of Several Basic Questions Concerning the Postwar International Situation,' by Lu Ting-yi," *China White Paper*, 710–19.

15. CIA, "Implementation of Soviet Objectives in China," Sept. 15, 1947, CIA Electronic Reading Room, CIA FOIA.

16. "Cable, Stalin [Kuznetsov] to Mao Zedong [via Terebin]," June 15, 1947, CWIHP.

17. Westad, *Decisive Encounters*, 150–54; Sidney Rittenberg, *The Man Who Stayed Behind* (New York: Simon & Schuster, 1993), 117–18.

18. Chassin, *Communist Conquest of China*, 111–13.

19. Westad, *Decisive Encounters*, 168–71; Stuart to SecState, Sept. 20, 1947, *FRUS*, Vol. 7: 1947, 234.

20. Chassin, *Communist Conquest of China*, 132–36; Siebens to SecState, Nov. 25, 1947, *FRUS*, Vol. 7: 1947, 294.

21. Spence, *In Search of Modern China*, 474–75.

22. John Leighton Stuart to SecState, Nov. 26, 1947, *FRUS*, Vol. 7: 1947, 377–78; Ward to SecState, Nov. 26, 1947, *FRUS*, Vol. 7: 1947, 378–80.

23. Taylor, *Generalissimo*, 381–82; Ringwalt to Butterworth, Jan. 12, 1948, *FRUS*, Vol. 7: 1948, 29–31.

24. "Mukden Is Prepared for Street Fighting," *New York Times*, Feb. 27 1948.

25. Taylor, *Generalissimo*, 381–83; Stuart to SecState, Mar. 17, 1948, *FRUS*, Vol. 7: 1948, 153–54.

26. Short, *Mao*, 411–13.

27. "Cable, Stalin [Kuznetsov] to Mao Zedong [via Terebin]," Apr. 20, 1948, CWIHP; "Soviet Military Order from Foreign Operations Section Chief to Commander of East-Asian Operation Section Managarov," May 22, 1948, CWIHP.

28. Jung Chang and Jon Halliday, *Mao: The Unknown Story* (New York: Knopf, 2005), 306–8; Henry Lieberman, "Changchun Left to Reds by Chinese," *New York Times*, Oct. 7, 1948.

29. Levine, *Anvil of Victory*, 134–36.

30. Edmund Clubb to SecState, Oct. 21, 1948, *FRUS*, Vol. 7: 1948, 398.

31. Angus Ward to SecState, Oct. 22, 1948, *FRUS*, Vol. 7: 1948, 401.

32. John Leighton Stuart to SecState, Oct. 29, 1948, *FRUS*, Vol. 7: 1948, 419.

33. Westad, *Decisive Encounters*, 199–204; Seymour Topping, *On the Front Lines of the Cold War* (Baton Rouge: Louisiana State University Press, 2010), 25; Henry Lieberman, "China Reds Pursue Isolation Tactics," *New York Times*, Nov. 28, 1948.

34. Henry Lieberman, "Life Grows More Eerie Day by Day in Nanking," *New York Times*, Nov. 28, 1948.

35. Henry Lieberman, "Peiping Like a Doomed City," *New York Times*, Dec. 18, 1948.

36. "Cable, Mao Zedong to Stalin," Dec. 30, 1948, CWIHP.

37. "Memorandum of Conversation Between Anastas Mikoyan and Mao Zedong," Jan. 20, 1949, CWIHP.

38. Westad, *Decisive Encounters*, 205–10.

39. Taylor, *Generalissimo*, 397–98; Chiang quotes from Taylor.

40. Chassin, *Communist Conquest of China*, 209–11.

41. John Leighton Stuart to SecState, Jan. 25, 1949, *FRUS*, Vol. 8: 1949, 79–80.

42. Spence, *In Search of Modern China*, 484–86; Lieberman, "Life Goes On, Wearily, in China," *New York Times*, Apr. 17, 1949.

43. Topping, *On the Front Lines of the Cold War*, 62–65; Henry Lieberman, "Riot Interlude in Nanking," *New York Times*, Apr. 24, 1949; John Leighton Stuart to SecState,

Apr. 22, 1949, *FRUS*, Vol. 8: 1949, 312; John Leighton Stuart to SecState, Apr. 23, 1949, *FRUS*, Vol. 8: 1949, 314; John Leighton Stuart to SecState, Apr. 23, 1949, *FRUS*, Vol. 8: 1949, 317.

44.   Chassin, *Communist Conquest of China*, 222–23; "Shanghai Troops Wrecked Suburbs," *New York Times*, May 26, 1949; Walter Sullivan, "Nationalists Cling to Lines Guarding Shanghai Retreat," *New York Times*, May 26, 1949; John Cabot to SecState, May 25, 1949, *FRUS*, Vol. 8: 1949, 403.

45.   "Cable, Mao Zedong [via Kovalev] to Stalin," June 14, 1949, CWIHP.

46.   CIA, "Prospects for Soviet Control of a Communist China," Apr. 15, 1949, CIA FOIA.

47.   Westad, *Decisive Encounters*, 252–55.

48.   Short, *Mao*, 419–20.

49.   Westad, *Decisive Encounters*, 297, 287.

50.   Ibid., 311, 316.

51.   CIA, "Indications of Chinese Communist Intentions Toward Southeast Asia," Jan. 27, 1950, CIA FOIA.

52.   John Cabot to SecState, May 31, 1949, *FRUS*, Vol. 8: 1949, 424.

53.   Chen Jian, *China's Road to the Korean War*, 3, 5.

CHAPTER 4: INTERVENING IN KOREA, 1945–1950

1.   Baldwin, "Tense Lands in China's Shadow."

2.   David Rees, *Korea: The Limited War* (New York: St. Martin's Press, 1964), 90.

3.   T. R. Fehrenbach, *This Kind of War: The Classic Korean War History* (Washington, DC: Brassey's, 2000), 5.

4.   "City of the Bell," *Time*, Oct. 8, 1945.

5.   Michael Hunt and Steven Levine, *Arc of Empire* (Chapel Hill: University of North Carolina Press, 2012), 128–29.

6.   Michael Fry, "National Geographic, Korea, and the 38th Parallel," Aug. 4, 2013, http://news.nationalgeographic.com/news/2013/08/130805-korean-war-dmz-armistice-38-parallel-geography/.

7.   Leffler, *A Preponderance of Power*, 89; Hunt and Levine, *Arc of Empire*, 128–29.

8.   Gregg Brazinsky, *Nation Building in South Korea* (Chapel Hill: University of North Carolina Press, 2007), 16–17.

9.   Dae-Sook Suh, *Kim Il-sung* (New York: Columbia University Press, 1988), 4, 8, 34, 47.

10.   See Charles Armstrong, *The North Korean Revolution* (Ithaca: Cornell University Press, 2002).

11.   Cumings, *Korean War*, 121, 128–30; Muccio to SecState, Apr. 9, 1949, *FRUS*, Vol. 7: 1949, Part 2, 214.

12.   Allan R. Millett, *The War for Korea, 1950–1951: They Came from the North* (Lawrence: University of Kansas Press, 2010), 167–71; Mydans, *The Violent Peace* (New York: Atheneum, 1968), 112.

13. Brazinsky, *Nation Building in South Korea*, 25; Callum MacDonald, *Korea, the War Before Vietnam* (New York: Free Press, 1987), 41.

14. Cumings, *Korean War*, 139–43.

15. CIA, "Chinese and Soviet Aid to Korean Communists," Dec. 30, 1949, CIA FOIA.

16. Dae-Sook, *Kim Il-Sung*, 113–14, 120–22.

17. Zubok, *A Failed Empire*, 78–80; "Telegram from Tunkin to the Soviet Foreign Ministry in Reply to 11 September Telegram," Sept. 14, 1949, CWIHP.

18. "Remarks by Dean Acheson Before the National Press Club," Jan. 12, 1950, Korean War and Its Origins Research File, Truman Library, https://www.trumanlibrary.org/whistlestop/study_collections/koreanwar/documents/index.php?documentid=kr-3-13&pagenumber=2.

19. William Stueck, *The Korean War: An International History* (Princeton: Princeton University Press, 1997), 35–36, 41–42.

20. "A Report to the National Security Council—NSC 68," Truman Papers, President's Secretary's Files, Meetings: 55, Apr. 12, 1950, https://www.trumanlibrary.org/whistlestop/study_collections/coldwar/documents/index.php?documentid=10-1.

21. David Halberstam, *The Coldest Winter* (New York: Hyperion, 2007), 54–55, 57; Millett, *War for Korea, 1950–1951*, 50.

22. Fehrenbach, *This Kind of War*, 44, 46, 71–76.

23. Leffler, *A Preponderance of Power*, 361, 366–67.

24. "Intelligence Estimate Prepared by the Estimates Group, Office of Intelligence Research, Department of State," June 25, 1950, *FRUS*, Vol. 7: 1950, 148–51.

25. Acheson, "Secretary of State to the Embassy in the United Kingdom," June 27, 1950, *FRUS*, Vol. 7: 1950, 109; Sebald to Acheson, June 25, 1950, *FRUS*, Vol. 7: 1950, 73.

26. Leffler, *A Preponderance of Power*, 367; Gaddis, *We Now Know*, 74; Shen Zhihua, *Mao, Stalin, and the Korean War* (New York: Routledge, 2013).

27. Chen, *China's Road to the Korean War*, 129–30.

28. Gaddis, *We Now Know*, 78; Jung Chang and Jon Halliday, *Mao: The Unknown Story* (New York: Knopf, 2005), 354.

29. "Letter from Filipov (Stalin) to Soviet Ambassador in Prague," Aug. 27, 1950, CWIHP.

30. John Garver, "The Opportunity Costs of Mao's Foreign Policy Choices," *The China Journal* 49 (Jan. 2003): 127–36.

31. Cumings, *Korean War*, 65.

32. MacDonald, *Korea*, 31–32; Cumings, *Korean War*, 13.

33. Hastings, *Korean War*, 59–60; Fehrenbach, *This Kind of War*, 59–60.

34. Clay Blair Jr., *The Forgotten War: America in Korea, 1950–1953* (New York: Times Books, 1987), 122–24.

35. Ibid., 124–25.

36. Fehrenbach, *This Kind of War*, 65–71, 105–7.

37. Halberstam, *Coldest Winter*, 143.

38. Millett, *War for Korea, 1950–1951*, 190.

39. Truth and Reconciliation Commission, Republic of Korea, "Truth and Reconcilia-

tion: Activities of the Past Three Years" (Seoul: Truth and Reconciliation Commission, 2009), 69.

40. Cumings, *Korean War*, 175–76.

41. MacDonald, *Korea*, 41–42.

42. "GIs Tell of a U.S. Massacre in the Korean War," *New York Times*, Sept. 30, 1999. The incident at No Gun Ri unleashed a firestorm of political debate when it was reported in U.S. newspapers in 1999. Allegations of the Korean War's "My Lai" elicited a fierce response from defenders of American and UN forces in the war, including a book-length study by an army officer teaching at West Point that sought to refute the Pulitzer Prize–winning AP report. Arguments over the details of the story, precise numbers, and the credibility of witnesses overlooked the larger point, however. While noncombatants had always suffered during warfare, the battlefields of the Cold War further blurred the distinction between civilian and soldier. To South Korean security forces and American soldiers, nearly any civilian could be a Communist agent; likewise, almost any civilian could appear as a counterrevolutionary to North Korean forces. In a civil war between Communists and anticommunists, citizens represented one of the more significant prizes to be fought over and won. By this same logic, political opponents could be viewed as targets to be eliminated. Compounding matters, the ferocity of modern, mechanized warfare expanded the scale of destruction. The conflict in Korea was merely a showcase for the devastating potential of warfare in the post-1945 era. A subsequent *New York Times* article explained, "Despite the new questions, senior Defense Department officials said . . . that an Army investigation has confirmed the central element of the [AP] report, that American troops fired on refugees, resulting in what the Pentagon calls the 'tragic death of hundreds of civilians.'" *New York Times*, May 13, 2000. For a refutation of the original AP story, see Robert Bateman, *No Gun Ri* (Mechanicsburg, PA: Stackpole Books, 2002).

43. See Tirman, *Deaths of Others*, 106.

44. Choe Sang-Hun, "Unearthing War's Horrors Years Later in South Korea," *New York Times*, Dec. 3, 2007.

45. "Text of MacArthur's Report," *New York Times*, Sept. 19, 1950.

46. Hastings, *Mao*, 90–92; Richard Johnston, "Refugees Stream into South Korea," *New York Times*, July 26, 1950; Richard Johnston, "South Korea Hard Pressed to Feed 2,000,000 Refugees," *New York Times*, Sept. 1, 1950.

47. Hastings, *Coldest Winter*, 82, 84–86.

CHAPTER 5: REHEARSING FOR WORLD WAR III, 1950–1954

1. Douglas MacArthur, *Reminiscences* (New York: McGraw-Hill, 1964), 350; Halberstam, *Coldest Winter*, 293–96.

2. Fehrenbach, *This Kind of War*, 165–68; Mydans, *Violent Peace*, 121.

3. Hastings, *Korean War*, 109; Cumings, *Korean War*, 187–88.

4. Roy Appleman, *South to the Naktong, North to the Yalu* (Washington, DC: U.S. Army Center of Military History, 1992), 523.

5. W. H. Lawrence, "Infantrymen Go In," *New York Times*, Sept. 25, 1950.

6. W. H. Lawrence, "Seoul Reds Make a Counter-attack," *New York Times*, Sept. 26, 1950.

7. MacDonald, *Korea*, 209.

8. "Marines Become Groggy from Guns," *New York Times*, Sept. 27, 1950.

9. "Rout," *Time*, Oct. 9, 1950.

10. Millett, *War for Korea, 1950–1951*, 256; Hastings, *Korean War*, 112.

11. Halberstam, *Coldest Winter*, 323, 329; Rosemary Foot, *A Substitute for Victory* (Ithaca: Cornell University Press, 1990), 25.

12. "Memorandum by the Executive Secretary of the National Security Council," *FRUS*, Vol. 7: 1950, 685–90; Stueck, *The Korean War*, 89.

13. Fehrenbach, *This Kind of War*, 273; Appleman, *South to the Naktong*, 608, 623.

14. Chen Jian, *Mao's China and the Cold War*, 87.

15. Short, *Mao*, 426–28.

16. Stueck, *The Korean War*, 93–94, 97.

17. Halberstam, *Coldest Winter*, 364–65.

18. Ibid., 365–69; "Substance of Statements Made at Wake Island Conference," Oct. 15, 1950, *FRUS*, Vol. 7: 1950, 680.

19. "Air Observer Sees a Dead Pyongyang," *New York Times*, Oct. 19, 1950; "Substantial Citizens," *Time*, Oct. 30, 1950.

20. Hastings, *Korean War*, 124; Hugh Deane, *The Korean War* (San Francisco: China Books & Periodicals, 1999), 101.

21. Fehrenbach, *This Kind of War*, 290–92; Chen, *China's Road to the Korean War*, 91.

22. Salisbury, *The Long March*, 191–92; Short, *Mao*, 429.

23. Cumings, *Korean War*, 19–20.

24. Chen Jian, *China's Road to the Korean War*, 211.

25. Millett, *War for Korea, 1950–1951*, 318–19.

26. Hastings, *Korean War*, 130–31.

27. Cumings, *Korean War*, 26–28.

28. Hastings, *Korean War*, 140; Stueck, *The Korean War*, 112.

29. MacArthur to JCS, Nov. 28, 1950, *FRUS*, Vol. 7: 1950, 1237–38.

30. Jessup, "Notes on NSC Meeting," Nov. 28, 1950, *FRUS*, Vol. 7: 1950, 1246.

31. CIA Memorandum, Dec. 2, 1950, *FRUS*, Vol. 7: 1950, 1308–10.

32. Editorial Note, Nov. 30, 1950, *FRUS*, Vol. 7: 1950, 1261–62.

33. Cumings, *Korean War*, 192–97.

34. Deane, *Korean War*, 101.

35. Cumings, *Korean War*, 29, 149–52, 158–60.

36. Halberstam, *Coldest Winter*, 431; Hastings, *Korean War*, 149, 157–58, 164.

37. Note from General Collins, dated Dec. 7, 1950, *FRUS*, Vol. 7: 1950, 1469.

38. MacDonald, *Korea*, 69–70; Truman, *Memoirs*, 2:387–88.

39. Millett, *War for Korea, 1950–1951*, 412–15.

40. Bruce Cumings, *Origins of the Korean War* (Princeton: Princeton University Press, 1990), 2:750.

41. "Text of MacArthur Statement," *New York Times*, Feb. 14, 1951; "M'Arthur Insists on Victory in Asia," *New York Times*, Feb. 26, 1951; "Text of MacArthur Statement on Korea," *New York Times*, Mar. 8, 1951; "Force Insufficient to Hold Parallel, M'Arthur Asserts," *New York Times*, Mar. 16, 1951; "To the Parallel: No End in Sight," *New York Times*, Mar. 18, 1951.

42. "Text of MacArthur's Korea Statement," *New York Times*, Mar. 24, 1951.

43. Hastings, *Korean War*, 201; Robert Ferrell, *Harry Truman*, 332–33; see also H. W. Brands, *The General vs. the President* (New York: Doubleday, 2016).

44. "Historical Notes: Giving Them More Hell," *Time*, Dec. 3, 1973.

45. Chang and Halliday, *Mao*, 366–67.

46. MacDonald, *Korea*, 249.

47. Stueck, *The Korean War*, 362.

48. Brazinsky, *Nation Building in South Korea*, 26.

49. Fehrenbach, *This Kind of War*, 658.

50. Millett, *War for Korea, 1950–1951*, 159.

51. MacDonald, *Korea*, 258.

CHAPTER 6: FRENCH INDOCHINA AND THE DEATH OF COLONIALISM, 1945–1954

1. Paul Kratoska, ed., *South East Asia, Colonial History* (London: Routledge, 2001), 4:358–59; Spector, *In the Ruins of Empire*, 102.

2. Marilyn Young, *The Vietnam Wars* (New York: HarperPerennial, 1991), 10; Christopher Goscha, *Vietnam: A New History* (New York: Basic Books, 2016), 191.

3. David Marr, *Vietnam 1945* (Berkeley: University of California Press, 1995), 98–105, 208.

4. Mark Lawrence, *Vietnam War* (New York: Oxford University Press, 2008), 30.

5. Fredrik Logevall, *Embers of War: The Fall of an Empire* (New York: Random House, 2012), 93–98.

6. David Marr, *Vietnam: State, War, and Revolution* (Berkeley: University of California Press, 2013), 184–87, 203.

7. Logevall, *Embers of War*, 156–58, 161, 144.

8. William Duiker, "Ho Chi Minh and the Strategy of People's War," in *The First Vietnam War: Colonial Conflict and Cold War Crisis*, ed. Mark Atwood Lawrence and Fredrik Logevall (Cambridge, MA: Harvard University Press, 2007), 160–62; Tuong Vu, *Vietnam's Communist Revolution: The Power and Limits of Ideology* (New York: Cambridge University Press, 2017).

9. Cecil B. Currey, *Victory at Any Cost* (Washington, DC: Brassey's, 1997), 7, 12, 52.

10. Duong Van Mai Elliott, *The Sacred Willow: Four Generations in the Life of a Vietnamese Family* (New York: Oxford University Press, 1999), 200.

11. William Duiker, *Communist Road to Power in Vietnam* (Boulder, CO: Westview Press, 1996), 141–42, 150, 156–57.

12. Jules Roy, *Battle of Dienbienphu* (New York: Harper & Row, 1965), 14–15, 17.

13. Bernard Fall, *Street Without Joy* (Harrisburg, PA: Stackpole, 1963), 315–17; Bernard Fall, *Hell in a Very Small Place* (New York: Da Capo Press, 2002), 43–44; Logevall, *Embers of War*, 381–83, 355; Goscha, *Vietnam*, 261.

14. Logevall, *Embers of War*, 390, 393–94, 448.

15. Ibid., 446, 450.

16. Fall, *Hell in a Very Small Place*, 407, 410, 484.

17. "Vo Nguyen Giap Assesses Dienbienphu's Importance," in *Major Problems in the History of the Vietnam War*, ed. Robert McMahon (New York: Houghton Mifflin, 2008), 85–86.

18. Mark Bradley, *Vietnam at War* (New York: Oxford University Press, 2009), 67–68.

19. Qiang Zhai, *China and the Vietnam Wars, 1950–1975* (Chapel Hill: University of North Carolina Press, 2000), 50–51, 53–55, 62, 64.

20. Jeremy Friedman, *Shadow Cold War* (Chapel Hill: University of North Carolina Press, 2015), 5.

21. CIA, "Evaluation of Leadership of Chinese Communist Party," Jan. 12, 1954, CIA FOIA.

22. Lorenz Lüthi, *The Sino-Soviet Split: Cold War in the Communist World* (Chapel Hill: University of North Carolina Press, 2015), 2.

23. Frank Dikötter, *Mao's Great Famine* (New York: Walker & Co., 2010), ix–xii.

24. Friedman, *Shadow Cold War*, 93–94, 86.

25. As one historian has argued, "The Sino-Soviet Split was one of the key events of the Cold War, equal in importance to the construction of the Berlin Wall, the Cuban Missile Crisis, the Second Vietnam War, and Sino-American Rapprochement." Lüthi, *The Sino-Soviet Split*, 1.

PART II: THE INDO-ASIAN BLOODBATHS AND THE FALL OF THIRD WORLD COMMUNISM, 1964–1979

1. For more on Soviet development, see Westad, *The Global Cold War*, 166–69.

2. John F. Kennedy, "Inaugural Address," Jan. 20, 1961, https://www.jfklibrary.org/Asset-Viewer/BqXIEM9F4024ntFl7SVAjA.aspx.

3. Michael Latham, *Modernization as Ideology* (Chapel Hill: University of North Carolina Press, 2000), 170, and *The Right Kind of Revolution* (Ithaca: Cornell University Press, 2011).

CHAPTER 7: MAKING A QUAGMIRE IN VIETNAM, 1961–1965

1. Peggy Durdin, "Saigon in the Shadow of Doom," *New York Times*, Nov. 21, 1954.

2. "Hanoi Acclaims Vietminh Troops," *New York Times*, Oct. 10, 1954; Tillman Durdin, "Hanoi Celebrates Vietminh's Entry," Oct. 12, 1954; Lien-Hang Nguyen, *Hanoi's War* (Chapel Hill: University of North Carolina Press, 2012), 31.

3. Dwight D. Eisenhower, "The President's News Conference," Apr. 7, 1954, *Public Papers of the Presidents of the United States* [hereafter *PPP*], 1954; and Eisenhower

news conference, Apr. 7, 1954, Editorial Note, *FRUS*, Vol. 8: 1952–54, 716; George Herring, *America's Longest War: The United States and Vietnam, 1950–1975* (Boston: McGraw-Hill, 2002), 51.

4. Edward Garvey Miller, *Misalliance* (Cambridge, MA: Harvard University Press, 2013), 33–34, 37–39, 48.

5. Quoted in Seth Jacobs, *Cold War Mandarin* (Lanham, MD: Rowman & Littlefield, 2006), 38–40.

6. Jessica Chapman, *Cauldron of Resistance* (Ithaca: Cornell University Press, 2013), 14–17; Lawrence, *Vietnam War*, 61; Jacobs, *Cold War Mandarin*, 62.

7. Chapman, *Cauldron of Resistance*, 108, 110–11; Jacobs, *Cold War Mandarin*, 102.

8. Latham, *The Right Kind of Revolution*, 135–36, 138–39; Bradley, *Vietnam at War*, 87.

9. Nguyen, *Hanoi's War*, 34–35.

10. Ibid., 17, 31–33.

11. Pierre Asselin, *Hanoi's Road to the Vietnam War* (Berkeley: University of California Press, 2013), 64, 87–89.

12. *Victory in Vietnam: The Official History of the People's Army of Vietnam, 1954–1975*, trans. Merle Pribbenow (Lawrence: University Press of Kansas, 2002), 55, 82–83.

13. William Taubman, *Khrushchev: The Man and His Era* (New York: W. W. Norton, 2004), 487; "Current Intelligence Weekly Review," Jan. 26, 1961, *FRUS*, Vol. 5: 1961–63, 15.

14. Kennedy, "Inaugural Address," 1–3.

15. Editorial Note, *FRUS*, Vol. 1: 1961–63, 2; Rostow to Bundy, Jan. 30, 1961, *FRUS*, Vol. 1: 1961–63, 4.

16. Latham, *The Right Kind of Revolution*, 136.

17. Andrew Preston, *The War Council* (Cambridge, MA: Harvard University Press, 2006), 76–77.

18. "1961 Rusk-McNamara Report to Kennedy on South Vietnam," *New York Times*, July 1, 1971.

19. Herring, *America's Longest War*, 91, 96–98; Taylor to Kennedy, Nov. 3, 1961, *FRUS*, Vol. 1: 1961–63, 210.

20. Herring, *America's Longest War*, 99–101.

21. William Turley, *The Second Indochina War* (Lanham, MD: Rowman & Littlefield, 2009), 63–64, 67–70.

22. Lien-Hang Nguyen, *Tet 1968* (New York: Random House, 2018).

23. Young, *The Vietnam Wars*, 89–90; Neil Sheehan, *A Bright Shining Lie: John Paul Vann and America in Vietnam* (New York: Random House, 1988), 208.

24. Sheehan, *A Bright Shining Lie*, 211–12, 262–64, 277.

25. Bradley, *Vietnam at War*, 77, 101–3.

26. Lodge to Bundy, Oct. 25, 1963, *FRUS*, Vol. 4: 1961–63, 216.

27. Miller, *Misalliance*, 292–93, 311–12.

28. Ibid., 319–24.

29. Asselin, *Hanoi's Road to the Vietnam War*, 78–79, 166, 180–81; Qiang, *China and the Vietnam Wars*, 119–20, 125.

30. CIA, "China's Growing Isolation in the Communist Movement," *Current Intelligence Weekly: Special Report*, Aug. 5, 1966, CIA FOIA.

31. Nguyen, *Hanoi's War*, 64–65.

32. Fredrik Logevall, *Choosing War* (Berkeley: University of California Press, 1999), 76–77.

33. John Prados, "Essay: 40th Anniversary of the Gulf of Tonkin Incident," Aug. 4, 2004, National Security Archive, https://nsarchive2.gwu.edu//NSAEBB/NSAEBB132/essay .htm; Johnson, "Radio and Television Report," Aug. 4, 1964, *PPP*, 1964, p. 498, http:// www.presidency.ucsb.edu.

34. Logevall, *Choosing War*, 411–12.

35. Young, *The Vietnam Wars*, 135–37.

36. Mark Clodfelter, *The Limits of Air Power* (New York: Free Press, 1989), 133–36.

CHAPTER 8: THE MASSACRE OF THE INDONESIAN PKI, 1965

1. Bradley R. Simpson, *Economists with Guns: Authoritarian Development and U.S.-Indonesian Relations, 1960–1968* (Stanford, CA: Stanford University Press, 2008), 5, 14, 127. My special thanks go to Bradley Simpson for his comments on this chapter.

2. Robert McNamara, *In Retrospect: The Tragedy and Lessons of Vietnam* (New York: Times Books, 1995), 214–15.

3. Harold Crouch, *The Army and Politics in Indonesia* (Ithaca: Cornell University Press, 1988), 24–25, 94.

4. Quoted in Simpson, *Economists with Guns*, 129, 144.

5. Douglas Kammen, *The Contours of Mass Violence in Indonesia, 1965–68* (Honolulu: University of Hawaii Press, 2010), 13.

6. Neil Sheehan, "A Simple Man in Pursuit of Power," *New York Times*, Aug. 15, 1965.

7. Adrian Vickers, *A History of Modern Indonesia* (Cambridge, UK: Cambridge University Press, 2005), 158–60; Kammen, *Contours of Mass Violence*, 14–15.

8. Westad, *Global Cold War*, 187.

9. NIE, "Prospects for Indonesia," July 22, 1964, *FRUS*, Vol. 26: 1964–68, 56.

10. Johnson to Embassy in the United Kingdom, Jan. 25, 1965, *FRUS*, Vol. 26: 1964–68, 102.

11. Crouch, *The Army and Politics in Indonesia*, 63.

12. Sherman Kent, "Principal Problems and Prospects in Indonesia," Special Memorandum Prepared by the Director of the Office of National Estimates of the Central Intelligence Agency, Jan. 26, 1965, *FRUS*, Vol. 26: 1964–68, 103.

13. Memorandum Prepared for the 303 Committee, "Program Report on [less than 1 line of source text not declassified] Covert Action in Indonesia," Feb. 23, 1965, *FRUS*, Vol. 26: 1964-68, 110.

14. Editorial Note, *FRUS*, Vol. 26: 1964–68, 120.

15. Telegram from the Embassy in Indonesia to the Department of State, June 5, 1965, *FRUS*, Vol. 26: 1964–68, 124.

16. Arthur Barber to John McNaughton, "Indonesian Claims on Nuclear Capability," Aug. 11, 1965, *FRUS*, Vol. 26; 1964–68, 133.

17. Crouch, *The Army and Politics in Indonesia*, 67–68.

18. Green to DOS, Telegram from the Embassy in Indonesia to the Department of State, Aug. 8, 1965, *FRUS*, Vol. 26: 1964–68, 131.

19. Simpson, *Economists with Guns*, 197.

20. Special NIE, "Prospects for and Strategic Implications of a Communist Takeover in Indonesia," Sept. 1, 1965, *FRUS*, Vol. 26: 1964–68, 137.

21. John Hughes, *The End of Sukarno* (London: Angus & Robertson, 1968), 30, 43–44.

22. John Roosa, *Pretext for Mass Murder* (Madison: University of Wisconsin Press, 2006), 34–36, 38, 41.

23. Crouch, *The Army and Politics in Indonesia*, 101–6.

24. Kammen, *Contours of Mass Violence in Indonesia*, 76–77.

25. Vickers, *A History of Modern Indonesia*, 161.

26. Memorandum of Telephone Conversation Between Acting Secretary of State Ball and Secretary of State Rusk, Oct. 2, 1965, *FRUS*, Vol. 26: 1964–68, 145.

27. Quoted in Simpson, *Economists with Guns*, 177.

28. Marshall Green to DOS, Oct. 5, 1965, *FRUS*, Vol. 26: 1964–68, 147.

29. DOS to Jakarta, Oct. 6, 1965, *FRUS*, Vol. 26: 1964–68, 148.

30. Andrew Tully, "CIA Forced Reds' Hands in Indonesia," Oct. 25, 1965, CIA CREST Files, CIA-RDP67B00446R000500030001.

31. Kammen, *Countours of Mass Violence*, 80, 83–84, 88–89.

32. Editorial Note, *FRUS*, Vol. 26: 1964–68, 162.

33. Rusk to Jakarta, Oct. 29, 1965, *FRUS*, Vol. 26: 1964–68, 163.

34. D. E. Nuechterlein to [Alvin] Friedman, "Establishment of Inter-Agency Working Group on Indonesia," Oct. 30, 1965, *FRUS*, Vol. 26: 1964–68, 164.

35. David Cuthell to William Bundy, "Indonesian Army Attitude Towards the United States Government," Nov. 3, 1965, *FRUS*, Vol. 26: 1964–68, 167.

36. Geoffrey Robinson, *The Dark Side of Paradise* (Ithaca: Cornell University Press, 1995), 297–99, 303.

37. Robert Cribb, *The Indonesian Killings of 1965–1966* (Clayton, Vic., Australia: Centre of Southeast Asian Studies, Monash University, 1980), 7–8, 10, 15, 170–73.

38. Quoted in Kammen, *Countours of Mass Violence*, 93–94.

39. Marshall Green to DOS, Dec. 2, 1965, *FRUS*, Vol. 26: 1964–68, 179.

40. Editorial Note, *FRUS*, Vol. 26: 1964–68, 185.

41. Marshall Green to DOS, Dec. 22, 1965, *FRUS*, Vol. 26: 1964–68, 186.

42. Kammen, *Contours of Mass Violence*, 95.

43. Robert Komer to LBJ, Mar. 12, 1966, *FRUS*, Vol. 26: 1964–68, 201.

44. CIA, "Peking's Setbacks in Indonesia," Special Report, Apr. 1, 1966, CIA FOIA.

45. Westad, *Global Cold War*, 185.

46. Kammen, *Contours of Mass Violence*, 11. For more on the massacre's role in consolidating the New Order in Indonesia, see Cribb, *Indonesian Killings*, 28, 56; Crouch, *The Army and Politics in Indonesia*, 134.

47. Simpson, *Economists with Guns*, 159.

48. Quoted in Cribb, *Indonesia Killings*, 5; see also Simpson, *Economists with Guns*.

CHAPTER 9: THE TET OFFENSIVE AND USSURI RIVER CLASHES, 1967–1969

1. For more on Indonesia's impact on Vietnam, see Simpson, *Economists with Guns*, 172.
2. Gregory Daddis, *No Sure Victory* (New York: Oxford University Press, 2011), 69–72, 95.
3. Herring, *America's Longest War*, 186, 189–91.
4. Daddis, *No Sure Victory*, 99, 102.
5. Nick Turse, *Kill Anything That Moves* (New York: Metropolitan Books, 2013), 45–46, 59–60.
6. Ibid., 2–5; William Allison, *My Lai* (Baltimore: Johns Hopkins University Press, 2012), 41–43.
7. Michael Sallah and Mitch Weiss, "Rogue GIs Unleashed Wave of Terror in Central Highlands," *Toledo Blade*, Oct. 19, 2003; John Kifner, "Report on Brutal Vietnam Campaign Stirs Memories," *New York Times*, Dec. 28, 2003.
8. Turse, *Kill Anything That Moves*, 208–15, 249–50.
9. Kifner, "Report on Brutal Vietnam Campaign Stirs Memories."
10. Lawrence, *Vietnam War*, 117; McNamara to Johnson, Nov. 1, 1967, *FRUS*, Vol. 5: 1967, 375.
11. Melvin Small, *Antiwarriors* (Wilmington, DE: Scholarly Resources, 2002), 75–76, 82, 101.
12. Nguyen, *Hanoi's War*, 90–92.
13. James Willbanks, *The Tet Offensive* (New York: Columbia University Press, 2007), 31, 34; Young, *The Vietnam Wars*, 217.
14. Nguyen, *Hanoi's War*, 91, 106; Bradley, *Vietnam at War*, 152.
15. Herring, *America's Longest War*, 232–35, 241–43.
16. Ronald Spector, *After Tet* (New York: Free Press, 1993), 213–14, 285–90.
17. "Phoenix: To Get Their Man Dead or Alive," *New York Times*, Feb. 22, 1970; Avery Plaw, *Targeting Terrorists* (New York: Routledge, 2008), 103; for a positive assessment of the program, see Mark Moyar, *Phoenix and the Birds of Prey* (Annapolis, MD: Naval Institute Press, 1997).
18. Spector, *After Tet*, 312–14.
19. Herring, *America's Longest War*, 249–51.
20. David Taylor, "The Lyndon Johnson Tapes: Richard Nixon's 'Treason,'" BBC, Mar. 22, 2013, http://www.bbc.com/news/magazine-21768668; Christopher Hitchens, *The Trial of Henry Kissinger* (New York: Twelve/Hachette, 2002), 13–14.
21. Jeffrey P. Kimball, *Nixon's Vietnam War* (Lawrence: University Press of Kansas, 1998), 73–74, 76.
22. Quoted in Edward Judge and John Langdon, eds., *The Cold War: A Global History with Documents* (New York: Rowman & Littlefield, 2017), 217.
23. Yang Kuisong, "The Sino-Soviet Border Clash of 1969," *Cold War History* 1, no. 1 (Aug. 2000): 25.
24. "Soviet Report to East German Leadership on Sino-Soviet Border Clashes," Mar. 2, 1969, CWIHP.

25. Kuisong, "The Sino-Soviet Border Clash of 1969," 25–26.

26. "Mao Zedong's Talk at a Meeting of the Central Cultural Revolution Group," Mar. 15, 1969, CWIHP.

27. Kuisong, "The Sino-Soviet Border Clash of 1969," 34.

28. U.S. State Department Memorandum of Conversation, "US Reaction to Soviet Destruction of CPR [Chinese People's Republic] Nuclear Capability; Significance of Latest Sino-Soviet Border Clash . . . ," Aug. 18, 1969, NSA, Doc. 10, http://nsarchive .gwu.edu/NSAEBB/NSAEBB49/.

29. State Department cable 143579 to U.S. Mission to NATO, Aug. 25, 1969, NSA, Doc. 11, http://nsarchive.gwu.edu/NSAEBB/NSAEBB49/.

30. Memorandum from William Hyland, National Security Council Staff, to Henry Kissinger, "Sino-Soviet Contingencies," Aug. 28, 1969, NSA, and accompanying note, Document 14, http://nsarchive.gwu.edu/NSAEBB/NSAEBB49/.

31. Memorandum from Miriam Camps, State Department Planning and Coordination Staff, to Under Secretary of State Elliot Richardson, "NSSM 63—Meeting with Consultants," Aug. 29, 1969, NSA, Doc. 15, https://nsarchive2.gwu.edu/NSAEBB /NSAEBB49/.

32. State Dept. INR—Denney to Acting Secretary, "War Between Russia and China: A Communist Nightmare," Sept. 23, 1969, NSA, Doc. 23, https://nsarchive2.gwu .edu/NSAEBB/NSAEBB49/.

33. "The CCP Central Committee's Order for General Mobilization in Border Provinces and Regions," Aug. 28, 1969, CWIHP.

34. Although he was at the time under house arrest, Chen Yi would be partially restored after 1971. As Westad argues, Mao would "take up many of Chen's 'wild ideas'" in the coming years. Odd Arne Westad, *Restless Empire* (New York: Basic Books, 2012), 361–62.

CHAPTER 10: SELECTIVE GENOCIDE IN BANGLADESH, 1971

1. For more on the formation of the U.S.-Pakistani relationship, see Robert McMahon, *The Cold War on the Periphery* (New York: Columbia University Press, 1997), and Andrew Rotter, *Comrades at Odds* (Ithaca: Cornell University Press, 2000).

2. "Pakistan Death Toll 55,000, May Rise to 300,000," *New York Times*, Nov. 17, 1970; Sydney Schanberg, "Pakistan Survivors Face Hunger and Burning Sun," *New York Times*, Nov. 21, 1970.

3. Srinath Raghavan, *1971: A Global History of the Creation of Bangladesh* (Cambridge, MA: Harvard University Press, 2013), 4, 9.

4. Archer Blood, *Cruel Birth of Bangladesh* (Dhaka: University Press, 2002), 77, 116, 119, 121.

5. Henry Kissinger Memorandum to Nixon, Nov. 20, 1970, *FRUS*, Vol. E-7: 99.

6. Shuja Nawaz, *Crossed Swords: Pakistan, Its Army, and the Wars Within* (New York: Oxford University Press, 2008), 261–62; Ray Cline to William Rogers, "Intelligence Brief INRB-217," Dec. 8, 1970, *FRUS*, Vol. E-7: Documents on South Asia, 1969–72, 104.

7. Blood, *Cruel Birth of Bangladesh*, 196; Quoted in Raghavan, *1971*, 148; Sydney

Schanberg, "Artillery Used," *New York Times*, Mar. 28, 1971; Sydney Schanberg, "Heavy Killing Reported," *New York Times*, Mar. 30, 1971.

8. Simon Dring, "How Dacca Paid for a 'United' Pakistan," *Washington Post*, Mar. 30, 1971, reprinted in *Bangladesh Documents*, ed. Sheelendra Kumar Singh (New Delhi: Ministry of External Affairs, 1971–73), 1:345–47.

9. George Allott, "Fact Sheet on Incidents and Information Collected by Americans in Dacca," in Singh, *Bangladesh Documents*, 1:353.

10. Blood, *Cruel Birth of Bangladesh*, 206–7; Archer Blood to DOS, "Killings," Telegram 986, Mar. 30, 1971, *FRUS*, Vol. E-7; Allott, "Fact Sheet on Incidents and Information Collected by Americans in Dacca," 1:354.

11. Archer Blood to DOS, "Selective Genocide," Telegram 959, Mar. 28, 1971, *FRUS*, Vol. E-7: Documents on South Asia, 1969–72, 125.

12. Sydney Schanberg, "Foreign Evacuees from East Pakistan Tell of Grim Fight," *New York Times*, Apr. 6, 1971.

13. "Britons Tell of Killings," *New York Times*, Apr. 4, 1971.

14. Gary J. Bass, *The Blood Telegram: Nixon, Kissinger, and a Forgotten Genocide* (New York: Alfred A. Knopf, 2013), 54, 72, 91.

15. Radio Address by Tajuddin Ahmad, "To the People of Bangla Desh," Apr. 11, 1971, in Singh, *Bangladesh Documents*, 1:282–86.

16. Pakistan became a member of the Southeast Asia Treaty Organization the same year.

17. Robert McMahon, "The Danger of Geopolitical Fantasies," *Nixon in the World*, ed. Fredrik Logevall and Andrew Preston (New York: Oxford University Press, 2008), 254–55. On the U.S. tilt toward Pakistan, see McMahon, *The Cold War on the Periphery*.

18. Bass, *The Blood Telegram*, 64–65; Nixon and Kissinger Telecon, Mar. 29, 1971, *FRUS*, Vol. 11: 1969–76, South Asia Crisis, 1971, Louis J. Smith ed., 14; Nixon and Kissinger Telecon, Mar. 30, 1971, *FRUS*, Vol. 11: 1969–76, South Asia Crisis, 1971, 15.

19. Archer Blood to DOS, "Dacca 1138, Subj.: Dissent from U.S. Policy Toward East Pakistan," Apr. 6, 1971, *FRUS*, Vol. 11: 1969–76, South Asia Crisis, 1971, 20.

20. Kissinger and Rogers Telecon, Apr. 6, 1971, *FRUS*, Vol. 11: 1969–76, South Asia Crisis, 1971, 20.

21. DOS to Dacca, Telegram 58039, Apr. 7, 1971, *FRUS*, Vol. E-7: Documents on South Asia, 1969–72, 129.

22. Archer Blood to DOS, Telegram 1249, Apr. 10, 1971, *FRUS*, Vol. E-7: Documents on South Asia, 1969–72, 130.

23. Special National Intelligence Estimate 32-71, Apr. 21, 1971, *FRUS* Vol. E-7: Documents on South Asia, 1969–72, 131; Paper Prepared by the National Security Council's Interdepartmental Group for Near East and South Asia for the Senior Review Group, Undated, *FRUS*, Vol. E-7: Documents on South Asia, 1969–72, 132.

24. McMahon, "Danger of Geopolitical Fantasies"; Saeed Ahmed, "In Bangladesh, Ted Kennedy Revered," CNN, Aug. 27, 2009, http://www.cnn.com/2009/POLITICS/08/27/bangladesh.kennedy.impact/.

25. Benjamin Welles, "U.S. Continues Aid to Pakistan Army," *New York Times*, Apr. 10, 1971.

26.   Transcript of Conversation in Oval Office, "Editorial Note 25," Apr. 12, 1971, *FRUS*, Vol. 11: 1969–76, South Asia Crisis, 1971, 25.

27.   Harold Saunders and Samuel Hoskinson to Kissinger, "SNIE on Prospects for Pakistan," Apr. 16, 1971, *FRUS*, Vol. 11: 1969–76, South Asia Crisis, 1971, 27.

28.   Saunders to Kissinger, "Pakistan—A Personal Reflection on the Choice Before Us," Apr. 19, 1971, *FRUS*, Vol. 11: 1969–76, South Asia Crisis, 1971, 33.

29.   Nixon underlined the word "Don't" three times. Kissinger to Nixon, "Policy Options Toward Pakistan," Apr. 28, 1971, *FRUS*, Vol. 11: 1969–76, South Asia Crisis, 1971, 36.

30.   Conversation Between Nixon and Kissinger, June 4, 1971, *FRUS*, Vol. E-7: Documents on South Asia, 1969–72, 136.

CHAPTER 11: THE INDIA-PAKISTAN WAR, 1971

1.   Raghavan, *1971*, 56, 59–60.

2.   Bass, *The Blood Telegram*, 47–48, 92–94.

3.   Anthony Mascarenhas, "Genocide," *Sunday Times*, June 13, 1971, reprinted in Singh, *Bangladesh Documents*, 1:358–73.

4.   Sydney Schanberg, "India: Three Million Links in a Chain of Misery," *New York Times*, May 23, 1871; Sydney Schanberg, "Disease, Hunger and Death Stalk Refugees Along India's Border," *New York Times*, June 9, 1971.

5.   Sydney Schanberg, "The Only Way to Describe It Is 'Hell,'" *New York Times*, June 20, 1971.

6.   "Letter from Indian Prime Minister Gandhi to President Nixon," May 13, 1971, *FRUS*, Vol. 11: 1969–76, South Asia Crisis, 1971, 46.

7.   Theodore Eliot to Kissinger, "Contingency Study for Indo-Pakistan Hostilities," May 25, 1971, *FRUS*, Vol. E-7: Documents on South Asia, 1969–72, 133.

8.   Kissinger, Lakshmi Jha, and Samuel Hoskinson Memcon, May 21, 1971, *FRUS*, Vol. 11: 1969–76, South Asia Crisis, 1971, 52.

9.   Nixon and Kissinger Conversation, May 26, 1971, *FRUS*, Vol. E-7: Documents on South Asia, 1969–72, 135; Bass, *The Blood Telegram*, 142–44.

10.   "Bengal the Murder of a People," Aug. 2, 1971, *Newsweek*, reprinted in Singh, *Bangladesh Documents*, 1:427–31.

11.   Bass, *The Blood Telegram*, 146–48, 156, 177; Kissinger and Farland, "Memorandum of Conversation," May 7, 1971, *FRUS*, Vol. 11: 1969–76, South Asia Crisis, 1971, 42.

12.   Malcolm Browne, "East Pakistan: Shades of the Vietnam War," *New York Times*, Aug. 1, 1971.

13.   Richard Sisson, *War and Secession: Pakistan, India, and the Creation of Bangladesh* (Berkeley: University of California Press, 1990), 182, 184–85, 210–12.

14.   Nawaz, *Crossed Swords*, 282–84.

15.   CIA Memorandum, Sept. 22, 1971, *FRUS*, Vol. E-7: Documents on South Asia, 1969–72, 144; Bass, *The Blood Telegram*, 236.

16.   "India's Foreign Minister's Address to the National Press Club," June 17, 1971, in Singh, *Bangladesh Documents*, 1:686–95.

17. "Minutes of Washington Special Actions Group Meeting," Oct. 7, 1971, *FRUS*, Vol. 11: 1969–76, South Asia Crisis, 1971, 159.

18. Kenneth Keating to DOS, "Risks of War in Indo-Pak Confrontation," Oct. 12, 1971, *FRUS*, Vol. 11: 1969–76, South Asia Crisis, 1971, 167.

19. Herbert Spivack to DOS, "East Pakistan Insurgency—Escalation," Oct. 20, 1971, *FRUS*, Vol. 11: South Asia Crisis, 1971, 170.

20. "Memorandum for the President's File," Nov. 4, 1971, *FRUS*, Vol. 11: 1969–76, South Asia Crisis, 1971, 179.

21. Conversation Between Nixon, Kissinger, and Haldeman, Nov. 5, 1971, *FRUS*, Vol. E-7: Documents on South Asia, 1969–72, 150.

22. Kissinger to Nixon, "Maury Williams' Views on Pakistan," Nov. 16, 1971, *FRUS*, Vol. 11: 1969–76, South Asia Crisis, 1971, 188.

23. Ibid.; Kissinger to Nixon, Nov. 22, 1971, *FRUS*, Vol. 11: 1969–76, South Asia Crisis, 1971, 195.

24. "Minutes of Washington Special Actions Group Meeting," Nov. 24, 1871, *FRUS*, Vol. 11: 1969–76, South Asia Crisis, 1971, 198.

25. Nixon, Kissinger, and Rogers Conversation, Nov. 24, 1917, *FRUS*, Vol. E-7: Documents on South Asia, 1969–72, 156.

26. Joseph Farland to Kissinger, Nov. 30, 1971, *FRUS*, Vol. 11: 1969–76, South Asia Crisis, 1971, 210.

27. Nawaz, *Crossed Swords*, 295.

28. "Minutes of Washington Special Actions Group Meeting," Dec. 3, 1971, *FRUS*, Vol. 11: 1969–76, South Asia Crisis, 1971, 218.

29. Nixon and Kissinger Telephone Conversation, Dec. 3, 1971, *FRUS*, Vol. 11: 1969–76, South Asia Crisis, 1971, 216.

30. Nixon and Connally Telephone Conversation, Dec. 5, 1971, *FRUS*, Vol. E-7: Documents on South Asia, 1969–72, 159.

31. CIA, "Moscow and the Indo-Pakistani Crisis," Intelligence Memorandum, Dec. 3, 1971, CIA FOIA.

32. "Prime Minister Indira Gandhi's Broadcast to the Nation Soon After Midnight," Dec. 3, 1971, in Singh, *Bangladesh Documents*, 1:209.

33. "President Yahya Khan's Broadcast to the Nation," Dec. 4, 1971, in Singh, *Bangladesh Documents*, 1:211.

34. Pran Chopra, *India's Second Liberation* (Delhi: Vikas Pub. House, 1973), 163–67.

35. Sydney Schanberg, "Indian Advance Leaves Bengali Village in Ruins," *New York Times*, Dec. 6, 1971.

36. Sisson, *War and Secession*, 213–14.

37. Robert Jackson, *South Asian Crisis: India, Pakistan, Bangla Desh* (New York: Praeger, 1974), 112–13.

38. Chopra, *India's Second Liberation*, 170–73; Henry Kamm, "Pakistani Forces Take Ghost Town in Kashmir," *New York Times*, Dec. 13, 1971.

39. Fox Butterfield, "Battle at Kashmir River Said to Leave 900 Dead," *New York Times*, Dec. 12, 1971.

40. Jackson, *South Asian Crisis*, 119–20.

41. Nawaz, *Crossed Swords*, 300–302.

42. Sydney Schanberg, "A Village Ablaze, a Blown Bridge," *New York Times*, Dec. 21, 1971.

43. Joseph Farland to Kissinger, Dec. 7, 1971, *FRUS*, Vol. 11: 1969–76, South Asia Crisis, 1971, 242.

44. Nixon and Kissinger Telephone Conversation, Dec. 5, 1971, *FRUS*, Vol. 11: 1969–76, South Asia Crisis, 1971, 229.

45. "Minutes of National Security Council Meeting," Dec. 6, 1971, *FRUS*, Vol. 11: 1969–76, South Asia Crisis, 1971, 237.

46. Nixon and Kissinger Conversation, Dec. 6, 1971, *FRUS*, Vol. E-7: Documents on South Asia, 1969–72, 162.

47. "Minutes of Washington Special Actions Group Meeting," Dec. 1971, *FRUS*, Vol. 11: 1969–76, South Asia Crisis, 1971, 248.

48. "Editorial Note," *FRUS*, Vol. 11: 1969–76, South Asia Crisis, 1971, 251.

49. Jackson, *South Asian Crisis*, 130–31, 134–35.

50. Kissinger to Nixon, "Information Items," Dec. 10, 1971, *FRUS*, Vol. 11: 1969–76, South Asia Crisis, 1971, 267.

51. "Editorial Note," *FRUS*, Vol. 11: 1969–76, South Asia Crisis, 1971, 266.

52. Kissinger to Nixon, "Information Items," Dec. 11, 1971, *FRUS*, Vol. 11: 1969–76, South Asia Crisis, 1971, 275.

53. "Editorial Note," *FRUS*, Vol. 11: 1969–76, South Asia Crisis, 1971, 281.

54. Ibid., 283.

55. James Sterba, "Dacca at War," *New York Times*, Dec. 11, 1971.

56. "Battle for City Starts," *New York Times*, Dec. 15, 1971.

57. Herbert Spivack to DOS, "Niazi Cease-Fire Proposal," Dec. 14, 1971, *FRUS*, Vol. 11: 1969–76, South Asia Crisis, 1971, 300.

58. Joseph Farland to DOS, "Discussion with President Yahya re Ceasefire," *FRUS*, Vol. 11: 1969–76, South Asia Crisis, 1971, 301.

59. Sydney Schanberg, "2 Men at a Table," *New York Times*, Dec. 17, 1971.

60. "125 Slain in Dacca Area Believed Elite of Bengal," *New York Times*, Dec. 19, 1971.

61. James Sterba, "In Dacca, Killings Amid the Revelry," *New York Times*, Dec. 18, 1971.

62. "Letter from Pakistani President Bhutto to President Nixon," undated, *FRUS*, Vol. 11: 1969–76, South Asia Crisis, 1971, 330.

63. Author interview with Ali Ahmed Ziauddin, New York, Aug. 30, 2016.

64. Author interview with Dr. Nuran Nabi, telephone conversation, Oct. 7, 2016; see also Nuran Nabi, *Bullets of '71: A Freedom Fighter's Story* (Bloomington, IN: AuthorHouse, 2010).

CHAPTER 12: THE FALL OF PHNOM PENH AND SAIGON, 1975–1979

1. Seymour Topping, "Cambodia: Calm Land Under War Pressures," *New York Times*, Jan. 9, 1966.

2.   David P. Chandler, *Tragedy of Cambodian History* (New Haven: Yale University Press, 1991), 14–15.

3.   Ibid., 125–27.

4.   Philip Short, *Pol Pot: Anatomy of a Nightmare* (New York: Henry Holt, 2005), 50–51, 66, 70.

5.   Ben Kiernan, *How Pol Pot Came to Power* (London: Verso, 1985), 123.

6.   Short, *Pol Pot*, 100, 140–41.

7.   Historian Ben Kiernan argues that it may have been Sar himself who betrayed Samouth and, in effect, used state police to orchestrate a coup against his mentor. Ben Kiernan, *The Pol Pot Regime* (New Haven: Yale University Press, 2008), 13n30.

8.   Chandler, *Tragedy of Cambodian History*, 126–28.

9.   Philip Sprouse to DOS, Nov. 13, 1963, *FRUS*, Vol. 23: 1961–63, 111.

10.   Komer to Bundy, Dec. 2, 1963, *FRUS*, Vol. 23: 1961–63, 127; Short, *Pol Pot*, 155–56.

11.   Chandler, *Tragedy of Cambodian History*, 140, 146.

12.   Elizabeth Becker, *When the War Was Over: Cambodia and the Khmer Rouge Revolution* (New York: Public Affairs, 1998), 87, 90, 119–20.

13.   Chandler, *Tragedy of Cambodian History*, 152–53, 156, 189.

14.   Short, *Pol Pot*, 165–69.

15.   Becker, *When the War Was Over*, 104–5, 106–7.

16.   James A. Tyner, *The Killing of Cambodia*, 69; Aldrich to Bundy, Sept. 11, 1967, *FRUS*, Vol. 27: 1964–68, 208.

17.   Short, *Pol Pot*, 174–75.

18.   "Discussion Between Zhou Enlai and Pham Hung," June 19, 1968, CWIHP.

19.   Becker, *When the War Was Over*, 110–11.

20.   William Shawcross, *Sideshow: Kissinger, Nixon, and the Destruction of Cambodia* (New York: Simon & Schuster, 1987), 68–71; Bowles to DOS, Jan. 12, 1968, *FRUS*, Vol. 27: 1964–68, 229; Bundy to Rusk, May 27, 1968, *FRUS*, Vol. 27: 1964–68, 234.

21.   Henry Kissinger, *White House Years* (Boston: Little, Brown, 1979), 240, 250–51.

22.   Shawcross, *Sideshow*, 28–30.

23.   Chandler, *Tragedy of Cambodian History*, 184–85, 187.

24.   Becker, *When the War Was Over*, 115–17.

25.   "Discussion Between Zhou Enlai and Pham Van Dong," Mar. 21, 1970, CWIHP.

26.   Arnold Isaacs, *Without Honor* (Baltimore: Johns Hopkins University Press, 1983), 200–203.

27.   Memorandum of Meeting, Apr. 28, 1970, *FRUS*, Vol. 6: 1969–76, 267; Richard Nixon, "Address to the Nation on the Situation in Southeast Asia," Apr. 30, 1970, *PPP*, 1970.

28.   Shawcross, *Sideshow*, 150; Wilfred P. Deac, *Road to the Killing Fields* (College Station, TX: Texas A&M University Press, 2000), 78.

29.   Deac, *Road to the Killing Fields*, 74–76; Becker, *When the War Was Over*, 125.

30.   Chandler, *Tragedy of Cambodian History*, 200–201, 206–7.

31.   Becker, *When the War Was Over*, 130–31.

32.   Shawcross, *Sideshow*, 202–4.

33. Chandler, *Tragedy of Cambodian History*, 214–15; Nixon, "Presidents News Conference," Nov. 12, 1972, *PPP*, 1972.

34. Short, *Sideshow*, 215–18.

35. Becker, *When the War Was Over*, 133–35.

36. Deac, *Road to the Killing Fields*, 127–30.

37. Short, *Pol Pot*, 224, 229, 231.

38. See Paul Chamberlin, *The Global Offensive* (New York: Oxford University Press, 2012), 87–88.

39. Nguyen, *Hanoi's War*, 233–34, 243–45.

40. Lawrence, *Vietnam War*, 154–55.

41. Bradley, *Vietnam at War*, 167–69.

42. Larry Berman, *No Peace, No Honor: Nixon, Kissinger, and Betrayal in Vietnam* (New York: Free Press, 2001), 246.

43. On the decent interval versus permanent war debate, see Kimball, *Nixon's Vietnam War*; and Berman, *No Peace, No Honor*, as well as the series of exchanges in the March 2002 issue of *Passport: Newsletter of the Society for Historians of American Foreign Relations*.

44. "Discussion Between Zhou Enlai, Le Duan, Pham Van Dong, and Le Thanh Nghi," June 5, 1973, CWIHP.

45. Shawcross, *Sideshow*, 272–73, 280–81.

46. Becker, *When the War Was Over*, 17–18.

47. Chandler, *Tragedy of Cambodian History*, 225, 231–32.

48. Short, *Pol Pot*, 262–65; "Robert Thompson's Report," Secret, Cable, 000668, Feb. 17, 1975, NSA.

49. Lawrence, *Vietnam War*, 166–68.

50. Spector, *After Tet*, 315.

51. Le Duc Tho and Kissinger, Memorandum of Conversation, Feb. 21, 1970, *FRUS*, Vol. 6: Vietnam, 190.

CHAPTER 13: THE CAMBODIAN NIGHTMARE, 1975–1979

1. Becker, *When the War Was Over*, 19; Shawcross, *Sideshow*, 365–67.

2. On the ethnic dimensions of the Khmer Rouge, see Kiernan, *Pol Pot Regime*.

3. Sydney Schanberg, "Cambodia Reds Are Uprooting Millions as They Impose a 'Peasant Revolution,'" *New York Times*, May 9, 1975.

4. Kiernan, *Pol Pot Regime*, 43, 45, 48.

5. François Ponchaud, *Cambodia: Year Zero* (New York: Holt, Rinehart and Winston, 1978), 40–44.

6. Chandler, *Tragedy of Cambodian History*, 254–55.

7. Short, *Pol Pot*, 286–89.

8. "Conversation Between Chinese Leader Mao Zedong and Cambodian Leader Pol Pot," June 21, 1975, CWIHP.

9. Kiernan, *Pol Pot Regime*, 55–57.

10. Becker, *When the War Was Over*, 148–50, 173–76.

11. Ponchaud, *Cambodia: Year Zero*, 55–56, 58–59.

12. "Decisions of the Central Committee on a Variety of Questions," Mar. 30, 1976, in *Pol Pot Plans for the Future: Confidential Leadership Documents from Democratic Kampuchea 1976–77*, ed. and trans. David Chandler, Ben Kiernan, et al. (New Haven, CT: Yale University Southeast Asia Studies, 1988), 18.

13. "Excerpted Report on the Leading Views of the Comrade Representing the Party Organization at a Zone Assembly (*Tung Pedevat* June 1976)," in Chandler, Kiernan, et al., *Pol Pot Plans for the Future*, 9–35.

14. Short, *Pol Pot*, 291–93, 295.

15. Ibid., 293–94.

16. "Excerpted Report on the Leading Views of the Comrade Representing the Party Organization at a Zone Assembly (*Tung Pedevat* June 1976)," 19.

17. "Preliminary Explanation Before Reading the Plan (Party Center, Aug. 21, 1976)," in Chandler, Kiernan, et al., *Pol Pot Plans for the Future*, 124–27.

18. Kiernan, *Pol Pot Regime*, 16–67.

19. Chandler, *Tragedy of Cambodian History*, 259–60.

20. "Cambodia Perspective," Mar. 1975, Internal Paper, John O. Marsh Files, Vietnam Supplemental Military Assistance (1), Digital National Security Archive [hereafter DNSA].

21. "Minutes of the Secretary of State's Staff Meeting," Apr. 30, 1975, *FRUS*, Vol. E-12: 1973–1976, 65.

22. "Research Study Prepared by the Central Intelligence Agency," Dec. 1976, *FRUS*, Vol. E-12: 1973–76, 95; see also CIA, "Democratic Kampuchea: An Experiment in Radicalism," Dec. 1976, CIA FOIA.

23. Scowcroft to Ford, May 10, 1976, *FRUS*, Vol. E-12: 1973–76, 89.

24. Peter Maguire, *Facing Death in Cambodia* (New York: Columbia University Press, 2005), 51–52.

25. "Secretary's Meeting with Foreign Minister Chatchai of Thailand," Nov. 26, 1975, National Security Archive Electronic Briefing Book No. 193, NSA.

26. Becker, *When the War Was Over*, 435.

27. David Chandler, *Voices from S-21* (Berkeley: University of California Press, 1999), 14–15, 16, 20–22, 27–28.

28. Ibid., 32, 38–39, 110.

29. Ibid., 139–40.

30. Short, *Pol Pot*, 352–53, 355, 357–61.

31. Kiernan, *Pol Pot Regime*, 313–14, 316–17, 321, 325, 338; Becker, *When the War Was Over*, 217, 265.

32. Nayan Chanda, *Brother Enemy* (San Diego: Harcourt Brace Jovanovich, 1986), 12–14; Kiernan, *Pol Pot Regime*, 358.

33. Chanda, *Brother Enemy*, 193–94.

34. "Discussion Between Hua Guofeng and Pol Pot," Sept. 29, 1977, CWIHP.

35.　Chanda, *Brother Enemy*, 196, 206–7.

36.　Kiernan, *Pol Pot Regime*, 392–400; Becker, *When the War Was Over*, 310–12.

37.　Kiernan, *Pol Pot Regime*, 393–94.

38.　Chanda, *Brother Enemy*, 216–19.

39.　"Speech Made by Pham Van Dong," Sept. 5, 1978, CWIHP.

40.　"Letter, Chen Chu to H. E. Baron Rudiger Von Wechmar," Dec. 11, 1978, CWIHP.

41.　CIA, "Another Cambodian War," Dec. 15, 1978, CIA FOIA.

42.　Becker, *When the War Was Over*, 432–33.

43.　Chandler, *Voices from S-21*, 1–3.

44.　"Chinese Foreign Ministry's Note to the Vietnamese Embassy in China Protesting Against Viet Nam's Military Provocations," Feb. 12, 1979, CWIHP.

45.　"Memorandum of the Ministry of Foreign Affairs of the Socialist Republic of Viet Nam on the Chinese Authorities' Intensified Armed Activities on the Viet Nam Border and their Frantic War Preparations Against Viet Nam," Feb. 16, 1979, CWIHP.

46.　"Statement by Xinhua News Agency upon Authorization," Feb. 17, 1979, CWIHP; Chanda, *Brother Enemy*, 35–58.

47.　"Notes on a Meeting in the Great People's Palace in Peking on Apr. 30, 1979 at 9 a.m.," Apr. 30, 1979, CWIHP; see also "Notes on a Meeting Held During the Secretary-General's Visit to Peking, 1 May 1979," May 1, 1979, CWIHP.

48.　CIA, "China-VN-USSR Triangle and US Policy," Apr. 10, 1979, CIA FOIA.

49.　Estimates of the death toll in the Second Indochina War range from 1 million to 4 million. Robert McNamara calculated the number of deaths at 2,358,000 (Tirman, *Deaths of Others*, 167–68). Walter LaFeber cites 4 million in "An End to Which Cold War." For Indonesia, Adrian Vickers cites general agreement of "at least half a million" with the highest estimates reaching up to 1 million (*A History of Modern Indonesia*, 159). Estimates of the Bangladeshi killings vary widely. The Pakistani government placed the number at 26,000 killed while Bangladesh cites 3 million killed. Indian estimates range from 300,000 to 1 million; American reporters suggested that as many as 1 million had been killed (Bass, *The Blood Telegram*, 350–51n6). Kiernan cites a figure of 1.67 million killed in Cambodia (*Pol Pot Regime*, 458).

PART III: THE GREAT SECTARIAN REVOLT OF THE LATE COLD WAR, 1975–1990

1.　Jeffrey Byrne, "The Cold War in Africa," in *Routledge Handbook of the Cold War*, ed. Artemy Kalinovsky and Craig Daigle (New York: Routledge, 2014), 155–57. See also Westad, *The Global Cold War*, and Piero Gleijeses, *Visions of Freedom: Havana, Washington, Pretoria, and the Struggle for Southern Africa* (Chapel Hill: University of North Carolina Press, 2013).

2.　See Greg Grandin, *Empire's Workshop*; Walter LaFeber, *Inevitable Revolutions* (New York: W. W. Norton, 1983); and Hal Brands, *Latin America's Cold War* (Cambridge, MA: Harvard University Press, 2010).

3.　On the debates over the definition of sectarianism, see Ussama Makdisi, "Moving

Beyond Orientalist Fantasy, Sectarian Polemic, and Nationalist Denial," *International Journal of Middle East Studies* 40, no. 4 (Nov. 2008): 559–60; Ussama Makdisi, *Culture of Sectarianism* (Berkeley: University of California Press, 2000).

4.   CIA, "Resurgent Islamic Nationalism in the Middle East," Mar. 1981, CIA FOIA.

5.   Robert Dreyfuss, *Devil's Game* (New York: Metropolitan Books, 2005), 240.

6.   U.S. Mission to NATO, "Islamic Fundamentalism and the Soviet Union," July 30, 1979, DNSA.

7.   Edward O'Ballance cites a Reuters number of 130,000 killed in his *Civil War in Lebanon* (New York: St. Martin's Press, 1998), 216. Robert Fisk estimates the death toll at "about 100,000" (*Pity the Nation* [New York: Nation Books, 2002], 389). For the Iran-Iraq War, Pierre Razoux estimates around 680,000 dead and missing (*The Iran-Iraq War* [Cambridge, MA: Belknap, 2015], 569). Anthony Cordesman cites figures of between 600,000 and 1.07 million killed (*Lessons of Modern War: The Iran-Iraq War* [Boulder, CO: Westview Press, 1990], 2:3). For Afghanistan, Artemy Kalinovsky estimates 800,000 to 1.2 million killed (*A Long Goodbye* [Cambridge, MA: Harvard University Press, 2011], 1). Rodric Braithwaite estimates 600,000 to 1.5 million killed (*Afgantsy* [New York: Oxford Unviersity Press, 2011], 331).

CHAPTER 14: THE LEBANESE CIVIL WAR, 1975–1978

1.   See James Stocker, *Spheres of Intervention* (Ithaca: Cornell University Press, 2016).

2.   On the multiple and at times conflicted notions of "moderate" Arab states, see James Stocker, "Diplomacy as Counter-revolution?" *Cold War History* 12, no. 3 (Aug. 2012).

3.   John Kifner, "Where Fashion Gives Way to Filth," *New York Times*, Aug. 18, 1982.

4.   Fawwaz Traboulsi, *A History of Modern Lebanon* (London: Pluto, 2007), 161.

5.   See Chamberlin, *The Global Offensive.*

6.   Itamar Rabinovich, *The War for Lebanon, 1970–1985* (Ithaca: Cornell University Press, 1985), 76.

7.   Ibid., 61–66.

8.   Most of the details are disputed: Palestinian spokesmen claimed the bus had been carrying families, Phalangists insisted that it was carrying guerrillas. Death tolls vary, from fourteen to twenty-seven. The names of the dead were apparently not released. Theodor Hanf, *Coexistence in Wartime Lebanon* (London: I. B. Tauris, 2015), 204; O'Ballance, *Civil War in Lebanon*, 1.

9.   "Battered Beirut Hopes for New Cabinet," *New York Times*, June 30, 1975.

10.   James Markham, "Violent Episodes Plague Lebanon," *New York Times*, Sept. 4, 1975; Markham, "Shooting Goes on in Lebanese Port," *New York Times*, Sept. 9, 1975.

11.   O'Ballance, *Civil War in Lebanon*, 27–29.

12.   Ibid., 30.

13.   Jonathan Randal, *Going All the Way: Christian Warlords, Israeli Adventureres, and the War in Lebanon* (New York: Viking, 1983), 75–76.

14.   David Hirst, *Beware of Small States* (New York: Nation Books, 2010), 111; James

Markham, "Panic Grips Beirut Amid New Killings and Kidnappings," *New York Times*, Dec. 7, 1975.

15. Yezid Sayigh, *Armed Struggle and the Search for State* (New York: Oxford University Press, 1997), 372–74.

16. Ibid., 375–76; Randal, *Going All the Way*, 89–90.

17. See Patrick Seale, *Asad of Syria* (Berkeley: University of California Press, 1989), 226–49.

18. William Harris, *Faces of Lebanon* (Princeton, NJ: Markus Wiener Publishers, 1997), 164–65.

19. Hanf, *Coexistence in Wartime Lebanon*, 214–15.

20. Rabinovich, *War for Lebanon*, 49, 54–55; Kissinger, *White House Years*, 1046–47.

21. Avi Shlaim, *Iron Wall* (New York: W. W. Norton, 2001), 342–43; Benny Morris, *Righteous Victims* (New York: Knopf, 1999), 500–501.

22. "Minutes of Washington Special Actions Group Meeting," Apr. 22, 1976, *FRUS*, Vol. 26: 1969–76, 286.

23. "Memorandum of Conversation," Apr. 13, 1976, *FRUS*, Vol. 26: 1969–76, 285; Robert Freedman, *Soviet Policy Toward the Middle East Since 1970* (New York: Praeger, 1982), 24–42.

24. O'Ballance, *Civil War in Lebanon*, 54, 56–57; Tony Walker and Andrew Gowers, *Arafat* (London: Virgin, 2003), 153; Sayigh, *Armed Struggle*, 398, 401.

25. Hanf, *Coexistence in Wartime Lebanon*, 224–26.

26. Morris, *Righteous Victims*, 383–85.

27. Hanf, *Coexistence in Wartime Lebanon*, 226–28.

28. Fisk, *Pity the Nation*, 137.

29. Shlaim, *Iron Wall*, 351–53.

30. Patrick Tyler, *Fortress Israel* (New York: Farrar, Straus and Giroux, 2012), 273.

31. Fisk, *Pity the Nation*, 127, 132, 136–37; Noam Chomsky, *Fateful Triangle* (Cambridge, MA: South End Press, 1999), 192.

CHAPTER 15: THE IRANIAN REVOLUTION, 1978–1979

1. Gary Sick, *All Fall Down* (New York: Random House, 1985), 164.

2. See Roham Alvandi, *Nixon, Kissinger, and the Shah* (New York: Oxford University Press, 2014).

3. James Clarity, "Rich but Underdeveloped, Iran Seeks More Power," *New York Times* June 3, 1975.

4. Robert Fisk, *Great War for Civilization* (New York: Vintage, 2007), 122–23.

5. For the CIA's secret internal history of the coup, see CIA Clandestine Service History, "Overthrow of Premier Mossadeq of Iran, November 1952–August 1953," Mar. 1954, by Dr. Donald Wilber, National Security Archive, http://www2.gwu.edu /~nsarchiv/NSAEBB/NSAEBB28/; for secondary works on the operation, see Stephen Kinzer, *All the Shah's Men* (Hoboken, NJ: John Wiley & Sons, 2003); James Goode,

The United States and Iran (New York: St. Martin's Press, 1997); Mark Gasirowski, U.S. Foreign Policy and the Shah (Ithaca, NY: Cornell University Press, 1991).

6. James Bill, The Eagle and the Lion (New Haven: Yale University Press, 1988), 3, 208–9.

7. Fisk, Great War for Civilization, 98–99, 111–12.

8. Said Arjomand, The Turban for the Crown (New York: Oxford University Press, 1989), 75–87.

9. Bill, The Eagle and the Lion, 148.

10. Baqer Moin, Khomeini (New York: Thomas Dunne Books, 2000), 83–84, 87–88.

11. Ibid., 89, 104, 107–8, 111–12, 122–21; CIA, "Security Situation in Iran," June 13, 1963, CIA FOIA.

12. William Sullivan to DOS, "Serious Religious Dissidence in Qom," Jan. 11, 1978, NSA; Charles Kurzman, The Unthinkable Revolution in Iran (Cambridge, MA: Harvard University Press, 2004), 33–34, 37–38.

13. William Sullivan to DOS, "Iran: Understanding the Shi'ite Islamic Movement," Feb. 3, 1978, NSA.

14. Michael Metrinko to DOS, "Rioting and Civil Insurrection in Tabriz," Feb. 23, 1978, NSA.

15. Michael Axworthy, Revolutionary Iran (London: Allen Lane, 2013), 105–9.

16. Ervand Abrahamian, Iran Between Two Revolutions (Princeton: Princeton University Press, 1982), 513–16.

17. Jack Shellenberger, Memcon, "Iran's Political Crisis," Oct. 25, 1978, NSA.

18. Kurzman, The Unthinkable Revolution in Iran, 77–79, 105–7.

19. William Sullivan to DOS, "Thinking the Unthinkable," Nov. 9, 1978, NSA; CIA Intelligence Memorandum, "The Politics of Ayatollah Ruhollah Khomeini," Nov. 20, 1978, NSA; David Mark, "The Gathering Crisis in Iran," Nov. 2, 1978, INR.

20. CIA, "The Opposition to the Shah," Nov. 3, 1978, CIA FOIA; CIA, "Iran: The Tudeh Party and the Communist Movement," Dec. 8, 1978, CIA FOIA.

21. Bill, The Eagle and the Lion, 248–52.

22. Ibid., 252–59; Precht to Saunders, "Seeking Stability in Iran," Dec. 19, 1978, NSA.

23. Arjomand, Turban for the Crown, 120–21; Kurzman, The Unthinkable Revolution in Iran, 107–8, 111.

24. Nicholas Gage, "Ruler Goes to Egypt," New York Times, Jan. 17, 1979; R. W. Apple Jr., "Khomeini Arrives in Teheran, Urges Ouster of Foreigners," New York Times, Feb. 1, 1979.

25. Moin, Khomeini, 200–201, 204–6.

26. CIA Intelligence Memorandum, "The Radicals in the Opposition," Jan. 12, 1979, NSA; U.S. Embassy Tehran, "Iran: A Comment on Terrorism in a Revolutionary Situation," Feb. 28, 1979, NSA; see the heavily redacted CIA, National Foreign Assessment Center, "Iran: Communist Activities," Feb. 15, 1979, NSA; William Sullivan to DOS, "Islamic Revolution: Turning Sour," Mar. 8, 1979, NSA.

27. Nikki Keddie, Modern Iran (New Haven: Yale University Press, 2006), 245–46.

28. Arjomand, Turban for the Crown, 137–39.

29. CIA Foreign Assessment Center, "Iran's Ayatollahs," Mar. 20, 1979, NSA.

30. Sick, *All Fall Down*, 160, 165; "CIA Director Fears Leftists May Gain Control in Iran," *Chicago Tribune*, Mar. 18, 1979.

31. Mark Bowden, *Guests of the Ayatollah* (New York: Grove Press, 2007), 6–7, 13.

32. Ibid., 34.

33. Sick, *All Fall Down*, 207–9.

34. Fisk, *Great War for Civilization*, 127.

35. Axworthy, *Revolutionary Iran*, 169–72.

36. Bill, *The Eagle and the Lion*, 300–301.

37. Paul K. Davis, "Observations on the Rapid Deployment Joint Task Force," P-6751, RAND Paper, 1982, https://www.rand.org/content/dam/rand/pubs/papers/2005/P6751.pdf.

38. William E. Griffith, "The Revival of Islamic Fundamentalism: The Case of Iran," Confidential, Report, Apr. 23, 1979, NSA; James H. Madden, "Islamic Fundamentalism and the Soviet Union," Confidential, Report, July 30, 1979, NSA; CIA, National Foreign Assessment Center, "Iran and the USSR After the Shah," Aug. 17, 1979, NSA; Malcolm Toon, "Soviet Policy Toward Iran," Sept. 10, 1979, NSA; Grummon to DOS, "Situation in Iran and Afghanistan," Sept. 24, 1979, NSA.

39. CIA, "Iran: The Shia Revolution and Iran's Neighbors," Oct. 1979, CIA FOIA.

CHAPTER 16: THE SOVIET INTERVENTION IN AFGHANISTAN, 1978–1979

1. Ali Ahmad Jalili and Lester Grau, *The Other Side of the Mountain* (Quantico, VA: U.S. Marine Corps Studies and Analysis Division, 1999), xiii.

2. Nikita Khrushchev, *Khrushchev Remembers* (Boston: Little, Brown, 1970), 298.

3. Olivier Roy, *Islam and Resistance in Afghanistan* (New York: Cambridge University Press, 1990), 75–76.

4. Bruce Riedel, *What We Won: America's Secret War in Afghanistan, 1979–89* (Washington, DC: Brookings Institution Press, 2014), 15–16.

5. Barnett Rubin, *The Fragmentation of Afghanistan* (New Haven: Yale University Press, 2002), 105.

6. "Political Letter from USSR Ambassador to Afghanistan to Soviet Foreign Ministry," May 31, 1978, CWIHP.

7. "Journal of Soviet Ambassador Puzanov, Memorandum of Conversation with N. M. Taraki and Delegation of the Soviet Academy of Sciences," July 11, 1978, CWIHP.

8. Saunders to SecState, "Situation in Afghanistan," Apr. 30, 1978, DNSA.

9. Eliot to DOS, "Six Weeks after Afghanistan's Revolution," June 13, 1978, DNSA.

10. Adolph Dubs to DOS, "Khalqi Regime Identifies Afghan Revolution as an Extension of the USSR's October Revolution," Nov. 15, 1978, DNSA; Dubs to DOS, "Afghan Leadership Underscores Ties to USSR," Nov. 16, 1978, DNSA.

11. Rubin, *The Fragmentation of Afghanistan*, 115–16.

12. "The Political and Military Situation in Afghanistan," 1979, DNSA.

13. J. Bruce Amstutz to DOS, "Death of Ambassador Dubs," Feb. 14, 1979, DNSA.

14. Cyrus Vance to U.S. Embassy in Kabul, "Press Coverage," Feb. 18, 1979, DNSA.

15. Warren Christopher to U.S. Embassy in Kabul, "AFP: Afghan Rebels Report Fierce Fighting with Military," Mar. 13, 1979, DNSA.

16. Gilles Dorronsoro, *Revolution Unending: Afghanistan, 1979 to the Present* (New York: Columbia University Press, 2005), 99–101.

17. "Transcript of Telephone Conversation Between Soviet Premier Alexi Kosygin and Afghan Prime Minister Nur Mohammed Taraki," Mar. 17, 1979, CWIHP.

18. "Record of Conversation Between L. I. Brezhnev and N. M. Taraki," Mar. 20, 1979, CWIHP.

19. Edward Girardet, "A Grim Chapter in Afghanistan War," *Christian Science Monitor*, Feb. 4, 1980.

20. J. Bruce Amstutz to DOS, "Current Status of the Insurrection in Afghanistan," June 4, 1979, DNSA.

21. "Soviet Communication to the Hungarian Leadership on the Situation in Afghanistan," Mar. 28, 1979, CWIHP.

22. "CPSU CC Protocol #152/159, 24 May 1979, and Instructions to Soviet Ambassador in Afghanistan," May 24, 1979, CWIHP.

23. "Draft Instructions to the Soviet Ambassador in Kabul with Appeal of the CC CPSU Politburo to the CC PDPA Politburo," June 28, 1979, CWIHP.

24. Robert Gates, *From the Shadows* (New York: Simon and Schuster, 1996), 146.

25. Riedel, *What We Won*, 98–99.

26. J. Bruce Amstutz to DOS, "Afghanistan's Khalqi Regime at 18 Months," Nov. 20, 1970, DNSA.

27. Braithwaite, *Afgantsy*, 59, 66, 73–74.

28. Ibid., 56, 76–78.

29. "Directive No. 312/12/001 of 24 December 1979 Signed by Ustinov and Ogarkov," Dec. 24, 1979, CWIHP.

30. Gregory Feifer, *The Great Gamble* (New York: Harper, 2009), 59–60, 62, 64–65.

31. Braithwaite, *Afgantsy*, 96–99.

32. Summary, National Security Council, "Summary of Conclusions: SCC Meeting on Soviet Moves in Afghanistan," Dec. 26, 1979, NSA.

33. CIA, "Tribalism Versus Communism in Afghanistan," Jan. 3, 1980, CIA FOIA.

34. Zbigniew Brzezinski to Jimmy Carter, "Reflections on Soviet Intervention in Afghanistan," Dec. 26, 1979, NSA.

35. Cyrus Vance, "Our Assessment of Recent Events in Afghanistan," Dec. 28, 1979, DNSA.

36. "Summary of the President's Telephone Conversation—Mrs. Margaret Thatcher, Prime Minister of Great Britain," Dec. 28, 1979, NSA.

37. Jimmy Carter, "Address to the Nation on the Soviet Invasion of Afghanistan," Jan. 4, 1980, *PPP*; "Talking Points for Telephone Calls on the President's Speech," Jan. 1980, DNSA; see also CIA, "The Invasion of Afghanistan: Implications for Soviet Foreign Policy," Jan. 1980, CIA FOIA.

38. Bruce Palmer, "Major Estimates of Soviet Military Capabilities in Situations Less than General War," Jan. 22, 1980, CIA FOIA.

39. Jimmy Carter, "State of the Union Address," Jan. 23, 1980, *PPP*.

40. DIA, "The Soviet Invasion of Afghanistan," Feb. 1980, DNSA.

41. Riedel, *What We Won*, 28–29.

42. The Russian General Staff, *The Soviet-Afghan War*, trans. Lester Grau and Michael Gress (Lawrence: University Press of Kansas, 2002), 17–19.

43. Ibid., 19–20.

44. Feifer, *Great Gamble*, 117, 129.

45. M. Hassan Kakar, *Afghanistan: The Soviet Invasion and Afghan Response* (Berkeley: University of California Press, 1995), 114–18.

46. Jalili and Grau, *Other Side of the Mountain*, xviii–xix.

47. Alfred (Roy) Atherton to DOS, "Egypt Takes Strong Measures in Response to Soviet Invasion of Afghanistan," Jan. 7, 1980, DNSA; Atherton to DOS, "Al Azhar Attacks Soviets," Jan. 20, 1980, DNSA.

48. Riedel, *What We Won*, 58–60.

49. Ibid., 60–63.

50. Harry Kreisler, "The Rise of al Qaeda," Conversation with Steve Coll, Conversations with History, Institute of International Studies, UC Berkeley, http://globetrotter.berkeley.edu/people5/Coll/coll-con5.html.

51. Gilles Kepel, *Jihad* (Cambridge, MA: Belknap, 2003), 143–44.

52. Rubin, *The Fragmentation of Afghanistan*, 197–98.

53. Peter Bergen, *Holy War, Inc.* (New York: Free Press, 2001), 71–72; State INR, "The Afghan Resistance Movement," Mar. 16, 1982, DNSA.

54. J. Bruce Amstutz, *Afghanistan* (Washington, DC: NDU Press, 1986), 112–15.

55. Vahid Brown and Don Rassler, *Fountainhead of Jihad* (New York: Columbia University Press, 2013), 4–6, 38, 40, 62.

56. "Report by Soviet Defense Minister Ustinov to CPSU CC on 'Foreign Interference' in Afghanistan," Oct. 2, 1980, CWIHP.

57. "Intelligence Note Concerning Actions by the US in Aiding the Afghanistan Rebel Fighters," Sept. 1, 1980, CWIHP.

CHAPTER 17: THE MIDDLE EAST AT WAR, 1980–1982

1. CIA, "Resurgent Islamic Nationalism in the Middle East," Mar. 1981, CIA FOIA.

2. Michael Kaufman, "Influence of Rebels in Afghanistan Is Still Growing, Diplomats Report," *New York Times*, Nov. 11, 1980.

3. Russian General Staff, *The Soviet-Afghan War* (Lawrence: University Press of Kansas, 2002), 20–21, 23–24.

4. Riedel, *What We Won*, 44.

5. Braithwaite, *Afgantsy*, 131–34.

6. Ed Girardet, *Afghanistan: The Soviet War* (London: Croon Helm, 1985), 33–35.

7. David Thurman to DOS, "Soviet Offensive in Kunar Province," Mar. 6, 1980, DNSA.

8. Tanner, *Afghanistan*, 246–47.

9. Diego Cordovez and Selig Harrison, *Out of Afghanistan* (New York: Oxford University Press, 1994), 59.

10. "Report of Military Leaders to D. F. Ustinov," May 10, 1981, CWIHP.

11. Ibid.

12. CIA, "Afghanistan: Iran's Role in the Crisis," July 1980, CIA FOIA.

13. CIA, "China's Afghanistan Policy," Jan. 28, 1982, CIA FOIA; Riedel, *What We Won*, 107.

14. Jeri Laber and Barnett Rubin, *A Nation Is Dying* (Evanston, IL: Northwestern University Press, 1998), 9–11.

15. Jalili and Grau, *Other Side of the Mountain*, xix.

16. Edward Girardet, "Afghan Refugees: The Palestinians of Asia?" *Christian Science Monitor*, July 9, 1982.

17. Barrington King to DOS, "Afghan Refugee Situation—An Overview," Dec. 9, 1982, DNSA; see also Sarah Kenyon Lischer, *Dangerous Sanctuaries* (Ithaca: Cornell University Press, 2005), 44–73.

18. Braithwaite, *Afgantsy*, 205, 215–19.

19. Edward Girardet, "Guerrillas Survive Biggest Attack Yet as Soviets Roar into Panjshir Valley," *Christian Science Monitor*, June 22, 1982.

20. Feifer, *Great Gamble*, 157–58, 173–75.

21. Robert Rakove, "The Central Front of Reagan's Cold War" (forthcoming; shared with author June 2017).

22. Dilip Hiro, *The Longest War* (New York: Routledge, 1991), 40–41.

23. Conflict Records Research Center Document (CRRC), "Saddam and His Advisers Discussing Iraq's Decision to Go to War with Iran," Sept. 16, 1980, CWIHP.

24. CIA, "The Implications of an Iraqi Victory," Sept. 26, 1980, CIA FOIA.

25. CRRC, "Saddam and High-Ranking Officials Discussing Khomeini," Feb. 20, 1979, CWIHP.

26. Phebe Marr, *The Modern History of Iraq* (Boulder, CO: Westview Press, 2012), 172–73.

27. Ibid., 180–82; CRRC, "General Military Intelligence Directorate Report Assessing Political, Military, and Economic Conditions in Iran," Jan. 1–June 30, 1980, CWIHP.

28. Axworthy, *Revolutionary Iran*, 192–94.

29. Keddie, *Modern Iran*, 251.

30. Edward O'Ballance, *The Gulf War* (London: Brassey's Defence Publishers, 1988), 37–41; "Youssef Ibrahim, "Iraqis Still Battle for Khurramshahr," *New York Times*, Oct. 5, 1980; Youssef M. Ibrahim, "In Khurramshahr's Port, Iraqis Watch for Snipers," *New York Times*, Oct. 8, 1980.

31. John Kifner, "Iraqis, On the Move, Place More Bridges on the Way to Abadan," *New York Times*, Oct. 13, 1980; John Kifner, "Iraq's Troops Move to Edge of Abadan," *New York Times*, Oct. 17, 1980; O'Ballance, *The Gulf War*, 37–41.

32. Stephen Pelletiere, *The Iran-Iraq War* (New York: Praeger, 1992), 37, 40–41.

33. Hiro, *The Longest War*, 52–54.

34. Kenneth Pollack, *Arabs at War* (Lincoln, NE: University of Nebraska Press, 2002), 195–202.

35. Cordesman, *Lessons of Modern War*, 136–39; Henry Tanner, "Iran's Recovered Port City," *New York Times*, June 4, 1982.

36. Charles Tripp, *A History of Iraq* (Cambridge, UK: Cambridge University Press, 2007), 226–29.

37. CIA, "Whither Iran," Dec. 6, 1982, CIA FOIA.

38. CIA, "Agenda for NIC Warning Meeting," June 14, 1982, CIA FOIA.

39. Axworthy, *Revolutionary Iran*, 226–29.

40. O'Ballance, *Gulf War*, 93–97.

41. James Blight et al., *Becoming Enemies* (Lanham, MD: Rowman & Littlefield Publishers, 2012), 104–5.

42. "Document 3-1: Discussion Paper for Senior Interdepartmental Group (SIG) on Policy Options for Deal with the Iran-Iraq War, mid-1982," and "Document 3-2: William P. Clark Memorandum for the President," c. July 1982, reproduced in Blight et al., *Becoming Enemies*, 309–11.

43. Department of State Briefing Paper, "Soviet Perspective on Iran/Iraq War," Sept. 24, 1980, DNSA; Christopher Andrew and Vasili Mitrokhin, *The World Was Going Our Way* (New York: Basic Books, 2005), 188–89.

44. Andrew and Mitrokhin, *The World Was Going Our Way*, 190–91.

45. CRRC, "Saddam and His Inner Circle Discussing the United Nations, the Soviet Union, and the United States," undated, circa 1981, CWIHP.

46. Nicholas Gage, "Beirut Regaining Prewar Glory, But Gaiety Has Hysterical Edge," *New York Times*, June 17 1980.

47. Sayigh, *Armed Struggle*, 447–55.

48. Morris, *Righteous Victims*, 507–8.

49. Seale, *Asad*, 316–17, 320–21, 329.

50. Ibid., 332–34.

51. Thomas Friedman, *From Beirut to Jerusalem* (New York: Anchor Books, 1995), 90.

52. Shlaim, *Iron Wall*, 395–98.

53. Randal, *Going All the Way*, 115–16, 118, 135–36.

54. Morris, *Righteous Victims*, 511–14; on Haig's "green light," see Seth Anziska, "Camp David's Shadow: The United States, Israel, and the Palestinian Question, 1977–1993," PhD diss., Columbia University, 2015.

55. Tyler, *Fortress Israel*, 303–5; Hirst, *Beware of Small States*, 135–38.

56. John Bulloch, *Final Conflict* (London: Century, 1983), 21–22, 60–63.

57. Zeev Schiff and Ehud Ya'ari, *Israel's Lebanon War* (New York: Simon & Schuster, 1984), 181.

58. Rashid Khalidi, *Under Siege* (New York: Columbia University Press, 1986), 87–89, 93, 95–99.

59. "The Israelis, Too, Are Outraged," *New York Times*, Aug. 13, 1982; "Dare Call It Terrorism," *Times* (London), Aug. 7, 1982; Ronald Reagan, *An American Life* (New York: Simon & Schuster, 1990), 428.

60. Morris, *Righteous Victims*, 538, 726n247; Sayigh, *Armed Struggle*, 538, 540.

CHAPTER 18: REAGAN'S WAR FOR THE MIDDLE EAST, 1983–1987

1. CIA, "Soviet Forces and Capabilities in the Southern Theater of Military Operations," Dec. 1983, CIA FOIA.

2. Fritz Ermarth, "Soviet Strategies in the Southern Theater," Aug. 1, 1984, CIA FOIA.

3. CIA, "Islam and Politics: A Compendium," April 1984, CIA FOIA.

4. State–INR, "The Afghan Resistance Movement in 1981: Progress, but a Long Way to Go," Jan. 19, 1982, DNSA; Casey quote in Steve Coll, *Ghost Wars* (New York: Penguin Press, 2004), 97.

5. Lawrence Freedman, *A Choice of Enemies: America Confronts the Middle East* (New York: Public Affairs, 2008), 114.

6. Feifer, *Great Gamble*, 146.

7. Braithwaite, *Afgantsy*, 146–47.

8. John K. Cooley, *Unholy Wars* (London: Pluto Press, 2002), 135–36.

9. Laber and Rubin, *A Nation Is Dying*, 10–11, 16, 18, 35, 42.

10. Braithwaite, *Afgantsy*, 232–33.

11. James M. Scott, "Reagan's Doctrine? The Formulation of an American Foreign Policy Strategy," *Presidential Studies Quarterly*, 26 no. 4 (Fall 1996): 1047–50; NSDD-75, "U.S. Relations with the USSR," Jan. 17, 1983, http://fas.org/irp/offdocs/nsdd/nsdd-75.pdf; Charles Krauthammer, "The Reagan Doctrine," *Washington Post*, July 19, 1985.

12. NSDD-166, "U.S. Policy, Programs and Strategy in Afghanistan," Mar. 27, 1985, http://fas.org/irp/offdocs/nsdd/nsdd-166.pdf.

13. Coll, *Ghost Wars*, 11, 149–50.

14. Schiff and Ya'ari, *Israel's Lebanon War*, 230–36.

15. Friedman, *From Beirut to Jerusalem*, 157–59; Ihsan Hijazi, "Israeli Looted Archives of P.L.O. Officials Say," *New York Times*, Oct. 1, 1982.

16. Morris, *Righteous Victims*, 543–44.

17. Fisk, *Pity the Nation*, 359–61, 382, 390; Seth Anziska, "A Preventable Massacre," *New York Times*, Sept. 16, 2012.

18. George Shultz, *Turmoil and Triumph* (New York: Scribner's, 1993), 111.

19. "Report of the Commission of Inquiry into the Events at the Refugee Camps in Beirut—8 February 1983," http://www.mfa.gov.il/mfa/foreignpolicy/mfadocuments/.

20. Freedman, *A Choice of Enemies*, 138.

21. Patrick Tyler, *A World of Trouble* (New York: Farrar, Straus and Giroux, 2009), 291–92, 296–97.

22. Friedman, *From Beirut to Jerusalem*, 201–2; Reagan, *An American Life*, 452–53.

23. Augustus Richard Norton, *Amal and the Shi'a* (Austin: University of Texas Press, 1987), 48–49, 55.

24. Augustus Richard Norton, *Hezbollah* (Princeton: Princeton University Press, 2014), 33–37.

25. Nicholas Blanford, *Warriors of God* (New York: Random House, 2011), 59; Anonymous (Michael Scheuer), *Imperial Hubris* (Washington, DC: Brassey's, 2004), 112; Matthew Levitt, *Hezbollah: The Global Footprint of Lebanon's Party of God* (Washington, DC: Georgetown University Press, 2013), 28–29.

26. Reagan, *An American Life*, 465–66.

27. Robin Wright, *Sacred Rage* (New York: Simon & Schuster, 2001), 105; CIA, "Hizballah's Rise: The US Stake," Oct. 21, 1986, CIA FOIA; CIA, "Lebanon: The Prospects for Islamic Fundamentalism," July 1987, CIA FOIA.

28. Wright, *Sacred Rage*, 101–4.

29. Rex Brynen, *Sanctuary and Survival* (Boulder, CO: Westview Press, 1991), http://prrn.mcgill.ca/prrn/papers/sanctuary/ch8.html.

30. Blanford, *Warriors of God*, 88–92.

31. Cordesman, *Lessons of Modern War*, 154–55.

32. Pollack, *Arabs at War*, 206–7; R. W. Apple Jr., "Iranian Officers, Seeking Revenge, Talk of Pursuing Enemy into Iraq," *New York Times*, Nov. 7, 1982.

33. Hiro, *The Longest War*, 96, 119–22.

34. O'Ballance, *Gulf War*, 142–47.

35. Cordesman, *Lessons of Modern War*, 191–96.

36. Nicholas Veliotes and Jonathan Howe to Lawrence Eagleburger, "Iran-Iraq War: Analysis of Possible U.S. Shift from Position of Strict Neutrality," Oct. 7, 1983, CWIHP.

37. CIA, "Iran: Outlook for the Islamic Republic," May 24, 1983, CIA FOIA.

38. CIA, "Prospects for Iraq," July 19, 1983, CIA FOIA.

39. CIA, "Iraq: Social and Political Factors Deter Religious Revival," Nov. 1983, CIA FOIA.

40. P. Wilcox, Top Secret Internal State Department Paper, "Iran-Iraq War: U.S. Responses to Escalation Scenarios and Threats to Persian Gulf States," Mar. 20, 1984, NSA.

41. CIA, "Iraq's Shias," Nov. 1984, CIA FOIA.

42. Jonathan Howe to George Shultz, Information Memorandum, "Iraq Use of Chemical Weapons," Nov. 1, 1983, CWIHP.

43. Defense Intelligence Agency, Defense Estimative Brief: Prospects for Iraq," Sept. 25, 1984, NSA.

44. Henry Kam, "In Iraqi Port, Sullen Mood Amid Shelling," *New York Times*, Mar. 7, 1984.

45. Pollack, *Arabs at War*, 217–19.

46. Shultz, "[George Shultz Opposition to NSC Operation with Iran]," Secret Memorandum, Dec. 1986, NSA.

47. Lawrence Walsh, *Firewall* (New York: Norton, 1997), 7–8; "Address to the Nation on the Iran Arms and Contra Aid Controversy," Nov. 13, 1986, *PPP*, Ronald Reagan Presidential Library, http://www.reagan.utexas.edu/archives/speeches/1986/111386c.htm.

48. CRRC, "Saddam Discussing 'Irangate' (Iran-Contra) Revelations with his Inner Circle," undated (c. late 1986), CWIHP.

49. Walsh, *Firewall*, 531.

50. Shultz, *Turmoil and Triumph*, 926, 931.

51. David Crist, *The Twilight War: The Secret History of America's Thirty-Year Conflict with Iran* (New York: Penguin Press, 2012), 222–27.

52. Freedman, *A Choice of Enemies*, 203–6.

53. CIA, "Soviet Policy Toward the Middle East," Dec. 1986, CIA FOIA.

54. CIA, "Islamic Fundamentalism in the Middle East and South Asia," Dec. 1986, CIA FOIA.

55. Ayatollah Khomeini, "We Shall Confront the World with Our Ideology," *Middle East Research and Information Project*, No. 88 (May/June 1980), http://www.merip.org/mer/mer88/khomeini-we-shall-confront-world-our-ideology.

CHAPTER 19: "YOU ARE CREATING A FRANKENSTEIN," 1988–1990

1. CIA, "Islamic Fundamentalism: Implications for the Arab World and the United States," Dec. 1987, CIA FOIA.

2. Robert Suro, "At the Front in the Gulf War," *New York Times*, Jan. 28, 1987; Bernard Trainor, "At the Front in Iraq," *New York Times*, June 8, 1987; John Cushman Jr., "In the Trenches in Iraq," *New York Times*, Aug. 25, 1987.

3. Bryan Gibson, *Covert Relationship* (New York: Praeger, 2010), 208–9.

4. P. Maher–INR, "HLDG Briefing: Iran/Iraq War," Ankara, Apr. 12, 1988, NSA.

5. Hiro, *The Longest War*, 203, 206; U.S. Embassy in Baghdad to DOS, "Iraq Exults in Fao Victory, Barely Mentions U.S. Actions," Apr. 19, 1988, NSA.

6. Fisk, *Great War for Civilization*, 259–60, 263–64.

7. Blight et al., *Becoming Enemies*, 345–47, 276.

8. Human Rights Watch, "Genocide in Iraq," July 1993, http://www.hrw.org/reports/1993/iraqanfal/.

9. Ibid.

10. Morton Abrahamowitz–INR to SecState, "Information Memo: Swan Song for Iraq's Kurds," Sept. 2, 1988, NSA; Abrahamowitz–INR to SecState, "Iraq: Status Report on the Kurdish Situation," Sept. 13, 1988, NSA.

11. Bureau of Near Eastern Affairs, Department of State, "Overview of U.S.-Iraqi Relations and Potential Pressure Points," Secret, Internal Paper, Sept. 9, 1988, NSA.

12. Samantha Power, *A Problem from Hell* (New York: Basic Books, 2002), 204, 223, 228–29.

13. April Glaspie, "After U.S. Actions, Saddam Changes His Tone," Sept. 12, 1988, NSA.

14. Melvyn P. Leffler, *For the Soul of Mankind: The United States, the Soviet Union, and the Cold War* (New York: Farrar, Straus and Giroux, 2007), 366, 369, 371.

15. Kalinovsky, *A Long Goodbye*, 74, 83.

16. CPSU CC Politburo Meeting Minutes, Nov. 13, 1986, CWIHP.

17. Feifer, *Great Gamble*, 217–18.

18. Notes from Politburo Meeting, Feb. 23, 1987, CWHIP.

19. Kepel, *Jihad*, 144–48.

20. Brown and Rassler, *Fountainhead of Jihad*, 71–75.

21. Kalinovsky, *A Long Goodbye*, 96–98.

22. Coll, *Ghost Wars*, 147–49.

23. "Record of a Conversation of M. S. Gorbachev with the General Secretary of the Central Committee of the People's Democratic Party of Afghanistan Cde. Najib," July 20, 1987, CWIHP.

24. Braithwaite, *Afgantsy*, 214–15.

25. "Conversation between M. S. Gorbachev and Ronald Regan on Afghanistan (Excerpt)," Dec. 9, 1987, CWIHP; "Conversation between M. S. Gorbachev and Vice President George H. W. Bush," Dec. 10, 1987, CWIHP. My thanks to Robert Rakove for his thoughts on this as well.

26. Kalinovsky, *A Long Goodbye*, 168.

27. For estimates of those killed in the war, see Kalinovsky, *A Long Goodbye*, and Braithwaite, *Afgantsy*.

28. CIA, Special NIE, "USSR: Withdrawal from Afghanistan," Mar. 1988, CIA FOIA, https://www.cia.gov/library/readingroom/docs/DOC_0005564723.pdf, and quoted in Coll, *Ghost Wars*, 172–73.

29. O'Ballance, *Civil War in Lebanon*, 185–88.

30. Hanf, *Coexistence in Wartime Lebanon*, 574–75.

31. Hirst, *Beware of Small States*, 211–13; "Ta'if Accord," Nov. 4, 1989, http://www.al -bab.com/arab/docs/lebanon/taif.htm.

32. Harris, *Faces of Lebanon*, 264, 276–77.

33. Hanf, *Coexistence in Wartime Lebanon*, 337.

34. Fawwaz Trablousi, *A History of Modern Lebanon* (London: Pluto, 2007), 232–35.

35. Mark Hosenball, "War on Terror: The Road to September 11," *Newsweek,* Sept. 30, 2001.

36. Jeremy Scahill, *Dirty Wars* (New York: Nation Books, 2013), 21–22.

37. Siobhan Gorman, "CIA Man Is Key to U.S. Relations with Karzai," *Wall Street Journal,* Aug. 24, 2010, http://www.wsj.com/articles/SB10001424052748704741904575 409874267832044.

38. Ann Scott Tyson, "Sorry Charlie. This Is Michael Vickers's War," *Washington Post*, Dec. 28, 2007.

39. Joby Warrick, *Black Flags* (New York: Doubleday, 2015), 51–52.

INDEX

ABOUT THE AUTHOR

Paul Thomas Chamberlin is an associate professor of history at Columbia University. He previously taught at the University of Kentucky and has held fellowships at Yale University and Williams College. He is also the author of *The Global Offensive: The United States, the Palestine Liberation Organization, and the Making of the Post–Cold War Order.*